A TERRIBLE GLORY

Custer and the Little Bighorn—
The Last Great Battle of the American West

Selected by *American Heritage* as
a Notable Book of the Year

"A riveting and highly readable account of the battle that marked the Native Americans' final triumph in the Sioux War of 1876. . . . Donovan has produced a fresh interpretation of one of the Army's most controversial commanders and one of this nation's most famous battles. Well-balanced and informative, *A Terrible Glory* comes closer to deciphering exactly what happened on the banks of the Little Bighorn River than any recent account. Monumental in its scope and gripping in its narrative, *A Terrible Glory* is history at its best."
—Col. Cole C. Kingseed, USA Ret., PhD, *Army Magazine*

"In this labor of love, Donovan collects the multiple threads that led to the 1876 massacre at Little Big Horn. . . . Exhaustive research, lively prose, and fresh interpretation make for a valuable addition to literature on this historical event." —*Publishers Weekly*

"*A Terrible Glory* is probably as close as we're going to get to knowing what really happened. . . . Gloriously free of the sociopolitical agendas and rhetorical cant that re-forms around Custer and the battle with each new decade. . . . One of the best things about *A Terrible Glory* is its lack of agenda."
—Allen Barra, *Los Angeles Times*

"James Donovan's expansive approach to the battle has resulted in the most memorable, readable, maybe best book on it to date. . . . The author is an adept biographer [and] provides astute portrayals of Custer and his engaging wife. . . . The Custer battle has never been as vividly and comprehensively told as in *A Terrible Glory*."

—Dale L. Walker, *Dallas Morning News*

"Donovan, a skilled writer and researcher, has sifted through a wealth of data to glean the best material [on Little Bighorn] available today . . . and written a fresh and compelling narrative. . . . The author's style of writing is engaging and reflects a mastery of the subject matter. This is a cohesive, fast-paced read and well worth picking up." —Erik F. Nelson, *Fredericksburg Free Lance–Star*

"Sifting through recently surfaced documents while aggressively reinterpreting the known record, Donovan breathes fresh life into this classic Western Iliad. And, like all fine narrative history, *A Terrible Glory* is a great pleasure to read."

—Hampton Sides, author of *Blood and Thunder*

"James Donovan's *A Terrible Glory* is exemplary. The research into firsthand sources is broader and deeper than I have ever seen."

—Robert M. Utley, author of *Lone Star Lawmen*

"James Donovan uses a plethora of primary and secondary sources to write a comprehensive study of the events leading up to the battle, the fight itself, and its aftermath. . . . Mr. Donovan's description of the battle is first-rate. Relying not only on some of the well-known soldier and Indian accounts, he also uses current scholarship and recent archaeological discoveries to clear up some of the mysteries of the fight. . . . *A Terrible Glory* is a great read and is destined to become one of the classic books of the Indian Wars."

—Steve French, *Washington Times*

"Recent decades have seen important new findings regarding the Battle of the Little Bighorn. What has been needed next is a clear narrative for scholars and lay readers alike embracing all of the recent research; Donovan has written just that. . . . An excellent starting point for those seeking an understanding of the Battle of the Little Bighorn."

— Stephen H. Peters, *Library Journal* (starred review)

"There have been so many books written about the battle of the Little Bighorn that it's natural to ask: why another? James Donovan's marvelous narrative puts that question to rest after only a few paragraphs. Its clarity and scope, its careful and unbiased assessments, and its gripping readability make us feel that we're encountering this astonishing American story for the very first time."

— Stephen Harrigan, author of *The Gates of the Alamo*

"Comprehensive. . . . Donovan is no agenda-laden, blind defender of Custer; he carefully notes the results of the inquiry that followed the famed slaughter. . . . His thoroughgoing account lends considerable humanity to all involved." — *Kirkus Reviews* (starred review)

"Enthralling. . . . *A Terrible Glory* is not another version of the Custer's Last Stand legend nor is it an unquestioning reappraisal based on Native American oral history. Donovan has recreated this epic clash with a cogent grasp of the issues leading up to the battle, astute analysis of tactics, weapons, and topography, and empathetic insight into the lives of the Lakota Sioux, Cheyennes, and the troopers of the U.S. 7th Cavalry. . . . *A Terrible Glory* will endure as one of the most solidly researched and moving accounts of Custer's death ride and the Plains Indians' last victory that we are likely to have for a long time to come." — Ed Voves, *California Literary Review*

Also by James Donovan

Custer and the Little Bighorn:
The Man, the Mystery, the Myth

A TERRIBLE GLORY

Custer and the Little Bighorn—
the Last Great Battle of the American West

JAMES DONOVAN

BACK BAY BOOKS
Little, Brown and Company
New York   Boston   London

Back Bay Books / Little, Brown and Company
Hachette Book Group
237 Park Avenue, New York, NY 10017
Visit our Web site at www.HachetteBookGroup.com

Originally published in hardcover by Little, Brown and Company, March 2008
First Back Bay paperback edition, May 2009

Back Bay Books is an imprint of Little, Brown and Company. The Back Bay Books name and logo are trademarks of Hachette Book Group, Inc.

Maps by Jeffrey L. Ward

Library of Congress Cataloging-in-Publication Data

Donovan, James.
A terrible glory : Custer and the Little Bighorn: the last great battle of the American West / James Donovan. — 1st ed.
p. cm.
Includes bibliographical references and index.
ISBN 978-0-316-15578-6 (hc) / 978-0-316-06747-8 (pb)
1. Little Bighorn, Battle of the, Mont., 1876. 2. Custer, George Armstrong, 1839–1876. 3. Indians of North America — Government relations — 1869–1934. 4. West (U.S.) — History, Military — 19th century. 5. United States. Army — History — 19th century. 6. United States — Military policy — 19th century. I. Title.
E83.876.D66 2008
973.8'2 — dc22   2007026156

10 9 8 7 6 5 4 3 2 1

RRD-IN

Design by Renato Stanisic
Printed in the United States of America

To my mother, Alyce Helen Carmen,
who nightly from an old black binder
read her favorite story poems, hand-copied,
to her four children:
"The boy stood on the burning deck . . ."

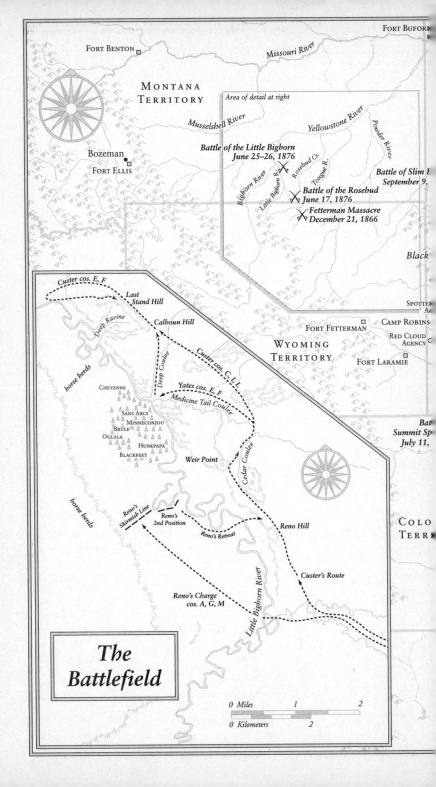

FORT BUFOR▸

FORT BENTON

Missouri River

MONTANA
TERRITORY

Area of detail at right

Musselshell River

Yellowstone River

Powder River

Bighorn River

Little Bighorn R.

Rosebud Cr.

Tongue R.

Battle of the Little Bighorn
June 25–26, 1876

Bozeman
FORT ELLIS

Battle of Slim ▸
September 9,

Battle of the Rosebud
June 17, 1876

Fetterman Massacre
December 21, 1866

Black

SPOTTE▸
A▸

FORT FETTERMAN

CAMP ROBINS▸

RED CLOUD
AGENCY C

WYOMING
TERRITORY

FORT LARAMIE

Custer cos. E, F

Last
Stand Hill

Calhoun Hill

Deep Ravine

Deep Coulee

Custer cos. C, I, L

horse herds

CHEYENNE

SANS ARCS

MINNECONJOU

BRULE

OGLALA

HUNKPAPA

BLACKFEET

Yates cos. E, F

Medicine Tail Coulee

Weir Point

Cedar Coulee

Bat
Summit Sp
July 11,

COLO▸
TERR▸

horse herds

Reno's
Skirmish Line

Reno's
2nd Position

Reno's Retreat

Reno Hill

Custer's Route

Reno's Charge
cos. A, G, M

Little Bighorn River

The
Battlefield

0 Miles   1   2

0 Kilometers   2

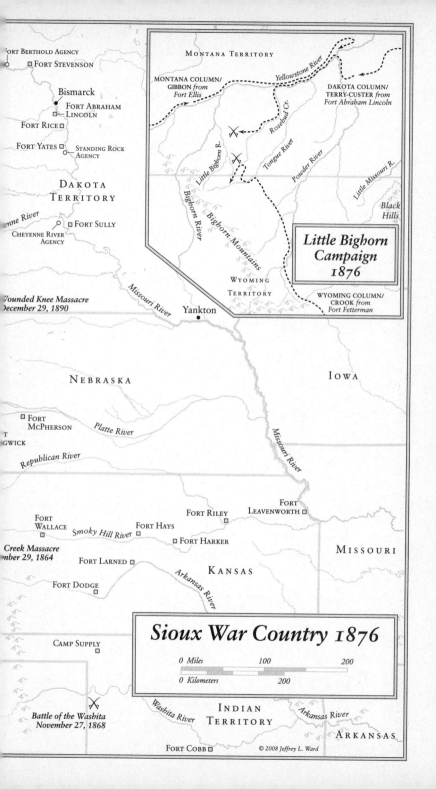

FORT BERTHOLD AGENCY
□ FORT STEVENSON
○

Bismarck
FORT ABRAHAM
□ LINCOLN

FORT RICE □

FORT YATES □   STANDING ROCK
○   AGENCY

DAKOTA
TERRITORY

enne River
○   □ FORT SULLY
CHEYENNE RIVER
AGENCY

Wounded Knee Massacre
December 29, 1890

Missouri River

Yankton ●

NEBRASKA

IOWA

□ FORT
McPHERSON   Platte River

GWICK

Republican River

Missouri River

FORT
LEAVENWORTH □

FORT RILEY

FORT
WALLACE   FORT HAYS
□   Smoky Hill River □

□ FORT HARKER

MISSOURI

Creek Massacre
mber 29, 1864   FORT LARNED □   KANSAS

FORT DODGE □   Arkansas River

Sioux War Country 1876

0 Miles   100   200
0 Kilometers   200

CAMP SUPPLY
□

Battle of the Washita
November 27, 1868   Washita River   INDIAN
TERRITORY   Arkansas River

FORT COBB □   © 2008 Jeffrey L. Ward   ARKANSAS

Little Bighorn Campaign 1876

MONTANA TERRITORY

Yellowstone River

MONTANA COLUMN/
GIBBON from
Fort Ellis

DAKOTA COLUMN/
TERRY-CUSTER from
Fort Abraham Lincoln

Rosebud Cr.

Little Bighorn R.

Tongue River

Powder River

Little Missouri R.

Bighorn River

Bighorn Mountains

Black
Hills

WYOMING
TERRITORY

WYOMING COLUMN/
CROOK from
Fort Fetterman

CONTENTS

AUTHOR'S NOTES

SOURCES AND ACCURACY

I have relied on primary accounts (rather than secondary accounts, interpretations, or hearsay) almost exclusively in the following narrative. But not all such accounts are created equal, and I have tried to be rigorous in their use. The just-surrendered Lakota leader fearful of retribution; the trooper or warrior whose faulty memory attempts to remember events of fifty or more years ago; the officer concerned with avoiding blame and thus subtly altering his version of those same events—the difficulties inherent in these kinds of accounts and others, such as faulty interpreters or overly dramatic reporters, have complicated the job of anyone trying to find the truth of what happened along that river on June 25, 1876. Combined with the all-too-human propensity for viewing and remembering the same event differently, the historian's task in this case is made surprisingly difficult considering the multitude of eyewitness accounts. Fortunately, the broad brushstrokes of history here are not in question, though many of the details certainly are. In such instances, where there is disagreement over what occurred, I have endeavored to examine the evidence objectively before making a decision as to the most likely course of action. (Any such examinations or discussions, moreover, are confined to the notes.)

All dialogue appearing within quotation marks comes directly from primary sources—accounts written or given by eyewitnesses or others who interviewed them. Those sources include trial transcripts, letters, interviews published in newspapers, et cetera, and unpublished participant interviews and accounts.

In only one area have I employed anything other than the strict historical record: that part of the battle dealing with the movements of Custer's battalion after trumpeter John Martin gallops away with a message from his commander as Custer leads his men down into Medicine Tail Coulee. We will never know, without a reasonable doubt, what happened to Custer and his 210 men. That is because no white observer saw any man of that contingent alive again, and the accounts of those who witnessed its movements—the Sioux and Cheyenne who defeated Custer—are, for many reasons, sketchy and often contradictory. But there is knowledge to be gleaned from a careful sifting of those accounts. The stories of those eyewitnesses, checked against each other and against the known positions of the troopers' bodies and the extensive archaeological and forensic work completed over the last quarter century, enable one to determine, to a reasonably accurate degree, the actions (and by extension some of the thoughts) of Custer and a few of the men in his battalion. Though others may interpret the same record differently, I believe that given the information available, the actions of Custer and his subordinates as related herein during that time are those most likely to have occurred.

SIOUX TRIBAL STRUCTURE

The people known to the whites as Sioux were divided into three related groups, each of which spoke a slightly different dialect. The largest and westernmost were the Lakota (Teton), consisting of seven major tribal divisions (Hunkpapa, Oglala, Minneconjou, Brulé, Blackfeet, Two Kettle, and Sans Arcs) that lived west of the Missouri River and north of the Platte River. The easternmost group were the Dakota or Santee (further divided into the Mdewakanton, Wahpeton, Wahpekute, and Sisseton), in Iowa and Minnesota west of the Red River. Between them—between the Missouri and the Red Rivers—were the Nakota or Yankton (comprising the Yankton and Yanktonai). There are many variant spellings of some of these (Uncpapa, Minnecoujou, and so forth), and there are also Siouan versions. In almost every case, I have employed the most common and traditional forms for familiarity, regularity, and simple ease of reading.

ARMY RANK

During the Civil War, a Union officer could actually hold as many as four ranks: his permanent ("full") rank in the Regular Army, a full rank in the Volunteers, and brevet ranks in both. A brevet rank was an honorary promotion given an officer for battlefield gallantry or meritorious service and was often awarded for much the same reasons medals are given out today (our modern system of medals did not exist until several decades after the Civil War). After the war, when the Volunteer army was disbanded, brevet promotions were still awarded, but less frequently. Though except in rare instances it imparted little authority and no extra pay, an officer was entitled to be addressed by his brevet rank. For the sake of clarity, I have refrained from that practice—with one exception. Despite his Regular Army rank of Lieutenant Colonel, George Armstrong Custer was referred to by one and all of the men under him as the General, in honor of his Civil War brevet ranks of Major General in both the Regular Army and the Volunteers. I have followed that custom frequently in this book.

A TERRIBLE GLORY

PROLOGUE

A Good Day to Die

Wolf Mountains, Montana Territory
June 25, 1876, 3:00 a.m.

The night was pitch-black and cool as the small party of scouts reined their horses off the creek and up into the hidden hollow between the hills. They picked their way through juniper trees, up the westernmost ridge, until it became too steep for horses. Second Lieutenant Charles Varnum dismounted, threw himself on the ground, and fell asleep instantly. The young West Pointer had ridden close to seventy miles since early that morning, almost twenty-four hours nonstop. He was bone tired.

All six of the Arikara Indians followed the officer's lead, for they had been in the saddle just as long. But two of the five Crow Indians, along with the dapper scout "Lonesome" Charley Reynolds, left their horses and climbed the steep slope to a ridge overlooking the pass that crossed the divide between the Little Bighorn and Rosebud valleys. The Arikaras were only along as couriers; their homeland lay on the Missouri River, almost three hundred miles to the east. This was Crow country, and the Crows had often used the hollow to conceal their horses while scouting the area during Sioux pony raids. From the lookout, they could usually see for a great distance in both directions.[1] But not this night, not now. The thin crescent moon had set before midnight, and only starlight illuminated the sky.

An hour later, the diminutive half-breed guide Mitch Boyer shook Varnum awake.[2] There was light in the sky, and the Crows wanted their chief of scouts on the hill. The hatless Lieutenant—he had lost his hat fording a stream along the way—and the scouts scrambled up through the buffalo grass to the top.

At the far edge of the bluff, the Crows pointed west, near the horizon, beyond the intervening ridges. They signed to the Arikaras—the two tribes spoke different languages—that they could see the Sioux camp. Charley Reynolds looked for a while, then peered through his field glasses a while longer. Finally, he nodded. Red Star, the youngest Arikara, nodded also; he could see the light smoke of morning cookfires, and beyond that black specks he thought were horses. White Man Runs Him, the young Crow who had led them here, even claimed he could distinguish some white horses among the herd.

Varnum shook his head. His eyes were inflamed from exhaustion and the hard, dusty ride. Even after an Arikara handed him a cheap spyglass, he could not make out anything resembling a village. *Look for worms crawling on the grass,* the scouts told him—that was the immense pony herd. He saw neither worms nor horses, nor the rising smoke they said betrayed the hundreds of cookfires of a large village. But the scouts and their trained eyes convinced him: less than twenty miles west, most likely in the valley of the Little Bighorn, was the large gathering of nontreaty Indians—"hostiles," as they were called by the U.S. government—that the six hundred men of the Seventh Cavalry had trailed for three days.

The scouts continued to scan the western horizon; perhaps the increasing light would aid visibility. Eventually, Varnum pulled out paper and pencil and scribbled a quick note about the discovery, folded it, and handed it to Crooked Horn. In turn, the older Arikara selected Red Star and Bull to carry the message back to camp. As the two saddled up, Crooked Horn pointed to the east, where smoke from the Seventh Cavalry's breakfast fires rose some eight miles away. Varnum could hear the anger in the Crows' voices: did the white officers think the Sioux were blind? But the smoke made the way back easier for Red Star, and he made good time on the creek-side trek. He carried the message himself—a great honor for the young man—and paid little attention to his companion. Soon Bull lagged far behind on his undersized pony.

When Red Star rode into camp a couple of hours later, his tribesman Stabbed met him, saying, "This is no small thing you have done." As the youth rode by, Stabbed turned and called out to the other scouts, waking them. Red Star dismounted, unsaddled, and told Bloody Knife, the half-Sioux, half-Arikara who was the General's favorite, of the big village to the west. The message delivered, Red Star looked up to see the one they called Son of the Morning Star heading his way along with Frederic Gerard, the interpreter.

George Armstrong Custer, it appeared, had found his Indians.

I

APPROACH

ONE

The Divine Injunction

Again, we come to the great law of right. The white race stood upon this undeveloped continent ready and willing to execute the Divine injunction, to replenish the earth and subdue it. . . . The Indian races were in the wrongful possession of a continent required by the superior right of the white man.

CHARLES BRYANT, *HISTORY OF THE GREAT MASSACRE BY THE SIOUX INDIANS* (1864)

Philip Henry Sheridan, tough, fearless, and tenacious, like the bulldog he resembled, faced a thorny problem in the fall of 1875—several thousand of them, actually.[1] A small contingent of Plains Indians, roaming the same lands they had occupied for generations, refused to bow to the manifest destiny of the nation he had so devoutly served for more than twenty years.

Sheridan's dilemma was a multifaceted one. From his headquarters in Chicago, he commanded the Division of the Missouri, by far the largest and most problematic military region in the country. It comprised the Great Plains and more—indeed, almost half the nation's territory, from the Canadian border to the tip of Texas, from Chicago to the Rockies. That expanse included most of the western states, five territories, a growing number of whites, and approximately 175,000 Indians of many different tribes. Over the past half century, most of those Indians had been herded onto reservations set aside for their use, both to keep them away from the westering whites and to facilitate the effort to make them, as much as possible, white people. The problems stemming from these relocations were monumental, though they were perceived by most whites as more humane, and considerably less expensive, than the alternative: war.

The U.S. government soon found out that it was one thing to assign tribes to reservations and quite another to keep them there—especially when the food rations and supplies promised them by treaty were delayed, stolen, inedible, or simply never delivered. What had been presented as a policy designed to prevent bloodshed soon became yet another rationale for it.

Sheridan's dilemma was shared by his immediate superior, General of the Army William Tecumseh Sherman, President Ulysses S. Grant, and several high-ranking members of Grant's administration. For years the two Generals had advocated all-out war on the Indians, with Sheridan, who had branded the uncooperative elements of the Plains tribes "hostiles," especially single-minded on the subject. But certain legal and moral niceties, which Sheridan found supremely irritating, precluded such belligerence. Grant's infernal "Peace Policy," which stressed humanitarian reforms before military intervention, was one. Treaties made with various Indian tribes were another. A third (and particularly galling) obstacle was that weak-kneed portion of the eastern intelligentsia whose naive, romantic view of "Lo the poor Indian" (a phrase from a poem by Alexander Pope, which led to the use of "Lo," with heavy frontier wit, as the generic name for the Indian) was formed by such unrealistic sources as the novels of James Fenimore Cooper and the poetry of Henry Wadsworth Longfellow.

But that November, at a high-level meeting at the White House, a bold solution to the Indian problem would be revealed.

UNTIL A FEW YEARS PREVIOUS, the Plains tribes had roamed at will. During the warmer months, they followed the buffalo, or bison, their source of food, clothing, shelter, and virtually every other material (and spiritual) need. Before the unforgiving winter swept down, they gathered up their stores of meat and then holed up in sheltered valleys along moving water to wait out the weather, as close to hibernation as a people could get. Until the new grass appeared in the spring, their ponies grew considerably thinner, surviving on the bark of riparian cottonwoods. The Indians, too, were vulnerable in winter, but they knew the *wasichus* (whites) were reluctant to launch any extended large-scale campaign then. A plains winter could turn deadly in a matter of hours, and heavy supply trains to feed men and mounts slowed a column even in the best of weather. The white soldiers had waged winter war once or twice, but that kind of campaign was difficult to muster and coordinate.

As emigrant travel through the heart of Sioux country increased, the monumental job of protecting incoming miners, farmers, ranchers, tradesmen, stockmen, railroad surveyors, lawmen, barbers, saloon owners, and others in an area of more than a million square miles fell to Sheridan, who commanded almost a third of the shrunken remnants of the victorious Federal army. More than two million men had served the Union during the Civil War, but more than half had mustered out a year after its end, and the regular army had gradually been trimmed to 25,000 enlisted men by the early 1870s. The nation was understandably tired of war, and a southern-controlled Congress found the idea of a large standing army distasteful. Undermanned, underpaid, undersupplied, undertrained, and underfed (a decade after Appomattox, Civil War–era hardtack was still being issued to frontier troops), the army Sheridan served faced a warrior culture that trained males from early childhood to fight, ride, and survive better than anyone else in the world. These people knew every hill and valley and water source in their wide land and eluded their pursuers with ease.

The job, Sheridan knew, had been easier, or at least simpler, a half century earlier. All that was necessary then was to push the Indians west, beyond "The Line"—wherever it was at the time.

The Line, which had existed almost since the white man had begun to penetrate the vastness to the west, was the result of more than three centuries of clashes between Europeans and the native population. Spanish conquistadors had clashed constantly with the native inhabitants of Florida during their many expeditions in search of gold and other treasures. In the epic Battle of Mabila in 1540, in the area later known as Alabama, Hernando de Soto and several hundred Spaniards had destroyed an entire army of thousands of Indians to the last man. To the north, in the swampy Tidewater region of Virginia, the two-hundred-village-strong Powhatan Confederacy had aided the ill-prepared English settlers at Jamestown since their arrival in 1607. The generous Indians had brought food to the starving colonists, given freely of their considerable agricultural knowledge, and generally made it possible for the English to survive the first few years of the settlement's existence. (They also taught the whites how to cultivate a cash crop called tobacco, which would enable the foundation and rapid rise of several more southern colonies.) Their generosity was not repaid in kind. The settlers were soon told by their superiors—who were, after all, directors of a for-profit joint-stock company—to do whatever it took to acquire all the land they could. Indian tempers grew short after a series of humiliations and attacks (no doubt aided and abetted by the Spaniards to the south), and fifteen years later they mounted a large-scale surprise assault on the colony that resulted in 347 English deaths in a matter of a few hours. The surviving colonists vowed revenge, and fifty years of almost constant eye-for-an-eye warfare followed. By 1671 the Virginia governor could report to London that "the Indians, our neighbours, are absolutely subjected, so that there is no fear in them"[2]—in no small part because there were only a few thousand of them left in the face of 40,000 Englishmen.

Over the next century, until the American Revolution, white men wrested North American territory from the Indians by treaty, sale, or sheer force—sometimes, truth be told, in concert with tribes seeking an advantage in Indian vs. Indian warfare.[3] From the very beginning, the Europeans, with few exceptions, had perceived America's native inhabitants as no more than savages—romantic, perhaps, in their primitiveness, and occasionally charming, or worthy of pity, but savages nonetheless. Whites had little respect for Indian cultures, their ways of life, or their concepts of government and landownership—the latter being particularly antithetical to white views. Indians did not develop the land, nor did they measure and mark what they owned; they simply did not understand land as private property. One could no more own the earth than the sky, the Indians reasoned. Rather, their land was commonly owned and used. To the ceaselessly toiling New World colonists, whose way of life was rooted in property ownership, this outlook was positively sacrilegious. This difference, more than anything else, would lead to the struggles between the two peoples.[4]

For the British, the end of the French and Indian War in 1763 resulted in huge additions of contested western territories ceded by the defeated French. But the excitement on the part of the colonials—who felt somewhat justifiably that they, not their distant British landlords, had "won" the new lands and should have the right to develop them—was dampened by George III's Royal Proclamation of 1763. The new law forbade settlement on "any Lands beyond the Heads or Sources of any of the Rivers which fall into the Atlantic Ocean from the West and Northwest," including the verdant Ohio Valley and all of the territory from the Ohio to the Mississippi rivers—roughly anything west of the Appalachians, from the southern limits of the province of Quebec in the north to Florida in the south. This area was referred to as "Indian territory," and all Englishmen were directed to abandon it immediately, regardless of title changes ("great Frauds and Abuses have been committed in purchasing Lands of the Indians . . . to the great Dissatisfaction of the said Indians"). All Indian peoples were declared to be under the protection of the King, and provisions for royal posts along the boundary were made.

The motivations behind the King's proclamation were more practical than humanitarian. Relations between the Indians and the colonists were already poor. Most of the Indian tribes had sided with the French during the war, and by placating the natives, the proclamation would, it was hoped, reduce the costs of defending the frontier. The boundary and the Indian preserve it established were meant to be temporary, the first step in a controlled, deliberate settlement plan. Five years later, after considerable colonist lobbying, the Indian Boundary Line was established farther to the west and formally agreed to in treaties with the Indians. But later that same year, due to a change in the British ministry, the Crown discontinued maintenance of the plan.[5] The increasingly restive colonists believed that the edict had another purpose: to keep them close to the eastern seaboard and easier to control—and away from the lucrative fur trade farther west.

The Proclamation of 1763 represented the last time that Indian sovereignty in the interior of the new land was considered important to the causes of peace and trade. Settlers and land speculators alike ignored the decree[6] and worked to open the western frontier and claim the Indian lands. Thirteen years later, two of the many grievances listed in the Declaration of Independence addressed the Crown's protection of "the merciless Indian savages, whose known rule of warfare, is an undistinguished destruction of all ages, sexes, and conditions" and royal resistance to "new Appropriations of Lands." (A year earlier, at the dawn of the American Revolution, the Continental Congress had instituted an Indian policy, largely to maintain peaceful relations during the ensuing war, though most eastern Indian tribes predictably sided with the British.) Once independence was established, however, the young Republic's first President, George Washington, sought to apply solid moral precepts to all dealings with the Indians: "The basis of our proceedings with the Indian nations," he said, "has been, and shall be *justice*."[7] The Northwest Ordinance of 1787 pledged goodwill and respect for the Indians' property, rights, and liberty. One of Washington's first acts as president was to issue the Proclamation of 1790, which forbade state or private-sector encroachments on all Indian lands guaranteed by treaty with the new country.[8] But while Washington believed in the sovereignty of Indian nations and tried hard to prevent outright confiscation, states and individuals alike ignored the federal law in order to satisfy the enormous demand for land dictated by an ever-increasing number of immigrants. As the new nation set to work exploring and settling beyond that short-lived Proclamation Line, land was acquired through bloodshed, treaty, crooked deals, or a mix of all three, and the absence of European powers meant that the Indians could not play one colonial interest against another.

The new century saw The Line move west quite a distance. After the Battle of Fallen Timbers in 1794, when General Anthony Wayne crushed Little Turtle's previously invincible Miami Indians,[9] the Ohio Valley was opened to settlers. Around 1803 President Thomas

Jefferson decided to relocate all eastern tribes beyond a Permanent Indian Frontier, extending from Minnesota to Louisiana west of the ninety-fifth meridian—a scheme made viable with the Louisiana Purchase that year—to an "Indian Country" of their own, far away from civilization. Reports from the explorations of Lewis and Clark (1804–1806) and Zebulon Pike (1806–1807) portrayed the lands beyond the Mississippi as mostly desert and "incapable of cultivation," unfit for white people. The idea of the "Great American Desert" was reinforced by Major Stephen H. Long's 1823 report, which first used that phrase and characterized the Great Plains as "almost wholly unfit for cultivation and of course uninhabitable by a people depending upon agriculture for their subsistence."[10] Just two years later, in 1825, President James Monroe began forcing tribes west of the Mississippi to this designated Permanent Indian Country.

The movement picked up full steam after the Indian Removal Act of 1830, passed soon after Andrew Jackson became President. The War of 1812 hero had caused an international incident when he had pursued Seminole Indians into Spanish Florida in 1818, and he still thought little of Indian sovereignty, referring to "the farce of treating with Indian tribes."[11] Jackson envisioned a confederacy of formerly southern Indians in the West that would one day take its place in the Union—after they became fully civilized, of course.[12] Some tribes went quietly, but others, chiefly the Seminoles in Florida and the Sauks and Foxes of Illinois, resisted mightily but futilely against the relentless whites. The pressure came from all directions. It mattered not a whit, for example, that the U.S. Supreme Court found the acts of the State of Georgia against the Cherokee nation unconstitutional and in violation of legally binding treaties; Jackson simply refused to support the decision.[13] The forced eviction of the Cherokees from their native Georgia and their march west to Indian Territory (present-day Oklahoma)—which reduced their population by more than 30 percent—came to be known as the Trail of Tears.[14] They and the rest of the so-called Five Civilized Tribes (the Cherokees, Chickasaws, Choctaws, Creeks, and Seminoles) lost all their land throughout the South and ended up on reservations in Indian Territory, as did many other vanquished tribes.

"Indian Country" had been officially defined by the Indian

Intercourse Act of 1834 as "all that part of the United States west of the Mississippi; and not within the states of Missouri and Louisiana, or the territory of Arkansas."[15] Congress decreed that white men were forbidden to travel beyond The Line without a license (though this and similar provisions in subsequent treaties were rarely, if ever, enforced),[16] and a line of forts was constructed to prevent whites from passing to the west and Indians from attacking to the east. In 1835 Jackson promised the Indians that their new lands would be forever "secured and guaranteed to them."[17] By 1840 Indian removal was largely complete.

Shortly thereafter, several nearly simultaneous events combined dramatically to change the situation. The first wagon train carrying white emigrants reached the Platte River in modern-day Nebraska in 1841, along what later became known as the Oregon Trail.[18] Many more followed, straight through the heart of the Lakotas' favorite hunting grounds. These first migrants over the Great Plains were greeted with more curiosity than hostility. The Indians allowed them through and traded with them for goods that the tribes quickly became dependent on; the Indians sometimes even guided and aided the migrants. Until the mid-1840s, there was only one reported death involving the overland migrants, and that was an Indian. But the number of annual emigrants rapidly increased more than tenfold, from 5,000 in 1845 to 55,000 in 1850. The wagon trains, and the settlers and miners they carried, drove away the buffalo and depleted the wood and grass along the way. The constant stream of invading whites also spread epidemic diseases such as cholera, smallpox, measles, and venereal diseases to the Indians, who had developed no immunity to these illnesses. Some tribes, particularly the Cheyennes and the friendly Mandans and Arikaras along the Missouri River, were decimated. The epidemics were viewed by some Plains Indians as the white man's black magic, and in response, depredations against the invaders began to occur more frequently.

The Mexican War of 1846–48 added most of the West and Southwest to the United States, and the settlement of the Oregon Territory boundary dispute with England clarified the country's holdings in the Northwest. In little more than fifty years, the original thirteen colonies hugging the Atlantic coast had become one of the largest nations on earth, stretching to the far Pacific in a wide swath from Canada to the Rio Grande. Settlement was already increasing when gold was found at Sutter's Mill in 1848, just after California had been acquired from Mexico. The rush toward the Pacific over the next few years triggered a boom in westward expansion, and the cry of manifest destiny—Americans' belief that they had a divine right to the undeveloped lands to the west, first enunciated in a New York newspaper, the *Democratic Review,* in 1845—provided a handy, Creator-approved rationalization for seizing Indian territories.[19] The Indian question became the Indian problem, and despite attempts by various interest groups to prevent widespread subjugation, one tribe after another was conquered: the Apaches and Navajos in the West, the Comanches, Kiowas, and Southern Cheyennes on the southern plains, and many smaller groups such as the Pitt River Indians and Yumas in California.

In the Northwest, stronger tribes such as the Yakimas and their allies put up a stiffer fight. The Yakima and Rogue River wars of 1854–1856 resulted in U.S. troops being rushed to the Oregon and Washington territories to stamp out resistance. Not until 1858 did forces led by General George Wright eradicate the threat through an unbeatable combination of superior firepower and widespread hangings of suspicious parties. Among his soldiers was a young Lieutenant fresh from West Point named Philip Sheridan.

The darkly handsome native of Ireland spent six years helping to tame the Cascade and Yakima Indians, and even learned the Chinook language, no doubt assisted by the pretty young Indian woman who kept his house, cooked for him, and shared his bed, a common arrangement at the time. The dashing dragoon courted several young white women in the area, but for about five years he lived with Sidnayoh, known to the whites as Frances.[20] She was the daughter of Chief Quately of the Klickitat tribe, allies of the Yakimas. But when Sheridan left in 1861 to defend the Union and make his name, he never returned to the Northwest. After the war, Sidnayoh, her brother, and two friends visited him in Washington. He never acknowledged or spoke of her, and in 1875 he married another woman, the daughter of a U.S. Army General.[21] Sheridan called the natives in the Northwest "miserable wretches" and seemed to care little that their sad plight was due to white malfeasance.[22] The man who would one day utter the phrase, "The only good Indians I ever saw were dead"—later modified to become the harder-hitting "The only good Indian is a dead Indian"—would espouse total war, and even extermination, against Sidnayoh's people.[23]

During the gold rush, fortune-seeking miners, settlers, and recently discharged soldiers with an itch for adventure surged west, and it was soon clear that The Line was not an effective solution to the Indian problem. As the 1850s dawned, an idea that had been implemented on a small scale in the East became U.S. government policy. Reservations—well-defined "colonies" of land set aside for the different Indian tribes, where they could learn how to farm, adapt to the ways of the whites, and, most important, keep out of the settlers' way—were established. The next two decades witnessed a frenzy of treaties as the government methodically seized—sometimes via forced agreements, other times via force alone—virtually all of the land it wanted. Treaties had been made almost since the first white colonists had disembarked in the East, but rarely of the scope and frequency seen from the 1850s on. In 1851 alone, treaties involving 139 tribes and bands were concluded.[24]

In 1851 at Fort Laramie in southeast Wyoming Territory, 10,000 Plains Indians representing nine major tribes, some of them mortal enemies, gathered at the behest of an honorable Indian agent, a former mountain man named Thomas Fitzpatrick. He had convinced Congress that funding such a conference was worthwhile, particularly if the resulting treaty could ensure the safety of emigrants traveling through the Indians' lands. The meeting constituted the greatest assemblage of Indians ever seen on the continent. Somehow, government negotiators convinced representatives of each tribe present to sign a treaty that set boundaries for their various hunting areas, established the right of the U.S. government to construct roads and forts in their territories, and set up a system of annuities to last fifty years. Using a shameful ploy that would be repeated in years to come, the U.S. Senate reduced the time span to ten years, without telling the Indians, before ratifying the treaty.

The Fort Laramie peace would be destroyed three years later in August 1854 by an incident involving a hotheaded young army Lieutenant named Grattan. When an emigrant wagon train outside the fort complained that a cow had been stolen and slaughtered by Indians (the animal was probably lame and may have been abandoned), Grattan set out with thirty men to arrest the culprit, hoping for a confrontation. He found the Indian camp and demanded that the Lakota warrior be turned over.

These Lakota Sioux (*Sioux* being a bastardized French word that they despised) were smart, fearless, and wealthy by the standards of the Plains tribes — rich with horses, buffalo skins, and even guns and ammunition. They had originated in the woodlands of Minnesota.[25] Their move westward had begun in the second half of the 1700s, abetted in no small part by the introduction at the dawn of that century of guns and horses. Both had been given to the Indians by whites — horses by the Spanish conquistadors and guns soon after by trappers and explorers. Horses increased the Indians' hunting range dramatically; guns did the same for their firepower. As the creeping tide of whites pushed eastern tribes, particularly the Chippewas, westward onto traditional Lakota hunting grounds, the Lakotas ranged steadily west, onto the Great Plains, beyond the Missouri River, in pursuit of buffalo, which were also leaving the eastern plains. Over the next century, this happy confluence of events made these latecomers to the plains rich and powerful, as they roamed north to Canada, land of the Great White Mother, and west almost to the Rockies. Along the way, they developed a warrior culture in which male status derived from war honors, and a society that revolved around the hunt and battle against neighboring peoples. The Lakotas fought every tribe they encountered and pushed most of them out of their ancestral lands, establishing a hegemony on the northern plains that would be challenged but not rivaled. Only the ferocious Cheyennes, after some initial clashes, became their allies sometime around 1826.

The Lakotas refused Lieutenant Grattan's demands after offering to pay for the cow, and the detail fired a volley into a group of Lakotas. Hundreds of nearby warriors observing the parley fell upon the detachment, and in the battle that followed, all of the soldiers were killed, including Grattan.

The punitive columns sent out in response to the killings put an end to the Fort Laramie peace. But many of the tribes, unwilling or unable to understand the abstract legal boundaries that prevented them from traveling where they pleased, had returned to intertribal warring even before that.[26] A year after Grattan's death, an army column led by General William S. Harney, dubbed "the Butcher" for the harsh way in which he dealt with the Indians, destroyed a Brulé camp and killed eighty-six men, women, and children. Harney's revenge delivered a message that the bluecoats were a force to be reckoned with.

Under the direction of the Bureau of Indian Affairs, organized in 1824 as part of the War Department and transferred to the new Department of the Interior in 1849, the treaties proved highly effective in gaining for the United States dubiously legal claims. Government officials became increasingly skilled at the bait and switch, the obfuscating explanation, the manipulation of pliable Indian chiefs partial to their cause—anything to gain the ostensibly legal cession of lands.

At Fort Wise, Colorado, in 1861, Cheyenne Indians met with federal commissioners to discuss their territorial boundaries. The Cheyennes were not nearly as populous as the Lakotas—cholera and smallpox had ravaged them—but they made up for their small numbers with an unequaled fearlessness, ferocity, and pride. They warred with almost as many tribes as the Lakotas, though they had formed truces with some, such as the Kiowas and Comanches to the south. They also got along well with the sedentary, agricultural river tribes of the Missouri—the Arikaras, Mandans, and Hidatsas. But their only long-term allies were the Arapahos, a smaller, more peaceful tribe that nevertheless fought alongside the Cheyennes in many battles. The two had camped together and supported each other for several decades, and there was much intermarriage between them.

Like the Lakotas, the Cheyennes were recent immigrants to the plains, having lived along the Missouri for many years and in Minnesota long before that. They, too, had followed the buffalo out onto the vast expanses of the plains soon after acquiring horses and guns. Their lands lay between the Platte and Arkansas rivers, all the way to the Rockies. Several large-scale attacks by the U.S. Army had reduced their numbers but hardened their resolve.

The Cheyennes agreed to a reservation south of the Arkansas River but in the process gave up virtually all the lands recognized as theirs in 1851. Shockingly, only six of the forty-four Southern Cheyenne and Southern Arapaho chiefs took part in the talks. Many of their brethren were furious with them for having "touched the pen" and refused to be bound by the treaty.

This was not an entirely uncommon phenomenon. The U.S. government never seemed to understand that the "chiefs" who put pen to paper rarely represented their tribes completely, in the way of traditional white representatives. Indians who did not sign a particular treaty felt no compunction to follow the treaty's dictates, much as the government expected them to. Since the government needed someone to sign each treaty, in some cases government representatives anointed a chief if one did not exist, which usually resulted in tribal strife. And treaty chiefs often misunderstood what they had signed, further complicating compliance. Faulty interpreters also ensured failure.[27]

Compounding the U.S. government's deceitful tactics was the fact that its adherence to the treaties was arbitrary, even when the agreements were changed to the benefit of the whites after the tribal representatives had signed them. Along with the treaties, a system of annuities was developed, guaranteeing regular (usually annual) payments of money, food, and supplies, including arms and ammunition, designed to discourage the buffalo-hunting lifestyle and result in the purchase of additional Indian land over a period of years. Traders and agents hired to control annuity payments were seldom incorrupt. They took advantage of the Indians in many ways, from charging them with made-up debts for extended credit and delivering inferior goods to shorting them during the distribution of supplies— sometimes with the help of equally corrupt chiefs. The fact that these men were appointed by members of Congress initiated a widespread patronage-for-payment arrangement that further ensured an under-the-table and unfair distribution of funds. With regard to the Santee, or Dakota, Sioux, for example, little of the money promised to them by the terms of the 1851 treaty was ever paid. Most of the Plains Indians took poorly to their new farming life, if they took to it at all. The sedentary agricultural life seemed unnatural to them, and to make matters worse, many of the agency lands were not well suited for agriculture. The only alternative to starvation was to leave the reservation to hunt for game, which they did in great numbers.

Most treaties were violated almost immediately, on both sides. But for the most part, the situation was tolerable, as long as the Indians were powerful enough to respect and major warfare was avoided. Thomas Fitzpatrick, the principled Indian agent, decried the system as "the legalized murder of a whole nation"[28] as early as 1853, but it was already too late. The treaties had accomplished their main goals: the seizure of Indian lands under quasi-legal agreements, the avoidance of widespread bloodshed, and the removal of the Indians to modest-size reservations as far away from emigrant routes as possible. Subsequently, via steamboats up the Missouri and other waterways, and railroads and wagons along regular routes and trails across the plains, a never-ending flow of settlers penetrated the land of every tribe in the West.

ONE SUNDAY in August 1862, in the frontier state of Minnesota, four young Dakota Sioux warriors returning home from a hunting trip worked themselves into a fury in an argument over some hen's eggs spotted on a white man's farm. The Dakotas were starving; that year's annuities were overdue—again—although the agency warehouses were full of food and other supplies. The Dakotas had already suffered through a decade of disruption, having ceded 24 million acres of their ancestral hunting grounds for $1.6 million and the promise of cash annuities. One unsympathetic storekeeper, Andrew Myrick, summarized the feelings of many whites when he advised the Indians to eat grass or their own dung.[29]

The warriors shot and killed the farmer, his wife, his daughter, and two neighbors. When they returned to their village and confessed what they had done, the Dakota chiefs decided after a long night's deliberation to proceed with an all-out, preemptive war and pressured Little Crow, an elderly peace chief—who regularly attended a nearby Episcopal church and wore white men's clothes—to lead them. A surprise attack on a nearby settlement at dawn the next morning ignited a frenzy of massacres in the area. By the end of the day, four hundred settlers had been brutally murdered. Before the uprising was over, more than eight hundred lay dead. Myrick's lifeless body was later found outside his store, his bloody mouth stuffed with grass.

The Minnesota Massacre, as it was called, was the first sign of large-scale, organized resistance to the relentless white incursions into the Indians' lands and the indignities heaped upon them under the reservation system. State and national authorities responded immediately. General John Pope, in charge of the Department of the Missouri, vowed, "It is my purpose to utterly exterminate the Sioux. . . . They are to be treated as maniacs or wild beasts." (In later years, Pope's views toward the Indians would soften, but his words were an accurate reflection of the views of most whites along the frontier.) A month later, General Henry Sibley and 1,500 troops defeated the Santees at Wood Lake. The most recalcitrant among the Indians escaped to the west into Dakota Territory and north into Canada, but 2,000 were captured, and 38 of them were hanged the day after Christmas in 1862. (The death toll would have been much higher — 307 had been sentenced to death — had President Abraham Lincoln not intervened and commuted all the sentences except for those of proven rapists and murderers.) In addition, the Dakotas paid for their actions with the loss of their strip of land on the Minnesota River, and they were moved to another reservation farther west, on the Missouri River.

But the seed had been sown. Sioux resistance spread westward with the fleeing Dakota warriors, and the next few years saw a steady increase in hostilities and depredations throughout the Great Plains. The endless stream of emigrants (300,000 during the Civil War alone)[30] up the Missouri River and along the main trails west — the Oregon, Bozeman, Bridger, and Santa Fe — angered the Sioux, who fought back the only way they knew how, with scattered raids throughout the area.

During the Civil War, army regulars on the frontier were moved to theaters of war back east, and volunteer militia took their place. These westerners were personally motivated to wreak revenge, and at dawn on November 29, 1864, they got their chance. Led by a former Methodist minister, Colonel John M. Chivington, the Third Colorado

Cavalry militia regiment surrounded and fell upon peace chief Black Kettle's sleeping Cheyenne village of about one hundred lodges on Sand Creek, 175 miles southeast of Denver in Colorado Territory. The fanatical Chivington had ordered women and children destroyed—"Nits make lice," he pointed out—and his seven hundred volunteers enthusiastically obeyed orders, chasing down, killing, and then carving up the Cheyennes, who had believed themselves to be under army protection. By day's end, approximately 150 Indians, most of them women and children, were dead, many of them hideously mutilated. Chivington's men later marched triumphantly through the streets of Denver, proudly displaying Cheyenne body parts.

White settlers in the area applauded and made Chivington a hero. Meanwhile, the Indian survivors made their way to other Cheyenne camps, and word of the massacre spread quickly across the plains. Over the next few months, enraged Cheyenne, Sioux, and Arapaho warriors raided towns, stage stations, ranches, and wagon trains, burning, looting, and killing wherever they could. Then, in late winter, they moved north to join their kinsmen in the Powder River country—that area between the Black Hills and the Bighorn Mountains which the Lakota considered theirs, though in fact they had wrested it from the Crows only a few decades before.

The end of the Civil War saw thousands more volunteer troops shifted to the frontier and the debacle known as the Powder River campaign of 1865, a largely fruitless effort to clean out the marauding Indians. That foray into the Sioux homeland by 6,000 soldiers in three columns stirred up the entire Lakota nation for good—particularly a tall, charismatic Oglala chief named Red Cloud, who had earned his reputation by collecting more than eighty coups from the time he was sixteen. (A warrior counted coup when he touched an opponent with his hand or a coup stick. Such bold acts were a measure of one's bravery and were tallied carefully.)

Over the next few years, the cunning and unrelenting Red Cloud rained havoc on any whites foolish enough to enter the Powder River country. Through the heart of this country ran the Bozeman Trail, the best route to the Montana gold mines. An attempted parley at Fort Laramie in June 1866 fell flat when the whites' talk of peace was revealed to be just that—talk. In the middle of the parley, a battalion of regular U.S. Army infantry marched into the post on their way to build more forts on the Bozeman. Red Cloud and almost all the Sioux promptly decided to leave after warning the whites to stay off the trail. Only the Brulé Sioux, led by the opportunistic Spotted Tail, and some minor chiefs signed the treaty, which was good enough for the government—any signature or mark was deemed legally binding. But the document was effectively meaningless, since the signees had no stake in the Powder River lands.

As the soldiers began building three forts along the Bozeman, they were constantly harassed by Red Cloud's warriors. In December 1866, a large force of Oglalas, Minneconjous, Cheyennes, Hunkpapas, and even two friendly Crows[31] bore down on Fort Phil Kearny. On December 21, they lured William J. Fetterman, a young Captain with little regard for the Indians' fighting ability, out of the fort with an eighty-man detail made up mostly of raw recruits. The soldiers charged over a long hill in pursuit of a small band of Indians led by an audacious young warrior. At the most opportune moment, the warrior let out a war whoop, and hundreds of braves hidden in the gullies and woods along the trail swarmed upon the stunned bluecoats. In less than an hour, it was all over. Few of the Indians had guns; most of them relied on bows and arrows, lances, stone clubs, and knives, and most of the fighting was at close range. The Sioux lost twelve warriors,[32] but Fetterman and every one of his men were killed. Earlier, Fetterman had been heard boasting, "Give me eighty men and I would ride through the whole Sioux nation."[33]

Legend has it that the bold war chief who lured Fetterman to his death was a young Sioux named Crazy Horse. One writer would later call him "the strange man of the Oglalas." It was an appropriate description, for Crazy Horse went his own way.

This warrior-mystic was born in the late fall of 1840 near Bear Butte, outside modern-day Sturgis, South Dakota, on the northern edge of the Black Hills.[34] His father, also named Crazy Horse, was an Oglala holy man; his mother, Rattle Blanket Woman, a Minneconjou.[35] His actual birth name was Light Hair, for his fine, sandy brown locks. His light hair, combined with his light complexion and sharp features, caused more than one settler to mistake him for a white child. An uncle died when the boy was about four, and his mother, grief-stricken, committed suicide. More than most Lakotas, Crazy Horse's life would be colored by the loss of those close to him.

When Crazy Horse was a boy, he went by the name of Curly, and he was known for his shy personality. Like all young Lakota males, he was regaled with stories and songs that celebrated the cult of the warrior and progressed from paternal instruction and childhood games that emphasized war skills to buffalo hunts and war parties, during which older boys assisted seasoned fighters with relatively safe duties such as tending the packhorses and equipment. Curly became an expert with horses at an early age, and as an adolescent he began a close relationship with a renowned warrior named Hump, who may have been an uncle. Hump became Curly's mentor, and soon the two were nearly inseparable.

As a young man, Curly was introverted and somewhat antisocial, to the point that others in his tribe considered him peculiar. Almost all Lakotas danced and sang socially, but Curly never would. "He never spoke in council," said a longtime friend, He Dog. "He was a very quiet man except when there was fighting."[36] He took to the life of a warrior naturally. When he came of age and displayed conspicuous bravery in a fight with an enemy tribe, his father passed on his own name, Crazy Horse, to his son and took the name Worm for himself.

When fully grown, Crazy Horse was five feet seven inches tall,[37] slight, and wiry. He had a narrow face, a straight nose, and "black eyes that hardly ever looked straight at a man," according to a close friend.[38] When the wife of a white scout encountered him in 1877, she thought him "a very handsome young man,"[39] despite a noticeable scar on his left cheek.

Throughout the late 1850s and early 1860s, in dozens of raids and fights against enemy tribes such as the Crows and the Shoshones in and around the Powder River country, Crazy Horse proved his worth as a warrior. His reputation was so secure that sometimes he would drop back and allow others to count coup; once he did this for his younger brother, Little Hawk. He always led his men from the front, and unlike most Lakotas, he dismounted to fire his rifle. He used good judgment and planned soundly. In battle he eschewed ostentatious dress. Instead, he wore a simple eagle feather upside down on the back of his head, a cotton shirt and breechcloth, and moccasins. His waist-length hair was braided down both sides. With one finger, he would draw a zigzag streak of red earth down the center of his face. As a good-luck talisman, he wore a small white stone in a bag under his left arm. Whether due to this amulet or not, Crazy Horse was rarely injured, though nine horses were shot out from under him in battle. Only once was he badly wounded, in the leg, and that was before he began carrying the stone.

Most of the warfare Crazy Horse participated in during this time was intertribal, but that changed in the mid-1860s. The opening of the Bozeman Trail and the army's three forts made it clear to Crazy Horse and several thousand other Lakotas that they would never walk the white man's road. For most of the decade, any soldiers or travelers along the Bozeman ran the risk of attack by a Lakota war party.

When the news of Fetterman's defeat reached the East, there was an immediate clamor for retaliation, particularly in the army. General William T. Sherman, Civil War hero and now commander of all military forces on the Great Plains, called for total extermination, if necessary. But a burgeoning peace movement, which had gained full steam after the Sand Creek Massacre and which comprised many humanitarians who had campaigned against slavery and were now turning their attention to the plight of the Indians, lobbied for a less bellicose solution. Their efforts, combined with the realization of the precarious positions of the three isolated forts and the fact that hostilities had reduced the traffic on the Bozeman to almost nothing, paid off. After much saber rattling and throat clearing in Congress, and an abortive campaign on the plains, President Andrew Johnson called for a peace commission to convene in the fall of 1867 at Medicine Lodge Creek, Kansas (with the southern Plains tribes), and in April 1868 at Fort Laramie (with the northern Plains tribes). Sherman was one of three generals named to the commission.

The discussions at Medicine Lodge led to the permanent establishment of many reservations in Indian Territory, as, for the first time, the idea of one big Indian reservation was abandoned. Plans also were made for the education and assimilation of the Indians into white culture via agency schools, the encouragement of farming and Christianity, and eventually individual landownership. At Fort Laramie, the government bowed to the dictates of the resolute Red Cloud, agreeing to abandon the three forts along the Bozeman and to concede the country to the Powder River tribes. Only when the soldiers had left and the forts were put to the torch did Red Cloud put pen to paper. The trail itself was closed, and no whites were allowed in this territory.

Red Cloud's was the only war with the United States that western Indians ever won. Even then, the victory proved illusory. The Fort Laramie Treaty of 1868 established the Great Sioux Reservation west of the Missouri in Dakota Territory, and Red Cloud and most of his followers soon became, in effect, reservation Indians. Now the government could more easily control them, which was the point. An "unceded territory" outside the reservation, where nonreservation Indians could hunt "so long as the buffalo may range thereon in such numbers to justify the chase," had been granted to the Sioux, but in classic treaty double-talk, another article dictated that the Indians were not allowed to "occupy" those lands. (Sherman was reassured by his fellow commissioners that the buffalo would not last long enough for the clause to be a problem.)[40] Thus, the very territory that Red Cloud and his countrymen had fought so hard to defend — the hunting grounds along the Powder and Bighorn rivers — would only momentarily remain theirs.

The U.S. government pledged to provide supplies and annuities while the tribes adjusted to their new homes. The treaty also allowed the construction of a railroad to the Pacific — and virtually anything else the government decided was necessary — through the heart of Lakota country. Some of the treaty's terms were vague, confusing, and somewhat contradictory, and only a few Indians at best understood them.[41] In a few years, the unceded territory especially would prove to be a sticking point for the U.S. government, when the rights of tribes there — particularly the nonreservation bands who lived and hunted there year-round and had never signed any agreements — clashed with the inexorable white tide working its way west. And the treaty's essential ineffectiveness was underlined less than four months after its proclamation by a general order from Sheridan, at Sherman's direction, that any Sioux found outside the reservation would be considered "hostile."[42] (Sherman, after returning east, wrote to his brother with chilling clarity: "The Indian war on the plains need simply amount to this. We have now selected and provided reservations for all, off the great roads. All who cling to their old hunting grounds are hostile and will remain so till killed off.")[43]

For a few years, a shaky peace held sway over the northern plains. At the same time, a stunning cavalry victory on the Washita River and the subsequent roundup of most of the warring Cheyennes largely eliminated hostilities to the south. The peace-seeking atmosphere in the East was augmented by the election of General Ulysses S. Grant, the architect of the Union victory in the Civil War. Grant felt sympathy for the Indians' plight. He told a friend that "as a young lieutenant, he had been much thrown among the Indians, and had seen the unjust treatment they had received at the hands of the white men."[44] In 1853 he had written, "The whole race would be harmless and peacable if they were not put upon by the whites."[45] Soon after taking office in 1869, he halted the army's offensives against the Indians and implemented his own Peace Policy.

Grant's policy consisted chiefly of moving all of the nomadic tribes onto reservations away from white expansion and attempting to civilize them. The difference was that now the government would attempt to do so nicely—"conquer with kindness," as officials phrased it—without resorting to the brute force usually used. In an attempt to eliminate the rampant corruption in the Bureau of Indian Affairs, Grant's administration hired churchmen, mostly Quakers, as Indian agents.[46]

The War Department disagreed vociferously with Grant's plan and proposed keeping the peace by instilling fear in the Indians. They wanted to wage war at the first sign of hostilities, since dead Indians would require no annuities—and thus no crooked traders and contractors.[47] For a while, the two policies worked well in tandem, at least on the southern plains. Indeed, the combination of humane treatment of reservation Indians and hard war on recalcitrants had tamed most of the southern tribes.[48] In the north, however, it was a different story.

*   *   *

IN 1871, LARGELY DUE TO A SQUABBLE between the Senate and the House,[49] Congress forbade the making of any more Indian treaties. As an alternative, President Grant was forced to make "executive agreements" with the tribes, which would be ratified by both houses of Congress. These were essentially treaties under another name, but this time the House had a say in their approval. The most unfortunate result of the new agreement system was the change in attitude toward the Indian nations. No longer would they be considered sovereign powers, but orphans or wards to be treated as any domestic group of Americans might. It was a subtle but important difference, and the government would seek to justify its actions in the following years.

It also became increasingly clear that filling agency posts with religious men would not stem the tide of corruption. The few safeguards fortifying the Peace Policy were circumnavigated fairly easily, and even some of the churchmen were unable to resist the lure of easy fortunes.[50] By the final years of Grant's presidency, the Bureau of Indian Affairs was marked by as much scandal as the rest of his administration, and his well-intentioned Peace Policy was completely discredited.

Into the early 1870s, the northern plains remained relatively quiet and peaceful. But the Bureau of Indian Affairs' turpitude steadily increased the natives' ire, and starving warriors stepped up their raiding. In addition to the lack of annuities and the poor quality of the rations delivered, two transcontinental railroads, the Union Pacific and the Kansas Pacific, had recently been completed and carried even more emigrants into Indian lands. Even worse, the great buffalo herds were almost gone, scared off by the railroads and then killed off—gradually at first and then more quickly. Sherman and Sheridan's troops aided the annihilation, visiting the same "total war" of food-supply destruction upon the Plains Indians as they had upon the Confederacy.[51] Hide hunters slaughtered more than a million buffalo a year in the early 1870s. As the plains were emptied of this great animal, whites and Indians alike broke treaties. For their part, the nonreservation Sioux and Cheyennes retreated into the Powder River country and rarely ventured out of it, limiting their attacks primarily to white incursions into their lands and occasional cattle raids.

The fuse to the northern plains powder keg was lit in a remote area of the Great Sioux Reservation in western Dakota Territory. The Indians named this place Paha Sapa, "Hills That Are Black," for the peculiar dark green coloring of the craggy rocks that encircled it and the pine trees that packed its slopes. Rumors of gold in the Black Hills had circulated for decades, including stories of Indians appearing at nearby trading posts with large nuggets and gold dust. Then, in 1857, an army expedition detailed to explore the region discovered gold "in valuable quantities," findings corroborated two years later by another military force.[52] After the Panic of 1873 (the country's most serious financial crisis up to that point), desperate men turned miners began sneaking into the Black Hills. Far from discouraging them, the army decided to send a reconnaissance expedition to find the best location for a fort, an idea Sheridan had been pushing for a few years. Two prospectors and four newspaper correspondents accompanied the large column. The Black Hills Expedition of 1874 was led by Lieutenant Colonel George Armstrong Custer, the colorful wartime cavalry hero who had become one of Sheridan's—and the nation's—favorite Plains Indian fighters.

Custer's column comprised 110 supply wagons, hundreds of cattle, a battery of Gatling guns, 10 companies of the Seventh Cavalry, 2 companies of infantry, almost 100 Indian scouts, interpreters, and scientific observers, and even a photographer—more than a thousand men in all. One of the strongest military forces to roam out onto the Great Plains, it wound its way southwest from Fort Abraham Lincoln, on the Missouri River five miles south of Bismarck, Dakota Territory, into the Black Hills three hundred miles away. The army expected—and perhaps hoped—to meet Indian resistance. Technically, according to the terms of the Fort Laramie Treaty of 1868, the United States was within its rights—Article II allowed "such officers, agents, and employees of the government as may be authorized to enter upon Indian reservations in discharge of duties enjoined by law"—but it is highly doubtful that the Indians had ever understood the terms to allow such a massive military force. The year before, Custer and most of his regiment had accompanied a railroad survey party along the Yellowstone River and deep into Montana Territory, and they had twice skirmished with the Sioux. But this summer there was little sign of the Sioux, although the Black Hills, their ancestral hunting grounds, were sacred to them. As a result, the expedition evolved into a three-week picnic. Still, Custer kept up his customary brisk pace, and his reports featured a rapturous if repetitious litany of verdant valleys, crystal-clear streams, picturesque campsites, abundant game, and—of considerably more interest to the nation—gold. Custer had requested a geologist for the trip, and two miners were hired at his expense.[53] That spring he had written to his good friend the renowned tragedian Lawrence Barrett, that "for many years it has been believed from statements made by the Indians that the Black Hills are rich in minerals," and there is little doubt which mineral he meant.[54] The Dakota territorial legislature, after all, had officially petitioned Congress more than once for a scientific survey of the Black Hills, chiefly to determine the truth of the reports of gold.[55]

In his first dispatch, Custer reported that both of his prospectors had discovered the metal "in paying quantities," but he judiciously tempered his remarks. He warned the newspapermen who accompanied him against exaggeration,[56] although soon after striking gold, he sent a well-dressed, soft-spoken scout and legendary hunter named "Lonesome" Charley Reynolds through 150 miles of Indian country with the news. Custer's second report stated that "men without former experience in mining have discovered [gold] at an expense of but little time or labor," a claim that the hordes of out-of-work men still reeling from the Panic of 1873 found irresistible.

By the time Custer returned to Fort Lincoln, his restraint had disappeared. He told a reporter there that the Black Hills would rival "the richest regions in Colorado," and other officers with the expedition and all of the news correspondents supported his claims.[57] (Later he would call for the extinguishment of Sioux title to the region "for military reasons" and declare that the Indians had no real need for the Black Hills.)[58] When these reports of gold were played up by newspapers from coast to coast—and especially after a follow-up expedition the next summer "confirmed in every particular" Custer's dispatch[59]—men from all over the country headed for the Hills, precipitating the biggest gold rush since the one in California in 1849.

Through most of 1875, only a few hundred miners could be found digging into the sacred land of the Sioux. By the spring of 1876, however, there were more than 10,000. The army was directed to expel trespassers, but there weren't nearly enough troops for the job, although they did give it a try. Since the punishment was usually no more than expulsion, many of the miners escorted from the Black Hills merely turned around and headed back. The soldiers sympathized with the prospectors, and some of Custer's men at Fort Lincoln even deserted to join them.

Since the military was unable to control the region, some people in the government began to consider another option: buy the Black Hills from their owners. After all, jobs were scarce, other western mining fields had cooled, and an infusion of gold would be good for the precarious economy. The Panic of 1873 had ushered in a depression, and bankruptcies were frequent, crime rates up, and farm prices down, in no small part due to one of the most severe grasshopper plagues ever to hit the Midwest. Hundreds of thousands of out-of-work men, many of them Civil War veterans, were desperate for employment. There was a clamor from both the public and many in the press to open the Black Hills, as unrestrained newspaper accounts embellished and trumpeted potential fortunes, even going so far as to claim that Black Hills gold could pay off the national debt, then more than $2 million.[60]

There was one slight problem. The Black Hills belonged to the Lakota Sioux, not only by birthright but also by treaty, and they did not want to sell their land. Red Cloud and Spotted Tail, the two most prominent peace chiefs, made that clear when they were summoned to Washington in the spring of 1875 to negotiate. They remained adamant in the face of veiled threats that included the withdrawal of food rations at their agencies and suggestions that the government might not continue to keep miners out of the region.

Red Cloud and Spotted Tail returned home without signing an agreement, but that September a commission was sent west to negotiate a lease. About 5,000 Lakotas gathered to meet with them near Red Cloud Agency in northern Nebraska. The hard-core nontreaty faction led by Crazy Horse and the Hunkpapa Lakota Sitting Bull did not attend, but they sent word that the Black Hills were not for sale and would be defended to the death. By this time, however,

Red Cloud and Spotted Tail could see that they had no choice—the whites would take what they wanted, deal or no deal—and they were ready to strike a bargain. When the United States refused to meet their price—$70 million—negotiations broke down. Some of the nontreaty Indians from the north then made their belligerent presence known. A Minneconjou named Lone Horn rode up and delivered a fiery speech against some of the Lakotas for trying to sell his country.[61] They succeeded in stirring up enough trouble that the commission members barely escaped with their lives. "The Commission were the gladdest people to get away from that part of the country that had ever visited there," observed General George Crook.[62] They returned to Washington in high dudgeon, recommending that Congress simply fix a fair value on the region and "then notify the Sioux nation of its conclusions."[63]

Thus, President Grant in 1875 found himself on the horns of a dilemma. What was good for the nation—and virtually demanded by a desperate public, particularly in the frontier states and territories—would constitute a direct repudiation of the high moral ground underlying his Peace Policy. How could he justify such a brazen seizure of lands solemnly ceded to the Lakotas by treaty?

The answer came in November. Sheridan had been in San Francisco on a five-month honeymoon with his new wife when he was summoned to an executive meeting at the White House. He took a train east, picking up General Crook in Omaha.[64] On November 3, the two met with the President and his top advisers on Indian affairs. Grant was persuaded—or decided, no one knows for sure—to follow a new course. The army was secretly ordered to no longer bar any settlers from entering or remaining in the Black Hills. To protect U.S. citizens from the sure-to-be-furious Lakotas, Grant would rely on an edict built on tenuous moral and legal grounds: the government would maintain that the 1868 treaty had been abrogated by the Sioux. Of course, some depredations had occurred, but Sheridan had reported that 1874 had seen relatively few Indian problems, and the Commissioner of Indian affairs had proclaimed that the Sioux had been more peaceful in 1875 than in any year for more than a decade.[65] Nevertheless, a report issued a week after the November 3 meeting by a Bureau of Indian Affairs inspector cited various trumped-up accusations and smoothly worded falsehoods regarding Indian violations. The inspector concluded: "The true policy, in my judgement, is to send troops against them in the winter, the sooner the better, and *whip* them into subjection."

The army had been itching for an excuse to make all-out war on the last unyielding Indians on the plains, but their hands had been tied by the Peace Policy and by the Bureau of Indian Affairs. Here was justification for Sheridan's winter campaign and the seizure of the Black Hills all wrapped up in one tidy report. Still, a further coloring of legality was needed. An ultimatum would be delivered to all the "wild" Lakota bands in the Yellowstone and Powder river country. Unless they left their hunting grounds in the unceded territory and arrived at the Great Sioux Reservation by January 31, 1876, they would be declared hostile. The U.S. government would then make war on them until they returned to the reservation to learn the white man's ways or were exterminated.[66]

Runners were sent from the Sioux agencies out to the hunting bands near the end of December, but by then winter had set in on the northern plains. Even if the Lakotas had wanted to come in to the agencies, it would have been impossible to do so before the ultimatum expired. The weather, their weakened ponies, and their women and children precluded their compliance. "It was very cold," one Oglala warrior said later, "and many of our people and ponies would have died in the snow. We were in our own country and doing no harm."[67] Furthermore, most Lakotas had little desire to live on the reservation, especially this winter, when worse than usual ration deliveries had led to famine and supreme distrust of any promise from the whites. Even Sheridan admitted that the ultimatum "will in all probability be regarded as a good joke by the Indians."[68]

So the deadline came and went, but only a few small bands arrived at the agencies. On February 1, 1876, the Interior Department announced that since the nontreaty Sioux had not complied with the ultimatum, they were now considered hostile and would be turned over to the army "for such action as the Secretary of War might deem proper under the circumstances."[69] Preparations for an immediate winter campaign moved forward quickly, built around a three-pronged attack to encircle and capture or destroy the hostiles.

All the while, whites continued to sweep across the country, beyond the Missouri River and the Great Plains, into and through the valleys bordering the Rocky Mountains, over the continent's spine to the Pacific: settlers, miners, and adventurers; men, women, and children, tearing up the country, scaring off the buffalo and other game, chopping down the forests, destroying the grass with their cattle and other livestock, and desecrating the most sacred Indian places. Only a few tribes of the northern plains stood against them—the Lakotas, Cheyennes, and Arapahos—and only a hard-line contingent of each tribe, around 3,000 Indians (no more than 800 warriors), were unwilling to abandon the only way of life they had ever known.

To be sure, these three tribes did not present a united front. Most of their people lived most of the year on reservations and were not interested in war—or at least not a year-round war. They had become too dependent on the white man and his wares, or too tired of fighting him. But their situation was far more fluid than was generally known. Quite a few of the agency Indians would spend the winter on their reservations, drawing supplies, arms, and ammunition, and then journey out in the spring, spending half the year following the buffalo and raiding their traditional Indian enemies in quest of battle honors, which led to prestige and status. That had been their life for generations, and the *wasichu* threat to their homelands and their way of life would not interrupt it.

AGAINST THESE SUPERB guerrilla fighters defending their lives, lands, families, and way of life, Sheridan could muster less than 3,000 U.S. soldiers in his two northernmost military areas: the Departments of Dakota and the Platte.[70] This tiny force, ill trained and badly equipped by a miserly Congress, was scattered across the frontier in dozens of garrisons large and small. Regiments spent little time together in training or maneuvers, and most soldiers spent little or no time improving their execrable marksmanship or devising tactics suited to fighting Indians. Most did not care. Aside from an educated officer corps—many of whom were graduates of West Point—the enlisted ranks were not composed of the best and the brightest. "All the really valuable survivors of the volunteer army had returned to civil life," wrote one historian. "Only the malingerers, the bounty-jumpers, the draft-sneaks and the worthless remained. These, with the scum of the cities and frontier settlements, constituted more than half of the rank and file on the plains."[71]

Another major problem—or blessing, given these sentiments—was desertion. As many as a third of the enlisted men in the 1870s took the "grand bounce" before settling into their new lives in frontier garrisons. The reasons were many: poor pay ($13 a month), inferior food, poor sanitation, harsh discipline, immediate danger, and, not to be underestimated, sheer boredom. Another temptation was gold. Many of the enlistees were unemployed and unemployable in the hard times following the Panic of 1873, and some of them, particularly those recruited in the big cities of the East, saw enlistment as transportation west. Once there, they skedaddled to the mining regions to make their fortunes.

To lead these troops, Sheridan could call on a handful of former Civil War Generals who were vying for the few top-ranking positions in the shrunken postwar army. Chief among them were George Crook, Nelson Miles, John Pope, John Gibbon, Eugene Carr, Wesley Merritt, and Ranald Mackenzie. And then there was his favorite, the man who had been his peerless troubleshooter and attack dog ("Sheridan's pet," said some) during the latter days of the Civil War; the man who had blazed the "Thieves' Road" through the Black Hills, the heart of the Lakota holy country: George Armstrong Custer.

TWO

"The Boy General of the Golden Lock"

G. A. Custer, Lieutenant-Colonel Seventh Cavalry, *is young,* very *brave, even to rashness, a good trait for a cavalry officer.*

WILLIAM T. SHERMAN

George Armstrong Custer's first charge as a General, on the second day of the Battle of Gettysburg, was a disaster, and he barely managed to escape with his hide (though not his horse). His final charge, against a large Plains Indian village on the banks of a winding river, was also calamitous. Between the two, he led a charmed life, attributable by some to chance—"Custer's luck," as he and both friends and enemies termed it—and by others to good fortune's true components: preparation, analysis, confidence, and decisive action.

His detractors claimed that he loved nothing better than a charge. They were right. They also accused him of recklessness, of acting without thought or deliberation. They were wrong about that. Custer had an uncanny ability to process what he saw, what he heard, and what he knew—the intelligence available in a situation—and then make a considered decision in an incredibly short amount of time. "He was certainly the model of a light cavalry officer," said one of General Wesley Merritt's staff members, "quick in observation, clear in judgment, and resolute and determined in execution."[1] Time and again in the last two years of the Civil War, after his promotion to

Brigadier General, his subordinate officers observed "the Boy General" decide on a split-second course of action that turned out to be the right thing to do at the time. It did not take more than a charge or two to make a believer out of nearly anyone. By war's end, only a few skeptics remained, and they tended to be resentful officers who were older and less successful. The men who served under Custer swore by him and claimed that they would follow him into hell itself.

FROM THE BEGINNING of his life, Custer never lacked for confidence. Its source, as with anyone, can only be guessed at — what a man is born with, what he develops, what he is accorded — but a good portion of Custer's share of that attribute likely was his upbringing. A middle child of a large family, he was loved, encouraged, and admired by his parents and all of his siblings.

Custer was born on December 5, 1839, in the western Ohio hamlet of New Rumley to Emmanuel Custer and his new wife, Maria Kirkpatrick. Both Emmanuel and Maria had been married before (both of their spouses had passed away), and each had brought young children to the marriage. Their first two children conceived together died soon after birth, so George Armstrong — or "Autie," as his family called him after his own toddler mispronunciation of his middle name — became the instant darling of the blended family and his father's constant companion.[2] Emmanuel Custer was a blacksmith of German stock, from Maryland originally, and a staunch Jacksonian Democrat who loved to talk politics. He and his selfless wife added four more children after Armstrong, and all of them mixed together as one mutually supportive clan. The family that lived in the plain, two-story, clapboard house was a rambunctious, happy one in which horseplay and practical jokes were as common as kisses and conveyed the same message. Armstrong became the new brood's leader, though his younger brother Tom was always to be found nearby.[3] Half sister Lydia Ann, fourteen years his senior, helped her frail mother raise the bunch, and young Autie became especially close to her.

Emmanuel Custer attended New Rumley militia meetings religiously — he had been elected Captain[4] — and often brought along little Armstrong. Clad in a soldier's uniform made by his mother, Autie would march along with the militia, his father beaming as he went through the manual of arms with his toy musket on his shoulder. The elder Custer had in mind a clergyman's life for his son, but Armstrong never cottoned to that dream.[5] Like most young boys of the day, he was raised on tales of chivalry and knights of old, and thus dreamed of a soldier's glory.

The family was far from well-to-do, but Emmanuel was a hardworking provider, and he eventually saved enough to sell his shop and buy an eighty-acre farm when Armstrong was nine. Between chores and school, Armstrong honed his riding skills. A cousin remembered that "he would show what a good horseman he was by riding standing up on the horse and running it around in a circle in the barnyard."[6] At twelve, after finishing the customary six years of basic lessons, Armstrong was sent to live with Lydia, who had married David Reed and moved to Monroe, Michigan, 120 miles northwest. She was lonely for her family, and the Custers would be hard-pressed to pay for any further schooling for Autie. While in Michigan, he attended the well-regarded Stebbins Academy for Boys. He was no scholar, preferring mischief and practical jokes, but he learned to read well enough to devour popular novels in class during lessons, his head buried under his raised desk lid.[7] He was usually the leader of any disruptive behavior, though seldom the one to be punished for it.

In 1855, when Armstrong was fifteen, the Stebbins Academy closed, and he returned to the family farm in New Rumley. Intelligent and curious, he was reluctant to become a farmer. He continued his education at a local school designed to train teachers, and before he was sixteen, he accepted a teaching position at a township seventy-five miles away while continuing his studies. He also began courting young women, particularly Mollie Holland, with whose family he boarded for a while.

In the spring of 1856, Custer tried to obtain an appointment to the U.S. Military Academy at West Point, New York. Not only would this serve his fondness for the military, but the academy's scholastic reputation was excellent, and he would likely be able to land a good position in the private sector after his service. Then sixteen, he wrote to John A. Bingham, the local Congressman, who had the power to make such appointments, usually as rewards for political patronage. Custer had been raised by his father as a die-hard Democrat, and Bingham was a Republican, a member of the new party barely two years old. Armstrong boldly—or foolishly, or both—made his political affiliation clear in his letter. Fortunately for him, Mollie Holland's father was determined to put a stop to his daughter's romance, and he likely interceded on Custer's behalf with Bingham, who happened to be his friend. The Congressman requested the appointment, and it was granted in January 1857. Armstrong's father gave his permission, borrowed the $200 required for admission, and in June, with the rest of the family, saw him off on a train bound for New York.

SINCE ITS FOUNDING in 1802, the U.S. Military Academy at West Point had seen its share of lollygaggers. Armstrong Custer would put them all to shame.

The education a young man received at the Point was as good as or better than that received at most of the young country's universities. The Corps of Engineers ran the school, and it turned out top engineers—essential to an expanding nation. But the academy's primary goal was to build military officers out of the rough materials provided. To that end, discipline and drill reigned, and even slight transgressions of the countless rules and codes earned cadets demerits. These demerits, or "skins," were closely tabulated. If a cadet earned two hundred a year, he would probably be expelled. Custer, whose curly golden hair earned him the nickname "Fanny," quickly began compiling skins at a record rate. Most of them were for seemingly insignificant infractions, such as tardiness, an untidy uniform, inattention, or boyish conduct. Others were the result of mischief making, and several southern boys in his circle (most of his close acquaintances were from the South) were his coconspirators. One, a Virginia-born Texan named Thomas Rosser, was likely his best friend.

Though the cause of much annoyance to his instructors, Custer soon became one of the most popular cadets ever to attend the academy. His sunny disposition and love of a good laugh proved magnetic, and though some judged him an unlikely soldier, "we all loved him," said one classmate.[8] Custer ignored rules and school-work and reveled in after-dark adventures, some to Benny Havens's tavern in a small town a mile away. He became a genius at managing his demerits; when he approached the limit, he would straighten up until term's end. He would also walk endless extra-duty guard tours to remove some minor breaches from his record. Still, by the time he graduated in 1861, he possessed more skins than anyone else in his class. Somewhat inexplicably, he avoided expulsion. When thirty-three cadets were declared academically deficient in January 1861, they were allowed to take a reexamination; only Custer was rein-stated. Though Custer gained a reputation for cleverness, it was only for his inventive pranks; his grades were almost never better than average and frequently worse. (One day in Spanish class, he asked the instructor to translate "class is dismissed" into Spanish. When the teacher complied, Custer led his classmates out of the room.) But he read voraciously—mostly martial romances, Sir Walter Scott's Waverley novels, and James Fenimore Cooper's Leatherstocking Tales—and began a lifelong habit of unceasing correspondence with friends and family that reflected his steady improvement as a writer. (He particularly enjoyed writing poetry to girlfriends back home, for he had acquired a healthy fondness for the fairer sex, judg-ing from the fact that he was treated for gonorrhea in August 1859 after returning to the Point from a two-month furlough.)[9]

The school's rigorous curriculum offered classes in all of the major subjects, such as mathematics, English, history, art, philoso-phy, and geography, and was supplemented by French, Spanish, eth-ics, astronomy, dancing, and much more. Military subjects ranged from infantry, artillery, and cavalry tactics to ordnance, gunnery, fortification, swordsmanship, and horsemanship (at which Custer excelled). Despite his mediocre grades, some of the learning stuck with him, and Armstrong was aware of its importance. To his older sister he wrote, "I would not leave this place for any amount of money, for I would rather have a good education and no money than a fortune and be ignorant."[10] Overall, however, he scraped by, noting later, "My career as a cadet had but little to commend it to the study of those who came after me, unless as an example to be carefully avoided." He seemed content with his class rank, and almost proud of it. He told one classmate that there were only two positions in a class worth noting, and since he was not interested in the "head," he had aspired to the "foot."

Armstrong's strongest attribute was a valuable one: more than anything else, he excelled at making friends. Upon arriving in 1859, one plebe remembered hearing the crowd around him shout, "Here comes Custer!" and turning to see the object of everyone's attention—a slim fellow with a gangly walk. "He was beyond a doubt the most popular man in his class," remembered one friend at the Point. One of his roommates called him "one of the best-hearted and cleverest men that I ever knew," but added, "The great difficulty is that he is too clever for his own good."[11]

After Abraham Lincoln's election to the presidency in November 1860, several cadets departed the Point. Even more resigned when South Carolina seceded on December 20, 1860, to be followed by six other states (Georgia, Florida, Alabama, Mississippi, Louisiana, and Texas) in the next few weeks. In February 1861, the Confederate States of America was formed, and that prompted the departure of most of the remaining southerners, who returned to their home states to take up positions in volunteer units. In all, thirty-two cadets separated from the academy because of the war, almost half of the graduating class.[12] Custer, still a staunch Democrat like his father, sympathized with his southern classmates, but he would remain loyal to the oath he had taken more than four years earlier and to his home state, Ohio. When Lincoln was inaugurated on March 4, 1861, hostilities seemed imminent. Six weeks later, Confederate cannon bombarded Fort Sumter. The President issued a call for 75,000 volunteers, and the nation entered a civil war.

At that time, the Point's course of studies lasted for five years. The class of 1861 graduated several weeks ahead of schedule in early May. Custer's class of 1862 was supposed to graduate thirteen months later, but there was a great demand for trained officers, even untested ones, to drill the tens of thousands of enlistees. Most believed this would be a short war, maybe even nothing more than one decisive battle. As a result, it was decided that the class of 1862's course work would be accelerated and its members graduated as soon as possible. On May 6, 1861, they began an abbreviated slate of classes that compressed an entire year's worth of instruction into little more than a month. The exhausted cadets studied in and out of the classroom almost around the clock, but their hard work was rewarded: they graduated on June 24 as the second class of 1861. There were thirty-four graduates. Final examinations put George Armstrong Custer at the bottom of his class. He earned his worst grades in cavalry tactics.[13]

Earlier, Custer had written to the governor of Ohio offering his service in the volunteer army, hoping for a temporary transfer from the regular army and a higher rank.[14] Nothing had come of that, and now, appointed a Second Lieutenant along with his classmates, he awaited his orders at the Point as the rest of his class left for their assignments. After a brief delay — he was court-martialed and reprimanded for not breaking up a fight while he was officer of the day — he received his orders and hopped a train for Washington on July 18. He stopped in New York just long enough to buy a uniform, a saber, and a revolver, and he reached the capital two days later, to find the city seething with activity. Arriving at the Adjutant General's office at the War Department for his orders, he found he was assigned to the Second Cavalry, which was with General Irvin McDowell's army in Centreville, Virginia. The army was located just east of a steep-banked creek called Bull Run, the likely location of an impending battle.

The young Lieutenant found a horse in Washington, a near-impossible task (in the process of searching stables, he met an enlisted man he knew from West Point who had an extra mount), and rode most of the night twenty-five miles out to Centreville, joining his unit before dawn. The Second Cavalry spent the next day assigned to support artillery batteries in the rear. From a hill, Custer watched an apparent Yankee victory quickly become a rout when the Rebels, aided by fresh reinforcements in midafternoon, outflanked the Union army. All through the rainy night, he retreated with the rest of the bluecoats back to Washington. It was suddenly clear that the war would last longer than one battle.

Custer's company saw no action that day. Although he would

later admit to the same fears that almost every soldier feels in his first engagement, Custer comported himself well while directing his men in a rearguard action and was cited for bravery. By all accounts, it appears he took to war like a duck to water. His regiment remained on duty in Washington, and he saw little of the hostilities that continued throughout the year. But he was not idle. West Point graduates were in great demand as staff officers, and Custer served as an aide to several minor Generals, learning leadership skills at their sides. Still, paperwork was not what Custer wanted, and throughout 1862 he volunteered for every chance for combat he could. He participated in the occasional skirmish and reconnaissance mission, and several commendations followed. In May 1862, his fearlessness in crossing a river to scout the enemy's lines impressed Major General George B. McClellan, commander of the Army of the Potomac. Little Mac offered him a spot on his staff as aide-de-camp and a brevet, or temporary rank, of Captain.

Custer seized the opportunity and quickly made himself indispensable to McClellan, whom he had worshipped from afar. The young Captain thrived in his new responsibilities, which sometimes involved acting as his commander's representative with units in combat and gathering and relaying intelligence, often from reconnaissance he conducted himself. It was valuable experience for the twenty-two-year-old. But when McClellan was relieved of his command less than six months later on November 7, Custer was left without a position. When winter conditions put an end to large-scale military operations on both sides, he spent most of that winter back in Monroe, flirting with the young ladies of the town and having a grand old time. He also met a dark-haired beauty named Elizabeth "Libbie" Bacon, the daughter of a judge who disapproved of the attentions paid her by a lowly blacksmith's son. From their first meeting on Thanksgiving Day, Armstrong was entranced by her combination of sophistication, vivacity, and sensuousness. He began courting her the next day and continued through the holidays. Libbie was initially cool—she had plenty of better-appointed suitors—but she quickly warmed to him in spite of, or perhaps because of, her father's opposition. Before the end of the year, they talked of marriage.

When he returned to the Army of the Potomac in the spring of 1863—his rank reverted to Lieutenant—the recent Union defeat at Fredericksburg had sparked another change in command. Major General Joseph Hooker had taken over from Major General Ambrose Burnside. Hooker would not last long either, but he did make some important organizational changes, particularly in regard to the cavalry. Up to this point, the Union horsemen had been ill used, performing chiefly in small units as couriers, escorts, and sentries for the infantry, with the occasional short-range reconnaissance mission thrown in. The Rebel cavalry—led by the daring James Ewell Brown "Jeb" Stuart—had literally run rings around the Federal army. Operating as large strike forces, guided by daring and initiative, Southern cavalry units seemed to roam the Virginia countryside at will. But Brigadier General Alfred Pleasonton, a martinet with seventeen years' dragoon experience, believed that, with the proper organization, training, and leadership, the Yankees could hold their own and more, and he recommended a unified cavalry corps comprising several divisions.

Hooker took his advice in February 1863 and appointed Pleasonton to lead one of three divisions. Pleasonton took Custer onto his staff, and the exacting older man and the eager young one got along well, with Custer again making himself invaluable to a General. In several battles that spring, he established himself as a natural combat leader. Through several scrapes and skirmishes, as well as the occasional raid, he furthered his reputation for fearlessness and having a nose for battle. "He was always in the fight, no matter where it was," recalled Custer's orderly, Joseph Fought.[15]

Pleasonton was given command of the entire cavalry on June 22 (meaning Custer also gained a grade) and decided he needed a few young brigade leaders to inject some vigor into his corps—"officers with the proper dash to command Cavalry." He picked three young officers who had served on his staff: Custer, Elon Farnsworth, and Wesley Merritt. On June 28, the Army of the Potomac's new chief, Major General George G. Meade, appointed them Brigadier Generals. While Pleasonton's other two choices might have been, at least in part, politically motivated, Custer's promotion could only have been the result of merit—and no small amount of affection.[16]

During the first two years of the war, while on the staffs of these general officers and a few others, Custer had absorbed firsthand the elements of command. From each he had learned something valuable about leadership. He had gained confidence in his ability to gather intelligence, assess it accurately and quickly, intuitively make the right decision, and then implement the proper action—and make sure the job got done. "He was true as steel," remembered an officer who served through the war with him. "He was depended upon for great things because he was dependable."[17] He had also learned, particularly from Pleasonton and McClellan, the value of tooting one's own horn, whether it was in a personal letter, an official report, or an account given to a newspaperman.[18] Finally, he had come to love battle as few other men did. Armstrong Custer felt truly happy, truly alive, only in war. He had found his calling, and he was damned good at it.[19]

Very few Generals led their men into battle, preferring to direct from the rear. Custer had an idea that if his men saw their commanding officer share the danger, they would fight even harder. Upon receiving his promotion, Brevet Brigadier General Custer and his bugler-adjutant pieced together a nonregulation uniform that was ridiculed by some: "a velveteen jacket with five gold loops on each sleeve, and a sailor shirt with a very large collar that he got from a gunboat on the James. The shirt was dark blue, and with it he wore a conspicuous red tie—top boots, a soft hat, Confederate, that he had picked up on the field, and his hair was long and in curls almost to his shoulders."[20] Custer's chief intention, he would explain, was conspicuousness: he wanted his men always to know where he was. Soon the men of his command began copying his red tie and even his long hair.

The twenty-three-year-old Custer (he was the youngest General in the Federal army for a while) barely had time to learn his subalterns' names before entering the crucible of Gettysburg just a few days after his appointment. Custer's division commander was an excitable little West Point classmate named Judson Kilpatrick, nicknamed by his troopers "Kill-Cavalry" for the senseless charges he often ordered his men into. Kilpatrick sent Custer's brigade to charge an unscouted Rebel position on the second day of the battle, south of

Hunterstown. Custer, eager to impress his new command, trotted to the front of the foremost company, turned to his men, and declared that he would lead them. They charged down a road and were met with furious fire. Custer's horse was hit, and he was thrown to the ground, stunned. A Private galloped up, shot a Rebel aiming his carbine at Custer, pulled his commander onto his own horse, and carried him to safety. Custer's first charge as a brigadier was a failure, but he had shown his mettle to his men.[21]

The next morning, the third day of the battle, General Robert E. Lee sent Stuart's feared cavalry—his "Invincibles"—north around the Union's right flank in an attempt to wreak havoc on its center rear while General George Pickett made his ill-advised charge on their front. In the area were the gun batteries that were doing significant damage to Pickett's advance. As part of the Union line was about to be overrun, Custer led the Seventh Michigan Regiment against Stuart's troopers with the cry, "Come on, you Wolverines!" His men drove the Rebels back until Confederate reinforcements arrived. Custer led his men back to safety before Stuart sent a wide formation of eight regiments forward in intimidating fashion. There was only one intact regiment, the First Michigan, and Custer again galloped to the head of the column, gave the same rallying cry, and led his men straight into the center of the eight Southern regiments. The resulting collision was like a train wreck, riders and their mounts crashing into and over each other, sabers clashing and pistols blasting at short range, bluecoats from either flank jumping in to help break the Rebel charge. Stuart withdrew, no doubt wondering who the fearless opponent in blue velveteen was. It was the first time the Federal horsemen had stopped Stuart's cavalry and held the field.

Triumph followed triumph for the Boy General and his Michigan Brigade, which quickly earned a reputation as the best brigade in the cavalry corps. "I believe more than ever in Destiny," Custer wrote a few weeks after Gettysburg.[22] He had good reason to do so. Pleasonton remarked in private that he thought Custer was "the best cavalry General in the world."[23] Culpeper, Brandy Station, Yellow Tavern, Haw's Shop, Cold Harbor, Trevilian Station—these battles and other lesser engagements honed Custer's tactical and leadership skills to a sharp edge. They also gained for him no small degree of fame. His style of dress and command, and his victories, made great copy, and his likeness began showing up in newspapers and weekly magazines. He was becoming famous.

He also became a husband. Over the previous year, he had mounted a full-scale charge on Libbie Bacon and her father and step-mother. Libbie had decided quickly that she loved him; her parents took a bit longer. Through occasional visits and constant correspondence, Armstrong had gotten one and all to agree to a marriage, and on February 9, 1864, Armstrong and Libbie tied the knot in a grand wedding that included hundreds of guests. After a honeymoon trip that included stops at West Point, New York City, and Washington, D.C., the General returned to his troops, accompanied by his bride. Until war's end, she followed him as closely as possible and stayed with him at his brigade headquarters whenever she could. Libbie was often the only officer's wife with the command, granted special dispensation by Philip Sheridan, who was inordinately fond of Custer, whom he called "youngster."[24]

Thanks to yet another round of command changes, the pugnacious Sheridan was now in charge of the cavalry. In the spring of 1864, Ulysses S. Grant was appointed General in Chief of the Federal army. He had been extraordinarily successful in the western theater, conquering Vicksburg and Chattanooga, and seemed to be the leader Lincoln had been looking for since the war's beginning. Grant came east and brought with him several of his favorite officers. One of them was a stocky man who wore a perpetual scowl — a tremendous leader, inspiring and audacious, whose men loved him. He had led infantry troops in the West, but now Grant put him in charge of the Cavalry Corps, relieving Pleasonton, much to Custer's dismay. But Custer liked his new commander immediately, for Philip Henry Sheridan was an Ohio man after his own heart. The son of a laborer, Sheridan had battled his way through West Point as an Irish Catholic outsider several years before Custer. The squatty Sheridan and the taller Custer were physically distinct, but both were mercurial, emotional, and demanding of the men they led.

In August 1864, Grant gave Sheridan command of his own Army of the Shenandoah and ordered him to crush the Confederate troops under the ill-tempered General Jubal Early that had been threatening Washington. Sheridan's 40,000 troops were to destroy Early's forces and wage total war on Virginia's fertile Shenandoah Valley, the "Breadbasket of the Confederacy," by burning or seizing all crops, livestock, and stores—anything that could feed the Rebel army. "Such as cannot be consumed, destroy," his orders read. As part of his command, Sheridan was given the First Cavalry Division, which included Custer's brigade, and the cavalrymen embarked from Harpers Ferry, West Virginia, on August 9, 1864. Over the next ten weeks, Sheridan's army brought the conflict home to the valley's civilian inhabitants, causing severe damage to their homes, crops, buildings, animals, and morale. "It was a phase of warfare we had not seen before," a Federal cavalryman later recalled.[25] The new doctrine would ultimately win the war for the Union.

The Army of the Shenandoah fought a series of running battles with Early's meager forces. The Rebels held their own for a few weeks, but after a two-week respite, the hostilities heated up in mid-September. At Winchester, Virginia, on September 19, Custer respectfully refused an order by Sheridan to make a charge into a heavily manned enemy position. When the Rebel units shifted, he led an attack that broke a superior infantry force and drove it from the field. The victory was his swan song with the Wolverines; at the end of the month, Sheridan rewarded him with a division of his own. Both the enlisted men and the officers of the Michigan Brigade were stunned and despairing at the news, and 472 of them signed a petition requesting transfers.[26] But Custer's new command, the Third Cavalry Division, was elated, and many of its members donned red neckties in his honor.

Once the Federals had driven the Rebels out of the Shenandoah Valley, Sheridan began withdrawing his forces north through the valley, the cavalry acting as a rear guard, burning and pillaging a swath thirty miles wide as they went. A fresh force of Rebel cavalry led by Custer's old West Point friend Tom Rosser nipped at the Union army's heels as it retreated. Custer begged to fully engage the Confederates, and Sheridan granted his wish. At Tom's Brook, the first major battle in which Custer led his new command, two brigades of the Third turned and attacked a larger division led by Rosser, smashing it so hard that the Union cavalry pursued the Rebels for twenty miles.

Ten days later, on the foggy morning of October 19, a brilliant surprise attack by Early's forces on the unsuspecting Union army's camp at Cedar Creek routed three entire divisions. Custer's Third Division, on the army's right flank, was one of the few commands that did not retreat in disarray. The men of his division and one other held firm until Sheridan, after his storied eleven-mile ride from Winchester the following morning, rallied the Union troops and swept the field. Custer's division delivered the death blow, and the battle essentially ended the fighting in the valley. It was clear to all that the Union cavalry had fought in the forefront, and to reward Custer and Merritt, his best cavalry leaders (Farnsworth had died at Gettysburg), Sheridan recommended their promotion to Brevet Major Generals. The brevets were awarded a few days later.

Through the rest of the year, the cavalry stayed in the field, busy with raids and reconnaissance in the valley against the never-say-die Rosser and his Laurel Brigade. The Texan gained a measure of revenge on December 21, 1864, when he surprised the Third Division at Lacey's Springs in a predawn attack after Custer had pulled his pickets in early, after reveille. The division regrouped quickly and counterattacked with minimal damages, but a shaken Custer—who had barely escaped from the inn that he had commandeered—ordered the Third to retreat back down the valley to Winchester. After criticism and questioning from Sheridan, Custer would twist the facts in his official report to avoid taking responsibility—a common tactic among Civil War commanders, and one that Custer would occasionally use in the future.[27]

In late February 1865, after a long, cold winter of work, the cavalry rode south to join up with Grant and the Army of the Potomac in their hammering of the remnants of General Robert E. Lee's Army of Northern Virginia, still entrenched in Petersburg and Richmond, Virginia. At Waynesboro in early March, the Third overwhelmed Early's forces and routed them, destroying what was left of the little Rebel army. A few weeks later, the cavalry reached Grant outside Petersburg. The Union commander gave them the task of riding around Lee's army and capturing his supply and escape routes, the Richmond & Danville and Southside railroads. The half-starved

Southerners could ill afford that blow, so Lee sent almost 20,000 men to block the Union troops. The two armies met at a crossroads named Five Forks. Over the previous two days, Custer's division had been detailed to guard and help the baggage train through thick mud, but he moved his men quickly up to the front just in time to bolster the sagging Union line. The next day, the Third played a large part in a furious Federal victory. The loss of many thousands of troops and the two railroads broke the back of the Confederacy.

The following day, Lee's Rebels made a run for North Carolina in an attempt to reach General Joseph Johnston's Confederate army there. Grant sent Sheridan's cavalry to head them off. Over the next eight days, Lee did his best to evade the Federals, avoiding major confrontations whenever possible, but his ragged troops were starving, exhausted, and dispirited, and the fight had largely gone out of them. On April 6, one wing of the Rebel army made a stand at Sayler's Creek but ultimately gave in to the constant pounding by the superior Union force. As usual, Custer and his Red Tie Boys, as they were now known, were in the thick of things.

Two days later, it was all over. At Appomattox Courthouse, Custer's Third Division seized four trains of Rebel munitions and supplies. The next morning, after some skirmishing, a single Confederate officer rode up to Custer waving a white towel. Lee wanted an end to the hostilities. That afternoon Lee met Grant at Wilmer McLean's house at Appomattox to negotiate the surrender. Outside, Custer wandered among the Confederate officers, talking with those he knew from the Point. Sheridan paid McLean $20 for the small table on which the conditions of surrender had been signed and gave it to Custer as a gift for Libbie. In a note to her he wrote, "There is scarcely an individual in our service who has contributed more to bring about this desirable result than your gallant husband."[28]

The war was finally over, and everyone in the Union army was thankful, including Custer, scarecrow gaunt after the final exhausting campaign—or at least so he told Libbie: "Thank God PEACE is at hand," he wrote her two days later.[29] But on some level, he must have been disappointed. He had rhapsodized in his letters about the glory of war, and it must have been clear to him after four years of almost constant fighting that he was a born warrior. Never again would he be as happy as when he was leading devoted soldiers into battle for a great cause. Of the Union's Generals, only Grant, Sherman, and Sheridan were thought of more highly by the American public. Among Custer's peers, only the jealous would whisper that such a meteoric rise was undeserved. There was still plenty of boy in him, but he had matured. He seemed to many, inside the army and out, to be the very model of noble knighthood. Custer's praise and concern for those serving under him filled his reports—to the virtual exclusion of any feats of his own. His men responded in kind, and anecdotes of his gallantry and modesty became the stuff of legend. After Custer's death, one soldier who had been shot in the leg and helped off the field by the Boy General summed up the admiration his men felt for their commander when he said, "I would have given my right arm to save his life—aye, I would have died in his place!"[30]

Custer spent much of the next year in Texas and other parts of the South with a cavalry division assigned to Reconstruction duty—and the not-so-hidden job of ostentatiously displaying America's martial might for the edification of Emperor Maximilian of Mexico, whose French puppet masters had violated the Monroe Doctrine by putting him in power. Custer's troopers were Northerners, volunteer remnants of the great Army of the Republic, and they could not have cared less for the idea of another campaign, however justified it might be. They had done their jobs and saved the Union, and now they just wanted to go home, as most of their fellow soldiers had. And they wanted no part of the harsh West Point disciplinary tactics that Custer believed in, including floggings, which had been abolished by the army in 1861, and even the execution of deserters, whose numbers were sky-high. Rations that were slow in coming or of inferior quality exacerbated the situation. After a grueling 150-mile march in August from Alexandria, Louisiana, to Hempstead, Texas, things got even worse. Most of the enlisted men in the division, and some of their officers, hated Custer. The commanding officer who had seemed so solicitous of his men during the war now seemed strikingly indifferent to their well-being. Sheridan encouraged Custer's strict discipline, and the local populace appreciated his efforts, but it earned him a reputation as a tyrant—a reputation that would linger, deservedly or not, to the end of his days and beyond.[31]

MAJOR GENERAL GEORGE ARMSTRONG CUSTER'S volunteer commission expired in January 1866, and he was mustered out of the army at the ripe old age of twenty-six. He and Libbie returned to Washington. By virtue of brevet — an honorary promotion granted to reward battlefield heroics or meritorious service, but all too often the result of staff connections — almost every officer in the service above the level of Lieutenant had commanded a regiment or battalion in the Civil War. The end of the war had seen virtually every one of them reduced to their regular army rank, usually several notches lower. Even Custer, one of the most accomplished Generals, could not avoid this fate. He was now only a cavalry Captain in the regular army, trying to decide what to do with the rest of his life. He explored civilian options, including several business opportunities in New York, with money and the means of earning it uppermost in his mind. Friends urged him to consider politics, but he decided against that after spending an unpleasant several weeks on President Andrew Johnson's campaign tour. Back in Washington, he seriously considered a lucrative offer from the Mexican government of a high position in the Mexican army. General Grant endorsed a year's leave of absence to pursue this opportunity, but Custer was still an officer in the U.S. Army, and the Secretary of State denied permission. To accept the offer, Custer would have to resign his commission, and who knew how long the job in Mexico would last? He turned down the post, his future still uncertain.

In July 1866, Congress decided to expand the mounted service and approved the creation of four more cavalry regiments bound for the western frontier. Custer was appointed Lieutenant Colonel of the Seventh Cavalry. (He had been offered the colonelcy of one of the two new black regiments, the Ninth, but had turned it down. He had specifically requested a command of white troops.)[32] Though no longer a General, he had a command again, since the regiment's Colonel would remain on detached duty. And he would see combat once more, this time against the original inhabitants of the continent.

OVER THE NEXT DECADE, Custer became the army's best-known — and, to many Americans of the time, best — Indian fighter. He fought Indians on both the southern and northern plains, though not nearly as often as his reputation suggested. He led the Seventh in only one major battle before 1876, and after that never engaged in more than a skirmish until the last day of his life. But a fawning press, still in love with the Boy General, embraced his new image, for no one looked better sitting on a horse, in a frontier scout's buckskins, than the tall, ramrod-straight soldier with the golden locks — and no one was more accommodating. Custer seemed to have an intuitive grasp of the importance of celebrity. On his frequent leaves of absence, which often stretched to months, he socialized with prominent actors, writers, politicians, businessmen, other military men, and the occasional society belle, for his wife did not always accompany him on his trips to New York or Washington. Newspapers and magazines responded enthusiastically. And of course there was Custer's own scribbling: the former schoolteacher had become a good writer, fashioning a clean style that was far less ornate than that of the typical scribe of the period. Before long, articles detailing his frontier experiences began appearing under a nom de plume, and by 1872 he was publishing regularly under his own name.

For these reasons and others, he was in the public eye more often than his counterparts, and — his ambition, ego, and confidence boundless — he enjoyed his celebrity enormously. There were other fine fighting leaders in the field, all former Union Generals, including George Crook, Eugene Carr, Ranald Mackenzie, and Nelson Miles. But none captured the fancy of the American public like George Armstrong Custer.

In October 1866, Custer and his wife traveled to Fort Riley, Kansas, to organize and train his new regiment. The regiment's commanding officer, the older Colonel Andrew Jackson Smith, was soon given an administrative position (in the small postwar army, a lot of doubling up occurred), as was his successor, Colonel Samuel D. Sturgis. For the next decade, Custer assumed de facto command of the Seventh. Several of his officers were men who continued to serve with him to the last day of his life. All of his senior officers and most of his Lieutenants were Civil War veterans. Most were older than he, and drinking men, as was a good portion of the "Old Army" of the next few decades.

Captain Frederick Benteen, five years older, was a cantankerous, moonfaced Virginian who was much like Custer in several ways— brave to a fault, confident in his opinions, and possessed of a healthy libido.[33] Brevetted a Colonel for bravery in the war, he had served under General James H. Wilson, a bitter rival of Custer's. Wilson had recently recommended Benteen for an appointment in the regular army,[34] and the grateful Captain planned to name his firstborn son after his former commanding officer (CO). Not surprisingly, Benteen took an instant dislike to Custer upon their first meeting in January 1867, put off by what he perceived to be the bluster and braggadocio of a press-created peacock.[35] What Benteen saw as a tactless put-down of Wilson during their initial conversation likely didn't help matters. It galled the Virginian to lead a mere company when others he felt were inferior to him led regiments, and that bitterness would infect the entire Seventh. (Benteen, ironically, had refused a Major's post in the Ninth Cavalry, the same black regiment Custer had refused to command.)

Benteen liked his whiskey, but he was not a particularly heavy drinker. Some of the other officers made up for his measured approach. Captain Myles Keogh, an Irish soldier of fortune, had served in the Pope's Irish Battalion before coming to America and joining the Union army. He and Custer had served together briefly on McClellan's staff. Handsome, brave, and a bit of a dandy, he drank too much and occasionally became melancholy, though he largely kept that trait hidden. As tough a critic as the abstemious Libbie Custer found the Irishman charming, even when he was in his cups.[36] Keogh was a more than capable officer, and most of the men in his troop appreciated his colorful antics. Captain Thomas Weir was another steady imbiber, but as a University of Michigan graduate, he was prized by many of the Seventh's officers and their wives for his engaging conversation. He became a good friend of Custer's and, some would later claim, even more intimate with Libbie.[37]

These were the civilized drinkers; there were plenty worse. One officer would even kill himself within a few months in a fit of delirium tremens.[38] The rare individual who did not imbibe at all was often the subject of ridicule among his fellow troopers. Whiskey was also one of the chief "medicines" prescribed by the army's doctors. Payday on a post was usually the scene of unbridled drunkenness, with virtually every trooper not on duty thoroughly inebriated and penniless in no time.[39]

The Seventh's job was to establish the young country's presence on the frontier and to protect settlers and railroad crews pushing westward. Early in the spring of 1867, the Seventh joined General Winfield Hancock's 1,400-man expedition of foot, horse, and artillery troops. The westward-heading campaign was intended as a show of force and to punish any raiding Indians, if necessary. But the effort was an abject failure, compounded by the heavy-handed Hancock's mishandling of a potential peace parley when he ordered a deserted Sioux-Cheyenne village destroyed. The result was increased hostilities and months of futile Indian chasing throughout western Kansas, Colorado, and Nebraska.[40]

This was Custer's first experience with an enemy that could not be caught and would not stand and fight if it were. Supply problems, inferior rations (some of the hardtack they were given had been boxed before the war), increased desertion (thirty-five men in one twenty-four-hour period),[41] unbearable heat, a deceitful half-Indian guide,[42] and Custer's increasing worry and longing for his wife (during their three-year marriage, they had never been separated for this long) exacerbated the situation. A moody Custer again imposed strict discipline, and officers and even a newspaper correspondent took notice of his tyrannical ways. In mid-July, he left his command at Fort Wallace and galloped eastward with an escort of seventy-six troopers. Fifty-seven hours and 150 miles later, he burst into Fort Riley and promptly leaped upstairs to his quarters for an ecstatic reunion with his wife. The official CO of the Seventh Cavalry, Colonel Smith, preferred several charges against him — "absent without leave from his command" and "conduct to the prejudice of good order and military discipline" among them—and another Seventh officer, already under charges preferred by Custer for repeated instances of drunkenness on duty, filed even more, including the accusation that Custer had ordered that deserters "be shot down" without trial.[43] Custer's defense was shaky. Although he would later claim that he was worried about his wife's safety because of a cholera epidemic spreading through the area and the threat of Indians, it appears that the real reason for his wild ride was simply a desire to see her—and perhaps his fear that Libbie was spending too much time with the engaging Captain Weir.[44]

A court-martial was convened two months after the event. Custer pleaded not guilty to all charges. (As a defense for riding so far from his command, he claimed that before the campaign, General Sherman had told him that "he was not to restrict himself to any orders. . . . he could go to hell if he wanted to.")[45] It appears that few of the officers—many of whom he had alienated over the previous several months with his imperious command style—were willing to speak up for him.[46] Both he and Libbie professed the charges to be a plan by Hancock to cover up the failure of the expedition— "the trial has developed into nothing but a plan of persecution for Autie," she wrote to a friend—and others also spread this rumor. But though it was true that several of the court's members were on Hancock's staff, or below Custer's rank, Custer's errors were well documented, and the conspiracy would need to have been wide-ranging indeed. (His claim of innocence is contradicted by a letter from Libbie to a friend in which she admitted that "when he ran the risk of a court-martial in leaving Wallace he did it expecting the consequences.")[47]

The court bent over backward to grant Custer every allowance available to defend himself, but after almost a month of deliberations, Custer was found guilty on all but three charges. The court ruled that he should be "suspended from rank and command for one year, and forfeit his pay for the same time." All things considered, it was a relatively mild sentence, since he could have been dishonorably discharged. After reviewing the verdict, President Grant termed it "lenient" and added that "the court must have taken into consideration his previous services."[48] Custer reacted by charging one of his officers with drunkenness on duty, and in that trial the regiment's officers were further forced to take sides in the manner of their testimony. The resulting rent would never be completely mended as long as Custer commanded the Seventh.[49]

AT THE TIME, a court-martial was not the career-ending humiliation it would later become, but a much more common occurrence that usually involved significantly less important charges. After coming to terms with the sentence, the Custers treated it (or at least pretended to) like a yearlong vacation. While they wintered at their friend General Sheridan's quarters at Fort Leavenworth and then headed east to Monroe in the spring, the relative peace that followed the Medicine Lodge Treaty of 1867 began to fracture just months after its signing. In July 1868, the Southern Cheyennes, angry at the government's initial refusal to issue their annuities and likely frustrated by the increasing number of whites in their country, raided, killed, and raped at white Kansas homesteads and along trails. As summer turned to fall, the attacks increased, and the army seemed powerless to stop them. In August the Seventh, along with other army units, was ordered out after the marauding bands, but by mid-September the campaign was over, virtually barren of results. If anything, raiding increased in the area.

The chief reason for the failure was ineffectual leadership. The Seventh's new field commander, Major Joel Elliott, had earned brevets for bravery as an officer of volunteers during the war. Later, as a member of Custer's staff, he had impressed Custer so much that Custer had endorsed his application for a commission in the regular army. Elliott had repaid him by testifying on his behalf at his court-martial. Major Elliott was handsome and smart; legend had it that he had scored so high on the application tests that despite his lack of experience, he had been given a Major's commission in the Seventh.[50] (The fact was that the governor of his home state had secured Elliott's commission before his board examination.)[51] Elliott clearly had a bright future ahead of him, but he was young and inexperienced, and he found few Indians on the plains of Kansas. Subsequently, Lieutenant Colonel Alfred Sully, a veteran of the botched

1865 Powder River campaign on the northern plains, was assigned command and ventured afield with a force of cavalry and infantry. But Sully was equally ineffectual, returning after only a week, most of it spent issuing orders from an ambulance wagon.

A desperate Phil Sheridan—the new commander of the Department of the Missouri—needed someone to get the job done. Since August 1868, 110 whites had been killed, 13 women had been raped, more than a thousand head of livestock had been stolen, and much personal property had been destroyed.[52] Sheridan requested that the rest of Custer's sentence (two months) be remitted so he could assume command of his regiment. Sheridan's superior, Sherman, sent a telegram to the Adjutant General near the end of September: "Gen. Sheridan needs active young field officers of cavalry and applies for the restoration to duty of Gen. Custer."[53]

In the meantime, Sheridan sent a telegram to Custer in Monroe that read: "Generals Sherman, Sully, and myself, and nearly all the officers of your regiment have asked for you, and I hope the application can be successful. Can you come at once?" Custer had been so disillusioned of soldiering that he had asked banking tycoon John Jacob Astor for an agent's job abroad. (Astor's reply was sympathetic but negative.)[54] Upon receiving the request, an ecstatic Custer packed quickly and took the next train west.

Sheridan gave him carte blanche, according to Custer: "I rely on you in everything, and shall send you on this expedition without orders, leaving you to act entirely on your own judgment."[55] With a command, on his own hook—that was how Custer liked it.

He found eleven companies (all but one) of his demoralized regiment at their camp forty-two miles south of Fort Dodge. They were clearly in need of the kind of leadership that only he could provide. Most, if not all, of his officers and men were happy to see him, and Custer apparently mended bridges with one officer who had spoken out against him during his court-martial.[56] Benteen and Weir were there, but Keogh was on detached service with Sully's staff. Several other officers who would serve with Custer until the end also were present. The tough and capable Lieutenant Myles Moylan was a "ranker" who had joined the army as a Private and worked his way up to officer not once but three times. Moylan had fought alongside

Custer in the war, and after he had enlisted in the Seventh in 1866, Custer had recommended him for a commission—and requested that he be given a second chance at the officer's examination after he failed it the first time. He was an able officer but for some reason beyond mere snobbery was not well liked. Second Lieutenant Algernon "Fresh" Smith had been severely wounded in the war and left with limited mobility in one arm. He had joined the Seventh the previous year, and soon after his comrades had given him the moniker "Fresh" to differentiate him from another Seventh Second Lieutenant who had once been a merchant seaman, H. W. "Salty" Smith. "Fresh" and his wife, Nettie, were part of the extended Custer family.

Second Lieutenant Edward Mathey was French-born but had served with distinction in the war. He was nicknamed "Bible Thumper" for his fondness for profanity. Captain George Yates, reliable and efficient, was a Monroe friend of Custer's who had served with him on General Pleasonton's staff. Custer had been instrumental in furthering his career. First Lieutenant William Cooke was another of Custer's friends—a tall Canadian from a wealthy family who had fought with the cavalry in the war. At twenty, the good-looking Second Lieutenant Francis Gibson was one of the youngest officers in the regiment and was known for his sense of humor. First Lieutenant Edward Godfrey was only a year out of West Point, but previous to that he had served as a Private during the early part of the war. Although he was still a bit of a pup as an officer, he was smart and not the type to take sides in regimental politics. Another First Lieutenant was a familiar face: Custer had wrangled a transfer in late 1866 for his brother Tom, who, like so many of his fellow officers, had acquired a wretched drinking habit.[57]

These men and others in the Seventh saw a different Custer upon his return. Whether it was the ten months of idleness or plenty of time to see the error of his ways, their commander was a changed man—energetic, purposeful, and itching to find some hostile Indians again. He made peace with the officer who had preferred charges against him and instituted a regimen of drilling, target practice, and tough scouting expeditions to sharpen the Seventh into a crack outfit. Sheridan provided Custer with everything he requested: plenty of fresh recruits; new horses, rifles, pistols, and equipment; winter clothing; and more than enough ammunition.[58] The new Custer was still a disciplinarian. When a few officers were tardy in getting ready to move out, he had their tents set on fire. "After that there was no tardiness," remembered Custer's wagon master.[59] A month after his arrival, they set out.

Sheridan's plan was perceived (by him at least) as something of a novelty: a winter operation. Although U.S. troops had directed winter attacks deep into enemy territory before, with varying degrees of success, Sheridan seems to have been unaware of them, as he always spoke of the strategy as a new one.[60] Overriding the protests of guides and advisers, such as the legendary mountain man Jim Bridger, who believed that the harsh blizzards of the plains would swallow up soldiers unused to such conditions, he decided to send three columns from different directions into the heart of the Indians' cold-weather sanctuary. Sheridan figured that the army could not catch the Indians during the summer, when their ponies were well fed, so striking them while they were settled into riverside campsites was a risk worth taking. In addition, the southern plains hostiles, having spent several months living on pemmican and other stored foods and rarely venturing far from the warmth of their tepees, also would be more vulnerable than they would be come the spring's first shoots of grass.

Sheridan wanted to visit a kind of "total warfare" on the Indians, much like he and Sherman had inflicted on the Confederates in the war. The army's crippling dependence on supply wagons would be solved by setting up and stocking a base camp much closer to Indian country. From the camp, the strike forces, headed by the Seventh Cavalry, could sally forth relatively unfettered. The Seventh Cavalry reached the chosen site within six days and erected Camp Supply in less than a week. Custer had carried out Sheridan's directives in the Shenandoah Valley with grim efficiency, and Sheridan hoped for the same on the southern plains.

On the morning of November 23, in the midst of a heavy snowstorm, the eight hundred men of the Seventh set out with a small supply train of about thirty-six wagons. Their orders were simple and direct: "proceed South in the direction of the Antelope Hills, thence toward the Washita River, the supposed winter seat of the hostile tribes; to destroy their villages and ponies, to kill or hang all warriors, and bring back all women and children." Four experienced scouts and a dozen Osage guides, bitter enemies of the Cheyennes, would assist in locating the enemy.[61]

A few days later, an advance scouting party led by Major Elliott, now Custer's second in command, hit a fresh trail—a war party of at least one hundred Cheyenne warriors[62] heading southeast, no doubt returning from a raid into Kansas. The command left all but eight wagons behind and rode in pursuit over rolling hills covered with thick snow. Just after midnight, they reached the valley of the Washita River and quietly followed it for several miles until a halt was called. Beyond the next ridge, the Osage scouts had found a village sheltered in a wooded bend of the river. No one was absolutely sure that the camp was hostile, but the war party's trail had led them to it, and that was enough for Custer.[63] Over the next few hours, he deployed squadrons to surround the encampment of fifty-one tepees and what they presumed were about one hundred fighting men, though Custer's scouts did not reconnoiter farther afield. The near-frozen troopers were enjoined from even stamping their feet to keep warm, for fear of being discovered.

Just before dawn, a squadron led by Captain Albert Barnitz descended a butte to find themselves beset by four howling fox-hounds—probably Custer's—which had escaped from the wagon train back on the Canadian River and pursued the column's trail. Followed by the baying dogs, the troopers continued their approach to the sleeping camp, which was apparently oblivious to their presence.[64] Minutes later, at daybreak, a shot from an Indian rifle rang out, followed by the trumpeters sounding the charge and the regimental band playing one feeble strain of "Garry-Owen," a favorite of Custer's, before their spittle froze. Custer led the charge from the north into the village—"He would allow no one to get ahead of him," remembered scout Ben Clark[65]—and the regiment galloped through the tepees from several directions, firing indiscriminately and killing men and women alike.[66] Within ten minutes, the bulk of the camp was secured. Most of the warriors were either dead or fleeing to the surrounding ravines and woods, or to the banks of the river to attempt resistance. Few of them carried guns, and the frigid weather made it difficult for them to wield their bows and arrows.[67] Some of the troopers began herding the women and children together.

By midmorning, mopping up had commenced. Then Custer was alerted to two alarming developments. Major Elliott was enterprising and, in the words of a fellow officer during the war, "brave as a lion." He also had something to prove, having lost command of the Seventh. Earlier, Elliott had galloped off downstream to the east with the regiment's Sergeant Major and sixteen troopers to pursue a group of fleeing Indians. None of them had returned. Even worse, Lieutenant Godfrey, in pursuit of ponies and Indians, had ridden about three miles downstream and discovered tepees "as far as I could see down the well wooded, tortuous valley. . . . Not only could I see tepees, but mounted warriors scurrying in our direction."[68] The village they had attacked was only one of several. Downriver lay several larger encampments, a danger that proper reconnaissance would have revealed.

As more than a thousand armed warriors from downstream began surrounding the troopers,[69] Custer ordered the village burned, the herd of almost nine hundred ponies destroyed, and the fifty-three captives mounted. Meanwhile, Custer sent a detail a few miles downriver to search for Elliott,[70] to no avail. (When Custer and the Seventh returned to the site with Sheridan two weeks later, they found the bodies of Elliott and his men in a circle miles from the camp, frozen solid, riddled with arrows and badly mutilated.)

With his supply train several miles behind him, darkness coming on, and the enemy pressing his position, Custer mounted his command and brazenly marched downriver toward the other campsites. As he had hoped, the Cheyenne warriors retreated before this show of force. As soon as it was dark, Custer quickly reversed direction and stole away. Accompanied by his prisoners, all women and children, the regiment marched until after midnight and reunited with the supply train the next afternoon. The Seventh paraded into Camp Supply a day later in a grand display of pageantry that, to one officer, "rivaled and no doubt was the prototype of the modern Wild West Shows."[71] Custer and his command were warmly congratulated by

Sheridan for the complete destruction of what they learned was a Cheyenne village under the rule of the peace chief Black Kettle, who had been killed with his wife while trying to escape on horseback early in the attack. Black Kettle had remained friendly despite enduring the Sand Creek Massacre four years earlier, during which his wife had been shot nine times. Ironically, his village had been situated several miles away from the main body of Cheyennes precisely because he had dreaded a repeat of Sand Creek.[72]

The military, most of the government, and the western populace echoed Sheridan's assessment: the Battle of the Washita was heralded as a major triumph against the hostile Indians of the southern plains. Many eastern newspapers agreed, calling Custer a great Indian fighter. Other newspapers, as well as humanitarians and Indian sympathizers (including the Bureau of Indian Affairs), expressed outrage and denounced the action as an attack on peaceable and defenseless Indians. Some compared it with Chivington's Sand Creek Massacre, persuaded no doubt by the presence at both of Black Kettle. But while most of the camp was peaceable, there seems to be little doubt that some of the warriors there had participated in depredations to the north.[73] Unfortunately, Black Kettle's innocent followers paid the price for associating with the guilty.

Before the battle, Custer had ordered any shooting to be limited to the "fighting strength"[74] of the village, but in the frenzy of the attack, some noncombatants had been killed—some deliberately, some unavoidably. According to the Cheyennes' own count, of the 30 to 40 Indians killed, approximately half were nonwarriors,[75] and some of those had taken up arms and fought back.[76] Custer reported a total of 103 warrior deaths, likely a classic example of military exaggeration. The true death toll was probably somewhere in between. Though there were a few instances of indiscriminate killing by the troopers, most of the innocent deaths were inflicted by the Osage scouts.[77] The Battle of the Washita was harsh war but no massacre. Custer had himself halted the shooting of some Indian women and assigned men to protect them.[78]

Whatever the truth, Custer's superiors were pleased with the result. Custer had done a superb job of whipping his troops into shape and marching deep into Indian country in severe weather, then hitting the unsuspecting Cheyennes hard on their home ground—a feat never accomplished before. Custer restored himself to the good graces of his superiors, and the victory restored some much-needed credibility to the army, both in Washington and on the plains, after the previous two years' failures. The unseasonable attack shocked and demoralized the southern Plains tribes. No longer could they depend on their winter hideouts for safety.

Over the next four months, Custer and the Seventh endured severe weather and a life-threatening lack of provisions as they tracked down and subjugated virtually all the remaining hostile bands. Near the end of one futile pursuit, they survived on horse-flesh and parched corn for several days, and on another occasion they lived on quarter rations of bread for ten days.[79] The campaign climaxed in a bold move whereby Custer, Lieutenant Cooke, and a few scouts rode into a large Cheyenne village to negotiate. They sat in the chief's lodge and smoked a peace pipe. A medicine man, the keeper of the tribe's sacred medicine arrows, tapped ashes from the pipe bowl onto Custer's boot as he told Custer in Cheyenne that if the General ever broke his oath of peace with the Cheyennes, he would die along with all those in his command.

When Custer returned to his command, he refused to attack the camp, much to the disappointment of the members of the volunteer Kansas regiment marching with him. One Kansan noted in his diary that his fellow soldiers called Custer "a coward and traitor to our regi-ment."[80] But Custer had ascertained that there were two white women captives within the Indian village, and an attack would almost guar-antee their deaths. After three days of delicate talks, Custer took three chiefs hostage and negotiated a swap.

Since the clash at Black Kettle's village, Custer and the Seventh had worked mightily to clear the southern plains below the Platte and above the Arkansas of hostile tribes. They had succeeded almost completely—all without a trooper or Indian being killed, a tribute to Custer's skillful work.

Of greater import to the Seventh and Custer, however, was the reaction of Captain Fred Benteen to Major Elliott's demise at Washita. Elliott and Benteen had served in the same unit during the war, and the irascible Benteen took his young comrade's death personally.[81] Soon after the engagement, he asked at least one person—the reliable scout Clark, well respected for his intelligence and honesty—if he would be willing to make a statement that Custer had "knowingly let Elliott go to his doom without trying to save him," Clark later reported. "I refused to have anything to do with the matter."[82] Benteen proceeded to write a letter to a friend that was published anonymously in a Missouri newspaper in February, then reprinted in the *New York Times* a week later. (Its florid, dramatic style makes it difficult to believe that it was not meant for publication.) In it he derisively accused Custer of the same charges of abandonment. When Custer read the letter, he called his officers together and, with a riding crop in his hand, demanded to know who had written it. He threatened to horsewhip its author. Benteen stepped up and admitted to the deed, and the confrontation ended with a flustered Custer walking away. His reaction may simply have been the result of pure shock. Benteen had been a frequent visitor to his tent and had kept his true feelings hidden, at least from Custer, who in a recent letter to Libbie had written at length of his high opinion of the Captain: "He is one of the superior officers of the regiment and one that I can rely upon."[83] Although Benteen would later brag that his commander had "wilted like a whipped cur," it is hard to imagine how else a responsible CO should have proceeded.[84]

Years later, Benteen would claim that Custer "had endeavored to the best of his ability to get Col. [Edward] Myers and myself killed at the Washita." He would also complain that Custer, in his official report, had not singled out Benteen for commendation by name, perhaps the true source of his disgruntlement. In fact, Custer had named not a single surviving officer, later claiming that it would have been unfair to single out individuals. This was a disingenuous explanation, since battlefield commendations influenced brevet promotions and medals, a fact that Custer, of all people, should have been aware of.[85] In any case, it is difficult to imagine what else Custer could have done on the Washita to aid Elliott. In the first place, Custer was friendly with Elliott and thought him an officer on the rise; why would he have deliberately sent the young man to his death? After Elliott's absence was discovered and Custer sent a search party downriver, darkness was approaching and the regiment found itself in a sticky situation: surrounded by a thousand furious warriors, without rations or overcoats, exhausted, and miles from their supply train. His primary responsibility was necessarily to the safety of his regiment. Apparently, Custer and many of his officers believed that Elliott's command had, upon returning, detoured around the formidable ring of combative Cheyennes and would be found on the main force's return to the wagon train, back at Camp Supply, or even at Fort Dodge.[86] Some of the enlisted men thought that Elliott's command was already dead and that Custer was perfectly justified in returning without recovering their bodies.[87]

Benteen had been an enemy of Custer's almost from the start, and new officers assigned to the regiment realized quickly that there was a Custer "family" and a small but active anti-Custer faction led by the cantankerous Captain. Most officers, like young Godfrey, remained neutral and got along with both sides.[88] But Benteen had never been as open about his feelings before. Elliott's death gave him a legitimate (at least to his mind) reason to loathe Custer, and he would continue to rail against him over the next seven years. His letter would guarantee that the regiment's officers would be sharply divided in their allegiance to Custer until his death, and beyond.[89]

THREE

Patriots

When we were young all we thought about was going to war with some other nation.

CHIPS, OGLALA SPIRITUAL MENTOR TO CRAZY HORSE

He was an old man now, stooped and almost blind, but a generation earlier he had been the most feared Indian on the northern plains. It had been his band of renegade Santee (Dakota) Sioux that had instigated the bloody Spirit Lake Massacre in 1857.

For more than four decades, he had been the leader of a small marauding band of Dakotas from near the homelands of all the Sioux, in southwestern Minnesota and northwestern Iowa.[1] One reliable source claimed that "many of the unpleasant incidents in frontier life from 1836 to 1857 in Minnesota and Iowa were directly chargeable" to him.[2] His name was Inkpaduta, translated variously as Red Top, Red Tip, or Scarlet Point—as in deer antlers red with blood.

Born around 1815, Inkpaduta was the son of Black Eagle, or Wamdesapa, a chief of the Wahpekute band of Dakotas, who had fought alongside the Americans in the War of 1812. Despite this, the Wahpekutes had a reputation for mischief going back as far as 1805.[3] Even then, their group had been made up of renegades banished from other bands.

The Wahpekutes, the smallest of the four eastern Dakota sub-tribes, never totaled more than 550 people. They hunted year-round on the rivers and streams of the area. But frequent warring with the Sauks and Foxes and other traditional enemies took its toll on the small band, and in 1839 an Indian agent wrote that "this ill-fated tribe, from being over warlike and a terror to their enemies have since 1812 nearly been exterminated."[4] A smallpox epidemic in 1837 reduced their numbers even further.

After Wamdesapa's death in 1846, the Wahpekutes separated into different bands, largely due to disagreements between various tribal leaders. When a Wahpekute chief and some of his adherents were murdered, Inkpaduta, now in his early thirties—tall and slender, with dark eyes set in a glowering visage pitted with smallpox scars—was held responsible and banished. He drifted southwest with his followers and large family (he would father as many as a dozen sons, including two sets of twins, and some daughters). They eventually settled along northern Iowa's Little Sioux River and its tributaries, where they found abundant game and fowl. Inkpaduta's band became known as a refuge for outcasts and undesirables from other tribes. They avoided whites and roamed the area for several years, hunting, trapping, fishing, and occasionally gardening in the summer, trading with fur buyers for supplies and arms and ammunition. They also warred against their traditional Indian enemies, since Inkpaduta believed that the lands he had come to belonged to the Wahpekutes by birthright.

Inkpaduta had not been included in Dakota negotiations with the U.S. government in 1851, which made it difficult to collect annuities. That exclusion also meant that, at least in Inkpaduta's mind, he was free to war when and against whom he wanted. After all, he had signed no treaties. When homesteaders began establishing small, isolated settlements and farms in the belief that the area would be opened up by treaty, the Wahpekutes tolerated them at first. But in the mid-1850s, Inkpaduta's band, called the Red Tops after the scarlet pieces of cloth they tied to the tips of their war spears,[5] began to display increasing hostility toward the homesteaders, taking captives, raiding, and generally annoying them. In 1854, after a run-in with a white whiskey trader and horse thief, Inkpaduta's brother, Sintomniduta, and his family were murdered. Inkpaduta's mother was among the victims. The Indians appealed for justice, but the trader went unpunished. The outraged Dakotas increased their plundering, though no whites were killed.

For both settlers and Indians, winters along the Minnesota-Iowa border were hard. The winter of 1856–57 was especially severe, and by the middle of February, the snow stood deep and the temperature plunged to thirty-seven below. Without annuities to fall back on, Inkpaduta's small band was barely surviving in the lake region of northern Iowa, subsisting on whatever food they could find, beg, or steal. White settlers in the area had experienced a poor harvest, and there was little extra food to go around.

Soon after one of Inkpaduta's grandchildren died of malnutrition in February, warriors from his band quarreled with white hunters over some elk they were both pursuing. The fearful whites took the Indians' guns, ripped down their tepees, and forced the Wahpekutes to leave their camp and travel through the deep snow along the Little Sioux River. In response, Inkpaduta and his warriors seized some guns from a white community and moved on in search of sustenance, raging at the whites who had invaded his land, murdered his mother, his brother, and other relatives, and were killing many of his people with smallpox and whiskey. Now they had expelled the Wahpekutes from their ancestral lands in the middle of a brutal winter, without food, shelter, or arms—an almost certain death sentence.

Inkpaduta had restrained himself from exacting revenge before, but he would do so no longer. On the morning of March 8, 1857, Inkpaduta and about fourteen warriors entered a cabin near Spirit Lake, Iowa, and killed everyone inside except a young girl named Abbie Gardner, whom they took captive. They moved on to other settlements and killed more whites. They bashed in the brains of small infants and shot men, women, and children, decapitating some and scalping others. Within a week, some forty settlers lay dead.[6] The Wahpekutes took three more women captive and moved north to Heron Lake in Minnesota. Two weeks later, they returned to Spirit Lake and murdered eight more whites at the nearby hamlet of Springfield. Few if any Indians were killed in return.

The renegade Wahpekutes then moved west, along the way killing two of the captives. The remaining pair, including the Gardner girl, were rescued when two friendly Wahpeton hunters (members of another Dakota subtribe) purchased their freedom. Army units failed to capture Inkpaduta, though they killed one of his sons, Roaring Cloud, in June. The government threatened the other Dakota bands with the loss of their annuities if they refused to help bring in Inkpaduta. So pressured, Little Crow, chief of the Mdewakanton (Dakota) tribe, led a hundred annuity Indians after him. They killed Roaring Cloud's twin brother, Fire Cloud, but Inkpaduta's band slipped away, moving farther west and joining a large Yanktonai (Nakota) camp in Dakota Territory. The government raised one more punitive expedition against the elusive renegade but failed to locate him.

Over the next several years, any Indian attack within hundreds of miles was attributed to Inkpaduta, the "savage monster in human shape, fitted for the dark corner of Hades," as Abbie Gardner described him. Indian portraits of Inkpaduta, and even some white remembrances, are far less severe: a half sister remembered him as a humble man who avoided trouble until repeatedly provoked, and another Indian said that he was gentle and kind to his family. A white settler said that he sometimes entrusted his own family to Inkpaduta and had learned Sioux from him. He considered the Indian chief a "good neighbor and true friend."[7] Whites throughout that part of the plains lived in fear that Inkpaduta—and his second set of vengeful and ferocious twin sons, Sounds the Ground as He Walks and Tracking White Earth—would return to lead an Indian uprising against them. His ability to elude white soldiers became legendary, and the former pariah gained stature among Indians for his fierce resistance. Though the degree of his involvement is unclear, it seems likely that Inkpaduta put aside intertribal differences and joined Little Crow's movement. When the reluctant Little Crow led the Great Sioux Uprising of 1862, which resulted in more than seven hundred white deaths, it was generally acknowledged by white observers that the government's inability to punish Inkpaduta for the earlier massacre was directly responsible for the distrust between the Indians and the whites that led to the later one.[8]

During the next year, Inkpaduta helped direct a series of running battles with the two-pronged army expedition led by Generals Alfred Sully and Henry Sibley that was sent out against Little Crow.

The Indians lost each standoff as they retreated up the Minnesota River valley and then west into Dakota Territory, thousands of them surrendering along the way. Some followed Little Crow north into Canada. But Inkpaduta and hundreds of others escaped across the Missouri and onto the Great Plains, there to spread the message of armed resistance to their western cousins, the Yankton and Yanktonai (Nakota) Sioux, and the Lakotas farther west.

Through the next decade, Inkpaduta roamed the northwestern frontier from the Canadian Rockies to the Mississippi River, hunting the buffalo and raiding whites in Minnesota, Iowa, and the Dakota, Nebraska, and even eastern Montana territories. He became a legend on the frontier—to whites, a phantom who was everywhere and nowhere, unable to be killed or cornered; to the Sioux, a brave patriot admired for his refusal to give in to the *wasichus*. His small band of refugee Wahpekutes and Yanktonais spent much time near the Canadian border, crossing over when army columns were sent into the field in pursuit. Sometimes they traveled alone, sometimes with a larger group of Sioux.

At the end of July 1864, an army column met a large force of Sioux from many tribes. Inkpaduta and his band were there, having joined the Hunkpapas earlier that summer (a daughter and a cousin had married Hunkpapa men). Near Killdeer Mountain in northwest Dakota Territory, 1,400 lodges and several thousand warriors gathered to fight the enemy. Though Inkpaduta's eyesight was deteriorating, the Sioux relied on his strategic advice. But the white soldiers and their superior weapons—the Indians had few guns, most of them carrying bows and arrows—overwhelmed them.[9]

Inkpaduta and his small band retreated to the northwest, and over the next twelve years, they wandered the upper Missouri country, hunting the buffalo and retreating into Canada when necessary. Sometimes they journeyed south and joined with the Hunkpapas to raid and fight against the whites invading their country. Inkpaduta had a crucial ally among the Hunkpapas, a warrior infuriated by the many white men who journeyed up the Missouri River to the goldfields at the river's headwaters. The two had met the year after the Great Sioux Uprising of 1862. They had fought together east of the river against the soldiers sent after the Lakotas. Years had passed since then, but Inkpaduta's friend was always glad to lend support to the old patriot. Sitting Bull respected a man who hated the whites as much as he did.

IN LATER YEARS, many whites believed that Sitting Bull was a medicine man. But he was more than that. He was a dreamer, a holy man, and a spiritual leader more concerned with the welfare of his entire tribe than with practicing the healer's art.

Sitting Bull was born about 1831 into a distinguished Hunkpapa family living on the upper Missouri River in what is now South Dakota.[10] The Hunkpapas, along with the Sans Arcs and Blackfeet (not to be confused with the Blackfoot tribe farther to the northwest), were the northernmost of the seven Lakota Sioux tribes. They were not large tribes and often traveled together over the northern Great Plains in pursuit of the vast buffalo herds. South of them lived the Minneconjous and Two Kettles, and even farther south roamed the Oglalas and Brulés. All seven were united by a common culture, language, and heritage.

Sitting Bull's father, a mystic, named him Jumping Badger, but he soon became known by the nickname Slow for his deliberate manner. Slow grew up like all Lakota boys, yearning to become a warrior, for the main preoccupation of the Lakotas was war. All of the tribes fought, and they fought frequently and for many reasons: plunder, horses, revenge, land. Intertribal war, however, did not consist of the full-scale pitched battles Europeans were accustomed to. Rather, elaborately planned raids on enemy villages were the norm. The primary reason they fought was for glory. With few exceptions, displaying bravery in battle was the only way a young man could gain prestige and honors, and only through war could a man rise to the level of chief. Before the whites invaded their lands, the Lakotas had battled enemy tribes. The presence of the whites did not change that.

As he grew older, Slow became proficient in the skills of a Lakota warrior. He was a fast runner and an accurate bowman. At the age of ten, he killed his first buffalo. When he was fourteen, he participated in his first battle, against his people's traditional enemy, the

Crows. A Lakota male often did not receive his permanent name until he had done something as an adult to earn it. But after this battle, Slow's proud father gave him his own name, Sitting Bull. Over the next several years, he forged a reputation as a brave warrior in battle after battle against the Crows and other Indian tribes, as well as against the whites encroaching on Lakota lands.

When he reached full physical maturity, he stood five feet ten inches tall and had a heavy, muscular frame. He dressed and bore himself humbly. His gaze was intense—his eyes dark and piercing—and his features were sharply defined. He took full advantage of his deep bass voice[11] and became a commanding presence. "He had some very indefinable power which could not be resisted by his own people or even others who came into contact with him," said a missionary who knew him well in his later years.[12] Legendary for his kindness to children and older people, he was also uncommonly gentle with women, and they responded: he married nine times.

By the age of twenty-five, Sitting Bull was a leader of one of the tribe's elite military societies, the Strong Hearts. Two other boys he had grown up with, Crow King and the orphan Gall, had also become noted warriors and belonged to the Strong Hearts. Every Plains tribe could boast of several of these *akicitas,* and in a culture that revolved around war, they played an important part in fostering a strong esprit de corps. Each society was a military fraternity of good fellowship, competing for battle honors. But the *akicitas* were also charged with maintaining civil order and took turns, usually for a single season, serving as camp police—guarding the village and supervising marches and communal buffalo hunts. Only young men who had demonstrated the right qualifications—a good war record, an outstanding "vision quest" that revealed some sort of supernatural power, or sometimes just membership in an important family— were asked to join an *akicita.*[13] Members of an *akicita* often became as close as brothers, and Sitting Bull's fellows in the Strong Hearts would follow him for decades.

As Sitting Bull continued to distinguish himself in battle and in the hunt, other Hunkpapas began to realize that he was more than just a military leader. He was that rare warrior who possessed each of the four cardinal virtues so valued by the Lakotas: bravery, generosity, fortitude (in regard to both dignity and the ability to endure physical hardship), and wisdom. The first three could be cultivated, in some individuals better than others. But the fourth was more difficult to acquire, springing in part from a combination of the first three but also from additional attributes—experience, intelligence, spirituality, and superior judgment in all matters—that could be fully developed only in a few rare souls. In Sitting Bull, each of the four virtues was developed to an extraordinary degree, and his kinsmen appreciated that fact. As a result, when he was in his late twenties, Sitting Bull was made a war chief of the tribe.

As Sitting Bull matured, he developed a remarkable kinship with the natural world—which, to the Sioux, was also the spiritual world. The two went hand in hand. Sioux pantheism celebrated an existence in which virtually every object, every occurrence, every force of nature contained a spirit, or deity, that could be good or bad. The young Hunkpapa understood these forces better than most, and with that knowledge came the ability to control, or predict to a certain extent, some of these forces. Even more important, others believed this to be true. Some of his tribesmen thought that he could interpret birdsong, for he became known for his singing and composing.[14] And his dreams sometimes proved prophetic. Based on this skill or gift, and others related to the Lakota religion which he was taught or simply intuited, he earned a reputation as a *Wichasha Wakan,* or holy man, before he was thirty.

By the late 1850s, the Lakotas understood that whites were a growing threat to their way of life. In the summer of 1857, six of the seven Lakota tribes—the Hunkpapas, Minneconjous, Two Kettles, Blackfeet, Sans Arcs, and Oglalas—gathered at Bear Butte, on the banks of the Belle Fourche River north of the Black Hills, for a special council convened to discuss the growing threat. (The Brulés under Spotted Tail were busy in the south, making war against the Pawnees on the Platte.)[15] For half a century, they had tolerated the infrequent forays by the *wasichus* into their lands, and even traded with them and treated with them. Sitting Bull himself had often associated with white traders at Fort Pierre, on the upper Missouri River, since his early youth. He had even worked for a French trader, buying furs, for a while.

At least 5,000 Lakotas pledged to resist white encroachment on their lands. A few days later, a band of them came upon an army survey party on the edge of the Black Hills. A chief allowed the *wasichus* to depart safely in return for one thing: the Lieutenant in charge would send a message to the white people and their President "that they could not be allowed to come into our country. . . . All they asked of the white people was to be left to themselves and let alone."[16]

In the 1860s, the discovery of gold in the Rockies turned the trickle of whites invading Lakota territory into a steady flow. When the Dakotas fleeing Minnesota after the Great Sioux Uprising of 1862 reached their Lakota brethren and spread the word of rebellion, army columns trailed after them. Dakotas and Lakotas united to fight the whites, gradually perfecting the hit-and-run guerrilla tactics that would prove so successful over the next decade.

Any ambivalent feelings on Sitting Bull's part disappeared by the end of 1864, after the bloody fighting at Killdeer Mountain in northern Dakota Territory, against the army column led by General Sully, and the running battles in the Badlands that followed. Over the next several years, he and the militant Hunkpapas kept up an ongoing guerrilla war against whites in the upper Missouri area. Their favorite target was Fort Buford, built in 1866 in the northernmost part of Dakota Territory, though other forts on the river also were targeted. Aside from occasional brushes with white traders who carried items the Lakotas needed, Sitting Bull and his followers avoided the *wasichus*—unless it was to actively resist their invasion. When Sitting Bull was approached to sign the Fort Laramie Treaty of 1868 and come in to the reservation, he refused, saying, "We do not want to eat from the hand of the Grandfather (the President). . . . We can feed ourselves."[17]

Soon after the treaty, certain high-ranking Lakotas realized the rapid changes occurring in their world and proposed an unprecedented solution: a supreme chief of all the Sioux. Up to that point, the proud and independent Lakotas had recognized few authority figures and maintained a most rudimentary and nonbinding political organization. Each tribe boasted its own old-man council of advisers, which recommended tribal actions rather than governed, and war chiefs who led by example. For many generations, the autonomous bands, or *tiospayes,* of each tribe had wandered separately, coming together only at the annual Sun Dance or on other special occasions. But the white threat to their existence, which necessitated interaction between the nontreaty Lakota tribes, required a high office that could make important, binding decisions.

At a special gathering in the Powder River country, backed by both older chiefs who recognized his superior leadership qualities and his adherence to the four cardinal virtues, and younger warriors respectful of his war record and his adamant opposition to whites, Sitting Bull was ceremoniously named supreme war chief of the entire Sioux nation.[18] Over the next several years, virtually all nontreaty Lakotas on the northern plains—the "hostiles," as the U.S. government branded them—gathered around him, at least in spirit. Most of the time, the tribes still roamed apart, but Sitting Bull's influence was felt, and his wishes were usually followed. While the majority of the Lakota became entrenched on reservations, Sitting Bull led the free roamers against the government, refusing all parleys and treaty invitations. He did not sign a treaty or even discuss one, nor did he enter a reservation to receive any annuity goods. He did not waver from that position for seventeen years, and when he finally buckled, it was only because his people were starving.

AFTER THE FETTERMAN MASSACRE had induced the United States to give in to Red Cloud's demands, Crazy Horse and several hundred Oglalas continued to roam the Powder River country, hunting and raiding against their traditional enemies as they had for generations. They had no interest in living on a reservation, eating food provided for them by the whites and trying to become farmers. They would live as Lakotas always had, free, following the buffalo through the country east of the Bighorn Mountains.

Crazy Horse's stature had steadily increased, and somewhere around 1865 he was awarded a rare privilege. He and three other young warriors who had proved themselves superior Oglalas were named Shirt-Wearers, the highest honor a Lakota could receive.[19] Besides certain governing and diplomatic responsibilities, a Shirt-

Wearer's duty was to put the interests of the tribe before his own and serve as an example of proper Sioux comportment. Crazy Horse assumed his new role readily, though his behavior—he was already well known for his generosity and kindness—changed little.

In the summer of 1870, Crazy Horse ran off with a married woman whom he had long cared for, disregarding all Lakota proprieties concerning such matters. Her enraged husband galloped after them and a day later burst into their tent. Before Crazy Horse could grab his knife, the warrior shot him in the face just below his left nostril. The attacker left, assuming he had killed Crazy Horse, and his wife ran away, though she was soon persuaded to reunite with her husband. Crazy Horse survived, sustaining only a broken jaw. But for his inability to rise above personal interest, Crazy Horse lost his Shirt-Wearer position. (He also gained a scar on his left cheek, which only made his face even more striking.) The incident did serious damage to tribal peace, and the office of Shirt-Wearer was never the same.

More misfortune followed. While Crazy Horse was still recovering from his jaw wound, his only brother, an impulsive young warrior named Little Hawk, was shot and killed during an attack on some miners. Then, on a badly planned raid against the Shoshones that fall, his close friend and mentor Hump was killed. Crazy Horse had wanted to abort the raid—rain had turned to snow, and the horses were having a hard time—but Hump had insisted, saying they would be laughed at if they turned back. Crazy Horse had reluctantly agreed, and the raid quickly turned into a fiasco. When Hump fell from his wounded horse, the Shoshones finished him.[20]

Sometime during the next year, 1871, Crazy Horse married a woman named Black Shawl. He may have been talked into it by friends—a war chief of his stature and age was badly in need of a wife, and his personal losses made it even more imperative. Like her husband, Black Shawl had waited longer than usual to marry. She bore him one child, a daughter named They Are Afraid Of Her, who looked like her father. The girl, Crazy Horse's sole offspring, lived only to the age of three, dying while her father was off on a raid against the Crows. The camp moved some seventy miles during his absence, and when Crazy Horse returned a few days later and heard the news, he rode two days through Crow country to find her death scaffold. (Plains Indians did not usually bury their dead, but left them on a platform high enough that wild animals could not reach them.) He mourned there with no food or water for three days and nights. That loss may have been the cruelest.

It was about the time of his daughter's birth that Crazy Horse met Sitting Bull. After 1870 the Hunkpapas had ceased raiding the upper Missouri forts and moved south and west into the Powder River country, content to battle their traditional enemies, the Crows, and wage a defensive war against white incursions into their country. Bitter winters and meager hunting forced Sitting Bull and his people to accept rations occasionally over the next couple of years. To the south, during the spring and summer of 1872, the Oglalas occupied themselves with hunting, making small raids on settlements and stations on the roads along the Platte River, and clashing with the Crows. In midsummer they moved north to the Powder River country. Crazy Horse's fierce opposition to the encroaching whites had by this time won him a large following of Oglalas, Brulés, and Minneconjous, his mother's people.

In August several thousand Lakotas gathered to hold their traditional Sun Dance—the annual tribal gathering that doubled as a rejuvenating religious ceremony and the year's largest social event—along the big bend of the Powder River in southeastern Montana. Two days after the Sun Dance, on August 14, 1872, Sitting Bull and Crazy Horse took part in an attack on army troops escorting a survey crew for the Northern Pacific Railroad, which was surveying its course west along the Yellowstone River. The army camp lay on the north bank of the river. Both leaders distinguished themselves that day, each in his own way. Sitting Bull halted an attack by a Lakota leader who had convinced seven young warriors that they were "holy" (bulletproof), while Crazy Horse earned many admirers for his daring as he rode out into the open. Indeed, his audacity may have compelled Sitting Bull to act. In the midst of the battle, the Hunkpapa leader walked out toward the soldiers' lines and sat down on the open plain within shooting distance of them. He calmly took out his pipe, lit it, and began to smoke. Four other Indians, two Sioux and two Cheyennes, joined him. As bullets kicked up dust around them, they all sat there quietly. Sitting Bull shared his pipe, and when it was empty, he cleaned it out with a stick. Only then did he walk back to his tribesmen two hundred yards away, followed quickly by the others. Inspired, Crazy Horse decided to make one more charge close to the army lines. On the way back, his pony was shot out from under him, and he ran back to safety.[21] Both men had covered themselves in glory.

Ten months later, in the late summer of 1873, an even larger survey expedition—almost 2,000 men—set out from Fort Rice, on the Missouri River. By August they had reached the Yellowstone again. In charge of the mounted contingent was Lieutenant Colonel George Armstrong Custer.

CUSTER AND HIS SEVENTH CAVALRY REGIMENT had recently been transferred to Dakota Territory and would now garrison a new post, Fort Abraham Lincoln, on the western bank of the Missouri, five miles downstream and across the river from the frontier town of Bismarck, which the Northern Pacific Railroad had just reached. Once the Northern Pacific route entered Montana Territory, it was to follow the Yellowstone River to the Rockies and a navigable pass through the mountains. The survey expedition kept to the north side of the river (though the railroad, when finally finished several years later, would run along the south).[22] The unceded territory's northern boundary was not defined in the 1868 treaty; the agreement also allowed for a railroad to be built virtually anywhere in Lakota country, reservation land or unceded territory. But of course Sitting Bull and the rest of the Powder River Indians had signed no treaty. These renegade Lakotas considered the valley of the Elk River—their name for the Yellowstone—theirs, for they had pushed the Crows out of the area almost a century before.

The first spark came on August 4, a brutally hot day. Custer was scouting ahead with two companies of cavalry several miles in advance of the main column. The Lakotas sent out a decoy party in an attempt to lure the bluecoats into a trap. Custer, reconnoitering on his own, galloped in pursuit but turned back just before it was too late, making it to his lines in the nick of time. Several hundred

Lakotas made it hot for the cavalry until the rest of the column appeared, then retreated to their camp. A week later, the Lakotas attacked the Seventh's bivouac, firing furiously from across the Yellowstone. Sitting Bull watched the battle from the bluffs on the south side of the river; it is not known whether Crazy Horse was present. The fight lasted most of the day. Groups of Sioux crossed the river and met mounted cavalry in a series of skirmishes, all to the strains of "Garry-Owen" played by the Seventh's band. Late in the day, the infantry showed up and blasted across the river with cannons, which sent the Lakotas galloping away. In accounts he later wrote, Custer seems not to have taken either encounter—or the Sioux's fighting capabilities—too seriously,[23] mistaking a calculated withdrawal for cowardice and lack of fighting spirit.

When the Northern Pacific went bankrupt later that year, inducing the Panic of 1873 and the severe depression that followed, all immediate plans to push the railroad west from Bismarck were canceled. But a year later, the Northern Pacific was no longer the chief grievance of the Lakotas. Another trespass would precipitate the final chapter of the Sioux War, and it would again involve the man they knew as Long Hair.

It mattered little to the Lakotas that they had wrested the Black Hills from the Cheyennes, who had taken them from the Comanches and Kiowas, who had ejected the Crows less than a century earlier. They did not care that each Indian landgrab had been even more direct than the whites'. The Lakotas viewed the region's lush valleys and heavily wooded hillsides as a "food pack" that they could access if necessary.[24] Bands led by Sitting Bull, Crazy Horse, and other leaders had kept busy over the past few years policing their lands, harassing white settlers and expeditions along the Yellowstone and on the edges of their territory. But actual attacks were sporadic and less serious than newspapers portrayed them to be. For example, the thousands of miners in the Black Hills faced only minor Lakota opposition, despite what the newspapers said.

Just as important to the Lakotas was making war on the Crows to the west. The Crow reservation below the Yellowstone as defined by the 1868 treaty extended east to the 107th meridian, near the Powder River's upper reaches. The Lakotas ignored such abstract boundaries and routinely engaged their worthy opponents in "civilized" intertribal warfare. Hunting territories had to be fought for, horses and women appropriated, honors won.

Many of the roaming bands had spent the long, cold winter of 1874–75 at the agencies. As spring arrived, they left for the north country, taking with them government-supplied arms, ammunition, and foodstuffs. The Black Hills lay along the trail north from two of the largest agencies, Red Cloud's and Spotted Tail's, and some of these young Lakotas made occasional raids into the hills to harass and sometimes murder miners and settlers. Free-roaming Lakotas from the Powder River country also trekked down to the Black Hills. Large groups of whites were safe, since the Lakota war parties were usually small; most of the deaths were of men traveling alone.[25]

At the end of 1875, the reservation Indians and some of the hunting bands returned to the agencies. Most of the 1,200 or so Northern Cheyennes wintered at Red Cloud Agency, although one large camp led by a chief named Old Bear remained in the Powder River country. So did the hard-line Lakota roamers under Sitting Bull, Crazy Horse, Lame Deer, and other leaders. These camps hunkered down in their fastnesses along the Tongue River and the Powder River and their tributaries, oblivious to the machinations of the whites in Washington and other points east. That winter was even more severe than the previous one. In December and January, runners were sent out from the agencies with the government's ultimatum—return to the reservations by January 31, 1876, or be declared "hostiles" subject to military action. The order (or invitation, as some viewed it) was generally ignored; only a few small bands returned to the agencies. Near the end of March, two lodges came in to Standing Rock Agency with a courier, who reported that others would come in when the weather permitted.[26] Sitting Bull knew that there was little or no food at the agencies; a number of young men from the reservations had journeyed north to his village for that reason. His people had little incentive to return to the agencies.

Save for the railroad survey parties, U.S. troops had not entered Sioux country eager to initiate hostilities in years. A few weeks earlier, agency Indians visiting their free-roaming brethren had warned, "Soldiers are coming to fight you."[27] But most of the nontreaty

Indians had scoffed. The treaty allowed them to hunt between the Black Hills and the Rockies, and they had been largely peaceful for quite a while. Why would the *wasichus* invade the Powder River country to find and fight them? It made no sense.

Old Bear's band of about sixty-five lodges, mostly Cheyennes with about fifteen visiting Oglala and Minneconjou lodges led by He Dog,[28] lay on the west bank of the upper Powder River in southern Montana. They were a peaceful group, heading leisurely in to their agencies, bivouacked along the river waiting for better grass and less severe weather. Early on a subfreezing morning in mid-March, a 400-man U.S. cavalry force fell upon the sleeping village. The inhabitants panicked and fled, but the 150 men in the village regrouped and fought back. The troops left several hours later with half the pony herd. Warriors followed and later that night managed to steal back most of their horses.

The Indians' casualties were light—only two dead and several wounded. But half of the village had been put to the torch, and most of Old Bear's band were without shelter and food. Guided by the visiting Oglalas, they trudged through the freezing night down the Powder until they reached Crazy Horse's small winter village a few days later. His Oglalas gave what they could, and the combined villages rode northeast to a larger camp led by Sitting Bull. The Hunkpapas also gave generously to the Cheyennes, sharing food, blankets, clothing, tepees, horses, even medicine pipes—anything they could spare. The old-man chiefs sat in council for three days and finally decided to travel together for protection. At a Sun Dance the previous summer attended by several Lakota tribes and Northern Cheyenne bands, Sitting Bull and Ice, a Cheyenne mystic, had bonded and sworn to support each other. Now the time had come to act on that allegiance. Sitting Bull counseled peace—or at least avoidance of the whites—with the firm caveat that the Hunkpapas would fight if their friends were attacked. He sent runners to the agencies calling for warriors to help fight the white troops.[29]

The large gathering of Cheyennes, Oglalas, and Hunkpapas moved north and then west in April and May. The Cheyennes considered themselves the people at war with the *wasichus* and so led the way. The Oglalas, their first friends, were next. The Hunkpapas, still desirous of peace, brought up the rear. The column was joined by other scattered bands of free roamers angry at the news of the cavalry attack—more Cheyennes and the Minneconjou, Sans Arc, and Blackfeet Lakotas. Some Assiniboines from the northwest also moved in, traveling and camping with the Hunkpapas and Blackfeet.[30]

Arriving from Manitoba in the Great White Mother's country to the north, with thirty lodges of refugees—Santees (Dakotas) and Yanktonais (Nakotas)—was the old patriot Inkpaduta and his long-time ally White Lodge. Two decades of wandering the plains had left Inkpaduta's small band almost destitute. They had no horses, only dogs to carry their small tepees and meager belongings. The women were poorly clothed, and the men wore so little that some of the other groups called them the No Clothing people.[31] But Inkpaduta, now almost blind, still hated the *wasichus*. He and Sitting Bull renewed their friendship—and their mutual desire to live as their ancestors had, free of the white man and his encumbrances.

By early June, the growing village numbered almost 500 lodges and nearly 1,000 warriors, and hundreds, even thousands, were leaving the agencies to join them. The warehouses at several agencies were bare, and reports of plentiful buffalo lured many Lakotas from the southernmost reservations, where the spring grass strengthened ponies earlier. Patriotism, too, played a part. Young men especially heeded the call to arms and the chance to gain glory and status on the battlefield in a great cause. In addition, Lakotas returning to the agencies from the Powder River country had spoken in glowing terms of the great spiritual powers of their charismatic leader, who could interpret the divine desires of Wakantanka, the Great Spirit, like no other.

Sitting Bull, Crazy Horse, Inkpaduta—few whites understood their importance to a Sioux nation that took its inspiration and direction, much like a warrior in battle, from their leaders. If they had, they would have realized that these three Sioux leaders shared one overriding trait—an unyielding insistence on defending their homelands, their families, and their way of life to the death.

FOUR

Outside the States

I expect to be in the field, in the summer, with the 7th, and think there will be lively work before us.

GEORGE ARMSTRONG CUSTER

L ife in Dakota Territory suited George Armstrong Custer.
A year and a half on Reconstruction duty in the backwater burg of Elizabethtown, Kentucky, had driven him to boredom. When not purchasing horses for the army, he had spent as much of his time as possible out of town. When he had been notified in February 1873 by his good friend Phil Sheridan that the Seventh was being ordered to Dakota Territory to escort a Northern Pacific engineering survey party into the Yellowstone region of Montana, then man a new fort in Indian country, his response, in a telegram to Libbie, was: "Regiment ordered to Dakota first of March this suits me. GAC."[1] He had hoped for a transfer to the plains two years before.[2]

Now, after two and a half years at Fort Abraham Lincoln, "the General"—as Lieutenant Colonel Custer was referred to, in honor of his wartime brevet rank—was largely content. For a man of his temperament and passions, life on an army post hundreds of miles from the States was an idyllic existence.

While the Seventh had been skirmishing with the Sioux along the Yellowstone in the summer of 1873, 150 carpenters and mechanics had worked steadily at Fort Lincoln to construct the spacious officers' quarters and relatively comfortable barracks of the enlisted men, using pine transported by train from St. Louis.[3] The result was one of the largest and perhaps the best-appointed post on the frontier, particularly after the buildings had been painted eggshell white and lace curtains had been hung in the seven houses on Officers Row. The monotony of garrison life at the fort was brightened by the frequent visits (some of them months long) of luminaries, friends, and acquaintances from the East—not a few of them attractive, young single women, whose long stays were encouraged by Armstrong and Libbie in an effort to enliven the officers' austere existence. All participated in a host of social activities, some manufactured, some spontaneous: frequent dances and parties, stage productions, large-scale hunts, baseball games, and endless rounds of charades. Virtually every day and evening saw a gathering of some sort at the two-story Custer quarters in the center of Officers Row. This was the largest and fanciest residence in Lincoln and, as the commanding officer's, the fort's center of social activity. Libbie felt an obligation to keep their doors open, and even her husband's regimental enemies admired her generosity. "In the evenings the house is crowded with company and they have dancing in the parlor. The Gen. has got a beautiful house with five servants and they live in high style," wrote one young visitor.[4] At least twice a week, the Custers hosted a ball for the officers and their wives that featured the regimental band playing waltzes, polkas, and square dances. The billiard room was also a popular hangout.[5] The Seventh's band was a particular source of pride to the music-loving Custer, for its leader, Felix Vinatieri, was a talented composer and arranger. He had been the bandleader of the Queen's Guard of Spagnis in Italy before coming to America and serving for a short time in the same capacity in the Union army. The General had heard him in Yankton upon first arriving in Dakota Territory three years before and had persuaded him to join the Seventh as chief musician. The diminutive Italian had immediately taken steps to improve the band's quality.[6] Since then their relationship had deteriorated, and Vinatieri had asked for a discharge in 1875, complaining, "I have not been treated with that amount of respect which I expected when I enlisted with the Regiment."[7] His request had been denied.

Custer usually made an appearance at an evening function, but he was just as likely to retire to his study to devote himself to one of his several indoor passions: taxidermy, which he had picked up during the 1874 Black Hills Expedition; studying the tactics of his favorite General, Napoleon, or other military texts; writing articles about his experiences for the *Galaxy* magazine; or reading for pleasure, perhaps a novel by Dickens or Ouida.[8] Libbie occasionally heard him laugh out loud while reading a book by Mark Twain, another favorite.[9] Somehow he found the time to write frequently to his parents and also to his beloved half sister, Lydia Ann, who had been a second mother to him. In fact, he was so fond of her only son, Harry Armstrong "Autie" Reed, that he had proposed adopting the boy years earlier, but Libbie had opposed the idea.

The days were always busy. There was the constant tedium of administering a large fort and three other Missouri River posts with the help of his longtime adjutant and close friend Lieutenant William Cooke. The tall Canadian with the long dundreary whiskers had been with him for a decade, since the founding of the regiment. As adjutant he handled the General's many administrative duties.

After two successive summers with large expeditions into Indian country, the summer of 1875 was relatively uneventful. The government had decided to send another expedition into the Black Hills to confirm the glowing reports of gold strikes Custer had sent in 1874, and Custer had been told that he would be its commander.[10] But another officer, Lieutenant Colonel Richard I. Dodge, had been assigned to lead it instead. After a careful exploration, Dodge's geologist, Walter P. Jenney, had confirmed Custer's claims but advised that extraction would be more difficult than previously reported. Nevertheless, the existence of gold in the Black Hills was now undeniable, and the resultant headlines lured even more miners.

Custer had spent some of his time the previous spring arranging a peace parley between several of the reservation Indian tribes in the vicinity. For almost a century, the powerful Lakota Sioux had preyed upon the smaller, friendly Arikara, Mandan, and Hidatsa (Gros Ventre) tribes to the north, which had banded together generations before after disease had decimated their numbers. After another recent raid, the peacefuls had begged for assistance from the government and headed south from their village on the Missouri in hopes of a parley. Arriving at Fort Lincoln in early March, they had asked the General to formally request help from the Sioux agents. "I trust and doubt not you will see the importance of encouraging the various bands under your charge to send their leading and influential Chiefs and head men," Custer had written in March 1875 to the Indian agent at Cheyenne River Agency on the Missouri River south of Fort Lincoln. That agency was home to several Lakota tribes. Custer continued:

> Not only would a treaty entered into in good faith between the Indians of the three Agencies named have a strong tendency to presume and maintain peace between the Indians themselves but between them and the people of the frontier. . . . Please say to them that as the representation of the Military in this vicinity and as one who earnestly desires to encourage the maintenance of peace not only among the Indians themselves but between the Indians and the white men I extend to them a cordial and friendly invitation to come to this post and take part in the proposed council.[11]

Treaties had been successfully concluded in May and June, with Custer presiding,[12] and in the Commissioner of Indian Affairs' annual report for 1875, he had specifically lauded Custer for his peacemaking efforts.[13] The *Bismarck Tribune* cast a more jaundiced eye on the results: "These treaties are all bosh, for as soon as members of either of these tribes get the other in a tight place, scalp lifting commences."[14]

When Standing Rock Agency's supplies and rations had failed to arrive that March, Custer had invited the agent there, Edmund Palmer, to bring his entire population, about 5,000 Sioux, up to Fort Lincoln, where the General would provide temporary rations. "The question of how these Indians are to be provided for threatens soon to become one not of establishing regulation—but of humanity," Custer wrote.[15] However, red tape between the Departments of War and the Interior prevented the rescue. Fortunately, a last-minute arrival of cattle alleviated the situation.[16]

That experience, and the visits of friendly Sioux leaders to Fort Lincoln pleading various causes, may have helped soften Custer's position on "the Indian question." In an unpublished article he would work on (but never complete) early in 1876, Custer stated his opposition to "exterminating the Indians" and declared that "no person who at all comprehends the necessities of the Indian question"—let alone anyone who belonged to "a Christian and civilized nation"—could "say a word in favor of extermination."[17] In this he diverged from his superiors, Generals Sherman and Sheridan, who had espoused just such a philosophy for years. Lest anyone confuse Custer with Bishop Henry Whipple, one of the leading voices in the east for Indian rights, he wrote an article published in the July 1876 issue of the *Galaxy* praising the "civilizing and peace-giving influence" of the railroad and its unique ability to promote progress in the west in general and the Black Hills specifically. The article made clear Custer's support of the opening up of the Hills to whites and the extinguishing of Indian title to the area granted in the 1868 treaty.[18]

Aside from these official and not-so-official duties were the pleasures of the outdoors. Despite the infrequent Indian attack (though the fort was far from the heart of Indian country, a raid occasionally occurred), there was the opportunity to hunt, and Custer liked few things more than hunting. He may not have been the peerless marksman he bragged about in his letters and articles, but he was a damn good shot—by most accounts one of the best in the army—and he complemented that with his trademark energy and endurance. Few men had ever been able to keep up with Custer in the saddle—there was more than one reason his men called him "Hard Ass"[19] behind his back—and even now, at the age of thirty-six, his energy and endurance seemed undiminished by fifteen years of soldiering, a good amount of it spent on campaign. True, his hairline was conducting a distinctly un-Custer-like maneuver—retreating—and his ruddy, lined face betrayed the hard years spent outside in the elements, but he was still lean and muscled, and strong as an ox.

Custer's idyllic life was not without problems. One constant irritant was his inability to advance in grade. But in the shrunken postwar army, every officer was affected. There were only eleven coveted generalships in the army, and the competition to obtain even a colonelcy was fierce. Seniority decided promotion through that rank, but the right combination of patronage (the support of an influential General or politician in Washington on the right side of the aisle, for example) and performance (nothing beat battlefield heroics) was necessary to kick an officer higher up the ladder. Witness Lieutenant Colonel George Crook: after a bravura performance in Arizona against the Apaches, he had been promoted over many more senior Colonels to Brigadier General.

Men accustomed to lightning-quick battlefield promotions during the Civil War often adjusted badly to an army in which attaining higher rank might take ten, fifteen, even twenty years. Only death, retirement, or transfer made the highest rank available. Consequently, the army's officer corps was rife with jealousy and infighting. A good many soldiers were still fussing over real or perceived slights dating back more than a decade—disagreement over proper credit for Civil War victories being the main culprit.[20] Some officers of Custer's generation would retire near the turn of the century at the same rank as, or only one higher than, their original commissions.

Nevertheless, the eternally optimistic Custer remained hopeful that he would receive a General's star, and with his old friend Sheridan lobbying for him, he was in a better position than most. At the very least, he was second on the army list behind his old rival Wesley Merritt for the next available colonelcy. A promotion seemed imminent, since a sixty-five-year-old Colonel named William Emory, West Point class of 1831, was slated to retire that fall.[21]

Another disappointment was his inability to make a strike in the financial world. America in the decade after the war seemed to brim with get-rich-quick opportunities, and a good many of them succeeded. But apparently "Custer's luck" did not extend to his business activities, for few things he touched turned to gold—or silver— despite the considerable time he spent on leave with the tycoons of Wall Street. He had embarked on several investment schemes (a Colorado silver mine he persuaded John Jacob Astor to invest in was the biggest and most disappointing, though Custer sold his promoter's shares before it went bust), but few, if any, paid off. While in New York over the winter of 1875–76, he had lost $8,500 in a wild stock speculation, a sum for which he had had to sign a six-month promissory note to a Wall Street brokerage firm[22]—and an amount more than twice his annual salary. His business affairs were in such dire straits that he had requested several extensions of his time off. Two were granted, but the third was denied peremptorily by Sheridan. "If I am forced to leave now I will be thrown into bankruptcy with a positive loss of over ten thousand dollars," Custer wired his superior. Sheridan still refused, prompting Custer to claim that "it will involve the loss of all I own if compelled to leave now."[23] Though his request was denied again, Custer somehow managed to stave off bankruptcy.

To be certain, Custer's failures dampened his spirits. But they were mitigated by the fact that he was almost always among friends. Indeed, Armstrong and Libbie were surrounded at Fort Lincoln by his favorite officers—his brother Tom, recently made a Captain; his brother-in-law James "Jimmi" Calhoun, the quiet, handsome Lieutenant who had married his sister Margaret (called Maggie) in 1872; and several others referred to by outsiders as part of the Custer "family." His youngest brother, Boston, was also there; sent west so that the fresh air of the plains could mend his consumptive tendency, he had worked for the regiment as a forage master since the Black Hills Expedition of 1874. The three brothers were constantly playing practical jokes on one another, and Boston as youngest was usually the hapless victim.

One of the reasons that Fort Lincoln seemed so much like one big family was that most of the anti-Custer faction was stationed elsewhere, no doubt deliberately, or on extended leave. None of the regiment's three Majors, each of whom was several years older than Custer, got along with their CO. This was somewhat extreme but not unheard-of. One, Lewis Merrill, was a good officer but on detached service as Chief of Staff to the President of the upcoming Centennial Exhibition in Philadelphia, General Joseph R. Hawley.[24] The senior Major, Joseph Tilford, was overweight and a heavy drinker, and he disliked the rigors of field duty. He was stationed at Fort Rice but on extended sick leave due to inflammatory rheumatism.[25] The junior Major was Marcus Reno, a West Point graduate from Illinois who had been appointed to the Seventh after the Battle of the Washita in

December 1868. A stolid, humorless officer, Reno had served in the Civil War with vague distinction, chiefly in staff roles, and near the war's end was still a Captain. But he had garnered a colonelcy and the command of a Pennsylvania volunteer regiment in the last few months of the conflict, most likely through political connections (his wife's family was one of the most prominent in Harrisburg), and by the time the war ended, he had been brevetted a Brigadier General.

Custer had initially been glad of Reno's appointment to the Seventh. He wrote to Libbie in early 1869, "Reno I know well, he is a finished gentleman and a most capable officer. He served in the Shenandoah and is a good friend of mine."[26] But his opinion of the man would change over the years. By the time he joined the Seventh, Reno had lost any knack he had of making friends, and most of his fellow officers in the regiment disliked him. Since the death in 1874 of his wife, who had seemed to temper his lack of sociability, his drinking had increased. He had missed the excitement on the Yellowstone in 1873 and the grand picnic in the Black Hills the next year, as he had been busy with two companies of the regiment escorting the Northern Boundary Survey Expedition. He had then taken a year's leave of absence to spend time with his only son, eleven-year-old Ross, after his wife's death. Now, in the spring of 1876, he was at Lincoln—his boy stowed safely with his in-laws—and chafing for a chance to prove himself and gain a command.

Captain Frederick Benteen, Custer's most open enemy in the regiment, was stationed twenty-five miles down the Missouri at Fort Rice, near Standing Rock Agency. Benteen and his wife, Kate, had just lost their fifth-born child to spinal meningitis, the fourth of their children to die of the disease they had inherited from their father; all four had perished before their first birthdays. The embittered Benteen's dislike of Custer had not abated since the Washita incident, but the two saw little of each other unless they were in the field. Though Custer was not a man who normally bore grudges, and did not in this case—"It seemed to me that Custer often went out of his way to mollify him," remembered one officer[27]—the arrangement suited both just fine. Benteen was an intelligent man, and a brave and inspiring leader, and was more like Custer than he would ever care to admit. But for all his smarts, he never indulged in the self-examination necessary to admit that jealousy was at the root of his hatred for his commanding officer.

In total, fourteen of the regiment's officers were on leave or detached service: recruitment service in one of the big eastern cities, art instruction at West Point, or, in the case of Captain Michael Sheridan, serving as aide-de-camp to his brother, General Philip Sheridan. Another officer was aide-de-camp to General William Sherman, and still another to General John Pope. The understaffed army was stretched thin, and the result was several companies of the Seventh commanded by Lieutenants.

Custer himself had long ago stopped worrying about whether his enlisted men, or even his officers, liked him. "I never expected to be a popular commander in times of peace," he had written his wife in 1869.[28] So he was probably unperturbed by the fact that he had made some enemies during the march up from Yankton in the summer of 1873. To straighten out what he no doubt saw as a slack command, Custer had decided to implement dozens of disciplinary orders. In the words of one officer, they were "annoying, vexatious, and useless orders which visit us like the swarm of evils from Pandora's box, small, numberless, and disagreeable."[29] Eleven of his subordinates had subsequently complained en masse to departmental headquarters during a series of courts-martial in which Custer continued to meddle.

Custer had eased off somewhat since then, but he was still a tough administrator and a by-the-book commander. While some of the enlisted men still swore by him, others swore at him. (The latter liked to cite the instance when, returning from the Black Hills in 1874, Custer had ordered sick men out of the ambulances and into heavy government wagons to make room for his dogs, whose paws were sore from prickly pear cactus.)[30] Few of his soldiers loved him as did those who had served under him during the war, but they respected him, if not for his formidable reputation, then for his strict but fair command style.

One who did love him unconditionally was his "darling durl," his "little gypsy," his "bunkey," Libbie. Though spoiled since birth and queen of the Custer court, she put on no airs at this frontier post. Twelve years of following her cavalier from battlefield to battlefield and then from post to post had tarnished somewhat her once radiant beauty, but she was still his soul mate, his confidante, the understanding angel he increasingly shared every concern with. When they were apart, he felt compelled to write her almost every day from waiting rooms, military offices, committee rooms, restaurants, anywhere he could find a moment's respite from his busy social schedule. The flirtatious Custer even regularly apprised her of the constant parade of attractive women he encountered. That their marriage had produced no children was a great disappointment to them, but it was one they had accepted and adjusted to. Their family comprised the always overstuffed menagerie of animals Custer acquired or adopted—dogs, wolves, mice, raccoons, wildcats, antelope, and many others—and the close-knit group of relatives, friends, and officers that surrounded them. They had weathered other marital problems—likely a sexual indiscretion or two on his part—and if anything, their love for each other had deepened over the years.[31] "Your magnificent letter of 42 pages sent me into the seventh heaven of bliss," Libbie wrote to her husband in July 1873 while he was in the field with the Yellowstone Expedition. Only a few days later, he wrote her an eighty-page missive, noting, "How we have managed to preserve the romance." No wife could be more supportive of her husband and his ambitions, and few men confided more completely in their wives. Both apparently obtained what they needed from the relationship.

ARMSTRONG AND LIBBIE had spent several months of the fall and winter of 1875–76 in New York, enjoying the social whirl that the General especially was addicted to: nights at the theater, where he would laugh and cry demonstrably; invitations to dinners, dances, and receptions at private clubs and tony mansions; and much time spent with his good friend, actor Lawrence Barrett. All this despite a singular lack of funds. (To save money, the Custers stayed in a room across from their usual quarters, the Hotel Brunswick, though they still received their mail and took their meals there.) Their financial future had, however, been brightened by an offer from a Boston speakers bureau: a lucrative series of lectures that could earn Custer up to $1,000 a week. The General hoped to begin the tour (with some coaching from Barrett and Libbie) after the summer campaign had concluded.

Custer had a good reason to delay his lecture series: he was convinced there would soon be a large-scale field operation against the nontreaty Sioux, and he was confident that the Seventh would be involved. In January he wrote to his brother Tom, "I think the 7th Cavalry may have its greatest campaign ahead."[32] The restless Custer remained disappointed that Lieutenant Colonel Dodge, not he, had accompanied the previous summer's expedition into the Black Hills to officially confirm the presence of gold. Sheridan had picked Custer to lead another expedition that season, this one up the Yellowstone, but that had been shelved indefinitely.[33] Custer was hopeful of action in 1876.

After Custer's request for a third extension of his leave was refused by Sheridan and Secretary of War William W. Belknap (Custer had no respect for the Secretary, suspecting him of crooked dealings, and had snubbed him socially during Belknap's visit to Fort Lincoln the previous year), the couple took the train to St. Paul, arriving there on February 15, the day Custer's leave officially ended. He spent the next two weeks at the Department of Dakota headquarters, conferring with General Alfred H. Terry.

Terry, a tall, gaunt man with gentle eyes, was soft-spoken, kind, and an excellent administrator. Before the Civil War, he studied law at Yale. He left after only a year and soon passed the state bar. To supplement his meager earnings as a lawyer, he became a court clerk in New Haven, Connecticut. At the onset of hostilities in 1861, he raised a regiment of state volunteers and entered the war as a Colonel. He soon found that he had an aptitude for command. After his brilliant assault on the nearly impregnable Fort Fisher in January 1865, he reached the rank of Brigadier General in the volunteer army, aided by a recommendation from Grant. When the war ended, he was rewarded with a regular army brigadiership and the command of the Department of Dakota. The forty-eight-year-old bachelor lived in St. Paul with his mother and four doting sisters and had become quite comfortable as an office administrator. Terry had no Indian-fighting experience to speak of and was glad to have Custer, an old hand at it, leading the expedition against the hostiles, although the younger officer's high-handed ways taxed Terry's patience at times.[34]

The two men differed on the answer to the Indian question. Although Custer was no proponent of extermination, in the spring of 1875 he had recommended to Sheridan that the Sioux be given a "sound drubbing" and that the Black Hills be opened. Terry, more sympathetic to the Sioux's plight, had disagreed,[35] at one point proposing that the region be settled with Indian farmers.[36] But the prickly and fruitless negotiations to obtain the Black Hills from the Sioux, a mid-December meeting in Chicago with Sheridan to discuss the situation, and Terry's appreciation of military hierarchy may have altered his views.[37] Sheridan had told him of the decisive conference at the White House on November 3, 1875, in which President Grant had been persuaded by the more hawkish elements of his Indian brain trust to allow miners into the Black Hills and provoke the Sioux hunting bands into war. Orders were orders, and the soft-spoken Terry was not one to challenge his superiors, who were delighted with his refreshing lack of aggressive ambition.[38]

And so the grand plan for a justified war lurched into motion. The predatory Indians—who had not been very predatory at all during the past year—had been given their chance to become "civilized."[39] Their refusal of this offer had forced the army to take action.

In the meantime, General Sheridan began to make plans for a quick winter strike at the hostiles, the majority of whom were reported to be near the mouth of the Little Missouri, a hundred miles from Fort Lincoln.[40] The same strategy had been successful in 1868, when Custer had overwhelmed Black Kettle's Cheyenne village and over the next several months had managed to help pacify the hostile Indians who remained on the southern plains.

In the earlier campaign, Custer had commanded one of three discrete columns attempting to converge on the hostiles from different directions. Sheridan's overall plan for the current campaign was very similar. Colonel John Gibbon would lead a force eastward from Fort Ellis in western Montana Territory. Brigadier General George Crook would move north from Fort Fetterman in Wyoming. Custer and the Seventh Cavalry, augmented by a battalion of infantry and artillery, would march west from Fort Lincoln. The key was to strike hard and strike soon, before the spring, while the Lakotas and their horses were at less than battle strength and disposition. The different bands tended to winter separately, and a quick attack could also catch the Indian camps before they were reinforced by the many Lakotas who left the reservations to hunt with their nontreaty brethren during the summer.

Sheridan contacted his departmental commanders, Terry and Crook, for reports on the feasibility of a winter campaign. Crook, who had been at the White House meeting, replied from his headquarters in Omaha that he had been making secret preparations and was ready to commence operations immediately. The considerably less bellicose Terry was unenthusiastic. The Great Plains had been ravaged by severe snowstorms, and it would be several months before his snowbound Dakota posts would be ready to march out, much less tackle the considerable logistical challenge of supplying a large column weeks out from their supply base without the aid of steamboats or trains. (Neither mode of transport could operate during the winter.) But Sheridan was adamant about the importance of a winter strike and told Sherman that "unless [the Indians] are caught before early spring, they cannot be caught at all."[41] On February 8, he wired Terry and Crook that operations against the hostiles had been ordered. Sheridan believed the nontreaties to be fairly few in number and regarded their fighting prowess and inclination so cavalierly that he gave no orders for coordinated actions to Crook and Terry. "I will hurry up Crook," he later wired Terry, "but you must rely on the ability of your own column for your best success. I believe it to be fully equal to all the Sioux which can be brought against it, and only hope they will hold fast to meet it."[42]

Only nine of the Seventh's companies were within Terry's jurisdiction; the remaining three—B, G, and K—were stationed with the Department of the Gulf on detached service. A day after Custer arrived in St. Paul, Terry asked Sheridan that the three troops be allowed to rejoin their regiment. Terry and Custer also requested recruits to fill out the thin ranks, the usual detail of Indian scouts to guide the column, and other necessities. By February 21, Terry was able to relate to Sheridan his strategy: "I think my only plan will be to give Custer a secure base well up on the Yellowstone from which he can operate, at which he can find supplies, and to which he can retire at any time the Indians gather in too great numbers for the small force he will have."[43] Several companies of infantry would accompany the Seventh to man the supply depots while Custer searched for the enemy, and steamers would freight supplies up the Missouri and Yellowstone Rivers. The Dakota column would leave Fort Lincoln on April 5.[44]

Custer also began to lay plans for press coverage, which was not unusual for a large-scale campaign. A few days after Terry's wire to Sheridan, he wrote to his friend Whitelaw Reid, editor of the *New York Tribune*: "Thinking you would like to have the Tribune represented, I write confidentially to say that the most extensive preparations are being made for a combined military movement against the hostile Sioux that have been attempted since the war." He went on to reveal the basic plan of three columns and concluded: "This I write for your personal information. The authorities have been laboring to keep all movements secret, but they will be made public perhaps by the hour this reaches you. If you send a special correspondent select some good man accustomed to roughing it."[45]

The Northern Pacific's regular operations west of St. Paul had been canceled until April due to the heavy snow, but the railroad—mindful of Custer's assistance and promotion, among other reasons—outfitted a special train with three engines and two snowplows to transport Armstrong, Libbie, and several others to Bismarck (along with plenty of merchandise for the boomtown's retailers). Also bound for Fort Lincoln was a contingent of artillerymen assigned to man a battery of Gatling guns to accompany the Dakota column.[46]

A raging blizzard hit the area on March 7, and at Crystal Springs, sixty-five miles short of Bismarck, huge snowdrifts stopped the train.[47] On board was a forty-two-year-old telegrapher turned newspaperman by the name of Mark Kellogg, a widower whose two young daughters lived with his dead wife's parents in La Crosse, Wisconsin. He was returning from a trip east—probably to visit his children—and was on his way to seek his fortune in the Black Hills, along with thousands of other desperate men, and possibly to renew his reporting for the *Bismarck Tribune*.[48] He had had some financial troubles since his wife's death in 1868, and he wanted very much to make enough money to educate and take care of his two girls.[49]

After a few days stuck in the stalled train, a pocket telegraph relay was found. Kellogg spliced into a nearby line and sent a message to Bismarck, prompting recently promoted Captain Tom Custer and a veteran stage driver to leave Fort Lincoln in a mule-drawn sleigh, pick up Armstrong and Libbie (and three of Custer's hounds), and deliver them safely to the fort on March 12.[50] The train and its passengers, including Kellogg, would not arrive until a week later after a thaw.

An enthused Custer set about preparing the regiment for its upcoming field operations. Supply logistics, troop drilling, target practice, the mustering of Indian scouts—there was much to do, and the bulk of the Seventh hadn't even arrived yet from their scattered stations. But he had barely unpacked before a telegram from Washington arrived three days later. Custer's presence was desired to testify before a committee investigating malfeasance by the office of Secretary of War William W. Belknap in regard to the appointment of traders at frontier forts. The proliferating scandals of President Grant's administration were about to engulf Custer and seriously hinder his hope of leading the last great Indian campaign.

FIVE

Belknap's Anaconda

It seemed to be [Grant's] wish to make every creature connected with him by blood, marriage or friendship the sharer of his good fortune.

NEW YORK HERALD, JULY 7, 1876

The public's respect and adoration for Ulysses S. Grant—a good-hearted, self-made man who seemed to personify the young American dream—had propelled him to two terms as President, and he was angling this centennial year for a third. The unpretentious General was a folk hero, almost a legend—the man who, especially after Lincoln's death, had saved the Union.

But by this time, seven years into his administration, an embarrassment of scandals had soured the public on Grant's presidency. Soon after his second inauguration, a steady stream of corruption involving Grant's relatives, friends, and appointees had turned into an unprecedented deluge. By the spring of 1876, it seemed that every day brought a new revelation of high-level dishonesty. For example, on March 30, the *New York Times* ran five lead stories on its front page; four of them involved cases of national fraud.

Relief from this constant barrage of iniquities came from two sources. First, there was the distraction of the centennial. To celebrate its first hundred years, the country had decided to mount the Centennial Exhibition in Philadelphia, to be held for six months from May to November. The expo would occupy 450 acres, jam-packed with exhibits celebrating both America's glorious past and its limitless future—a future symbolized by the gigantic Corliss engine, a forty-foot-high, steam-powered behemoth that powered 8,000 smaller machines. Many other inventions were featured, including an electric lamp, a typewriting machine, and a device that received little attention—Alexander Graham Bell's telephone.[1] Of the nation's 46 million residents, 8 million would visit the Centennial (as it quickly became known) that summer, almost one out of every five Americans, and it made an unforgettable impression on virtually everyone who attended. "Nothing but seeing it with your own eyes can give you any conception of its magnitude," wrote one visitor. "Everything that was grand, beautiful, useful and ludicrous is there, not only from our own beloved land, but also from every nation I ever heard of and some that I had not heard of."[2] The key-note speaker at the opening of this frenzy of self-congratulation was none other than the President of the United States. But Grant's stock had fallen so low that his short address received more hisses than hurrahs.[3]

The second distraction came from the sad fact that Grant was hardly alone in his perfidy. In the postwar Gilded Age, money and its pursuit were all-important. The confluence of technology, opportunity, and greed created a wide-open era of unparalleled upheaval and advances in massive new industries on an unforeseen scale. The Civil War had started many avaricious men—speculators, contractors, agents—on the road to riches. After the war, when these industries grew more quickly than any attempts to regulate them, these unprincipled schemers brazenly set forth to corrupt men at the highest levels of business and government—and succeeded in quite a few instances. The Tweed Ring, the Gold Ring, the Indian Ring, the Navy Ring, the Custom-House Ring—there was even a Moth Ring, involving almost half a million dollars paid to a firm for a worthless moth repellent. And there were regional rings, such as the Land Grab Ring on the Pacific coast and the Warren County Ring in New Jersey.[4]

Unfortunately for Grant, when a few honest men and the watchdog press began to investigate, his administration—or at least his appointees at its highest levels—seemed to be an integral part of many of the worst offenses. On the surface, Grant appeared to have triumphed over his humble beginnings. But his distrust of those better educated and more refined than he caused him to surround himself with men of similar background, primarily ex-soldiers who had fought their way up as he had, without the aid of higher education or the luxury of higher culture. Indeed, upon ascending to the presidency, Grant rewarded many of his closest associates—men who had served him well during the recent conflict—and an inordinate number of relatives (forty-two) with government positions. Many of these men were easily influenced, and some of them possessed principles that were less than finely honed.

Abel Corbin, the President's brother-in-law (one of three who caused Grant trouble and embarrassment),[5] was a perfect example. He had given the unscrupulous financiers Jay Gould and Jim Fisk inside information, with which they conspired to corner the gold market in the summer of 1869. Grant's decision to release enormous amounts of gold on the market foiled the plan and vindicated him. But the fact that he had known of the scheme in advance, and had even socialized with the schemers at their homes (and on Fisk's luxury steamer), tempered the public's forgiveness.

Though the worst aspects of the Crédit Mobilier scandal, in which Congressmen had sold their influence for kickbacks, had taken place in the previous administration, its exposure during the presidential race of 1872 only increased the distrust of the American people in their chosen leaders. (Both Grant's outgoing Vice President and his incoming Vice President were implicated.) In May 1875, Grant's private secretary, Orville Babcock, one of his oldest and closest friends, was revealed to have been taking bribes, though he avoided a jail sentence. Another swindle, known as the Sanford Contracts, involved tax fraud and featured the Secretary of the Treasury—whom the President fired and then immediately appointed to a judgeship on the U.S. Court of Federal Claims.

Nepotism and favoritism were standard tools of the spoils system before and after Grant, but never in the history of the Republic has a generous benefactor been repaid in such ungrateful coin. Yet the President had nobody to blame but himself, for he seemed to be completely incapable of recognizing a crook.[6] During the war, Grant had looked the other way while corruption occurred in the areas of supply and procurement, and he had stocked his headquarters with men of questionable morals.[7] One of his greatest assets, his loyalty, was also his greatest weakness. He discouraged, politicked against, and fired reformers who dared help prosecute his friends, and in at least one case, the Whiskey Ring, the President even perjured himself in a deposition made before the Chief Justice of the United States to keep Babcock out of jail.[8] (Grant's testimony was probably the principal reason his aide was found innocent.) In the face of mounting evidence of improprieties, Grant continued to support and defend these intimates to the bitter end and beyond—an admirable code of conduct for a friend, but deplorable in a President, whose higher duty is to the integrity of the nation.

Hot on the heels of the most damaging revelations of the Whiskey Ring, a conspiracy of hundreds of public officials and distillers who diverted millions of dollars in unpaid liquor taxes to their own pockets, came the first details of another high-level government scam. A law had been passed six years previously that granted the Secretary of War the power to appoint traders at frontier forts. Formerly, these traders, known as "sutlers," had been selected by local boards of army officers, who monitored their operations. That bit of legislation was the result of a struggle between the commanding General of the army, William T. Sherman, and Secretary of War William W. Belknap over a specific appointee—a conflict that also involved the duties and powers of the War Department and the Interior Department. These two government entities had been tussling since at least the Civil War for complete control of the country's Indian wards. Belknap's alliances in Congress had resulted in the 1870 military bill expanding his power, and the Secretary of War had initiated other new protocols that bypassed Sherman and weakened his authority. Grant had promised Sherman that he would rectify the situation, but he never did, and a disenchanted Sherman had cooled toward the President. Weary of Washington politics and especially the Secretary of War's continued appropriation of his powers, Sherman had relocated his headquarters to St. Louis in October 1874. It was a sad end to what had once been a close relationship, for Belknap had served under Sherman during the war and had landed his high office largely through a recommendation from his former commander.

Widespread fraud in the Bureau of Indian Affairs had long occurred on the agency level and was commonly known even in the ranks.[9] As early as 1865, General Alfred Sully had written, regarding Indian annuities, "It is my opinion that very little of it reaches the hands of the Indians," and claimed that the traders pocketed most of the money.[10] Custer had spoken out against the corruption in interviews, articles, and books, and had even forced the removal of two of Belknap's traders.[11] Other officers, foremost among them Colonel William B. Hazen and Colonel Ranald Mackenzie, had also testified to the problems, but it wasn't until the spring of 1876 that things came to a head. The upcoming election had increased the usual Washington feeding frenzy. Neither party offered a clear-cut frontrunner, and with Grant's plummeting reputation ending any plans of his running, the Democrats were excited about their chances of winning the presidency for the first time in twenty years.

Custer entered this quagmire at the end of March. Upon receiving the telegram requesting his testimony before the House Committee on Military Expenditures, chaired by Democratic Congressman Hiester Clymer, he had wired Terry (the former lawyer) for advice. The departmental commander was not happy about this hitch in plans, and when Custer told him that anything he could tell the committee would be mostly hearsay, Terry suggested that he ask if it were possible for him to answer questions by telegram. Custer did so, but he was clearly conflicted about his duty to speak out against corruption that harmed both the Indians and the soldiers on the frontier. Before he received a reply, he sent another telegram telling the committee chairman that he would come to Washington as requested.

Before he left, Custer directed Major Reno and Captain Benteen at Fort Rice, to place their garrisons "in efficient condition for prolonged service in the field." He also ordered supplies to be sent to the soldiers on the Northern Pacific train still stranded in the snow.[12] Then he boarded a stagecoach headed east.

A week later, on March 28, he arrived by train in Washington. Although the city had changed dramatically since the Civil War — approximately one-third of its 150,000 inhabitants were black, and large fields around the city that had once housed thousands of Federal troops now contained scattered wood-frame houses and shanties—some things remained the same. For instance, the half-finished Washington Monument still towered over the Mall. Begun in 1848, its construction had been abandoned in 1854 due to a lack of funds. The monolith would not be finished for another ten years.[13]

Belknap had already tendered his resignation in the face of potential impeachment. He had been implicated in the trading post scheme by Colonel Hazen four years earlier. Although the charges (which had caused the contentious Hazen to be banished to Fort Buford, widely known as the least hospitable frontier fort) had been ignored at the time, they had resurfaced after the *New York Herald* had published its investigative series on the subject. That investigation had been aided on the sly by Custer, a friend of *Herald* publisher James Gordon Bennett, who had sent an undercover reporter to Bismarck to look into widespread reports of corruption among Indian agency and military trading post appointments on the upper Missouri. Custer, who had railed against such injustices and illegalities in print[14] and had fed Bennett and other Democratic organs information injurious to the Republican administration,[15] had assisted the newspaperman.

When the Democrat-controlled House went after Belknap, Hazen, no friend of Custer's, supplied his name on a list of possible witnesses,[16] hence the telegram to Fort Lincoln. Also implicated was Orvil Grant, the President's brother, who later admitted his malfeasance to the Clymer committee on March 9 and even complained of the money he had lost, regretting (as one newspaper reported) "not the use of his influence, but disappointment in the smallness of the amount he made out of the traderships."[17]

Custer testified before the committee on March 29 and again on April 4. Most of his testimony was hearsay, and he admitted as much to the committee,[18] which was likely fishing for more information. He outlined for the committee members in both broad and specific terms how the scheme worked—how food meant for Indian agencies was resold to post traders, thus forcing the government to pay for the supplies twice and starving the Indians. He showed how the kickback scheme, in which the post traders paid a hefty part of their earnings to Secretary Belknap, worked on the post level and offered an example from his own Fort Abraham Lincoln. Custer also mentioned the already implicated Orvil Grant in a poor light and praised Hazen, with whom he had sparred in print for many years.

Custer's lengthy and detailed testimony caused the *New York Times* to editorialize, "Gen. Custer's testimony before Clymer's committee to-day reveals some of the bold rascalities of Indian and Army traders, and reflects severely upon the late Secretary of War. . . . No one who witnessed the earnest manner with which he gave testimony, doubts the sincerity of his convictions."[19] No less reliable an observer than Secretary of State Hamilton Fish called him "one of the most effective witnesses before Hiester Clymer's Committee."[20] Hazen had again testified against Belknap, by letter, as had two other army officers.[21] But testimony from the army's best-known Indian fighter about widespread corruption in the War Department's management of Indian affairs, whether hearsay or not, added significant credibility to the accusations.

An article in the March 31 issue of the *New York Herald* titled "Belknap's Anaconda" offered additional details and further entwined Belknap in the scandal. The story was uncredited, as was standard newspaper practice at the time, but rumors spread that Custer had written it, making him even more unwelcome in Republican circles.

Custer took advantage of his time in the capital. Before another House committee, he lobbied for better pay for the army's noncommissioned officers. He also testified twice against the Seventh Cavalry's Major Lewis Merrill, who was accused of receiving cash rewards from a state government for the Ku Klux Klan members his command captured and of accepting a bribe while acting as judge advocate in a court-martial.[22] Though Custer had earlier requested Merrill's presence with the Seventh, he had concluded that he had little use for Merrill. Neither, apparently, did Benteen, Reno, or most of the regiment's other duty officers, since Merrill had seen little service on the frontier in his eight years with the Seventh. Reno would later call him a "notorious coward and shirk,"[23] and Benteen would brand him a "chump,"[24] killing two reputations with one stone by declaring, "Poor a soldier as Reno was, he was a long way ahead of Merrill."[25] Custer's original request for Merrill had come about because the regiment was short on field-grade officers, and Custer had no faith in Reno's ability to lead much of anything. Merrill was an associate of Belknap's, and probably a Republican,[26] which points up Custer's desperation.

Merrill had been relieved of his duty at the Centennial Exhibition due to the charges, but a few days later, that order was rescinded by the President.[27] Though Custer claimed in the press that he had only been investigating the charges, in the pages of the semiofficial *Army and Navy Journal,* Merrill accused Custer of slander instigated with "cowardly purpose,"[28] and the investigation against him was soon dropped.

Another effort would bear fruit. Terry had asked more than once that the remaining three companies of the Seventh serving in the South be transferred to Fort Lincoln. The War Department had turned him down. But General Sherman, back from his self-imposed exile in Chicago, had warmed to Custer after his committee testimony. Sherman and Hazen were old friends, and he appreciated that Custer had defended and praised Hazen. Furthermore, Sherman had been aware of the trading post corruption[29] and was hostile toward Belknap, who had usurped his power ever since taking office.[30] While Custer stayed in Washington, he and Sherman dined together regularly, and when Custer asked about the availability of the three companies, Sherman saw to it that they were transferred.[31] He also personally requested recruits to replace seventy Seventh Cavalry troopers who were about to be discharged on May 1—another request of Terry's that had been ignored. In addition, Sherman introduced Custer to the new Secretary of War, Alphonso Taft, who had asked Sherman to return to Washington.

One of Custer's failings was his inability to anticipate or appreciate fully the reactions of others to his vocal opinions, and he ran true to form now. During his time in the capital, Custer wrote his "precious sunbeam" every two or three days. "I have done nothing rashly," he said in one letter. "And all honest straightforward men commend my course."[32] But while Custer may have gained a political friend in Sherman, his testimony had compromised relations with the man who had been his most loyal champion since the war. His longtime mentor, Sheridan, was furious about Custer's claim that Hazen's banishment to remote Fort Buford had been punishment for his daring to question the Indian Ring. He wrote to the War Department contradicting some of Custer's testimony, including the Hazen claim. So did his military secretary, James Forsyth, who kept Belknap abreast of War Department developments after his resignation and conspired with him to hurt Custer.[33] Sheridan, loyal to his old commander Grant and his administration—including his friend Belknap[34]—would no longer protect Custer as he had for more than a decade.

Custer's letters to Libbie told of how he socialized day and night with several prominent Democrats, including Clymer, who was apparently happy with his testimony. Though not strong enough to indict anyone, it had been corroborated by others. Clymer told him that Belknap might still be impeached despite his resignation, and if so Custer would likely be needed for more testimony. Belknap was indeed indicted for trial before the Senate, but Custer's mostly hearsay testimony would not be needed. He was released by the committee and left Washington on April 20.

Terry had originally planned for the Dakota column to depart while the Indians were still isolated in their winter camps and before the snow began to thaw enough to open supply routes, but he had been forced to delay the departure of the expedition until April 15, and then early May. Now time was of the essence, but instead of rushing to return to Fort Lincoln and his command, Custer went to New York, stopping on the way in Philadelphia to visit the Centennial Exhibition. In New York, he discussed business with his publisher, arranged with the *New York Herald* to submit unsigned dispatches from the field, and found time to attend the theater and dine with prominent Democrats. At one luncheon, when asked about the upcoming expedition, he boldly told a group that the Seventh could whip all the Indians on the plains. General G. M. Dodge, who had fought the Lakotas a decade earlier, was among the group. The next day in his office, he cautioned Custer against such hubris, but Custer shrugged off the warning.[35]

*   *   *

CUSTER HAD PLANNED on leaving New York for Fort Lincoln by train on the evening of April 24, but before he could depart, he received a summons from the Senate ordering him back to Washington for the possibility of further testimony in the Belknap trial. The summons had probably been engineered by the disgraced ex-Secretary himself, who still had close ties to the administration and was obsessed with revenge against those, such as Custer, whom he perceived to be responsible for his fall from grace.[36] A Chicago newspaper reported, "Belknap and his friends are collecting material to make out a case against Gen. Custer with a view to having him tried by court-martial before Gen. Terry at St. Paul." Although Belknap was studying Custer's various testimonies, the story claimed, "the General does not seem to be alarmed. He says he is willing to have his record examined with the closest scrutiny."[37]

A trip that Custer originally expected to last a week or ten days—including the quick jaunt to New York to tend to business matters—now had no end in sight. Stunned, he returned to Washington on April 27. The next day, he met with Secretary Taft and asked him to request his release by the impeachment committee. Taft promised to do so,[38] but he never wrote the letter.

"Do not be anxious," Custer wrote Libbie after seeing Taft. "I seek to follow a moderate and prudent course, avoiding prominence. Nevertheless, everything I do, however simple and unimportant, is noticed and commented on. This only makes me more careful."[39] It was far too late for prudence, however. Besieged Republicans were doing their best to smear Custer, accusing him of perjury with a view toward a court-martial and even providing the press with defamatory material.[40] Though not politically naive, Custer was out of his element in Washington. He clearly had no idea of the hornet's nest his testimony and actions had stirred up—or of Belknap's power or vindictiveness.

Custer was also about to encounter the wrath of Belknap's good friend the President. Grant had been cool toward Custer at least since his court-martial in the fall of 1867, and Custer knew it, but this new provocation was more than the President could take. Grant was furious over Custer's implication of his brother, his hurtful but unimpeachable testimony, and his general antiadministration comportment. (Custer had also once placed the President's son Captain Fred Grant under arrest for drunkenness.)[41] In Grant's eyes, he had only one recourse—total humiliation. At a cabinet meeting later that day, the President directed Taft to relieve Custer of command of the Dakota column and assign another officer in his place. The order went through the chain of command to Sherman, then Sheridan, and finally Terry.

When Custer was told, he quickly obtained permission from the Senate to leave for his post. (Belknap's impeachment trial was held, but the Senate fell short of the number of votes required to convict, with most senators considering the case outside their jurisdiction.) Per the demands of military protocol, he also received permission to leave from Sherman, who advised him to wait two days, until Monday, May 1, to depart, and to attempt to see the President and explain himself in order to regain command of the expedition.

Custer had called at the White House twice during the previous month, but Grant had refused to see him both times. Now Custer appeared at 10:00 a.m. Monday and presented his card. He sat in the anteroom for five hours and watched as others were ushered into Grant's presence. At 3:00 p.m., the President sent word that he would not see Custer. A desperate Custer then sent Grant a letter begging a brief hearing, to no avail. His options exhausted, he left.

He stopped by the War Department and received a letter from the Inspector General granting him permission to leave the city—"understanding that the general of the army desires you to proceed directly to your station"[42]—then boarded a train headed west that evening. He stopped in Monroe on the way back to Dakota Territory and spent most of a day there, "from the morning train until the evening only," remembered his father, Emmanuel Custer. "I remember he told me that Bloody Knife [an Arikara scout Custer had taken a liking to] had sent him word that he was going to take his scalp, and he laughed as he said it."[43] After bidding good-bye to his parents, he visited the home of his old friend attorney John Bulkley, his former seatmate at the Stebbins Academy. Several friends stopped by to wish him luck, and then the two retired to the library to sit and talk. When the subject of Grant's actions came up, Custer became philosophical. "Never mind," Custer said. "It is a long lane that has no turning. I don't believe that a man ever perpetrated a rank injustice, knowingly, upon his fellow man but that he suffered for it, before he died."[44]

When he left Monroe for St. Paul, he was not alone. With him was his favorite nephew, Autie Reed. Custer had arranged for Autie, who had just turned eighteen, to accompany the column as a beef herder. Autie was joined by Emma Reed, his teenage sister, who came along to stay with Libbie for the summer. Another young man, Dick Roberts (who was the brother of Annie Roberts Yates, one of Libbie's closest friends), would also be hired as a herder, with extra duties. While in New York, Custer had arranged with Whitelaw Reid for young Roberts to file dispatches for the *New York Tribune,* since Reid had declined to send one of his own reporters—a sign, perhaps, of how unimportant this latest Indian-hunting expedition was considered in the East. Both young men were excited about witnessing what promised to be the last great Indian battle.

The train pulled into Chicago on the morning of May 4. At the railroad station, an officer from Sheridan's headquarters, Custer's good friend Colonel Tony Forsyth, found Custer on the St. Paul train and handed him a message. By order of Sherman, but clearly the work of Grant, Custer was commanded to remain in Chicago until receiving further orders. His transgression? "He was not justified in leaving without seeing the President or myself," Sherman had telegraphed to Sheridan. "Let the Expedition from Fort Lincoln proceed without him."[45] Invoking a twisted, petty rationale, Grant had latched on to Custer's breach of protocol in leaving the capital without paying his respects to the President, despite his several attempts to do so.

A desperate Custer sent several telegrams to Sherman asking for justice and explaining in great detail how he had tried to see the president. He also pointed out that he had indeed procured permission to leave from Sherman. When that did not produce an answer, he asked that his detention be transferred to Fort Lincoln. The next day, his request was allowed, though he was still barred from the expedition. Custer's humiliation at the hands of Grant would now be even more exquisite: he would have no choice but to watch helplessly as his beloved Seventh Cavalry rode off to the last great confrontation with the Indians under another's command—Major Marcus Reno's, perhaps. As all of this was going on, the eastern papers were, for the most part, condemning the President's actions as tyrannical and partisan. "It seems strange a man should lose his position for emulating the boy 'who could not tell a lie,'" wrote one. "He was struck down for telling the truth," railed another. Some of the Republican papers supported Grant, though their defense consisted of ad hominem attacks on Custer that were usually riddled with errors.

Custer reached St. Paul on May 6 and found General Terry sympathetic to his plight. After Custer had been relieved of his command, Terry had suggested a few infantry Colonels in his stead, but Sheridan had decided that the best candidate to lead the expedition was the departmental commander himself. Apparently ignored was the regiment's official commander, fifty-four-year-old Colonel Samuel D. Sturgis, West Point class of 1846, who had been on recruiting duty in St. Louis for several years (and who had recently testified to the good character of Orville Babcock, who would soon be implicated—and again cleared of any wrongdoing—in another scandal, the Safe Burglary Conspiracy).[46] Sturgis had fought in the Mexican War along with most of his classmates, such as Grant, McClellan, Stonewall Jackson, and John Gibbon, and had spent several years fighting Indians before the Civil War. But he hadn't been in the field in years and was clearly on the downside of his career. Reno, who had little Indian-fighting experience, had wired Terry in early April asking for the command. When Terry had responded negatively, the Seventh's junior Major had gone over his head to Sheridan, who in a July 1864 endorsement of a brigadiership for Reno had lauded him as "one of the most promising young cavalry officers of this army" and opined that "the cavalry service has no better officer than Capt. Reno."[47] "Why not give me a chance," suggested Reno, "sending instructions what to do with Sitting Bull if I catch him." But "Fighting Phil" declined to interfere, shifting all responsibility back to Terry, who refused to reconsider his original decision.[48]

The last thing Terry wanted was to lead a military command hundreds of miles on horseback in the unrelenting summer heat against the fiercest Indians on the plains. Not only was he content to be a desk officer living with his sisters in St. Paul, but he had never campaigned against Indians. He desperately desired, and needed, Custer's experience. So did Sheridan and Sherman, who had received a tongue-lashing from Grant when a newspaper had quoted Sherman as saying that Custer "was not only the best man but the only man fit to lead the expedition now fitting out against the Indians."[49]

With tears in his eyes, Custer begged Terry for help.[50] The sagacious Terry and his humbled subordinate crafted a telegram to the President that wisely avoided mention of any transgressions and instead appealed to the old soldier's sense of duty.

To His Excellency the President, through Military Channels.

I have seen your order, transmitted through the General of the army, directing that I be not permitted to accompany the expedition about to move against hostile Indians. As my entire regiment forms a part of the proposed expedition, and as I am the senior officer of the regiment on duty in this Department, I respectfully but most earnestly request that while not allowed to go in command of the expedition, I may be permitted to serve with my regiment in the field.

I appeal to you as a soldier to spare me the humiliation of seeing my regiment march to meet the enemy and I not share in its dangers.

(Signed) G. A. Custer
Bvt. Maj. Gen. U.S. Army.[51]

Terry appended a letter of transmittal that humbly requested Custer's reinstatement and declared that "Custer's services would be very valuable with his command."[52] In Chicago, Sheridan also endorsed Custer's request, though in words disparaging to his subordinate. Clearly, though respectful of Custer's military skills, he remained angered by Custer's antiadministration activities. Sherman and Taft likely advised the same. With his top brass recommending clemency, no grounds on which to prefer court-martial charges, and most of the press castigating him for his partisan actions, Grant had little choice but to relent. Custer was at Terry's headquarters on the morning of May 8 when word came of the President's decision. A tele-gram from Sherman to Terry revealed the news: "General Custer's urgent request to go under your command with his regiment has been submitted to the President, who sent me word that if you want General Custer along he withdraws his objections. Advise Custer to be prudent, not to take along any newspaper men, who always make mischief, and to abstain from personalities in the future." Custer's luck, it seemed, had held fast.

An elated Custer left Terry later that morning to return to his room at the Metropolitan Hotel, just a few blocks away, where his niece and nephew waited. In the street, he ran into Captain William Ludlow, a longtime acquaintance who had accompanied the Yel-lowstone and Black Hills expeditions and who was now chief engi-neer on Terry's staff. According to Ludlow, Custer revealed his good news and then claimed that he would "cut loose" from Terry at the first available chance—that he had "got away from Stanley [Custer's commander on the 1873 Yellowstone Expedition] and would be able to swing clear of Terry."[53]

Custer may have been joshing affectionately with an intimate acquaintance or simply (and thoughtlessly) voicing the desire of every cavalryman—to be given a command of his own.[54] If he was serious, the statement was a sad indictment of the cocky Custer and his lack of gratitude. At any rate, Terry was planning to give Custer a good deal of freedom; he would be able to "swing clear" rather easily.

Custer, his niece and nephew, Terry, and several of Terry's staff members and two of his sisters left St. Paul by rail and arrived at Fort Lincoln on the evening of May 10. The Seventh's leader had been away from his command for seven weeks. The winter campaign was now a late-spring campaign. The advantage Sheridan had hoped for by pushing a winter strike, compromised by atrocious weather, had now been lost.

SIX

"Submitt to Uncl Sam or Kill the 7 Hors"

Our Skeleton Army! It seems like the dead
To the buzzards rapacious that wheel overhead,
Yet its nerve is of steel, and its eye is of fire
And the tattered old banner waves brighter and higher.

W. A. CROFFUTT

On a warm day in the middle of May, beside a river thirteen miles from Fort Lincoln, Libbie Custer wrapped her arms around her husband's neck and held him tight. Sobbing, she begged him to be careful. He promised her that he would. She was a soldier's wife, he told her, she must be brave. "Soon he'd be back and then we'd all have good times at Fort Lincoln again," remembered Custer's devoted personal orderly of six years, a taciturn Private named John Burkman, who held Libbie's horse. Aside from the same year of birth, the simple, illiterate striker (an army word for an enlisted man who worked as an officer's servant for extra money) had little in common with his CO except for their love of animals, but that had been enough to forge a curious codependency. The two would often argue heatedly over some matter but eventually make up, the Brevet Major General as often as not apologizing to the Private.

Custer was teary-eyed himself. He gently disentangled his wife's arms and watched as Burkman helped her mount. She leaned down and placed her hand on Burkman's shoulder and asked him to look after her husband. Then she joined the General's sister Maggie Custer Calhoun and his niece Emma Reed and rode away with the paymaster's wagon, her head bowed.

The General watched until his wife and the small party were just tiny dots on the endless prairie. He said softly, "A good soldier has to serve two mistresses. While he's loyal to one the other must suffer."[1]

In the week since his arrival at Lincoln with Terry, Custer had worked nonstop helping to oversee preparations for the expedition's departure. Dressed in his buckskin suit, he had been everywhere fine-tuning his regiment.[2] During his absence, Reno and his staff had acquired an impressive collection of white and Indian scouts, interpreters, and guides. Thirty Arikaras, including a few half-breeds (the term used for anyone of half-white, half-Indian ancestry) had been recruited as scouts and couriers from the Fort Berthold Agency, and because they were unfamiliar with the country west of the Little Missouri, four Lakota Sioux scouts also were brought along.

Bloody Knife, a half-Arikara, half-Sioux, was a favorite. The impudent scout's refusal to kowtow to the General had endeared him to Custer, who listed him as a guide with the Quartermaster Department so that he would be paid more than the other enlisted Arikaras.[3] He had led a curious life. Raised in his father's Hunkpapa village for the first sixteen years of his life, he had faced a good deal of ridicule for his Arikara blood—much of it from another youth, a burly boy named Gall. When he was sixteen, Bloody Knife's mother took her children and returned to her Arikara village on the Missouri River. As a grown man, Bloody Knife decided to visit his father's people. Upon reaching the Hunkpapa encampment, he was stripped and humiliated. Not long after that, Sioux raiders killed, scalped, and mutilated two of his brothers.

A few years later, Bloody Knife found an opportunity for revenge. Gall, now a tall, beefy warrior and the leader of his own small *tiospaye* (band), had become a scourge of the upper Missouri army forts, though he would sometimes camp near one for trading purposes, and even sign the occasional treaty. In November 1865, Bloody Knife led an army detachment to Gall's camp and identified him. When the Hunkpapa resisted arrest, the soldiers bayoneted him and left him for dead. But the hardy warrior somehow survived to continue his troublemaking ways.[4]

Bloody Knife had worked for the army as a courier, mail carrier, and enlisted Indian scout for more than a decade. In the past three years, he had become somewhat of a blood brother to Custer. He knew that Gall would probably be among the nontreaty Sioux they were after and was looking forward to finding the hostile camp.

The detachment of Indian scouts was led by Second Lieutenant Charles Varnum, West Point class of 1872, who had impressed Custer with his performance in the Yellowstone skirmishes. The appointment was a plum for a young officer without a troop, since the scouts were constantly in advance of the column and he was sure to be in the thick of things.[5] Varnum's tall, homely classmate, Lieutenant George Wallace, had held that position on the Black Hills Expedition but would now serve as the regiment's engineering officer, tabulating the mileage and keeping the official itinerary. Joining them would be "Lonesome" Charley Reynolds, the quiet guide whom the Arikaras called "Lucky Man" for his extraordinary hunting ability.[6] Reynolds was the best white scout in Dakota Territory. He had earned Custer's respect with his excellent work on the Yellowstone and Black Hills expeditions, and earlier that spring he had returned from a long trek into hostile territory to report to Custer that the Lakotas under Sitting Bull "were gathering in force."[7] They had been preparing for war by collecting Winchester repeating rifles and plenty of ammunition. The normally imperturbable Reynolds was convinced that the Lakotas were deadly serious in their intent to fight.[8]

As each Indian tribe needed a translator, two excellent ones were hired. The blue-eyed, fair-haired Frederic Gerard, a former trader once married to an Arikara woman, had been the Fort Lincoln interpreter for that tribe since 1872. As a youth years before, he had worked as a printer's devil in a St. Louis newspaper office, and at one time he had served as a correspondent for the *New York Herald*.[9] He had lived and worked in the upper Missouri area for almost thirty years, much of that time for fur companies around Fort Berthold, and Custer thought highly of him. "I consider his knowledge of Indians and the country west of the Missouri river invaluable," Custer told Terry. "He is an educated man and I have never met his equal as an interpreter."[10] The two had something else in common: their disgust with the fraud perpetrated by crooked Indian agents. While at Berthold in 1868, Gerard had complained to Washington about the agent there cheating the Arikaras out of their annuities. The agent had caused Gerard to lose his position.[11] His fortunes had declined since then—besides his interpreting duties, he sold butter and eggs to the Fort Lincoln soldiers—but he had somehow managed to send his three young half-breed daughters to a Benedictine school in St. Joseph, Minnesota, for a proper education.[12]

Despite the blunt refusals of Terry and Sherman, Reno had still expected to go out in command of the regiment before Custer's return. In anticipation, he had fired Gerard on May 6, telling the interpreter that he had to economize and could hire three teamsters at Gerard's salary. Gerard thought the reason suspect and the termination personal. Custer immediately reinstated him the day after his return.[13] Besides being a likable sort,[14] Gerard was capable, knowledgeable, and brave. He was admired by the Arikaras for his part in helping defend them against a Yankton Sioux attack, when he had held out in his trading post alone for ten days. Their nickname for him, for the number of Sioux he had killed, was "Seven Yanktons."[15] During one bartering session with Sitting Bull years before, the two had argued vociferously and wrestled over some Iroquois shells. The Hunkpapa had raised his double-barreled rifle toward Gerard, but Gerard had managed to push the gun away and knock the firing caps off with his thumb. Sitting Bull had later voiced his respect for the trader, and the two did business again.[16]

To handle the Sioux language, Custer had hired a tall, quiet black man named Isaiah Dorman, who had worked as an interpreter and courier for several years at Fort Rice. A former slave from New Orleans, Dorman had earned the respect of soldiers and civilians at the fort. He was married to a Dakota Sioux woman named Visible; they had no children. Not a young man, he signed on with the expedition because he loved the wild country and said he wished to see that western land once more before he died.[17]

The main body of the Dakota column comprised all twelve

companies of the Seventh Cavalry, three infantry companies, and a battery of Gatling guns. Accompanying the column in various roles were Boston Custer, hired, for no valid reason, as a guide[18] at $100 a month; Autie Reed and Dick Roberts, along for the fun of a summer expedition; Mark Kellogg, the sole newspaperman with the column, who had been more or less stuck with the Seventh since he had met Custer on the snowbound Northern Pacific train in March, his plans to return to the Black Hills put on hold when *Bismarck Tribune* publisher Clement Lounsberry had obtained permission from General Terry to send a correspondent;[19] four or five doctors;[20] and several teamsters overseeing the pack train.

The reputation of the "Fighting Seventh" — "the best cavalry in Uncle Sam's service," as Custer had proudly described it to his good friend Lawrence Barrett[21] — preceded it. In truth, however, its reputation was a hollow one. The Fighting Seventh had not fought anyone, much less Lakota Sioux, in three years. Their most recent action had consisted of two skirmishes on the Yellowstone in the summer of 1873. Four of the regiment's companies had not participated in either of those fracases and had no combat experience in the previous seven years, save some chasing after the Ku Klux Klan and moonshiners. The other eight troops could boast of only five skirmishes with an Indian foe during the same period.[22] Only about 172 men — 30 percent of the total — could claim to have fought Indians.[23]

Outside of the two Yellowstone encounters, in which a total of five soldiers had been killed, the Fighting Seventh had fought only one large-scale contest. The Battle of the Washita had made the regiment's name, but that had hardly been an epic contest, and few of those enlisted men were still around eight years later. Finally, there was the matter of recruits. The previous October, 150 new men had joined the regiment; 60 of these had served in the army previously. On May 1, barely two weeks before the departure date, 63 more had arrived at Fort Lincoln. The long, severe Dakota winter of 1875–76 had afforded few opportunities for cavalry training. Reno had ordered four to six weeks' worth of steady drill earlier that spring, but that instruction had been elementary, mostly company and battalion drill, with very little squad drill and little if any work in horsemanship or marksmanship.[24]

It certainly did not help matters that recruits received only the most basic instruction during their short time at Jefferson Barracks, Missouri, the cavalry's recruit depot. Training in marksmanship, horsemanship, skirmishing — any practical lessons that Indian fighting might actually involve — was virtually nonexistent. Formal military training of recruits consisted mostly of elementary drill aimed at making a grand appearance at dress parade.[25] After a week or two at most of close order drill and fatigue duty, they were sent directly to their units, presumably to learn the finer points of soldiering from company officers and noncommissioned officers. "Recruits are sent to the cavalry companies with practically no knowledge whatever of their duties," complained Major Lewis Merrill.[26] And with only fifteen rounds a month per soldier allotted for target practice (just increased from ten rounds the previous September),[27] which was highly irregular at best, few of the many recruits from the big cities in the East gained any kind of proficiency with a rifle or pistol. The Indians were aware of this. Remembering a fight against a group of plainsmen whose marksmanship was impressive, one Hunkpapa Lakota said, "The warriors knew that they were not fighting soldiers, because soldiers were poor shots."[28]

Individual combat training — learning how to fight a foe in close quarters — was virtually unknown. Horsemanship took the bulk of the enlisted men — mostly city boys — a long time to master. "Many of the men had never been on a horse," recalled one Lieutenant a few years later. Another complained that "the men are never drilled at firing on horseback, and the consequence is that the horses are as unused to fighting as the men themselves, and become unruly in action."[29] With horses new to the cavalry and untrained in battle (either to gunfire in general or against Indians in particular) — the case with half the Seventh's mounts — the regiment's effectiveness was further decreased.[30]

It should come as no surprise, then, that the fighting ability of the Seventh, and of virtually every cavalry unit on the plains, was questionable. Any tactics discussed at the officer level reflected the military's preoccupation with a European-style war involving massed forces battling in a straightforward manner. This "conventional" warfare was dramatically different from the guerrilla warfare conducted by the Plains Indians. The recent Franco-Prussian War of 1870–71 occupied the minds of the army's higher-ranking officers, as several of them had traveled to Europe to observe a few battles. (Upon his return, Sheridan had told Armstrong, "Custer, you with that Third Division could have captured King William six times over.")[31] Indian warfare was not taken seriously enough to inspire any kind of accepted, widespread doctrine. Commanders on the plains learned as they went along, and such knowledge was rarely shared with anyone outside their units. Frontier duty was viewed in the East as a kind of police action, with little chance of glory and an excellent chance of either disappointment when the Indians couldn't be caught or embarrassment when they were.

As mediocre as the soldiers' training and fighting ability was the caliber of their character. One general officer said, "The enlisted personnel consisted largely of the dregs from the Union and Confederate Armies and of recent immigrants from Europe." A cavalryman remembered that "criminals and semi-criminals made up a large part" of the one hundred men in his group of enlistees, and he described them as "the toughest sort of city rowdies."[32] One Seventh Cavalry Private, who at the age of sixteen had abandoned his six months' pregnant wife to enlist, claimed that "some of the hardest cases that I ever came across are at present serving in this company."[33] Another described his comrades in arms as "vile and wicked . . . a set of thieves and gamblers yea murderers."[34] This was not the army of a dozen years earlier, composed of motivated young volunteers from all walks of life and almost all levels of society, and all dedicated to "the cause." The country was still reeling from the Panic of 1873, and a third of the workforce could not find a job. Many of the unemployed joined the army solely to get fed, housed, and paid $13 a month. The military's desertion rate was so high—about 30 percent for much of the 1870s—and the reenlistment rate so low that recruiters largely ignored mental and physical requirements. If a man could mount a horse and carry a gun, he was good enough for the cavalry. Age mattered little. One man two weeks shy of his forty-first birthday enlisted at the "official age" of eighteen.[35] One older trooper, John Armstrong, had returned home from the Civil War to find his wife living with another man and in a family way, and had immediately reenlisted.

Foreigners made up almost half of the Seventh's ranks, with the United Kingdom and Germany contributing the lion's share. Most of the Germans, ironically, had fled to the United States to avoid conscription into the Prussian army. Some of these foreign-born men became excellent soldiers. Many joined to survive while they learned their new country's language. The Scottish-born John Forbes was using an assumed name, John Hiley, and keeping secret his noble birth. He had got into some trouble in his native country but had just received a letter from his mother telling him the problem would soon be settled and he could return. His five-year hitch would be up in January.[36]

There were some active young men of good character who had joined the army for the sake of adventure or for some other reason. Here and there in the ranks was a schoolteacher, a lawyer, or a trained artisan such as a stonecutter or watchmaker. But the position most frequently listed under "Previous Occupation" was laborer, which usually meant an unskilled, unlettered ruffian from a big city in the East. The overall caliber of the Army's enlisted ranks had deteriorated noticeably since the end of the Civil War. In the Seventh Cavalry alone, more than 10 percent of the men had enlisted under an alias.

The regiment's noncommissioned officers, fortunately, were overwhelmingly Civil War veterans, chiefly of Irish or German descent. But many of these grizzled veterans were absent on leave or detached service, weakening the ranks even further. One of the most experienced was Sergeant John Ryan, a young man who had joined the Union army at sixteen and had served with the Seventh almost since its inception, nearly a full decade. Ryan, who was often referred to as the handsomest man in the regiment, had witnessed the horrors of Antietam and was not impressed with the mettle of the enlisted men around him. "Individually the Indians were better soldiers than our troops, for every Indian was a perfect rider and a good soldier," he wrote later. "The regular army was composed mostly of green recruits and so unreliable that even Custer did not dare to fight them mounted on some occasions and had to turn his men into mounted infantry."[37] That Ryan was there at all was a surprise to some. He had just that spring been court-martialed at Fort Rice for harsh discipline and busted to Private. The acting post commander, Captain Benteen, could have mitigated the punishment but did not, likely due to bad blood between the two. Ryan's company CO, Captain Thomas French, had gotten Ryan reinstated by Major Reno just days before the regiment's departure.[38]

The officer corps could boast a bit more Indian-fighting experience than the enlisted men. Half of the twenty-eight officers had taken part in an actual battle with Indians. Ten had fought at the Washita eight years before, and four more had engaged the Sioux in the two skirmishes on the Yellowstone. Several of the Second Lieutenants were recent graduates of West Point: the diminutive, irrepressible Benny Hodgson, a favorite with everyone, who had been thinking about resigning—his father wanted to set him up in the sperm oil business in his hometown of Philadelphia[39]—until his good friend Lieutenant Varnum persuaded him to stick around for one last campaign; Lieutenant James "Jack" Sturgis, the unpretentious only son of the regiment's commander and a member of the most recent West Point graduating class; Lieutenant Luther Hare, the big, unassuming Texan who was as fine a horseman as General Custer; and Lieutenant Henry Harrington, who had been on leave with his wife and two small children in the East but had returned early to Fort Lincoln to ride out with his company.

These young West Pointers and others were well versed in drill and the essential elements of a gentleman's education but woefully inexperienced in campaigning and leading men into battle. Despite their shortcomings, many graduates of the Point had acquired an air of superiority regarding those officers who had not walked those hallowed halls: the "rankers," enlisted men who, through a demonstration of leadership or bravery, or simple diligence, had made officer grade during the war and had passed the tests for a regular army commission afterward; Civil War volunteer officers who had gained a regular army commission; and men appointed to the officer corps from civilian life, the result of superior test scores or influential patrons. Needless to say, this lack of respect was usually repaid in kind, and serious problems of cooperation, communication, and distrust sometimes developed between these two classes.

Despite the fact that the regiment's officers were generally of a better class than the enlisted men, they had their own moral and professional failings. The "Benzine Boards"—appointed to weed out the officer corps and named after a popular cleaning solvent—and attrition had purged most of the worst cases since the Civil War, but the army still had its share of "soldiers of fortune, drunkards, gamblers, and libertines," as one historian put it.[40] A variety of vices and weaknesses, among them sexual misconduct and abuse, theft, corruption, and racial prejudice, also damaged the leadership and cohesiveness of the regiment. Alcohol was the most prevalent problem. Many of the old-line officers who had fought in the Civil War had lost their illusions and ambitions in the decade since and now relieved their boredom and apathy the same way they had endured the horrors of the war—by turning to the bottle. Almost all of the officers imbibed, and many of them did so heavily. It was a drinking man's army, and a drinking man's regiment, despite the fact that its field commander abstained.

Other factors further impinged on performance. Fifteen of the regiment's officers were absent, several of its officers were assigned to companies they were unfamiliar with, and it had been two years since any substantial number of the twelve troops had served together as a body. As a matter of fact, all twelve had never been together before. Custer, desperately short several officers, had even allowed the temporary transfer in of a young infantry Lieutenant only a week before leaving. Second Lieutenant John Crittenden had flunked out of West Point—a disappointment, since he was from a long line of distinguished officers—but with the help of his father, Lieutenant Colonel Thomas Crittenden, he had secured a commission only seven months before. He had lost an eye in a hunting accident in October and now wore a glass one. He badly wanted some field experience, and his father had persuaded Custer to replace an officer on medical leave with his son. Young Crittenden was possessed of a delicate physique—his West Point classmates had called him "their baby" and relieved him of many of the harsher duties of cadet life.[41] But he was determined to make a career of the military and planned to enter artillery school after the campaign.[42] The Seventh's chain of command was shaky at best.

But with Custer at its head, supported by a mostly veteran officer corps and a solid group of noncoms, the Seventh managed to muster up an impressive degree of esprit de corps. "You felt like you were somebody when you were on a good horse, with a carbine dangling from its small leather ring socket on your McClellan saddle and a Colt army revolver strapped on your hip," observed Charles Windolph, a Private in Benteen's company. "You were a cavalryman of the Seventh Regiment. You were part of a proud outfit that had a fighting reputation."[43] The Seventh might have had its problems—problems endemic to virtually every regiment in the frontier army—but, like the rest of this glorified police force, it usually got the job done. More than anything, that was due to its field commander, to whom the regiment owed its identity and fame. Despite the grumbling in the ranks of both enlisted men and officers, Custer's reputation as a beau sabreur could still inspire. When he boasted that the Seventh could handle all of the Indians in the West, as he frequently did, most of them believed him, and with good reason. No disciplined force of soldiers larger than an eighty-man squadron—specifically, the one led by Captain William Fetterman in 1866 at Fort Phil Kearny that had been lured away from the fort and annihilated by some 1,500 warriors—had ever been defeated in battle by Plains Indians. Ever.

There were several reasons for this. To white thinking, "acceptable losses" were part of war and the cost of gaining an objective. Indians thought otherwise. The Sioux and their allies usually avoided any confrontation in which they did not possess an advantage in numbers—which sometimes coincided with the strength of their "medicine" on any particular day. "They will not venture an engagement unless they hold all the winning cards," noted an observant officer. "To risk as little as possible—such is their fundamental maxim."[44] The seminomadic life of the Plains Indian also dictated against protracted, costly stands. Since they had no permanent villages, they were not required to protect them unless completely surprised, as when Custer had surprised the Cheyenne camp on the Washita. Warriors were not required to follow leaders, who did not "command" in the sense whites understood it. Instead, they followed a man because of his reputation, which was based on personal skills and previous success in battle, charisma, and medicine. Good leaders planned their raids well, came home with more battle honors, sustained fewer casualties, and thus instilled confidence, the best medicine of all.

The Sioux and Cheyennes relied primarily on two basic strategies: the lightning strike and the ambush. In the Plains Indians' warrior culture, a man's status almost completely relied on honors gained in combat against either enemy tribes or *wasichus*. Once a group of warriors engaged in battle, every man's primary focus was on achieving as much personal glory as possible, and group strategy other than the most basic was almost nonexistent. Complicating this—at least to the ignorant white observer—was the Plains Indians' honors system of bravery. The highest honor involved disarming an enemy without hurting him, and killing ranked low on the bravery scale. The reasoning was based on degree of risk. Shooting someone with a rifle at long range involved none, at least to the Indians' way of thinking. Approaching close enough to insult the enemy by disarming or at least touching him with a hand or a stick held in the hand—counting coup—was a high honor. A warrior kept track of his coups, each of which required a witness for verification, and boasted of his deeds for years to come.[45] Whites often viewed the Plains Indians' style of fighting as cowardly. The warriors felt the same about the *wasichus'*.

The Indians also seemed incapable of driving home attacks in any sustained way, but there was a good reason for that. Battles against other tribes and the bluecoats had resulted in a low male-to-female ratio in the Indian population. A war of attrition had become a fundamental concept of the U.S. Army, but the Indians never seriously considered the thought of repeated attacks against an entrenched enemy until superior numbers won the day. When confronted with any force of regular army troops that held their ground, the Indians usually gave up after making one or two attempts at breaking their ranks. Then, in the words of one historian, "Plains Indians made a lot of noise, raised a lot of dust, but in the end fled or fired a few annoying, but generally harmless, long-range shots."[46] For example, seven months after the Fetterman Massacre, on August 2, 1867, in the vicinity of the same post, thirty soldiers and two citizen woodcutters had forted up behind fourteen wagon boxes placed in a semicircle and held off a small army of Sioux and Cheyennes led by Sitting Bull, Crazy Horse, Young Man Afraid of His Horses, and the Cheyenne chiefs Dull Knife and Little Wolf—at least five hundred warriors[47]—for six hours. The whites had lost only four men. The day before what became known as the Wagon Box Fight, some seventy-five miles up the Bozeman Trail as many as eight hundred warriors[48] had attacked a hay-mowing detail working in a meadow near Fort C. F. Smith. Ensconced behind a rudimentary corral of stacked logs, the twenty-one soldiers and nine civilians had fought off their attackers over several hours. Finally, there was the celebrated Battle of Beecher's Island in September 1868, when Custer's good friend Major George Forsyth and his handpicked company of fifty "first class hardy frontiersmen" had gone looking for hostile Indians and found plenty. Caught off-guard by six hundred or so Oglalas and Cheyennes, they had dug in on a small, brush-covered spit of sand in the middle of the dry Arikara Fork of the Cheyenne River. The veteran Indian fighters withstood several fierce frontal charges and then a weeklong siege that ended with a rescue by the buffalo soldiers of the Tenth Cavalry. Six of Forsyth's men (most notably, Lieutenant Fred Beecher, the nephew of the famed New York clergyman Henry Ward Beecher) were killed and fifteen wounded, but the battle was celebrated for years afterward as a triumph of grit and bravery over vastly superior numbers. These and other lesser-known engagements supported the belief that a well-armed and disciplined command could hold its own against an Indian force many times its size.[49]

The specific aim of the Dakota column—indeed, of the entire campaign—entailed far more than merely avoiding defeat. The hostiles were supposed to be chastised. The army was to punish them and force them onto their reservations. The three-pronged strategy had worked before; there was no reason to think it could not work again. And Custer, who had led the successful strike force at the Washita and then scoured the southern plains securing peace through war and treaty, could surely do the same on the northern plains.

Many of the men of the Seventh had written home, often sharing thoughts they could not within their companies. Irish-born Sergeant

William Cashan of L Company told his cousin, "If I will be lookey anoughf to get this thrue I will be a feerefull warrior Sutting Bulls scalp mus be mine if posible." A Scot in the same troop, Charles Scott, wrote his sister with details of the expedition: "We air going to what is cauld the Big Horn River . . . and will Be Gone 3 months."[50] Another Private in L, a farm boy named Ami Cheever, sent his mother $100 and told her, "I thought I would come home spring but changed my notions. I guess I will put it off awhile longer."[51] In a letter to his sister, a Private from Indiana named Marion Horn waxed dramatic about Sitting Bull and then offered a surprisingly accurate reason for it all: "I expect they will have a time to capture him for he is a notorious heathen scoundrel and has been commiting deprida- tion along this river for years and I hope they will scalp every one of them. . . . All the Indians along the River are all for war[;] there is one of the greatest Indian war expected this year that has been for years and it is all on account of them being frauded out of there rations and the miners going in the Hill."[52] And a blacksmith in I Company, Henry Bailey, summed up the feelings of many of the sol- diers in a letter to his sister: "We expect to go out after Sitting Bull and his cut throats, and if old Custer gets after him he will give him the fits for all the boys are spoiling for a fight."[53]

Some of the officers, however, seem to have foreseen that "old Custer" might not have things his own way. Captain Myles Keogh had suffered a variety of ailments over the previous year, and he had recently applied for one month's leave to begin October 1, provided the Indians were rounded up by then. Now he wrote a longtime female friend whose family the melancholy Irishman had grown close to: "I have requested to be packed up and shipped to Auburn in case I am killed, and I desire to be buried there. God bless you all, remember if I should die—you may believe that I love you and every member of your family—it was a second home to me."[54]

GENERAL GEORGE CROOK'S Wyoming column had not been the first in the field that year. That honor belonged to the battalion of the elderly Major James "Grasshopper Jim" Brisbin, so nick- named for his interest in and frequent discourse on the agricultural potential of his station in western Montana. Despite suffering from rheumatism so severe that he could not ride a horse or even walk without crutches, Brisbin had led a two-hundred-man cavalry force and a contingent of fifty-four Crow scouts from Fort Ellis to rescue a group of besieged traders and wolfers at Fort Pease, a recently constructed structure on the north bank of the Yellowstone, a few miles below the mouth of the Bighorn. Built in anticipation of increased river traffic and trade, the crude collection of log huts connected by a log palisade was no military post, and the angry Sioux began a series of attacks on the enterprise, killing six men and wounding eight. The Sioux had disappeared by the time Brisbin arrived, and he returned with nineteen citizens on March 17. That same day, more than a hundred miles to the southeast, Crook drew first blood.

Crook was tall, taciturn, and thoughtful, and a bit of an eccentric. He braided his long whiskers into two forks, and he liked to wear civilian clothes, sometimes donning moccasins and overalls, other times a canvas hunting suit and pith helmet. On this campaign, he wore a Private's uniform and overcoat with a high-crowned black hat. Like Custer, he neither smoked, drank, nor swore, and he often neglected to share his plans with his subalterns. Also like Custer, he had been a lackadaisical student. As a West Point classmate of Sheridan's, his immediate superior, he had ranked even lower than Custer, thirty-eighth in a class of forty-three. Both were publicity hounds and avid hunters with a passion for taxidermy, and both liked to ride far ahead of their columns, hunting for game—though unlike Custer, Crook preferred riding a mule to a horse while on campaign. He had developed meticulous and superior mule-packing techniques that greatly contributed to his success. One aide close to him, Lieutenant John G. Bourke, claimed that Crook "made the study of pack-trains the great study of his life."[55] His men liked serving under him and enjoyed his quirks.

Crook had risen to Major General during the Civil War despite a mixed record of achievement, and after the war and the usual reduction to regular army rank, his success in hunting down and fighting small bands of Apaches in Arizona had garnered him a coveted generalship and a transfer to the command of the Department of the

Platte. He had fought none of the horse tribes of the northern plains, but he was eager to begin.

Crook launched his expedition from Fort Fetterman, Wyoming Territory, on March 1, the day after a heavy snowstorm. His force was relatively small: two companies of infantry and ten troops of cavalry under fifty-five-year-old Colonel Joseph J. Reynolds, a man with some severe health problems. A longtime army veteran with service in both the Mexican War and the Civil War, Reynolds had been on the frontier for only a year.[56] But no one in the army was better at preparing an expedition than Crook, and his men were equipped with extra-heavy clothing and bedding. Crook hoped to surprise the hostile camps before spring, when warm weather saw the exodus of young warriors from the agencies.

A week out of Fetterman, to increase his mobility, Crook sent the wagon train and infantry back with all of the tenting and bedding save for two blankets a man. The weather had been bitterly cold, but in a few days it plunged to twenty-three degrees below zero and remained there or lower for a week. Soldiers had to break up bacon with an ax before heating it, and often the ax broke first. The stripped-down column continued north.

On March 16, scouts reported two Sioux hunters nearby, a likely indication of a camp. Crook split his command, giving Reynolds a strike force of almost four hundred men and remaining behind with four companies and the pack train. Reynolds pushed forward on the hunters' trail through falling snow, guided by the astonishing tracking abilities of Frank "the Grabber" Grouard, a half-Polynesian, half-white scout who had recently returned from spending eight years with the Sioux, most of them as an adopted brother of Sitting Bull and later as a friend of Crazy Horse. The next morning at sunrise, they found an unsuspecting camp of about sixty-five lodges nestled on the west bank of the Powder River. The temperature was forty or fifty degrees below zero, and a thick fog covered the river bottoms.

Though information from his scouts led Reynolds to believe that the camp was Crazy Horse's, it was actually a Cheyenne band of fifty lodges led by Old Bear, who planned to lead his band into its agency come spring, and about fifteen lodges of He Dog's Oglalas with some Minneconjou traders.[57] They were working their way slowly toward the agencies and were planning to visit Crazy Horse's camp down-river in the next few days.[58] Reynolds divided his command into three squadrons and attacked at midmorning. The soldiers quickly routed the Cheyennes from their tepees and secured the pony herd, but the village's 150 warriors regrouped and counterattacked, and Reynolds panicked and botched the withdrawal. After they torched the camp, the exhausted troopers hastily left at noon with most of the horses to rendezvous with Crook. The Cheyennes followed the force deep into the night and eventually recovered most of their mounts and seventy cavalry steeds after Reynolds neglected to post a guard over the herd and refused to send a force in pursuit.[59]

Reynolds returned almost devoid of results, with only a small por-tion of the Indian ponies. He had destroyed much of the village, true, but that included buffalo robes and furs and large stores of meat that could have been used by Crook's hungry and freezing men.[60] Only one Sioux and one Cheyenne had been killed. It was barely a tactical victory and in no way a strategic one, and the starving Wyoming col-umn returned to Fort Fetterman low on supplies and morale. Three dead troopers had been abandoned in the village, and, worse, one wounded man had been left behind to the mercy of its inhabitants.[61] Crook's expedition and the high expectations accompanying it were finished. Sheridan's hopes of a successful winter campaign, hitting the smaller villages before the spring brought hundreds more war-riors from the agencies, were dashed.

Crook was "terribly incensed at the blunders made by the imbe-cility of Reynolds," according to one of the correspondents with the column,[62] and immediately filed charges against him. Reynolds then did the same to two of his subordinates. After an acrimonious court-martial, Reynolds was convicted of "conduct to the prejudice of good order and military discipline," though there was some disagreement as to what his exact orders had been. He was suspended from rank and command for one year, and his subordinates in the battle were convicted of similar offenses.

Crook didn't take the field again until more than two months later, heading north on the old Bozeman Trail on May 29 with a force of almost 1,100 men and no Indian scouts. His attempt at Red

Cloud Agency to procure Lakotas for that purpose had been singularly unsuccessful. Lieutenant Colonel William B. Royall—a tall, handsome Virginian with a full gray mustache, bright blue eyes, and a Rebel saber scar at the apex of his forehead[63]—commanded fifteen companies of cavalry, and five companies of infantry were attached.[64] A week out of Fetterman, couriers delivered a dispatch from Sheridan informing Crook "that all able-bodied male Indians had left the Red Cloud Agency."[65] Crook knew that the annual spring departure for the nontreaty camps was in full force, exacerbated by problems with the delivery of agency ration supplies, and he was eager to find the village before it was reinforced by the agency warriors. John Finerty, a *Chicago Times* reporter with the column, wrote that "Crook was bristling for a fight."[66]

General Terry had planned for the expedition to leave on Monday, May 15, but a huge downpour on Sunday postponed the departure until May 17. The day before, a telling scene occurred in the Custer home. Custer brought his wife into the living room, where Terry was. Custer shut the door and turned to the tall, thin man with the dark beard and soft eyes.

"General Terry," he said, "a man usually means what he says when he brings his wife to listen to his statements. I want to say that reports are circulating that I do not want to go out to the campaign under you. But I want you to know that I do want to go and serve under you, not only that I value you as a soldier, but as a friend and a man."[67]

That night Custer visited with the Arikara scouts. He recognized several from previous campaigns—some of them had accompanied the Seventh on the Yellowstone Expedition of 1873 and the Black Hills Expedition of 1874. To Bloody Knife, still his favorite, Custer presented a medal he had procured in Washington and a black handkerchief spotted with blue stars. He told the scouts that this would be his last campaign and emphasized the importance of a victory over the Sioux.[68]

When reveille sounded at 4:00 a.m. the next day, the men of the

Dakota column woke to a cold, foggy dawn. By six o'clock, after a quick breakfast of bacon, hardtack, and coffee, the wagons, more than 150 in all, were packed and started on the trail leading from the river to the prairie above the post. Three companies of infantry, about 140 soldiers, and an artillery detachment of four guns and 34 men followed as an escort.[69]

Terry and Custer had decided that a formidable display of bravado might allay the anxiety of the family members left behind, so the Seventh marched through the mist toward the fort, like most frontier posts an unstockaded one. By 7:00 a.m., they were marching around the parade ground in company column of fours, led by Custer and his regimental staff, accompanied by Libbie, Maggie Calhoun, and Emma Reed.[70] The band, mounted on its white horses, came next, playing "Garry-Owen," the regiment's unofficial battle tune. The forty Arikara and four Sioux scouts (most of them married to Arikara women),[71] led by the prematurely balding Lieutenant Varnum — "Peaked Face," they called him, for his high forehead and large, sharp nose, accentuated by his thick mustache — sang their melancholy war songs and beat on small drums; as they passed their quarters, the women, old men, and children joined in. Small boys banging on tin pans and waving flags made of handkerchiefs marched alongside in a column of their own. When the companies passed Suds Row — the name given to the married enlisted men's quarters, due to their wives' work as laundresses — women and children stood outside and sobbed for their husbands and fathers. Libbie Custer recalled the scene years later: "Mothers, with streaming eyes, held their little ones out at arm's length for one last look at the departing father. . . . The grief of these women was audible and was accompanied by despondent gestures."[72]

Just outside the fort, the column was halted, and married officers were permitted to leave ranks to say good-bye to their families. Some loved ones stayed inside, tear-filled eyes watching from behind curtains. When the men rejoined their companies, the two-mile-long column marched westward over the hill behind the fort to the strains of another regimental favorite, "The Girl I Left Behind Me," which was almost drowned out by the many wagons, horses, and mules and the bawling of the cattle herd accompanying the expedition.

> If ever I get off the trail and the Indians don't find me,
> I'll make my way straight back to the girl I left behind me
> That sweet little girl, that true little girl,
> The girl I left behind me.

Bringing up the rear were almost eighty fresh recruits without mounts, sentenced to trudge along behind their comrades until horses were obtained for them.

Near the front of the column, Custer turned frequently to admire his men, calling Libbie's attention to their grand appearance. Each company rode horses of the same color, making the regiment even more distinctive. As the column mounted the prairie hill, Libbie, on Custer's horse Dandy, looked back toward the fort. The early-morning mist hanging over the Missouri River floodplain broke, and she saw a mirage appear "which took up about half of the line of cavalry, and thenceforth for a little distance it marched, equally plain to the sight on the earth and in the sky."[73] To anyone aware of the regiment's fate, the sight might have seemed a premonition: the Seventh Cavalry's troopers floating above the ground, halfway to heaven.

II

ADVANCE

SEVEN

"The Hide and Seek for Sitting Bull"

The Game of War is carried on very much on the principle of
"Blindman's Buff." The Indians can always, in summer, avoid a
single column, or select their own time and place for meeting it.

COLONEL JOHN GIBBON

Major Marcus Reno, West Point class of 1857, was not a happy man as the Dakota column made its way westward over the rolling prairie. He had commanded Fort Lincoln as its acting regimental CO since the previous November, covering Custer's lengthy absences that winter and spring. Custer, upon his return, had rescinded a few of Reno's orders and also rearranged the Seventh's regimental assignments, creating two wings consisting of two three-company battalions each. Reno would lead the right wing, Captain Benteen the left.

Custer had directed Reno to get the regiment in shape for "prolonged service in the field" against the hostile Indians, and he had had two months to do it. By all accounts he had not done a satisfactory job. Before previous campaigns, Custer had implemented an intensive regimen of morning and afternoon skirmish drill and target practice,[1] and he liked to take the regiment out for a two-week march to shake the rust off. Reno had begun daily hour-long target practice on March 6[2] (trimmed to a half hour on April 3)[3] and instituted daily morning drill, but he had neglected extended marches

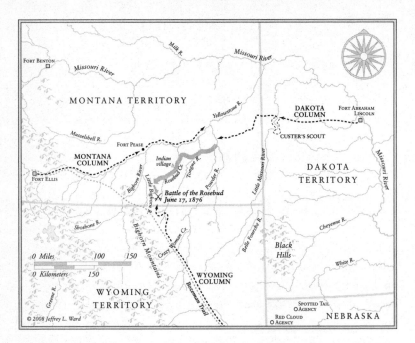

and other matters designed to increase the regiment's efficiency.[4] These actions, and his clear disloyalty in strenuously attempting to obtain command of the regiment during Custer's troubles in Washington, increased the coolness between the two.

Reno's dislike of Custer was shared, of course, by Benteen. But the two men were not friendly with each other either. One night years before, in the officers' club room of a post trader's store, Benteen had slapped the Major in the face in front of a group of officers, called him a son of a bitch, and dared Reno to challenge him to a duel, an offer Reno had declined.[5] That episode had most likely been fueled by alcohol. Even before his wife's death in 1874, Reno had been a fairly heavy drinker, but since then his intake had increased. Most of the regiment's officers did not like him, an attitude that was shared by many of the enlisted men.[6] Some of the officers purportedly asked Custer to keep Reno away from any kind of command.[7]

Reno had met and courted his wife, Mary Hannah Ross, in the fall of 1862 while stationed in Harrisburg, Pennsylvania, to purchase cavalry mounts.[8] Back then he had been young and somewhat dashing in appearance, and he had swept the pretty, impressionable eighteen-year-old off her feet. The two had been married the next fall. Besides an attractive wife, Reno had gained valuable political connections, for Mary's family was one of the most prominent in town. Over the next decade, Reno's social ineptitude and introverted manner had been offset by his wife's outgoing personality,[9] but her death in 1874 had clouded his situation. Mary Reno's health had been fragile since the difficult birth of their son, Ross, in 1864, and she had died at the age of thirty while Reno was in command of a Seventh Cavalry squadron protecting the Northern Boundary Survey Expedition. His request for leave to return to Harrisburg had been refused by General Terry. More than two months had passed before he had arrived in Pennsylvania, and his in-laws had found it difficult to understand the reasons for his absence. Reno had taken his son on a long trip to Europe and then arranged for his wife's cousin to become Ross's legal guardian. He had not returned to active duty at Fort Lincoln until November 1875.

Reno's parents had died when he was young, and he did not stay in close contact with his siblings. The sudden loss of his wife, the estrangement of his in-laws, and the surrender to her family of his only son all contributed to an increase in his drinking and a darkening of his already dour personality. He had nothing left except his army career, and his actions in the spring of 1876 suggest a desperation to improve his standing in any way he could. Reno's Indian-fighting experience was almost nil. He had chased various depredatory bands of Shoshones in Oregon Territory before the war but had come into actual contact with only two warriors, whom he had personally captured with the help of a Sergeant and promptly hanged.[10] He had also spent several weeks chasing but not finding belligerent Sioux tribes in 1870. Perhaps if the current expedition encountered Sitting Bull's camp near the Little Missouri, where Terry suspected it to be, there would be an opportunity for action and recognition.

BUT THE INDIANS were not on the Little Missouri, the first of several waterways west of Lincoln that flowed north into the Yellowstone. The Sioux always camped near one of these streams, but it would take several weeks, and much scouting, to discover which of them Sitting Bull had chosen this summer.

At the column's first campsite out of Fort Lincoln, Custer directed the paymaster to tender the men their wages. Terry and Custer had decided that these troopers would receive their long-overdue pay[11] away from the saloons and fleshpots of Bismarck's Fourth Street or the ramshackle collection of seedier gin mills and "hog ranches" of Whiskey Point, situated across the river from Lincoln with the express purpose of emptying the eager enlisted men's wallets. The risk of hangovers, desertions, and absences due to alcohol was too high. (More than one soldier had drowned trying to swim across the Missouri after "Taps" was sounded.) The men received their pay and immediately stepped over to the table of the post sutler, John Smith, who had accompanied the paymaster specifically to settle debts.

Two weeks of marching took the column westward over the flat, grassy Dakota prairie toward the Little Missouri River. On the march, the four battalions of the Seventh constituted the points of an elongated diamond, between which trudged the infantry, the long wagon train (which included the only woman with the expedition, Custer's personal cook, a black woman named Mary Adams; both she and her sister Maria worked in the Custer household), and the horse and beef herds. Mail carriers and message couriers operated between Fort Lincoln and the column. The scouts roamed miles ahead in search of hostile Sioux and camped separately from the soldiers, who rarely saw them except to buy the game they had bagged that day.

Though this was enemy country, no sign of Indians was seen except for the warm embers of a few small campfires—until May 23, five days out. The General had been chasing an elk far ahead of the column, his usual place, when he came upon an abandoned campfire still burning. That evening at dusk, Indians were seen on a bluff three miles away, observing the expedition. Their tribal identity was unknown, but it was clear that the column's progress was being monitored.

Ten days and almost 150 miles out of Lincoln, the Badlands of the Little Missouri, a harsh landscape of deep ravines and sparse vegetation, came into sight. After three days of tortuous maneuvering up and down the canyons, the expedition made camp on the east bank of the river, and orders were issued forbidding the discharge of any firearms: this was a favorite wintering area for the nontreaty bands.

Terry's intelligence, garnered from reservation agents and Indian and white scouts, had been contradictory and distorted. Terry had written to Sheridan two days before the column's departure:

> Information from several sources seems to establish the fact that the Sioux are collected in camps on the Little Missouri between that and the Powder River. . . . It is represented that they have 1,500 lodges, are confident, and intend to make a stand. Should they do so, and should the three columns be able to act simultaneously, I should expect great success.[12]

The next day, Terry wired that he had "no doubt of the ability of my column to whip all the Sioux we can find"[13] and suggested that Crook's column be moved up as quickly as possible. Sheridan replied, somewhat peremptorily:

> I will hurry up Crook, but you must rely on the ability of your own column for your best success. I believe it to be fully equal to all the Sioux which can be brought against it, and only hope that they will hold fast to meet it. . . . You know the impossibility of any large number of Indians keeping together as a hostile body for even one week.[14]

No one—not Sheridan, not Terry, and certainly not Custer—fretted over fighting the Sioux. To catch them before they scattered—that was the only worry, one voiced by everyone. During the harsh winter of 1875–76 at Fort Lincoln, while the troopers had huddled around their stoves, old-timers among them had told Indian-fighting stories. "About all there was to it," remembered one recruit, "was to surprise an Indian village, charge through it, shooting the Indians as they ran, and then divide the tanned buffalo robes and beaded moccasins before burning the lodges and destroying the supplies."[15]

Terry's belief in the proximity of the Sioux could not have been shared by many; even the enlisted men suspected that their trek would take them as far west as the Little Bighorn River.[16] Custer's own reconnaissance certainly didn't dispel their suspicions. He led four troops on a scout twenty miles upriver and returned the same evening. Not only were there no Indians, but all signs indicated that no large number of Sioux had passed through the area in the past six months. Any hopes of a quick strike within reasonable distance from Lincoln were dashed. A disappointed Terry apprised Sheridan of the situation and moved on, angling southwestward toward the Powder River, the bounteous region that many of the hunting tribes considered home. "I did hope . . . that we should find the Indians here in force prepared to fight but now I fear that they have scattered and that I shall not be able to find them at all," Terry wrote to his sisters.[17] The command left the Badlands a few days later, after a sudden snowstorm on June 1. They reached the Powder River on June 7 without seeing a single hostile Indian.

UNBEKNOWNST TO TERRY, weeks earlier and more than a hundred miles to the west, a small detachment of soldiers and Crow scouts from the Montana column had discovered the main camp of the hostiles.

General John Gibbon's Montana column had been operating along the Yellowstone River for more than a month, ordered to head east from Fort Ellis in eastern Montana with five companies of infantry and four cavalry troops under Major James Brisbin. The column, comprising about four hundred men, was accompanied by two Gatling guns, fifty-four Crow scouts, and twenty-five white scouts and guides, and its mission was to find and engage nontreaties. Gibbon, the commander of the military District of Montana, had proved himself a true hero in the Civil War, leading the famed Iron Brigade in the war's early years and then breaking Pickett's Charge on the third day of Gettysburg. A war injury led his Crow guides, who had hired on for three months as Privates at the standard $13 a month, to call him "Limping Soldier" or "No-Hip-Bone."

On the morning of May 16, a conscientious young Lieutenant under Gibbon named James Bradley, in charge of a mounted detachment of twelve infantry scouts, lay atop a lookout bluff thirty-five miles down Rosebud Creek. He spotted an immense Lakota camp along the river about eight miles distant. Bradley, his men, six Crow guides, and a half-breed interpreter stole quietly away and made for the Yellowstone as fast as they could ride.

Upon hearing Bradley's report of a large hostile village a day's march away, Gibbon ordered his command to cross the Yellowstone and strike at the encampment. On May 17, the same day the Dakota column commenced its march hundreds of miles to the west, the crossing began. The fast-flowing Yellowstone made it difficult for the small boats carrying the troopers, who led swimming horses behind them. After an hour, only ten horses had crossed, and when four drowned, Gibbon canceled the movement. Another factor in his decision was the sight of a Lakota party on the high bluffs across the river watching the attempted crossing. Clearly, a surprise attack would now be impossible.

The Lakotas continued to monitor Gibbon's column, occasionally swimming the river to steal government horses. They also harassed hunting parties, killing and scalping three of Gibbon's men.

On May 27, Bradley returned to his previous lookout point. The village he had spied eleven days earlier had now grown to almost five hundred lodges and had moved from the Tongue River to the Rosebud, the next waterway of any size to the west. But when he delivered his startling news to Gibbon, there was no response. The chief of scouts and others were puzzled by Gibbon's refusal to take action,[18] though Bradley later surmised that the number of Indians—possibly twice Gibbon's four hundred men—might have had something to do with it. More puzzling was the fact that just hours after hearing Bradley's news, Gibbon wrote to Terry but only mentioned this important news—the sighting of a large enemy village—offhandedly, in a postscript: "P.S. A camp some distance up the Rosebud was reported this morning by our scouts. If this proves true, I may not start down the Yellowstone so soon."[19]

Gibbon's report was delivered by courier to Terry a week later. Terry, meanwhile, had ordered Gibbon to move east down the Yellowstone toward the Little Missouri, where the hostiles were mistakenly believed to be gathering, and to meet and cooperate with the

Dakota column, which had already turned south and then southwest to canvass the area between the Little Missouri and the Powder. The next afternoon, an anxious Terry took two companies of the Seventh and rode north toward the Yellowstone in search of Gibbon and desperately needed information.

ACCOMPANIED BY FIVE NEWSPAPERMEN (to the Dakota column's one), George Crook headed north, reaching Goose Creek on June 11 and establishing a base camp there. The column was bolstered by the addition of a group of 65 discouraged Montana miners who had joined it on June 8 and the long-awaited arrival of 260 Crow and Shoshone scouts (both tribes longtime foes of the Sioux) on June 14. Crook left the wagon train and the pack train with a guard of a few soldiers and some 200 packers and teamsters and continued north with four days' rations early in the morning of June 16 with about 1,300 men, including 175 infantrymen mounted on green wagon mules. This large force was confident of victory should they find the Indians.

But where were the hostiles? Throughout the march, the soldiers had observed smoke signals daily, and small groups of warriors had harassed the column, sniping at the fringes and trying to stampede the horses. The location of their village, however, remained a mystery. The Crows had reported to Crook their belief that the enemy was located somewhere on the Tongue River or thereabouts. But now Grouard read signs that indicated to him that they were on Rosebud Creek.[20] As it turned out, he was right—the large gathering of nontreaty Indians was camped about fifty miles away from Crook's camp. By this time, plenty of agency Indians had come into the village bringing news of the belligerent soldiers. So the Indians packed up their tepees and moved west over the divide into the valley of the Little Bighorn River on June 15. Another, much smaller band of Cheyennes under Magpie Eagle also was in the area.

On the afternoon of June 16, two Cheyenne hunting parties stalking a herd of buffalo came upon Crook's Wyoming column. The Cheyennes returned to the nontreaties' village—and its almost 1,000 warriors[21]—located to the northwest on a creek that emptied into the Little Bighorn. The chiefs of all the tribal circles met in one large council and after discussion advised prudence. But the younger warriors overwhelmingly pushed for an immediate attack, and finally that course of action was decided on. Throughout the evening, groups of Lakotas and Cheyennes from every camp circle ate a quick meal of roasted buffalo meat and prepared themselves spiritually for the battle, then rode south to check the column before the soldiers found the village and its women and children.

These preparations were sometimes quite elaborate. White Bull, nephew of Sitting Bull and a celebrated Minneconjou veteran of many battles, wore a pair of dark blue woolen leggings decorated with beads, beaded moccasins to match, a red flannel breechcloth reaching to his ankles, and a shirt. Around his waist he wore a folded black blanket, and over it a cartridge belt with one hundred bullets. He hung over his right shoulder a small thong that supported his war charms: four small leather pouches of "medicines" (earths of various kinds), a buffalo tail, and an eagle feather. The final touch, worn just for its beauty, was a long bonnet of red and white eagle feathers that reached to the ground. Fine war clothes made one more courageous, and if he died, he did not want people to think he was poor.[22]

The Indian force comprised at least seven hundred warriors[23]— some had remained with the village—and Sitting Bull and Crazy Horse rode with them. But Sitting Bull would not participate in the battle, and for good reason.

SITTING BULL and his one hundred lodges of Hunkpapas, with some Cheyennes and Oglalas, had wintered on the Yellowstone near the mouth of the Powder, midway between Forts Peck and Berthold on the Missouri.[24] They had traded at both places and continued to pressure the traders and wolfers at Fort Pease, the misguided trading post recently erected opposite the mouth of the Bighorn. By March they had moved up the Powder. Most of the other hunting bands also were camped along the river or a few miles up one of its tributaries.

The village, which had by then grown to 235 lodges, had followed the buffalo west from the Powder to the Tongue and then the Rosebud, where, as word of the Powder River attack on Old Bear's village spread, other hunting bands joined the camp: the Minneconjous of Lame Deer, Fast Bull, and Hump; the Sans Arcs of Spotted Eagle; the Blackfeet of Kill Eagle; and even Sitting Bull's old friend Inkpaduta, now very old and almost blind, down from his refuge in Manitoba. With him were his twin sons, the warriors Tracking White Earth and Sounds the Ground as He Walks, an attractive daughter,[25] and thirty lodges of Dakotas and Nakotas. They were poor and ragged, and some were even without horses. But they were ready to stand with their brethren if necessary.

By mid-June, the village had swelled to 450 lodges—all the non-treaty bands and the first trickle of agency warriors and families. For over a month now, they had been harrying the white soldiers on the north side of the Yellowstone (Gibbon's Montana column), and some Cheyenne hunters had reported another force of soldiers advancing from far to the south, on the Tongue. As they had with Gibbon's troops, scouts kept track of Crook's column, occasionally trying to stampede the horses.

Around the same time, at a site almost fifty miles south of the Yellowstone, something momentous occurred. Sitting Bull's village had been slowly ascending the Rosebud for a couple of weeks, stopping to make several camps as they journeyed south. (The waterways of the region flowed north to the Yellowstone.) The long, brutal winter had finally subsided. The green grass fattened the ponies, and there were plenty of buffalo. The time was right: Sitting Bull decreed that the Hunkpapas would hold an early Sun Dance.

This most sacred of Lakota religious ceremonies, held every summer to purify and strengthen tribal unity and faith and to test the manhood and dedication of young warriors, lasted for several days. Only Hunkpapas participated this time, but many from the other tribes came to look on as young men endured various traditional ordeals to prove their fortitude and courage in hopes of achieving warrior status, while older men, through suffering and self-torture, hoped to induce a prophetic vision from the gods. Sitting Bull, who a few weeks earlier had received a vision from Wakantanka of a great Indian victory over the soldiers, was among them. Surrounded by dancing warriors, he sat with his back against the tall central lodge-pole as his adopted brother, Jumping Bull, used an awl to remove fifty small pieces of flesh from one arm, then fifty from the other. Afterward, Sitting Bull danced around the pole for hours, his face raised to the heavens. Eventually, he stopped and stood motionless, still gazing upward, until Black Moon and others helped him to the ground.[26]

He described the vision he had just received. Many soldiers and horses above an Indian village, all falling into the village upside down. Some of the villagers were upside down, too, but not many. It would be a great victory. But, Sitting Bull added, a voice had warned him that his people were not to loot the soldiers' bodies.

Sitting Bull's village — by now consisting of virtually every Cheyenne and Lakota nontreaty band — derived even more confidence and strength from his prophecy. With the conclusion of the Sun Dance, they continued up the Rosebud, then decided to follow the buffalo herds that their scouts had sighted to the west, in the valley of the Greasy Grass, the river the whites called Little Bighorn.

So when the warriors rode from their camp on a creek just east of the divide, Sitting Bull accompanied them. His arms still swollen and painful from his ordeal a week earlier, he would not fight but only ride among his men giving them encouragement and instruction. Besides, his family was represented by younger men — Jumping Bull and Sitting Bull's adopted son One Bull — and that was honor enough for one *tiospaye*. Nobody expected an old-man chief of forty-five to ride into battle unless it was in direct defense of Sioux women and children.

CROOK HAD MARCHED north from Goose Creek, a hard thirty-three miles, and bivouacked just a few miles from the Rosebud. At six the next morning, June 17, the column moved out. After a ride of an hour or so, the Rosebud — here just a thin stream flowing through boggy lowlands surrounded by broken terrain and bluffs — came into sight. Crook called a halt; he was convinced that the Indian camp was only eight miles away, at the other end of a canyon the creek entered a couple of miles downriver, and Indian scouts were sent ahead to reconnoiter.

Crook's men took full advantage of the midmorning break. After unsaddling and picketing their horses on either side of the creek, they relaxed, some erecting tent shelters against the warm sun, others making coffee. Crook settled into a game of whist with his staff officers, and the Shoshones and Crows raced ponies—odd behavior for a command believing itself in close proximity to a large hostile camp.

Less than an hour later, gunshots were heard from the north. Scouts rushed in yelling of approaching Sioux: "Lakota! Lakota!" The Shoshones and Crows jumped on their mounts and galloped toward the front. Crook ordered pickets sent out in the same direction, and his men ran to their horses and saddled up. The Battle of the Rosebud had commenced.

Sitting Bull's men had traveled all night, stopping only at dawn to rest their horses and apply their war paint. Each warrior wore his best clothing. The paint was part of their "medicine," and would protect them, but the clothes reflected more earthly concerns: in case of death, every man wanted to look his best.

After their final preparations, they continued south until they ran into Crook's Indian scouts, who, via an undisguised return to camp, led them straight into the soldiers. The Sioux and Cheyenne warriors found the *wasichus* twenty-five miles from their village in the Little Bighorn Valley—less than a day's ride away.

Over the next six hours, a furious contest between the 1,300-man column and the 700 or so nontreaties raged over the meadows, hills, and ravines of the area. The warriors fought with no grand strategy, but as individuals in quest of war honors, as they always did, though they employed some group tactics. Finerty, the newspaperman from Chicago, reported that one chief "directed their movements by signals made with a pocket mirror or some other reflector."[27] To the constant roar of 8,000 pounding hooves and perhaps 1,500 guns, and the shrieks of eagle-bone whistles, a constant ebb and flow of horsemen swept over the broken ground. "There were charges back and forth," remembered Wooden Leg, a noted Cheyenne warrior who was eighteen at the time. "Our Indians fought and ran away, fought and ran away. The soldiers and their Indian scouts did the same. Sometimes we charged them, sometimes they charged us."[28] Sitting Bull's men fought with a persistence previously unseen. Usually they broke off an attack after their initial charge, as Plains Indians almost always did when they owned no clear-cut advantage in numbers, tactics, or firepower. But this day was different. They charged into the soldiers head-on and "were extremely bold and fierce," said the reliable Lieutenant Bourke, who took notes during the fighting, "and showed a disposition to come up and have it out hand to hand. . . . They advanced in excellent style."[29] The fractured battle seemed to consist of countless smaller clashes as small flocks of individual warriors and groups rode at breakneck speed up and down the ravines and ridges north of the creek. A unit of soldiers would successfully drive the Indians before them, only to find that the warriors had quickly deployed to attack their flanks after the troopers were separated by the terrain.

The Shoshone and Crow scouts fought tenaciously, and Indians on both sides made many daring rescues. A veteran Cheyenne warrior named Chief Comes in Sight was one of the first to charge the soldiers. As he was making a bravery run back and forth in front of them, his pony was killed from under him. From the Indian lines, a rider raced through the soldiers' rifle fire up to Chief Comes in Sight, stopped and pulled him up behind, and safely galloped off. The rider was his sister, Buffalo Calf Road Woman, and afterward the battle was always spoken of by the Cheyennes as "Where The Girl Saved Her Brother."[30] The rescue was a classic example of how the smaller Indian ponies—one or two hands shorter than the big cavalry mounts—were superior in quickness and agility.[31]

Crook had rushed to a nearby hill to establish a command post, and after a few hours he thought the battle was under control. He still believed the Indian encampment to be nearby, perhaps six or eight miles downriver—the ferocious attack of the nontreaties, clearly launched to provide the women and children time to escape, seemed proof of it—and he ordered half his cavalry out of the fray and down the Rosebud to attack the village. But the premature withdrawal inspired the Lakotas and Cheyennes, who fell upon the battalion as it followed the creek curving north and then massed on Crook's central position. A countercharge by Crook's Shoshones put an end to the immediate threat, but another problem had developed: a battalion led by Lieutenant Colonel Royall, Crook's cavalry commander, was surrounded after cavalierly chasing some warriors. Royall had mishandled what should have been an easy job of rejoining the main force. Crook quickly realized the precariousness of the situation.

As the detached battalion followed the creek bend north, the troopers could see that the canyon narrowed somewhat to about a half mile wide, its sloping sides thick and dark with pine trees. Before they could continue, an adjutant arrived with orders to return to the battlefield. The battalion turned west into the hills west of the creek, returning to the battlefield through the flanks and rear of the surprised hostiles. The Indians began retreating through the ravines and hills to the north. Crook ordered a pursuit, but his men soon gave up and returned.

Crook now led a march downstream in search of the elusive village. (Since he had preferred charges against Reynolds two months earlier for not securing the Indian camp on the Powder River, he surely felt obligated to find this one and attack it.) But his scouts balked at the entrance to the narrowing canyon, fearing a classic Sioux ambush, and convinced Crook to fall back. Though Crook and his subalterns would enthusiastically embrace this entrapment danger in their reports, the Sioux force was in fact miles away, returning to their camp in jubilation over their success. They had halted fighting because they were afraid that the Crow and Shoshone scouts would make for their village.[32] Besides, they were hungry, and their horses were tired. They knew that it had been a good day of many coups and much glory.

The Wyoming column was obviously less happy, and the men spent the night on the battlefield after burying their dead comrades. Crook would officially report ten dead, including one young Shoshone scout. Burdened with more than twenty wounded and low on rations and ammunition—his men had expended 25,000 cartridges to inflict about a hundred casualties, a telling example of army marksmanship, or the lack thereof—Crook saw no choice but to turn south. Ironically, Crook's reputation in Apache country had been made with the use of finely tuned pack trains, which had enabled him to remain in the field to hound his quarry. Against the larger Plains tribes, he had ventured out from his base camp without a pack train, carrying only four days' rations and not enough ammunition, and thus could not pursue the enemy. The next morning, he returned to his wagon train at Goose Creek.

Within a few days, the Crow scouts and all but a few of the Shoshones left for their homes, disgusted with the white man's style of fighting—the Crows called Crook "Squaw Chief"[33]—and the wagon train with the wounded returned to Fort Fetterman, 175 miles to the southeast. Crook and his men remained in camp at Goose Creek for almost six weeks, waiting for supplies and reinforcements that he now professed to need. "It was patent to every one," observed Bourke, "that not hundreds, as had been reported, but thousands of Sioux and Cheyennes were in hostility and absent from the agencies."[34] While waiting, Crook and his men spent much of their time fishing, hunting, prospecting, even playing baseball. "My note-books about this time seem to be almost the chronicle of a sporting club," Bourke wrote.[35]

News of the debacle reached Chicago on June 23. In his report to Sheridan, Crook claimed a victory—after all, he asserted, he had driven the hostiles from the field "in utter rout."[36] If so, it was a hollow one, which Sheridan was quick to recognize; his official report called the victory "barren of results."[37] Strategically, Crook had lost, for he had retreated the next day and abandoned his mission. The newspapermen saw through the pretense. Finerty noted the General's dissatisfaction, and another reporter termed the retreat "cowardly."[38] In regard to the Plains Indians, Crook changed his tune. At the campaign's outset, he had predicted that "they would never stand punishment as the Apaches had done."[39] Now he insisted on reinforcements and the construction of several forts in the area before commencing any further operations.

As the weeks passed, Crook's attempts to track the large Indian force or locate their village were minimal. It was not until July that a detachment led by Grouard headed out in search of signs.[40] And Crook made no attempt to communicate to Terry or Gibbon to alert them of the numbers, ferocity, or firepower of the enemy, despite his personal complaint that no news was heard from the Generals and their commands.[41] Though he would notify Sheridan on June 19 of the battle and his withdrawal, that valuable intelligence would not reach Terry for weeks—July 9, to be exact. Never before on the plains had such a large force of Indians attacked an even larger force of soldiers, or fought with such cohesion and tenacity, and that knowledge would almost certainly have altered Terry's plans. True, there were plenty of hostiles somewhere to the north, but two weeks previous, Grouard and three civilian scouts had traveled three hundred miles in that direction to the Crow Agency west of the Little Bighorn and returned safely with 175 Crow allies.

Crook's reports to Sheridan late in July reveal his helplessness and his true concern: his own reputation. He referred to a plot to "do the command and myself great injustice" through "most villainous falsehoods" published in the *New York Herald*. He also wrote that the correct account, by the *New York Tribune* reporter, "never reached its destination and it is supposed here that it was suppressed in the telegraph Office, at Fetterman."[42] Crook would eventually admit a kind of failure by blaming the disappointing results at the Rosebud on some of his officers, notably Lieutenant Colonel Royall, expressing regret that he had not had them court-martialed.[43] But that would occur ten years later. Now he cast about for someone to excoriate.

When the news reached the East, at least one newspaper fastened on the root of the problem. On June 27, the *New York Herald* opined:

> When Crook, with thirteen hundred men, was unable to follow up a fight with Sitting Bull we may well be anxious over the fate of either of Terry's detachments, numbering less than seven hundred men, if they should meet them single handed. If Crook, with even his present forces, could be sent forward to the support of Custer and Terry it might, although still at great risk, end the difficulty. Reinforcements for both columns should be swiftly hurried forward.

Sheridan had expressed his hope that the columns would operate independently but eventually effect a juncture. The strongest arm of the campaign was out of action, the nontreaties were numerous and determined to fight, and Terry knew none of it. He was more in the dark than he realized.

THE LAKOTAS AND CHEYENNES returned to their village also believing that they had triumphed. About twenty warriors had been lost, and many more had been injured.[44] But with a fighting force little more than half that of the *wasichus,* they had checked the threat to their village and forced the soldiers to retreat. "We knew that we had defeated him because he turned back," said the Oglala He Dog.[45] Many warriors had earned great honors on the field of battle, and despite the mourning for the dead, there were four days of celebrating, feasting, and dancing in the tribal circles after the village had moved down the creek into the beautiful valley of the Greasy Grass. Clearly, Sitting Bull's medicine was strong, and the confidence of the Lakotas and Cheyennes soared as even more of their brethren from the agencies joined the camp. If the whites were foolish enough to come again, let them.

EIGHT

The Fruits of Insubordination

*Faint heart never won fair lady, neither did it ever pursue and over-
take an Indian village. . . . Few officers have ever had such a fine
opportunity to make a successful and telling strike and few have
ever failed so completely to improve their opportunity.*

GEORGE ARMSTRONG CUSTER

At the outset of the campaign, Terry had ordered Gibbon's
smaller command to move down the Yellowstone to the mouth
of the Bighorn River, prevent any Indians from getting away to the
north, and strike a hostile camp only if the opportunity arose. His
Montana column had been encamped some twenty miles east of the
mouth of the Bighorn since April 20. The next day, a dispatch from
Terry reached him with orders to stay put until the weather-delayed
Dakota column got under way—most likely in a few weeks. Gibbon moved his command downstream to the mouth of the Rosebud
a month later, on May 21, four days after the failed river crossing, in
response to his scouts' report of a large body of Indians headed that
way. He found no Indians but established a new camp there. A week
later, pursuant to fresh orders from Terry to move east toward the
Little Missouri, he began marching downriver to join the Dakota
column against the hostiles then believed to be in that vicinity.

The Dakota column had reached the wide and shallow Powder
River a few miles below the Yellowstone late on June 7, after several

days of hard marching through the rugged Badlands. A week earlier, a freak snowstorm had halted its progress for two days; when the march was resumed, three scouts from Gibbon's command rode up and delivered the news that the Indians were in considerable force south of the Yellowstone. They also brought word that the supply depot established at Stanley's Stockade, a crude fort built during the 1873 Yellowstone Expedition at the confluence of Glendive Creek, had received supplies from the paddle steamers *Far West* and *Josephine,* chartered by the government for the duration of the campaign.

After more than five weeks on the Yellowstone, Gibbon's command of almost five hundred men had accomplished little. True, it appeared that no large force of hostiles had escaped across the Yellowstone, but the Indians, far from planning an escape, seemed indifferent to the soldiers to the north and unfazed by the potential danger, as they crossed to the north side of the river frequently. They had intermittently harassed the base camp and had even inflicted the ultimate humiliation by absconding with all of the Crow scouts' thirty-two horses. (The seventeen Crows, master horse raiders themselves, wept copiously in anger and embarrassment upon waking one morning to find themselves mountless.)[1] Two half-breed interpreter-guides even conducted a conversation with some Sioux warriors across the river using sign language and dialogue. The Sioux told the guides that they had left the agencies because they were starving and were now out hunting food. They said that they did not want to fight white men and asked to be left alone.[2]

Terry sent Gibbon's couriers back with orders to halt where he was and directed the Captain of the *Far West* to proceed to the mouth of the Powder River with a company of infantry to establish a new supply depot there. The couriers were turned back by hostiles — or at least they thought they were: the large party of Indians they sighted were actually Crow scouts attached to Gibbon's command.[3] The *Josephine* returned downstream, but the *Far West,* piloted by the knowledgeable Grant Marsh,[4] arrived at the Powder on June 6 with a company of infantry aboard to wait for Terry.

Captain Marsh had already made quite a reputation for himself as the best riverboat Captain on the upper Missouri. It was said

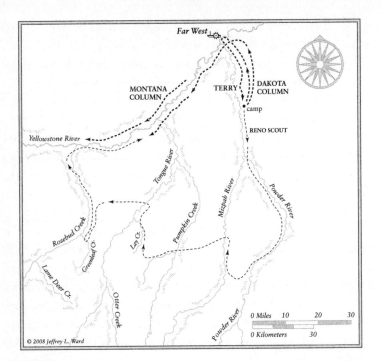

© 2008 Jeffrey L. Ward

that he could navigate a boat on heavy dew and once had "actually walked his boat half a mile over dry land."[5] Marsh had been traveling the region's waterways for thirty years, ever since he had signed on as a twelve-year-old cabin boy on a steamer in Pittsburgh. He was the only man ever to have navigated the upper reaches of the Yellowstone—he had guided a steamer to explore up the river for the army the previous summer and had reached a spot 250 miles from the Powder's confluence. No one knew the river better.

In late May, less than two weeks before, the *Far West* had been docked at Fort Lincoln, taking on supplies, and Marsh had entertained the officers' wives on board the boat one afternoon. He had dissuaded Libbie Custer and Lieutenant Algernon "Fresh" Smith's wife, Nettie, from accompanying him upriver to meet their husbands. (Mindful of the dangerous territory, Marsh had suggested that the ladies would be more comfortable on the passenger steamer *Josephine,* which they might board when it next came downriver.) Libbie and her husband had planned such a reunion before the column's departure, and she had been counting on it. Ever since he had left, she had been visited by premonitions as never before. For his part, Custer missed Libbie so badly that a few days out of Lincoln, he proposed in all seriousness to hand-deliver dispatches back to the fort "just for the sake of getting home again for a few hours."[6]

UPON ARRIVING AT THE POWDER, Terry sent Arikara scouts downstream to the new depot at the mouth of the river to contact the *Far West*. They returned late the next morning having accomplished their mission and bringing the erroneous news that Gibbon's couriers had encountered forty Sioux and had returned to the boat with Terry's new orders. But the vital answers to many questions were still unanswered: Where exactly was Gibbon? Where was the hostile village, how large was it, and which way was it headed? Was the new depot sufficiently stocked to begin long-range operations? During the three-week journey, Terry's impatience had increased. He had recently written his sister of his worry that the Indians "have scattered and that I shall not be able to find them at all. This would be a most mortifying & perhaps injurious result to me."[7] At one point on the difficult descent to the valley of the Powder, he had uncharacteristically grabbed a pick and shovel to help blaze the trail. Terry decided to waste no more time resting in camp with the column and waiting for dispatches to arrive. He left at half past noon with an escort of two companies of the Seventh and rode the twenty-two miles down the Powder River to its juncture with the Yellowstone. He would commandeer the *Far West* and steam upriver to find Gibbon himself, if necessary.

Before he left, Terry ordered the wagon train mules out of their harnesses and refitted to carry pack saddles in preparation for a scout by the entire Seventh Cavalry up the Powder.[8] Though Crook had made his reputation with the help of mule trains, they had never been used in the Department of Dakota. The process provided some sorely needed levity. The entertainment of the past five weeks had chiefly been limited to the sight of Custer's staghounds attempting to bring down elusive rabbits and fleet-footed antelope, a nightly serenade by the Seventh's band, and the occasional evening poker game. As the stubborn, bucking mules resisted their training, there were many scenes of swinging hooves and flying troopers. Custer, left in command of the column, spent much of the day in his tent writing his latest article for the *Galaxy,* one of several about his Civil War experiences.

Terry reached the Yellowstone that evening to find the *Far West* already moored there. On board he discovered that his message ordering Gibbon to halt had not been delivered, and that Gibbon had continued his leisurely march down the Yellowstone and was even now just a day and a half away. Terry sent couriers upstream to stop Gibbon's progress and summon him down to the steamer to report. Early the next morning, June 9, Marsh steamed upriver with Terry to meet Gibbon. They hailed Gibbon five miles downriver from the Montana column's camp. Gibbon came aboard, and he and Terry conferred for two hours. When Terry learned from Gibbon of the large Indian village sighted on May 26 by Lieutenant Bradley just eighteen miles up the Rosebud, he ordered Gibbon to retrace the fifty-five miles back to his recent camp at the Rosebud's mouth. Gibbon's four companies of cavalry, under the direct command of the ambulance-bound Brisbin, prepared to move out that afternoon, but a heavy downpour delayed them until the next morning. While the *Far West* ferried infantry troops and supplies from Stanley's Stockade to the new depot at the mouth of the Powder, Terry returned to the Dakota column. Neither column had received word from Crook, who was known to be marching north from Fort Fetterman. If he had encountered the hostile camp, the Indians might at this moment be heading down the Rosebud to escape across the Yellowstone into the rugged country north of the upper Missouri.

From the fresh intelligence now available to Terry, it appeared that the hostiles were somewhere to the west, along the Rosebud or one of the next rivers, either the Bighorn or its tributary the Little Bighorn. But since no one had seen the hostile camp in two weeks— Gibbon apparently had not even kept it under observation—the village may have moved east. Thus, before heading west, a reconnaissance in search of any scattered Sioux along the Powder, the Little Powder, and the Tongue was uppermost in Terry's mind.

But Terry needed a guide who knew the area. Capable Charley Reynolds may have been the best hunter on the northern plains, but he was unfamiliar with the country south of the Yellowstone. He had led the Dakota column astray in the Badlands east of the Powder, though Custer, who had a knack for pathfinding, had found an acceptable trail to the river. So when Terry left the *Far West* to return to the Dakota column, with him rode Michel "Mitch" Boyer, a half-Sioux, half-French scout who had been trained by the legendary Jim Bridger himself. He and Bridger had led the Raynolds-Maynadier Expedition of 1859–60, which had mapped some of the country south of the Yellowstone, and he had scouted for the army in the area during Red Cloud's War a decade earlier. Boyer had been Gibbon's main guide through this rough region and had performed impressively. Married to Magpie Outside of the Crow tribe, and the father of her four children, Boyer spoke English, Sioux, and Crow. He was soft-spoken and hesitating in his speech and on the short side.[9] He dressed like a white man and wore a hat, though he looked more like an Indian with his dark skin. Gibbon judged him the best guide in that part of the country, second only to Bridger.[10] Having guided immigrant trains and army expeditions in the area for almost twenty years,[11] he had performed such valuable service that the Sioux had sworn vengeance against him — a fact that Boyer had mentioned to Gibbon more than once.[12] Sitting Bull, he claimed, had offered one hundred ponies for his head.[13] But Boyer had shrugged off the threat. "If the Sioux kill me," he said, "I have the satisfaction of knowing I popped many of them over, and they can't get even now, if they do get me."[14]

Upon his arrival back at the Dakota column, Terry gave orders for the reconnaissance. He had now decided that only the right wing, six companies, of the regiment would go — under Major Reno. It appears that Custer had expected to lead the scouting expedition, as he had led every other during the march from Fort Lincoln.[15] But Custer had tested Terry's patience more than once on the march, and Terry may have wanted to show him who was in command. Besides, it seemed unlikely that there was any large body of hostiles in the area.

This was what Reno had been waiting for: an independent command and a chance to show what he could do. Before they had left Lincoln, Custer, the regiment's acting Colonel and field commander, had directed Reno to perform the duties of Lieutenant Colonel, but those duties had been few thus far.[16]

Custer thought the scout unnecessary and made his feelings clear in an anonymous dispatch to the *New York Herald*.[17] Not only did he believe that the Indians were farther to the west, but he feared that the reconnaissance would alert them of the column's proximity, thus inciting the tribes to flee and compromising the success of the expedition.[18] Captain Frederick Benteen shared Custer's fears. He thought that Reno's scout would "precipitate things," he wrote to his wife, and "cause the Indians to cross the Yellowstone before we can get in striking distance—and per consequence, prolong our stay in this country."[19] True, he admitted, the scouting expedition might make contact with Crook somewhere to the south, but time was of the essence. Should a reconnaissance that was not expected to find the main body of Indians delay operations for almost two weeks? After all, Terry had ordered twelve days' rations for the detachment. The most recent confirmed sighting of the village had been on the lower Rosebud, two weeks previous. Why not implement an operation that would center on that area, or send the Seventh Cavalry reconnaissance in force now, or send out small scouting parties to locate the camp first?

If any of these alternatives was presented to Terry, he was not persuaded. His written orders called for Reno to ascend the Powder "to the mouth of the Little Powder. From the last named point he will cross to the headwaters of Mizpah Creek, and descend that creek to its junction with the Powder River. Thence, he will cross to Pumpkin Creek and Tongue River, and descend the Tongue to its junction with the Yellowstone."[20] There he would rejoin the Dakota column, which would then move out immediately. Reno's written orders were precise and detailed, and allowed little room for improvisation. Terry also instructed Reno verbally to stay away from the Rosebud, clearly to avoid tipping off the hostiles, who were most likely there.

The right wing left at 3:00 p.m. on June 10, under clearing skies. Reno's troopers were accompanied by a Gatling gun and its crew and a pack train of about seventy mules. The rest of the command marched north down the Powder to the Yellowstone, to the new supply depot there. The map Reno carried was the same used by all components of the campaign, one prepared in 1872 from the Raynolds-Maynadier Expedition. It was hardly complete. The threat of hostile Indians had prevented the two army engineers from surveying the entire lengths of all the rivers. The unplatted rivers were represented by lightly drawn lines indicating the probable courses of the streams. The Powder was fairly well represented, as was the Bighorn far to the west. But the country between, and the many waterways therein that drained into the Yellowstone or one of its larger tributaries, was largely unmapped. Only a short distance of the Tongue, Mizpah, Pumpkin, Rosebud, and Tullock's had been explored, no more than thirty miles. The Little Bighorn had not been platted at all and thus was only a light, projected line on the map.[21]

Reno's guide through this semi–terra incognita was Boyer— "the Man in the Calfskin Vest," as the eight Arikara and Lakota scouts accompanying the force called him. (The Arikaras' name for Reno was "the Man with the Dark Face." He had threatened to shoot one Arikara in an argument before the wing's departure, and only the timely intervention of Bloody Knife had prevented bloodshed.)[22] Several of Custer's favorite officers rode with Reno: the likable Lieutenant Henry Harrington, commanding C Company in place of Tom Custer, who was serving on his brother's staff as aide-de-camp;[23] Captain Myles Keogh and his I Company; Lieutenant Algernon Smith and the "Gray Horse Troop," E Company; Lieutenant Jimmi Calhoun, who had just been transferred to the command of L Company; and Captain George Yates and his spiffy "Band Box Troop," F Company. The sixth troop in the right wing was B Company, led by the easygoing Captain Tom McDougall.

Reno rode his men hard through scattered showers—some rain would fall every day of the scout[24]—and over rough, slippery ground, but the command made good time, slowed only by the Gatling gun battery and its infantry detachment. The heavy gun and its ammunition and accoutrements was mostly pulled by two "condemned" cavalry mounts judged not fit to carry troopers, but it needed the occasional hauling by hand through some of the rougher ravines. (The gun would eventually upset and injure three men.) After two days of marching, the force bivouacked at a point some twenty miles from the mouth of the Little Powder; from there Reno sent his Indians upriver to scout the area. The next day, he marched west toward Mizpah Creek, which paralleled the Powder. Reno's orders directed that he descend the Mizpah a long way until it joined the Powder before turning to the west. But from the divide between the two, Reno could see a considerable distance down the valley. No Indian signs or smoke could be seen. He decided to take a chance and deviate from his orders. The wing turned west toward Pumpkin Creek, another of the many tributaries draining north into the Yellowstone or one of its feeder streams. Then, after just a single day's march down the Pumpkin, he veered west again to the Tongue. Boyer guided the wing to the village site Lieutenant Bradley had spied on May 16 and found evidence of some four hundred lodges.

Finally, Reno had acquired some previously unknown information—confirmation of Bradley's count of the hostile lodges. But Boyer undoubtedly told Reno of the more recent camp on the Rosebud that Bradley had discovered. The large village would have moved since then, probably more than once, since the needs of grazing, hunting, and sanitation demanded it. But a reconnaissance of the area might be able to determine which way it had moved, vital information to Terry's plans.

With Boyer as his guide, Reno decided to deviate from Terry's orders again. On its seventh day out of camp, the wing rode west again to Rosebud Creek. Four miles short of that valley, Reno sent Indian scouts to reconnoiter. They returned with reports of two old encampments and a large lodgepole trail leading south. (Each Lakota and Cheyenne family, like most of the Plains Indians, carried their belongings on a travois consisting of two of their tepee's lodge-poles tied to a horse and dragged behind. Most of the family's camp possessions could be transported this way.) The command reached the Rosebud and the higher abandoned campsite around midnight and bivouacked. The next morning, June 17, they followed the wide, heavily marked trail upstream and found another deserted campsite, this one fresher and just as large. Clearly, the village was moving south up the Rosebud valley. Reno ordered a halt here, increased perimeter security, and forbade any loud noises or bugle calls. This was good procedure but, unknown to the Major, unnecessary on this day, as most of the warriors from the hostile camp now situated in the valley of the Little Bighorn were at that moment engaged in the battle with Crook's Wyoming column.

Boyer and the Indian scouts continued up the creek. Twelve miles on, they found another large campsite, this one even fresher. They followed the trail another seven miles to a large bend of the Rosebud, made sure the trail didn't leave the valley there, and rode back to the soldiers.[25] Along the way, they examined travois trails that appeared to be even fresher than the village sites. Clearly, other bands were moving after the main camp.

Reno listened to Boyer's report and his claim that the hostile village lay no more than a day or so's march away, and considered following up.[26] But their rations were low, their horses were tired and weak (the long marches over rough terrain had taken their toll, and the animals had been rationed for only two pounds of oats a day, one-sixth rations, during the scout), and the Arikaras were not confident. If the hostiles were found, a battle was likely, and "if the Dakotas see us, the sun will not move very far before we are all killed," declared the senior Arikara scout, Forked Horn.[27] Reluctantly, Reno was persuaded to turn back.[28]

A hard march that afternoon and another the next day brought Reno's weary command to the mouth of the Rosebud. A mile down the south bank, they stopped and camped just above Gibbon's column across the river. The two commands communicated by the army code of flag signals, then a Crow swam the wide, fast-moving river to bring a written message to Reno. The next morning, his troopers continued downstream toward the rendezvous point at the Tongue, where the main part of the Dakota column awaited.

WHILE RENO WAS SEARCHING for Indian sign, Custer had marched his men to the supply depot on the Yellowstone on June 11 and rested them in camp. When the *Far West* arrived with sutler John Smith, who quickly set up a makeshift bar of planks and barrels to ply a good portion of the regiment with dollar-a-pint whiskey, "some of the boys got gloriously drunk," remembered one trooper.[29]

A man in a yawl had also arrived to sell beer at two bits a small glass.[30] Since there had been little for them to spend their money on besides poker games and meat bought from the Arikara scouts, heavy drinking was inevitable. In the absence of a guardhouse, the worst cases of inebriation were herded out onto the open prairie to sober up. Custer was disappointed to find no Libbie aboard the *Far West*, as they had planned.

On June 15, after drawing supplies and loading them on the pack mules, Custer led the left wing of the regiment—stripped down and ready for action—up the south bank of the Yellowstone to the Tongue, where they would wait for Reno. The whiskey trader accompanied them, to the delight of the troops.

The *Far West* followed the command upstream and now lay moored off the Yellowstone's south bank. The ground the regiment was encamped on had been occupied by the Indians the previous winter. "A number of their dead, placed upon scaffolds, or tied to the branches of trees, were disturbed and robbed of their trinkets. Several persons rode about exhibiting trinkets with as much gusto as if they were trophies of valor, and showed no more concern for their desecration than if they had won them at a raffle," remembered Lieutenant Edward Godfrey, who kept a diary on the campaign.[31] Young Autie Reed, Custer's nephew, snagged a bow, some arrows, and a pair of moccasins.[32] Reed should have been left at the Powder River depot with the other herders, but he rode with his three uncles. His fellow herder Dick Roberts had wanted to go also, but his pony, Humpty Dumpty, had given out and stranded him at the depot. His brother-in-law Captain George Yates had promised to send for him when another horse was found.[33] Also left at Powder River (on Terry's orders, despite Custer's wishes)[34] were the musicians, whose horses were given to some of the unmounted troopers. Felix Vinatieri would not have the opportunity to lead the band in "Garry-Owen" while the regiment rode into battle, as he had three years earlier on the Yellowstone.[35]

The rest of the walking cavalry, which included most of the new recruits, also remained at the Powder River depot, along with a few dozen others who were sick or detached for various details—a total of about 150 troopers. Finally, the regiment's sabers were boxed up and left behind. Only one officer, Lieutenant Charles DeRudio, carried his on a pack mule. He claimed it came in handy for killing snakes.[36]

At the new campsite, Custer ordered Isaiah Dorman, the interpreter, to pull down one particularly fragrant burial scaffold and throw the corpse in the river. Later, when the Arikaras saw Dorman fishing near the same spot, they suspected him of using the corpse as bait—a bad omen in their eyes. Other troopers threw Sioux bones into the Yellowstone.

Some of the officers played whist on the boat, and the Custer brothers fished soon after arriving at the Tongue.[37] Custer was in an expansive mood. "We are living delightfully," he wrote to Libbie on the 17th. "We are expecting the *Josephine* to arrive in a day or two. I hope that it will bring me a long letter from you, otherwise I do not feel particularly interested in her arrival—unless, by good-luck, you should be on board; you might just as well be here as not."[38]

Near sunset on the 19th, two Indian couriers from Reno arrived in the idle camp with a letter from Gibbon and a terse report from Reno, which read in part:

> I am in camp eight miles above you. I started this a.m. to reach your camp, but the country from the Rosebud here is simply *awful*. . . . I enclose you a note from Gibbon, whom I saw yesterday. I can tell you where the Indians are not and much more information when I see you in the morning. . . . My animals are leg weary and need shoeing. We have marched near to 250 miles.[39]

An angry Terry, who had by now transferred his headquarters to the *Far West,* read this cheeky, ill-phrased message, which admitted disobedience of orders but included no justification for it. Custer had followed his own lead more than once on the march from Lincoln; now Reno had done the same. As rumors of "hot Indian trails" and "plenty of Indians not far to the south and east" began to circulate through camp,[40] Terry sent his brother-in-law and aide-de-camp, Captain Robert Hughes, upstream to acquire more information and to tell Reno to remain where he was. Hughes returned that night. Terry wrote to his sisters:

> It appears that he [Reno] had done this in defiance of my positive orders not to go to the Rosebud, in the belief that there were Indians on that stream and that he could make a successful attack on them, which would cover up his disobedience. . . . He had not the supplies to enable him to go far and he returned without justification for his conduct, unless wearied horses and broken-down mules could be justification. Of course, the performance made a change in my plans necessary.[41]

On June 20, the day after Reno's message arrived, the Dakota column marched upstream to join Reno, with Terry and the *Far West* following them up the Yellowstone. When Custer and Terry heard Reno's report in person, a frustrated Custer questioned his junior Major sharply, upbraiding him for not acquiring more information, such as the direction the Indians were taking. Reno replied tersely, but before the argument got out of hand, "Terry interposed and smoothed the matter over," remembered one trooper.[42]

Custer continued to voice his disapproval in a more public way, via a scathing anonymous dispatch to the *New York Herald* penned two days later.

> Reno, after an absence of ten days, returned, when it was found, to the disgust and disappointment of every member of the expedition, from the commanding General down to the lowest private, that Reno, instead of simply failing to accomplish any good results, has so misconducted his force as to embarrass, if not seriously and permanently mar, all hopes of future success of the expedition. He had not only deliberately and without a shadow of excuse failed to obey his written orders issued by General Terry's personal directions, but he had acted in positive disobedience to the strict injunctions of the department commander. . . . Had Reno, after first violating his orders, pursued and overtaken the Indians, his

original disobedience of orders would have been overlooked, but his determination forsook him at that point, and instead of continuing the pursuit, and at least bringing the Indians to bay, he gave the order to countermarch and faced his command to the rear . . . and reported the details of his gross and inexcusable blunder to General Terry . . . who informed Reno in unmistakable language that the latter's conduct amounted to positive disobedience of orders. . . . The details of this affair will not bear investigation. . . . A court-martial is strongly hinted at, and if one is not ordered it will not be because it is not richly deserved.[43]

Custer's in-print criticism of a fellow officer echoed an earlier instance of the same—Benteen's caustic missive castigating Custer's actions at the Washita. When Custer had denounced that anonymous letter after seeing it in a St. Louis newspaper, he had considered it a heinous, dishonorable act and threatened to horsewhip the author. Benteen's letter had been vitriolic and opinionated, but Custer's printed, albeit anonymous, censure of an officer directly under his command was certainly less than honorable. And whether accurate or not, it was another case of Custer expecting others to follow rules that did not apply to him. Reno's initiative had achieved results, and he had done what Custer would likely have done in his place, though Custer would just as likely have pursued and attacked the village and its fighting force despite its vast size advantage. Reno, by contrast, had listened to the counsel of his scouts and officers, exercised discretion, and returned without the loss of a single trooper.

Curiously, in a letter to Libbie the day before, Custer had voiced his worry that Reno's wanderings had alerted the hostiles to the soldiers' presence. "Think of the valuable time lost!" he wrote, and then added, in a typical display of enthusiasm, "But I feel hopeful of accomplishing great results. I will move directly up the valley of the Rosebud."[44] That sentence, in Custer's last letter delivered to Libbie before he headed south from the Yellowstone after the hostiles, points up the value of Reno's disobedience. Though Terry was furious at Reno's insubordination, he quickly realized the worth of Reno's intelligence. Since the Indians were obviously not on the lower Rosebud, a new plan was needed. As the cool night fell and the *Far West* steamed up the Yellowstone, General Terry and his aides aboard the stern-wheeler pulled out the Raynolds-Maynadier maps and began revising their strategy.

There was another reason for revision, though Terry was not yet aware of it. Far to the east, the army was finally receiving accurate reports from its posts near the agencies—reports that spoke of much larger numbers of hostiles. From Sheridan's divisional headquarters in Chicago, a message to Terry was dispatched on June 6.

> Chicago, June 6th. Courier from Red Cloud Agency reported at Laramie yesterday that Yellow Robe arrived at agency (six days from hostile camp). He says that eighteen hundred lodges were on the Rosebud and about to leave for Powder River, below the point of Crazy Horse's fight, and says they will fight and have about three thousand warriors. This is sent for your information.

The numbers were exaggerated, but the message here and in other reports coming into army headquarters was clear: young warriors from the agencies were on the move—and likely headed toward Sitting Bull's camp. (Sheridan, in Wyoming Territory later in the month, would be sufficiently unsettled by the absence of young men at the Indian agencies to order the capable Lieutenant Colonel Eugene A. Carr and his Fifth Cavalry north to reinforce Crook's column.)[45] This was significant information and would necessitate a radical change in Terry's plans.

The June 6 dispatch had been telegraphed to Fort Lincoln with instructions to send it to Terry in the field "by boat" or any other opportunity.[46] The fort's commanding officer in Custer's stead, Captain William McCaskey, Twentieth Infantry, forwarded the message by the steamer *Yellowstone* that morning. He also planned to forward copies by two other government-contracted steamers, the *Key West* and the *Josephine*, once they arrived at the fort. The *Key West* departed three days after the *Yellowstone;* the *Josephine* left for the Yellowstone and the supply depot on the 15th.

The *Josephine* arrived at the Powder River depot on June 24, and

Arikara scouts carried the message on horseback with the rest of the mail 120 miles up the Yellowstone to Terry's camp at the mouth of the Bighorn. By then, however, Terry was gone. He would not receive the message until the last day in June—much too late to affect his new plan.

NINE

The Seventh Rides Out

Before many days you will hear of a big fight or a lively foot race.
LIEUTENANT GEORGE WALLACE

G eneral Alfred Terry was proud of his new plan to catch the hostile Indians—this despite the fact that, if one looked closely, the new plan was very much like the old plan.

Terry had transferred his headquarters to the *Far West* before her departure from the mouth of the Powder on June 15, a week earlier. The steamer had subsequently moved up the Yellowstone. After unloading supplies for Gibbon's command, Terry had moored two miles east of the mouth of the Rosebud, where the Seventh Cavalry had just arrived to set up camp on the south side of the larger river. Gibbon's Montana column had been dispatched upstream toward the Bighorn, pursuant to Terry's new plan, the broad outlines of which he and his aides had finalized by then.

Terry hosted Gibbon, Custer, and Brisbin in a conference room of the *Far West* about two o'clock in the afternoon of the 21st[1] as the Seventh Cavalry prepared to move out the next day. The men sat around a table, upon which the Raynolds-Maynadier map[2] of the area was spread, and over the next few hours, Terry outlined his plan and the commanders worked out the final details.

Since the Indians were believed to be on the headwaters of either the Rosebud, Bighorn, or Little Bighorn—Terry's Crow scouts had reported seeing smoke in the valley of the Little Bighorn[3]—Terry had in essence merely shifted the movements of his forces to the west a stream or two. Instead of two equal forces converging on a known location, however, this time a larger, faster strike force would seek the Indians and then drive them against a smaller blocking force—Gibbon's Montana column. Custer and his entire regiment would ride up the Rosebud to its headwaters, continue south past the Indian trail if it was found to diverge westward (to give Gibbon time to reach the Little Bighorn and to make sure no Indians escaped south or east), and then move over to the Little Bighorn and down that river. Gibbon and his less mobile Montana column (he had several infantry companies) would march up the Yellowstone to the mouth of the Bighorn, where the *Far West* would ferry them across to the south side. They would then proceed up the Bighorn to the Little Bighorn and hasten up its valley to block the hostiles' escape to the north, while the steamer made its way up the uncharted Bighorn as far as possible.[4] Terry estimated that Gibbon's slower-moving command could reach the mouth of the Little Bighorn by the 26th, four days after the Seventh Cavalry's departure. The two columns would rendezvous there, hence Custer's instructions to proceed farther south than the Indian trail.[5]

Sitting Bull's specific location was unknown and would probably shift within a few days, so a simultaneous attack on a predetermined date by two separate columns that were operating in unknown territory was an impossibility. A flexible plan was needed: thus Custer's more mobile strike force and Gibbon's slower blocking force—the hammer and the anvil, though each was considered strong enough to handle an Indian contingent of any size. No one knew the exact whereabouts of Crook's Wyoming column, but he was believed to be marching north from Fetterman toward the Rosebud. With any luck, his force would be able to participate, and at the very least block any hostile flight to the south. "I only hope that one of the two columns will find the Indians," Terry wrote in a dispatch to Sheridan the next morning.[6]

For his part, Custer was undoubtedly elated to lead his own command—to be able to "swing clear" of Terry—and obtain the honor of striking the Indians first. Glory was hard to come by when fighting Indians—Gibbon would later describe it as "a term upon the frontier, which has long since been defined to signify being shot by an Indian from behind a rock, and having your name spelled wrong in the newspaper"[7]—and here was a golden opportunity to gain some, possibly the final such chance, since Sitting Bull's Lakota camp contained what was thought to be the country's last large gathering of hostile Indians.

Gibbon was disappointed, or at least claimed that he was later. He had shown little desire for chasing Indians while guarding the Yellowstone for two months, but he expressed chagrin at now being relegated to a mere blocking force, and so did his subordinates, younger men who had had few chances for battle accolades since the Civil War. They had been in the field chasing the hostiles since February and had developed a proprietary feeling for their opponent.

At one point during the conference, the commanders called in George Herendeen, a seasoned frontiersman attached to the Montana column, and asked him for information about the area of Tullock's Creek, west of the Rosebud—the valley of which included a well-used Indian trail—and about the Little Bighorn. Herendeen had recently hired on with Gibbon, who was much impressed with him.

As Herendeen stepped up to the table, Custer put his finger on the map. "Do you know that place?"

The scout said he did.

"You are the man I want," said Custer.[8]

Satisfied that Herendeen knew the country, the commanders agreed that he would deliver a dispatch to Terry from Custer after the Seventh had scouted the head of Tullock's Creek. He would receive $200 upon completion of this hazardous mission. Brisbin told Herendeen that the scout could find his cavalry near the mouth of the Little Bighorn in a few days.[9]

At some point during the conference, Brisbin's four Second Cavalry companies were offered to Custer, a clear indication that the Seventh was expected to hit the Indian village first. That would have left Gibbon with only a small, two-hundred-man force of infantry and artillery. Custer declined, stating his confidence that the Seventh could handle any Indians they came across. His feelings were echoed by Mark Kellogg, the *Bismarck Tribune* correspondent, who had taken a cabin on the *Far West* when the Dakota column had reached the Yellowstone. Kellogg's dispatch written after the council of war summarized the plan and mentioned the fighting force of the Indians as numbering 1,500.[10] He most likely received this new total from Custer, who seems to have been the only officer at the conference who thought there might be that many warriors.

Terry's grand strategy no doubt appeared reasonable in the *Far West*'s cabin, the light of the oil lamps illuminating a map with pushpins in it signifying rates of march. But the Sioux village and its several thousand inhabitants were not permanent map markings to be approached, captured, and herded at the will of Terry and his subordinates. No one knew their present location, which in a few days would probably be their old location. It was highly doubtful that they would remain in one place, waiting patiently for the blue-coats to find and attack them. The last village site Reno's scouts had reached was now almost two weeks old. Up to that point, its size had remained steady for several weeks at about four hundred lodges—almost all the nontreaty Sioux and Northern Cheyennes. Whether Sitting Bull had been joined by agency Indians, and if so by how many, was unknown. But at the time, little thought was given to their numbers. The overriding concern, wrote Gibbon later, was "to prevent the escape of the Indians, which was the idea pervading the minds of all of us."[11]

Terry's number-one priority remained the same: find the hostiles and engage them. There would be a battle, or at least an attack. The option of approaching the Indians to discuss their surrender and return to the agencies apparently never came up.

Custer's understanding of his mission was somewhat different. As he described it in a last-minute dispatch to the *Herald* the next morning, he would take up the Indian trail on the Rosebud that Reno had abandoned and "follow the Indians as long and as far as horse flesh and human endurance could carry his command."[12]

Custer refused Terry's offer of the Gatling gun battery. Each of these heavy, hand-cranked weapons could fire up to 350 rounds a minute, an impressive rate, but they were known to jam frequently. Besides, Reno had taken one along, and it had been nothing but trouble. And during the Black Hills Expedition two years earlier, a Gatling gun had turned over, rolled down a mountain, and been demolished.[13] Each gun was mounted on large wheels and drawn by four condemned horses and would surely have been difficult to maneuver. Custer wanted nothing to impede his progress. He planned "to live and travel like Indians; in this manner the command will be able to go wherever the Indians can," he wrote in his *Herald* dispatch. When Lieutenant William Low, commander of the artillery detachment, heard that he would not be part of the strike force, he almost wept.[14]

When the conference ended, Gibbon told Custer not to be selfish and to give the Montana column a chance to get into the fight. Custer just laughed.[15] Terry and Gibbon walked Custer to his tent, pitched just a few feet from the *Far West*. The three men talked for a few minutes, then Custer had officers' call sounded as the other two commanders returned to the boat.[16]

Custer's briefing to his officers was terse and brusque, as usual—he was not known for his effusiveness when issuing orders. The command would strip down to the essentials. The pack mules would carry fifteen days' rations of hardtack, coffee, and sugar, twelve days' of bacon, and fifty extra rounds of ammunition per man. (Gibbon's men would draw only six days' rations before marching up the Bighorn, since they would not be ranging far from the stores on the *Far West*.)[17] In addition to ammunition, each trooper would carry twelve pounds of oats for his horse. Custer also recommended that extra forage be carried on the pack mules. Finally, all battalion and wing organizations were canceled; each troop commander would be directly responsible only to Custer. Supplies would be off-loaded from the *Far West* the next morning.

After Custer dismissed his officers, Lieutenant Godfrey and Captain Moylan, the ranker who had once been the General's adjutant, remained behind. The two pointed out the weakened condition of the pack mules that had accompanied Reno's strenuous scout and noted that they might break down, especially if they carried extra forage. An impatient Custer replied, "Well, gentlemen, you may carry what you please. You will be held responsible for your companies. The extra forage was only a suggestion, but this fact bear in mind, we will follow the trail for fifteen days unless we catch them before that

time expires, no matter how far it may take us from our base of supplies. We may not see the supply steamer again." Before entering his
tent, he added, "You had better carry along an extra supply of salt.
We may have to live on horse meat before we get through."[18]

Later that evening, Lieutenant Winfield Edgerly, West Point
class of 1870, walked up to regimental headquarters and visited
with Cooke, the tall Canadian adjutant. Tom Custer sat down for
a while, smoking, until Boston Custer and Autie Reed came by and
convinced him to join them at the river for a bath. Custer emerged
from his nearby tent.

Edgerly said to him, "General, won't we step high if we do get
those fellows!"

"Won't we!" Custer replied. "It all depends on you young officers. We can't get Indians without hard riding and plenty of it."[19]

Later on, several officers of the two columns gathered to discuss
the possibilities. Custer and Benteen soon were trading gibes, though
the exchange seems to have been initiated by Benteen, who said that
if a fight occurred, he hoped he would be supported better than he
had been at the Washita. Custer in turn taunted Benteen about killing a young boy in that battle, which led Benteen to explain that
he had had to do so to protect his own life. The discussion became
rather heated. "It was plain to be seen that Benteen hated Custer,"
remembered a second lieutenant who was present.[20]

Custer returned to his tent to prepare for the next day's departure. Late that night, he started a letter to Libbie. Outside, the
General's striker, John Burkman, walked guard duty in front of
his commander's tent under a moonless, cloudy sky. Wind gusted
through the trees nearby, and scattered raindrops pattered on pup
tents. Down at the Indian scouts' camp, they wailed their death
songs. Early the next morning, Burkman found Custer asleep on his
cot with just his coat and boots off and his pen in hand.[21]

After briefing their Sergeants, the officers returned to their tents,
some to write last letters home, others to make out their wills or
dispose of some belongings. Lieutenant Cooke entered Lieutenant
Gibson's tent and asked "Gibby" to witness his will.

Gibson laughed. "What, getting cold feet, Cookie, after all these
years with the savages?"

"No," said the tall Canadian, "but I have a feeling that the next fight will be my last."

Jack Sturgis fell on Gibson's cot, laughing. "Oh, listen to the old woman. Bet he's been to see a fortune teller," he said.[22] Within a few days, Sturgis would be the recipient of another officer's will—that of his troop commander, Thomas French.[23]

Others had the same idea as Cooke. Myles Keogh had already entertained sufficient misgivings, even before leaving Fort Lincoln, to make arrangements for his burial. Now he stepped aboard the steamer and sought out Lieutenant John Carland, a Sixth Infantry officer he knew assigned to the *Far West*. Carland had been a lawyer, and Keogh asked him if he could draw up a proper will.

"I don't know what may happen to me, and as I have not disposed of some things I have I want to make a will," he told Carland. After the will was drawn up, signed, and sealed in an envelope, Keogh handed it over and said, "If anything should befall me open the envelope and send the papers to my sister."[24]

Not all of the Seventh's officers would be marching out with Custer the next day. Keogh's good friend and fellow Seventh Cavalry officer, Lieutenant Henry Nowlan, was also on the *Far West,* but he would not accompany his comrades. A fellow Irishman and a graduate of Sandhurst, England's elite military academy, the handsome Nowlan had been decorated for gallantry in the siege of Sebastopol (1854–55). Like Keogh, he had arrived in New York in 1862 and fought in the Civil War, and each had served with the Seventh since its inception.[25] Nowlan had served Custer splendidly as the regimental quartermaster for several years—a position his father had held in the British regular army[26]—and General Terry had appointed him to the same position for the entire expedition. He wanted badly to go with his regiment—also like Keogh, he had done much Indian chasing but little actual fighting—but he would remain with Terry and his staff on the boat.

THE NEW REGIMENTAL ARRANGEMENT left Reno without a command of his own. Now it was likely that any glory garnered by the regiment would accrue to its commander, known for leading his men from the front, and not its acting Lieutenant Colonel. After making his preparations for the next day's march, he began drinking heavily.[27] That evening he ended up on the deck of the *Far West* harmonizing on the lugubrious "Larboard Watch" with Carland and a few other officers, arms about each other's shoulders.[28] Mitch Boyer got good and drunk, too, and bragged to another Crow interpreter how he was going to slaughter the Sioux, his mother's people.[29]

Mark Kellogg, the only reporter on the scene, was up until after midnight finishing his final dispatches and preparing for the journey, for he had just that night decided to ride with Custer and received permission to do so.[30] In two canvas saddlebags, he packed his pencils and paper and plenty of sugar, coffee, and bacon. He was well liked by the officers of the expedition and had been given the run of headquarters. In response, his stories extolled everyone he wrote about, with the singular exception of Major Reno after his disobedient jaunt up the Rosebud. Kellogg's weapon of choice was a Spencer carbine, and he knew how to use it.

The indefatigable Captain Marsh was up early the next morning, hours before sunrise, directing the off-loading of supplies from his boat. He ran into Charley Reynolds, whom he had given a cabin. The soft-spoken scout had twice had a presentiment of his own death[31] during the march from Fort Lincoln and had become convinced that he would not return from the expedition. His friend Fred Gerard had finally persuaded him to ask General Terry for permission to leave the column. Terry had talked him out of it. Reynolds's haggard face betrayed his pain and lack of sleep; for some time now his left hand near his thumb had been badly infected, and it had not improved despite the efforts of the column's acting assistant surgeon, Dr. Henry Porter of Bismarck. Marsh tried to talk Reynolds out of going, to no avail. Later that morning, he attempted the same with Boston Custer, whom he had taken a shine to. Bos seemed persuaded by the Captain, but by the time he returned to his cabin to finish a letter to his mother, he had changed his mind. "I am feeling first-rate," he told her. After relating the Seventh's plans, he continued:

> I hope to be able to capture one or two Indian ponies and
> a buffalo robe for Nev [the fourth and remaining Custer

brother, a farmer in Monroe]. There are something like eight hundred Indians and probably more, But be the number great or small I hope I can truthfully say when I get back that one or more were sent to the happy hunting-grounds. . . .

Autie Reed is going. He will stand the trip first-rate. He has done nicely and enjoying it. . . . Tell Annie [Autie's mother, Lydia Ann] he is standing the trip nicely and has not been sick a day. . . .

Goodbye my darling mother. This will probably be the last letter you will get till we reach Lincoln. Goodbye and believe me

Still your affectionate son

Boby[32]

His brother Armstrong was finishing his letter to Libbie at mid-morning when one of Terry's aides delivered the General's written orders. The former lawyer had crafted a carefully worded set of instructions — a curious combination of specific directives and sur-prising largesse that reflected the uncertainties involved. Whereas Terry's orders to Reno twelve days earlier had been terse and direct, with repeated use of the common military imperative "You will," these seemed more like suggested movements couched in flattering language designed to placate his subordinate, whose feelings and reputation had so recently been battered by Grant and his allies in the press.[33] Terry could hardly give Custer free rein after the Presi-dent had made clear his views of his subordinate's behavior. Terry needed to retain responsibility — or at least its appearance.[34] But the inexperienced Terry also felt that he had to trust a subordinate more knowledgeable in Indian fighting to make the right decision if the opportunity arose. Whatever the reasoning, Custer was so pleased that he copied some of the orders into Libbie's letter:

"It is of course impossible to give you any definite instructions in regard to this movement, and, were it not impossible to do so, the Department Commander places too much confidence in your zeal, energy and ability to impose on you precise orders which might hamper your action when nearly in contact with the enemy."[35]

The day before, Boyer had helped select six of Lieutenant Bradley's best Crow scouts to accompany Custer's command, leaving Gibbon without a guide who knew the country. (Since the Montana column was following known waterways to the mouth of the Little Bighorn, it was assumed they could get by.) The Crows knew the area much better than the Arikaras, who were hundreds of miles away from home. They were familiar with some of the trails along the Yellowstone, however, and would act as couriers and outriding scouts on the flanks of the column. The hostile Sioux were likely on Crow land, as granted to the Crows by the Fort Laramie Treaty of 1868. The upper reaches of the Rosebud lay on the western edge of the reservation, although Sitting Bull and his free-roaming brethren had previously pushed the Crows west beyond the Bighorn River.

No tribe on the northern plains had resisted the Sioux invasion as the Crows had, even after the Sioux had permanently driven them from the Powder River country. Though the Sioux outnumbered them dramatically—the Crows counted between 4,000 and 5,000 men, women, and children[36]—they were prodigious warriors. They had been fortunate to avoid most of the cholera and smallpox epidemics that had ravaged the sedentary Missouri River tribes such as the Arikaras, whose population had declined by almost 90 percent to less than 1,000, and left them helpless before the raiding Sioux. (These diseases had almost halved the Sioux population, too.) Almost every spring or summer in the past decade or so, the Crows and Sioux had met in battle in this area, almost as if by tradition. Though large, the fights were rather mild, with few serious casualties. It appeared that more than anything, the clashes provided an opportunity for young warriors to increase their stature by winning honors. Except for those instances in which there were vastly superior Sioux numbers, the Crows gave as good as they got.

Besides the Sioux, the Crows were surrounded by other enemies, so much so that white fur traders had years ago written the Crows off as being doomed and had abandoned their forts in Crow country. But the Crows had survived. They had seized their hunting grounds from the Shoshones a century earlier and had fought that tribe since, although the two nations had recently made peace. Another traditional enemy, the Blackfoot, lay to the west.[37]

The Crows had befriended the whites from the beginning, since the first French fur traders met them in the mid-eighteenth century. Indeed, many whites in southern Montana Territory saw the Crows as their protectors against the Sioux. One business firm wrote to the Crow agent begging him to supply the Crows with plenty of ammunition, and in 1871 a Bozeman newspaper praised them for their resistance against the Sioux.[38] Most of the Crows still avoided whiskey and punished those who used it. And their standards of cleanliness and deportment were somewhat closer to white expectations, unlike, say, the Arikaras, who were compared to "antiquated Negro washerwomen" by General Gibbon.[39]

The six Crow scouts — Half Yellow Face (their leader), White Swan, Goes Ahead, Hairy Moccasin, White Man Runs Him, and the youngest, White Swan's eighteen-year-old cousin Curly[40] — were ferried across the river on the *Far West,* then escorted to Custer's tent. He shook hands with each and welcomed them. The scouts were dressed in their traditional native garb, but each wore a red armband above their right elbow to help the soldiers differentiate them from the hostiles. The Crows were tall, with features closer (compared to other Indians) to what whites considered handsome, and they bore themselves proudly. Custer was much impressed; in a letter he wrote the next day to Libbie, he called them "magnificent-looking."[41] They were equally impressed with him, especially after Custer told them (via their interpreter, Boyer, since none of the Crows spoke English) that he was known as "Charge the Camp," that he had "cleaned up" an Indian village down south years ago and would do the same to the Sioux, and that the Crows could keep all the horses they could capture.[42] Custer reminded the Crows that they would not fight, only scout, which was the standard arrangement with Indian "wolves," as scouts were known.

The Crows had not been pleased by what they had perceived as Gibbon's reluctance to fight, and when they heard that Custer followed an enemy trail to its end, they were overjoyed. "There is a kind, brave, and thinking man," Curly thought when he met the General, and noticed that "Son of the Morning Star" — their name for him — had "kind eyes."[43]

The taciturn George Herendeen would also ride with Custer.

He was a highly capable, jack-of-all-trades frontiersman who had spent the previous winter wolfing and living in a dugout up on the Yellowstone near Fort Pease, the crude little civilian stockade that its founders, Herendeen among them, hoped would develop into a successful trading settlement as steamboats ventured farther up the river. Before that, he had embarked on a variety of schemes that had invariably intruded into Sioux territory and as a result usually involved Indian fighting. Herendeen was a good man with a gun and dependable in a tight spot.

After the supplies had been strapped to the pack mules and the men downed a late breakfast of bacon and coffee, the regiment formed and marched in column of fours through sagebrush toward the Rosebud. Custer rode ahead and fell out next to Terry, Gibbon, a few of their staff officers, and Kellogg. He was in high spirits, chatting freely, evidently proud of his regiment's appearance as it passed by.[44] The Arikaras, who had just finished the customary singing of their death songs, led the procession. They were happy to be following Long Hair, for he understood them. On the march from Fort Lincoln, Custer had often come to their bivouac to eat meat and talk with them. "Custer had a heart like an Indian; if we ever left out one thing in our ceremonies he always suggested it to us," remembered one Arikara.[45]

A band of trumpeters sounding a march came next, wheeling out of the column as they came up and continuing to play as the command passed by. The pack train followed the regiment, and a rear guard was last.[46] Terry, thoughtful as ever, addressed each officer pleasantly as he returned their salutes.

After the last trooper had passed, Custer shook hands with the two commanders and mounted his horse Dandy, one of two he had brought with him. Terry said, "God bless you," and then Custer galloped after his column.

As he left, Gibbon called out, "Now Custer, don't be greedy, but wait for us."

Custer laughed as he had the evening before when Gibbon had said much the same thing, then waved and replied, "No, I will not."[47]

Right behind him rode Kellogg, his two canvas saddlebags bouncing atop the mule he rode. (The 175 pack mules, many of them still weary from the Reno scout and most determinedly uncooperative, gave evidence of future problems from the start: several packs fell off before they got out of camp.) Trotting along beside the column were two of Custer's favorite dogs, Tuck and Blucher, and a small yellow bulldog named Joe Bush that belonged to Keogh's I Company.[48]

Back on the boat a few minutes later, Terry said to interpreter Fred Gerard, who had stayed to start some Arikara couriers to the Powder River depot with the mail, "Custer is happy now, off with a roving command of fifteen days. I told him if he found the Indians not to do as Reno did, but if he thought he could whip them to do so."[49] Terry knew his subordinate and also knew that no written suggestions would prevent Custer from following a fresh Indian trail if he happened to strike one.

TEN

The Trail to the Greasy Grass

We marched 12 Miles and went into Camp every man feeling that the next twenty four hours would deside the fate of a good manny men and sure enough it did.

PRIVATE THOMAS COLEMAN

In the early spring, Sitting Bull had sent word out to all the agencies: come join us on the Rosebud, for the white soldiers are on the move.[1] Some of the Lakotas had become too accustomed to their new lives, wretched as they were, to fight again, and few of the Dakotas and Nakotas east of the Missouri answered the call; only some of the renegades under the allegiance of the aged Inkpaduta joined their brethren.[2] Most of the Indians at the two big agencies below the Black Hills remained there in allegiance to their chiefs, Red Cloud and Spotted Tail, who had pledged peace and would keep their word. Crazy Horse's close friend Touch the Clouds, the tall Minneconjou chief by birth who had spent many years roaming the country with him, had elected to remain at the Cheyenne River Agency with his band and negotiate a peace with the *wasichus*.[3] But hundreds of lodges from those agencies and others made the journey west and north and reached the village after the great victory on the Rosebud.

The camp remained at that site on the Greasy Grass—what the whites called the Little Horn or the Little Bighorn—for six days, a

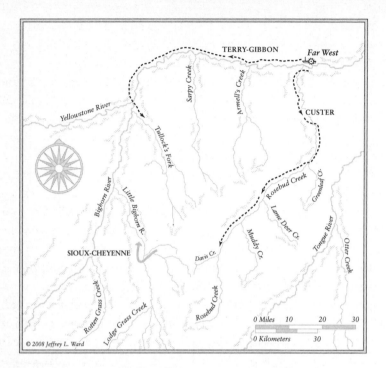

long time for such a large gathering, since the needs of sanitation, grazing for the huge pony herd, and game to feed so many stomachs necessitated frequent moves. A shift up the valley toward the Bighorn Mountains was planned, but then scouts brought reports of many antelope in the other direction. Thus, on the sixth morning, the Cheyennes on the lower end led the Sioux tribes north down the valley. Eight miles away, beside the river swollen with snowmelt, a new village was established, with six large tribal circles, five Lakota and one Cheyenne. Here the stream, from thirty to fifty feet wide and four to five feet deep, ran cold and clear as it snaked its way past frequent clumps of cottonwoods and scattered ash and willow trees. To the west, the valley stretched flat for almost a mile to low grass-covered benchlands, where many of the horses could graze. The terrain on the east side offered a contrast: sheer, rugged cliffs two hundred to three hundred feet high, looming above the water, cut through here and there by deep ravines and coulees. The steep bluffs hid most of the village from anyone approaching from the east. The only significant relief near the camp was a flat area with an easy ford giving access to the center of the village, which stretched almost two miles along the banks, its northern end nestled above a large loop of the river that extended almost halfway across the valley.

Arrivals within the past week had almost doubled the size of the gathering to more than a thousand lodges and a few hundred wickiups (small, temporary shelters made with bushes stuck in the ground, their tops fastened together, over which the Indians draped canvas or buffalo robes or blankets) containing single men—at least 8,000 people in all and 2,000 men of fighting age.[4] Most of the greatest leaders and bravest warriors of the Sioux and Northern Cheyenne nations were there. Many of the older fighters were veterans of more than a decade of constant battling and skirmishing with the whites and their soldiers. All but the very youngest had gained combat experience fighting traditional enemies such as the Crows and other tribes on the northern plains.

Two of the Hunkpapas' most respected warriors had just arrived. Gall, the tough, stocky subchief who had been a friend of Sitting Bull's since childhood, had spent a good part of the previous year drawing rations at Standing Rock Agency.[5] Though not the recalcitrant free roamer that Sitting Bull was, Gall was nonetheless recognized as fearless and ferocious. The tall, fiery Crow King was equally respected. His band of eighty warriors[6] included several of his brothers. Gall and Crow King led 120 lodges between them.

Another Hunkpapa present was Rain in the Face. He had been arrested by Tom Custer the previous year for killing two civilians during the 1873 Yellowstone Expedition. After three months of imprisonment at Fort Lincoln, he had escaped—almost surely with the help of one of the guards or a white prisoner. Rain in the Face had vowed vengeance on Tom and his brother the General.

Some Assiniboines, longtime enemies of the Lakotas and Cheyennes, had intermarried with Nakotas and Dakotas fleeing from the Minnesota uprising years before and were now encamped with the Hunkpapas.[7] A few warriors from other tribes that had sided with the Sioux, such as the Gros Ventres, were also there. The only Arapahos present were a small war party of five men looking for Shoshones to fight. When they rode into camp, they were thought to be scouts for the *wasichus*. Their guns were taken, and they were made prisoners. Only after Two Moon, a Cheyenne war chief, intervened were their lives spared and their arms returned. They were not, however, allowed to leave the village.[8]

Every tribe of the Lakotas, a few of the eastern Nakotas and Dakotas, and perhaps a hundred lodges of Northern Cheyennes were there. Their leaders were Big Road, Crazy Horse, and Knife Chief of the Oglalas; Black Moon, Gall, Crow King, and Sitting Bull of the Hunkpapas; Hollow Horn Bear, Low Dog, and Little Hawk of the Brulés; Lame Deer, Hump, and Fast Bull of the Minneconjous; Spotted Eagle, Red Bear, and High Bear of the Sans Arcs; Runs the Enemy of the Two Kettles; Scabby Head of the Blackfeet; and Inkpaduta with his ragged Wahpekute and Yanktonais. Those leading the Cheyennes included Dirty Moccasins, Old Bear, Ice, Brave Wolf, and Lame White Man, a brave Southern Cheyenne war chief who had lived a long time with his Northern brethren. Only the *tiospayes* of Dull Knife and Little Wolf were missing, and the latter was expected to arrive soon.

Though most of the men in the village still carried the bow and arrow in battle and on the hunt, over the past decade the sale and trade of arms to the Indians had increased significantly. Some guns issued to agency Indians for hunting had made their way to their free-roaming brethren, but there were many other ways a warrior could acquire a rifle. Post traders on some reservations supplied illegal arms to nontreaties; so did unlicensed traders—primarily the half-breed Canadian Métis gunrunners to the north and unlicensed white traders in the desolate area known as the Burning Grounds below the Black Hills. The latest Winchester magazine rifles were available for the right price: a horse or mule for a repeater, and buffalo hides for ammunition. Many men carried older guns—muzzleloaders, for which some molded their own bullets; Henry and Spencer repeaters; Springfield, Enfield, and Sharps breechloaders; and many different makes of pistols. All told, between one-third and one-half of the gathering warriors owned a gun.[9]

All of those present acknowledged Sitting Bull as their spiritual leader. His crowded lodge stood on the southern edge of the Hunkpapa tribal circle, his *tiospaye* blessed with the addition of his two twin sons born just a few days earlier.[10]

Throughout the afternoon and early evening, women and children attended to the many chores involved in erecting the lodges and preparing camp. Young boys herded their families' horses away from the village, mostly to the low hills to the west and north where the grazing was good. Some warriors rode out in groups to hunt buffalo and antelope—a gathering this huge required constant game to supply the Indians' heavy meat diet.

As the sun dipped toward the western horizon, Sitting Bull took his nephew and adopted son One Bull (nineteen years before, the grieving holy man had taken him into his lodge at the age of four after his own young son had died of disease) across the river and climbed a high hill overlooking the bustling village. There he stood and prayed to Wakantanka, offering several possessions—a buffalo robe, buckskin-wrapped bundles of tobacco—as he beseeched the Great Spirit to save his tribe. The victory over the bluecoats a week earlier had been glorious, but Sitting Bull's vision of soldiers falling into camp had not been fulfilled, and troops were known to be in the area. He left the offerings on the hill and returned to the village with One Bull.

The Sioux and Cheyenne chiefs met in council that evening. Scouts had reported soldiers somewhere to the northwest. Sitting Bull's fighters had galloped out to meet troops a week earlier; they decided that this time they would wait for the enemy to approach. If the whites wanted to talk peace, the chiefs would listen. If they wanted war, the Indians would oblige.

As darkness descended, a group of about twenty young Sioux and a few Cheyennes, most of them in their teens, pledged to die in the next battle. One of these "suicide boys," Noisy Walking, the son of Ice, was only fifteen. Some of them had lost relatives in the Rosebud fight and had decided to avenge them in death. As the young men prepared to dance and sing in the Dying Dancing, people gathered around the dance circle to honor these brave young boys.[11] Men sang their strong-heart songs, and women trilled their accompaniment, while an old man encouraged the boys. Should they die fighting, he said, their names would be remembered for a long time.[12]

After sundown, two young Cheyenne cousins, Wolf Tooth and Big Foot, took their horses north of the village and hobbled them, then returned to camp. The Kit Fox *akicita,* the warrior society assigned as camp police that day, had sent lookouts to high points up and down the river to prevent eager young men from slipping away and attacking the whites on the Rosebud too early, before it was known what they wanted.[13] When it was fully dark, the two Cheyennes sneaked back to their ponies, quietly made their way down to the river, and hid in the brush along the east side. The next morning, they would make a circuit north and then east around the camp. If the soldiers on the Rosebud came this way, they would earn the honor of striking them first—or at least warning the camp.[14]

A CAVALRY REGIMENT was authorized to have almost 900 officers and enlisted men—not counting the 17 band members[15]—but between those deserting, mustering out, and on detached service, no regiment was anywhere near full strength. The Seventh's numbers had been further depleted by the 150 troopers left at the Powder River depot on the Yellowstone. When the regiment left the camp on the Yellowstone on June 22, Custer rode at the head of 31 officers, 578 enlisted men, 45 scouts and guides, and several citizens in various capacities—all told, about 660 men.[16] Over five strenuous weeks, they had covered 350 hard miles. A color Sergeant carrying the General's personal headquarters flag—a swallow-tailed guidon of red over blue with crossed swords, the same he had used during the Civil War—followed him closely. Thirty-seven Arikaras, four Sioux, and a few half-breeds scouted on the flanks, while the six Crows, more familiar with the country, ranged far ahead.[17]

As a rule, dress regulations were relaxed in the field, and the Seventh was no exception. Even a disciplinarian like Custer realized the foolishness and impossibility of adhering to such rules when far from even the crude civilization of a frontier post. Except for the company guidons and the standard-issue dark blue flannel blouses that most of the troopers wore—by this time usually stained green or purple by rain and sweat—an observer might have initially mistaken the column for a band of brigands. They sported hats of several colors and styles. Many of the men—Privates, noncoms, and officers alike—had recently bought light straw hats from a trader who had floated down the Yellowstone with a boatful of goods in search of a quick profit. Others wore standard-issue black wool campaign hats or more expensive store-bought slouches, usually gray. Their sky blue pants were by this time badly faded and worn, usually reinforced in the legs and seat by whitish canvas. Some had replaced ragged shirts with checkered hickory shirts bought from the trader, and others doffed their heavy blouses and wore only long-sleeved gray undershirts under their suspenders. Beards and shaggy hair were the rule rather than the exception.

Custer wore a fringed buckskin jacket and pants—six or seven other officers and both of his brothers wore similar coats—and a dark blue, wide-collared "fireman's shirt," like most of the officers. His trademark red scarf encircled his throat, and a light gray, broad-brimmed hat sat atop his reddish blond hair, which had been cropped short before leaving Fort Lincoln. Many of his officers had followed suit and cut their hair short as well.[18]

On a sling hooked to his horse, each enlisted man carried the regulation single-shot, breechloading, 1873 Springfield carbine—a solid weapon with superior range and stopping power, though its soft copper cartridges would occasionally heat up and jam upon firing and need to be pried loose. The Springfield had won out over many other American and foreign rifles, some of them repeaters, after extensive testing supervised by an army board that had included Marcus Reno and Alfred Terry. Army appropriations were at an all-time low, and a key factor in the Springfield's favor was its low production cost. The standard-issue sidearm was the reliable Colt .45 pistol. Each man carried 100 rounds of carbine ammunition and 24 pistol cartridges with him—as many as 50 on a belt or in a pouch and the remainder in his saddlebags.[19] (The pack train mules carried 26,000 more carbine rounds.) Some of the higher-ranking officers and a few Sergeants supplied their own, more expensive arms. Custer carried a Remington sporting rifle, a hunting knife in a beaded scabbard, and two stubby English revolvers on his belt. He thought the handle of the .45 was too short.[20]

Despite the regiment's ragged appearance and thin ranks, the somber thoughts and forebodings of the night before had seemingly been abandoned. The men were eager, excited, and confident.

A fresh Indian trail lying not too far ahead would likely lead to a large village of hostiles. Within the next few days, the soldiers would probably engage these warriors in battle. Few of them had fought Indians before, but they were part of a proud regiment of the U.S. Army. They had been chosen to strike the enemy first, and the man who led them was one of the most celebrated Generals of the Civil War, a seasoned Indian fighter, and seemingly invincible. If Custer had been a Lakota warrior, his tribesmen following him into battle would have thought him bulletproof.

The column proceeded at a leisurely pace down the western side of the clear-running Rosebud, only a few feet wide and a few inches deep, until the bluffs closed in and forced them to the left. A thick tangle of wild rosebushes covered the banks, and cottonwoods and willows lined the sides of the bluffs. The rain the night before had moistened the ground and made progress more difficult. The column marched some distance away from the Rosebud, occasionally traversing ravines and small tributaries and crossing the stream now and then. At four o'clock, twelve miles upstream on the east side of the river, Custer called a halt. The pack train was still giving fits, largely due to the several crossings, which caused the most trouble. The last of the mules straggled into camp around sunset.[21]

The horses were tended to first, in a routine even the greenest recruit had memorized by now: loosen the saddle girth and remove the saddle; have a noncom inspect how wet the horse's back was to decide if the blanket should be taken off or kept on; clean the saddle, bridle, and other equipment; sponge the horse's eyes and wisp its head and mane; inspect and clean the hooves and shoes; feed, water, and groom the mount; and finally picket it in the area designated for his company. Only after all this could a trooper see to his own needs. Bed blankets and tent flies had been left behind, save for the officers', so each man would wrap himself in his saddle blanket and overcoat (using his saddle as a pillow) after eating.[22] Each company's cook began to prepare the typical supper for a soldier in the field: hardtack, bacon, and coffee.[23] (Mary Adams, Custer's personal cook, had been left behind on the *Far West*. The danger to her of accompanying the General into battle was deemed too great.)

After his command had settled in after supper, Custer issued a silent officers' call at his bivouac. Squatting around the General's small tent shelter, the officers talked in low tones. Custer began. First on his mind was the pack train. Unhappy with its performance, he told Lieutenant Mathey to oversee the 175 mules and the 70 troopers and 6 civilian packers assigned to it. He discussed a few other details, emphasizing caution and vigilance in camp and on the march: the hostile Indians could be anywhere, a surprise attack was always a possibility, and their success depended on remaining undiscovered for as long as possible. Until further orders, there would be no trumpet calls except in emergencies.

Then Custer's briefing took an unusual turn. He told the group that he expected to meet at least a thousand hostile fighting men;[24] with the extra warriors from the agencies, there might be as many as 1,500, but no more.[25] Explaining his refusal of the Gatling gun detachment and the Second Cavalry battalion, he convolutedly reaffirmed his confidence in the Seventh's ability to defeat any number of Indians they would find. If the hostiles could whip the Seventh, he said, they could defeat a much larger force. (Custer's logic, of course, was founded on the belief that U.S. cavalrymen could not be beaten by an undisciplined force of Indians, no matter how big, but his knotty justification of the Seventh's limits opened a door to the notion that failure might be possible.) He intended, he said, to follow the trail until they came upon the Indians, even if it took the regiment to the Indian agencies in Nebraska or on the Missouri River. That could mean being out longer than the time for which they were rationed, so troop officers were advised to husband their rations and the strength of their mules and horses. He also went to great lengths to emphasize his reliance on their judgment, discretion, and loyalty, and he stressed the importance of obeying orders without complaint—especially since some of his actions in the past had been criticized. Benteen, catching a drift, asked him who exactly he was accusing. Custer insisted that none of his remarks had been directed toward him.

Custer did not tell his subordinates of the grand strategy devised by Terry. His officers, much less the enlisted men, knew little or nothing of the plan to meet the Montana column somewhere near the mouth of the Little Bighorn on the 26th. They were on the trail of the hostiles and ordered to follow them until they were found. That was all they were told[26]—though some of the officers had surely gleaned some or all of the plan from fellow officers the evening before.

Custer ended the conference by soliciting suggestions from any and all officers, even the most junior of Second Lieutenants, then or at any time in the future. This was a request Custer's subordinates had never heard from him before. They were accustomed to his taciturn style—he usually issued orders tersely, without much explanation, and invited no debate, expecting his directives to be carried out without discussion. Now he seemed to be asking for help. The un-Custer-like tone—unsure, beseeching, even somewhat depressed—made an impression on all present. Whether this attitude was due to a legitimate or imagined slight or to the General's appreciation of the magnitude of the mission and its potential effect on his career, no one knew.

After synchronizing their watches—they operated on Chicago time, about an hour and a half later than local time, there being as yet no national system of time zones[27]—the group broke up, with the officers scattering to their troops to attend to their duties. Ten of the officers gathered around Lieutenant Edgerly's shelter tent and sang for about an hour. Lieutenant Calhoun told them that his wife had sent him a large cake, which was with the pack train. The day after the fight, he intended to send a piece around to each officer in the regiment.[28]

Lieutenants McIntosh, Godfrey, and Wallace walked back to their bivouac. They were silent for a while, then Wallace said, "Godfrey, I believe General Custer is going to be killed." The tall, gangly Wallace was known to be somewhat superstitious.

"Why, Wallace, what makes you think so?" Godfrey asked.

"Because I have never heard Custer talk in that way before."

Godfrey returned to his troop to brief his Sergeants, then walked to the herd to check on their security. At the bivouac of the Indian scouts, he saw Mitch Boyer, Bloody Knife, and some other Indians talking, some of it in sign language. He stood watching for several minutes, until Boyer turned to him.

"Have you ever fought against these Sioux?" the half-breed guide asked.

"Yes," said Godfrey.

"Well, how many do you expect to find?"

"It is said we may find between one thousand and fifteen hundred."

"Well, do you think we can whip that many?"

"Oh yes," said Godfrey. "I guess so."

Boyer turned to the Indians and interpreted the conversation. Then he said, with a great deal of conviction, "Well, I can tell you we are going to have a damn big fight."[29]

Before he turned in, Charley Reynolds pulled out the small leather notebook a friend had given him three days before leaving Fort Lincoln. Though he could hardly bear down on the pencil because of his painful infection, he slowly wrote a few details of the day's march, then ended with this: "The Indians seemed to be traveling leisurely along. Last camp found was probably 12 days old."[30] It would be the last entry Reynolds would make.

THE NEXT DAY was warm and sunny. The column headed out at 5:00 a.m. up the quarter-mile-wide Rosebud Valley. The Crows rode ahead, the Arikaras on the flanks. Benteen had been assigned with three companies to follow up the pack train and assist its movement and to guard against a rear attack. But every time the column crossed the Rosebud, the untrained pack mules balked—and the stream was traversed several times that day.

A few hours' march brought them to a deserted village site. Custer was in the advance and called a halt. He summoned Varnum, overseeing his Indian scouts, and said, "Here's where Reno made the mistake of his life. He had six troops of cavalry and rations enough for a number of days. He'd have made a name for himself if he'd pushed on after them."[31]

They came upon the remains of two more large campsites in the next twelve miles. At each, the pony droppings, lodge circles, and lodgepole trails were examined in an attempt to determine the size of the village and how recently it had been there. Many wickiups were still present. (Though they were likely shelters for single warriors from the agencies, some of the Seventh's officers thought they were built for dogs.) At one point near the great bend of the river, George Herendeen showed Custer the place where he and 149 other Bozeman men prospecting and exploring up the Rosebud in the spring of 1874 had fought off five hundred or six hundred Sioux warriors.[32] This was further proof to the Seventh's commander that a well-organized force of whites would emerge victorious in a battle with three or four times as many Indians. After all, if a group of 150 civilians could accomplish so much, what was a disciplined army regiment four times its size capable of?

After a long, hot day's march, the command had made about thirty-three miles before going into camp at 4:30 p.m. along a plain on the east side of the Rosebud. Once again, the last of the pack mules got into camp near sunset, even though a halt had been called earlier specifically to allow them to catch up.

Even more deserted camps were seen the next day, the 24th, another warm and clear day. The column was barely under way when Custer called Herendeen over to him. Custer told Herendeen that he thought it was time to send the frontiersman with Charley Reynolds to the head of Tullock's Creek—the valley that Terry had wanted Custer to scout. But Herendeen told him it was too early and called to Mitch Boyer for confirmation.

"Yes, further up on the Rosebud we come opposite a gap, and there we could cut across and strike Tullock's in about fifteen minutes' ride," said the guide.

"All right," said Custer. "I could wait."[33]

Later that morning, in a large deserted camp, the scouts found a white man's scalp hanging from the center pole of a Sun Dance lodge frame. The Arikaras examined the remains of the camp carefully and interpreted many signs there to mean that the Lakotas knew the enemy was coming and that they would triumph in battle. The Lakota medicine, they decided, was strong.[34] At one point, while Custer was inspecting the area, his color Sergeant stuck the staff of his battle flag in the ground. When it fell down and pointed to the rear, the superstitious Lieutenant Wallace remarked that it boded ill for the General.[35]

After a half hour at the Sun Dance camp, they rode on, in two parallel columns to reduce the thick, choking dust clouds stirred up by the horses. At one o'clock, a halt was called, and Custer summoned his chief of scouts. Varnum's contingent had begun to discover signs of fresher trails that branched off the main one, and Custer wanted no trail overlooked. Herendeen and then Godfrey had just reported that a large path had gone up a branch stream leaving the valley about ten miles back. Varnum protested; besides the Arikaras and Crows, he had the half-breeds Billy Jackson and Billy Cross and interpreter Fred Gerard assisting, and he was confident of their thoroughness. His scouts could not have missed a trail. But Custer directed the weary lieutenant to take some Arikaras and investigate. He also assigned the young Second Lieutenant from Godfrey's K Troop, Luther Hare, to assist Varnum with the scouts. Hare, a tall Texan recently graduated from the Point, was well liked by his men, and he came from a long line of soldiers; his father had fought for the Confederacy. Varnum left some Arikaras with Hare, grabbed a fresh horse, and headed downstream. During his absence, the command rested and ate dinner.

The trail would turn out to be a detour that rejoined the main route a short while later. But while Varnum was gone, Custer sent the Crow scouts far ahead to investigate. They returned at four o'clock to report a fresh Indian campsite about twelve miles ahead, at the forks of the Rosebud where a creek joined the stream from the divide to the west. All signs indicated that the massive Indian camp was no more than thirty miles away.

The march was resumed at five o'clock, Varnum taking the left front and Hare the right. The command rode through the remains of several more large campsites. Some of the fires were still smoldering,[36] and the entire width of the valley was scarred from the thousands of trailing lodgepoles dragged along by the Indians. There were a great many of them not far ahead.

Herendeen rode up to Custer, for the best route to Tullock's Creek was coming up on the right. "General, here is where I leave you to go to the other command," he said. Custer knew the deal: this was the agreed-upon juncture from which Terry was expecting Herendeen to return with the latest intelligence. (Herendeen also wanted to collect his $200.) But Custer just stared at him before looking away. The frontiersman said nothing and after a while fell back to the main column.[37]

At 7:45 p.m., the Seventh bivouacked on the grassy west side of the Rosebud, two miles below the forks, after marching twenty-eight miles that day. Custer chose a spot particularly pleasant—a level plateau between the stream and a sheer bluff, surrounded by rosebushes in full bloom. Men, horses, and mules were weary, for the troopers had been almost constantly in the saddle and on the march for fifteen hours, in sapping heat and choking dust. After the horses were unsaddled, fed, and rubbed down, most of the men ate a meager supper and began spreading their blankets.[38]

Custer still hadn't grasped the meaning of the diverging trails the command had thus far encountered. The scouts knew and discussed it over supper: these paths were not diverging, but converging. The fresh side trails represented agency Indians finally joining the large camp. But Custer, along with virtually every other soldier on the expedition from Terry on down, seemed too obsessed with the hostiles scattering to conceive of anything else.

The General had again sent the Crow scouts ahead, and at nine o'clock they rode into camp with momentous news: The trail turned west off the Rosebud along the other creek and crossed the divide toward the valley of the Little Bighorn. The trail was fresh enough to indicate that the hostiles were nearby and on the lower part of that stream, not farther up as Terry had supposed.

Terry's instructions had been clear, at least in one part of his orders: if the trail was found to turn away from the Rosebud, he wanted Custer to proceed southward to the headwaters of the Tongue before turning west to the Little Bighorn to descend that stream. But the Indians were so close that detection of the Seventh was now much more likely. If the hostiles had not already discovered the column's presence—the scouts had found several signs of Sioux, from distant signal fires to fresh horse tracks and footprints—hunting or scouting parties or other agency bands probably would. A mounted six-hundred-man force was hard to hide in this country, dust clouds or not. Besides, if Custer continued south toward the headwaters of the Tongue, at least another thirty miles, and then headed west and north, he would not reach the village until the 27th, or even later. Terry had hoped to be in the valley of the Little Bighorn on the 26th. What if the Indians were on the lower reaches of the river? And who knew where they would be by then? No, there was only one way the Seventh could be there on time.

Custer had already disobeyed one of Terry's directives by not scouting the upper reaches of nearby Tullock's Creek or bothering to send Herendeen down it to Gibbon's column. His next act of disobedience would be more significant. Terry's orders had dictated that Custer "should conform to them unless you shall see sufficient reason for departing from them"—and here was the opportunity of a lifetime: the chance to surprise a large village of hostiles, the object of the entire campaign. Ridicule had been heaped on commanders who had allowed Indians to escape, and some had been court-martialed—Reynolds on Powder River being only the most recent example. The hostile camp was likely a day's march away. Custer and the Seventh Cavalry would follow their trail.

ELEVEN

On the Jump

We scouts thought there were too many Indians for Custer to fight. . . . It was the biggest Indian camp I had ever seen.

WHITE MAN RUNS HIM, CROW SCOUT

Charles Varnum, West Point class of 1872, prided himself on his thoroughness. He took his job as chief of scouts seriously, and he had spent most of June 24 far in advance of the column with his Crows and Arikaras, talking to his charges through interpreters Isaiah Dorman, Frederic Gerard, and Mitch Boyer, making sure they did not miss any Indian sign.[1] Now, about an hour after making camp, the exhausted Second Lieutenant was eating supper and looking forward to some much-needed rest and sleep after a day's hard riding of sixty miles or so.

Then came the summons from the General.

Upon returning from their reconnaissance, the Crows had told Custer of a high hill, on the divide between the Rosebud and the Little Bighorn, from which they had just returned. There was a hidden hollow near the summit, perfect for concealing horses and men, that the Crows often used on horse raids against the Sioux when near the Little Bighorn. From the top, a good deal of country could be seen in several directions, but especially toward the west. If Sitting Bull's camp was on the Little Bighorn, the sign of smoke from early-morning campfires could be seen in the clear light of dawn. Judging by the trail they had picked up, the scouts believed the Sioux were on that river — Crow land, according to the 1868 treaty.

Now, when Varnum reached Custer's bivouac, the General told him of the lookout the Crows had mentioned. He said he wanted an intelligent white man to go with them and send back word of what they found.

"Well, I guess that means me," Varnum said.

"Not at all," replied Custer. "After what you've done today, you can't stand it."

Varnum reacted to this jab the way his CO knew he would. He was chief of scouts, he told Custer. He objected to anyone else going unless Custer had lost faith in him.

A satisfied Custer said he had figured that was about what Varnum would say and told him to go. Varnum would leave about 9:00 p.m. with the Crows, a few Arikaras, and their interpreters and get to the lookout before dawn. The lieutenant asked for a white man to talk to — Charley Reynolds was his choice, which Custer okayed. The General told him that the regiment would move out at 11:00 p.m. and camp near the lookout hill.[2]

On a flat below a bluff on the east bank of the Rosebud, the weary troopers finished their cold supper after tending to their mounts. Fires were limited to one per company, for coffee only, dry wood to be used, flames quickly extinguished. Most of the men lay down to sleep, but some walked over to the Rosebud and went for a swim.

Not far away from the stream, Mark Kellogg was working on another dispatch: "We leave the Rosebud tomorrow and by the time this reaches you we will have met the red devils, with what results remain to be seen. I go with Custer and will be in at the death."[3]

At the scouts' bivouac, talk was of the massive village not far ahead. The mood was somber.

"We are going to have a big fight," said Bloody Knife. "I know what is going to happen to me. I shall not see the sun."

Benteen, escorting the pack train, rode into camp late, but his friend Keogh hailed him, using the moniker given him by the enlisted men. "Come here, Old Man, I've kept the nicest spot in the whole camp next to me, for your troop," he said, "and I've had to bluff the balance to hold it, but here it is, skip off."

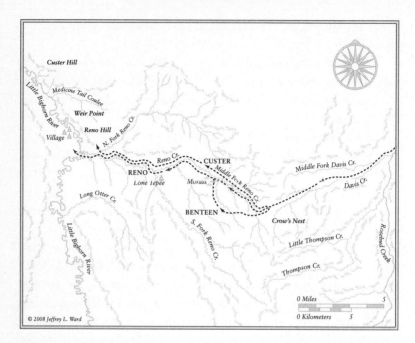

The white-haired Captain bivouacked his troop and found some grub, then lay down under a bullberry bush and pulled off his boots. Keogh settled down near him, under a tent fly. Nearby a few of the other officers were listening to Lieutenant Charles DeRudio tell stories of Italian derring-do.

Benteen interrupted. "See here, fellows, you want to be collecting all the sleep you can, and be doing it soon, for I have a 'pre' that we are not going to stay in this camp tonight, but we are going to march all night." He added, in a clear hint, "So good night."[4]

A moment later, the orderly trumpeter appeared to notify them of officers' call at headquarters at once. The officers stumbled over sleeping men and through horse herds to the only light in the valley—a candle at Custer's bivouac.

At about 9:30 p.m., not long after Varnum's departure, the General informed his officers of the Crows' discovery. He told them of his decision to cross the divide later that night, conceal the column during the next day while he thoroughly reconnoitered the exact location and particulars of the village, and attack the following morning, the 26th, at daylight. He issued orders to be ready to move out at 11:00 p.m.

After the conference, a group of the younger officers gathered to harmonize on a few songs—the wistful "Annie Laurie," followed by others of the same pensive nature. They ended with the doxology, then added a round of "For He's a Jolly Good Fellow" to end on a lighter note before saying their good-nights and settling down for a brief rest.[5] As if to counter the effort, a clear voice singing the hymn "Nearer, My God, to Thee" could be heard in another part of the bivouac.[6]

Soon the word was passed along from group to group—no trumpet calls now—to saddle up. The command moved out about 11:30. Half Yellow Face, the Crow leader, guided the column through the Stygian darkness and choking dust away from the Rosebud and up the creek heading west, on a gradual climb toward the divide. Custer tried to keep the pace at a trot, but the march through occasional timber and up hills and down gullies—some of them dry, some not—was difficult. The barest sliver of a moon had just set, and the night was so black that some of the men and officers did not know they had left the Rosebud Valley. Men and horses slipped and fell into ravines. Troopers followed the sounds of rattling carbines and tin cups deliberately banged by the last men in the company ahead and knew they had strayed off the trail if the air was clear of dust. The progress for all was slow, but the pack train in particular struggled, quickly falling far behind. Keogh and his company had been assigned escort duty, and the Irishman's fervent cursing of the exhausted mules and packers could be heard loud and clear as he and his men aided the animals across the muddy Rosebud. When packs loosened, the men cut them off as ordered and left them where they fell.

Gerard rode with Bloody Knife and Custer at the head of the column right behind Half Yellow Face. Custer told him to be sure the scouts followed up any trail, no matter how small. He wanted to make sure any and all camps, from four lodges to four hundred, were driven down the Little Bighorn. Gerard told the Arikara this.

"He needn't be so particular," said the dour Bloody Knife. "We'll get enough when we strike the big camp."

Custer asked Gerard how many Indians he thought they might find. Not less than 1,500 to 2,000 fighting men, the interpreter told him.[7]

Eventually, Lieutenant Mathey, in charge of the pack train, galloped forward and told Custer how far behind the mules had fallen. Custer stopped the column soon thereafter, about 2:00 a.m. They had made only eight miles, about five miles short of the crest of the divide.

Most of the men dismounted and dropped to the ground where they were to sleep, their reins in their hands, managing only to loosen their saddle girths and slip the bits from their horses' mouths. Some unsaddled and used their saddles for pillows. Custer ducked under a bush, pulled his hat over his eyes, and slept for a while. When daylight came about 3:00 a.m., fires were started for coffee, though the water from the closest stream was so alkaline it was almost undrinkable. The men had "a hearty breakfast," remembered Sergeant John Ryan ruefully: "some raw bacon, hard tack and cold water."[8]

John Burkman carried some coffee and hardtack over to the General. When the striker called, Custer did not stir. Burkman woke him and gave him his coffee.

Custer drank some and returned the cup. "Thanks, John," he said. "I'll tell Miss Libbie when we get back how well you've been taking care of me." Then he closed his eyes again for a while.[9]

VARNUM AND HIS SCOUTS made their way for several hours along the right bank of a timbered stream west up toward the divide, the Crows stopping a few times in the tangle of undergrowth to smoke cigarettes. Just short of the divide, the group splashed across the creek and rode almost a mile south before reaching the hill about 2:00 a.m. They led their horses into the sheltered pocket just below the top and unsaddled them. The spot reminded Varnum of a similar one at West Point, known as the Crow's Nest. While a few of the scouts climbed to the top of the steep ridge, Varnum dropped to the grass at its base and slept among the scattered pine and juniper trees. Boyer woke him about an hour later, and he scrambled to the summit with the other scouts.

Two of the Crows pointed toward the west. In the clear, early light of dawn, they detected signs of a large village—columns of smoke from breakfast fires and part of a large pony herd on the far side of the valley. Using a small telescope, the man the Arikaras called Peaked Face looked in the direction of the Little Bighorn. A few miles away, he could easily see two tepees along a creek that wound its way west. But try as he might, he could not see anything in the valley far to the west, some fifteen miles away.

One of the Crows said something, and Boyer interpreted. "Don't look for horses, look for worms," he said. "At that distance horses look like worms crawling on the ground."

Varnum had been in the saddle and up and down the hot, dusty trail for more than twenty-four hours, and his vision was blurry from lack of sleep. He still couldn't see what the trained eyes of the scouts, including Boyer and Reynolds, could spot so clearly. But if they were convinced, he was convinced.

The lieutenant wrote a short memo to Custer, and a little before 5:00 a.m. the two Arikaras, Red Star and Bull, set out for the column with the note, guided by the smoke of the soldiers' coffee fires clearly visible against the eastern sky. The Crows on the hill were aghast. Did the whites think the Sioux were blind?

The Arikaras were finishing their breakfast of boiled pork and crackers when Red Star, who had outdistanced Bull and his slower mount, rode into camp about 7:30 a.m. Isaiah Dorman escorted him to Custer's bivouac, next to the scouts'. The General signed to the young Arikara, asking him if he had seen the Sioux. Red Star assured Custer that he had, then he handed Custer Varnum's note telling him of the big village on the Little Bighorn. Custer jokingly gestured to Bloody Knife in sign language about how scared his brother Tom, standing nearby, was. Then he jumped on a horse and rode bareback around the camp to his officers, spreading the news and issuing orders to be ready to march at 8:00 a.m. When he returned, he summoned the Arikaras, who squatted around him. He told them that when they got to the Sioux camp, he wanted them to run off all the horses they could.

The Arikaras looked nervous, and Custer appeared distracted until a remark from Bloody Knife caught his attention.

Custer asked Gerard, "What's that he says?"

"He says we'll find enough Sioux to keep us fighting two or three days," the interpreter replied.

Custer smiled. "I guess we'll get through them in one day."[10]

Custer took Gerard, Bloody Knife, and a few Arikaras and rode to the hollow four miles away to see the village. Varnum had not actually seen the encampment, and Custer wanted a look for himself—every scrap of information would be valuable when formulating strategy.

Behind him the column prepared to move out. No word had been given to Major Reno, who had no command of his own. Custer had not consulted him since the departure from the Yellowstone, nor given him any orders, and Reno had not marched toward the front with Custer. He had done little except unhappily exercise the duties he imagined were those of a Lieutenant Colonel.[11] This morning march came as a surprise to him.

The column moved out at half past eight at a lively walk. As they paced forward, the men discussed the impending confrontation. One old soldier declared that the campaign would end just as soon as they could catch Sitting Bull.

"If that is all, the campaign will soon be over," said another, "and Custer will take us all with him to the Centennial."

"Of course," said a third, "we will take Sitting Bull with us."

Roars of laughter ensued.[12]

NOT LONG AFTER the two Arikara couriers, Red Star and Bull, had headed back to the main column, Varnum and his scouts spotted two Indians. They were about a mile to the west, an older one riding a pony and leading another on a lariat, a young boy behind him, also mounted, whipping the led pony along. They were headed east. If they continued, they would pass close to the hollow and proceed directly toward the column. It was clear what had to be done. Varnum, Reynolds, Boyer, and two Crows began making their way down through the trees and ravines to intercept and kill the two Indians.

Before they had gone very far, they heard a series of crowlike calls. Varnum's two Crows answered in similar fashion. The party returned to the hill to find that the two Indians, apparently Sioux, had changed their course. But soon after, they turned and headed east again, following the lodgepole trail, and soon disappeared from sight. By this time, dust clouds stirred up by the approaching column were visible. It appeared the hostiles had discovered the troops.

A short time later, Varnum and his group saw seven Indians to the north, riding single file toward the Rosebud on the crest of a ridge parallel to the column. They disappeared in a flash, then a small dark spot reappeared on the ridge. These hostiles, too, had likely been alerted to the presence of the soldiers and were now watching them.

About nine o'clock, Custer's party came into sight, and the lieutenant went down to meet it.

"Well, you've had a time of it," said the General.[13]

Varnum agreed he had. He led Custer up toward the Crow's Nest, filling him in as they climbed to the crest.[14] Once there, Custer sat down and scanned the landscape to the west, then through Boyer talked with the Crows. The sharp light of the early dawn was now hazier, but they tried to show him what they could see. Reynolds and Gerard both tried to direct Custer as he searched without success for signs of the village.

"I've been on the prairie for many years. I've got mighty good eyes, and I can't see anything that looks like Indian ponies," he said.

A frustrated Boyer knew what was on the Little Bighorn, and he knew how big it was. He had been telling Custer since they had left the Yellowstone. "If you don't find more Indians in that valley than you ever saw together before, you can hang me," the scout now said.

Custer jumped to his feet and gave a short laugh. "It would do a damn sight of good to hang you, now wouldn't it?" he said testily. Varnum had only heard him swear once before, and that had been on the Yellowstone in 1873 while in a hot fight with some Sioux.[15] Finally, Reynolds offered his field glasses, and after looking through them, Custer finally nodded, now able to make out a large, dark mass and dust rising—clear indications of a huge pony herd.

When the Crows had told Custer of the nearby Sioux and the distinct probability that his command had been discovered, he had refused to believe them. Though they had originally favored his plan to keep the column concealed until the next day while the scouts made a full reconnaissance, they now pressed for an immediate attack, insisting in no uncertain terms that the Sioux had spotted them. Custer finally agreed.[16]

Nevertheless, he remained on the hill for almost an hour, studying the terrain, before leading the entire group down to the command, which had marched to within a mile or so of the divide and was now hidden in a large ravine sheltered on two sides by hills. As he did so, Tom Custer rode toward his brother with more bad news.

Indians had been sighted on their back trail. It seemed that a Sergeant of F Troop had requested permission from his company commander, Captain Yates, to ride back to find some personal belongings of his that had gone missing. Yates had told him to take a detachment of four men with him. Upon cresting a knoll after a few miles on the back trail, they had come upon three warriors several hundred yards away, opening boxes of hardtack that had fallen off the pack mules. The troopers had fired upon them, and the hostiles had disappeared into the hills.

Then Herendeen, who had been out on the flanks, told the General he had seen a couple of Indians not far from the column. They had quickly fled and might even now be riding to alert the village. Boyer had seen them also.[17] Sure enough, fresh pony tracks were found up a ravine.

Custer immediately had his trumpeter blow a soft officers' call, the first trumpet notes since they had left the Yellowstone three days earlier. While the other officers gathered around the General, Varnum, who had not eaten anything since the morning before, ignored the meeting to hunt for some food and drink.

Custer now felt he had no choice. The Seventh had been chosen as the attack force, and Terry's orders had directed him to "proceed up the Rosebud in pursuit of the Indians." If Custer knew how to do one thing, it was pursue an enemy. A day of invaluable reconnaissance — and much-needed rest for the men, horses, and mules — would have to be scratched.

Custer told the officers gathered about him that the scouts had discovered a large village about fifteen miles away on the lower reaches of the Little Bighorn. He had not personally seen the camp, he said, but Boyer and the Indian scouts had. The regiment had been discovered by hostiles, who were likely riding fast to warn the village. The Seventh would move out immediately and attack. Custer told the company commanders to assign five or six men and one noncom each to the pack train.[18] All told, about 130 troopers and packers—20 percent of the command—would ride with the mules to protect the supplies and extra ammunition.[19] The officers were ordered to ascertain the readiness of their companies; troops would march in the order that they reported them ready.

Herendeen spoke up. "General, the head of Tullock's Creek lies just over those hills yonder." His journey to Gibbon and Terry was now a fifty-mile ride, a distance unforeseen when the commanders had been huddled over the sketchy map in the cabin of the *Far West*.

"Yes, but there are no Indians in that direction—they are all in our front," Custer said impatiently. He had scouted the country to the north while up on the Crow's Nest and had seen no trails or Indians. "And besides, they have discovered us. It will be of no use to send you down Tullock's Creek. The only thing to do is to push ahead and attack the camp as soon as possible."[20] Though Terry expected the scout's arrival, there now seemed little point in sending Herendeen through that valley to tell Terry long after the Seventh had made the attack that there were no Indians in it.

Charley Reynolds chimed in, saying this was the biggest bunch of Indians he had ever seen.[21] Then Boyer repeated his warning to Custer: "I have been with these Indians for thirty years and this is the largest village I have ever known of," he said.[22] Custer wasn't worried much about the size of the Indian camp; striking before it scattered was his overriding concern. Custer and everyone else on the campaign wanted to avoid a long chase after many smaller bands that would take the entire summer, perhaps longer.

Custer told Boyer that since he was not a soldier, he did not have to go in with the regiment. Boyer replied hotly that he wasn't afraid to go anywhere Custer did, but there were more Indians down there than they could handle, and if they went down into the valley of the Little Bighorn, they would both wake up in hell the next morning. Then the guide turned and walked away.[23]

The meeting broke up, each troop commander returning to his bivouac. Benteen had walked only a few yards when he turned on his heel and reported his company ready. Custer, a bit taken aback, said, "The advance is yours, Colonel."[24] The honor of taking the lead would belong to H Company.

Captain Tom McDougall had overslept and was the last to report, so B Company was given the pack train escort detail. Some of his disappointed troopers, doubtful they would see any action, wept at this.[25]

Custer turned to John Burkman and told him to saddle Vic (short for Victory). He had taken his older horse, Dandy, to the Crow's Nest and wanted a fresh mount. Moments later he swung into the saddle, then leaned over and put his hand on his striker's shoulder and told him to ride with the pack train. There would be no led horses with the advance. "You're tired out," he said. "But if we should have to send for more ammunition you can come in on the home stretch."[26]

Varnum reported for duty, and the General asked him if he felt able to continue scouting. The lieutenant said he had to continue riding anyway, and one place was as good as another. He was told to go ahead, so he took the left front of the advance, with the Arikaras, and sent Lieutenant Hare to the right with the Crows.[27]

The interpreters translated the orders to the Indian scouts and emphasized their role in the coming battle. The General did not expect them to fight, and had told them so, but he did want them to capture as much of the pony herd as possible—Sioux Indians without a good supply of ponies were easier to catch. As they began their battle preparations, an older Arikara named Stabbed, their second in command, exhorted his younger tribesmen to be brave. Then he prayed and rubbed a special clay—earth he had brought with him from their country along the Missouri—on their bodies for good medicine.

The regiment saddled up, and the word was passed to mount. There was not much talking now. The men were confident of victory, but word had spread of the massive village of hostiles, and the General had been unusually serious and businesslike since the Yellowstone—no cutting up with his brothers as he had on the journey out from Lincoln. And, of course, most of the men had not slept for more than a few hours; they were tired and dirty and hungry. But that, they knew, was the life of a soldier on the trail.

The command moved out in column of fours, fifty feet between each company, following the lodgepole trail west over the divide through a narrow valley, the northern end of the Wolf Mountains and the Crow's Nest on their left. Custer led, accompanied by his adjutant, the dundreary-whiskered Lieutenant Cooke, and followed closely by his two color-bearers, his chief trumpeter, and his orderly for the day, a young Italian trumpeter from H Company named Giovanni Martini (now known as John Martin). Martini had been a drummer boy with Garibaldi a decade earlier. He had immigrated to the United States from Italy in 1873 and enlisted a year later. His English was not very good, but he was a feisty little fellow. Inevitably, some of the troopers called him "Dry Martini."[28]

Burkman, back with the pack train waiting to pull out, watched the battalions ride away. He had to hold Custer's two dogs, Blucher and Tuck, by their collars while they whined to follow. I Company's little yellow dog, Joe Bush, ran along after the troops. Burkman whistled at him, but he didn't stop.[29] The striker had had similar luck in persuading Autie Reed to stay with the pack train.

The regiment began a gentle descent along a small creek that wandered toward the Little Bighorn. Reno rode with Moylan's troop, about halfway back. A few minutes after noon, almost a mile farther on, Custer called a halt to make battalion assignments. He and Cooke rode off a ways to talk, the adjutant scribbling in his notebook, probably assessing the strengths of various divisions.

There were several factors to take into consideration. When many bands of Indians gathered, they usually spread out along a watercourse for sanitation and grazing purposes. Sometimes they were so far separated as not even to be within sight of each other. At the Washita in 1868, Custer had not reconnoitered the area completely before the battle and had almost been surprised by hundreds of warriors from several large villages a few miles downstream. Now he knew he needed a force both to scout the valley above the camp and to drive any Indians there downstream. A small squadron could accomplish the first task, but a larger force — at least two or three companies — was needed for the second. And he would likely need to strike the village from more than one direction, especially if its occupants attempted to scatter. One final consideration was the pack train. It was apparent after three days that it could not keep up with the column even at a walk, much less at the faster pace needed now. To lose the ammunition it carried, 26,000 rounds, would be disastrous.[30] That, too, had almost happened at the Washita.

Custer took the right wing—the same troops that Reno had led on his scout down the Tongue, minus McDougall's B Troop, now plodding miserably beside the pack train. Those five companies, C, E, F, I, and L, happened to be some of his favorites, led by officers close to him: Yates, Smith, Calhoun, Keogh, and Tom Custer. The General would retain direct command of the entire battalion, though the two senior officers, Keogh and Yates, would each command a wing, with Yates taking the smaller one.[31] (The right wing's horses were the most fatigued of the command, as they had gained little rest since the grueling Reno scout.) To Reno, Custer detailed three troops—A, G, and M, the commands of Captains French and Moylan and Lieutenant McIntosh. To Captain Benteen, he assigned three—D, H, and K, the commands of Captain Weir and Lieutenant Godfrey, along with Benteen's own. Each of the General's four senior subordinates would lead a battalion.

After Custer gave the battalion orders, Half Yellow Face spoke though Boyer. "Do not divide your men," he said. "There are too many of the enemy for us, even if we stay together. If you must fight, keep us all together."

Custer was in no mood to hear dire predictions. "You do the scouting, and I will attend to the fighting," he said.

The Crow began to strip off his clothes and paint his face. Custer asked what he was doing.

"Because you and I are going home today, and by a trail that is strange to us both," said Half Yellow Face.[32]

DURING THE HALT along the small creek, Custer noticed a line of bluffs only a mile or so to the southwest.[33] The Little Bighorn valley, and quite possibly more Indian camps, lay somewhere just beyond them.[34] He ordered Benteen to take his battalion of 118 men and move toward the bluffs—and, as Benteen later remembered it, to "pitch into anything" he came across and send word back to the

General. If no Indians were found, then as soon as he was satisfied that any further movement in that direction was useless, he was to rejoin the main command as quickly as possible.[35] Custer apparently expected Benteen's battalion back soon—in an hour or so—if it did not become engaged.

None of the three doctors with the column rode with Benteen, a fact hinting that Custer doubted it would see any action. Instead, Henry Porter and James DeWolf, two civilian contract surgeons, rode with Reno, and George Lord, the regimental surgeon, remained with headquarters. Lord had been indisposed since the Yellowstone—probably dysentery, a common cavalryman's ailment, usually due to bad water—and had not been able to eat since then, barely keeping up with the column. Custer suggested that he remain with the rear guard, but the dutiful Lord refused to relinquish his position.[36]

Benteen was not happy with his new assignment. The honor of leading the regiment and striking the enemy first had now been replaced by a secondary mission with little chance for glory. Custer, he was sure, had engineered this as a personal vendetta. He could have assigned any other battalion, or even a lesser force. But the Captain had no choice in the matter. He turned his battalion off to the left.

Custer led his five companies at a fast walk down the right side of the creek. Reno and his three companies proceeded down the left, gradually falling behind the General. The Indian scouts ranged ahead of the column, riding back and forth with news, the smaller Indian ponies having to gallop to stay ahead of the soldiers. A few miles down the trail, the creek bottom began to widen a good deal. Custer called another halt, and he and Varnum momentarily trained their field glasses on the valley ahead. Then the march continued. The day was heating up quickly, and most of the men removed their heavy blouses. As the afternoon wore on, many of them discarded overcoats and other spare clothing, haversacks, forage sacks, and the like to get down to fighting trim.[37] The ground was very dry, and as the command advanced, the horses stirred up large clouds of dust. The pack train's exhausted and sloppily packed mules fell behind and were soon lost from sight.

Mark Kellogg kicked his mule forward until he reached Gerard at the head of the column. Would Gerard lend him his spurs? Gerard handed them over but advised the reporter not to put them on and instead to fall back with the main command and stay there. Kellogg replied that he was "expecting interesting developments" and wanted to keep up with the scouts.[38] He remained near Custer.

A little before two o'clock, about ten miles beyond the divide, Herendeen, Hare, Varnum, his orderly, and some of the scouts came upon the remnants of a large campsite that extended half a mile along the north side of the creek. At the far end were two tepees, one collapsed and the other still standing, opposite a high, chalk white bluff upon which were Boyer and the Crows, who waved the newcomers up. They scaled the hill and peered down the valley. On a rise two or three miles to the west was a group of about fifty warriors riding away amid a cloud of dust. The Crows had been watching them for a while.[39] From the still-warm ashes in the fires down below, it was apparent that these Indians had just left their camp of the night before and were heading toward the larger one, no doubt warned of the soldiers' approach by some of the Indians seen that morning. The scattering had begun, and when the hostiles in sight reached the village and warned it, the huge gathering would disperse into thin air.

Varnum and his orderly continued down the creek. Hare dispatched an Arikara with a note to Custer. Then the remaining Arikaras charged down to one of the tepees and ripped it open with knives. Inside, upon a scaffold, was the wrapped body of a dead warrior, surrounded by his possessions and weapons.[40] The other tepee also contained a few dead bodies.[41] A few minutes later, Custer, at the head of the Seventh, rode into view of the standing tepee. Down the creek beyond it, he could see the cloud of dust. After examining the lodge and its occupant, the General told his orderly to set it on fire.[42] He turned and with a wave of his hat summoned Reno and his column across the creek. A moment later Gerard, on a low knoll closer to the tepee, waved his hat toward Custer and yelled, "There go your Indians, running like devils!"[43]

Custer had expected the Arikaras to continue on to the Sioux camp and make away with some of the pony herd, but as he looked around, he found them making a big fuss over the two tepees in the abandoned campsite, again making lengthy preparations for a fight by stripping off their soldier blouses and greasing themselves and singing. "We are going to have church," remarked one lieutenant upon hearing the death songs this Sunday morning.[44]

Almost two hours had passed since Benteen had turned left off the trail on what Custer hoped would be a short scout, and neither he nor a messenger was anywhere in sight. But there was no time to lose. Custer ordered the Arikara scouts after the fleeing village. They refused: not without soldiers. The General accused them of cowardice and threatened to take away their guns and horses. The Arikaras objected, and one replied with a similar insult to the soldiers, after which the other scouts laughed. As the rest of the command entered the campsite, Gerard rode up and assured the Arikaras of soldier support. But Custer had already turned to Cooke. Since the Arikaras would not move out, he told the Canadian, Cooke should order Major Reno and his battalion after the escaping Indians.[45]

When Reno and Hodgson reached the head of the column a few minutes later, Cooke relayed Custer's orders: "The Indians are about two and a half miles ahead—they are on the jump. Go forward as fast as you think proper and charge them wherever you find them and he will support you."[46]

Reno crossed back to his command and moved out down the creek. As he passed the General some thirty yards away, Custer yelled, "Take your battalion and try and overtake and bring them to battle and I will support you."[47] As Reno rode ahead, Custer added, "And take the scouts along with you."

There was no mention of any overall plan—unsurprising, since the huge village they had been tracking for days had still not been seen—and Custer sent no one to deliver word of these new developments to Benteen, out of sight somewhere to the left, or the pack train, far behind them on the trail. For that matter, Reno had only the vaguest idea of what Benteen was up to. When Benteen had turned off the trail to the left, Reno had asked him where he was going, and the Captain had only replied that he was to drive everything before him.

The erosion of order—and the fragmentation of the command— continued. Mitch Boyer told the Crows to stay with Custer.[48] The

General had sent a couple of them over a ridge to find the village, but as Reno's battalion started down the creek, in the confusion they followed the Major.[49] Gerard called out to Dorman and the Arikaras to join him with Reno's battalion. Then, as Reno led his three companies out at a trot, Varnum and his orderly returned from scouting the left front. When Custer asked him what he had seen, he replied that the village was out of sight behind the bluffs — only a few tepees were visible — but the valley was full of Indians.[50] Varnum asked where Reno's squadron was going.

"To begin the attack," said Custer. He told Varnum that he could accompany them if he wanted to and ride with the scouts.[51]

Varnum called back to Wallace, his gangly West Point classmate. As acting engineering officer, he was riding with the General. "Come on, Nick, with the fighting men. I don't stay back with the coffee coolers."

Custer shook his fist, laughed, waved his hat, and told Wallace he could go.[52]

Reno led his battalion in column of twos on a fast trot down the creek. "Keep your horses well in hand, boys," he said, as some of the beasts threatened to get away from their inexperienced riders. With about 140 troopers and 35 scouts — every Arikara and all of the rest, save 4 Crows and Mitch Boyer — he led a fighting force of 175. As Reno rode after the fleeing Indian camp, Adjutant Cooke and Captain Keogh rode with him, though it was not clear whether they were to join the attack or observe and report back.

Meanwhile, Boyer and the four remaining Crows rode up into the hills ahead to the right. Custer led his men at a walk past the burning lodge and down the creek after Reno.[53] His nephew Autie Reed rode with him, as did the newspaperman Kellogg. His brother Boston was on his way back to the pack train to exchange his horse for a fresh one.

Less than a half hour later,[54] at about 3:00 p.m. Chicago time, Reno's battalion came within sight of the Little Bighorn after a ride of three miles. Indians could be seen far down the valley on the other side.[55] The creek Reno's men had been following led them to a natural ford that was clearly an Indian crossing. The river here was thirty to fifty feet wide and three to four feet deep, cool and clear, about belly high to the horses. Most of the Arikaras climbed the farther bank first, while Reno and his command began to wade over, some of the troopers stopping to water their mounts. Downstream, pony herds were grazing on both sides of the river. Several of the Arikaras turned and galloped along the east side toward them.

Cooke and Keogh pulled up and sat their horses on the bank of the stream. As Sergeant Ryan and a group of M Company troopers galloped past them, Cooke called out, "For God's sake, men, don't run those horses like that; you will need them in a few minutes."[56] Keogh and then Cooke soon turned and headed back toward Custer.[57]

Lieutenant DeRudio rode into the river behind the command. He surged toward Reno and Gerard, who were watering their horses. Reno was drinking from a flask of whiskey. As the Italian neared him, his horse splashed the Major, who said, "What are you trying to do? Drown me before I am killed?"[58]

As Gerard came up out of the river, the two Crow scouts riding ahead and to the left yelled something. Herendeen heard this and hollered back toward him, "Hold on—the Sioux are coming."[59] He couldn't see them, but the Crows could.

"Hell, Custer ought to know this right away," said Gerard to no one in particular, "for he thinks the Indians are running. He ought to know they are preparing to fight. I'll go back and inform him." With that, Gerard rode back to Reno.

"Major, the Indians are coming up the valley to meet us," he announced when he reached Reno.

Reno only stared dully at Gerard, whom he had fired at Fort Lincoln, then looked across the river and down the valley. A moment later he yelled, "Forward!"[60] and the three companies cleared the fringe of timber onto the prairie, where the men dismounted briefly to tighten their girths and prepare for battle before swinging back into their saddles. Reno re-formed the command in column of fours, with A and M companies in the front and G in reserve in the rear. As the men formed in line, someone said, "There goes Custer," and sure enough, there he was on the hills to the right, moving at a fast trot.[61]

Gerard recrossed the river and headed back up the creek after Cooke to deliver the news.[62]

*   *   *

RENO'S DEPARTURE with a quarter of the regiment had left Custer with 220 men, give or take a trooper—five seriously understrength companies, to be sure, but not unusual in this army. More serious was the battalion's thin officer corps. Though each company was authorized three officers, none of them had more than two. Making things even worse, several officers had been assigned to companies other than their own in an attempt to cover the paltry distribution. Incredibly, one company, C, was led by a Second Lieutenant, Henry Harrington, who had no combat experience. (The troop's assigned Captain, Tom Custer, was riding with his brother as aide-de-camp.) F Company was led by Second Lieutenant William Van Wyck Reily, who had been in the army less than eight months and had only recently mastered the fundamentals of horsemanship, much less cavalry tactics in a combat situation. (The troop's veteran Captain, George Yates, was leading a wing.)

Captain Myles Keogh led I Troop and had been given command of Custer's other wing, but another young and untested Second Lieutenant, James Porter, assisted him. Porter's wife had just given birth to their second child in March, and he had requested a transfer to the general staff for a more settled life. Since his graduation from the Point in 1869 and his marriage to his wife, Eliza, later that year, the couple had moved fourteen times. His request had been endorsed by several senior officers but was still going through channels when the expedition had left Fort Lincoln.[63]

It was similar all down the line. First Lieutenant Jimmi Calhoun, commanding L Company instead of his own C, was a veteran of the Civil War and the skirmishes with the Sioux on the Yellowstone. His only subaltern was Second Lieutenant John Crittenden, the frail young infantry officer with only one good eye. First Lieutenant Algernon Smith, another experienced Indian fighter, led E Troop instead of his own A. His junior officer was Second Lieutenant James "Jack" Sturgis, the son of the regiment's nominal commander, Colonel Samuel Sturgis. Young Jack had been with the regiment since the previous October, after graduating from West Point just months earlier.

Just as worrisome was the shortage of noncommissioned officers, the veteran soldiers who interacted with the enlisted men much more than the officers and knew their strengths and weaknesses—and provided bedrock confidence in battle. To a large degree, each troop's day-to-day activities were handled by the First Sergeant and his duty Sergeants and Corporals. In point of fact, they ran the company.[64] Of the thirty Sergeants authorized to the five companies, fully half were absent, either with the pack train or on detached duty.

Despite these serious shortcomings, Custer remained confident. The men with him were overwhelmingly veterans—only 15 percent of them had less than a year's military experience, and none had been with the regiment less than six months. Virtually every troop commander with him was a friend and admirer. Each one of them, and a few of the junior officers, wore a buckskin jacket like the General's, though most had by now stripped down to their wide-collared "fireman's shirts."[65] They were men he could count on to do what was needed, do whatever he asked of them. Though few of his troopers or officers could claim any Indian-fighting experience, Custer still expected them to acquit themselves proudly when the time came. He had often boasted that his regiment could whip and defeat every Indian on the plains,[66] and if his scouts were correct in their claims of the large number of Indians ahead, today he could make that brag fact.

From the bluffs ahead, Boyer and the four Crows could see some lodges downstream that indicated the large village they had expected. Boyer reported them to Custer.[67] Varnum had noted much the same thing to the General before he had left with Reno.[68] That meant the main camp was downstream as well, apparently all on the west side of the river, and the Indians Reno was chasing were not the majority, but a smaller group moving in that direction. Benteen was blocking the Indians' escape south, and Terry and Gibbon were somewhere downstream to the north. With any luck—Custer's luck, which had never failed the General before—the massive village was still intact and vulnerable. The battalion continued at a trot down the lodgepole trail toward the valley of the Little Bighorn.

Some twenty minutes later, Keogh and then Cooke came galloping back with the news from Gerard. Reno had followed the hostiles across a well-used ford about a mile away.[69] But the enemy was not retreating; instead the Indians were riding up the valley to meet him. Custer was never one to follow another man's charge, and he decided to implement an age-old cavalry maneuver that he had used time and again in the war and on the plains: hit the enemy's flank while the main attack occupied his front. Since he had not specifically told Reno that he would follow him across the river, this new plan called for a messenger to be sent to inform the Major of the change. Whether he believed Reno would understand once he saw the battalion on the bluffs, or whether he reasoned that he would reach the scene sooner than a rider could overtake Reno, Custer sent no courier.[70] He turned right and led his five companies north, following another trail of lodgepole tracks out of the ravine and over the rolling hills.[71] A few minutes later, he stopped to water the horses. The early-afternoon heat was stifling, and the General pulled off his buckskin coat and tied it behind his saddle.[72] He warned his men not to let the horses drink too much—they had a lot of traveling and a lot of fighting to do that day.[73]

Sergeant Daniel Kanipe of C Troop, a tall, twenty-three-year-old farm boy from North Carolina, noticed between fifty and seventy-five Indians on a higher hill to the north. When Custer was told, he ordered the command up the slope at a fast trot. The battalion followed him, the five companies in column of twos and riding abreast—ten men across and twenty men deep.[74]

AFTER DELIVERING THE NEWS of the hostiles' offensive movement to Cooke, Gerard headed back to the river. Before he got there, he passed a trooper—Private Archibald McIlhargey, Reno's striker, the owner of a fast horse[75]—riding back along the trail with much the same message from Reno to Custer: the Major now had the enemy to his front and in strength. When Gerard reached the Little Bighorn, he could see Reno's battalion moving at a fast walk down the valley between the winding, tree-lined river flanked by high bluffs on the right and low plateau hills almost a mile to the left, where large pony herds were visible.[76] He splashed across the stream and galloped after the command, on the way passing yet another courier, Reno's cook, Private John Mitchell, bearing a similar message from Reno to Custer.

Gerard caught up to Reynolds, Herendeen, Dr. Porter, and some of the Arikara scouts behind the battalion on the left. The command's trot soon became a slow gallop.[77] The ground before them was flat and open, dotted with sagebrush, and the grass had been cropped by Indian ponies and trampled to dirt by their hooves. M and A companies rode in line of battle spread across the valley, with G Company in their rear, toward about fifty hostiles up ahead and a large cloud of dust about two miles beyond—all they could see of the small village they had been ordered to pursue. Once or twice, the troopers saw Custer's battalion on the bluffs across the river, moving downstream. Some of the men began to cheer and wave their hats, but Reno, now in the rear of A Company, shouted, "Stop that noise!" Then he yelled "Charge!" At least one A Company trooper heard the order slurred and glanced back to see the Major drinking from a half-full flask and passing it to Benny Hodgson.[78]

One hundred and fifty men rode down the valley of the Little Bighorn.[79]

III

ATTACK

TWELVE

The Charge

When you run from an Indian you are his meat.

R. J. SMYTH, FRONTIERSMAN

By the time Custer's battalion had reached the high ridge where one of his men had earlier sighted fifty or so Indians, the enemy had vanished. But there were plenty of other things to notice.

Below, nestled along the other side of the river and stretching for almost two miles downstream, was the largest gathering of Indians that Custer had ever seen. The bluffs and the trees, and a thick cloud of dust, hid some of it, but most of the village's thousand-odd lodges were visible. The camp was in a frenzy as women and children rode and ran north, while hundreds of warriors rushed to find their horses in the herds to the west and north. Those already mounted galloped in circles and back and forth before the village to stir up dust and shield the fleeing families.

Almost directly across the river, Reno's command could be seen galloping down the valley, approaching a large wooded bend of the river, beyond which the village lay. Custer's troops began to yell at the sight of the camp and their charging comrades, and some of the horses caught the excitement and bolted ahead of the General.

During the war, Custer had often made light of a grim situation to inspire the men behind him.[1] Here was just such an opportunity.

© 2008 Jeffrey L. Ward

He yelled, "Boys, hold your horses—there are plenty of them down there for us all."[2]

There was no sign of other villages, as at the Washita; all of the Indians seemed to be encamped in one place. But Custer had almost lost his supply train at the Washita, and he wanted to safeguard against that. They needed all the troops and the pack train up now, he told Cooke. The adjutant turned to Tom Custer and asked for a courier.

Tom motioned forward one of his Sergeants. Daniel Kanipe trotted up.

"Go back to McDougall," Tom told him. "Tell McDougall to hurry the pack train straight across the country to Custer and if any of the packs get loose, cut them and let them go—do not stop to tighten them." As Kanipe headed his horse around, Tom added, "And if you see Benteen, tell him to come on quick—a big Indian camp."[3] The view from the bluffs made it clear that there were no other camps to the south within supporting distance, so the fight was in front of them. Benteen's men were needed here.

Kanipe saluted, then turned his horse south. He was disappointed; he would miss all the action. But he rode quickly along the back trail until he saw a dust cloud over to the left. It could only be Benteen or the pack train. He spurred his horse across the hills in that direction.

CHARLES VARNUM, LUTHER HARE, and the scouts preceded Reno's battalion down the valley. After they had gone about a mile, they could see a great many horses ahead of them. Up on the left, near the foothills, a few young Sioux herders led a large group of ponies toward the village.[4] More than a few horses straggled behind. The Arikaras on the left made for these and began herding a great number of them back toward the river. They had not gone far before mounted Sioux thundered down the valley to cut them off. The Arikaras released part of their quarry, which the Sioux slowed to recover, and the scouts made the ford safely.[5] Another group of Arikaras spied a herd of about two hundred ponies downriver beyond the bluffs and gave chase, cutting some of them out of the pack. They exchanged their worn-out mounts for fresh ones, then headed back into the hills. Before they left, they overtook several Sioux women, perhaps ten, and killed them in a ravine on the east side of the river.[6]

Not all of the Arikaras split off to gather horses as Custer had wanted. Some of them, perhaps as many as ten, elected to stick with the soldiers and battle their blood enemies, though their duties as scouts did not usually include line fighting.[7] Another eleven of them never even made it across the river. Their smaller ponies had to work harder to keep up with the army mounts, and some of them played out, stranding their riders.

About a mile down the valley, Reno ordered G Company to move up to his right flank. By this time, the command was moving at a gallop in line of battle across the valley: M on the left, then A, then G along the timber. Ahead was an expanse of open prairie and about fifty Indians—the same ones they had been chasing for more than half an hour—galloping to and fro, back and forth, raising a massive cloud of dust, behind which little could be seen. Beyond them in the distance were other Indians, and the closer the soldiers approached, the more Indians they could see. There was still no support from Custer, though many men riding with Reno had seen his command on the bluffs on the east side of the river, a ways behind them. Reno, in command and likely inebriated to some extent,[8] was becoming increasingly anxious.

The next mile brought another problem. Several hundred yards ahead was a shallow ditch that had once been part of the river's course but was now a dry ravine about five feet deep and ten feet wide. Indians could be seen pouring out of it. If the command continued at a gallop, every horseman would hurtle into the ravine, experienced and inexperienced alike, and would likely be thrown off his mount. Discipline and momentum would be completely lost, and they would be extremely vulnerable to enemy attacks.[9]

As the battalion neared a timbered bend of the river that looped almost halfway across the valley, a somewhat clearer view of the village emerged, at least from the left side of the line. This was no sleeping camp of fifty-one lodges, like the one on the Washita that the Seventh Cavalry had charged and taken within minutes. The heavy dust still obscured the village's full dimensions, as did the wooded bend, but now Reno could see that there were at least four hundred tepees in several large circles, and riding forth in increasing numbers were hundreds of painted, screaming warriors, most of them naked save for a small breechcloth.[10] Though Custer had accomplished the rare feat of surprising a large Indian village at midday, the Sioux and Cheyennes were quickly mobilizing to defend their families.

Plains Indians could be surprisingly lackadaisical when it came to guarding their camps, and an effective attack could be achieved if a village could be closely approached before charging. Such was the case on another hot Sunday afternoon, in July 1869, at the Battle of Summit Springs in Colorado. There Major Eugene Carr and 300 men of the Fifth Cavalry, supplemented by a battalion of Pawnee scouts, had charged into a sleeping camp of 500 Cheyenne Dog Soldiers and routed them. In the process, they had killed the Cheyennes' leader, Tall Bull, and fifty-one others. Army casualties had amounted to a scratch to one trooper's cheek. In another attack near the headwaters of the north fork of the Red River in Texas, Colonel Ranald S. Mackenzie in September 1872 had led five companies of the Fourth Cavalry against a Comanche village of 262 lodges—at 4:00 p.m. Thirty-two Comanches had been killed and 124 captured, with the loss of only 4 troopers.[11]

This day would not see a charge the likes of those. Another cavalry officer with more dash, more experience, or more confidence and faith in his CO might have continued into the village, regardless of the odds. But Marcus Reno had never demonstrated much élan, during the Civil War or after.

Custer had shared no overall strategy with Reno, nor told him exactly what he planned to do. If his experience fighting Plains Indians had been greater, the Major might have known that the surest method of panicking them was a headlong, disciplined charge into their village. By this time, Reno also might have surmised his commander's ploy, since Custer and his battalion had been sighted riding downstream on the other side of the river. One of the most common cavalry tactics was a pincer movement—striking an enemy from two directions at the same time. The Seventh had employed it successfully on the Washita, albeit against a much smaller gathering.

Perhaps the Major assessed the situation properly and decided that a charge into a camp this large by three depleted companies was suicidal. Or perhaps Reno's liquid courage had lost its effect. Custer had ordered the Major after an escaping camp of Indians, not a large standing village, and had promised to support him. Now the situation had changed dramatically. If the General had decided on a new plan, he was obligated to tell Reno. No courier had arrived with a message of any change in plans. At any rate, and for whatever reason, he called out, "Battalion halt—prepare to fight on foot—dismount."[12] His adjutant, Benny Hodgson, relayed the order to G Company on the extreme right.[13] It was not quite 3:30 p.m.

The troopers reined in their horses and began to dismount a half mile or so from the nearest tepees.[14] A few uncontrollable M Troop horses continued to gallop down the valley toward the hostile lines about a thousand yards distant, despite their inexperienced riders' frenzied attempts to stop. Two Privates, James Turley and George Smith, galloped straight ahead and into the dust cloud. They were never seen again. Another Private, Roman Rutten, managed to steer his steed in a wide circle right through the timber to safety, while a fourth rode straight into the Indians and somehow shot his way out.

The rest of the command dismounted smoothly enough and assumed skirmish intervals—though the nervous troopers made the standard five-yard distance between them closer to five feet in most cases.[15] After a ten-man detail from M Company had canvassed the woods for Indians, every fourth trooper[16] took his comrades' horses (each linked to the next by its "skirmish link," the snap ring on the bridle strap) and led them behind the line into the timber along the river, just below the large wooded loop. Orderlies with their own horses and those of their officers accompanied the horse holders.

Left on the thin blue line were less than a hundred troopers stretched out across 250 yards of prairie, halfway to the hills on the left. These soldiers now walked down the valley, shooting feverishly at hundreds of Indians, some of them as close as five or six hundred yards away, within range of their breechloading Springfields.[17] After they paced forward a hundred yards, the order came to stop. The soldiers promptly kneeled or lay prone on the ground, some of them using the mounds of a prairie dog town as breastworks. The officers walked behind them, cautioning them to stay cool and fire low, though most of the troopers managed neither. Beyond this cursory advice, little fire control was exercised, partly because the officers were too busy admiring their own marksmanship. Captain Thomas French, the thickset Irish immigrant's son with a high-pitched voice and excellent aim, called attention to an Indian he knocked from his horse with his Long Tom infantry rifle. After eight or ten rounds, a few of the troopers' carbines developed cartridge extraction problems, common to the Springfield (the extractor would tear into the soft copper shells), leaving the men to use knives to laboriously pry the empty shells out of the chambers.[18]

WATCHING RENO'S TROOPS from a high ridge along the edge of the bluffs were the General, Cooke, and Tom Custer. Through field glasses they could see a wide cloud of dust several miles to the southeast that indicated Benteen's battalion and the pack train not far behind it.

After Kanipe had galloped away, Custer led his five companies downstream along the edge of the bluffs at a stiff trot. The strenuous pace began to take its toll on the horses; several gave out and forced their riders to dismount and lead them back the way they had come. After traveling a half mile farther downriver, Custer called a halt.

Now Custer and Cooke doffed their hats and waved them at Reno and his command, who had dismounted and were hotly engaged with several hundred Indians down in the valley more than a mile away. The General turned in his saddle and looked at his men. "Courage, boys, we've got them!" he shouted. "We'll finish them up and then go home to our station."[19] The troopers responded with a loud cheer.

From here the full extent of the village could be seen: more than a thousand lodges in several large circles. With Lieutenant Charles DeRudio's Austrian field glasses—more powerful than the standard 5X issued to officers[20]—the General could see that there were few warriors in the village itself. Those with horses had galloped toward Reno, and others were running to the west, toward the huge pony herd. More dust and movement from the far end of the village undoubtedly signified a large group making its way north—women, children, and older men, no doubt, heading for safety.

Custer watched Reno's battalion move off the skirmish line into the timber with little or no loss. The northern edge of the woods was only several hundred yards away from the closest tepees. That threat would keep a good many of the Indians occupied. There was no time to lose.

The General turned to Boyer and through him told the Crows that they were dismissed—they had done their job.[21] Then he led his troopers east in column of twos down a narrow ravine lined with small cedars. The Crows remained behind. Curly turned south to find water for himself and his horse. White Man Runs Him, Hairy Moccasin, Goes Ahead, and Boyer moved farther downriver along the bluffs. Upon reaching two close peaks with a sugarloaf in between, they dismounted and fired a few shots into a small Sioux camp below them on the east side of the river, on the flats.[22] Across the river, hundreds of Sioux and Cheyennes were massing around the woods.

*   *   *

AFTER TAKING A FEW POTSHOTS at some of the Indians far ahead and to the left of them, Varnum, Hare, Wallace, the scouts, the doctors, and their orderlies had moved into the timber and picketed their horses soon after dismounting. Fred Gerard joined them, having reached the command just as they had dismounted, but Isaiah Dorman and the mixed-blood scout Billy Jackson, at sixteen the youngest man in the command, remained on the line. Varnum glanced up as he made his way down the line to see Custer's battalion almost straight across the Little Bighorn, moving at a trot along the bluffs back a ways from the river.[23] He assumed that they were riding downstream to attack the lower end of the village.[24]

The left end of the line was now anchored by Bobtail Bull, the leader of the Arikara scouts. The troopers continued to fire into the Indians, though most of the hostiles remained out of reach. Reno, after another nip from his flask,[25] accompanied McIntosh and G Company into the woods after a soldier reported Indians infiltrating from the river. Moylan moved his A troopers toward the woods to fill the gap.

ALMOST BLIND and barely able to walk, old Inkpaduta was no longer a warrior. But he was still a canny strategist.

He was fishing with his two young grandsons, sitting on the west bank of the Greasy Grass east of their lodges near the Hunkpapa circle at the upper end of the village, when one of them noticed the dust cloud moving down the valley toward them. Inkpaduta knew what it meant: bluecoats were coming to kill them.

The two boys helped their grandfather return to the camp as fast as they could to alert their people. Others had seen the dust—some women who had been out digging wild turnips south and east of the camp were also sounding the alarm, and a herd of Indian ponies and their herders were already moving down the valley. A group of Sans Arcs—mourners for their chief, She Bear, who had been mortally injured in the Rosebud battle—had just arrived from their previous night's bivouac a few miles back on the lodgepole trail. As they approached the village and spread the word, about fifty warriors rode out and began galloping back and forth to create a masking wall of dust as the noncombatants of the great camp retreated from the bluecoats. The Indians had known of the approximate location of the large force of soldiers to the east, but no one except Box Elder had expected them to attack so soon. The blind old Cheyenne had had a vision of *wasichus* coming and had sent a crier to tell his people to hold their horses in the village.[26]

Inkpaduta remained near the line of attack, encouraging the warriors riding forth. Gall, the boyhood friend of Sitting Bull who had grown into a barrel-chested warrior and respected leader of his own band, soon arrived from finding his horse down the valley. After assessing the situation, he told Inkpaduta to keep the soldiers on the retreat, then turned and galloped north to the village with the old chief's twin sons, the warriors Tracking White Earth and Sounds the Ground as He Walks.[27] There Gall found his two wives and three of his children dead. With a feeling beyond words, he threw down his rifle and took his hatchet in his hand. He now had only one thing on his mind: revenge.

Inkpaduta eventually made his way back to camp, then aided in shepherding the women and children to safety. Everywhere there were people running: children looking for their mothers, mothers seeking their children, young boys sprinting out to the herds to bring horses to warriors preparing for battle. Women packed small bundles to flee with, then gathered the nonwarriors in their families to move northward to the low hills beyond the Cheyenne camp, some crossing the river there.[28]

Wooden Leg, still basking in the hard-earned glories won in the Rosebud fight a week earlier, had danced until dawn and met many young women. He had woken up late and gone swimming with his older brother Yellow Hair, for the midday sun was already hot. They joined many frolicking children and other adults in the cool waters of the Greasy Grass. Afterward the two dozed under a tree on the riverbank.

The two brothers awoke to a great commotion and the distant sounds of shooting, and they joined hundreds of others running to their lodges. Everyone was shouting about the soldiers charging down the valley. The brothers ran north toward the tribe's pony herd below their camp circle, arriving just in time to find the horses being driven back to the Cheyenne camp. An exhausted Wooden Leg walked back to his lodge. His father had caught his favorite horse and now helped him get ready for battle. Wooden Leg pulled on a new pair of breeches, a good cloth shirt, and a nice pair of beaded moccasins. Then he painted his face; tied back his hair (he would have oiled and braided it also, but his father was urging him to hurry); grabbed his horse (his father strapped a blanket onto its back and fixed its lariat bridle), six-shooter, and bullets; and galloped upriver through the camp after all the other young men.[29]

Beyond the large Hunkpapa circle and the adjacent, smaller Blackfeet one were hundreds of Indians on horseback, racing back and forth, raising a thick dust cloud before a long line of dismounted soldiers a thousand yards distant. Some warriors were making bravery runs, galloping closer to the soldier line, concealing their bodies on the far side of their mounts and firing their weapons under their horses' necks.

The Cheyennes learned of the attack minutes after it was launched, thanks to the warnings of the camp criers. Lame White Man had just begun a bath in a friend's sweat lodge down by the river after following the "suicide boys" parading through the village. He was proud of the five young Cheyennes who had vowed to die fighting. "I must go up there and ride down in the parade with my boys," he had told his wife.[30] Now he and the other men crawled out of the sweat lodge and ran to their lodges and families. Some of the horses had been brought in that morning to be staked out near the camp in case of emergency, and Lame White Man helped get his family started north to safety. Once they were on the way, he decided there was no time to don his war clothes or prepare properly. He wrapped a blanket around his waist, threw on his moccasins, grabbed his ammunition belt and gun, jumped on his horse, and rushed to the wide ford across from the village.[31]

By now the Hunkpapa camp was filled with a chaotic mix of women and children screaming, men yelling for their horses and arms, and the roar of guns. Old men sang death songs to encourage the warriors and helped them prepare for battle. Women trilled the tremolo to inspire their men. Dust was everywhere. The gunfire coming from the soldiers in the timber was high, though some bullets shattered the lodgepoles. Several horses fell. Hundreds of warriors—many of them until now asleep after a long night of dancing, others eating a late breakfast—grabbed their arms, poured from their tepees, and began frantically searching for their horses. The fortunate ones had tethered their mounts nearby for just such an emergency. Women and young boys helped others catch theirs. In ragged clusters, the mounted men rode south through the lodges to defend their village and their families.

Sitting Bull was lying in his lodge on the southwest side of his tribal circle[32] when word of the attacking soldiers arrived. His nephew One Bull had just returned from the herd with horses, and he and Sitting Bull quickly took the family and other villagers into the low hills beyond the Cheyenne circle, then returned to the Hunkpapa camp. Sitting Bull helped his nephew prepare for battle, giving him a stone-headed war club and his own rawhide shield; then he buckled on his cartridge belt and went outside. He mounted a black horse and rode off to encourage those gathering to counterattack. While One Bull and other warriors charged the far end of the soldier line, Sitting Bull, White Bull (another nephew), and other Lakotas moved forward to a shallow draw that ran across the valley just south of the camp. From there they traded furious fire with the bluecoats, who had dismounted and planted three guidons out on the prairie.

Amid the mayhem, some Arikaras on the far end of the soldier line moved closer to the camp. Their gunfire killed several women and children in the Hunkpapa lodges before mounted warriors moved to repulse them. The Arikaras pulled back and galloped toward the woods.

The dead women and children were not the only losses. Four Lakotas galloped close to the soldiers, and only one came back.[33] But as more warriors joined the first defenders, the Lakota line was extended to the west and then around the flank of the bluecoats, who fled into the timber behind an old riverbank and formed a new, shorter line facing west at its edge.

Then word spread quickly: "Crazy Horse is coming! Crazy Horse is coming!"

*   *   *

WITH NO CASUALTIES bar those from the runaway horses at the beginning of the battle, the troopers were still in good spirits, talking and laughing and confident of victory.[34] But after some fifteen minutes on the line, the number of Indians increased significantly — four or five hundred of them, maybe more. Some began to ride around the line's left flank; Captain Myles Moylan counted at least two hundred.[35] Realizing that Custer was nowhere in sight, Wallace asked Moylan if they could send a messenger to the General. Moylan asked Billy Jackson if he could go back. Jackson looked around, then waved his hand to the left and rear and told them there were too many Indians to get through.[36] Moylan sent for Reno and told him of the Indians reaching their rear.

The Major commanded the line to swivel right and draw back to the timber, yelling, "Retreat to your horses, men!" without arranging a rearguard action. As he passed into the trees, he took a big swig of whiskey that emptied his flask.[37] Some of the troopers started rushing toward the trees. Captain French quickly ordered, "Steady there, men! I will shoot the first man that turns his back on the enemy — fall back slowly. Keep up a continual fire, you damned fools!"[38] The men retreated to the timber slowly and steadily. One man did not obey: Miles O'Hara of M Company, a young Ohio lad, had just earned his Sergeant's stripes a few days before, replacing a man whose term of service had expired and who had been left back at the Powder River depot. Slumped motionless on the ground, he had taken a round through the breast and was likely already dead. His head would be found in the village two days later.[39]

The timber in the old river bottom was on ground lower, by ten feet or so, than the prairie. The line of troopers retreated to the dry riverbed's near embankment, on the fringe of the woods, their backs to the river, and continued to fire into the hundreds of Indians galloping closer. The air was thick with dust and black powder gunsmoke, the constant fire of hundreds of rifles, the high-pitched yells of warriors, the shrieks of eagle-bone whistles, the screams of injured and panicked horses, the shouts of soldiers excited or scared or injured. "It was one long continuous roar," remembered one trooper.[40]

The scouts — with Varnum, Herendeen, and Reynolds — moved to the extreme right of the new line, now only 150 yards long. Varnum heard someone mention that G Company was going to charge a part of the village down through the woods and decided to go with them. Back near the river, among the large cottonwoods and dense underbrush, lay an open glade where most of the horses had been led. Beyond the clearing, Varnum could see the stream, and on the other side was part of Sitting Bull's village.[41] Several narrow animal paths wound through the trees, and Varnum followed one into the glade to find Reno and Lieutenant Donald McIntosh directing the men of G Troop against the infiltrating Indians.

"How are things on the line?" asked Reno.

"I don't know," said Varnum.

"Find out and let me know," ordered the Major.[42]

Varnum dismounted, tied his horse, and returned to the line to find Moylan complaining that his men were nearly out of ammunition — the fifty rounds that each man had carried on him were almost gone.[43] Though exhausted and operating only on nervous energy, Varnum volunteered to bring the horses up. He made his way back to the opening and retrieved A Company's mounts, bringing them and a good deal of the rest of the men back to the line. Moylan's men fell back in alternate fashion to get ammunition from their saddlebags.[44]

CRAZY HORSE was not to be rushed. The Oglala war chief had been bathing when the first shots had been heard upriver. He had taken time to apply his paint and prepare himself properly for battle.[45] Other warriors waited impatiently for him. Finally, he emerged, leaped onto his pinto pony,[46] and led a horde of mounted Oglalas up the valley. Other men, even a few Cheyennes, joined him. There were many great fighters in the camp, but no one's medicine was as strong as Crazy Horse's. Within minutes, hundreds of warriors, perhaps a thousand, surrounded the wooded loop sheltering the bluecoats. Those without horses moved up the river and across it to fire into the trees from the east and north.

AS REYNOLDS AND GERARD entered the timber, a despondent Reynolds told Gerard that he had never felt so depressed and discouraged in his life. (The night before, the scout had distributed his belongings among his friends.) He needed something to stimulate him—the nasty abscess on his left hand was causing him great pain. Did Gerard have anything with him? Gerard pulled out a flask and passed it to Reynolds, cautioning him not to drink too much. Then they took positions on the edge of the old riverbank and fired on the Indians for twenty minutes or so.

Now, as Varnum dropped down next to him, Gerard pulled out his flask again and said, "Well, I've got a little whiskey left. We'll take one last drink together."[47] Charley Reynolds took a swig and passed it to Varnum, who partook himself.[48]

The men in the woods began to yell something about charging, and in response Varnum and most of the others jumped up and ran in search of their horses.

"What damn fool move is this?" Gerard asked Reynolds, next to him.

"I don't know," the scout replied. "We will have to go. We'll have to get out of this." Reynolds jumped up and went for his horse.[49] Gerard moved off the edge of the hill with him.

Meanwhile, Reno continued to direct the fire of G Troop toward the Indians infiltrating the river side of the woods. They were everywhere, with more of them arriving every minute. Arrows whistled past and smashed into trees; bullets zipped by, raining twigs and branches down onto the men. Gray clouds of gunsmoke hung in the air, and the noise from hundreds of rifles was deafening. Reno had seen Custer atop the bluffs across the river and upstream a ways waving his hat—his battalion was stirring up quite a cloud of dust[50]—and that meant he must have chosen a flank attack in support. But where was he now? All the Major could see were high, sheer cliffs across the river—surely a crossing was not possible anywhere nearby.[51] And where was Benteen? No sign of either column, not even a messenger with some kind of news or fresh orders.

Then someone told Reno that several of the horses had been shot in the rear of their position in the woods. To the Major, the situation now seemed close to untenable. The ammunition was about half-gone. Unless they got out now, there would be no getting out at all. It was time to find a more defensible position, one closer to the rest of the regiment and away from the large village that could be glimpsed through the trees. The command was virtually surrounded by hostile Indians, and a movement in any direction would likely incur casualties, probably deaths. But some, perhaps most, of the men would survive—if they left now.

Reno ordered Moylan and McIntosh to mount and form in column of fours, then sent Hodgson to tell French, closer to the edge of the woods with M Troop. But neither Reno nor Hodgson relayed that order to a trumpeter—chiefly because G Company, still scattered throughout the woods, didn't have one that day and Reno had not assigned a trumpeter to attend him. (Of G Company's two trumpeters, one had been detailed as an orderly to General Custer, and the other was on detached service.) As the order descended from the Major down the ranks to the lowest Private, it was lost. Only those men within earshot or fortunate enough to hear the order passed knew of Reno's command.[52] Quite a few troopers, mostly from G Company, did not.[53]

Near pandemonium reigned as dismounted troopers yelled the names of their number four men with their horses and Indian bullets continued to zip among them, accompanied by high-pitched war cries. Varnum attempted to stay the developing stampede, yelling, "For God's sake, men, let's don't leave the line. There are enough of us here to whip the whole Sioux nation." That brought a few men back, but not for long.[54] Reno asked Moylan his opinion as to where they should go, then pointed out a high point on the bluffs across the river, right where he had last seen Custer. They would go there to regroup, thought Reno, await further developments, and with any luck rejoin the regiment.[55]

Varnum entered the glade and yelled to Reno, asking where the company was going. Reno did not answer; he was trying to communicate with Bloody Knife, a few feet from him, asking him through sign language where the Indians would go once the command left the trees. Some of the mounted men—mostly those G troopers who had heard the order—replied for Bloody Knife: "They're going to charge!"

Over among the soldiers on the left of the line, Sergeant John Ryan told his troop commander, French, "The best thing that we can do is to cut right through them."[56] French yelled, "To your horses, men!"

One trooper without a mount grabbed Private William Morris's and relinquished it only after the young redheaded recruit leveled his carbine at the man's head and said, "Let go, or I will blow your head off!"[57] A good many troopers mounted and began to ride in random directions until Ryan got them in some kind of order.[58]

Due to the sudden exodus from the line, the firing had greatly slackened. This emboldened the Indians, who now surged closer. A moment later, a volley erupted from a group of Indians who had reached some bushes in the rear, not more than thirty feet from the soldiers.[59] One round hit Bloody Knife in the back of the head, and as he threw his hands up and fell over, his blood and brains spattered Reno's face and front. The Arikara had been wearing the kerchief given to him by his friend Custer. A soldier hit with the same volley screamed, "Oh my God, I've got it," then slumped forward and slid off his horse.[60] Reno, startled, wiped bits of bone and blood off his face and gave the order to dismount—thick woods and underbrush were no place for mounted men to fight Indians on foot and at close range. But the hostiles appeared to have retreated after the single volley, so he quickly ordered his men to mount again, once more without bugle calls.[61] The rapid-fire orders may have made sense to Reno, but they didn't to his troopers, and further confusion set in as some obeyed and some did not.

Private Morris had just mounted his horse when French's striker, a German immigrant named Henry Klotzbucher, was shot through the stomach. Klotzbucher yelled and toppled to the ground. French told Morris to dismount and take care of him. Morris and another trooper began to lift Klotzbucher onto Morris's horse, but the pain was too much. "Leave me alone, for God's sake!" the wounded man shrieked, refusing to stand. Morris and the trooper dragged Klotzbucher back into some thick underbrush and braced him against a tree.[62]

Many of the men were still on foot when Reno yelled, "Any of you men who wish to make your escape, draw your revolvers and follow me." Reno spurred his horse out of the woods, down the dry riverbed a short way, and up onto the prairie.[63] He made no arrangements for any rearguard action to cover the retreat—standard military procedure and more than warranted in this situation—and he paid little heed to the state of his command before galloping off. His wounded, and those men who had not heard the order to mount and charge, would have to fend for themselves.

Reno's panic spread through most of the command. Someone hollered, "Every man for himself,"[64] and desperate troopers jumped on any horse they could find, leaving others without mounts. Through thick underbrush and then suffocating clouds of dust, those men who had found horses followed the Major, climbing up the embankment and onto the prairie in a semblance of column of fours. A Troop was right behind them. Captain French made sure the men of M Troop got out of the timber, then followed them.[65] Some of G Troop followed in ragged fashion.

Morris still remained with the wounded Klotzbucher. It seemed every other soldier had left, and it was all he could do to keep his horse from running after them.

Klotzbucher said, "Go on, don't mind me, you can't do me any good."

"Captain told me to take care of you," said Morris, holding his horse's reins.

"Go on, you cannot do me any good."

"All right," said the young recruit. "If you say so, I'll go." He left Klotzbucher a canteen of water, then attempted to mount. Unable to get near his frenzied horse's stirrup, he hurled himself up and grabbed the pommel of his saddle. The horse took off, Morris on his stomach across the saddle, holding on for dear life as he galloped up the embankment and after the command.[66]

"THE SIGHT that greeted my eyes was certainly very discouraging," wrote one recruit years later of the exodus from the woods. "Not over two hundred yards away was a large and constantly increasing number of Indian warriors coming toward us as fast as their ponies could travel, a whooping, howling mass of the best horsemen, the most cruel and fiercest fighters in all our country, or any other."[67] The hundreds of hostiles fell back at first in the face of this unexpected movement in their direction. They parted as Reno led the fleeing men in a file of ones and twos up the prairie. But as they realized that the soldiers were not riding toward them but past them, the warriors turned and whipped their horses after the bluecoats, along their flanks. As the soldiers spurred their tired mounts by, those Indians with rifles started shooting, their Winchesters lying across their saddles pumping bullets, into the men. Some of the bolder Indians galloped into the soldiers' ranks, though most stayed a safe distance—at least fifty yards—away from the six-shooters.[68] Once a trooper stopped firing his revolver, the Indians rode closer to shoot him or knock him off his horse with stone clubs. Some Indians on the east side of the stream also fired into the long line of soldiers.

Death came swiftly and frequently. One rider's horse broke from the ranks and galloped directly into the Indians; the soldier did not return.[69] A Corporal from G Troop had his horse shot out from under him and was soon surrounded by the enemy. Private Roman Rutten galloped toward him, yelling, but the dismounted trooper never emerged.[70] An Indian put an arrow into the back of a soldier's head, but somehow the corpse remained mounted, the dead man galloping across the prairie. Only after another arrow went into his shoulder did he tumble to the ground.[71]

Some of the ground the battalion rode over was the site of a prairie dog village, and the holes and mounds presented a nasty obstacle course for horse and rider. More than one horse stepped into a hole and threw its rider, mount and man careening over the prairie.[72] Doughty George Herendeen, one of the last to leave, had just cleared the woods when his horse fell, throwing him off, and ran away. The scout turned and made for the timber, barely avoiding about twenty Indians bearing down on the troopers. Herendeen had been in several large fights with the Sioux and knew of their reluctance to charge into woods.

On the way, he saw Charley Reynolds mounting his horse. Herendeen yelled, "Charley, don't try to ride out. We can't get away from this timber."[73] But Reynolds ignored him and galloped away until his horse was shot and he went down. He knelt on the ground behind his horse and fired as many shots as he could before a Sioux round killed him.[74]

Upon reaching the woods, Herendeen ran into Lieutenant Charles DeRudio and about a dozen other soldiers, some with horses, some

George Armstrong Custer, "the Boy General of the Golden Lock."

Libbie Bacon Custer: intelligent, beautiful, and besotted with the Boy General.

President Ulysses S. Grant, whose wrath Custer incurred when he testified before a House committee about corruption in the Grant administration.

Commanding General of the Army William T. Sherman.

Gen. Philip Sheridan, Custer's mentor.

Maj. Marcus Reno, Custer's second-in-command on the expedition.

Capt. Frederick Benteen chafed at
serving under Custer, whom he despised.

Gen. Alfred Terry, commander of the
expedition, would have preferred remaining
in his comfortable office in St. Paul.

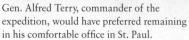

The sole newspaperman with the expedition,
Mark Kellogg: "I go with Custer and will be at the
death." *(Courtesy Sandy Barnard)*

The four Crow scouts who rode with Custer's battalion (left to right): White Man Runs Him, Hairy Moccasin, Curly, Goes Ahead.

Capt. Tom Custer, wearing his two Medals of Honor.

Mitch Boyer, the halfbreed scout mentored by Jim Bridger, knew the Powder River country like the back of his hand.

Boston, the youngest Custer brother, hired as a scout for no apparent reason.

Just turned eighteen, Harry Armstrong "Autie" Reed rode with his three uncles to see the last big Indian battle.

Frederic Gerard, Arikara interpreter, knew Sitting Bull only too well.

Unflappable scout George Herendeen had fought the Sioux two years before.

Custer's favorite Indian scout, the Arikara Bloody Knife, had a personal score to settle with the Lakota Sioux.

"Lonesome" Charley Reynolds, the soft-spoken scout and legendary hunter—and scion of a well-to-do family in the East.

Pvt. John Burkman, Custer's striker, with the general's two favorite mounts, Dandy and Vic (for Victory).

Lt. George Wallace, the regiment's engineering officer. Custer's last-minute decision saved his life.

Lt. Charles Varnum was in charge of Custer's Indian scouts, who called him "Peaked Face."

Lt. Luther Hare, the self-proclaimed "fighting son of a bitch from Texas."

Dr. Henry Porter, the only one of the three surgeons to survive, performed heroically on the hill.

Lt. Edward Godfrey: his skillfully directed rearguard retreat of Company K probably saved the rest of the regiment.

Lt. Donald McIntosh, the halfbreed officer who commanded Company C.

Capt. Thomas Weir, a part of the "Custer clan" despite a rumored romance with Libbie.

The "Adonis of the Seventh," Lt. James Calhoun married Custer's younger sister, Margaret.

Capt. George Yates commanded Company F, known as the Band Box Troop for its sharp appearance.

Lt. Algernon Smith commanded Company E, the Gray Horse Troop.

Lt. William Cooke, Custer's adjutant and close friend; the tall Canadian known for his elegant dundreary whiskers was the regiment's fastest runner.

Capt. Myles Keogh, Irish soldier of fortune and commander of Company I.

Lt. James Sturgis, son of the regiment's actual commander, Col. Samuel Sturgis, who was on detached service.

Pvt. John Martin, the trumpeter who was sent to the rear with Custer's last message.

Sitting Bull, spiritual leader of the Plains Indians, had been a renowned warrior in his prime.

Gall, the powerfully built Hunkpapa warrior who lost two wives and three children in the battle.

Spotted Eagle, Sans Arc war chief.

Low Dog, Oglala war chief.

Crow King, Hunkpapa war chief.

Wooden Leg, noted Northern Cheyenne warrior.

White Bull, nephew to Sitting Bull and a great warrior in his own right.

Hunkpapa warrior Rain in the Face.

The three members of the Reno Court of Inquiry. Above Left: Col. John King, presiding officer. *(Courtesy U.S. American Military History Institute)* Above Middle: Col. Wesley Merritt, friend and rival of Custer's. *(Courtesy U.S. American Military History Institute)* Above Right: Lt. Col. William Royall. *(Courtesy U.S. American Military History Institute)*

Lt. Jesse Lee, Recorder of the Reno Court of Inquiry. *(Courtesy U.S. American Military History Institute)*

Capt. Frederick Benteen with Lyman Gilbert, Reno's counsel. *(Courtesy U.S. American Military History Institute)*

A newspaper cut, from a photograph, of deliberations of the Reno Court of Inquiry. The three members of the Court — Merritt, King, and Royall — sit at left. The stenographer, H. H. Hollister, sits at the center table. Recorder Lee questions Lt. DeRudio at right, and Frederick Whittaker takes notes in the right foreground. Reno sits facing left at the window at right center.

Officers of the Seventh Cavalry, including four survivors of the Little Bighorn battle, a few days after the Wounded Knee massacre. Seated in front (left to right): Capt. Winfield Edgerly, Capt. Charles Ilsley, Capt. Henry Jackson, Capt. Charles Varnum, Col. James Forsyth, Maj. Samuel Whitside, Capt. Myles Moylan, Capt. Edward Godfrey, unidentified.

on foot. They had not heard the order to mount. (DeRudio had stopped to pick up the company guidon, which had been thrown away by a panicked Sergeant.)[75] Herendeen told them to stay in the woods and conceal themselves.

Dorman, the black interpreter, was surrounded by Indians a short distance from the timber. He turned in his saddle and shot one through the heart, but his horse, riddled with bullets, went down.[76] The big man dropped to one knee and began firing into the Indians with his sporting rifle. When his friend Rutten galloped by, Dorman yelled good-bye to him. Soon Dorman was surrounded by hostiles while the command passed him by. A bullet found him. Mortally wounded but still alive, he sat on the ground, his life flowing from him.[77]

MORE THAN ANYTHING, the Indians all agreed later, the battle resembled a buffalo chase.

The warriors pursued the column to the Greasy Grass and into the fast current. Sioux on the eastern bluffs just downstream took aim on soldiers in the water and on the banks. Sitting Bull followed his warriors, shouting encouragement and advice. Women and young boys who had not retreated to the hills ran among the downed soldiers, finishing off those still alive, mutilating the dead as was their tradition, and plundering their bodies.

Just a hundred yards southeast of the timber, along the trail of dead, Sitting Bull rode up to where several Lakotas were gathered around the wounded black man sitting in the dirt. He was known to them as Teat, married to a Hunkpapa woman named Visible. He was clearly close to death, a gunshot wound to his breast.

"My friends," Teat said, "you have already killed me, don't count coup on me."

"Don't kill that man, he is a friend of mine," said Sitting Bull, remembering the day years before when the black man had given him some food.[78] Sitting Bull dismounted and gave the dying man some water, then rode off toward the river.[79]

A Hunkpapa woman named Eagle Robe, mourning for her ten-year-old brother just killed by the *wasichus*, rode up and jumped to the ground.

"Do not kill me, because I will be dead in a short while anyway," said Teat.

"If you did not want to be killed," said the woman, "why did you not stay home where you belong and not come to attack us?" Her brother's name was One Hawk. He had gone to the east with another man very early that morning looking for a horse that had strayed from the family herd. They had discovered the soldiers and then made for the camp as quickly as they could. They had just reached the Greasy Grass when some Arikara scouts ahead of the soldiers had killed him. The other man had escaped to warn the camp.

Eagle Robe raised a revolver and shot Teat in the head.

After killing him, Eagle Robe continued to the river, where she killed two more wounded soldiers. She shot one with her revolver and dispatched the other with her sheath knife. Behind her, other women began to mutilate Teat. They drove a picket pin through his testicles into the ground, slashed his body, and cut off his penis and stuffed it into his mouth.[80]

ABOUT TWENTY YARDS from the river, Rutten saw the buckskinned McIntosh having some difficulty. He had become separated from his orderly, who held his horse, Puff, and had appropriated one of his troopers'—to his great dismay, since the animal refused his lead. The Indians were soon upon "Tosh" in force, twenty or thirty of them circling the half-breed lieutenant. They pulled him from his mount and shot him repeatedly until he fell dead.[81] Rutten frantically galloped right through them and followed the command toward the water.

Three troopers became separated from the command and galloped upriver toward the original crossing. One soldier turned east and escaped into the timber along the river, while the other two continued southward. One turned right and made for the hills to the west, where he climbed a draw before he was overtaken and killed. The other reached the timber near the first ford, dismounted, and made a stand, wielding his six-shooter. The Indians surrounded and killed him.[82] He was joined in death by fifteen of Reno's men. The Major and his troops had been forced past one large loop of the river and around another. At one point, about twenty troopers broke off from the column and headed straight into the second loop, splashing through the water twice. The Indians pursued them. Only five soldiers survived to rejoin their comrades.[83]

The stream was forty feet wide and four feet deep at the point Reno reached, and the near bank was high, five or six feet above the water. The far bank was even higher—eight feet at least—and jutted sharply into the river. The only easy egress was a narrow buffalo ford that angled into the fast-rushing water and that quickly became clogged with frantic men and mounts trying to climb out. As the column reached the riverbank, the horses jumped in and surged across. Several men lost their seats in the process and had to swim across. Indians gathered on the bank and the bluffs above and shot down into the roiling mass of soldiers and horses. Streams of blood soon streaked the water. Some warriors jumped into the strong current to pull men from their mounts. One used a captured Springfield to club two troopers off their horses.[84]

Most of the Crow and Arikara scouts at the tail end of the column veered left to ford the river below the soldiers. Bobtail Bull made it to the east side and climbed up to the flat. There a Cheyenne warrior charged toward the Arikara leader, and the two fired their rifles at the same moment. Both pitched off their mounts, dead.[85] Another Arikara, Little Brave, took a gunshot to the right shoulder but managed to cross the river downstream, take cover behind a low knoll, and begin firing at the enemy warriors. He killed one before several Cheyennes circled around and rushed him from the rear, beating and stabbing him to death.[86]

Just as Hodgson—"the Jack of Clubs," as the enlisted men called the jaunty young officer[87]—plunged into the stream, a shot felled his horse. Hodgson dismounted and tried to stand, the water around him red with blood. He reached for a nearby trooper's stirrup but couldn't catch it, then lunged for Private Morris's, begging, "For God's sake, don't leave me here—I am shot through both legs." As Hodgson seized Morris's stirrup with both hands, Morris grabbed the lieutenant by the collar. Ahead of him two troopers were trying to climb through the narrow cut; Morris yelled at them to hurry. One made it out of the water, only to be killed.

The next made it up safely. Morris's horse lunged more than half-way up the bank before Hodgson was shot fatally in the head and slipped free.[88]

Varnum had been one of the last to leave the woods. He, too, was surprised to see the column veering left away from the enemy. His Kentucky thoroughbred quickly carried him the half mile to the river. By then he was near the head of the retreating column. Just before reaching the stream, he stopped and tried to control the frenzied abandonment, yelling, "Hold on, men, what's the use of this? We've got to get into shape to fight it out. You can't run away from Injuns."

On his right, a voice interrupted. "I'm in command here, sir," Reno announced.[89]

Reno may have been in command, but he had not been in control for some time. He halted on the near bank only a moment before jumping his horse into the cold water and crossing, again neglecting to order any covering fire for those men bringing up the rear. The Major scaled the far bank and crossed a scrub-covered flat area of a hundred yards or so. Then he scrambled up a ravine that led up along a series of steep bluffs, which ran back a quarter mile from the river and two hundred feet above it. The remnants of his battalion followed him, and the narrow exit from the stream was widened when enough horses' hooves caved in the earth on either side. Under continuous fire, few troopers stopped after reaching the east bank. Instead, they goaded their weary mounts over to the bluffs and began the steep climb up one of the ravines.

Some men dismounted to lead their panting horses to the summit, while others grabbed the tails of their mounts as they struggled up the steep incline. Most who remained seated held on to their horses' necks for dear life. At least one exhausted horse refused to budge another inch even after its owner jabbed the trembling animal with his gun and delivered a final, furious kick before grabbing his carbine and attacking the bluff on foot.[90]

Varnum and his orderly began climbing a ravine a few ridges downstream but stopped when they heard men yelling at them and pointing to Indians lying in wait near its crest. They descended and found another draw that led to the top. Not far ahead of them were

Reno and Moylan. On the way up, the orderly was hit, and Varnum dismounted to kneel beside him. He heard the men yelling again and turned to see Dr. DeWolf and his orderly taking the route he had tried first. The Indians above were training their rifles on them. As a teen-age Corporal at Second Bull Run, James DeWolf had been wounded badly enough to be discharged with a pension. He had resigned his pension to reenlist as an artilleryman and had fought out the war. The next day, June 26, would have marked a year since his gradu-ation from Harvard Medical School.[91] Below on the flats, Wallace and Reno's orderly, Private Edward Davern, fired on the hostiles,[92] but before DeWolf reached the summit, he was shot dead.

About two-thirds of the way up a ravine, Private Morris stopped to catch his breath and looked back down the valley. Bodies of sol-diers and horses marked a bloody path from the timber to the water below. Dead troopers floated down the river. Smoke reached toward the sky where the Indians had set the prairie on fire in an attempt to flush the soldiers from the woods.

Morris said to another Private a few feet away, "That was pretty hot down there."

"You'll get used to it, shavetail," said the trooper, an Englishman named Gordon who had a few years' service on Morris. A moment later, there was a volley of gunfire from a group of Indians on the bluffs to the right, and Gordon fell dead with a bullet through his neck. Another man near him, named Bill Meyer, was killed by a shot through his eye. Morris received a round in his breast but managed to grab his horse's stirrup and reached the top, bleeding profusely.[93]

The majority of what was left of the sodden, exhausted battal-ion finally reached the summit a few minutes after four o'clock. Var-num, still making his way up, yelled, "For God's sake, men, don't run, we have got to go back and get our wounded men and officers!" When Luther Hare scaled the hill, he echoed the Lieutenant, hol-lering, "If we've got to die, let's die like men. I'm a fighting son of a bitch from Texas." To Moylan's troop, which was following its Cap-tain away from the river, he added, "Don't run off like a pack of whipped curs!"[94]

Their appeals roused Reno enough to tell Moylan to dismount

his men. The Captain managed to convince enough of his demoralized troopers to throw out a skirmish line just below the edge of the hill, though the Indians below and on the nearby bluffs had begun to withdraw even before the deployed men began to fire at them.

That action and the remonstrances of Varnum and Hare stopped most of the men from running any farther, especially since the Indians were not pursuing them up onto the bluffs. Many of the men flopped to the ground to rest. Some descended the hill to the river to fill their canteens. One trooper, Private John Wallace, reached the crest clutching a Sioux scalp, taken from a dead Indian he had come across on the side of the hill. Meanwhile, Captain French found his guidon-bearer, eighteen-year-old Private Frank Sniffin. "You damned fool, where are your colors?" he snarled. The other two companies in the valley fight had lost theirs. Sniffin reached under his shirt and pulled them out—he had torn the guidon from the staff and stuffed it close to his chest during the frenzied retreat. The Captain affixed the colors to a carbine and stuck it into the ground.[95]

When Dr. Porter reached the summit, he saw Reno walking around excitedly with a red bandanna wrapped around his head. Porter said to him, "Major, the men were pretty well demoralized, weren't they?"

"That was a charge, sir!" was the Major's strange reply.[96]

About half of Reno's shattered column had made it to the bluffs unscathed. Twenty-nine enlisted men and three officers lay dead in the valley below, where at that moment, all along Reno's route to the river, Indians in plain view were ransacking their bodies for clothing, ammunition, and other possessions, scalps included.[97] Nearly twenty others were missing, quite possibly still in the timber, maybe dead. Seven wounded men[98] would eventually make it to the temporary hospital area Dr. Porter was establishing. None of the white scouts and only a few of the Indian scouts were on the hill. Ammunition was low, and so was morale. No other soldiers were in sight, and Reno and his men had just been chased up the bluffs by a thousand Indians, some of whom had repeating rifles and had put them to good use.

But for some reason, the enemy had quit the battle. Most of the Indian horsemen were now galloping north down the river, some pointing, others yelling at their comrades.

Finally, there was a ray of hope for the beleaguered cavalrymen. Ten minutes or so after regrouping, they saw a column of bluecoated horsemen approaching from the south along the bluffs, a sight that raised a hoarse cheer from most of the men.

AS THE BLUECOATS dragged themselves across the flats and up the steep bluffs beyond, Lakotas a few hundred yards downstream yelled over to the warriors near the water, and some waved blankets: other soldiers to the north were riding toward the village, down a large coulee that widened as it approached the river, and they were after the women and children. Within minutes, hundreds of warriors, all save a few, turned and galloped downstream—some arcing around the bend, some splashing through the woods and water, and some crossing the river and climbing to the ridgetop on the east side of the Little Bighorn.

"They seemed to fill the whole hill," remembered a Two Kettle chief named Runs the Enemy, speaking of the soldiers. "It looked as if there were thousands of them, and I thought we would surely be beaten. As I returned I saw hundreds of Sioux. I looked into their eyes and they looked different—they were filled with fear."[99] After Sand Creek and the Washita, as well as other smaller battles with the bluecoats, every warrior knew what could happen if their families fell into the hands of the *wasichus:* death, injury, imprisonment, or dishonor. It was time to see whose medicine was stronger.

THIRTEEN

"The Savior of the Seventh"

Come on. Big village. Be quick.

GEORGE ARMSTRONG CUSTER

Custer halted his battalion where the narrow ravine turned north and dumped into a larger one that appeared to head toward the river. The troopers dismounted and adjusted their saddles and girths—both men and animals were sweating in the torrid heat. The General turned to his adjutant, Cooke, and instructed him to write a message to Benteen. He needed the Captain's men and the pack train with its ammunition.

"Orderly," Cooke said as he ripped the page out of a small notebook and handed it to John Martin, "I want you to take this dispatch to Captain Benteen and go as fast as you can. Take the same trail we came down. If you have time, and there is no danger, come back, but if there is any danger or Indians in the way stay with your company."

Martin's horse was tired, but he turned and rode back up the ravine. When he looked back, Custer and his command were headed down toward the river. They were galloping.[1]

He reached the high ground a few minutes later. To his left, some Indians fired at him, but he spurred his horse faster, and they did not pursue.

Then he saw Boston Custer riding hard toward him. They both stopped.

"Where's the General?" asked Boston.

"Right behind the next ridge you'll find him," said Martin, gesturing.

Boston pointed out to Martin that his horse was limping. Then, anxious not to miss the action, he dashed down the ravine after his brothers.[2]

Boyer had watched Reno's panicked retreat from the ridge where Custer had left him and the Crow scouts. Figuring that the General would want to know of this turn of events, Boyer told the three Crows to leave, then rode past the grassy peaks and down into the wide coulee below to find Custer. He reached him at about four o'clock. The news called for a change in strategy.

Eight years earlier on the Washita, taking fifty-three captives had helped Custer keep a thousand warriors at bay and had enabled the Seventh Cavalry to retreat safely. That might work here, but Reno's predicament presented a dilemma. They needed to move farther north to cut off the families and corral them, but the Major's beleaguered battalion needed immediate help. After the Washita, Custer had been criticized by some for not making a stronger effort to find and rescue Major Elliott's contingent. That could not happen again.

Boston Custer galloped up soon after, bearing good news. He had passed Benteen's battalion on the lodgepole trail less than an hour before, and the pack train had been only about a mile behind. The courier Martin was making good time on the back trail and would likely deliver the message safely.

Custer needed a lookout point to reassess the situation. He took his command across the wide ravine and onto the ridge on its north side and called a halt.[3] From the elevation, he could see a good deal of the village — which he now realized was even more extensive than he had first thought — and, four miles or so to the south, a dust cloud that must be Benteen's battalion. That meant it was a good bet that Benteen would be up in a half hour at the most, if he accelerated his pace as ordered.

Last Stand Hill

Deep Coulee

South Branch

North Branch

YATES

ford

CUSTER

Medicine Tail Coulee

Cedar Coulee

Weir Point

RENO

Reno Hill

SIOUX

Little Bighorn River

BENTEEN

Reno Creek

0 Miles   1   2

0 Kilometers   2

© 2008 Jeffrey L. Ward

The situation called for a gamble, and Custer had always been a gambling man, whether it was a horse race, a poker game, or a battle. He instructed his old friend George Yates to take his two companies—Keogh's seniority dictated that he lead the larger wing, of three troops—and ride swiftly over the hills down to the river a mile away. There, with a big show, he would feign a crossing into the village and secure the ford until Benteen arrived and Custer, with six companies, joined Yates to storm into the camp. The demonstration would draw a good portion of the hostiles from Reno. Meanwhile, the General and Keogh's troops would wait for Benteen and join him in riding toward the ford and the village. If Benteen did not arrive soon, they would ride north along the high ground, keeping an eye out for him and a clear path for his 125 men. A volley of rifle fire would signal Yates to leave the ford and move north across the hills to rendezvous with Keogh's right wing on the high ground about a mile and a half northeast, where a long ridge a half mile back from the river ran northwest. The closer end of that ridge would be their rendezvous point.[4]

Victory could still be seized if Custer stayed on the offensive, but not with a retreat. Fortune favored the bold—everyone knew that—and boldly was the only way Custer knew how to fight. Splitting his battalion once again was risky, but there seemed to be no other way to assist Reno while the rest of the command united and rode into the camp to secure noncombatant hostages.

Captain Algernon Smith and young Jack Sturgis led E Company over the hills along the coulee toward the river. Yates and his only Lieutenant, the green but game Willie Reily, followed with F Company. Custer watched the seventy-six troopers leave.[5]

IN LATER YEARS, Fred Benteen would claim that Custer's orders to him were vague and "senseless"[6]—"valley hunting *ad infinitum.*"[7] But on this day, dissent was not an option. He may have despised the former Boy General, even hated him—he derisively referred to Custer's recently published book as "My Lie [rather than "Life"] on the Plains"—and he disagreed with him about the strategy he had decided on. But Benteen was a good soldier, so he followed Custer's orders—up to a point.

The scouts all swore there was a very large Indian camp up ahead, with more hostiles than Custer had ever seen, and Benteen tended to believe them. The cherub-faced Captain had been ordered by Custer to take his three-company battalion and ride toward the southwest "to see if the Indians were trying to escape up the valley of the Little Big Horn, after which we were to hurry and rejoin the command as soon as possible," Benteen's subaltern, Lieutenant Frank Gibson, remembered soon after the battle.[8] Every cavalry attack on an Indian camp produced some attempt to flee to safety, and if these Indians tried to escape, the south had to be blocked—to the west lay the country of the Crows, blood enemies of the Sioux, and to the north was Terry's battalion.

Benteen led his men out toward the bluffs at a brisk walk. His bay mount, Dick, was a fast walker, and some of the horses had to trot to keep up. Per Custer's instructions, he ordered Gibson to ride ahead with the Captain's French field glasses and six additional troopers. The small detachment would scale the bluffs when they reached them and inspect the valley on the other side. That would relieve the rest of the battalion and its tired horses from doing the same, since they could skirt the ridges and avoid the steep hills.

Further instructions were delivered by the two messengers—first the regimental chief trumpeter, Henry Voss, and then Sergeant Major William Sharrow—sent by Custer soon after his battalion had proceeded down the trail a ways and he was able to see more of the country into which Benteen was riding. Voss arrived as Benteen neared the base of the hills and ordered him to move into the valley beyond. Sharrow reached him fifteen minutes later and told him that Custer wanted him to move even farther, to the second line of bluffs, and look into the next valley. If no Indians were discovered, Benteen was to look into the valley after that. What was initially expected to be a quick reconnaissance in force to the nearby valley of the Little Bighorn[9] was becoming a longer and, to Benteen's mind, aimless scout. Convinced that there were more than enough Indians to the north to pose a challenge to the entire regiment, he did not like Custer's orders. Benteen acknowledged them, and as he watched Sharrow ride away after Voss, he glimpsed the main column, or at least E Company, the Gray Horse Troop, almost two miles to the north, galloping down the lodgepole trail.

Benteen's battalion moved forward, wending its way through ravines and up and down hills, as Gibson and his men guided their horses up the first bluffs, which were not as steep as expected, more like rolling hills. "Gibby" signaled that there were no Indians to be seen from the highest point, then descended into the rough terrain beyond. He rode up the next line of bluffs, descended, and yelled to his Captain that there was no valley to be seen, only more intervening hills. He climbed the next line of bluffs, then the next—at least four altogether.[10] From the final ridgeline, a higher divide almost five miles from where they had left the main column, Gibson finally gained a good view of what he was sure was the upper valley of the Little Bighorn and examined it with the glasses. There were no Indians to be seen.[11]

Benteen had already decided that he had gone far enough, and Gibson's report confirmed his decision to return to the trail. This felt like a wild-goose chase, and perhaps, he thought, that had been the plan all along: to keep him out of the fight and away from any attendant glory.[12] Besides, the horses were tired and thirsty, not having been watered since the evening before, and that water had been heavily alkaline. He ordered a right oblique—a forty-five-degree turn—and moved his men north through the hills back to the trail. The battalion moved at a slow walk, the horses having become jaded after the two-hour off-trail march.[13] Since he had been specifically ordered to send a messenger only if he found any signs of Indians, he sent none, although a reconnaissance usually called for a report by courier, and an anxious Custer (he had, after all, sent two follow-up orders regarding Benteen's mission) would certainly have appreciated knowing there were no Indians upstream.

Four or five miles later, the battalion reached the Indian trail and turned to trot west along the right bank of the creek, less than a mile ahead of the slow-moving pack train. Benteen was now only a few miles behind the main column—less than an hour's walk.[14] A half mile later, in a large depression surrounded by low hills, they stopped at a morass that covered the trail to water the thirsty, tired horses. The men filled their canteens as their mounts drank, and some took off their heavy blue coats, for the heat was stifling. The break continued for twenty minutes or so. Some of the officers discussed why Benteen didn't order them out. "I wonder what the Old Man is keeping us here for?" said one.[15] As the watering continued, the buckskinned Boston Custer rode into view from the rear on his fresh mount.[16] He gave Lieutenant Winfield Edgerly a cheery salutation as he trotted by to rejoin his brothers ahead.

Among those impatient with the long break was Captain Thomas Weir. He approached Edward Godfrey and suggested that they petition Benteen to move forward, but Godfrey demurred, unwilling to incur the Old Man's wrath. We ought to be over there, said Weir, and being at the head of the column, he mounted his troop and started off down the trail with his men. Benteen immediately ordered the rest of the battalion to follow.[17] As the last of the troopers moved out, the van of the pack train reached the area, the thirsty mules plunging into the water despite all the attempts of the packers to restrain them.[18] The lead mules quickly became bogged down, slowing the pack train's progress to a standstill.

Benteen quickly caught up with the insubordinate Weir and passed him without a word. They soon encountered the lone tepee, still burning, at the abandoned Indian camp about a mile west of the morass. Benteen dismounted to inspect the lodge, then remounted and continued down the trail, a few hundred yards in advance of his battalion. Gunfire could now be heard, and it soon became constant and furious. A mile or so farther on, a rider approached waving his hat. It was Sergeant Kanipe, with a message from the General for the pack train to move forward at a faster pace. To Benteen he said, "They want you up there as quick as you can get there—they have struck a big Indian camp." He made no mention of the division of the regiment into two more battalions. Benteen directed him toward the back trail, where he would find the pack train in about a mile or so. Kanipe rode past the column, yelling, "We've got 'em, boys!" and added, "They are licking the stuffing out of them." Benteen's troopers now had the impression that Custer and his eight companies had attacked and captured the village.[19] All the glory work, it appeared, had been done.

Despite the order to hurry—and Benteen's original orders to hurry back after accomplishing his mission—the column continued to move at a fast walk.[20] The horses were tired, but none had fallen out due to exhaustion, and they were capable of a faster gait. Benteen would have none of it.

Apprehension increased as they rode down the trail. Even the horses felt it and became anxious, as weary as they were. The gunfire had become sporadic. Was the battle finished? Few of these troopers had fought before; some could barely shoot their guns, much less attempt to do so from horseback. But they unholstered their pistols and checked their chambers. An Indian attack could come from anywhere, particularly from the hills to the right of the trail. And there was still the hope of some Indians left to charge, if Custer had not rounded them all up.

A mile or so after they encountered Kanipe, another horseman came into sight, galloping over the hills to the right—a trooper again, this one Private Martin, the young Italian whose English was not so good. He was one of Benteen's own men, picked to go with Custer as a regimental orderly that morning. As he reined in, the excited trumpeter was almost jumping out of his skin and had failed to notice that his spent horse was bleeding from Indian gunfire. Martin bore a written message from Custer that he gave to Benteen, who was now riding a few hundred yards in advance of his battalion. Written in Cooke's hasty pencil scribble, it read:

> Benteen
>   Come on. Big
> village. Be quick.
> Bring pack.
>   W. W. Cooke
> PS bring pacs.[21]

Benteen found the message confusing. Bring the packs? Clearly Custer meant the ammunition boxes—or did he? He knew where the pack train was, not far behind them—they could see the dust it kicked up about a mile back—and no Indians had as yet been seen. To wait for the pack train to arrive, or even to go back for it, made no sense if they were needed. How could he do that and "come on" and "be quick" at the same time? Which did Custer want, the packs or Benteen's men?

Benteen handed the slip of paper to Weir as he rode up, followed by Gibson, Godfrey, and Edgerly. They all read it, but no one offered an opinion.

"Where is General Custer?" Benteen asked Martin.

"About three miles from here," said Martin in his thick accent, full of relieved and nervous laughter after his dangerous ride. He said he supposed by this time the General had made a charge through the village, since they had found all the Indians asleep in their tepees, and that Major Reno was charging the camp and killing men, women, and children right and left.[22] Benteen did not question the trumpeter as to why Reno was attacking and not Custer.

The Captain pointed out where Martin's horse was bleeding. Godfrey concluded that the fight was over and there was "nothing to do but go up and congratulate the others and help destroy the plunder." His feelings were doubtless shared by many.[23]

"Well!" Benteen said. "If he wants me to hurry, how does he

expect that I can bring the packs? If I am going to be of service to him I think I had better not wait for the packs."[24] Besides, if the Indians were already scattering, there would be less need of the supplies, there being no pitched battle.[25]

Benteen sent Martin back to McDougall with an order to bring up the pack train; Martin did so and returned to Benteen's company.[26] Benteen led out, finally increasing his gait to a trot.[27] A short while later, they came to a point on the main trail where it was clear that part of the column had split off over the rolling hills to the right, following another large lodgepole track.[28] Fresh horse droppings and shod hoofprints bore off in that direction as well as straight ahead.

Benteen reined in his horse. "Here we have the horns of a dilemma," he said.[29]

Gibson suggested taking the right-hand trail; Weir pushed for the left, toward the river, particularly since firing could be heard in the distance. Apparently, no one thought to ask Martin, who had just come back that way to meet them. After some discussion, Weir led his troop to the left, and the rest of the battalion took the trail to the right. Benteen and his orderly rode between them.

As the battalion proceeded, the gunfire from beyond the bluffs to the right increased, so much so that it sounded as if it were getting closer—Indians retreating before Custer's attempt to reach the pack train, perhaps.[30] The men formed a line, and the command broke into a gallop. Moments later they came into view of the Little Big-horn valley.

Downstream, heavy smoke curled up from the burning prairie to join clouds of dust, and hundreds of horsemen, close to a thousand, filled the landscape below. Indians seemed to be swirling around a dozen or so dismounted men on the valley floor near the river, about two miles away. On a bluff about as far down, a group of men could be seen, though whether friend or foe, it was impossible to tell.

Some of the Crows with a few captured ponies came into view on the bluffs to the left, in the direction of the river. Benteen angled over to them. The scouts told him, *"Otoe Sioux, otoe Sioux"*—many Sioux.[31] Another said, "Soldiers," and pointed to the men in the distance. Benteen led his battalion down the bluffs.

As they approached, a much-excited Reno, red handkerchief tied around his head, rode out to meet them. "For God's sake, Benteen, halt your command and help me," he shouted. "I've lost half my men." He told the senior Captain what had happened. "We are whipped," he said.[32]

Benteen drily replied, "I guess not,"[33] then showed him the written order from Cooke. It made little impression on Reno, who said he knew nothing of Custer's present whereabouts. The last he saw of Custer, Reno said, he was on the crest of the hill they were now on. Custer had waved his hat after seeing Reno engaged, which Reno had taken as a sign of approval.[34] Benteen said, "Well, let us make a junction with him as soon as possible."[35] But Reno insisted that they wait for the pack train and its supply of ammunition. Some of his men had expended half their cartridges in the valley.

Though the note from Cooke relayed direct orders from Benteen's commanding officer to "come quick," the Captain now decided to halt and join Reno's command. He may have assumed he had fulfilled his orders by reporting to Reno, his superior officer, and conveying the orders to him—or he may not have given it any thought, perhaps feeling obligated to obey Reno's plea for help. Whatever the reason, any further compliance with Custer's orders stopped then and there.[36]

Reno's troopers were still climbing up to the summit of the hill, some on horseback, some afoot. Most of the men were scattered about in the buffalo grass; some of the wounded were crying for water. A few Indians were firing on them from nearby bluffs and ravines. Weir, having met up with the rest, ordered his company to deploy in a skirmish line, and the Indian sharpshooters soon left. By Benteen's orders, Godfrey dismounted his troop and formed a line along the bluffs on the river side. Soon the hundreds of warriors in the valley had inexplicably withdrawn and could now be seen riding downstream. Despite their departure, Reno turned and discharged a revolver at some Indians about a thousand yards off—about nine hundred yards out of pistol range. (He had lost his own carbine and sidearm during the retreat, possibly due to the spirited horse he rode.)[37]

Charles Varnum, overwhelmed by a severe lack of sleep, swore and cried as he borrowed Wallace's rifle—a particularly fine .45-caliber Springfield[38]—and fired fruitlessly in the same direction as Reno had.[39] Sergeant Thomas McLaughlin of H Company told Reno that he thought someone should be sent to rescue the wounded down in the valley. Troopers at the hill's edge could plainly see warriors scalping and plundering the bodies of the fallen troopers on the retreat line and gray-haired men and women mutilating them. Reno replied that the Sergeant could get a detail up and rescue them himself if he wanted. Word of his answer quickly spread and caused some demoralization as the men watched their comrades being killed and carved up.[40]

It seemed that just about every man on the hill was thinking the same thing: *Where is Custer?* A rumor began circulating that Custer had abandoned them as (at least according to the accusations of Benteen and a few others) he had Elliott at the Washita. But before long, firing could be heard somewhere downstream, and it gained in volume, soon erupting into loud volleys.

As Varnum returned Wallace's carbine to him, he said, "Jesus Christ, hear that—and that."[41] Then, referring to the rumors, "How's that for abandonment, eh?"[42] To a Sergeant nearby, he remarked that Custer must be heavily engaged, which seemed obvious, even to Reno.[43]

Edward Davern, Reno's orderly, noticed a large body of Indians circling around far downstream, a half mile or so beyond where the valley skirmish line had been. The Irish-born Private called it to Weir's attention. "That must be Custer fighting down in the bottom," he said.

Weir looked to where Davern was pointing. "Why do you think so?"

"I hear the firing and see the dust and see the Indians have all left us."

Weir said, "Yes, I believe it is."[44] But he said nothing to Reno or Benteen, his superiors, and the command remained where it was as the distant volleys degenerated into a constant, dull roar of gunfire.

FOURTEEN

Soldiers Falling

We circled all around them — swirling like water round a stone.

TWO MOON, CHEYENNE

At the Rosebud eight days earlier, the young Cheyenne warrior White Shield had added to his renown, killing a Shoshone and several soldiers, including one with three yellow stripes on his arms. He had also counted many coups and saved Young Two Moon, a full day's work and glory to last a lifetime. On this day — windless, clear, and already quite hot — he planned to relax.[1]

He had been fishing in the river's cool water with his half brother and his son when they became aware of shooting upstream, then saw people making for the hills below their camp to the northwest. White Shield ran to his lodge, where his mother was waiting with his warhorse. As he prepared himself for battle, he looked across the river.

Along the rugged hills on the north side of the wide coulee across from the Cheyenne camp he could see several groups of soldiers.[2] One bunch rode white horses and were moving toward the river. White Shield mounted his pony and crossed to join four other Cheyennes on the far bank. There Lame White Man — older, and one of the wisest and bravest chiefs in the camp[3] — counseled the warriors to resist charging the soldiers; there were too many. Near a low ridge by the water's edge, the Cheyennes stopped and dismounted.

The soldiers had ridden down into the streambed of the wide

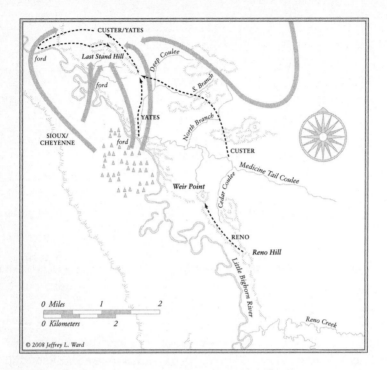

coulee and were now chasing five Lakotas on foot.[4] As the soldiers approached, the Lakotas veered away up into the hills. The blue-coats, led by the white horse company, kept toward the river. When they were a couple of hundred yards away, a bugle sounded, and they dismounted and spread out on a bench back from the water's edge.[5] The company behind them did the same. From behind the low ridge, White Shield and his tribesmen began firing at the soldiers. The five Lakotas ran behind them and joined in the shooting.[6] More warriors began to arrive, some of them from the battle upstream, others who had just retrieved their horses. They began to cross the stream and fire on the soldiers. More appeared on the bluffs overlooking the ford and opened fire on the *wasichus* below. A group of them rode down the hillside and made a charge on the soldiers. Everywhere, white cottonwood blossoms fell softly from the trees along the water.[7]

From up the coulee three or four loud volleys of rifle fire could be heard. The soldiers nearest the river pulled back to their gray horses and began to retreat, ascending a narrow ravine that angled north from the crossing. The second group of bluecoats fired past them into the warriors,[8] who pursued and shot at the retreating troops. A few whites pitched from their horses, one of them apparently an officer, judging from his buckskin attire and the field glasses and compass in a wooden box found on him later.[9]

Hundreds of warriors crossed up and down the river wherever they could. Many of them followed the bluecoats up the small ravine into the hills above. Others galloped downriver in the direction of their women and children. Sitting Bull urged them on, then rode toward the hills on the western side of the valley to join Inkpaduta and the older men to protect the families.[10] There were more than enough men of fighting age.

A MILE TO THE EAST, Wolf Tooth and Big Foot had found what they wanted.

At sunrise the two young cousins had carefully made their way downstream away from the village and out of sight of the *akicita*. They worked their way downriver until they ran into more young warriors with the same idea, and then some more—almost fifty men had evaded the lookouts. A couple of miles north of the village, they turned east and followed a creek a few miles.

They were making their way up a hill when they heard someone yelling behind them. They turned to see a Lakota horseman about a mile back, waving at them to return. When they reached him, he told them that the soldiers were already riding down to the village. They all galloped back up the creek until they found a ridge they could follow south toward the camp. In a few minutes, they could see soldiers ahead of them. They decided to split up, with half of them riding around the north side of the bluecoats to intercept them and the other half riding south and then west to follow them. When they were several hundred yards away, the soldiers dismounted and started shooting, and the warriors pulled up and returned fire, then retreated back to the hills. Soon the *wasichus* moved north.[11]

"GENTLEMEN," SAID CAPTAIN MYLES MOYLAN as he and most of the other officers stood near the edge of the bluffs overlooking the valley, "in my opinion General Custer has made the biggest mistake of his life, by not taking the whole regiment in at once in the first attack."[12] They watched the Indians across the river at their work of plunder and mutilation, some with stone hammers crushing the heads of the dead and the wounded, others with knives gashing the bodies, hacking off heads, private parts, and extremities.[13] These Indians were not Sitting Bull's warriors; they were women and old men. About a quarter of an hour after the arrival of Benteen's battalion, virtually every one of the hundreds of horsemen had turned and galloped down the valley out of sight. The gunfire downstream had become quite heavy, and almost everyone commented on it—even the half-deaf Godfrey. Behind Moylan, the noncoms of M, A, and G took roll call and checked on the condition of their remaining troopers. Dr. Porter tended to the seven or so wounded men who had made it to the summit, only to slip from their mounts.[14]

The subject of riding toward the gunfire was raised. Benteen spoke against it.[15] Custer could take care of himself, everyone agreed. But why hadn't he sent word to them? What were they supposed to do? Reno and Benteen conferred for a few minutes. Reno made Luther Hare his acting adjutant and then ordered Benteen's battalion to share its cartridges with his own. (He would later claim that his men were almost out of ammunition, though little or none had been expended on the retreat to the ford.) As Godfrey observed, "The men gave up their ammunition ungraciously."[16] But in the absence of orders, Reno made no effort to "ride to the sound of the guns" or communicate in any way with Custer's force downstream. Whether because of alcohol, shock, or the simple inability to command, he had not even sent a reconnaissance detachment toward Custer to assess the situation. Instead, he had decided that something else was more important.

Over the next thirty minutes, while half the Seventh Cavalry did almost nothing but listen to the steady roar of gunfire from Custer's battalion downstream, Reno took a dozen troopers and Dr. Porter down the bluffs to find his closest friend in the regiment, Benny Hodgson. Reno's adjutant had been reported dead, but the Major wanted to make sure. They found the unmutilated body of the "Jack of Clubs" by the river. Reno recovered Hodgson's class ring and some other personal items, but a few Indians fired on them, persuading him not to carry the body up the steep incline.

In the half hour Reno was gone, three of Custer's dismissed Crow scouts—White Man Runs Him, Hairy Moccasin, and Goes Ahead—made their way upstream to Reno's command.[17] They stayed there for less than an hour, then left to go home, to their village on the Yellowstone. They had seen enough of this expedition. Some of the Arikara scouts rode up with their purloined ponies. They, too, left in a few minutes, riding hard on the back trail toward the Powder River depot, where Custer had told them to go.

Upon scaling the hill and finding the pack train still not arrived, Reno sent Hare to hurry it up and bring a few mules with ammo boxes ahead. By plan or serendipity, he picked the right man for the job. The lieutenant was the best horseman outside of Custer in the regiment, and he actually had some experience with hostile Indians, albeit as a child. In Texas, when Hare was three, an Indian had attempted to kidnap him, pulling him onto his pony. Young Luther's screams had brought his mother running with a gun, and when she had started shooting, the warrior had dropped the boy and disappeared.[18]

Hare's horse had been shot in the jaw, so he borrowed the mount of his troop commander, Godfrey, and galloped off. Then Reno ordered Varnum to go down and bury Hodgson. Varnum told him that he would do so as soon as the pack train arrived with the regiment's few shovels.

Weir's D Troop had been standing beside their horses for a long while after driving away the Indians on the bluffs to the north. The Captain had been pacing anxiously for several minutes, impatient to do something. When the thunderous crash of two or three distinct volleys could be heard—a signal of distress to some—his Second Lieutenant, Winfield Edgerly, said to him, "We ought to get down there."

Weir asked his subaltern what he thought they should do.

"Go get Custer, of course," said Edgerly.

The heavy firing continued, as did Weir's pacing. His First Sergeant, Michael Martin, approached Edgerly.

The Lieutenant noticed a cloud of dust to the north and pointed it out to the Sergeant. "There must be General Custer. I guess he is getting away with them," he said.

Martin said, "Yes sir, and I think we ought to go there."

Edgerly made no answer.[19]

CAPTAIN GEORGE YATES had been gone only a few minutes when a group of Indians—about fifty, it looked like—appeared several hundred yards to the north of the ridge where Custer and his three companies were positioned. The General ordered his troopers to dismount and fire on them. The warriors fell back and scattered into the hills. After about fifteen agonizing minutes, Custer could wait for Benteen no longer. Through his field glasses, he could see a growing number of Indians pressuring Yates and his two companies at the ford. He ordered several volleys of rifle fire by the entire battalion to signal Yates to move to the rendezvous point, then led his headquarters staff and Keogh's right wing down a ravine and up onto another ridge.

Custer's men moved north along the rise, stopping to fire at the increasing numbers of Indians encroaching from the south and east, who sent up showers of arcing steel-tipped arrows that fell upon the three companies. A few troopers were hit and fell from their mounts.[20] As the men neared the south end of the long, high ridge, the left wing could be seen approaching up a coulee that snaked from the river. Indians followed behind them and on their flanks, though they kept their distance.

Yates led his men up out of the shallow coulee and reported several dead, among them Jack Sturgis, the son of the regiment's commanding officer, shot from his horse at the river. If Custer had been unsure of what to do before, he was not anymore. He could not return to Fort Lincoln with nothing to show for his efforts but the Colonel's dead son.

There was still no sign of Benteen, and the hundreds of hostiles on almost every flank, especially those riding downstream, represented a serious threat. Custer convened a brief officers' call and outlined his plan. Keogh and his three companies would hold this high point, both to act as a beacon for Benteen and to protect the General's rear. Custer would take Yates's smaller wing, ride down the ridge to its end, and then head west to the river to find the noncombatants. A bold offensive thrust to seize the women and children was now the only chance for success. To dig in or to retreat would signify surrender and renounce any hope of victory.

With Yates's two companies, his regimental staff, and the others—his brothers Tom and Boston, his nephew Autie, correspondent Kellogg on his mule, the ailing Dr. Lord, and Mitch Boyer—behind him, Custer led the wing northwest along the half-mile-long ridge. Covered with sagebrush and grass, the surface was not steep, and a horse could gallop over any part of it.[21]

The superior view revealed the daunting size of their task. On the other side of the river were thousands of Indians—probably women, children, and older men—streaming into the hills and ravines north and west of the village. Custer had corralled only fifty-three of them on the Washita; the job at hand would require more than two depleted and tired companies missing several officers and Sergeants.

When Custer and the eighty-odd men behind him reached the far end of the ridge, they continued down into a swale and then turned left toward the Little Bighorn.[22] Behind them a group of Indians rode to the crest line they had just left and fired down at them as they galloped away.[23]

A few minutes later, the wing reached the river—what looked like a good crossing—and ran into strong resistance.[24] The brush on the west side of the water was thick with warriors, and they fired arrows and bullets into the soldiers. Custer halted the command and traded fire while he assessed the enemy's strength. He realized quickly that there were too many hostiles and that he needed reinforcements, and soon. He turned and led his men back toward the high ridge. More than halfway there, on a flat rise a few hundred yards short of it, he ordered a halt. They would wait there for Keogh and Benteen before proceeding. Meanwhile, Dr. Lord, though weak himself, could attend to the casualties. Kellogg was nowhere in sight—when last seen, he had been down by the river, desperately spurring his mule to keep up with the large army mounts.[25]

The General raised his field glasses, looked upstream, and saw nothing but thick clouds of dust. Keogh was out of sight a mile to the southeast, somewhere below the long ridge. The constant roar of gunfire from that direction could only be his three companies.

Whether he realized it or not, Custer had now surrendered the offensive to the enemy. The Indians, not the white men, would decide the course of this battle.

AT THE FAR END of the ridge, Myles Keogh had deployed his forces around the base of the hill. Keogh divided his strongest company, Jimmi Calhoun's forty-four-man L Troop, into two platoons and ordered them along the crest of a spur running off the ridge. As the officers and Sergeants yelled orders and the horse holders in each set of four gathered their mounts and moved to the rear, about eighteen troopers in each platoon moved down the slope, extending the skirmish line about a hundred yards. The company's two officers stood in the rear to direct fire. Calhoun, who had fought as an enlisted man during the Civil War, stood behind one line. His second in command, young John Crittenden, scion of a long line of military men but a West Point reject and an infantry officer for only a few months, stood thirty feet away behind the other. Keogh placed C Company, with the most inexperienced men, behind Calhoun. He pulled his own I Company back in reserve, in a swale below the eastern side of the crest line.

Even before he had finished his deployment, the Indian fire had increased. Most used bows and arrows, but plenty of the hostiles carried rifles. From the sound of the reports, they seemed to be of every sort: old muskets, some army Springfields and other breechloaders, and quite a few magazine guns, probably Winchesters, Henrys, and Spencers, though the repeaters were not very accurate outside a couple of hundred yards. Few of the Indians approached within that range, but over the next half hour, they surrounded the position, using gullies, bushes, and the occasional rock to close in on the soldiers on their flanks and in their front.

When a group of mounted warriors emerged from a large coulee and made a charge toward the command, several volleys drove them back, but more intimate action was needed to clear the ravines of Indians encroaching from the Little Bighorn. Keogh ordered the only officer present with the company, Second Lieutenant Henry Harrington, to lead a skirmish line of C troopers down along a ridge toward the river, just past Calhoun's L Company. Anchoring the line were three Sergeants: First Sergeant Edwin Bobo, a veteran of the Washita; Jeremiah Finley, an Irishman who had served in the Civil War and another Washita veteran; and George Finckle, a tall German who had once been a Captain in the Prussian army.[26]

The tactic was effective, but not for long. As Harrington's group advanced, the Indians retreated to safer positions, but they soon reemerged in overwhelming numbers and surrounded the line. Every available rifle was needed, so each trooper held his own reins with one hand. As arrows rained down into their position, the injured horses bucked and kicked, making it increasingly difficult to shoot with any accuracy or to reload. Some of the thirsty horses broke free and made for the river. Soon the men began to drop. Finley and Finckle remained on the line and fell fifty yards from each other; half of their company died with them. As Indians began to overrun the position, some troopers turned and galloped north to Calhoun's company and beyond. Harrington and Bobo retreated with them.

But Calhoun's position had also been taking casualties. Indians waving blankets and screaming got close enough to stampede the soldiers' horses. From a ridge a few hundred yards to the east, several Indians with repeaters fired into L Company, aiming for the small clouds of gray smoke belching from the soldiers' Springfields.

AS HUNDREDS MORE WARRIORS arriving from the valley forded the river and made their way up the ravines and over the hills east of the Cheyenne camp, Crazy Horse galloped downstream. He had made a brief stop at his lodge to make his medicine strong and do the same for about ten of the younger men who had vowed to follow him anywhere in battle.[27] Some of his Oglalas had become impatient at his lengthy prayers to Wakantanka, but now these and other warriors followed him with bold assurance. At a point about a mile north of the Cheyenne circle, they splashed across the river and up a deep, wide ravine.[28] Almost half a mile east, where the coulee forked, they turned right. When it narrowed a quarter mile farther, they dismounted and walked their ponies. Crazy Horse stopped and gave his horse to his cousin Flying Hawk to hold. Then he crawled up out of the gully. When he reached the top, he could see a line of soldiers just south of him. He aimed his Winchester and shot at them as fast as he could.[29]

Other warriors carefully crawled from one ravine to another, hiding behind bushes and hills as they approached the soldier lines. Gradually, they made their way closer. Most of them had no guns, but from the protection of the gullies, they arced thousands of arrows into the bluecoats. As they got within range, more and more found their marks, and soldiers fell as frightened horses reared and kicked, many of them breaking loose and galloping away toward the river.

The Hunkpapa Crow King, a celebrated fighter and the leader of a band that included eighty warriors, was known for a temper so fierce that he had once killed another Lakota in a fit of rage.[30] He had ridden up the coulee behind the Cheyennes and worked his way north toward the *wasichus*. Two of his brothers had died in the fight upstream, and Crow King wanted revenge. Now he and his men readied their ponies for a charge.

Though they were not without fear, they knew their medicine was good that day. After all, they had defeated the soldiers to the south, and only a few brave warriors had just turned back a much larger force at the river. Now there were many more fighting men. How could the *wasichus* withstand them?

To bolster their courage, each man whipped another's horse as they charged upon the bluecoats, whooping and blowing their eagle-bone whistles. Low Dog, a fearless Oglala warrior and leader of his own band, yelled to the men around him, "This is a good day to die—follow me!" and rushed forward.[31]

Lame White Man had also made his way close to the soldiers. When forty of the bluecoats charged down the ridge and dismounted, he had retreated with the others. But they soon began moving forward again, and the endless stream of arrows and bullets took its toll as the soldiers started falling. Now, to the warriors gathered around him, Cheyenne and Lakota, Lame White Man said, "Come. We can kill all of them," and he led a charge against what remained of the bluecoats on the hill.[32]

From the east, the west, and the south, the Indians converged on the soldiers and overwhelmed them, shooting and clubbing the few who remained. Then they stormed through the next group of blue-coats to the north, who had made a good stand for a long while. Many coups were counted in the close fighting. A violent roar filled the air: horses screaming, hooves pounding, warriors and soldiers yelling, skulls and bones breaking, flesh tearing, and over it all the deafening roar of close-quarters rifle and pistol fire. The two officers at the rear of the soldier lines bravely stood their ground and died facing the onslaught.

One soldier, a balding, heavyset man with side-whiskers and yellow stripes on his arms, took off southwest toward the river. Several warriors galloped after him. He was almost to the wide coulee a mile away when a bullet dropped his mount and threw the soldier to the ground. He knelt near his horse and began firing his rifle at his pursuers, hitting several of them. He kept the warriors at bay for a while, but several surrounded him and crept closer until one shot him from behind.[33]

KEOGH HAD NO CHOICE but to eke one last ounce of strength out of Comanche. The tough little horse already bore several wounds but responded gamely as Keogh whirled him around once again to rally the men running madly up the ridge—the remnants of C and L spreading confusion and panic among his own I Troop. Everything was falling apart. The best he could hope to do now was to get the men north to consolidate with Custer on the far end of the ridge.

A bullet smashed into Keogh's left knee—the knee that had been giving him trouble for years. The round went clear through his leg into Comanche's body. Both went down.[34]

With that, any hope of an orderly withdrawal was gone. His two Sergeants, Varden and Bustard, came off the line to help him. His trumpeter stayed with him, too, relaying orders that amid the chaos went unobeyed. The bulk of I Troop was still clustered around its Captain when the wave of Indians swept over them all.

WHITE BULL had worked his way around the soldiers to the east. Most of the fighting there was still at a distance. Several Lakotas with magazine rifles lay behind a ridge a couple of hundred yards away and poured a steady fire into a group of about sixty blue-coats north of the others, making their way along the east side of the long ridge.[35] White Bull joined them and put his seventeen-shot Winchester to good use. But he soon grew impatient; there were no opportunities for coups in this kind of fight, and therefore no glory won. With perfect timing, Crazy Horse, who had just skirted the soldiers' position, challenged White Bull to a bravery run to cut off the large group of bluecoats before they all turned and galloped north.

White Bull cried, "Only heaven and earth last long!" and the two warriors whipped their horses forward, across the hills and up the east side of the ridge, through a gap between the soldier groups. They leaned down over the necks of their ponies, and bullets whizzed by them as they crested the grassy ridge and rode over it, then turned around and galloped back.[36]

Having done it once, they decided to do it again. As they did so, others followed them, and the army horses stampeded and ran for the river. The bluecoats fired at the horsemen, and when they stopped to reload, the rest of the warriors, mounted and afoot, charged in among them, fighting hand to hand. The soldiers threw down their rifles and used their pistols against the warriors' toma-hawks and clubs. Many coups were counted during that charge as the Indians pulled men off horses and ran down others on foot.[37] An officer rallying his troops near the rear of the column was shot off his claybank horse, and several soldiers with yellow stripes on their sleeves futilely surrounded him before hundreds of warriors over-whelmed the whites, killing them all.[38]

Scores of exulting Lakotas and Cheyennes joined in from the south. Warriors stopped to grab rifles, pistols, and ammunition from the dead and their horses. Then it was another buffalo stampede as they chased the line of soldiers fleeing northwest along the ridge. Some of the mounted *wasichus* escaped their pursuers, but most of them were brought down before getting too far, shot or chopped or bludgeoned.

One officer on a powerful horse galloped through the dark clouds of dust and gray gunpowder and headed west over hills and down ridges for a mile or more. Several warriors on ponies chased him, but eventually they gave up one by one. The last man had just reined in his horse and was about to turn around when he saw the soldier shoot himself in the head with his pistol and pitch from his mount. The warrior rode up and counted coup on the dead soldier, then stripped him of ammunition and valuables, took his horse, and returned to the battle.[39]

EVEN WITH DERUDIO'S EXCELLENT FIELD GLASSES, Custer still could not tell how things were going at the far end of the high ridge. Keogh had apparently placed his troops on the spurs below the southern end, but only a haze of gunsmoke and dust and the steady crackle of gunfire indicated action. It was clear that Benteen had not arrived, since the General could see no cavalry movement toward him.[40]

Things were heating up around Custer, too. As yet there were only a few Indians closer than a couple of hundred yards — just out of range of arrows and of all but the most accurate marksmen, which excluded most every Indian as well as most troopers. But slowly, inexorably, hundreds of warriors were surrounding the position on all sides. Below the wide ridge to the south, scores could be seen running up the large ravines that snaked from the river and moving over the hills. To the north and east, several groups had begun sniping from a distance. Others approached from the crossing to the west. Action was necessary.

A large ravine a couple of hundred yards to the south seemed to be the main avenue of infiltration. Custer ordered Algernon Smith to take E Company and move down toward it to form a skirmish line along the coulee and drive the hostiles back.

As Smith and his troopers moved down into the basin below and extended a line almost halfway to the river,[41] Custer led the regimental staff and F Company up to the high ground at the end of the hogback ridge. The Indians at its crest quickly mounted and galloped down the far slope to a hill two hundred yards farther east. There they took up prone positions and resumed firing their rifles at the soldiers.[42]

In the green buffalo grass near the top of the ridge, on its western slope, Custer deployed his men. The position was vulnerable, with little or no cover, but it was the high ground. He ordered almost all the horses shot in a rough semicircle facing the warriors attacking from the west and southwest—primitive breastworks and, given a cavalryman's dependence on his mount, a stark declaration of the seriousness of the situation. On the summit, four or five more animals were felled. There, on a narrow flat area, Custer set up his command position. Around him were his brothers, his nephew, and his regimental staff. Sergeant Robert Hughes planted Custer's personal guidon, its red and blue swallowtails fluttering in the sporadic breeze.

The men on the side of the hill and on its crest threw themselves down behind the dead horses and resumed firing. They were now fighting for their lives, and they knew it.

The troopers of the Gray Horse Company dismounted at skirmish intervals. Holding their reins, they fired into the Indians in and around the ravine. Their fire forced the warriors to retreat—for a while. Then a group of about twenty young Indians galloped boldly down into them from the ridges to the northwest and shattered the line, killing several where they stood and stampeding their horses. Some of the soldiers managed to drop a few of the Indians, but more warriors rushed toward them. Many of the troopers ran or jumped or even galloped down into the deep ravine they had just cleared out and made for the river. At a point where the gully deepened to twenty feet with steep sides, men and horses bunched up. Indians ran to the edges and shot down at them; one or two eager warriors fell in and were killed also. Soon the bottom was a mass of dead men and horses. One Private was just a stone's throw from the river when he was overtaken and killed.[43]

Only a few of the exhausted cavalrymen managed to stagger up the slope to safety,[44] Algernon Smith among them. He settled in near his commanding officer. No report was necessary. There was no further strategy to discuss. They could only try to expend their cartridges judiciously—a difficult proposition when sitting on an open hill surrounded by more than a thousand hostile Indians—and hope they could withstand the enemy until Benteen and Keogh arrived.

THE FIRING FROM THE NORTH had almost stopped completely. Weir asked Edgerly if he would be willing to ride in that direction with their troop even if the other companies would not go. Edgerly assented. So did their First Sergeant.

Weir walked over to where Benteen and Reno were. He and Reno detested each other. At Fort Lincoln, before Custer had returned from the East, Reno had preferred charges against Weir for insubordination, though General Terry had refused to pursue the matter. Now Weir's request for permission to ride quickly devolved into angry words, arm waving, and gesticulating.[45] In a few minutes, he came back and without a word mounted his horse and with an orderly rode off in the direction of the firing. Edgerly assumed Weir had received permission; he mounted his troopers and set out after the Captain.

Weir rode northeast along the crest of the bluffs, with his men following in a shallow ravine to the right. They made for the highest point in the area, a trio of peaks a mile away, the two on the right connected by a sugarloaf ridge. Almost an hour had passed since Reno's command had reached the hill.

CUSTER'S HOPE OF RELIEF from Benteen and Keogh was soon quashed. Along the ridge from Keogh's position came several troopers, most of them C Company men on sorrels and a few afoot, gasping their way toward the General, a horde of Indians behind them. A volley of covering fire drove back the warriors. As the last of the troopers reached safety, their mounts were shot, their carcasses forming a small redoubt facing south down the ridgetop. About fifty men now occupied the position.

From the ridges to the east and the north, Indians kept up a relentless fire. From the wide ridge the column had just left, and from the ravines and ridges to the southwest, arrows rained down on the few still alive.[46] The troopers hunkered down behind their makeshift breastworks and returned the fire, but the Indians were difficult targets, raising their heads from cover only to shoot a quick round, then ducking down to move to another spot before the soldiers could aim below the small burst of telltale black powder smoke. The bowmen remained well hidden in the gullies and behind the ridges surrounding the hill. Horsemen circled the hill at a distance; beyond them, even farther out of range, a crowd of women, old men, and young boys gathered on horseback, the outcome no longer in doubt. An occasional warrior galloped up near the hill, then angled off, the soldiers picking off one or two as they emerged from the thick cloud of dust and gunpowder, but that was little help given the situation.

The dead horses provided meager protection from the hail of bullets and arcing arrows. Men yelled and screamed as casualties began to mount. It was impossible to keep the Indians at a distance. There was simply not enough firepower. They had too few guns and too few men to use them efficiently. There were some accurate shots on the hill, and the General was putting his Remington sporting rifle to good use,[47] but the fact was that most of the troopers had never had the training or the practice to develop into marksmen. Anything beyond point-blank range was a guess for the Indians, since they knew little of making adjustments for wind and distance, but the number of their weapons made up for their poor shooting.

Custer took a shot in his left breast that knocked him back. He dropped his rifle and drew his English bulldog pistols. Many of the men around him were dead when another bullet smashed into his left temple and killed him instantly. Mitch Boyer jumped up, yelled to the remaining men, and headed down the slope toward the river. Most of the survivors who could walk—no more than ten men total—threw down their rifles, pulled out their Colts, and followed him. Tom Custer lay motionless, but Boston and his nephew Autie ran down the hill. They got only a hundred yards before they were shot dead. Boyer and some of the troopers somehow made it halfway to the Little Bighorn before they were overcome. Warriors wielding clubs and revolvers fell upon them from all sides. A few of the men reached the deepest part of the ravine and were killed among their comrades. As had happened on other parts of the field, some of the soldiers killed themselves just to get it over with. No white man wanted to be alive when he fell into the hands of Indians.[48]

WHEN THEY REACHED the sugarloaf ridge, Weir and Edgerly ascended the south crest and dismounted. The men were deployed in a skirmish line around the heights, and they strained to see what was going on. There was some kind of commotion on a long ridge about three miles north. They could only glimpse hundreds of horsemen on and around the far end of the ridge—"a great many," remembered Edgerly, "riding around and firing at objects in the ground and several guidons flying."[49] But they assumed it was Custer's rearguard action they were witnessing, and that the General was escaping north toward Terry and Gibbon.

Weir sent Edgerly and his troopers another half mile out, where they deployed in a skirmish line.[50] Then he scanned the area to the north again. "That's Custer over there," he declared, and mounted and prepared to ride in that direction.

One of his Sergeants, a tall Civil War veteran named James Flanagan, said, "Here, Captain, you had better take a look through the glasses; I think those are Indians."[51]

Through the binoculars, Weir could see that the figures were indeed Indians, riding around and firing at objects on the ground.[52] He dismounted and stood on the hill. Custer had never lost a flag during the war; a unit's colors were protected at the cost of life itself. If those objects were cavalry guidons, then the General had suffered a serious setback, probably the loss of at least two or three of his companies.

Then they spied a single trooper galloping away from the commotion. A group of Indians cut him off and felled him from his horse.[53] Not far behind them were more Indians starting south toward the cavalry, a huge mass of warriors two or three miles away.

AFTER THE LAST of the *wasichus* ran down from the hill, hundreds of warriors overwhelmed the position, counting coup and finishing off the wounded. Just below the hill, White Bull leaped from his horse to wrestle a big soldier who threw his pistol at him when it jammed. After a fierce struggle, White Bull finally smashed the soldier's skull several times until he let go, then counted first coup and shot him. It was one of seven coups he earned that afternoon.[54]

Crazy Horse also reached the area before the fighting was over. When a soldier lit out east on foot, Crazy Horse jumped on his pony, galloped after the soldier, and took him down.[55] Gall, too, arrived on the hill just in time to help dispatch the last of the wounded soldiers. Many of the "suicide boys" had died in the charge they had made that had broken the bluecoat line. Lame White Man was found a short distance down the ridge, dead and scalped by a Lakota who had mistaken him for an Arikara army scout.[56]

One of Inkpaduta's sons, Sounds the Ground as He Walks, insisted that the fine-looking sorrel he claimed was Long Hair's. Though none of the warriors present had ever seen Long Hair, they had heard of this great fighter. But they could not find anyone on the hill dressed as an officer with long blond locks.

They stripped the bodies and scalped some of them, though most of the soldiers had hair too short for the effort. Then, as the men of the village threw themselves on their ponies and rode south toward the bluecoats standing on the high point near the river, the women, boys, and old men who had waited on their ponies out of range arrived to help kill the wounded and begin the important task of mutilation. Many warriors had died, but far more *wasichus* lay dead along this ridge. There were skulls to crush, eyes to tear out, muscles and tendons to sever, limbs to hack off, and heads to separate from bodies.[57] These soldiers would not move through the next world in comfort.

FIFTEEN

The Hill

The men expected orders every minute to march toward the firing.

SERGEANT STANISLAS ROY

Varnum had commandeered some troopers and a couple of spades from the first two mules and begun descending the bluffs toward the river to bury Benny Hodgson. Before he reached the river, he saw Herendeen leading eleven thankful troopers, most of them from G Company, up to safety. The frontiersman had persuaded them to wait in the timber for a better chance to escape. A few of them had been badly wounded, and they had only five or six mounts. After things had cooled down and most of the Indians had cleared off, Herendeen had carefully led them out of the woods and across the river upstream.

Benteen had seen Weir's company riding north and assumed the entire command was moving out. After his men had restocked on ammunition—Hare had returned in twenty minutes, followed by two mules carrying ammo boxes, and some cartridges had been distributed—he ordered H, K, and M companies after Weir. Captain French also led his men north, the only company of Reno's battalion to do so. If Reno was issuing orders, no one was noticing or obeying them.

Captain McDougall, with B Company and Mathey's pack train, reached the Major a few minutes later. An apparently inebriated

Reno saluted Mathey by raising a flask of whiskey. "Look here, I got half a bottle yet," he said, though he didn't offer any to the Frenchman.[1] McDougall mentioned that he had just heard the two loud volleys. Reno paid no attention, replying, "Captain, I lost your lieutenant, he is lying down there."[2] McDougall left the Major and ordered his troop to throw out a skirmish line, since no one had replaced Weir's after he had left.

Varnum had no sooner reached Hodgson's body than Lieutenant Wallace called him back. Varnum and his detachment made the long climb back to the bluffs to find that all except Moylan's company — A, to which Varnum belonged — had moved out. He stayed with his troop commander and helped with the wounded. Meanwhile, a mile north at the promontory, Hare arrived with an order from the Major: Weir was to open communications with Custer. Reno would follow as soon as the pack train arrived. To the north, Hare could see about 1,500 warriors moving in their direction.

On the bluffs behind them, Reno ordered a trumpeter to sound the command to halt, and he did so continually. Weir ignored the order, as did Benteen and his officers, who continued toward Weir with their companies. When there was no reaction to his order, Reno commanded the remaining troops, including the pack train and the injured, to move north after Benteen and rode forth himself. McDougall's company and then Moylan followed, his men carrying the seven casualties on horse blankets, six men to a blanket. A few other wounded troopers managed to mount and ride.[3]

WHEN BENTEEN AND HIS THREE COMPANIES arrived at the peaks a mile to the north, he ordered his men to dismount and deployed them in a skirmish line on the ridges around the area. The Captain climbed to the top of the left hill. On the ridge to the north, the air was full of dust, but now there was only the occasional shot. Benteen took his troop guidon and jammed it down into some stones. If anyone was alive in that direction, they might see it and the horses and make for them.

It quickly became apparent that the only people coming toward them were more of Sitting Bull's warriors, and they were coming fast.

"This is a hell of a place to fight Indians," said Benteen. "I am going to see Reno and propose that we go back to where we lay before starting out here."[4]

With that, he descended the hill and led his troop back toward the Major, who was about half a mile back, in front of the pack train and Moylan and the wounded. Weir followed him, alone, leaving his troop in the care of Edgerly. French, the only senior officer left, remained with his company.

The closest Indians were now about seven hundred yards away and closing fast on the regiment's forward position. The two companies under Edgerly and French dismounted in a skirmish line around the forward peak. Many of the men, understandably unnerved, began to shoot. The Indians, now armed with two hundred additional Springfields, returned their fire.

When Benteen reached Reno, he suggested that they fall back to their previous position, because Weir's hill, despite its superior height, was a poor one for defensive purposes. There was little or no cover, since no part of it was completely protected. Reno agreed and began issuing orders to withdraw to their previous position. But perhaps because nobody trusted Reno any longer, no trumpeter blew the recall, and Reno himself did not bother to order a rear guard.

As Benteen neared the position, McDougall rode up to him. After talking with another officer, he had decided that Reno was completely incompetent and drastic action needed to be taken. "Say old man," he asked Benteen, "what is going to be the outcome of this unless we have a commanding officer here pretty damn soon? You are the senior captain, and we would like to see you take the lead in affairs." If they were not careful, McDougall added, there would be a second Fort Phil Kearny affair, referring to the Fetterman Massacre.

Benteen only smiled and said nothing. But he followed McDougall's suggestion, and when they reached their position, he directed his men to set up a defense on one side of the site and then helped form the defense on the other side—Reno's side.[5] From that point on, Benteen quietly and unobtrusively took control of the command from Reno. Henceforth, most of the orders regarding the defense of the hill, whether they came officially from Reno or Benteen, were suggested by Benteen.[6]

The retreat went smoothly for the most part. One runaway mule loaded with ammunition tore off and made it halfway toward the oncoming Indians. Only the quick pursuit of Sergeant Richard Hanley and Private John McGuire of C Company prevented the animal from falling into enemy hands.[7]

Edward Godfrey's company was in line along a ridge closer to the river and south of Weir's position on the hill. He had been so busy instructing his men that he was startled to realize that Reno, Benteen, and the command were out of sight over the hills to the south; he had expected them to be deploying to fortify this new defensive position. Hare rode over and delivered the retreat order to Godfrey,[8] who pulled his men in, got them mounted, and began to march south.

In the confusion, French had received no orders to withdraw, but he finally mounted his men, yelled over at Edgerly to retreat, and led his company at a gallop over the bluffs past Godfrey. Edgerly's troop followed soon after, though the lieutenant and his orderly, Private Charles Sanders, remained behind on top of a hill. Some two hundred Indians were swarming over the ridges the soldiers had just abandoned, and Edgerly could not resist taking a shot at one. He missed, and the rifle report startled his horse, which kept swinging away when he tried to mount. The closest Indians were only twenty paces away and firing at the lieutenant and his orderly, who grinned broadly the entire time. With Sanders's help, Edgerly finally got on his horse, and the two galloped away. (When the lieutenant found time the next day to ask Sanders what he'd been smiling at, the trooper replied that it had been the atrocious marksmanship of the Indians when so close to them.)[9]

Edgerly and Sanders had only made a couple of hundred yards when they came upon the troop farrier, redheaded, Swiss-born Vincent Charley, crawling on his knees and one hand. He had been shot through the hips and unhorsed, and his head was bleeding where he had hit the ground. He begged them not to leave him. Edgerly stopped and told him to find a ravine to hide in, and he would come back for him as soon as they could get reinforcements. Then the Lieutenant and his orderly rode away south after his troop. After riding a while, they looked back and saw the Indians finishing up Charley.[10]

Indians appeared on the top of the hill and started down the slope, firing into the retreating troopers. Godfrey was only a short distance from the hill, and almost half a mile from Reno and the bulk of the command, when M and D troops passed him at a full gallop. The Indians were close behind them.

Godfrey had graduated from West Point in 1867 and had served with the Seventh Cavalry since then. He had not made much of an impression his first year or so. His company commander had said of him, "He is very slovenly and lazy and unmilitary . . . of very little account in the company."[11] But "God," as his friends called him, had shaped up as an officer. He had fought Indians with Custer on the Washita and the Yellowstone, and he had learned a few things along the way—particularly about retreat tactics. During the Battle of the Washita in 1868, with only a platoon of men facing hundreds of attacking Indians, he had handled a tricky rearguard action and come through with no casualties. He was well aware that Indians liked few things better than chasing down a fleeing enemy. He knew that if a proper rear guard was not implemented, the command's retreat could turn into another buffalo chase, much like Reno's in the valley below.

Godfrey turned to Hare. "If this continues, the Indians will follow us right into the main camp, and I am going to try and stop it."

Hare hesitated—his position as orderly required him to return to Reno's side—and then said, "All right, adjutant or no adjutant, I'm going to stay with you."

"I may need you," said Godfrey. He had been told of Reno's disorganized retreat from the valley, and it was vivid in his mind.

Godfrey dismounted his thirty-odd men—all but the number fours, whom he sent with the horses back to the main command. He quickly formed the remaining twenty-two troopers into two squads, each under the direction of an experienced noncom. As the first of the Indians galloped toward them over a rise, he ordered his men to fire into the approaching hostiles, who held up and retreated to cover. Godfrey withdrew his men methodically, by the book, pulling each platoon back a short distance, alternately halting, kneeling, and firing as he had at the Washita. Despite his discipline, the men started to panic and bunch up, and then some began to run through the knee-high grass. Only with Hare's help was Godfrey able to halt them and organize the lines. When the Indians started forward again, another volley drove them back to cover.

As all this was going on, a messenger from Reno galloped up with orders to hurry back. Godfrey yelled, "Double time, march!" then watched his men ignore him and start off like sprinters. He pulled his revolver and swore at his troopers, threatening to kill any man who ran away. The men turned and looked at him for a moment, but they obeyed. He managed to organize an orderly retreat, continuing to fire at the growing number of Indians.

A few hundred yards from the safety of the regiment's position, the small rear guard began to pass a high ridge over toward the river. Godfrey noticed some Indians making for it and realized that its superior height would make it an excellent defensive site. He ordered Hare to take ten of the men and hold the hill. But just as the detachment began to move in that direction, a trumpeter rode up with orders from Reno to fall back as quickly as possible. Godfrey recalled Hare and shouted, "Every man for himself and hurry back!" They needed little encouragement. A few minutes later, the men tumbled past the perimeter Reno had set up, without a single casualty.[12] Behind them galloping over the hills came a thousand or more Indians.[13]

SIXTEEN

"Death Was All Around Us"

We were thus surrounded and our little squad of men being killed and wounded by twenty times their number of Indians, and with no prospect of relief and expecting every moment to be murdered and, perhaps, tortured and burned.

DR. HENRY R. PORTER

K Company's measured rearguard action had bought precious time for the rest of the regiment, enabling Benteen and Reno to deploy their troops fairly well as they filtered into the lines. Benteen took one side, Reno the other, and they detailed each company to a length of the perimeter, though for the most part each commander handled his own once locations were assigned.[1] Wallace was among the first officers back to position, and Benteen ordered him to place his company on the line.

"I have no troop," said the Lieutenant, "only three men."

"Well, stay here with your three men," said Benteen, "and don't let them get away. I will have you looked out for."[2]

The area the command occupied was a large saucerlike swale bordered on the north and south by two low, roughly parallel ridges. On the west side, the rough, steep bluffs dropped gradually down to the river a quarter mile away. In the depression in the middle, within a circle of mules, Dr. Porter's hospital was established.

The position wasn't a perfect one for defense: some points several hundred yards to the north, east, and south were slightly higher and within effective rifle distance. The superior height of the enemy positions wasn't the only problem. As many as half the men stationed themselves below the crest of the low ridge on the perimeter, thus severely restricting their fields of fire—at some points less than thirty feet and rarely more than twenty-five yards. This would enable some of Sitting Bull's warriors to advance close enough to toss dirt clods, rocks, and even arrows among the troopers.[3]

As each company took its place, the officers yelled at the men to lie flat on their stomachs and stay down to avoid exposing themselves. They threw themselves on the ground at regular intervals; on the east and south sides, between twenty and twenty-five feet separated the men. The ammunition boxes were also placed at intervals within the perimeter. Many of the officers and Sergeants limited the fire of their troops, and some, like Godfrey, allowed only the best shots to fire at will. There was little natural cover—no trees, rocks, mounds, or such, just an occasional scraggly sagebrush or prickly pear cactus, along with knee-high grass that was quickly trampled flat. Some men grabbed anything at hand to use as breastworks: saddles, boxes of hardtack, sacks of bacon, bags of forage. None of this offered much protection, but it was better than nothing. There was no time to entrench, and besides, there were only three spades in the entire command.[4]

GODFREY'S TROOPERS HAD MANAGED to dash over the low rim and turn to join the troopers facing north moments before the mass of mounted Indians charged. Several volleys into the attackers' ranks repulsed the initial wave, but as the Indians fell back, they began to occupy every high point around the command. Along the east flank, the warriors made several charges; each one was turned back by furious fire. Sergeant Ryan was on this side, and he carried his own rifle, a Sharps carbine with a telescopic sight. When an accurate Indian sniper quickly took the lives of two troopers and injured another, Ryan, French, and several others jumped up and poured a volley into his location, to the cheers of the surrounding troopers. The bullets seemed to silence the Sioux marksman.[5]

On the south flank, Benteen's H Company occupied slightly higher ground—a tail-like ridge that ran out to a small hill on the edge of the bluffs—and was more vulnerable to enemy fire. Small groups of Indians would sneak up close to the soldier lines and blaze away, using all kinds of tricks to draw their fire. Occasionally, a shower of arrows would arc into the position,[6] though few found warm human targets. The highly visible horses and mules, however, were downed by the dozens. Their carcasses were dragged into place around Dr. Porter's hospital.

As the minutes passed, more lives were lost. Godfrey was standing over his First Sergeant, DeWitt Winney, giving an order, when a bullet went through the noncom. Winney gave a quick jerk, said, "I am hit," and looked up at his commander. Godfrey told him to lie down and be quiet until the attack was over and they could carry him to the hospital. The Sergeant turned, fell onto his elbows, and died.[7]

One trooper at Benteen's position threw himself down behind a box of hardtack, only to be killed instantly when a bullet ripped through the box into his head. "Strange as it may sound here, nearly every man who saw this laughed," wrote Edgerly.[8] Not far away, another man, trumpeter Julius Helmer, took a shot through the bowels. Godfrey told him that they would get him to the doctor as soon as the firing cooled. The eleven-year veteran, in great pain, was quiet for a while but then began to yell and scream as his suffering increased, begging his comrades to kill him and put him out of his agony. Every outburst brought a volley in his direction. Reno and Weir lay a few yards away, and finally Weir said to Helmer, "Don't scream, my man. The noise gives direction to the shooting and may cause the death or wounding of others." Not another sound came from the trumpeter. When the fire cooled somewhat, Godfrey went up to help carry him to the rear, and Helmer's silence was explained by the utter stillness of his body.[9]

As the afternoon stretched on, a pattern emerged. The Indians would pour a heavy fire into the position, their guns emitting a thick ring of smoke surrounding the regiment. Then they would work their nerve up to make a charge, at which time the troopers would pop up and fire, scattering them back to the hills. This went on until sunset and beyond.[10]

By the time darkness descended upon the bluffs and the Indian fire slackened, twelve troopers had been killed and twenty-one more wounded.[11] Only the poor marksmanship of the Indians had prevented more casualties. At the center of the swale, Dr. Porter had his hands full with almost thirty injured troopers, the more able of whom helped him with those in dire need. Porter had erected several fly tents as shelter for the casualties. Every so often a bullet would zip through the canvas.[12]

When the enemy fire stopped, all were still. Then, as the men gradually realized that the Indian fire seemed to be finished for the day, they began to move around freely. Pickets were set out—at some points, three hundred yards beyond the perimeter[13]—and Reno ordered all the companies to dig entrenchments. They had incurred more than thirty casualties in only three hours. If precautions weren't taken, the next day's toll would be even worse—if they managed to survive at all. They had almost no water, and no easy access to it; a limited supply of ammunition; and an inferior defensive position surrounded by thousands of enemy warriors, many of whom bore excellent arms. The odds seemed fearful.

The men started scraping the ground with tin cups and plates, spoons, knives, pieces of hardtack boxes, and anything else hard enough to dig into the heavy clay. Most of the troopers worked on the entrenchments in pairs, or threes and fours, until some rudimentary rifle pits were gouged out of the heavy clay. They also threw more bulky items onto the barricades. By morning every troop except Benteen's had created some kind of rifle pits a foot or so deep, or at least shoveled some dirt in front of where they lay. Benteen had allowed his men to rest instead. He had a feeling the Indians would not be returning.

Night also brought time to reflect on the many exemplary feats of heroism accomplished that afternoon by the enlisted men. There was Sergeant Benjamin Criswell, who had ridden his horse down the bluffs to Benny Hodgson's body before the command had been completely engulfed by warriors. He had picked up the lieutenant's body, taken the ammunition from the saddlebags of several dead horses, and returned to the hill under heavy fire. There was also Corporal Charles Cunningham, who had been shot through the neck but had refused to leave the line. Another trooper, Private Henry Holden, had withstood a storm of bullets to bring ammunition repeatedly to his comrades on the line.

Some of the officers—Varnum, French, Weir, Godfrey, Hare, and Wallace, especially—had also acquitted themselves well. But others had failed to rise to the occasion. Captain Moylan had spent much of the time dug in behind a mule pack, earning him the sobriquet "Aparejo Mickie," after the Spanish word for "pack."[14] Benteen's First Lieutenant, Frank Gibson, had been just as bad. "He did not get up off the ground the whole time the battle was fought," wrote one trooper. "Captain Benteen told the men to charge right over him."[15] Reno had made a round or two of the lines but had spent most of the time in his bedding, in the depression near the makeshift hospital.[16] When Benteen returned from one visit to the Major, he told a Sergeant, "I found him lying in the same place where I saw him before."[17]

Through it all, Benteen had been magnificent. With bullets whistling all around him, he had strolled along the line oblivious to the rain of enemy fire, encouraging the men and helping them gauge firing distances. It had been clear to everyone present who was really in charge, and the men had been content with that. "He took absolute charge of one side of the hill," wrote a trooper years later, "and you may rest assured that he did not bother Reno for permission of any kind."[18]

Varnum had found Reno lying in a rifle pit with Weir—a bit odd, since the two couldn't stand each other, though perhaps their common love for the bottle explained it. The chief of scouts had volunteered to ride north and find Custer if he could find a good man to go with him. Reno had not replied for some time, but then had said he did not want to be without two good shots—besides, they would get killed anyway. When Varnum had continued to press his case, Reno had snapped, "Varnum, you are a very uncomfortable companion." A frustrated Varnum had walked away. Weir had found him afterward and said that Reno would let him send only Indian scouts.

Varnum had then found the few Arikaras who had not lit out for the Powder River depot near the north perimeter.[19] The two Crow scouts Half Yellow Face and White Swan were there, too. They had been among the last of Reno's men in the valley to reach the hill.[20] Both had fought well, despite White Swan's several wounds and a badly mangled right hand.[21] When Varnum talked to the scouts, they agreed to go, but they barely made it beyond the lines before returning. The Sioux were everywhere, they said.[22]

After the digging was done, many of the men fell asleep, a few snoring away as if they were back in their Fort Lincoln barracks. The night had turned cool, and some donned overcoats retrieved from their saddles. Others stretched their legs and walked about the position. A few of the hungrier ones gravitated toward the pack train area. All of the mules were jumbled together, and the supplies were in no order—some had been thrown up as barricades and others used as makeshift protection for the hospital area. The supply Sergeants had quite a time finding food for their companies. As a result, few if any rations were distributed, so any food had to be scrounged up by the soldiers themselves, without regard to whose packs were whose.[23]

Young Private William Taylor went looking for his Sergeant, the German-born Henry Fehler, who at forty was one of the older enlisted men in the command. He finally found him near the herd of horses and pack mules.

"What are we going to do, stay here all night, or try to move away?" asked Taylor.

Major Reno was standing nearby. He turned and said, "I would like to know how the hell we are going to move away." He had finally left his sheltered spot once darkness had descended and now was walking around with a bottle of whiskey, from which he took an occasional sip.[24]

Taylor was surprised but unfazed. "If we are going to remain here we ought to be making some kind of barricade, for the Indians will be at us, the first thing in the morning."

"Yes, Sergeant, that is a good idea," said Reno. "Set all the men you can at work at once."

The Sergeant proceeded to do so, and a crude barricade was erected across the lower end of the depression.[25]

Reno continued to drink during the night. After making a circuit of the lines, he returned to the pack train area sometime before ten to drive out men looking for food and water. He had done this several times already, his devotion to this duty possibly the greater because of the presence there of the keg of whiskey he had brought with him, from which he filled his flask.[26] On this particular occasion, he ran into two of the citizen packers, B. F. Churchill and John Frett, searching for their blankets and something to eat.

"Good evening," said Frett, a former St. Paul policeman and Civil War veteran.

Reno asked, "Are the mules tight?"

Frett, unclear as to whether the Major meant "tight" or "tied," said, "Tight? What do you mean by tight?"

"Tight, God damn you," said Reno, and slapped Frett across the face. As he did so, some whiskey from the flask he held splashed onto the packers. Frett moved to strike Reno, but Churchill held him back. Then Reno picked up a carbine, leveled it at Frett, and said, "I will shoot you."

Churchill grabbed Frett by the shoulders and pulled him away. Neither of them saw Reno again until the next day.[27]

Down in the valley, there was great activity. Large fires could be seen, and the beating of drums, singing, dancing, and occasional scattered rifle fire marked a great celebration that lasted late into the night—a revelry particularly unsettling to the troops on the hill above. Rumors circulated that comrades were being tortured or burned to death. Unknown to the soldiers, some of the wailing they heard was the death songs of relatives mourning for loved ones.[28]

The general belief among the men on the hill was that Custer and his command had been temporarily corralled by the Indians just as they were, or had retreated downriver toward Terry and Gibbon and the Yellowstone. But in the dark, certain occurrences persuaded some of the men, at least briefly, that the General had returned to save them. Large shadows were observed on the hills and ridges to the north (some no doubt thrown by the huge fires in the village), and several soldiers thought they detected the tramping of a large force of mounted men. When the sound of a trumpet was heard, some of the men began to cheer: "Custer is coming at last!" But when Reno ordered a trumpeter to return the call, it was not answered. Eventually, the men realized that some Indian had wrested an instrument from one of Custer's trumpeters and was trying it out.[29]

Later in the evening, clouds appeared overhead, and a slight rain fell. Some of the troopers stretched out pieces of canvas to catch the meager rainfall, which was barely enough to wet a man's lips.

At some point in the night, Reno approached Benteen with a grim proposition. He suggested that they take every man who could ride, destroy everything they could not carry, and make a forced march under cover of darkness to their supply camp on the Yellowstone at the mouth of the Powder River, about 120 miles away.

Benteen asked him what he proposed to do with the wounded.

Reno said, "Oh, we'll have to abandon those that cannot ride."

"No, Reno, you can't do that," said Benteen.[30]

Reno, perhaps realizing that Benteen's support of the plan would be necessary for its implementation, did not push it. But Weir, who had been sharing a rifle pit with Reno most of the evening, walked over to Godfrey's position that night. He had apparently heard of the idea from Reno or Benteen.

He said, "I want to thank you, Godfrey, for saving my troop." He paused, then said, "If there should be a conflict of judgment between Reno and Benteen as to what we should do, whose orders would you obey?"

"Benteen," said Godfrey without hesitation.[31] Apparently relieved, Weir left. The next day, rumors of the plan circulated among the wounded troopers in Dr. Porter's makeshift hospital, causing great consternation among those unable to mount a horse.

AT BENTEEN'S SUGGESTION, just before the first hints of dawn broke in the east, reveille was sounded to present a bold front to the enemy. Before the trumpet's last notes had died away, rifle fire began from all directions, scattered at first, then constant and heavy as the light improved and the Indian lines were reinforced by warriors from the village. As the day wore on and the sun grew hotter, the Indians tried anything to draw the soldiers' fire—including standing up in full view for just a moment, then dropping to a safe place before a volley of rifle fire reached them; raising hats and blouses on sticks; and strapping a dummy atop a horse and directing it to gallop in front of the lines. Such ruses became less successful once the return fire was restricted to the best shots in each company.

As the fighting dragged on, Benteen's company steadily lost men. As they had built no fortifications during the night, they were now exposed to several Indian positions, most seriously the high ridge several hundred yards north of the command. Soon after sunrise, the fire became so fierce that a number of the troopers left the line seeking safety in the hospital area. Some of the troopers were down to four or five cartridges. The men who remained on the line had no choice but to retreat from the advancing Indians, who sang as they rushed forward.

All the while, Benteen was trying to get some sleep, undeterred by a bullet through the heel of his boot that disturbed his slumber for a moment or two. Now informed of the situation, he got to his feet and made his way to the pack train, where he found more than a dozen skulkers avoiding the heavy rifle fire. He ordered them to carry to his position anything they could find as breastworks— sacks of bacon, boxes of hardtack, pack saddles—then turned them over to Gibson, telling him to hold the position at all costs and shoot the first man who left the line. Benteen left to find Reno and ask for reinforcements.

He found the Major still in the pit with Weir. "The Indians are doing their best to cut through my line, and it will be impossible to hold my position much longer," Benteen announced.[32]

Reno at first seemed not to notice the seriousness of the situation, replying that the Indians were pressing him, too, and he couldn't spare a company. But when Benteen told him that if H Company gave way, the entire position might be overrun, meaning the end of them all, Reno directed Captain French to take some of M Company to the south side as reinforcements. Reno himself didn't leave the rifle pit. French's men went, though they weren't happy about it. Why should they have to pay for H Troop's overnight negligence?[33] As they made their way back, Benteen found some more of his men in the pack train area and took them along.

At H Company's position, Gibson had held the line, but barely.

The Indians had approached close enough to throw dirt clods and arrows into the company's ranks, and they seemed to be readying for an attack, singing what were undoubtedly war songs.[34] One had even crept close enough to count coup on a dead soldier but was shot seconds later. Benteen told his men he wanted them to charge down the ravines just beyond their small hill as if their lives depended on it. It was time to turn the tables a bit. He led his men over the edge of the hill and down the gullies, everyone screaming as loud as they could, for almost a hundred yards. The surprised Indians hastily retreated, some of them "somersaulting like acrobats"[35] in their eagerness to escape, before the soldiers double-timed back to their positions.

One trooper was killed in Benteen's surprise maneuver, and his body remained partway down the ravine. Another shot in the action died a few minutes after they resumed their original position.[36]

Benteen was as much of an inspiration on this day as he had been on the previous. He remained on his feet the whole time, walking around the entire position with his shirttail hanging out, ignoring the bullets flying around him, and talking to the weary, thirsty troopers: "Men, this is a groundhog case. It is live or die with us. We must fight it out with them."[37] When Hare asked him if he was trying to draw the Indians' fire, Benteen told him, "If they are going to get you they will get you somewhere else if not here."[38] To another officer he said, "When the bullet is cast to kill me, it'll kill me, that's all."[39] Not only the enlisted men but also the officers were inspired by his confidence.

At one point after the charge, Benteen walked up to Private Charles Windolph, a young German whose former occupation was shoemaker and who was using the name Charles Wrangel at the time, since he had deserted from the infantry four years earlier. The Indian rifle fire had resumed and happened to be particularly fierce at the time. Benteen told the prone Private to stand up. Young Windolph hesitated, since two of his H Company comrades, Julien Jones and Thomas Meador, had only recently been killed beside him. He asked his Captain if it was really necessary that he stand.

"On your feet," ordered Benteen.

Windolph obeyed.

"Look at all those Indians," Benteen said. "If you ever get out of here alive, you will be able to write and tell the Old Folks in Germany how many Indians we had to fight today."[40]

As the onslaught continued, more soldiers went down, among them a Corporal named George Lell, who took a shot in the abdomen. A few other troopers dragged him to the hospital, but he was dying, and he knew it.

"Lift me up, boys," he told his comrades. "I want to see the boys before I go."

They helped him to a sitting position. Lell watched the battle, and the fight the regiment was putting up, and managed a weak smile. Then they lay him down. He died soon after.[41]

One of the citizen packers, Frank Mann, sat at Moylan's position facing the east, apparently aiming a carbine over a three-foot-high barricade. But he had been quiet and motionless for about twenty minutes. A trooper scrambled over to him and discovered he was dead. A bullet through the temple had killed Mann, leaving him frozen in position as if he were sighting his gun.[42]

Noticing that H Company seemed to be the target of many of the sharpshooters, Benteen suspected that the Indians had a ploy in mind. He walked up to find Reno again. He found him sequestered in the same pit on the north side of the line. Standing above him, a smile on his face as the bullets whizzed about him, Benteen told the Major that if steps weren't taken soon, the Indians would overrun the lines. Reno gave no reply.

"You've got to do something here on the north side pretty quick," Benteen said impatiently. "This won't do, you must drive them back."

Reno asked, "Can you see the Indians from there?"

"Yes," answered Benteen.

"If you can see them, give the command to charge."

Benteen walked to the highest position on Reno's side—every Indian seemed to be firing on him—and rallied the troopers in the area. "All ready now, men," he yelled. "Now's the time. Give them hell. Hip, hip, here we go!"

Reno managed to get up and leave his hole just in time to lead the charge.[43] Every man of the four companies on the north side but one (who stayed in his rifle pit crying like a child) jumped up and leaped over the ridge. The large group of Indians a few hundred yards away, who were clearly gathering for an attack, rapidly dispersed as the troopers strode forward, firing steadily. They advanced fifty yards or so before Reno called the command back. It was only fifty yards, but it was enough:[44] the Indians in their front quickly retreated to the hills behind them. Every man in the charge made it back to the lines alive. The trooper who had remained in his pit was shot in the head moments later and died instantly.[45]

This second charge ended about 10:00 a.m.[46] The sun was already beating down pitilessly, and the cries of the wounded men for water increased. Some men sucked on raw potatoes, which seemed to help a bit. Others put pebbles and even the lead from bullets in their mouths in hopes of inducing salivation. At least one trooper's lips were so dry and swollen that they cracked and bled.[47]

About eleven o'clock, Godfrey sent a detail down to the river with canteens to try to secure water, but the men came back empty-handed: the Indians in the brush on the opposite bank were too numerous. There was one other alternative. At the south end of the position, on the west side of the hill Benteen's men occupied, a steep draw crowded with thick underbrush and some scrub trees ran down to the flat at the river, about five hundred yards away. This was the same draw the Indians had crept up and been repulsed from earlier. Benteen called for volunteers, and almost twenty men stepped forward. He detailed a dozen to descend the irregular ravine. The twelve men would climb down and, in smaller groups, run across the thirty feet of exposed space to the river, where they would have to throw themselves down at the water's edge and reach down three feet to fill their canteens and camp kettles. Benteen assigned four of the best shots — Sergeant George Geiger and Privates Henry Mechling, Charles Windolph, and Otto Voit — to stand on the bluff above them and provide covering fire. The riflemen began to shoot, despite exposure to the higher ridge several hundred yards to the north. When the fire from the ridge got too hot, they scrambled over to the south slope of the hill, until the Indians to the south began firing on them, at which point they returned to the north slope. They repeated this maneuver for twenty minutes, until the water party finished their work. Somehow, none of the four was hit.[48] And while a few water containers were punctured, all of the troopers made it back alive, although one, Sergeant Mike Madden, was wounded and his leg broken. He had to lie in the gully partway up the hill for some time until he could be carried to safety. (His leg would be amputated the following day after gangrene set in. Madden so enjoyed the liberal dose of whiskey given to ease his pain that he offered his other leg for more.)[49]

Most of the water was delivered to the hospital, where Porter distributed it to his charges. Several other water parties were sent, and eventually the crisis was averted. But a mystery was born from the mission: someone with the Indians across the river had yelled at the water carriers in good English, "Come on over to this side, you sons of bitches, and we will give it to you! Come on over!" This and other observations would lead Reno, among others, to claim later that there were white men among the Sioux.[50]

By now, most of the Indians surrounding the command had left for the village, leaving only a contingent of warriors guarding the river. A brief resurgence of fire at about two o'clock lasted only a short while. By three o'clock, the firing had ended altogether, though a few groups of warriors remained in the valley, across the river. Later that afternoon, smoke began to rise from the valley floor. The Indians had set fire to the grass, a tactic sometimes used to mask a large movement.

About seven o'clock, most of the besieged Seventh Cavalry stood and watched as an immense cavalcade of people and horses began to move leisurely from the village up the valley, toward the Bighorn Mountains to the south. Men, women, and children were mounted, with travoises carrying equipment, provisions, and the occasional wounded warrior. A number of the women sang—some of the songs celebrating the great victory, others mourning the dead. The horse herd contained at least 20,000 ponies. Several of the soldiers later estimated that there were about 3,000 warriors and at least 7,000 people in all. Godfrey thought the column at least three miles long and three-quarters of a mile wide, and densely packed. The procession continued for several hours before it passed from sight. The warriors remaining across the river, now clearly identified as a flank guard for the village, stayed until nearly dark, then rode after their people.

As the majestic cavalcade made its way south, Reno turned to

Moylan and said, "For God's sake, Moylan, look what we have been standing off."[51] The men on the hill breathed a sigh of relief, and more than one uttered a fervent "Thank God," then they gave the departing Indians a full-throated three cheers.

Some had grave doubts that the Indians were gone for good. After all, Benteen's false "pre" was fresh in some of their minds. Maybe they were short on ammunition and were only moving their village before making one last attack. Maybe it was just a classic Indian ruse on a huge scale—they planned to ambush the command when it moved out. And maybe, just maybe, Custer had met up with Terry and had approached near enough to chase the Indians from the neighborhood.

No one knew for sure. But just in case, Reno decided to relocate the command to a position closer to the river for better access to it. Most of the men were eager to leave the overwhelming stench of the dead men and the fifty dead horse and mule carcasses festering in the hot sun. The move was conducted over the next few hours. New rifle pits were dug and barricades erected. Canteens and camp kettles were filled and the stock watered. Dead comrades were buried. Over the previous twenty-four hours, the regiment had suffered seventy casualties. To make matters worse, their ammunition was dangerously low.[52] The next charge might be the last.

Later that night, just before midnight, Gerard and Billy Jackson came through the lines. About three the next morning, Private Thomas O'Neill, followed closely by Lieutenant DeRudio, called out to the sentries and scampered into the position, to the delight of their comrades. All four had spent the previous thirty-some hours hiding in the timber and brush along the river and had narrowly escaped death several times. DeRudio immediately began regaling his fellow officers with his hair-raising adventures. Benteen and French, neither of them admirers of "Count No-Account," as Benteen labeled him, walked away in disgust. DeRudio said that he had returned to the timber to rescue his troop's colors. Some saw his claim as a weak attempt to explain his decision to hide like a coward instead of engaging the enemy.

The surviving horses and mules were led down to the river to be watered for the first time in thirty hours, then allowed to graze.

When that was finished, company cooks did the best they could to rustle up a meal for the troops. Then pickets were thrown out, and most of the men lay down to sleep. Without the ominous sounds of the celebrating Indian camp, their rest was somewhat easier. "We lay in the trenches with the Sky for a Covering and Slept Soundly until Morning," remembered Private Thomas Coleman.[53] But the mass grave into which they had placed their dead comrades was a grim reminder of the uncertainty of their situation. No one knew what the next day would bring.

SEVENTEEN

The Rescue

And Now comes the most hartrendering tale of all. . . . Oh what a slaughter.

PRIVATE THOMAS COLEMAN

After Custer had led the Seventh Cavalry up the Rosebud on the afternoon of June 22, Captain Grant Marsh cast off and guided the *Far West* up the Yellowstone. On board were General Terry, Colonel Gibbon, Major Brisbin, and some of Terry's staff. On the way upstream, as the paddle steamer churned against the strong current, Gibbon came down with a severe gastrointestinal ailment. By the time the boat reached the confluence of the Bighorn early in the morning of the 24th to begin ferrying the column across the Yellowstone, his condition had deteriorated. He was in great pain and unable to leave his bed. Terry placed Brisbin in command of Gibbon's troops.

For a variety of reasons, most of which reflected poor planning, the ferry operation did not begin until noon. Save for a single infantry company left at a base camp on the north bank, the entire command—four companies of cavalry, five infantry troops, and the artillery detachment—was ferried across the river by 4:00 p.m. With them went mules carrying rations for six days.[1] Clearly, the column was not expected to roam far from its Yellowstone base camp, which would be supplied by wagon trains from Fort Ellis almost two hundred miles to the west.

Terry's column, about four hundred men strong, began to ascend the Bighorn an hour later. Four miles upriver, they turned into the valley of Tullock's Creek, the tributary that ran due south and roughly parallel to the Bighorn. An hour later, they stopped for the day. Terry and Brisbin soon rode into camp; Gibbon remained on the boat, still incapacitated.

Terry expected George Herendeen to arrive at any hour, the frontiersman having specifically been sent with Custer to return with news of developments. There was also the chance that the Indians were camped along the stream. Lieutenant James Bradley's Crow scouts were sent up the valley fifteen or twenty miles to reconnoiter for both Herendeen and the hostiles. They returned around sunset without having seen either, or even any sign of a recent trail.

Terry became anxious.[2] Custer had been on the march almost three full days, and ever since the war, Custer on an enemy's trail had been known to be "like a hound on a rabbit," as one of Gibbon's officers put it.[3]

Terry had told Custer that he would have Gibbon's column at the mouth of the Little Bighorn on the morning of the 26th, and that point was some forty miles away.[4] The next day, the 25th, the command broke camp early and began marching upstream. They had made only two miles before Terry turned the command west, up a dry creek bed that ascended the divide between the valleys. Terry was acting on the counsel of Brisbin and another officer, who were in turn heeding the advice of citizen scout Muggins Taylor, filling in less than adequately for Mitch Boyer and the injured Tom Leforge. Taylor had lived near the frontier for many years, but mostly in small towns. He was not a frontiersman and was not familiar with the country he was now guiding the column through. (Indeed, the next day he would nearly get the command lost. Only the objections of an officer who had been through the area recently prevented it.)[5] The level plateau Taylor believed would be found crossing the divide was nowhere to be seen, and the terrain soon deteriorated into "a labyrinth of bald hills and deep precipitous ravines," in the words of Lieutenant Bradley, "entirely destitute of water. . . . A worse route could not have been chosen."[6] Bradley and his scouts, ranging several miles ahead of the column, had not been consulted on the change in direction. The rough country, combined with the suffocating heat and choking alkaline dust, quickly fatigued both infantrymen and cavalry mounts and made it almost impossible to retain the Gatling gun battalion. When Bradley's Crow scouts were finally reunited with the command, they adjusted the direction of march, but the improvement was minimal, and soon infantrymen began to fall out and collapse, some of them fainting.[7] They staggered into the valley of the Bighorn about 3:00 p.m. and after a two-hour rest marched on. The command stopped for the day at 7:00 p.m., after what Terry's infantry commander, Captain Henry Freeman, later described as "the hardest marching I ever made."[8]

The exhausted foot soldiers could go no farther; they would remain in camp until morning. But Terry had not forgotten his promise to Custer.[9] He asked Brisbin if the cavalry, even now preparing its dinner, could ride on that evening. Brisbin replied that it could. The call to boots and saddles was sounded, then to horse, and on the troopers rode, through a dark night marked by occasional showers and gusty winds. At one point, the Gatling battery was lost, then found a mile or so from the column — but only after repeated trumpet calls were sounded. A company of cavalry also got lost for a while.[10]

After several hours of slow progress, the head of the column found itself perched on the brink of a narrow precipice. On each side lay a deep, black chasm. Somewhere far below, a river roared through a canyon. The tired, wet command came to a screeching halt. The officers sat their mounts for several minutes, at a loss as to what to do. Finally, Bradley suggested to Terry that they call up an old Crow named Little Face, who had roamed the area as a boy a half century earlier and claimed that he knew every foot of it. Little Face was summoned. He said that he could find a way out, and a good campsite, and led off as if it were a bright sunny day. Soon enough he brought them to an inviting valley, where they halted around midnight, unsaddled, and dropped to the ground for a few hours' rest.[11] They had somehow made twelve more miles and were only about a mile and a half from the mouth of the Little Bighorn, which flowed into the Bighorn some forty miles south of the Yellowstone. Whether that satisfied Terry's obligation to Custer or not, it was as close as they could get before dawn.

The next morning, the Crow scouts were sent out. A few hours later, they came upon three of Custer's Crows — White Man Runs Him, Goes Ahead, and Hairy Moccasin — who after leaving Reno's command on the hill had worked their way east and then north of the Sioux encampment. When the three told their tribesmen that a legion of Sioux had defeated all but a small portion of Custer's command, and that those survivors had been surrounded and were still besieged, Bradley's Crows began a series of doleful cries and wailings. The interpreter explained that they were mourning for the dead.

Bradley and his soldiers were willing to accept that something dreadful had happened but thought the Crows were exaggerating. Custer and the Fighting Seventh badly whipped — an entire regiment almost wiped out? It was not possible.

Bradley reported the Crows' story to Terry, two miles on the back trail. The General was now accompanied by a shaky John Gibbon, recently arrived from the *Far West,* which was slowly making its way up the Bighorn over shallow rapids and through dangerous quagmires. Surrounded by several of the other officers, they listened to Bradley's report. Most of the men refused to believe the story, some even accusing the Crows of cowardice in fleeing the field before the battle was over.

As his subalterns argued, Terry sat his horse quietly, biting his lower lip, his eyes fixed on Bradley. Finally, he spoke. "I find it impossible," he said, "to believe that so fine a regiment as the Seventh Cavalry should have met with such a catastrophe."[12] Then he yelled, "Forward!"

The infantry had just come up, and now, following Terry's orders, the entire column continued on. On the horizon to the south rose heavy smoke — evidence of Custer burning the Indian village, it was surmised.

The Crow interpreter and all of the Crow scouts, Custer's and Gibbon's, were last seen galloping north in the direction of their agency a hundred miles away. The excuses provided later for their departure were unconvincing, ranging from worn-out horse hooves and White Man Runs Him's lack of sufficient clothing to a general belief that the fighting was over. As they left, the interpreter explained to Gibbon that the scouts had been out for too long and had "become hard up for women." He assured the colonel that they would be back.[13]

The column pushed over a divide and into the valley of the Little Bighorn along its west bank. About ten miles later, around noon, they crossed the cold waters, the chill more than welcome after so much time spent in the torrid heat.[14] After a rest of a few hours, the troops marched upstream on the Little Bighorn's east side. Up ahead, Bradley and his eleven men began to see Sioux in small groups and large. The column advanced in fighting order. A short while later, an advance troop ran into a "perfect skirmish line of mounted Indians"[15] arrayed across the valley. The Sioux did not move when they saw the troopers. When the troopers spotted, some distance behind the line, three or four hundred more figures, and what appeared to be a troop of cavalry in dark clothes and carrying a guidon, and then another troop, both in cavalry formation, the situation became perplexing.[16] It was only upon closer inspection that their true identity was revealed. They were Indians wearing the garb of cavalrymen—many cavalrymen.

The advance company retreated toward the main column, though the Indians did not pursue. With darkness approaching, Terry decided to bivouac for the evening—a decision not all of his men welcomed. He ordered camp set up in the form of a hollow square. Pickets were set out, and every man slept in his clothes with his rifle beside him. During the long night, the story of the three Crows was reevaluated. Something clearly had gone wrong. By now, most of the infantry officers believed the Crow story, but most of their cavalry counterparts still did not.

With the dawn came the realization that the body of warriors up the valley had disappeared. The command ate breakfast and resumed the march south in battle formation.

A couple of hours later, Gibbon's advance troop rounded a timbered bend of the Little Bighorn and, in a long, mile-wide valley, discovered signs of a large Indian village along the west bank. Now the actions of the Indians seen the previous day were made clear: they were a rear guard protecting the camp while it packed and made off. Most of the grass on the plain had been burned black and still smoldered. On the banks of the stream, a stray horse here and there nibbled at the few patches of green left. Two tepees still stood, each surrounded by a ring of dead horses. Inside each lodge were dead Sioux, five in one and three in the other, dressed in their finest clothes. Scattered robes, pots and pans, cookstoves, kettles, axes, lodgepoles, china dishes, and many more valuables strewn for miles along the river gave evidence of a hastily abandoned camp. When the troopers came across pieces of cavalry equipment—saddles, clothes, the feet of top boots—and then three severed heads of white men, they began to fear the worst.

As the rest of the column came up, they made more gruesome discoveries, including underwear belonging to the Seventh Cavalry's Lieutenant Sturgis, the gloves of Captain Yates, and Lieutenant Porter's buckskin jacket, with a bloody bullet hole under the right shoulder.

The command continued through the village and around a bend of the river. Now they began to find bodies of white men, all severely mutilated and covered with swarms of flies. Then, on the opposite side of the river, upstream a mile or so, they could see many figures standing on a bluff. Several officers trained their field glasses on the hill, trying to ascertain their identity. Some thought they were Sioux scouts.

Bradley and his men had been scouting on the east side of the Little Bighorn, along the low hills that sloped up and away from the river, and now rode up with grim news.

"I have a very sad report to make," he said, his voice quavery with emotion. "I have counted one hundred and ninety-seven bodies lying in the hills."

Someone asked, "White men?"

"Yes," said Bradley. "White men." He added that, though he had never met General Custer, from pictures he had seen, one of the bodies might be his. All along the crest of one hill and around it, on either side for more than a mile, were bodies of white men, stripped naked, most of them hideously mutilated.

It was about then that two horsemen could be seen riding toward them from the south.

When, about nine o'clock in the morning of the 27th, a pillar of dust was spied to the north of Reno and his command, their first thought was that the Indians were returning. That fear was put to rest when two officers with field glasses recognized the distant column as an army command. Whose troops they were—Terry's, Custer's, or Crook's—was still unclear, but there was a sense of relief that help was at last on the way. As the force in the valley slowly approached and it became clear that it was an army column—Crook's, they figured at first—the men on the hill gave cheer after cheer and waved blankets and hats and guidons. Reno sent two Arikaras to investigate. They were followed by Lieutenants Hare and Wallace, who were ordered to make contact with the troops.

The two Seventh Cavalry officers drew up riding bareback, greeting Terry and his men, and pointed out their position on the bluffs upstream.

"Where is Custer?" someone asked them.

"The last we saw of him," said Wallace, "he was going along that high bluff"—he indicated a point downstream from where he had located Reno—"toward the lower end of the village. He took off his hat and waved to us. We do not know where he is now."

His eyes filling with tears, Terry said, "We have found him."[17]

The two doctors with Gibbon's column were ordered ahead to Reno's position to help Dr. Porter with the fifty-four wounded men. When they reached the summit, Varnum recognized one of the surgeons. "Where is Custer?" he asked. "Is he coming with your column?"

The doctor told him what Bradley had reported. Varnum turned away and broke down, recalled the surgeon, "crying like a baby."[18] Many of the men did, too.

No one could believe it. "We were simply dumbfounded," remembered Godfrey.[19] The loss of their comrades was bad enough, but they also had to adjust to the realization that the epic two-day struggle for their lives was much the lesser story. There were few dry eyes on the hill as the news of the fate of Custer's battalion spread. As Gibbon and Terry approached, the men gave several cheers, but when Terry reached the summit and approached the men of the Seventh, his sad face, lined with tears, silenced everyone.

A skeptical Benteen asked Terry where Custer had gone. "To the best of my knowledge and belief," the General said, "he lies on this ridge about four miles below here with all his command killed."

Benteen was still unconvinced. "I can hardly believe it," he replied. "I think he is somewhere down the Big Horn grazing his horses. At the Battle of the Washita he went off and left part of his command, and I think he would do it again."

Terry had heard enough. He said, "I think you are mistaken, and you will take your company and go down where the dead are lying and investigate for yourself."[20] He ordered Lieutenant Bradley to guide Benteen to the battlefield. Then he rode over to the hospital, where he greeted every man there with a reassuring word and a handshake. As he made his way through the camp, almost every officer quietly thanked him.

John Burkman, Custer's devoted striker, was too numb to cry. He had kept busy for much of the siege dragging dead animals to fortify the breastworks around the hospital and tending to some of the live ones. Dandy, Custer's older mount, had been shot in the neck, and Burkman had taken special care of the little horse. Now he walked off a ways and looked out over the valley, talking to himself.

"Custer is dead," he said. "The General is dead." He recalled later that he thought, "Now I won't have to tell him that maybe Dandy's going to die." And he wished more than anything that he could have been along, that he could have been there at the last.[21]

BENTEEN MOUNTED AND RODE DOWNSTREAM, taking Weir, DeRudio, and Nowlan with him. Guided by Bradley,[22] they followed what appeared to be Custer's trail north across the bluffs, down a wide coulee to a ford at the river, up into a rough terrain of ravines and ridges, and then on to the south end of a long, high ridge. The first body they came across, not far from the river, was that of Calhoun's First Sergeant, James Butler. A horse lay nearby. Scattered about Butler's body were several empty cartridges, mute testimony to the spirited fight the man had put up. He had been known as a fine shot. Almost a mile farther to the northeast, at the southern end of a long, high ridge that ran parallel to the river, they found the remains of L Company, with the bodies of Calhoun and Crittenden just a few feet from each other. Calhoun was scalped, but not badly mutilated. The young infantry officer's body was shot full of arrows, including one that had stuck in his glass eye and splintered it.[23] North of them, in a swale on the east side of the ridge, was Myles Keogh. Close around him lay the dead troopers of I Company, including several of his noncom officers.[24] Keogh's body was naked, save for his socks, but otherwise untouched, and some kind of Catholic medal was still around his neck.[25] More corpses led to the far end of the ridge — more than two hundred all told.

Almost all of the bodies were stripped of their clothing, except for the occasional sock — though even in these cases, the names stitched in them had been cut out. Most were scalped and mutilated — heads, hands, feet, and legs cut off and scattered around the field. After two days in the blistering sun, they were swollen; some were discolored, almost black. Many of their legs had received a slash on the right thigh, the Sioux sign for marking their victims.

One of Benteen's troopers motioned him over to a group of bodies. The Captain rode over. On the flat crest at the far end of the ridge lay Custer, naked, leaning in a half-sitting position against two soldiers beneath him. His face wore a peaceful expression — "He looked as natural as if sleeping," remembered one officer[26] — and his body bore two gunshot wounds, one to his left temple and the other near his left breast. His right thigh had received the customary Sioux slash. He had not been scalped, probably because his recently trimmed hair was too short. Under his body and around him were about twenty cartridge shells, at least some of them brass casings from his Remington sporting rifle.[27] An arrow had been stuck into his penis.[28]

Benteen dismounted, walked over, and looked down. "By God, that is him," he said. Then he mounted and rode off.[29]

Surrounding Custer were five of his officers—his brother Tom, Yates, Smith, Reily, and Cooke, his face half torn off, with only one long dundreary left. On the slope below him were about forty troopers, most of them from F Company. Thirty-nine cavalry horses, some obviously shot to form a roughly circular breastwork, lay around them. Dr. Lord was there,[30] and Boston Custer and Autie Reed were found close together about one hundred yards downhill toward the river. Tom Custer's corpse was one of the most severely damaged. His head was smashed flat and scalped, his throat cut, his abdomen sliced open and entrails protruding, his genitals hacked off. Many arrows had been shot into his body; one embedded in his skull could not be pulled out. Only a tattoo on his arm—the initials T.W.C.—enabled him to be identified.

After litters were fashioned, the wounded were all moved down to the camp of the Montana column, near the woods Reno had retreated from two days before. Terry and his staff gave up their tents for the wounded.[31] The rest of the day was spent burying the hacked-up remains of the men who had died in the valley, among them Hodgson, McIntosh, Reynolds, Bloody Knife, Bobtail Bull, and Dorman, who might have been the worst-looking of all. One trooper described Dorman's body as "horribly mutilated; looked as though it went through a hash machine."[32] The soldiers were still interring their friends and destroying their unusable possessions when darkness descended over the valley.

Early the next morning, Terry sent several scouts out to look for any survivors. None were found. Detachments of the Seventh Cavalry marched to the battlefield and resumed burying their dead with the help of a few shovels and spades found in the abandoned village.[33] Benteen and Godfrey rode together, away from the rest of the command.

"Benteen, it's pretty damn bad," said Godfrey.

"What do you mean?" Benteen asked.

"Reno's conduct."

The moonfaced Captain turned in his saddle and faced Godfrey. "God, I could tell you things that would make your hair stand on end."

"What is it? Tell me."

At this moment, another horseman approached them. Benteen jerked his head toward the other rider and said, "I can't tell you now."

Godfrey said, "Will you tell me sometime?"

"Yes," said Benteen. Five years would pass before Benteen revealed to Godfrey how Reno had, on the night of the 25th, proposed abandoning the wounded and making a forced march back to their supply camp.[34]

As the Seventh's officers approached the area, they could see what appeared to be white boulders shining in the bright morning sun.

"What are those?" someone asked.

Godfrey took his field glasses and examined the objects. A moment later, he almost dropped them again. "The dead," he said.

Near him Weir said, "Oh, how white they look! How white!" He turned to Godfrey. "My, that would be a beautiful sentiment for a poem." He said no more, overcome by the thought.[35]

The troops divided up to cover different portions of the field. The dry soil made their digging difficult, and only the officers received anything more than a few shovelfuls of dirt and some sagebrush. "In a great many instances," remembered Sergeant Ryan, "their arms and legs protruded."[36] The stench of decaying bodies and horses was overwhelming, and more than one trooper ran to the river for a drink of fresh water after vomiting, particularly after the skin from one of their comrade's arms slid off.[37]

Twenty-eight dead troopers—most from Lieutenant Algernon "Fresh" Smith's E Company—were found in a deep ravine, halfway down to the river on the battle ridge's western slope. On the sides of the coulee, claw marks revealed a desperate attempt to scramble to safety. Most of the dead had been shot in the back of the head or in the side. They were left in the bottom, their interment consisting of several scoops and chunks of dirt thrown down on them from the edge of the ravine.

The bodies of Custer and his brother Tom were wrapped in canvas and blankets and buried side by side in the same grave, about eighteen inches deep, with a row of stones around the edge—"the best burial on the field," according to Ryan, who was in charge of the interment detail.[38] Each identified officer's grave was marked by his name on a piece of paper in an empty cartridge shell, which was then driven into the top of a stake;[39] the enlisted men were extended no such courtesy. The bodies of three of Custer's officers—Sturgis, Porter, and Harrington—were never identified, though the head of young Sturgis was discovered in the village.[40] And since Porter's buckskin jacket had also been found there, it was assumed that he had been mutilated beyond recognition and buried with the other unidentified troopers. No trace was found of Harrington.

Benteen counted seventy dead horses on the field, only a few of them Indian ponies. Now and then, troopers came upon a badly wounded horse, still alive. These were all destroyed except two. A gray horse near the river, named Nap, followed the command when it returned to the Yellowstone, then disappeared, only to show up at Fort Lincoln some time later.[41] The other was Comanche, Myles Keogh's mount, found wandering around the battlefield, bleeding heavily from seven wounds, three of them severe. Private Gustave Korn assumed care of the claybank gelding.

The Seventh troopers buried 204 men. Despite their best efforts, they missed some of their dead comrades, and over the next fifty years, the remains of several more were discovered on or near the battlefield.

A COMPANY OF THE SECOND CAVALRY was sent south to find where the Indians had gone. The troopers rode toward the Bighorn Mountains for about twelve miles and then found that the trail divided, one camp headed southeast and one southwest. They returned without engaging the hostiles.

Like the fish that got away, the number of Indian warriors the Seventh had faced seemed to grow larger with each telling. The 1,500 to 2,500 braves the regiment initially believed it had fought quickly doubled to 4,000, then became 5,000."[42] Two and a half years later, Benteen would testify that he had come to believe there were between 8,000 and 9,000 warriors, and Wallace would also claim 9,000.[43]

Since their rescue, Reno's subordinates had shared their experiences with their brother officers in Gibbon's column. Soon after arriving, Lieutenant Henry Nowlan had asked Mathey about Reno's conduct, having heard rumors about it from someone else.[44] Criticism of his performance, or lack thereof, was severe and frequent—the word "cowardice" was used[45]—and would continue in that vein for many months, both within the expedition and in the newspapers. The battle might have been over, but a long war of words against Reno had already begun.

Preparations had been made to transport the injured troopers to the *Far West,* which was then at the mouth of the Little Bighorn. Twenty-one men were so severely wounded as to need carrying; the others were able to ride.[46] The command moved out late in the afternoon, eight men to a litter, taking turns in shifts.

As the command made its way upstream, the body of newspaperman Mark Kellogg was found near the river, about three-quarters of a mile away from Custer. Save for a missing scalp and ear, he was untouched, probably dying so far from the main action and so early in the battle that he was forgotten and undiscovered when the mutilation and plunder began.[47]

The uneven ground made progress slow, and hard on the wounded. After dark the march became even more difficult. About midnight the command went into camp, having made only four miles or so. Most of the next day was spent fashioning a better method of carrying the wounded. Horse and mule litters built of lodgepoles were finally devised and worked fine. Early in the morning of the 30th, the steamer was sighted.

The men on the *Far West* already had an idea of the calamity. Three days earlier, about eleven o'clock in the morning of the 27th, the young Crow scout Curly had appeared on the shore near the boat, wearing a red Sioux blanket.[48] After boarding the steamer, he "gave way to the most violent demonstrations of grief."[49] The men around him looked on uncomprehendingly, for there was no interpreter aboard, nor anyone who could speak Crow. Someone thought to give him a pencil, and he dropped flat on the deck and began drawing a crude map—a small circle surrounded by a larger one. Between the two, he began making many small dots and repeating "Sioux! Sioux!" in a voice full of despair. When he had almost filled the space with dots, he began filling in the smaller circle with other dots, saying, "Absaroka! Absaroka!" Captain Grant Marsh had heard another Crow Indian refer to soldiers with that word (although it was much better known as the Crows' name for their people), and when Curly leaped to his feet and began imitating someone getting shot, it gradually became clear to his audience what he meant.[50] One skeptical officer thought to send Curly back to Custer with a dispatch bearing the location of the *Far West*. No amount of persuasion could convince the young Crow, and he refused to leave the boat. It was not until two scouts from Terry rode up in the evening of the next day that the news was confirmed.

Marsh and his crew prepared the vessel for the wounded, clearing space for a hospital and spreading eighteen inches of fresh grass on the deck, then covering that with a tarpaulin to create a massive mattress. A place was found for another passenger in the stern, between the rudders. Comanche was escorted aboard by Korn and several Seventh troopers, who were regarding him with reverence. As Korn led Keogh's mount across the gangplank, tears coursed down his cheeks and he said, "This is all that is left of Custer." The regiment's veterinarian surgeon, who had remained on board, extracted the several bullets and arrowheads and dressed the horse's wounds.[51]

Just after dawn, General Terry asked Marsh to report to his cabin. Terry told Marsh to use all his skill and caution to take the injured men—"the most precious cargo a boat ever carried"—down the several dangerous rivers to Fort Lincoln.

"Every soldier here who is suffering with wounds is the victim of a terrible blunder," Terry concluded. "A sad and terrible blunder."[52]

Marsh gave the order to cast off lines, then began to maneuver down the shallow river, frequently bouncing against the shore or the multitude of small islands and sandbars. For much of its distance, the Bighorn was little wider than a creek. About thirty miles downstream, it coursed into the much larger Yellowstone. There they tied up on the north side of the river, at Gibbon's base camp, to off-load supplies and army scout Muggins Taylor, who would ride west 175 miles to Fort Ellis to spread the news.

Terry and his troops arrived two days later, in the evening of July 2. The job of ferrying them across the river was finished the next morning, and the *Far West* started downriver. The badly injured White Swan was left with his Crow tribesmen, and fourteen of the injured men had recovered sufficiently to remain at the camp, leaving thirty-nine badly wounded troopers aboard. (One Corporal had died the previous night and was buried ashore.) Seven hundred miles away, down the Yellowstone to the Missouri, and down that river, lay Bismarck and Fort Lincoln. Marsh's orders were to reach them in the shortest possible time.

On board, with Captain Edward Smith, Terry's adjutant, was a bagful of letters from members of the expedition and a telegram to General Sheridan. On June 27, Terry had written two telegrams to Chicago in which he had related the results of the battle in factual, nonjudgmental terms. Muggins Taylor had taken them west with him. When Terry arrived at the supply camp on the Yellowstone on July 2, he wrote another telegram to Sheridan. The tone of this report was different. It began: "I think I owe it to myself to put you more fully in possession of the late operations." In the lengthy missive that followed, Terry went to great lengths to point out Custer's negligence and outright insubordination. The former lawyer used skillfully chosen language to suggest a different plan than that actually agreed upon—one in which Gibbon "would be able to cooperate with him [Custer] in attacking any Indians that might be found on that stream." The movements proposed for Gibbon's column "were carried out to the letter," he wrote, "and had the attack been deferred until it was up I cannot doubt that we should have been successful." He went on to list Custer's mistakes: his decision to veer from the proposed route, his refusal to scout Tullock's Creek.

> I do not tell you this to cast any reflection upon Custer. For whatever errors he may have commited [sic] he has paid the penalty and you cannot regret his loss more than I do, but I feel our plan must have been successful had it been carried out, and I desire you to know the facts. . . .
>
> I send in another dispatch a copy of my written orders to Custer, but these were supplemented by the distinct understanding that Gibbon could get to the Little Big Horn before the evening of the 26th.[53]

The age-old process of assigning and evading blame had officially begun.

IV

AFTERMATH

EIGHTEEN

"All the World Has Gone"

Long Hair has never returned,
So his woman is crying, crying.
Looking over here, she cries.
LAKOTA KILL SONG

Another trooper died soon after the *Far West* left the base camp on July 3. The next day, Captain Grant Marsh docked at the supply depot at the mouth of the Powder River—where 150 troopers without mounts, band members, and other Seventh Cavalry members had remained—and the body was taken ashore to be buried. Marsh delivered the news of the disaster—intimations of it had been passed on by Varnum's Arikara scouts, who had already rendezvoused there, per Custer's instructions—and relayed Terry's orders to move the depot to the new camp upstream. At Fort Buford, where the Yellowstone flowed into the broader Missouri, they put off a wounded Arikara scout, Goose, and took on wood. They made one more stop for wood at Fort Stevenson, then continued on a straight run down the Missouri to Bismarck. The boat's flag was lowered to half-mast, and black streamers adorned the pilothouse.[1]

At 11:00 p.m. on July 5, Marsh docked his boat at the Bismarck landing. He had made an astonishing 710 miles in 54 hours—a time never bettered before or since by any steamer anywhere on the Missouri or its tributaries. The paddle wheeler's constant whistle woke the town, and the news of its arrival and of the dark fate of the men of the Seventh quickly spread. Soon Bismarck's citizens were on the streets, and groups of men remained out and about until daylight discussing the disaster.[2]

Clement Lounsberry, the editor of the *Bismarck Tribune,* and a telegraph operator named J. M. Carnahan were quickly found and awakened. Captain Marsh, Dr. Porter, and others from the boat went with them to the telegraph office near the Northern Pacific freight office. The single wire was split at Fargo and was not available until morning; they spent the night sorting out Captain Smith's suitcase full of relevant field messages, newspaper dispatches, and Terry's official reports, which Lounsberry used to write his story. When the wire opened up in the morning, Carnahan began sending as fast as his fingers could tap.[3] Eventually, Lounsberry's article was transmitted — a complete account of 15,000 words, the last message of the day sent by the weary operator twenty-two hours after he had begun.[4] It cost the receiving party, James Gordon Bennett's *New York Herald,* $3,000, but that was a small price to pay for one of the biggest scoops in American newspaper history. (The *Herald* posthumously anointed Mark Kellogg their "special correspondent." Some time later, Bennett sent $2,000 to the dead newspaperman's two daughters.)[5]

Somehow, Lounsberry also found time to compose a story on the battle for his own *Bismarck Tribune.* The single-sheet extra came out the next morning. The oversized single-word headline, followed by ten subheads, read: MASSACRED.

Two hours after midnight, Marsh returned to his boat and cast off for Fort Lincoln, across the river four miles downstream.[6] After he docked there, the wounded and one more trooper who had expired the previous afternoon[7] were helped off and carried on stretchers up the hill to the hospital. Captain Smith walked over to Officers Row to deliver the dispatch and further news of the catastrophe to the post's commanding officer, Captain William McCaskey. The Captain briefed his stunned subordinates and asked the post surgeon, Dr. J. V. D. Middleton, and his adjutant, Lieutenant C. L. Gurley, to accompany him to the Custer quarters next door. It was just before 7:00 a.m.

*   *   *

SINCE THEIR HUSBANDS' DEPARTURE seven weeks earlier, Libbie Custer and the officers' wives at Fort Lincoln had passed the time worrying, supporting one another, and surviving the occasional false alarm of an Indian attack. But when word had come ten days earlier[8] that a large Indian force had checked Crook at the Rosebud and that he had been forced to retreat from the plan of operations, they began to be filled with dread. Arikara scouts had been sent west to Terry with the news, but everyone knew the trip would take a week or more. The women went to great lengths to bolster one another's spirits, gathering at the Custer home on Sunday, June 25, to sing hymns. Then, a few days later, there had been rumors and whispers among the friendly Indians at the fort of a great battle. Foreboding filled the air.

In the early hours of July 6, there was a knock at the back door of the Custer house, then footsteps that awoke Libbie. She put on a dressing gown and met Maria Adams, her housemaid, at her bedroom door. (Maria's sister Mary had accompanied the expedition as the General's cook and had just returned on the *Far West*.)[9] It was Lieutenant Gurley who had knocked, and he asked that Libbie, Maggie Calhoun, and Emma Reed come to the parlor. As Gurley walked down the hall to the front door to let Captain McCaskey and the doctor in, Libbie called out to him, asking the reason for such an early visit. He gave no answer.

In the parlor, the three men waited until all three women had gathered. McCaskey had been left in charge of Fort Lincoln when the Dakota column had left in May. He had served throughout the Civil War and seen action in twenty-eight engagements. He would retire a Major General in 1907, after commanding troops in two of the major battles of the Spanish-American War. But the hardest duty he would ever perform involved these three young women of the Custer family.[10] McCaskey told them the news about the expedition, and they wept with inconsolable grief.

In the slight chill of a Dakota summer's dawn, Libbie asked for a shoulder wrap, then walked outside with the men to help with the painful task of telling the many other widows that their husbands would not return.[11] She felt it her duty. The *Far West*'s whistle had awakened many in the fort, and men, women, and children were now running down to the dock for news of their loved ones.[12]

As McCaskey left the house, an uncomprehending Maggie Calhoun ran after him, crying out. She had lost three brothers, a nephew, and her husband. There was no consolation in the answer to her question: "Is there no message for me?"[13]

THE NEW YORK HERALD correspondent had found William Sherman at the Transcontinental, one of the two large temporary hotels erected near the entrance to the Centennial Exhibition. The sixth of July was a hot day in Philadelphia, and the commanding General of the army sat in an easy chair sans boots and coat, fanning himself by a window.

They were speaking of Custer and the stories that were starting to make their way east from their origin 2,000 miles away in the territories. Sherman had not received official news of a battle, let alone a disaster, and was skeptical.

"It seems almost too terrible to be entirely true," he said. "It must be exaggerated. I cannot believe that Custer and his command would be swept away. I don't think there were enough Indians there to do it like that."

He went on to give the newspaperman the latest official information, which for the most part consisted of Terry's dispatch of June 21, in which he had outlined the plan of action. There had been no word since then—at least nothing through military channels.

There had, Sherman knew, been a few unofficial stories. When Muggins Taylor had headed north to the Yellowstone and then west to civilization, or what passed for it in Montana Territory—Fort Ellis and nearby Bozeman—he had barely eluded Sioux pursuers before chancing on the Far West at the mouth of the Little Bighorn. Taylor had remained on board for three days, until June 30, when he had embarked on a marathon ride west.[14] When he had reached Bozeman on July 3, the story of Custer's defeat—or at least its rough outline—had been relayed to other settlements. That same day in Bozeman, and the next day in Helena, the local papers had issued special editions containing the general facts of the battle. These stories had been quickly telegraphed east, and the Associated Press had subsequently distributed a version to the papers along the eastern seaboard.[15]

The War Department in Washington and Sheridan's headquarters in Chicago had expressed skepticism over the initial reports. Sherman and Sheridan, both in Philadelphia for the Centennial's Fourth of July festivities, had individually dismissed them also.

Now, as Sherman explained to the *Herald* correspondent how an official dispatch would wend its way east from Fort Ellis, there was a knock at the door. It was a telegram from Sheridan at the downtown Continental Hotel, and it read:[16]

> Custer had a fight with Indians and was killed. Terry's detailed report has not been received. I will send you Terry's dispatch which is confidential. Terry with the wounded are at the mouth of the Big horn all right.[17]

There could be no more denying it. Apparently, the story was true.

THE OFFICIAL CONFIRMATION of the disaster hit the Centennial—and the rest of the country—like a thunderbolt. As the young nation celebrated its one hundredth birthday and the many technological advances made during its brief existence, the news that its best-known Indian fighter and 262 of his men, troopers of the glorious "Fighting Seventh," had been annihilated by a small tribe of savages one step away from the Stone Age was greeted with grief, outrage, and even disbelief by some. Not since Lincoln's assassination eleven years earlier had such a shocking story gripped the country.

In the next few days, as more was learned through accounts both official and unofficial, a more detailed picture emerged—clearer, perhaps, but in several ways inaccurate.

Terry's first official report, affixing no blame for the defeat, inexplicably sat on a desk in the Bozeman telegraph office for days, then was finally mailed to Chicago and made public on July 9. His second dispatch, of July 2, which blamed Custer for failing to adhere to Terry's "plan," was received on July 6 by Sherman, who read it and handed it to a courier for delivery to the Secretary of War in Washington. However, the courier happened to be a journalist, and most of the confidential report was quickly reprinted in newspapers throughout the country the next day.[18] Other reports of the battle—official dispatches and personal accounts and letters from officers of the expedition, such as Reno's official report, which included a listing of Custer's fatal mistakes—supported Terry's grand strategy. Custer was quickly painted as the scapegoat—a brave one, but foolish. The consensus was that a rash, glory-hunting Custer, smarting under Grant's opprobrium, had pushed his men and horses on exhausting forced marches—"he marched day and night without rest," reported one newspaper[19]—and attacked the village before Gibbon's column had a chance to reach the site in time to participate in a combined, and planned, strike. The facts of the matter—that the village's exact location was unknown, thus precluding any coordinated attack by two widely separated columns in a virtually uncharted region, and that the actual plan from the start had called for Custer to find and attack an unknown number of Indians, with the Montana column to act as a blocking force, if possible—were lost in the frenzy of lurid headlines splashed across the nation's newspapers. Prebattle reports and stories that discussed the selection of Custer's regiment as the attacking force gave way to the army's new company line.

The general opinion among army officers echoed the newspapers: Custer had been "rashly imprudent," and his defeat brought about by "foolish pride."[20] Sheridan issued a near-noncommittal public statement in which he termed the loss of Custer and his men "an unnecessary sacrifice, due to misapprehension and a superabundance of courage."[21] He initially accepted Terry's version of events, writing Sherman on July 7 that "Terry's column was sufficiently strong to have handled the Indians, if Custer had waited for the junction."[22] (Both men would later alter their opinions and temper their remarks after learning more of the facts.)[23] President Grant gave no official response to the disaster and would not speak publicly of it until two months later, but when he did, he blamed Custer for the debacle. In a newspaper interview, Grant concluded, "I regard Custer's massacre as a sacrifice of troops, brought on by Custer himself, that was wholly unnecessary—wholly unnecessary"[24]—an uncharitable and unsurprising utterance, given his treatment of Custer in May. Grant also mentioned that Custer had marched his weary men eighty-three miles in twenty-four hours, a grievous exaggeration, but one that would only contribute to the perception of Custer's rashness and glory seeking.

The truth was, as it often is, more complicated. Custer's marches, except those of the final night and morning, were hard but not severe. When he was fifteen miles from the battlefield, he originally planned to rest his force an entire day while reconnoitering the village. But once the column's presence was detected by the Indians, Custer saw no choice but to attack immediately—a decision that any aggressive cavalry commander would have made given the circumstances. And Terry's ill-advised march, away from Tullock's Creek across the divide's rough terrain, had been a disastrous choice. By the time his infantrymen had reached the valley of the Little Bighorn, they were exhausted and late. These and many other embarrassing facts—including Gibbon's unforgivable failure to keep tabs on the large Sioux village despite its sighting on two separate occasions by Lieutenant Bradley and his Crow scouts—were deliberately ignored in Terry's official reports, a tactic shared by his staff; Benteen, Reno, and other officers of the Seventh Cavalry; and the army's top brass. The natural human tendency to avoid blame after a mistake—developed to an especially fine point in the military—combined with other factors to obscure the truth. The complexities of the campaign were subsumed under a simpler message: blame the dead Custer, whose reputation for sudden charges conveniently dovetailed with the official story. (Terry made clear his feelings two months after the battle, while still in camp at the mouth of the Powder River. He showed a correspondent a copy of his orders to Custer and the accompanying maps and said, "General Custer arrived ahead of time. If he had lived he would, necessarily, have gone before a court-martial.")[25] To be sure, Custer had made mistakes on June 25. For example, his early division of the regiment into four widely separated bodies before accurately assessing the enemy's numbers, location, and disposition allowed the Indians to defeat him one contingent at a time. But these errors were not, ironically, those he was accused of.

Not every newspaper toed the line. A few questioned the quickness with which Terry blamed Custer.[26] The antiadministration *New York Herald*, which had led the way in reporting government scandals, wasted no time in lambasting the Grant administration and the scandal-ridden Bureau of Indian Affairs. The same day that the paper splashed the news of the tragedy across the front page, an editorial inside proclaimed: "It would hardly be too severe to say to President Grant, 'Behold your hands! They are red with the blood of Custer and his brave three hundred.'"[27] Nine days later, the paper asked, "Who Slew Custer?" and then provided the answer: "The celebrated peace policy of General Grant, which feeds, clothes and takes care of their noncombatant force while the men are killing our troops—that is what killed Custer. . . . That nest of thieves, the Indian Bureau, with its thieving agents and favorites as Indian traders, and its mock humanity and pretence of piety—that is what killed Custer."[28] Several other papers, many of them southern or western, followed the *Herald*'s lead. Later the army would attempt to blame the loss on inaccurate reports from the Indian agents, who benefited from underestimating their charges' defections. But the army knew full well that every spring saw an exodus of agency Indians to their free-roaming brethren to hunt and socialize, so that argument held little water. It was not the size of the hostile camp but the scattering of the bands that the top brass had been worried about.

Even the Seventh's commanding officer joined in the chorus, with coruscating ferocity. A week after the news reached the East, a St. Louis reporter interviewed Colonel Samuel Sturgis, the father of young James, who had died with Custer. The grieving Sturgis delivered a bitter diatribe against his second in command, accusing Custer of deliberately sacrificing young lieutenants first, since he preferred to keep the older officers as a guard for himself. He declared that Custer was no Indian fighter, contradicting a statement he had made years earlier that "there is perhaps, no other officer of equal rank on this line who has worked more faithfully against the Indians, or who has acquired the same degree of knowledge of the country and the Indian character."[29]

"He was guilty of disobedience and of sacrificing good men's lives to win notoriety for himself," the Colonel added. "If a monument is to be erected to Gen. Custer, for God's sake let them hide it in some dark valley, or veil it, or put it anywhere where the bleeding hearts of the widows, orphans, fathers and mothers of the men so uselessly sacrificed to Custer's ambition can never be wrung by the sight of it."[30] After his words saw print, Sturgis claimed in a letter to the editor that his strong language was "the result of an unfortunate misunderstanding," but then went on to criticize Custer once again.[31] He would never forgive Custer for his son's death.

SHORTLY AFTER THE BATTLE, the Seventh Cavalry and the combined Montana-Dakota column went into camp on the Yellowstone at the mouth of the Bighorn. While they awaited supplies and reinforcements, one of the Seventh's noncommissioned officers began a petition addressed to the President and the "Honorable Representatives of the United States" calling for Reno's promotion to Lieutenant Colonel of the regiment and Benteen's to Major. By the book, such promotions were strictly by seniority, but the petition noted that these officers had "by their bravery, coolness and decision . . . saved the lives of every man now living of the 7th Cavalry who participated in the battle." Two hundred and thirty-six signatures were affixed to it—about 80 percent of the battle's survivors—and the letter was sent downriver by the next steamboat on July 16. General Sherman denied the request in Washington a few weeks later, pointing out that the proper promotions had already been made by the President and approved by the Senate.[32]

Reno also wrote a letter on July 4, one to Sheridan that skipped regular military channels. In it he managed the neat job of castigating two of his superior officers on the expedition. "I think Custer was deceived as to the number of Indians and that he did not give consideration to the plan of campaign that the subject demands. He went in hastily and with one of his usual hurrahs . . . but after all, the expedition would not have been a failure had Gibbon used then the cavalry force at his disposal. . . . The truth is he was scared. . . . I have said this in my official report but I tell you it is true that he was stampeded beyond any thing you ever heard of." After more criticism of Gibbon, he returned to the subject of his commanding officer: "I think Custer was whipped because he was rash."

He also brought up the issue of "hard marching." "He runs his command down and attacked with tired and exhausted horses and men," he said of Custer, "a very large and strong village of Indians. . . . However strong as they were, I believe the 7th Cavalry would have whipped them properly handled—if I could stand them off with half the Regt. should not the whole whip them." There seemed little doubt whom he had in mind to handle the regiment properly.[33]

Reno's criticism bespoke a convenient disingenuousness or forget-fulness. In the middle of June 1870, Reno led four companies of cav-alry 60 miles in 20 hours after Indians in Nebraska and Kansas, from midnight until late evening of the following day. (He caught nary a one, though it must be added that he had no experienced guides.) He bragged about it in his report, writing that "the endurance of horse & man was put to the utmost."[34] From 5:00 a.m. in the morning of June 24 to about 3:00 p.m. the next day—about 34 hours—Custer led his regiment about the same distance. His troopers and mounts were certainly tired by the time they went into battle, but no more so than many another cavalry command's on an enemy's trail. Indeed, just a few months before, in early March, Crook's column had marched 54 miles in 24 hours in much more severe conditions—with temperatures of twenty-six degrees below zero and his men allowed only two blankets each. Three weeks after Custer's defeat, Lieuten-ant Colonel Wesley Merritt marched his Fifth Cavalry 85 miles in 31 hours to intercept Cheyennes heading northwest from Red Cloud Agency. In 1879 he would lead his command 170 miles in 66 hours.[35] Hard marching was to be expected occasionally when maneuvering against the enemy.

The military establishment did not object to Reno's excoriation of Custer; it had its own reasons for casting blame on a dead man. The calamitous results of the campaign—the lauded forces of two of the country's top Indian fighters checked or defeated within the space of eight days, leaving Crook and Terry paralyzed for a month or more while they awaited orders and reinforcements—could prove highly detrimental to the army. Every year the military's appropriations bill faced intense debate before it was approved, often after heavy budget cutting. Six days before the battle, the Democratic House had voted for a significant reduction in the army's numbers and budget. A nation still recovering from the grievous losses of the Civil War was not persuaded of the necessity of a standing army of any size. Any further light cast on the army's dirty linen—particularly its disastrous management at the highest levels of the recent campaign—could mean even more severe cuts. Far better to blame as much as possible a single man, a lightning-rod officer such as Custer, notorious for his "attack first" reputation. The army's precarious position was indicated by the fact that there was no move to hold a formal, internal inquiry into the reasons for the disaster, despite there having been such investigations following the Fetterman affair a decade earlier.

The plan worked: within a week of the news of Custer's defeat, despite opposition from some of the southern states, a new appropriations bill was approved that called for the addition of 2,500 soldiers and the construction of the two forts in Indian country Sheridan had been lobbying for since 1873. The military was given full control of the agencies, and an embargo on arms and ammunition sales to the Indians was immediately instituted. The ponies and guns of all Indians returning to their agencies were confiscated—and just for good measure, so were those of their reservation brethren. Conditions on the agencies deteriorated, and many formerly peaceful Sioux left to join their free-roaming friends before they lost their horses and arms. An Indian appropriations bill in mid-August tied the delivery of any further supplies to the agencies to several draconian conditions. These terms were presented without debate to a group of chiefs at Red Cloud Agency early in September. The agreement stripped the Sioux of a large chunk of their reservation, including the coveted Black Hills, and the unceded lands to the west. With legal backing for virtually anything it desired, the army proceeded to round up the "trespassing" Indians, many of whom were already straggling into the agencies to surrender. By the end of May 1877, only Sitting Bull would remain at large, in the British possessions to the north, the Great Mother's land.

DESPITE THE HARSH CRITICISM, there was also some outpouring of affection for Custer, as well as outrage at his manner of death. In certain ways, the charge of rashness seemed, if anything, to endear

Custer all the more to a public battered by scandals and starved for heroes. Volunteer troops throughout the country, many of them Civil War veterans on both sides, offered to organize and march against the Indians at a moment's notice. The U.S. Marines volunteered to send 800 to 1,000 men, almost half of their personnel, to join the forces in the West.[36] But the congressional appropriations bill obviated any need for militia groups. "Custer Avengers" joined the cavalry in impressive numbers and were quickly shipped west to join the fighting—some of them without arms until arriving at the main camp on the Yellowstone.[37] The stage was set for a major campaign that, in theory, would end the Indian problem once and for all. Whereas only a small-town stringer had accompanied Terry's column in May, reporters now flocked to be in on the kill. But there was little fighting to be had.

Terry's command remained at the base camp on the Yellowstone awaiting reinforcements, supplies, and orders until the end of the month, when they moved downstream to the mouth of the Rosebud. There they found a trader's store and made good use of it. Reno's heavy drinking apparently increased: in a twenty-two-day period beginning August 1, he bought an eye-opening seven gallons and two demijohns (four more gallons) of whiskey. No other Seventh officer came close, not even Lieutenant French, another heavy drinker, who purchased a gallon of whiskey and two quarts of brandy during the same period.[38] (French had found other ways to forget his problems. While on the Yellowstone, he had taken an overdose of opium that he had stolen from the farrier and had fallen down in front of Hare's tent and turned blue. Hare and his tentmate had thought he was dead, but he had recovered.)[39] The Major became more unpleasant as he drank. One fresh young Lieutenant described Reno charitably as "most unlovable" and remembered that Reno publicly ridiculed him because he did not drink.[40] Other officers of the Seventh who had survived the battle, including some who had petitioned for his promotion, grew unhappy with Reno for another reason: in his official report, he mentioned only one man, Benteen, and recommended not a single officer for a brevet.[41]

Benteen also indulged in the bottle. One day he called Sergeant Charles Windolph to his tent. He commanded Windolph to tell the other officers that they were all a pack of cowards, with the exception of Captain French. He then ordered Windolph to load his gun and shoot anyone who approached Benteen's tent.[42] (Windolph relayed the message, though no one was shot.) And after Thomas Weir rendered an opinion on the conduct of Reno and Custer during the battle, Benteen told Weir he was a damned liar. Weir said that meant blood. Benteen had been born and raised in Virginia, though he had fought gloriously for the North. Now the southerner, ill with dysentery, challenged Weir to a duel.

"Well, there are two pistols in my holsters on saddle, take your choice of them," Benteen said. "They are both loaded, and we will spill the blood right here!"

Weir declined, and the surrounding crowd of officers left, Weir with them. The challenge was a direct violation of the Articles of War and merited dismissal from the army. The next time they met, Weir graciously offered his hand to Benteen.[43]

Reno and Benteen were not the only ones drinking more than usual. There didn't seem to be much else to do, since there were no hostile Indians in the neighborhood and the biggest excitement in camp was the baseball games between the officers and the daily horse races, sometimes three a day, held on a course set up behind the cantonment.[44] E. A. Garlington, a newly commissioned Seventh Cavalry Lieutenant, remembered that three of the regiment's officers in succession reported for duty as officer of the day under the influence of liquor, only to be sent to their tents under arrest. And at one point during the summer, a court-martial was convened, with Captain Weir appointed President of the court. The session was held under a cottonwood tree, the members sitting on roots or stumps. Weir kept a two-gallon demijohn of whiskey between his knees and drank from it at regular intervals.

But Reno and his conduct during the battle were the center of discussion. Garlington noticed that "there seemed to be a suppressed feeling, at least among a portion of the officers of the 7th Cavalry, that Major Reno had not met the trying emergency suddenly thrust upon him with the most heroic spirit."[45] That opinion was echoed and given broader public exposure by Custer's former battlefield foe and longtime friend, Thomas Rosser, who wrote a letter published in the *St. Paul Pioneer Press and Tribune* that was reprinted three days later in the *New York Herald*. The Minnesota paper had blamed Custer for the debacle, citing his "reckless indiscretion"; Rosser rode to his friend's defense, referring to Terry's orders, then charged that Reno "took refuge in the hills, and abandoned Custer and his gallant comrades to their fate." He also mentioned Custer's military need to "strike them wherever he found them."[46]

Rosser's accusation did not reach the Seventh Cavalry, encamped on the Yellowstone, until late July. An annoyed Reno wrote a well-crafted reply that was published in the *Herald* on August 8. He defended his actions, pointing to the ten-to-one odds against his battalion—"overwhelming numbers" that forced him to retreat to a more defensible position.[47]

Another letter from Rosser was published two weeks later. Though Reno did not reply, the debate by that time had gained a momentum that would in time prove unstoppable. Over the next couple of years, it would be brought to a boil primarily by the efforts of two writers, one an Irishman, the other English-born.

The Irishman was a big, well-traveled man named James J. O'Kelly, correspondent for the *New York Herald,* who arrived at the expedition's new encampment on the Yellowstone on August 1 along with some Seventh Cavalry recruits. O'Kelly was no pasty-faced scribe. He had already fought as a soldier of fortune on three continents, both in the French foreign legion and the French army. Captured while fighting for Maximilian in Mexico, he had escaped, crossed the Rio Grande into Texas in a dugout canoe, and made his way back to Ireland. A few years later, he had arrived in New York and accepted a job with the *Herald*. After a thrilling adventure in Cuba, where he had barely avoided being shot as a spy, he had been assigned to cover the Sioux War.[48] The engaging veteran had little problem gaining the confidence of military men.

The day after his arrival, August 2, O'Kelly interviewed Terry about the new campaign—the reinforced expedition was to move up the Rosebud and join with Crook before pursuing the Indians—then talked to Reno. The newspaperman's initial assessment was favorable. "Colonel Reno is of middle stature," he wrote, "very strongly built, has a swarthy complexion and dark eyes, combined with a certain rapid action and frankness of manner which makes a favorable impression." He reported the Major's annoyance "at the unfair criticism passed on the surviving officers of the Seventh by the people who knew nothing of the battle," meaning Rosser's letter, though the only officer Rosser had criticized was Reno.[49]

But after spending several weeks with the men of the Seventh Cavalry and other commands[50]—the staff officers of Terry, Gibbon, and Nelson Miles, who had arrived with six companies of the Fifth Infantry—and listening to their candid off-the-record admissions, O'Kelly's opinion changed. The talk around the campfires—and there was a lot of it—dwelled largely on the battle and the performance therein of the Seventh Cavalry and its officers. On September 21, a lengthy opinion piece by O'Kelly appeared in the *Herald*. In no uncertain terms, and in language surprisingly direct, he wrote:

> No confidence can be placed in the official report of the battle of the 25th of June. It is full of inaccuracies, and has been read with something approaching astonishment by the men who took part in the fight. . . .
>
> If the public want to know the whole truth about the Custer Massacre, there must be a full and searching investigation where the witnesses will have to answer on their oath. If such investigation should be held, startling revelations may be looked for. . . . Your correspondent has gleaned some important facts which must compel further investigations, but the officers of the regiment will give no further information unless they are compelled to do so.

O'Kelly went on to speak of the officers who had clammed up and why: "Men there were who could tell the truth, but they were soldiers; it was their duty to be silent. . . . They were loyal to their regiment; there was a secret and they felt themselves bound in honor to be silent. It was also their interest." He also spoke of a less honorable reason for their silence: self-preservation. According to O'Kelly, some lieutenants were afraid of losing their commissions if they spoke the truth.

"There is buried with the dead a terrible secret," claimed O'Kelly, "but the witnesses still live, and the government can learn the whole truth if the government wants to know it."

The article was more than a vilification filled with flimsy conjecture. It thoroughly questioned the officially accepted version—Reno's primarily—of what had happened in the valley and of the command's inaction on the bluffs while the sound of heavy firing was distinctly audible. O'Kelly had also ferreted out the true nature of Weir's advance north—that it had not been ordered in that direction as Reno had claimed in his report. "What were seven companies of cavalry doing gathered upon a hill when four miles away their comrades were fighting desperately for their lives?" For good measure, he questioned Benteen's failure to hasten his command to the scene of the battle.[51]

O'Kelly's accusations seemed at the time to have little effect on public opinion and none on the government. But this story, and others appearing here and there (such as a packer's claim that Reno, "from the effects of liquor, was unable to direct his command"),[52] sowed the seeds of a public outcry for the truth.

THOUGH TERRY HAD MADE little effort to track the Indians, the last communication from Crook indicated that they had moved south toward the Bighorn Mountains. The reinforced command, now known as the Yellowstone column, moved up the Rosebud Valley on August 8 with thirty-five days' rations and forage. Two days later, they met up with the Wyoming column, which had only recently ventured away from its extended idyll at Cloud Creek Camp after being reinforced itself. The force was guided by William F. "Buffalo Bill" Cody, Crook's lead scout, who had left the stages of the East and his popular show "Buffalo Bill's Own" to join Crook's expedition back in June, before the battle.[53] He had guided one element of that command, the Fifth Cavalry, seven years earlier in their successful campaign against Tall Bull and his Cheyenne Dog Soldiers, and now he felt an obligation to rejoin his comrades[54]—and perhaps polish his reputation for frontier derring-do.

The combined force—now an unwieldy mass of more than 4,000 men—headed east and continued its pursuit of the hostiles through

August, slogging through heavy rain and mud to the Tongue and Powder rivers. Crook, chafing under Terry's control, broke away near the end of the month—decamping early one morning without even informing his superior—and headed farther east after the Indians who had embarrassed him on the Rosebud. Confident that he could overtake them in a matter of days, he left his supply wagons behind—along with his Shoshone and Crow allies, who went home fed up with the white man's way of fighting and eager to draw their forthcoming annuities. Only a few half-breed scouts, Frank Grouard among them, remained to guide the Wyoming column. In the interest of mobility, a mere two days' supply of food was taken.[55]

Crook's pursuit degenerated into a grueling trek dubbed the "Starvation March" after his men were forced to shoot and eat scores of their played-out horses and abandon hundreds of others.[56] The 2,000 wet, hungry, chilled, and altogether miserable troopers turned south on September 5. Three days later, at Slim Buttes in Dakota Territory, a 155-man detachment of cavalry sent ahead to find food discovered a small camp of about forty lodges of Minneconjous led by American Horse.[57] A dawn attack the next day secured the village, but hundreds of warriors from other camps in the vicinity, including Crazy Horse's, rushed to the scene to provide support. When Crook and his main force came up in midmorning, the two sides exchanged fire but did little damage. The Indians fell back before dark. After four hundred miles of hard marching and many days with only horsemeat to eat, neither the exhausted and dispirited soldiers nor their commander had the stomach for a major battle—or the rations for the pursuit that might follow. Crook made little effort to attack these several hundred Indians, who were clearly among those who had annihilated Custer.

The next day, the column headed south, away from the Sioux they had hunted for six months; the warriors harassed them as they marched away. The only material goods that came of the encounter were the herd of 200 Indian ponies and the 5,000 pounds of dried meat in the camp, enough to stave off starvation for a while. (Also found was a pair of gauntlets marked with the name of Captain Myles Keogh of the Seventh Cavalry, along with his I Company guidon.)[58] A few days later, Crook's men staggered into Custer City, a Black Hills mining settlement named after the late General. They were in no condition for anything much more strenuous than recuperation for some time afterward, thus effectively ending Crook's campaign. Aside from the capture of the small Minneconjou village, it had been a fruitless effort, a lumbering pursuit of a will-o'-the-wisp. One newspaperman attributed the "utter failure of the campaign" and the "humiliation of defeat . . . to the fact that the several commanders knew nothing of the work to be accomplished or the character to be traversed."[59]

Terry's column fared no better. On September 5, after weeks of marching about the country north and south of the Yellowstone near the Tongue without finding the Indians, he ordered his units back to their posts, with the Seventh Cavalry ordered to scout along the northern bank of the Yellowstone and then the Missouri on their way home. This was in response to reports of a large force of Sioux in the area—who were later found to have crossed the Missouri several days earlier on their way to Canada. Weir summed it up well: "As the Sioux have failed to find us, we are going home."[60]

The sense of anticlimax in the Seventh was palpable. When the regiment reached Fort Buford on the Missouri, Reno and his adjutant and quartermaster took advantage of a steamer heading downriver to leave the regiment and return to Fort Lincoln early. Weir, as senior Captain, was now in command, since Benteen had departed earlier in the month for recruiting duty in New York. Weir's excessive drinking—exacerbated by the trauma of the Little Bighorn—caused his physical condition to deteriorate significantly. Reno had confined him to his tent at one point, but hopes for an extended period of sobriety had been dashed when a kindhearted herder had smuggled him some alcohol.[61] Another officer described Weir as "terribly used up with liquor."[62] After the regiment reached Fort Stevenson, Weir got so drunk that he wandered off and was found later that night in a water hole. At the head of the command the next morning, remembered Garlington, "he presented a sorry spectacle; his clothes were all wet and wrinkled. . . . He always carried his shoulders very high, but this morning his head seemed to be buried in them." Even Weir's handsome black horse seemed humiliated.[63] Soon after the regiment's return to Lincoln, Weir left for New York, switching places with Benteen, who had experienced a change of heart and wrangled a release from the assignment.[64]

About noon on September 26, 131 days after leaving their station, the trail-weary Seventh reached Bismarck. Turning out to meet the regiment were quite a few saloonkeepers, bullwhackers, and gamblers.[65] "Tears came unbidden to many an eye," noted the *Bismarck Tribune,* "for Custer, the brave Custer, his noble brothers and fellows, were not there. . . . A few familiar faces were recognized, but those with whom Bismarck people were best acquainted lie in the trenches of the Little Horn."[66] At Fort Lincoln, no band greeted them with "Garry-Owen" or "The Girl I Left Behind Me." Instead, the doorways and windows of the officers' quarters—most of which had been vacated by the widows and orphans of the regiment—had been painted black in mourning.[67]

That evening, after bathing and donning a change of clothes for the first time in more than four months, quite a few cavalry and infantry officers gathered at the officers' club room for dinner and relaxation. After a goodly number of drinks had been downed, the talk turned to the battle. When an infantry lieutenant voiced his support of Rosser's criticism, Reno took offense. The two officers soon came to blows, rolling in the slop, spittle, and spilled liquor on the floor. When Reno tried to throw the lieutenant out of the room, Charles Varnum moved to break it up. Reno switched his fury to his subaltern.

"If you intervene, Mr. Varnum," said the Major, "I will make it a personal matter with you."

Weir stepped in to mediate this second altercation. He persuaded Varnum to extend his hand, but Reno would have none of it. "Don't you touch my hand," he said, and challenged Varnum to a duel. When a newly assigned lieutenant intervened, Reno pushed him away and shouted, "Who the hell are you?"[68]

The fracas was finally smoothed over, but with Reno's unfortunate talent for alienating acquaintances, it was inevitable that the kind of talk O'Kelly had only heard whispered back at the Yellowstone would grow louder behind the closed doors of the Seventh's own post officers' club room.[69]

*　　*　　*

THE INDIAN NATION that had turned back Crook and defeated Custer would never again approach that military high-water mark. "Custer's Last Stand" was theirs also.

In the wake of that battle, the name of Sitting Bull became synonymous with the hostile Sioux tribes. Whereas previously he had been "recognized as chief of all the wild Indian bands,"[70] now he was the military mastermind behind Indian victories whose "Napoleonic tactics and strategy" were trumpeted.[71] A public unable to believe that an unlettered aborigine had defeated the cream of the nation's military was inundated with sensational, often wildly inaccurate stories based on distorted dispatches from the frontier. The hostiles, it was claimed, had been advised by white frontiersmen or unrepentant Confederates, possibly reinforced by a horde of half-breeds. A persistent rumor claimed that Sitting Bull was really "Bison" McLean, a peculiarly hirsute graduate of West Point, where he had honed his military genius—and his resentment, after being denied his diploma for ungentlemanly conduct.[72] Though the Hunkpapa spiritual leader dominated the news, Crazy Horse, too, gained infamy. The Oglala leader had previously been almost unknown to the American public, since he never attended treaty talks or drew agency rations. Now his name began to appear more frequently as a principal Sioux leader and war chief.

A few days after the battle, having marched several miles south toward the Bighorn Mountains, the massive village had splintered into two main groups. The Hunkpapas of Sitting Bull, Crow King, and Gall, with some Minneconjous and Sans Arcs, rode east toward the Powder River and then north. Crazy Horse led his band of Oglalas and others northeast into the Powder River country,[73] then south toward the Black Hills.

For the rest of the summer, after the army reinforced, resupplied, and regrouped, the Sioux and Cheyennes led the forces on a wild-goose chase. But the constant movement took its toll. By the spring of 1877, it was clear that the continued existence of any nontreaty band off the reservation would entail a life of constant movement and serious food supply problems. The eternal vigilance and pressure to remain one step ahead of the *wasichus* provided no time to hunt and stockpile the meat necessary for their usual six months of hibernation. The days of the tranquil winter camp were gone. Non-treaty Indians would not be left in peace again.

AFTER DISBANDING HIS FORCES, Terry left Nelson Miles and his Fifth Infantry, reinforced by some troops of the Twenty-second Infantry, to winter on the Yellowstone, in a cantonment at the mouth of the Tongue River. Miles was a commander in the Custer mold: energetic (altogether too energetic, complained some of his own officers), resourceful, and aggressive. "If you hear of a fight, look out for Miles," wrote one correspondent.[74] He had done good work during the Red River War two years before, rounding up the recalcitrant Indians of the southern plains, though he had chafed at having to serve under officers whom he considered his inferiors. Now, given a virtual free hand, he took full advantage. His troopers skirmished with Sitting Bull's warriors a few times in mid-October and parleyed with the Hunkpapa leader twice. Sitting Bull refused to give in, but when it became clear that the well-supplied soldiers were determined to remain in the Indians' country and pursue them, other chiefs representing several hundred lodges, most of them Minneconjous and Sans Arcs, surrendered and were escorted in to their agencies.

Miles continued to send out well-outfitted expeditions throughout the winter, north into the country south of Fort Peck between the Yellowstone and the Missouri after Sitting Bull, and southwest after the Oglalas and Cheyennes under Crazy Horse, Two Moon, and others. His forces skirmished frequently with these Indians and kept them on the run. In early January, several hundred of them surrendered after a brief engagement with a force of about 350 soldiers under Miles, and in the early spring, two more bands numbering about 1,000 came in.[75]

During the retreat from Miles, Crazy Horse's people left behind many of their belongings, and the bitter cold and lack of provisions caused much suffering among them. There was little game to be found, and not enough grass or cottonwood bark for the ponies, many of which died and were eaten. There was talk of surrender. The failure to defeat the soldiers had crushed the Indians' confidence, and the hard winter had weakened them both physically and spiritually.

The *wasichus* had shown that they would continue to pursue and attack the Indians wherever they might hide. When news of the sale of the Black Hills and the unceded country to the west reached their camp, their spirits were further dampened. Sitting Bull and his bands found Crazy Horse's people in mid-January and brought with them a mule train of much-needed ammunition. The large village remained together on the Tongue River for about two weeks, then split again. Sitting Bull headed north, while Crazy Horse moved west into the valley of the Little Bighorn in search of buffalo.[76]

As the harsh winter continued, Crazy Horse began acting oddly — even more so than usual. "He was always a queer man, but that winter he was queerer than ever," remembered Black Elk, his cousin.[77] He spent most of his time out away from the village. "I am making plans for the good of my people," he told another relative.[78] But there was nothing he could do — or rather, only one thing. On May 6, 1877, after some negotiating over terms, Crazy Horse bowed to the inevitable and brought 889 Oglalas into Camp Robinson, Nebraska, near Red Cloud Agency. They surrendered 12,000 gaunt ponies and 117 arms.

Crazy Horse was allowed to settle on the reservation. He still commanded great respect from the Lakota people. With no desire for power, he did his best to avoid becoming swept up in agency politics and refused repeated entreaties to travel to Washington. He wanted a reservation of his own in Wyoming, and he repeated his request whenever he could to whomever he could, General George Crook included. But other Indian leaders, jealous of Crazy Horse, began to circulate rumors that he planned to leave the agency, that he and many warriors would go north and return to the warpath. The white authorities became increasingly suspicious. When some of Crazy Horse's followers left his camp, the Indian agent was sure that trouble was imminent. And when a jealous nephew of Red Cloud's revealed that Crazy Horse was planning to kill Crook at a council, Crook told a group of prominent Lakota leaders that they needed to arrest, and perhaps kill, the Oglala warrior. When Colonel Luther Bradley, the commander of Camp Robinson, heard of this, he ordered Crazy Horse arrested and sent to Fort Jefferson on the Dry Tortugas off Key West, Florida, where the worst Indian troublemakers were imprisoned, usually for a long time.

On September 3, about twenty followers of Red Cloud found Crazy Horse in the process of moving his camp to the quieter Spotted Tail Agency. He refused to leave with them, but after another confrontation, this time with Spotted Tail and hundreds of his men, he was convinced to return to Camp Robinson to discuss his move. Two days later, he was escorted by several of his friends and a growing group of Spotted Tail's warriors. A young army lieutenant temporarily assigned as Indian agent, Jesse M. Lee, also accompanied Crazy Horse at the Oglala's own request.

Word had spread of Crazy Horse's approach, and when he arrived at Camp Robinson, several thousand Lakotas were there to witness his arrest and subjugation. Though Lee had promised the Oglala that he would be able to speak his piece, Bradley refused to allow it and insisted that Crazy Horse be taken into custody. Bradley assured the Indians that no harm would come to him.

When Crazy Horse was told this, he voluntarily went with the officer of the day, who led him toward the guardhouse next door. He entered the jail but then realized what was about to happen. Drawing a hidden knife, he ran outside and made a wide sweep with the blade, cutting one Oglala behind him who had grabbed his arms; Little Big Man, a warrior who had fought beside Crazy Horse for many years but who now worked for the whites, fell to the ground. There was a rush on all sides toward Crazy Horse, and the officer of the day yelled, "Kill him! Kill him!" One of the surrounding soldiers lunged forward with his rifle and bayoneted the Oglala leader near his left kidney, in the back. Crazy Horse collapsed in the dirt. Amazingly, even with tensions high, no further bloodshed occurred, though his followers resisted an attempt to move him into the guardhouse. He was carried into the adjutant's nearby office, where a doctor gave him morphine as he drifted in and out of consciousness, comforted by his father and his old friend Touch the Clouds. About 10:00 p.m., he asked for Lieutenant Lee. Crazy Horse told Lee that he did not blame him for what had happened. The greatest war chief of the Oglalas, who only wanted peace and quiet after his surrender, died about midnight.[79]

*   *   *

WHEN CRAZY HORSE had decided to return to the reservation, Lame Deer had told him that he and his Minneconjous would not accompany him—they were going to hunt buffalo. The day after Crazy Horse surrendered, Miles hit Lame Deer's camp of three hundred. After Lame Deer and thirteen other warriors were killed, Miles induced most of the rest to relinquish their arms. Some members of the band escaped into the hills, eventually making their way in to the agencies. With this, all of the hostiles on the northern Great Plains had been rounded up—except for one large group.

Black Moon had led his fifty-two lodges across the Canadian border in December 1876. Four Horns, Gall, Crow King, and others had followed, until there were 3,000 Lakotas in Canada. In May 1877, after a miserable winter near Fort Peck, the trading post and agency sixty miles south of the border, Sitting Bull and a thousand hungry followers, most of them Hunkpapas with a few Minneconjous and Sans Arcs, joined the exiled Lakotas. Sitting Bull would remain in the Great Mother's land for four years. Though the Canadian authorities allowed him to stay provided he remained peaceful and treated him with compassion, they refused to grant him his own reserve.

The first year, buffalo were plentiful. But each summer his people saw fewer of them, and each winter the brutal Canadian blizzards weakened their bodies and their spirits. Various chiefs led their bands south to surrender to U.S. authorities and find a kind of peace on the reservation—Hump in the spring of 1877; Black Moon, Little Knife, Spotted Eagle, Rain in the Face, and Big Road in 1880; Crow King, Gall, and Low Dog in early 1881. In the spring of 1878, bolstered by the arrival of almost 250 lodges of Crazy Horse's band after their leader's death, Sitting Bull's village comprised about 800 lodges and 5,000 people.[80] Three years later, only a fraction of that number remained with him. His people were starving. For a man who loved women and little children as much as he did, that was enough to wilt his resolve. Although Sitting Bull had consistently resisted the unconditional surrender terms that would accompany his return to the United States and the Canadians had treated him well, he knew that they wanted him and his people to leave. On July 19, 1881, Sitting Bull led a destitute group of less than 200 followers, mostly old men, women, and children, and 14 gaunt ponies into Fort Buford.

The next day, he formally surrendered. "I wish it to be remembered that I was the last man of my tribe to surrender my rifle," he said.[81]

The Cheyennes' experience was similar. In late November 1876, after their village on the Powder River was overwhelmed by a force led by Colonel Ranald S. Mackenzie, most of them, about nine hundred under Dull Knife and Little Wolf, rode into Camp Robinson to give up.[82] And after a harsh winter of nearly constant pursuit by the army, including Miles's victory in the Wolf Mountains, Two Moon and his band surrendered at Fort Keogh in the spring of 1877. Other Cheyennes journeyed south to join their southern brethren in Oklahoma.

There were, however, some who had not surrendered. About 250 Sioux remained in Canada, most of them remnants of Inkpaduta's band.[83]

After Custer's defeat, the wily old Wahpekute and his tattered band traveled with Sitting Bull and his Hunkpapas, eventually turning north toward Canada. Since the great battle he had lost yet another son to the *wasichus:* Tracking White Earth, one of his two younger twins.[84] By September 1876, Inkpaduta and a Lakota chief named Long Dog left the main camp and made their way north to Fort Peck.[85] There they attempted to trade booty from the Little Bighorn—including Dr. Lord's surgical instruments—for food and ammunition.[86] Most of the group remained in the Missouri River bottoms below the fort throughout the fall, sometimes begging for supplies.[87] Before the end of the year, Inkpaduta led his *tiospaye* across the border into Canada. Eventually, he returned to the Oak Lake Indian Reserve in Manitoba, where he had lived before riding south to join Sitting Bull. There the instigator of the Spirit Lake Massacre, the scourge of the northern plains for twenty years, took up farming. He died in 1879, the only major Sioux chieftain never to make peace with, never to surrender to, and never to be captured by the United States government.[88]

THE INDIANS were not the only ones dispossessed.

After Libbie Custer had steeled herself to assist in breaking the news to the other widows of Fort Lincoln, she had helped minister to the wounded at the post hospital. Despite an amputation or two, all of the men would recover.[89] Then she had returned to her house and slipped into despondency. She had lost not only her husband but several in-laws and many friends—three of the five companies stationed at the fort had been almost completely annihilated with the General. She shared her grief with Maggie Calhoun, whose losses were, if such things can be measured, even worse—a husband, three brothers, and a nephew. And while the wives of the enlisted men, as laundresses, had some rights in the army's eyes, officers' wives did not. Whatever sympathy might be felt for them personally, officially there was none. The deaths of their husbands ended their military status, and they were required to leave their residences as soon as possible; other officers and their families would be arriving soon to take their place. Friends worried for Maggie's mental state.

As General Miles made his way up the Missouri to reinforce Terry with his Fifth Infantry, he stopped at the fort to pay his respects to Libbie. He had admired Custer, and he and his wife had enjoyed the Custers' company whenever possible. He found her in bad shape. "Mrs. Custer is not strong," he wrote to his wife, "and I would not be surprised if she did not improve. She seemed so depressed and in such disrepair."[90] During religious services one Sunday at the Custer quarters (the post had no chapel or chaplain), Libbie fainted; it took almost an hour to revive her.[91] Her brother-in-law David Reed arrived at Lincoln on July 13 to provide emotional support and help his sisters-in-law and daughter Emma with their leave-taking. Dick Roberts, Annie Yates's brother and the young tentmate of Autie Reed who had stayed behind at the Powder River depot, also lent assistance. Along with her personal items, Libbie took only her bedroom set and a few other pieces of furniture with her. (After Libbie left Lincoln, eight officers moved into the Custers' quarters, some of them sleeping on the drawing room floor in their field bedding.)[92] The Northern Pacific, mindful of the work done on its part by Custer and the Seventh Cavalry, provided the women transport (other railroads along the way followed suit), and on July 30 they boarded a special car in Bismarck and headed east. The progress of the party, which included Libbie, Maggie Calhoun, Emma Reed, Nettie Smith, and Annie Yates and her three small children, was reported in the newspapers, and sympathetic crowds met them at the stations where they stopped. In Fargo, a reporter watching Libbie enter a hotel noticed that she had "so little strength left that she could scarcely reach the top of the stairway."[93] In Chicago, the widows were graciously received by Potter Palmer, the hotelier, whose resplendent Palmer House, on the corner of State and Monroe, just a few blocks from Lake Michigan, had been rebuilt bigger and better than ever after the great fire of 1871. (It was proudly billed as the world's first fireproof hotel.) During their wait between trains, he allowed them the use of his private rooms, where they found an abundance of flowers sent by well-wishers.[94]

Libbie and the others—all but Nettie Smith, who had continued on to upstate New York to her parents' home—finally arrived in Monroe on August 4. They found the small town almost completely draped in black[95] and ready to welcome them with open arms.

The day the news of the debacle had reached Monroe, its leading citizens had been reluctant to deliver the news of the deaths of the four Custer men to Emmanuel and Maria Custer. A fifteen-year-old boy named James Barry was sent, and when he finally made Emmanuel understand that this message was not one of the many false reports of similar disasters he had received over the years, the old man's grief was such that he literally tore his hair out by the roots.[96] The mayor announced a public meeting that evening, and businesses closed early. As the news spread to every part of town, "all the bells began to toll—church bells, fire bells, every bell in town."[97]

By the time Libbie returned to Monroe, she had probably already decided on her life's mission—to restore the luster to her Autie's damaged reputation. She had become aware of the severe criticisms of her husband in the press—disobedience, rashness, selfishness—and had been shocked by them. But if she had ever had any qualms, newspaper stories such as O'Kelly's and talks with Weir and other officers had bolstered her opinion of her husband's innocence. Custer was not at fault for the disaster; therefore someone else must be. And Libbie had no doubts as to who the prime candidates were. Within a very short while, she would join forces with a man who shared her unstinting adulation of the General and would prove just as determined as she.

NINETEEN

The Lost Captain

Sapphire skies and seas cerulean,
Whiskered pirates fierce, Herculean,
Isles of coral;
Colored consorts of the pirates —
Practices, a Christian eye rates
Most immoral!

These, and other tales entrancing
Guide the summer hours, enhancing
Joys of living;
Stories that will chill and fright one—
Tales that hypnotize, delight one,
Pleasure giving.

Whittaker, thou rare raconteur. . . .
AL. W. CROWELL

Captain Frederick Whittaker, songwriter, poet, editor, and dime novelist extraordinaire, had fought gallantly in the Civil War. He had joined the Union army as a Private and been brevetted an officer by war's end. But he was no Captain.

Whittaker was born in London in 1838 to a successful solicitor and his wife. Young Fred's father, Henry, made the mistake of cosigning some financial papers for a nobleman, Lord Kensington; when his client defaulted, Henry fled England with his family to avoid debtors prison, first roaming through Europe and finally sailing for America in 1850. Two years later, he published a successful law reference volume that went into several editions. The Whittakers eventually settled in Brooklyn in 1858, where Henry built up a good law practice.[1]

Fred was eleven when the family arrived in America, and his early schooling was limited to six months. His older brother, Henry, was also a lawyer by this time, and Fred's father obtained a position for Fred as office boy in a New York law firm. The discipline didn't take, and by the eve of the Civil War, young Whittaker was working in an architect's office. A vision defect put an end to that career path, and when war broke out, he enlisted in the Sixth New York Cavalry. He served to the end, achieving the rank of Second Lieutenant after he was shot through the lung in the Battle of the Wilderness in May 1864.[2]

After the war, Whittaker pursued his true dream, one inherited perhaps from his father—writing. After working as a book salesman and schoolteacher, he began placing stories, songs, and poems in various publications. In 1870, with money inherited from English relatives, he bought a two-story cottage in Mount Vernon, Westchester County, just north of the Bronx. He also married a lovely schoolteacher named Elizabeth. A year later, he wrote the first of more than eighty dime novels, most of them for Beadle and Adams, the industry leader, and achieved a dubious fame as one of the best practitioners of that populist (and hugely popular) art, primarily stirring stories of adventure and romance in the old-fashioned sense aimed at boys of all ages.[3] He also began writing for the independent and influential *Army and Navy Journal,* penning a cogent analysis informed by his personal experiences titled "Volunteer Cavalry: The Lessons of a Decade." On the strength of that and other articles, he became an assistant editor at the weekly. As he continued to churn out dime novels such as *The Death's Head Rangers* and *The Corsair Prince,* his flair for romance began to extend to his own life, with *The Lost Captain* soon transmuting into the lost Captaincy. Whittaker was no longer content with the lieutenancy the army had given him at war's end. He adopted the self-conferred brevet rank of Captain, probably for the added prestige. No one, it seems, thought to question it.[4]

Though he had served in the same cavalry division of the Army of the Potomac as Custer had, Whittaker had met the man only once—in the spring of 1876, when Custer had visited the offices of Sheldon and Company, publisher of Custer's book *My Life on the Plains* and also the *Galaxy* magazine, where a series of Custer's war memoirs was then appearing. The meeting made an impression. Soon after the news of Custer's death reached the East, Whittaker wrote a fulsome eulogy for the fallen cavalryman, which the *Galaxy* published in September—the same month that the *Army and Navy Journal* ran his reverential poem "Custer's Last Charge." The article, though flagrantly admiring, did ascribe "impetuosity," "rashness," and "vanity" to the General, in addition to forced marches to his final battle. But the chief reason for the tragedy, Whittaker claimed, lay in the superior numbers of the enemy.[5]

Sheldon and Company was clearly impressed with the article, for at the end of July, the company announced that it would soon issue a biography of Custer. It would be a lavish, subscription-only volume, for which agents were being canvassed,[6] and

> the proceeds of which, after paying expenses, will be devoted to the benefit of Mrs. Custer. The work will be entrusted to Bvt. Capt. Frederick Whittaker, lately of the staff of the *Journal*. With a view to render this history as complete as possible, this gentleman requests that all who can furnish any information, personal anecdotes, etc., concerning Gen. Custer at any time in his career, will send the same to him, care of Sheldon and Co., 8 Murray Street, New York, promising to acknowledge the same with thanks, and use them in the memoir.[7]

Subscription sales represented an aggressive and potentially more profitable bookselling method that had recently been embraced by Samuel Clemens (Mark Twain), whose book *The Gilded Age* was the first subscription novel. Subscription books were unavailable in bookstores and were instead sold in advance by thousands of traveling canvassers—book agents, as Whittaker had briefly been before turning to writing—who worked door-to-door calling on homes and businesses in large cities and tiny hamlets throughout the country. Subscription books were sold for two or more times the going rate for a comparable trade book (a book intended for the general public and sold in bookstores) and were usually larger, thicker, and filled with woodcuts and steel engravings to justify the price.[8]

Whittaker took a leave of absence from the *Army and Navy Journal* and quickly began contacting potential sources. One of his first letters was to Libbie Custer, still in Monroe settling her husband's affairs and caring for his aged parents, Emmanuel and Maria Custer. Libbie soon realized the positive effect such a book could have on Armstrong's sullied reputation, and she agreed to assist him after they met.[9] She lent him personal letters and put him in touch with several Monroe citizens, whom he contacted during a visit there. Annie Yates was enlisted in the cause and gave Whittaker original material of her own to use. Lydia Ann Reed, the General's beloved half sister, lent Whittaker descriptive passages from Custer's letters to her.[10]

Using James O'Kelly's September 21 story in the *New York Herald* as a guide, Whittaker also queried several of the Seventh Cavalry's officers and others attached to Gibbon's column. Lieutenant John Carland, the Sixth Infantry officer from Fort Lincoln who had remained on the *Far West* during the battle, responded to the writer's inquiries about his good friend Custer.[11] One of Reno's subalterns showed Whittaker's letter to the Major, prompting Reno to write to Whittaker with a defense of his actions in the battle, buttressing his version with the claim that he had nineteen years' Indian-fighting experience under his belt.[12] From this new material derived from these and other participants, and influenced by a certain persuasive widow, Whittaker's perception of the battle changed significantly.[13]

Though armed with Libbie's approval, Whittaker received no answers to his letters sent to Captain Thomas Weir. It was not until late November, after the book was finished, that Whittaker finally tracked him down and found out why. Weir had arrived in New York City in October to begin his two-year detail at the Cavalry Recruiting Rendezvous in the Burton Mansion on Hudson Street and rented an apartment just down the street. Battle fatigue, the traumatic loss of so many close friends, the method of their destruction, the slander of Custer's good name—any or all of these had increased his dissipation. When Whittaker met him, Weir was not in good shape. He was rapidly destroying himself with alcohol and spent most of his days in a state of depression and nervous exhaustion, holed up in his room when not at his office. He had not replied to Whittaker because he believed that any information from him would be perceived as personally biased, due to his public clash with Reno, and thus would hurt the cause.[14] Even so, he had provided a few other newspapermen sworn to secrecy[15] with a good deal of information about the battle—and more important, a more jaundiced view of certain individuals' actions. Weir told Whittaker about his altercation with Reno on the bluffs, among other things, which only O'Kelly had hinted at in print previously.[16] Whittaker badgered Weir to sign an affidavit of the facts of the battle, which Weir steadfastly refused to do, though he gave Whittaker the names of Edgerly and Varnum as two officers whose testimony would corroborate his.[17] The writer soon wore out his welcome, though Whittaker told Libbie, "I feel no doubt that he will speak out when the fight begins."[18]

Whittaker somehow finished the massive manuscript by mid-November, and *A Complete Life of General George A. Custer* was published a few weeks later at the steep price of $4.25—double the price of most new hardbacks. Its official publication date was December 9, just in time for the gift-giving season. Captain Thomas Weir died the same day, of what his doctor officially listed as "congestion of the brain," with a secondary cause of "intemperance." On October 15, in his final letter to Libbie Custer, he had told her that he considered it his life's duty to vindicate the reputations of his friends who had perished in the battle. He had concluded with a promise to go to Monroe to see Libbie, Annie Yates, and Maggie Calhoun: "I know if we were all of us alone in the parlor, at night, the curtains all down and everybody else asleep, one or the other of you would make me tell you everything I know."[19] He never did.

Libbie Custer would later claim that she never read Whittaker's biography of her husband. True or not, she would have undoubtedly been pleased at the book's portrait of the General, if not its literary quality. The lavishly illustrated tome of 648 pages was an unabashed paean to, in the author's words, "one of the few really great men that

America has produced—a man who triumphed over great odds to reach the pinnacle of greatness." He continued:

> Few men had more enemies than Custer, and no man
> deserved them less. The world has never known half the real
> nobility of his life nor a tithe of the difficulties under which
> he struggled. It will be the author's endeavor to remedy this
> want of knowledge, to paint in sober earnest colors the truth-
> ful portrait of such a knight of romance as has not honored
> the world with his presence since the days of Bayard.[20]

That lofty estimate of his subject was maintained and often raised throughout the book, occasionally to absurd lengths,[21] and similar treatment was afforded his closest comrades-in-arms. "Custer and Custer's men were the flower of the Seventh Cavalry," gushed Whittaker.[22] Other players in the Custer saga were not so fortunate this time around. Grant, Benteen, and Reno were all castigated for their actions during the recent campaign, doubtless due to Libbie's influence and the information received from Weir and other officers of the regiment. Benteen was charged with disobedience, Reno with cowardice, and Grant with mean-spirited pettiness, their combined malfeasance resulting in Custer's defeat and death. Whittaker ended the book with a call for a court of inquiry (an army investigative body) to look into the matter. Whittaker's accusations might not have carried as much weight coming from the pen of a humble Second Lieutenant. But with "Captain" on the title page, they had to be taken more seriously. No longer was his bogus rank just a harmless piece of vanity. Now it conferred a spurious authority on the military judgments he was so noisily proclaiming. He claimed that many of the Seventh's officers had been deterred from speaking the truth "by fear of those superiors whom their evidence will impeach. . . . The nation demands such a court, to vindicate the name of a dead hero from the pitiless malignity, which first slew him and then pursued him beyond the grave."[23]

Whittaker's book betrayed scant evidence of an editor's judicious hand, likely due to the limited time available. Awkwardly padded with large chunks of Custer's own articles and *My Life on the Plains;*

relying heavily on the unreliable newspaper accounts of the battle; and larded with echoes of Horatio Alger's "pluck and luck" dime novels, Mark Twain's recently published *Tom Sawyer*, Cooper's frontier sagas, the Christ story, and the author's own romances,[24] the tome received mixed reviews. The *Nation* called it "a very good book, but repellently large and heavy. . . . It is well-written, without possessing any charm or style."[25] Even Whittaker's employer, the *Army and Navy Journal*, criticized the work for its excessive adulation, and the *Galaxy* reviewer, while praising much of the text, wrote that "the great fault of this otherwise attractive biography is the unwise partisanship."[26] Its influences did not go unnoticed: "Much of it reads like 'Charles O'Malley,' " said the *Chicago Daily Tribune*, citing a widely popular British martial romance that had enthralled boys for decades—including a young Michigan schoolboy named George Armstrong Custer.[27]

Though its publisher, Isaac Sheldon, wrote to Elizabeth Custer of the book's disappointing sales, the biography likely sold well enough and was reprinted. "The times have been adverse to its success," he wrote, "but I think it has even now earned some little profit, a share of which I have always intended should go to you so feel that you have always a little something to fall back on when necessary."[28] (Even as late as March 1877, the publisher ran ads for agents to sell the volume, calling it one of "the two best subscription books of the year," and the book was reissued in a popular, less expensive edition soon after.)[29] Despite these assurances, it is doubtful that any royalties made their way to Libbie as initially promised. (The book's actual sales figures are lost to history.) More important, despite its critical drubbings, the book played a large part in disseminating Whittaker's serious accusations and forming a public image of Custer, "the last cavalier," which was quickly embraced.

Whether motivated by honest indignation to clear Custer's name (as he claimed in letters to Libbie)[30] or cooling sales of his book (as some of his critics insisted), Whittaker was steadily lobbying behind the scenes for an investigation.[31] In May 1878, after failing to persuade the War Department to open an official inquiry into Reno's conduct in the battle, he wrote a letter to the congressional delegate from Wyoming Territory, W. W. Corlett, urging a congressional investigation and offering "a great amount of evidence, oral and written," and "the statements of an officer, since deceased, made to me a few days before his death," all of which would prove Reno's cowardice.[32] (Whittaker apparently had decided to focus his energies on Reno, Benteen's sins now having been reduced to "willful neglect." Furthermore, while Reno had few allies, Benteen was the acknowledged hero of the siege and admired by all, and there was little or no chance of anyone testifying against him.) A former Captain in Custer's Seventh, Satterlee Plummer, acted as go-between and gave the letter to the Congressman.[33] The sympathetic Corlett referred the matter to the House Committee on Military Affairs, which reported favorably on an inquiry, but Congress recessed before responding to the request. Whittaker then released the letter to the press in mid-June, and it was widely published, heaping further disapprobation on Reno.

THE LAST THING Marcus Reno needed right then was more damage to what was left of his reputation. His situation was bad enough as it was.

Upon the Seventh's return to Fort Lincoln in September 1876, the regiment had disarmed and dismounted the Sioux at the Standing Rock and Cheyenne agencies downriver, then scattered to various posts for the winter. Because Colonel Sturgis had assumed active command of his regiment at Lincoln, Reno had been assigned to Fort Abercrombie, a drab little two-company post 220 miles northeast on the Dakota-Minnesota border. There, on more than one occasion, the lonely Major forced his attentions upon a married woman of questionable reputation whose husband, a Captain in the Seventh Cavalry, was absent for a few weeks. The woman may have been unfaithful to her husband previously, but she was ultimately not interested in Reno. When she more than once rebuffed his physical advances, and in no uncertain terms, the socially inept Major responded by attempting to besmirch her reputation even further. One thing led to another, and when the woman's husband returned and was apprised of the situation, he pressed charges against Reno for "conduct unbecoming an officer and a gentleman."

A court-martial was convened on March 8, 1877. Reno hired two experienced attorneys, but despite their efforts and the testimony of three Seventh Cavalry officers—Benteen, Wallace, and Merrill—that the woman's reputation was indeed bad, Reno was found guilty. The court sentenced him to be dismissed from service, a verdict that was shortly thereafter confirmed by General Sherman. But the final review was left to the recently inaugurated President Rutherford B. Hayes, a former volunteer officer who had risen to the rank of General. After taking into consideration Reno's twenty years of service, he commuted the sentence to suspension from rank and pay for two years.[34]

After a weeklong visit with his teenage son in Pittsburgh, Reno took a room at one of the better Harrisburg hotels. He remained in Harrisburg for the duration of his suspension, living off funds from his late wife's estate and narrowly avoiding further charges of "conduct unbecoming" stemming from his drunken brawling the previous September at Lincoln. (Twelve officers of the Seventh—Moylan, McDougall, and DeRudio among them—endorsed the charges, but Sturgis and Terry disapproved of them, and the Adjutant General's office declined to accept the case.)

Of Whittaker's three principal targets in his Custer biography, Grant had ignored the book, at least publicly, and Benteen had written a single letter to the *Army and Navy Journal* ridiculing the writer's accusations (and criticizing Custer severely) soon after publication. The debate over Reno's part in the battle had cooled over the next year and a half, but by the time Whittaker's letter was widely disseminated in June 1878, Reno's stock had sunk so low that he could not afford to ignore any further slight to his name. In a widely published *New York Herald* interview with Sitting Bull the previous November, the Sioux chief had insulted Reno's performance at the Little Bighorn: "The squaws could deal with them," he had said of the troops on the bluffs. "There were none but squaws and papooses in front of them that afternoon."[35] A few days later, a *Herald* correspondent talked to Reno. "He is grieved," wrote the reporter, "that certain papers should charge him with enmity toward so brave and gallant a man as Custer. They were personal friends, he says, and were upon the best of terms, having been in the Military Academy at West Point together."[36] These were questionable statements (if accurately reported), especially the last. Reno had graduated in June 1857, before Custer's class of 1862 began its studies.

A desperate Reno traveled to Washington, D.C., to officially request the investigation Whittaker and others had called for. "I respectfully demand that I may have this opportunity to vindicate my character and record which have been thus widely assailed," he wrote to the committee.[37]

After Congress adjourned without taking action on the matter, Reno wrote another letter, this one to President Hayes, asking for a military court of inquiry. General Sherman approved the request on June 25, 1878, exactly two years after the first day of the battle. (Coincidentally, the statute of limitations under military law for a more serious court-martial was two years from the time of the offense for which a man was charged.) The Secretary of War concurred the same day and ordered a court of inquiry to be convened as soon as possible at Fort Lincoln. Since the Seventh was still busy mopping up after the Sioux War, and many of its officers would be required as witnesses, it was decided that as soon as the season of active operations was over, the Reno court of inquiry would convene in Chicago, headquarters of the Division of the Missouri.[38]

LIEUTENANT JESSE M. LEE, acting adjutant, Ninth Infantry, had joined the Union army in 1861 at the age of eighteen and by war's end had earned the rank of Captain of volunteers. After mustering out, he had been made a lieutenant in the Ninth Infantry, and from 1869 that regiment had carried out various duties on the frontier, mostly in Wyoming Territory.

The burly Lee was an industrious, intelligent young man with an intimate knowledge of hard work. He had toiled on the family farm in Illinois starting when he was very young, his father, a businessman and part-time lawyer, having died when Lee was three, leaving Lee's mother with eight children, one of them an invalid. "Much work and but little play. . . . Much self denial," he remembered years later. "Since boyhood, have had little time for play, fun, or frolic." Like George Armstrong Custer, he had taught school at age sixteen, and also like Custer, he was a Jacksonian Democrat.[39]

In the decade since the Civil War, Lee had earned a reputation as a dependable soldier and a fair and honest man. In March
1877, he was made acting Indian agent at Spotted Tail Agency and
was present when Crazy Horse was murdered. After fifteen months
at Spotted Tail, he railed against the previous agent's mismanagement and fraudulence in his official report. Though Lee's grandfather had, as a young man, been shot, stabbed, and scalped by
Indians in Kentucky (but lived to raise a large family),[40] Lee was sympathetic to the plight of his charges and was in turn greatly respected
by them.

In late 1878, Lee was notified that he had been appointed the
recorder for the court of inquiry investigating the conduct of Major
Marcus Reno to be held in Chicago the following January — likely
because his commanding officer, Colonel John King, had been
named President of the court. On the face of it, the duty assignment was a curious one, considering the importance of the case.
Such courts often employed a legally trained judge advocate in
the role of recorder. Most lieutenants had little legal experience to
speak of, save the occasional courts-martial that every officer was
required to attend and occasionally preside over. But Lee had been
detailed as Judge Advocate at least twice, and during one Civil
War–era court-martial, he had performed well enough to be complimented by the Judge Advocate General. The praise had led Lee a
decade later to seriously consider resigning from the army to become
a lawyer in his father-in-law's office. He had taken a six-month leave
to study law but had ultimately concluded that the profession was
overcrowded.[41]

A court of inquiry, however, was different from a court-martial,
in which a soldier was charged with a specific crime, prosecuted by
a Judge Advocate, and judged guilty or innocent. A court of inquiry
was a sort of grand jury, an investigative body that determined
whether the evidence warranted further proceedings (usually a
court-martial). Since the two-year statute of limitations had expired,
in this case a recommendation of a court-martial was unlikely —
although, as one officer pointed out, "if an officer . . . takes advantage of that regulation it is quite conclusive proof of his guilt."[42] A

censure was more likely—or, as Marcus Reno hoped, a finding of innocence.

ONE MEMBER OF THE COURT reached Chicago early. After a two-month leave, Colonel Wesley Merritt arrived with his wife on Wednesday, January 8, and took a room at the investigation's downtown venue. The Palmer House was the city's elite hotel and, at eight stories, its tallest structure. Just eight years after the great fire of 1871, Chicago had almost completely recovered and was bigger and better than ever. It was now the fourth-largest city in the country, with a population of half a million. The Palmer House's spacious rooms, luxurious appointments, and fine food made it a popular site for proceedings of this type. (A congressional investigation into a local judge was scheduled to open there a couple of weeks after the Reno inquiry.) Merritt knew Chicago well; he had served on Sheridan's staff for two years until July 1876, when Colonel William Emory had finally retired after forty-five years of service and Sheridan had given Merritt command of the Fifth Cavalry.

Merritt and the two other members of the court—they would arrive on Sunday, the night before the court was scheduled to convene—were a distinguished group. Commissioned an officer in 1837, Colonel King had served his country extensively and honorably for more than forty years. Lieutenant Colonel William B. Royall, Third Cavalry, also had achieved an excellent record over thirty-three years of service—if one did not count the dishonor General Crook had claimed that Royall had visited upon him at the Rosebud and that had (according to Crook) blown the chances of a clear-cut victory. These parallels to Reno's case were unknown outside a small group of officers, however, since Royall was not among those Crook had immediately criticized after the battle. Later in 1876, during Crook's "Starvation March," Royall and Merritt had clashed over what Merritt had seen as a lack of discipline on the older officer's part.[43]

Merritt—still youthful-looking at forty-four with a full, light brown beard—and Custer had been rivals since their promotion to

Brigadier General on the same day in late June 1863, but the two had remained on fairly good terms. Merritt was also familiar with Reno, who had served under him in the war. According to Edward Godfrey, Reno "did not have the confidence and esteem of his Division Commander."[44]

The Palmer House was, coincidentally, temporary headquarters for Sheridan's Division of the Missouri. Nine days earlier, on the afternoon of Saturday, January 4, a fire had roared through a section of downtown a few blocks from the hotel, engulfing the Honore block, which included the post office and Sheridan's third-floor offices. Though no records had been lost, the General and his staff had leased most of the rooms on the Palmer's second floor until they could find more permanent quarters.

Reno had retained the legal services of a young Harrisburg acquaintance, Lyman DeHuff Gilbert, at the time the Deputy Attorney General of Pennsylvania. The thirty-three-year-old Gilbert had grown up near the Ross and Haldeman families, Reno's in-laws. He had graduated from Yale in 1865 and founded a law firm in Harrisburg in 1871. He would not arrive until January 13, the court's first day. Reno took residence at the Palmer on Friday, January 10. He was running short of money and had requested that the army pay for his lodgings, which it did. After dumping his luggage and private papers in his hotel apartment, he granted a short interview to a *Chicago Times* reporter, answering his questions "politely but guardedly" as he briefly defended his actions in the battle.[45]

Several of the Seventh's officers—Benteen, McDougall, Wallace, Hare, and Varnum among them—left the same day from Bismarck on a Northern Pacific train for Chicago, a three-day journey.[46] Others would arrive in Chicago in the weeks to follow. Most would stay at the Palmer. Captain Thomas French had been scheduled to testify,[47] but his heavy drinking had resulted in several charges of drunkenness and conduct unbecoming, and he was involved in his own court-martial at Fort Lincoln, which had convened a week earlier than the Reno investigation. Like Thomas Weir, French had increased his consumption of alcohol and "stimulants" after the rigors and horrors of the summer of 1876. A doctor who had examined him a few weeks before had declared him "incurable by ordinary methods of treatment."[48] He was in such bad shape that for several days, he was unable to appear at his own trial, much less in a courtroom a thousand miles away.[49]

The only other officer surviving the battle who had not been called was Lieutenant Frank Gibson, who was on leave at the time—although Captain Myles Moylan, also on leave, would manage to return in time to appear. One reporter in Chicago noticed Gibson's absence, calling him a "forgotten witness. He is said to have in his keeping some interesting remarks Reno made about the time he ordered the boys to mount and gallop for the bluffs."[50]

In fact, none but his family knew that Gibson had been critical of the Major in a letter to his wife written days after the battle—"Reno didn't know which end he was standing on," he had told her[51]—but the reporter's statement was typical of the many stories swirling around the investigation. Just two weeks earlier, an article printed in many major newspapers had spoken of a damning, anti-Reno sworn statement by Weir. "It was given under the seal of secrecy not to be used until Weir was dead," related the breathless correspondent. The *New York Herald*'s James O'Kelly had reportedly secured the alleged affidavit from Weir and then entrusted it to Frederick Whittaker, who had placed it with "the proper authorities." The statement was presumed to reveal the true details of Weir's sortie north from the command's position and accused Reno of cowardice and inaction.[52]

But Reno's might not be the only reputation to suffer. "The one topic of conversation now at military headquarters is the forthcoming court of inquiry," noted a newspaper,[53] and at Sheridan's temporary offices on the second floor of the Palmer House, several staff officers confidentially voiced their belief that the vast amount of testimony would "result in the tarnishing of Custer's name and renown as a warrior."[54]

Twenty-three men would ultimately be called to testify at the inquiry, which would be in session daily except Sundays. For the army, far more was at stake than individual reputations. Once again, the future of the service could be affected. Lee's report of agent malfeasance had been quoted by Sheridan on January 2 in a supplement to his annual report that continued the General's running battle with the Bureau of Indian Affairs and the Department of the Interior. At the same time, a House committee was busy debating a new appropriations bill that would involve a major reorganization of the army. "Reduction of expenses" was the order of the day, and one of the proposals would lop off entire regiments in every arm, including two cavalry regiments. Another would set the line officers (those in the field) back a few years in promotion, from Major down. The total reduction in officers would be a staggering 406, almost 25 percent.[55] The last thing the military needed at this moment was confirmation of incompetency or cowardice—rumors of which were now circulating even more freely around the impending court of inquiry in Chicago.

TWENTY

For the Honor of the Regiment

It is already as tangled up as an English chancery suit, with about as slender a chance that an intelligent decision can ever be reached.

Chicago Times, JANUARY 27, 1879

Monday, January 13, 1879, dawned cold and clear. With only a few exceptions, the weather during the monthlong proceedings would remain frigid—a typical Chicago winter. The thermometer climbed to twenty-eight degrees by eleven o'clock, when the court convened in the smallish Room 14 on the entresol (mezzanine) level of the Palmer House—the same floor as Sheridan's temporary headquarters—with an adjoining chamber reserved for witnesses not testifying.

Lee had hired a stenographer out of Fort Leavenworth named H. C. Hollister, and he sat near the recorder. The tables had been arranged in the form of the letter T, with the three judges sitting along the crossbar of the letter with their backs to the windows. Colonel King, as President of the court, sat in the middle, flanked by Colonel Merritt on his right and Colonel Royall at his left. Lee and Hollister sat at the foot of the T, while Reno was at another table on one side of the room. Each officer wore his full-dress uniform, right down to his sword and white gloves—a sight that "excited the curiosity of even the chambermaids . . . passing the open door," read one newspaper account.[1]

On this day, only a few spectators were present, including an old friend of Custer's, Colonel Rufus Ingalls, and Captain Mike Sheridan, officially assigned to the Seventh Cavalry but in fact serving as aide-de-camp to his brother. The next day, the crowd would overflow into the hall and necessitate a move to a larger room.

The first day was spent discussing and agreeing on procedure. After the three officers of the court and the recorder were sworn in, it was decided that the proceedings would be open to the public, an option not always taken in such a case. The presence of about half a dozen reporters—four from Chicago papers and a few others—gave rise to the question of whether they should be allowed to take notes. Another question involved Whittaker. Lee suggested that the writer might be called to appear if he wished, to produce evidence or call witnesses. Reno objected, but after private consultation, the court decided that Whittaker would be called and that note taking would not be allowed. The latter decision was reversed three days later, after resourceful representatives of the press hid their notebooks in their laps, under their hats, or in their pockets and managed to scribble fairly accurate notes, which allowed them to write nearly verbatim accounts of the proceedings.[2]

Reno's counsel would not arrive until later that day—his train was behind schedule, Reno said[3]—so the Major requested the court's indulgence until the next morning. As only two of the subpoenaed witnesses had arrived and Lee had only that morning received papers he had requested from Washington, an adjournment was granted after an hour's deliberation.

BY THE FOLLOWING DAY, despite the subfreezing weather outside, the crowd had increased from a mere handful to thirty or forty, too many for the small room. Reno's counsel, the dapper, mustachioed Lyman Gilbert, made his first appearance—and a strong impression on the newspapermen. "A gentleman of pleasant address and quiet manners," reported the *Chicago Times,* "rather a young man and dressed in fashionable style . . . small in both height and frame, and a clear eye, with a tendency to a humorous twinkle at times."[4] Gilbert was unfamiliar with military law, but he had read the transcript of another court of inquiry to gain a sense of the procedure,[5] and he immediately began sparring with Lee and the court over various procedural and evidential matters. When he objected to the introduction of Whittaker's letter to Corlett, Colonel King made it clear that the letter was only a basis from which to proceed and the court would not be bound by it: "We shall not confine ourselves to that letter. We shall go outside of it. We intend to cover the whole ground." The entire battle would be investigated, not just Reno's conduct.

Lee led off by swearing in his first witness, Lieutenant Edward Maguire, Terry's engineering officer, who had overseen the survey of the battlefields. A copy of his map was introduced as evidence. The chief feature of the map was the degree of its imperfection, for virtually every officer of the Seventh and civilians besides would testify to its errors. But it was the only visual aid available, and every witness made reference to it during his testimony. The stocky Maguire was asked general questions about positions, conditions, and topography in order to establish a solid factual foundation for further testimony.

Wednesday saw the court moved to a larger room, a corner one on the third floor, which could accommodate one hundred people. Tall windows gave access to a sweeping view of the intersection of Monroe and State below. A gaslit chandelier with six mantled jets, suspended from the center of the high ceiling, would illuminate the proceedings on days when overcast skies made the room too gloomy. Along with the many old soldiers and ex-officers in attendance was Sheridan himself, who came up from his offices and occupied a seat to the left of the judges for much of the day. Also present was the Reverend Dr. Arthur Edwards, who had accompanied Reno as chaplain of his command during the Civil War. Years later, he would reveal that Reno had confided in him that he was drunk at the Little Bighorn, but he allowed no such revelations on this day.[6]

The Seventh's acting engineer officer on June 25, Lieutenant George Wallace, was sworn in. His testimony established the basic chronology of the battle, but more important, he bolstered Reno's claims of innocence. "The Effect of His Testimony Is That the Major Had All He Could Attend to Without Looking After Custer," read a *Chicago Times* subhead the next day. "It is evident from the

testimony of Lieutenant Wallace that there is going to be some difficulty in locating the blame in the case under examination," wrote the
Times reporter. Though the hearing was ostensibly for the purpose
of inquiring into Reno's conduct, the public focus was on assigning
blame for the fiasco.

Over the next two and a half days, Wallace uttered nary a word
against Reno and offered several slippery semitruths, particularly in
his account of the command's straggling forward movement from
the hill, led by the insubordinate Weir. Wallace's authority rested on
his assertion that he had been riding with Reno when Custer gave
him his attack orders, and thus he could support Reno's claims as
to the nature of those orders—even though he had actually been at
Custer's side, exactly where the engineering officer should have been.
But since he was presumably the only other surviving officer present at the time, his testimony was unassailable. Wallace also claimed
that he had not heard any firing when on the hill the afternoon of
June 25. The only other officers who would deny hearing gunfire
were Reno and Benteen. Furthermore, Wallace approved of Reno's
retreat from the timber. Otherwise, he said, "Major Reno and every
man with him would have been killed."[7] When asked about Reno's
behavior, he replied, "I could not find any fault. I think it was good."[8]
Wallace also bent the truth in several other answers concerning the
expenditure of ammunition in the valley, the condition of the horses,
the number of fresh recruits in his company, and other subjects.
Each was relatively minor, but cumulatively they supported Reno a
good deal.

On other matters, such as Weir's march north toward Custer,
Wallace's memory was not so good—or so he claimed. "That I don't
remember. I can't state for I don't recollect," he answered to a question about when Weir moved out. He did recall, however, that Weir
had marched forward on Reno's orders.[9] He also asserted that the
last he had seen of Custer was when Reno's command had been
ordered forward, three miles from the Little Bighorn—even though
at the time he had told members of Gibbon's column that he had seen
Custer on a bluff across the river, below their siege position, and that
Custer had waved his hat at them.[10]

Why Wallace went so far to protect Reno is a mystery that will likely never be explained, though he may have been convinced that he was defending the honor of the regiment.[11] But his testimony, and the confident way that he delivered it, made a powerful impression. He became the yardstick by which all other witnesses were measured.[12]

On Friday, after Wallace finished, the first citizen took the stand—interpreter Frederic Gerard. Despite their mutual dislike, Reno had sent for him upon his arrival in Chicago and treated him hospitably.

On the stand, the impression Gerard made was of "a very plain-looking man with a plain pepper and salt suit and short-cut hair and stiff beard"[13]—to the disappointed reporters, hardly the image of a frontier scout, which they continued to call him. By now the crowds had increased to the point that spectators crowded close to the witness stand and stood against the walls, while even more occupied the hallway. Gerard's antipathy toward Reno was well-known; one newspaper had labeled him "Reno's Enemy."[14] Though he had defended the Major at a campfire discussion with some officers several weeks after the battle, most present anticipated that he would criticize Reno severely here.[15]

Gerard, hoarse and suffering from a cold, was quickly led by Lee into a detailed account of the battle. He contradicted Wallace's story in several particulars. Wallace had claimed that Reno's battalion had been met by several hundred warriors; Gerard had seen no more than seventy-five in front of the skirmish line. In the timber, it was "every man for himself," and according to Gerard, there "appeared to be no command or order" to the retreat from the woods.[16] He offered his opinion that Reno's battalion could have held out in the timber "as long as their provisions and ammunition lasted if they were determined men."[17] He also asserted that the horses were not in any way fatigued, as Wallace had claimed. Finally, he mentioned hearing heavy fire from Custer's direction for at least two hours, whereas Wallace had claimed the battle couldn't have lasted more than a half hour.[18]

Earlier, in a private meeting set up by Reno, Gilbert had tried to get out of Gerard what his testimony would be, but Gerard had talked only in generalities. When Reno had returned to the room,

Gerard had heard the attorney say in a low voice, "This man is all right. He knows nothing that is damaging."[19] It was now clear that had been a miscalculation. On cross-examination during the next session, Gilbert tried to confuse Gerard to defuse his assertions. "I am endeavoring to answer you direct, but you are making me say things I didn't say," the interpreter claimed after a particularly tangled exchange.[20] Gilbert got Gerard to admit to what he hadn't the previous day — that the Indians were coming up the valley "in large numbers,"[21] not the forty or fifty he had first mentioned — and then for good measure, Gilbert emphasized the admission for the court.

Gilbert said, "So large as to excite your apprehension in regard to the ability of Major Reno to meet them?"

"Yes sir," answered Gerard.[22]

Gilbert now did everything he could to weaken Gerard's credibility. After the interpreter volunteered an account of drinking whiskey with Charley Reynolds, the attorney referred to it no less than six times in the space of a few minutes' questioning. He also brought up Reno's firing of Gerard several times. But his boldest move was his effort to paint Gerard as a "squaw man" and thus much less trustworthy than a gentleman.

"Married, are you?" he asked.

"I am, sir."

"To an Indian woman?"

"A white woman, sir."[23]

In fact, Gerard did have a white wife, but they had been married for only fourteen months. He had been previously married to an Arikara woman, by whom he had three daughters; he had also fathered a son by a Piegan woman. Gilbert clearly knew of one or both of these unions and their offspring, as was evident from an out-of-context question he sprang on Gerard later:

"Have you any Indian children, Mr. Gerard?"

Lee rose and objected to the question as irrelevant, though Gerard answered affirmatively. Both question and objection made clear to everyone in the room what the defense counsel had implied, but Gilbert hammered it home in his outrageous reply. He stood up. "I may as well state to the Court the purpose I had in asking the question," he said. "The witness had stated that he has had thirty-one years' intercourse with the Indians. I merely wished to see to what extent his intimacy extended."[24] The objection was sustained, but the aim had been achieved. Gerard's potentially damaging testimony had been compromised in several ways.[25]

That same day, the *St. Paul Pioneer Press* and some of the Chicago newspapers reprinted a story from the previous day's *Bismarck Tribune*.

> Capt. French, of the Seventh Cavalry, stationed at Fort Lincoln and a delayed witness before the Reno court at Chicago, stated in an interview to-day that he did not see Reno from the evening of the 25th until noon of the 26th, when the Indians were weakening. During the hardest portion of the fight Reno was hid. French was walking about most of the time and claims that he could not find any one who did see Reno.

French's assertion prompted little public comment and would never be mentioned during the Reno court of inquiry, and the "delayed witness" would never make it to Chicago. After a monthlong trial in which he was found guilty of three counts of drunkenness and one of conduct unbecoming, French would be suspended from rank for one year at half pay. In February 1880, a few days before he would have returned to active duty, he was retired by the army after a medical examination determined him to be "mentally unfit and physically incapable to perform any military duties."[26] He died of a stroke two years later. Like Weir, his breakdown was likely brought on by "soldier's heart," the era's phrase for combat fatigue or shell shock.

Charles Varnum, one of the two officers Weir had privately mentioned to Whittaker could corroborate his testimony,[27] was the next witness. He remained on the stand for the better part of three days. Almost completely bald by this time — one reporter described him as having "a four-inch part in his hair"[28] — the young lieutenant was a nervous witness, circumspect in his account while avoiding outright lies, criticizing no one. He claimed, for example, that the timber was difficult to defend, as there were not enough men to hold it. Varnum also avoided discussing Wallace's position when Reno had been ordered after the Indians, though years later he would reveal in three different accounts that Wallace had been riding with Custer, not Reno.[29] And when Varnum was asked by Lee if Benteen with his battalion could have crossed the river to Reno's aid, "the witness, after a good deal of circumlocution, and the manifestation of a desire not to rely on his own judgment, or to express any opinions about it, was finally brought to the assertion that he believed Colonel Benteen could have done it."[30] The lieutenant's 260-word answer to a simple yes-or-no question made clear his reluctance to assert an opinion on any part of the battle that was even remotely controversial.

Varnum did make one important admission: when he saw Custer's battalion on the bluffs during Reno's charge, he realized that Custer was en route to attack the village. That conclusion, surely, must have been shared by every man with Reno, including the Major himself. But curiously, nothing was made of it during the inquiry.

Frederick Whittaker—the "official accuser of Maj. Reno," as one newspaper referred to him[31]—arrived in town that day and granted an interview with a *Chicago Times* reporter at the Palmer that night. Whittaker absolved Benteen of his previous charges of disobedience, claiming that a recent talk with John Martin had convinced him that Benteen had made haste upon receiving Custer's last message. (While Martin may have told him this, a more likely deciding factor was the unanimous support for "the Savior of the Seventh" and the unlikelihood that anyone would testify against him.) Though Whittaker had recently been named editor of a new boys' magazine, he would continue to attend the court's sessions, sitting in the gallery with the other spectators. No mention would be made of the alleged Weir affidavit.

Halfway through the second week of the hearing, the proceedings had settled into a predictable rhythm. At eleven o'clock sharp each day—Reno walked in a few minutes late one day and was sharply rebuked by Colonel King—the court was declared in session. Spectators filled the room as each session proceeded, often standing against the walls. "Occasionally ladies come in—never more nor less than two," reported the *Chicago Daily News*. "They stay only a short time."[32] A meek orderly fetched witnesses and did the bidding of the court officers. The stenographer read aloud the preceding day's testimony, making changes when necessary as corrected by the witness. Less than a week into the investigation, Hollister began reading from the *Chicago Times* account instead of his notes and making corrections to it. He had planned to write up his official account in longhand, but he had fallen behind as the hearing progressed and received permission to insert the newspaper accounts — as much as half the testimony — into the official record.[33]

While Hollister took up to an hour reading the testimony, some of the officers perused the morning newspapers, which also carried the testimony and other stories of interest. Congressman Hewitt's army reorganization bill had been sent back to committee, and another one, less severe, was forthcoming. The Cheyenne outbreak near Fort Robinson was still unresolved. And a new invention called the telephone was now for sale: front-page ads in the *Inter-Ocean* touted its advantages for business use, guaranteeing its range up to one mile.[34] During the occasional short recess between witnesses, the officers of the court stretched their legs, often discussing matters other than the case — for instance, the fact that the Austrian opera star Minnie Hauk occupied the room on the opposite side of the hall.[35] The proceedings rarely lasted more than three hours, after which a plaintive look from Hollister indicating that he had more than enough notes to transcribe prompted King to call an adjournment until the next day.

Most of the witnesses took the opportunity to see the city. Benteen, however, avoided leaving the hotel. He had brought no civilian clothes with him and disliked being stared at in the street. He left only to shop for his wife and her friends and to visit a photographer to have his picture taken with Lyman Gilbert.[36]

As the hearing wore on, Lee's questioning showed marked improvement, particularly his cross-examination and redirect. Soon he was holding his own in clashes with Gilbert, who, while never having participated in a court of inquiry either, was the Deputy Attorney General of Pennsylvania and a savvy and tenacious trial lawyer. A week into the investigation, the *Inter-Ocean* noted that Lee "fences with all the urbanity and cleverness of his opponent."[37] But in terms of fixing guilt or otherwise, not much had been achieved. At least one newspaper noted the lack of substantial criticism of the Major, commenting on the "as yet rather fruitless search for cowardly conduct at the Little Big Horn fight."[38]

As each witness took the stand, told his story, rendered answers, and gave way to the next, it became increasingly evident, to some observers at least, that the truth—especially "the whole truth"—was not always supplied. One reporter wrote: "There was more the appearance among the soldiers of brother officers met in pleasant counsel than of the trial of one of the number for conduct unbecoming one adorned by sword and straps."[39]

This bonhomie might have been the result of Reno's largesse. He entertained often in his suite, and rumors spread of copious amounts of champagne and whiskey on tap, along with cigars and even, according to Whittaker, "ladies of pleasure."[40] Reno himself was perhaps not the most convivial of companions, but Benteen was on hand to smooth things over. He might be shy of strangers' stares in the street, but he showed no such self-effacement when it came to inveigling junior officers to join in the party atmosphere.

In later years, stories would spread that the Seventh's officers had agreed beforehand as to how they would testify, in some accounts even practicing their testimony privately. Godfrey hinted as much, telling how Benteen had urged him to join the merry drinkers and had tried to draw him out on his testimony concerning Reno's conduct. Both Gilbert and Lee conducted pre-interviews with some of the witnesses to help them prepare their testimony. Indeed, as the trial progressed, Lee noticed an alarming difference in what he was told outside the courtroom and what was testified to on the stand, and many years would pass before he would fully understand the reasons for it.[41] But suspicions remain that something more than preparation, and very like collusion, went on among the partygoers in Reno's suite. Most to their dying day denied such allegations indignantly. Only one officer admitted it: Charles DeRudio.[42]

CIVILIANS, OF COURSE, were outside the Palmer House charmed circle, though that did not make them immune to Palmer House pressure. Much later, Gerard claimed that any officer who made himself obnoxious to the defense would incur the wrath of certain officers in pretty high authority in certain department headquarters farther west than Washington and not as far west as St. Paul [Terry's headquarters; in other words, Sheridan's headquarters in Chicago]. . . . The trial had not proceeded far before it came to be known among the witnesses, including commissioned officers, some of whom were outspoken to me in confidence, that the way of the innocent and truthful could be made hard.[43]

Nevertheless, as Gerard had already demonstrated, civilian witnesses could be unpredictable—and damaging. The next witness called, Dr. Henry Porter, was just one such.

Like Gerard, Porter had been queried by Gilbert as to what information he could reveal on certain points. There were questions that Porter hoped he would not be asked.[44] While he intimated that Reno had "lost his grip," as the *Tribune* put it—Porter described the Major as "a little embarrassed and a little flurried. . . . He didn't hardly know whether to stay there or leave" the timber[45]—Gilbert on cross-examination made it clear that between tending to the wounded, his admitted fright, and his lack of military knowledge, the good doctor's conclusions were questionable.

Any minor damage done to Reno was mitigated by the next witness, Captain Myles Moylan, who appeared in civilian clothes, since he had just finished a leave of absence in the East. Though Moylan had expressed his low opinion of Reno before and would do so again,[46] his testimony on this day was nothing but complimentary. His story of the battle supported Reno in every instance, and the straightforward and confident manner in which he answered made a strong impression "not only upon the audience, but upon the court," observed the *Chicago Times* reporter.[47]

One exchange, however, was telling. Gilbert asked Moylan, "Wouldn't you sooner have been dejected on top of the hill than dead in the timber?"

"Well, I would rather be on the top of the hill than dead anywhere," said Moylan, and the room erupted in laughter.

A few minutes later, Lee took the witness. "In regard to your statement that you would rather be dejected on the hill than be dead in the timber," he said, "would it not have been better dead in the timber than dishonored on the hill as a soldier?"

After an objection by Gilbert and some hemming and hawing from Moylan, the Captain finally answered. "Very few men but would prefer to be dead in the timber than to be alive on the hill and degraded," he said. There was no laughter this time.

"Yes," said Lee, "that is just what I thought you would answer."[48]

Lee's pressing of Moylan, the most senior officer to appear so far and an intimidating presence, marked Lee's growing confidence. The examination also marked a subtle shift in his role. He was astute enough to have spotted the emerging strategy of the Reno camp: prove that Custer's fight was over quickly and therefore that Reno's actions could have done nothing to affect the outcome. This, however, meant trashing the performance of Custer's battalion. A panic rout was required, and a panic rout was duly supplied by the battlefield evidence cited by army witnesses.

To Lee, this was clearly distasteful. Moylan's evidence had carefully and conveniently exempted his own brother-in-law, Calhoun, from the general slur but had otherwise taken the party line: Custer had established no skirmish lines and therefore had presented no organized resistance. Lee now challenged Moylan and forced him to agree that the command "might have been fighting with all the courage and bravery possible, and still the position of the bodies might not indicate it."[49] From then on, Lee lost few opportunities to make similar interventions. If any witness pointed to the small number of cartridge cases found on Custer's field, Lee would immediately counter with, "Do you know or not know it was the habit of the Indians to pick up those shells?" He also forced more than one officer to admit that Custer could have escaped from the field but had elected to stay and fight.[50] If Custer's dead were to be put on trial here, Lee would see to it that they were not without a defense counsel.

The next Monday, Moylan answered one inconsequential question from Gilbert and gave way to George Herendeen. The scout painted a harrowing picture of a panicked command fleeing from the timber — "Everyone was running for his life," he said[51] — and claimed that Reno could have held the timber indefinitely with water and provisions. Gilbert did his best but could not weaken Herendeen's assertions.

Luther Hare took the stand for the last half hour. Though he, too, avoided any direct criticism of Reno, he reiterated that there was no attempt to provide cover during the river crossing on the retreat, a fact Moylan had also admitted under Lee's cross-examination.

The next day brought a surprise. As soon as Hollister finished reading Herendeen's testimony of the previous day, Lee arose to call the attention of the court to a document he held in his hand.

Frederick Whittaker had sat in the gallery on the other side of the room from Reno and watched quietly for four days. Though summoned by the court to appear, his participation had been limited to "side expressions of contempt or impatience"[52] at any mention of Reno's conduct. He had heard and seen enough. It was time to take matters into his own hands.

Lee stated that Whittaker had handed him a paper containing seven questions that he wanted the recorder to put to Herendeen. Whittaker had also requested that he be permitted to interrogate Herendeen or any other witness. In other words, he wanted to act as prosecutor, or Lee's assistant.

Lee was courteous in his response, but his irritation was clear. "As far as I am concerned as recorder, I have not considered that I was here as the prosecutor of Major Reno," he said, a fact he had made clear previously.[53] "I have desired to elicit all the facts in the case, whether they are for or against Major Reno; and while I have not a very exalted opinion of my own abilities in the matter, still I feel that I am, if I may be allowed to say so, competent to go on with the matter as I have done heretofore, because if I had not felt so, I shall have asked the Court before this time for assistance in this matter."[54] Gilbert examined the questions and voiced no objections, but the court ruled against Whittaker's request. It did, however, allow Lee to use the queries.

Reno edged forward in his chair and watched Herendeen intently as Lee posed the questions to him. Each involved Reno's conduct during the battle, and most centered on his actions just prior to leading the retreat from the timber. Herendeen's answers revealed that Bloody Knife's blood and brains had spattered onto the Major and that Herendeen believed that it had "demoralized him a good deal."[55] But he refused to be led into any statement of cowardice on the Major's part.

Over the next three days, the court heard from four more Seventh Cavalry soldiers. On Wednesday DeRudio took the stand, followed by Sergeant Edward Davern, Reno's orderly during the battle; Sergeant Ferdinand Culbertson of A Company; and trumpeter John Martin, the bearer of Custer's last message. Each commended Reno's personal conduct. DeRudio was the first Seventh Cavalry officer subpoenaed not by Reno but by the recorder. His opinion of Reno had improved noticeably in two weeks. The day he had left Bismarck for Chicago, he had granted an interview with a reporter and criticized the Major severely, alluding to Reno's "fatal mistake in retreating from the wood . . . nothing but fear could have prompted his retreat." DeRudio now claimed that he had been misquoted and went on to praise the Major effusively.[56]

An extra-large crowd was on hand for the proceedings of Saturday, February 1, to see the inquiry's star witness. Frederick Benteen had been called the previous afternoon, but the orderly sent to fetch him had failed to find him at hand. Word of his scheduled appearance had spread. Several women graced the courtroom—the Captain was widely acknowledged as the great hero of the battle, and his feelings regarding Custer were well-known.

Benteen did not disappoint. Over the next day and a half on the stand, he put on a show. He blithely ignored some of Lee's questions and answered others with non sequiturs. A seasoned trial lawyer would have had Benteen squirming in his seat as he attempted to defend testimony chock-full of holes, untruths, and contradictions. But Lee, despite his rapid improvement, was not experienced and was not expected to prosecute. He made few if any attempts to probe Benteen's testimony. When he did, asking the Captain three times where Reno had been when the column had begun to retreat from Weir's forward position, Benteen simply did not answer, though he implied that Reno had been with him. His testimony was laced with indirect criticisms of Custer and cleverly contrived to avoid overt disparagement of Reno, while making it clear that he, Benteen, was the better man. He contradicted his official report and (unknown to anyone in the room) private letters he had written to his wife just days after the battle. He offered outright lies, abundant sarcasm, and frequent obfuscation, all with a degree of wit. The audience loved him.

Benteen stumbled only once. On redirect the next day, Lee asked him, "When two columns, say that of General Custer and yourself at that time, are in quest of Indians, would it not be the duty of the one which found the Indians to notify the other?"

"Certainly," replied Benteen.

"Did you not receive such notification from General Custer at the hands of Trumpeter Martin?"

"I received an order to 'Come on, be quick, big village, bring packs.' He then had found them"—Benteen stopped in midsentence; Lee had led him to the point of admitting that he had disobeyed a direct order from his commanding officer—"but at the same time, I wish to say before that order reached me that I believe that General Custer and his whole command were dead. I mean before that order reached me."

That was an odd statement to interject at that moment, and it directly contradicted some of his testimony of the previous day—that he had believed Custer was still alive when he had planted the guidon on the high peak. But if Custer had died soon after sending the order, Benteen was technically not obliged, under the Articles of War, to obey it.[57] Neither Lee nor any officer of the court interrogated Benteen after this glaring contradiction.

After several more questions that Benteen answered in increasingly contemptuous fashion, Lee had one more matter to bring up.

He asked, "Were you on amicable terms with General Custer on the twenty-fifth of June 1876?"

The white-haired Captain again attempted a clever answer that would not be a direct lie. "As amicable then as I ever was," he said, in a statement classically Benteen—the truth but not the whole truth.

Lee understood Benteen's meaning—his feelings toward Custer were well-known in the army. "Were your relations with General Custer in accord at that time?"

Benteen replied in the same way: "As much so as they ever were."

Lee was not to be put off and finally asked the question in a way that would make it difficult for the Captain to evade the truth and yet remain faithful to himself: "Did you entertain a good or bad opinion of General Custer as a commander?"[58]

Gilbert had remained silent after the first two questions. But he must have realized Lee's intent and the possibility that Benteen—who had, after all, said that Reno's conduct was only "all right" and had also expressed his belief that the timber was a stronger position than the hill—might tell the truth and cast the shadow of personal vindictiveness on his supportive testimony. Everyone knew that Reno hated Custer; if Benteen admitted to the same feelings, it might seem conspiratorial. The lawyer broke in to object: the relations of General Custer with other officers, he said, were irrelevant to this inquiry.

Lee pointed out that Gilbert had gone into some matters of this type—Gerard's relationship with Major Reno, for one—and this was no different.

They argued back and forth for another couple of minutes. After a quick consultation, the court sustained the objection. After a few more questions, Benteen rose and walked out of the room.

And so it continued, witness after witness—Edgerly, Godfrey, Mathey, McDougall—all only mildly damaging. The two citizen packers, Frett and Churchill, told of their altercation with a drunken Reno. Gilbert tried to damage their credibility, but Frett in particular gave as good as he got, and Gilbert quickly called several officers to the stand who refuted their accusations. By the end of it all, the only thing that seemed conclusively established was that Reno drank too much.

Though by military law Reno was not required to testify, once the witness list was completed, he formally requested permission to take the stand. Late Friday morning, February 7, his examination began. He spent the rest of that day and all of the next in the witness chair. Though the crowd on Friday had been a good one, the spectators on Saturday spilled out into the corridor when news that Reno would take the stand hit the papers.

For the most part, it was a well-orchestrated defense of his conduct during the battle. As led by his counsel, Reno refuted the various charges made against him over the previous three weeks. He took a page from Benteen's testimony to explain his much-delayed march toward Custer on the hill in an attempt to make it sound like a well-coordinated movement that he had overseen in every way. Despite his statement in his official report that he had heard Custer's gunfire, he now claimed that he had not, and he refused to admit that anyone had brought it to his attention. The Major told the court that he had not drunk a drop from his bottle until long after the firing quit past midnight—two or three hours after his violent confrontation with Frett, which he weakly rationalized by saying that the man had had no business among the pack animals and had angered him enough to justify slapping him.[59]

On cross-examination, Lee displayed an edge not seen before. It was the closest he came during the trial to being a prosecutor. He pointed out contradictions between Reno's testimony and his official report, and then he asked Reno whether he distrusted Custer or had confidence in him.

"Our relations were friendly enough, and if my brothers had been in that column, I could not have done any more than I did," Reno said.

"The question is," said Lee, "whether you went into that fight with feelings of confidence or distrust?"

"My feelings towards General Custer were friendly."

This time the recorder would not be put off. He turned to the court. "I insist that the question shall be answered," he said.

"The witness will answer the question," said Colonel King.

"I had known General Custer a long time," Reno added warmly, "and I had no confidence in his ability as a soldier." His admission caused a sensation in the room.[60]

Later, Lee asked Reno what had become of the wounded men left behind in the timber.

"I suppose the Indians killed them," Reno said.

"What steps were taken to bring them out?"

"I could not make any efforts. None were made." Some of the spectators murmured at this.

"What became of the wounded men who were left in the bottom on crossing?"

"I do not know," said Reno, adding, rather too smartly, "The Indians would not permit me to take care of them." This, too, prompted mutterings in the room.[61]

Gilbert on redirect asked a final question: "Was there any communication on the part of anyone to tell you that General Custer's column had been seen while you were in the timber?"

Reno's answer was emphatic. "No, sir," he said. "Never."[62]

Reno's testimony was shot through with discrepancies and outright falsehoods. If anything, he had strayed farther from the truth than Benteen had. As he had done with the other witnesses, Lee refused to seize on these opportunities. Even so, Reno, it seemed, had done an excellent job of discrediting himself without Lee's help. The mood in the room was against him.

Reno was released from the witness chair on Saturday afternoon, February 8. Closing arguments began the following Monday morning, with Lyman Gilbert leading off. He began with an unsubtle appeal to the superior breeding of the officer class, complimenting "the greater impartiality which high rank confers." He heaped disdain upon the citizens who had testified against Reno. "Those who live in the suburbs of the Army," he said—in effect, anyone not an officer—"shall not be his [Reno's] judge in matters which concern his life or his honor." He went on to disparage the individuals in classic ad hominem fashion, using selective testimony from the Seventh's officers to rebut every criticism.[63]

One of Gilbert's last arguments was a nervy appeal to the memory of Custer that seemed to take hold among the officers of the court.[64] The attorney suggested that "if Custer could come back," he might say to the Seventh's survivors, "Our efforts failed to be mutual supports because of overwhelming force that confronted each one of us, and your honor takes no stain."[65]

Gilbert's performance was masterful. "Gilbert's Gloss," blared the Chicago Times headline the next day. "He Even Conjures Up Custer's Ghost to Corroborate His Statement in Full" read a subhead. "It was a careful analysis of the evidence of the past four weeks," wrote the Times reporter, "and abounded with passages of remarkable force and eloquence. It made a good impression on the court and audience."[66]

Lee gave his response the next day. His speech was somewhat shorter than Gilbert's. For an hour, while a light snow fell outside, he delivered a "cool, dispassionate review of the evidence."[67]

He began by criticizing Gilbert's attempts to attack the credibility of the nonofficers. "The evidence of even mule packers as to matters of fact . . . is as good as that of anyone, however exalted, until it is contradicted," he pointed out. Concerning Reno's flight from the timber and the approval of every officer present of the move, he observed that it was natural for every survivor of the retreat to "ultimately arrive at a conclusion that after all it was the best thing to do." Esprit de corps, he noted, "is a strong inducement to participants to do this."

Lee concluded that the Major's retreat was a contributing factor to the defeat of Custer's battalion, since Custer had logically expected Reno to hold the timber and continue to threaten the village. He also pointed out the undisputed fact that Custer had received no support whatever from Reno's seven companies, and Lee blamed this on indecision and tardiness. He stopped short of calling Reno a coward, though he provided multiple examples of his sorry performance. He also made it clear that he believed Reno to be lying when he testified that he had not heard Custer's gunfire downriver. Even the partially deaf Godfrey had heard it, said Lee.

Only once did he show passion. To the last, he did not forget his self-imposed duty to the memory of Custer's men. He had allowed Benteen to get away with stating that Custer's battle was "a rout, a panic, until the last man was killed."[68] Now he hit back with fiery eloquence. "Fighting to the last and against overwhelming odds," he said, "they died on the field of glory. Let no stigma of rout and panic tarnish their blood-bought fame." It was a sharp and courageous rebuke. Whatever the verdict on Reno might be, Lee had struck his final blow for a "not guilty" verdict on the dead.

The court was cleared and closed for deliberation. Lee and the members of the court consulted for two hours before finalizing their findings and opinion about five o'clock. The report would be sent to Washington the next day.[69] The War Department's Bureau of Military Justice would review the sealed verdict and opinion, then send it to the President for his approval.

That same day, a letter from Frederick Whittaker appeared in the *Chicago Times*. He was confident, he wrote, that "this trial has established facts which prove Custer to have been, not rash, but prudent; not defeated by the enemy, but abandoned by the treachery or timidity of his subordinates. . . . The charge of disobedience has yet to be met, and I promise the people of the United States it shall be met and refuted at no distant date, before Congress."[70]

No such investigation or refutation ever occurred. The various witnesses and officers of the court left Chicago the evening of the final day of proceedings or soon thereafter. The Seventh's officers returned to their assigned stations. Reno remained in town for a few days, then returned to Harrisburg.

By that time, the court's findings had been leaked to the press and appeared in many eastern newspapers: Reno had been found innocent. When the official report was released on March 6, it merely confirmed the rumors. The Major received the congratulations of his friends in Harrisburg and "congratulatory letters from all parts of the country," reported a local newspaper.[71] Reno and Gilbert discussed a libel suit against Whittaker's publishers, Sheldon and Company, but never followed through.[72] The Major would resume active duty on May 1, and he was looking forward to it.

The full text of the findings of the Reno court of inquiry was released to the public early in March. As endorsed by the Judge Advocate General, General Sherman, and the Secretary of War, and approved by the President, the report was in essence a complete exoneration of Reno's conduct. "No further proceedings are necessary in this case," it concluded. The only admonition, mild as it was, read: "The conduct of the officers throughout was excellent, and while subordinates in some instances did more for the safety of the command by brilliant displays of courage than Maj. Reno, there was nothing in his conduct which requires animadversion from this court."[73]

Years later, Merritt reportedly told his adjutant, "Well, the officers wouldn't tell us anything and we could do nothing more than damn Reno with faint praise."[74]

The official record of the proceedings—all 1,300 foolscap pages of it, half of them clipped accounts from the *Chicago Times*—was sent to Washington with the court's findings and put away under lock and key, not to be available to the public for almost three-quarters of a century.

*   *   *

WHITTAKER'S PUBLIC INVOLVEMENT comprised two more letters. He wrote a long one to the *New York Sun* after the leaked opinion first appeared. This missive was a bitter, almost hysterical diatribe against Benteen, Reno, Gilbert, Merritt, Mike Sheridan, and even the army Adjutant General that labeled the proceedings "the merest mockery of justice . . . a partial whitewash." He claimed to have overheard Merritt say, on the penultimate day of the investigation, "It is a pity that this thing was brought on now. It will hurt the army badly. It ought not to have been allowed to come out."[75] After an ex-officer acquaintance of Benteen's answered with a letter in the *Philadelphia Times* that denounced Whittaker's interest in the case as an advertising dodge for his biography of Custer and ridiculed the Weir affidavit he allegedly had, Whittaker wrote a letter to that paper and claimed that he had "never pretended to have an affidavit from Weir, and never caused such a statement to be made."[76] It was the last public statement Whittaker made on the subject.

THAT MILITARY COURTS could be manipulated, and had been, was nothing new.[77] And the top brass could not have been happy to have the Reno court of inquiry forced upon it, though that was surely preferable to a potential congressional hearing, which would have been much harder for the army to control.

On the unit level, there was good reason to downplay Reno's incompetence. A proven charge of cowardice on the Major's part would be a stain on the regiment and its officers—one that would never completely disappear. Regimental pride was more than enough reason for the Seventh's officers to stand shoulder to shoulder and defend their honor, even if in doing so they had to stand with someone most if not all of them despised.

But it was on the personal level that they may have felt most motivated. Few of the surviving officers could be completely proud of their own conduct during the battle. Many if not all of them had something to hide, whether it was disobedience, cowardice, incompetence, or insubordination: Benteen's dawdling on the back trail; Edgerly's abandonment of a trooper in his headlong retreat from the high peaks; Gibson, Mathey, and Moylan's hiding on the hill during the siege; DeRudio's questionable return to the timber; the shared failure to mount a rear guard during the retreat; leaving the wounded in the valley; most of the officers' heading north without permission and ignoring Reno's calls to retreat; and so on. A full confession of Reno's faults might have led to another, more comprehensive inquiry into the conduct of other officers, and who knew what might be discussed and discovered then? In addition, every officer knew that according to Article 121 of the Articles of War, testimony given in a court of inquiry could be admitted as evidence in a court-martial. The two-year statute of limitations had run out, but no one cared to muddy the waters.

At the deepest, most solitary level, each of the testifying Seventh officers must have confronted his own shortcomings, real or imagined, through the accusations made against Reno. That they rehearsed their stories beforehand is unlikely; all it took was a mutual agreement—one that made sense in so many ways—to defend the honor of the regiment by avoiding blame and refusing to brand Reno a coward. Every officer's greatest fear was breaking under pressure as Reno had. Even a veteran soldier of many a terrific battle like Moylan had displayed questionable courage. If it could happen to him, it could happen to anybody, at any time. Perhaps it was better to keep those innermost anxieties chained and submerged, in the deepest recesses of a man's psyche, and avoid a public questioning of another man's courage. The next time, it could be any one of them. Besides, the Lieutenants and Captains of the Seventh were testifying against their superior officer (or at least Reno would be again, after his sentence was up and he returned to active duty in six weeks), and who wanted to place himself in ill favor with a man who might be his commanding officer for a long time? Reno was a vindictive sort and might jeopardize a man's military career.[78]

The thin blue line had closed and apparently helped stave off reorganization. The army appropriations bill finally passed in early April with no amendments attached. The court's verdict seemed to satisfy the nation's outcry for an answer on the cause of the debacle. But human nature decreed that blame be placed somewhere, and a public unfamiliar with the complexities of the situation, and unable to examine the record, accepted Custer's guilt with satisfaction.

Someone needed to wear the goat's horns; if not Reno, then his commanding officer.

For a still vibrant and attractive widow struggling to make a living in New York, that would not do.

IN THE SPRING of 1877, Libbie Custer had moved from Monroe to New Jersey, then New York City. Liens against her husband's meager estate—from debts he had accrued as a result of his failed financial dealings—had left her with little money beyond a pension of $30 a month. Though President Grant had arranged for her to assume postmistress duties in Monroe, Libbie's pride had prevented her from accepting a favor from him. New York seemed the most likely place for a woman to find employment. She took a part-time job as secretary of a women's organization and began to make new friends.

In the summer of 1877, a contingent commanded by Captain Mike Sheridan and guided by George Herendeen trekked to the battlefield to recover the officers' remains and cart them back east. Despite doubts in some quarters as to the authenticity of her husband's remains, Libbie arranged for his burial at West Point. On October 10 of that year, she attended a funeral with full military honors, including a chapel packed with cadets and a cortege with a riderless horse bearing in its stirrups a pair of spurred cavalry boots, toes turned to the rear. The solemn ceremony and its respectful coverage in newspapers and magazines eased her mind a bit. Autie had always wanted to be buried at West Point.

In the two years since Whittaker's biography, he and Libbie had corresponded occasionally. Just months after the book's release in December 1876, Whittaker had counseled her through fits of despondency brought on by the ensuing publicity. He had advised her to write of her life with her husband, recommending it as a kind of catharsis, and had provided advice on the subject: "Use short sentences preferably. . . . Avoid using the dash. . . . Be careful of your pronouns."[79]

Libbie did not travel to Chicago for the hearing, and the news of Reno's exoneration only reinforced her feelings about Wesley

Merritt, whom she knew, in her own mind at least, to have been her husband's enemy since their days in the Army of the Potomac. (Her instincts may have been right. Upon hearing of Custer's death, Merritt had said, "Well, he hadn't anybody this time to help him out," according to one of his Fifth Cavalry troopers.)[80] She had hoped that Merritt had put aside his enmity and jealousy, but the court's decision convinced her that he never had.[81] As for Reno, she would always consider him "a coward who lost all control on [the] battlefield and took revenge on a soldier who could not reply."[82] But if the dead Custer could not reply, his widow could.

Whittaker had failed as knight-errant on Libbie's behalf: Reno had not, as she had hoped, been publicly disgraced, and her Autie had not been fully vindicated. As a guide and mentor, however, the Englishman was more successful than he could have anticipated. Libbie would heed his advice and eventually write three accomplished and successful books about her and her husband's adventures on the frontier that would remain in print for more than a century. She lived fifty-seven years more than her husband and devoted her life to polishing his reputation as a great cavalier and a perfect man and husband. Along the way, she used her popularity as an author to forge a successful career on the lecture circuit that provided a more than comfortable living for the permanent widow. And for more than half a century, she corresponded with Presidents, Generals, and anyone else who might help her in her quest for official vindication of her Autie. Most expressed sympathy and begged off. Those who aided her, such as Edward Godfrey, did what they could in the manner of letters, articles, and publications. Even her husband's enemies respected Libbie and refrained from causing her pain. Not until after her death in 1933 was any reappraisal of her glowing portraiture attempted, and then to devastating effect. The following year, novelist Frederic F. Van de Water's well-written but scathing biography of Custer, *Glory-Hunter,* hit the bookstores and the headlines and initiated decades of reexamination. But Libbie's efforts had ensured that George Armstrong Custer's name would live on in the consciousness of the American public and of the world. He was gone, but he would never be forgotten.

TWENTY-ONE

Ghosts Dancing

I have seen the wonders of the Spirit Land, and have talked with the ghosts.

KICKING BEAR, MINNECONJOU

In February 1878, Sheridan's office in Chicago forwarded to the Adjutant General's office in Washington a report of the total cost of the Sioux War in the Department of Dakota. As estimated by General Terry with disconcerting military precision, it was $992,807.78.[1]

After he and his ragged followers surrendered at Fort Buford, Sitting Bull was not allowed to settle at Standing Rock Agency with the rest of his people as he had been promised. Instead, he was sent down the Missouri River to Fort Randall. After twenty months of forced exile there with those who had followed him from Canada, Sitting Bull moved back to Standing Rock in May 1883. He spent most of the next seven years doing his best to peaceably resist the ways of the white man.[2]

It was only after Sitting Bull had settled at Standing Rock that he began to understand the futility of resistance. A large chunk of the Great Sioux Reservation had been lost in 1876 to the whites and never again would the Sioux roam where they wanted, following the buffalo in the warm months and semihibernating far from the white man during the long plains winters. Even the Sun Dance, the most sacred Sioux religious tradition, was prohibited; the last one was held in 1883. Worst of all, the Lakotas were beholden to the *wasichus* for most of their food and supplies.

Sitting Bull moved into a small cabin and attempted to till the soil just as most of the other Hunkpapas did. But he continued to fight the white man's persistent attempts to eradicate his people's way of life. The government—even those of its representatives who were kindly disposed to the Sioux—aimed to reduce the Indians' adherence to tribal authority and tradition. Their goal was Americanization and all it entailed: individual responsibility and landownership; allegiance to Christ, God, and the flag; and ultimately, when virtually every trace of Sioux culture was erased, citizenship.

Sitting Bull would have none of this. He settled in the southern part of the reservation, on Grand River, very close to his birthplace, and engaged only in those practices of the white man that he decided were tolerable. He sent all of his children to the day schools set up for them, but he did not convert to Christianity, though he acknowledged the noble work that some missionaries did. And he battled the shrewd and powerful Standing Rock agent, James McLaughlin, for control of the reservation's people. McLaughlin was honest and cared for his Indian charges, but he took an instant dislike to Sitting Bull's proud manner and intractable ways. When the holy man refused to bow to the agent's wishes, McLaughlin quickly decided that Sitting Bull was an active impediment to his plans and spread the word of the Hunkpapa's obstinacy and dangerous attitude. Realizing the power that Sitting Bull still wielded among his people, McLaughlin did his best to undermine him by dealing with other Lakota chiefs and appointing them to prestigious offices.

Sitting Bull traveled east several times, once in the summer of 1885 with Buffalo Bill Cody and his Wild West show, where the high point of the performance was a reenactment of Custer's Last Stand. He toured with the former scout for four months, during which Cody paid him well and treated him honorably. The holy man was dutifully impressed by the *wasichus'* wealth, power, ingenuity, and sheer numbers, but his friendship with the showman did not alter his views on the whites. "The white people are wicked," he told a missionary. "I want you to teach my people to read and write but they must not become white people in their ways; it is too bad a life. I could not let them do it.

"I would rather die an Indian," he declared, "than live a white man."[3]

As the decade progressed, Sitting Bull continued to rally his people against efforts to further destroy the traditional Sioux way of life, particularly government allotment of Sioux land in severalty (individual ownership), which would result in the loss of nine million acres—almost half of the Great Sioux Reservation. But his strenuous efforts to prevent his people's agreement to the Sioux Act of 1888 failed due to backroom dealings, factionalism, and whispered promises that were never fulfilled.

That year, reduced rations and a bad crop led to persistent hunger on the reservations, and diseases made things worse. As a new decade neared, the Lakota people were hungry, low in spirits, and desperate for any sign of hope. So when rumors and reports of a Sioux messiah in the West began to reach Dakota Territory in the summer of 1889, they created a welcome excitement. Lakota emissaries were sent to ascertain the truth; they returned in March 1890 with tremendous news. The messiah, they reported, was a Paiute holy man in Nevada named Wovoka. His religion was a mix of traditional Sioux beliefs and elements of Christian theology, and it promised a new world where every Indian and all of his ancestors existed in a bountiful paradise filled with all kinds of game, including buffalo. According to Wovoka, a huge wave of earth would come from the west and push the *wasichus* back over the ocean to where they had come from. Though the new religion espoused a new world without white people, it was otherwise peaceful.[4]

The Ghost Dance, as this faith came to be called by whites, caught on quickly at several of the Missouri River agencies, though Sitting Bull initially did not support it as it swept through Standing Rock. But another crop failure, combined with the loss of their land, short rations, and the usual miserable conditions on the reservations, intensified Sioux unrest. When word spread that believers would dance through the winter until the great change came the next spring, even Sitting Bull began to encourage the dancing. He refused white entreaties to disband the gatherings; he even forecast a mild winter to accommodate the ceremonies.

Not surprisingly, this new religion did not meet with approval from the vast majority of whites in the area. Many of them, particularly a few inexperienced Indian agents and residents of nearby white settlements, considered any Indian dance a war dance. The result was widespread fear of a full-scale Indian uprising. The government reacted accordingly. Nelson Miles, Custer's old friend and now commanding General of the Division of the Missouri (Phil Sheridan had assumed command of the army upon William T. Sherman's retirement in 1883 and had died five years later, at the age of fifty-seven, after a series of heart attacks), called for 3,500 troops to be activated and sent toward the Missouri reservations to head off any trouble. One of the regiments ordered to the area was the Seventh Cavalry.

Since the Sioux War of 1876 and the grueling Nez Perce campaign the following year, there had been little excitement for Custer's old regiment. There had been marriages: at least nine enlisted men had married their fallen comrades' widows. (One scout, Tom Leforge, had wed the wife of his best friend, Mitch Boyer, and raised Boyer's children as his own.) There had been decorations awarded: no fewer than twenty-four enlisted men had received the Medal of Honor for heroic acts during the Reno-Benteen siege, the most awarded for one action until a massive operation on Iwo Jima, sixty-nine years later.[5] But save for the occasional small-scale Indian outbreak that never amounted to anything and ended as soon as it began, the Seventh's twelve companies had spent the intervening dozen years garrisoning at many forts in the West. Only a handful of enlisted men and officers who had fought at the Little Bighorn still served. Edward Godfrey, Winfield Edgerly, George Wallace, and Charles Varnum had now joined Myles Moylan and Henry Nowlan as Captains; along with Lieutenant Luther Hare, they comprised the small core of veteran Indian fighters among the regiment's officers.[6]

Colonel James Forsyth, longtime aide-de-camp and then military secretary on Sheridan's staff, had commanded the regiment since 1886. He, like most of the enlisted men, had almost no experience fighting Indians. Few of his troopers had even been under fire, and about 20 percent of them were fresh recruits.[7]

The Seventh arrived by train from Fort Riley, Kansas, on November 26, 1890, and settled in at Pine Ridge Agency, about one hundred miles from their old nemesis, Sitting Bull, at Standing Rock. Their conduct at Pine Ridge would embroil the regiment in another controversial army investigation.

The army had asked the Indian agents to identify the chiefs — most of them Ghost Dance leaders — who were giving them the most trouble. Plans were made to arrest the worst of them to head off any large-scale outbreak. On December 10, General Miles issued orders to have Sitting Bull arrested and removed from the reservation. James McLaughlin thought it would be best handled by his Indian police and began to plan this delicate mission.

Sitting Bull had just decided to visit the Ghost Dance leaders of the Pine Ridge and Rosebud agencies to learn more about the religion. Though he defended the right of his people to dance, he was still somewhat skeptical about its legitimacy. Those leaders had taken their followers, about 1,200 Oglalas and Brulés, to an area called the Stronghold, a large mesa with almost sheer sides that rose hundreds of feet above the Badlands in the northwest corner of Pine Ridge. Sitting Bull planned to leave for the Stronghold on December 15; when McLaughlin and his Indian policemen found out, they sprang into action.

Just before 6:00 a.m. on the day of Sitting Bull's departure, a contingent of forty-four Indian policemen arrived at his cabin on Grand River. They pounded on his door, and when someone opened it, they burst in and demanded that Sitting Bull leave with them. At first he agreed, and they allowed him time to dress. Then, as he was escorted outside, where a large throng had gathered, he changed his mind after his teenage son chided him for submitting. He declared that he would not go. As the crowd surged forward, one of Sitting Bull's followers shot an Indian policeman, who staggered back and then fired his pistol at Sitting Bull, hitting him in the chest. Another policeman shot the holy man in the back of the head. A full-scale melee erupted. When the shooting was finished a few minutes later, Sitting Bull and six of his followers lay dead. Six Indian policemen also sustained fatal wounds. As Sitting Bull's two wives and daughters sang their mourning songs, his bloody corpse was thrown into a wagon and delivered to the Indian agent. Like Crazy Horse before him, this great Lakota leader was killed with the help of his own people. Many major newspapers, the *New York Times* among them, crowed that Sitting Bull was finally "a good Indian."[8]

ON THE NIGHT of December 23, soon after hearing of Sitting Bull's death, the old chief Big Foot and about 350 of his Minneconjou followers quietly slipped away from their Cheyenne River Agency and headed to Pine Ridge, one hundred miles south, to seek refuge with their Oglala brethren led by Red Cloud. The Minneconjous were worried about their safety: a large "camp of observation" had been set up near them by the army. The authorities thought that they might be headed toward the hostiles in the Stronghold and issued orders to apprehend them at all costs. But by the time Big Foot's band reached Pine Ridge, the Stronghold was virtually deserted— almost all the Ghost Dancers had been persuaded to return to their agencies—and the Minneconjous posed no threat.

Five days later, a battalion of the Seventh Cavalry chanced upon the Minneconjous about twenty miles east of Pine Ridge and just a few miles from where the troopers had bivouacked the night before in the nearby valley of Wounded Knee Creek. The bedraggled band of Sioux, its leader prostrate with pneumonia, surrendered and agreed to a military escort into camp. They pitched their fifty tepees[9] a couple of hundred yards south of the regiment's tents near a shallow dry ravine. Forsyth arrived with four more companies of the Seventh and an artillery battery that night. He carried orders to disarm the Minneconjous and escort them to a Nebraska railroad and thence by train to Omaha, where they would remain until the trouble had passed.

Until late in the evening, the Seventh's officers celebrated the capture of Big Foot's band, visiting at various tents to congratulate one another. The night was clear and cold, but a keg of whiskey warmed them and made the occasion more convivial. A few of the officers grabbed some of the Minneconjou warriors and interrogated them as to which ones had been in the Custer battle fourteen years before.[10] In fact, more than one newspaper had reported a desire for revenge by the regiment. One had written a few weeks earlier, "It is well-known that the Seventh Cavalry is fairly itching to be away and pursue the poor Indians. . . . Many of the present officers were with Reno on that day, only four miles distant, and it is safe to say the Sioux will receive no quarter from this famous regiment should the opportunity occur to wreak out vengeance for the blood taken at the battle of the Little Big Horn."[11] Another quoted Captain George Wallace as saying, "The Seventh has a bloody score to settle with them."[12]

The next morning, December 29, was cool and clear. The Minneconjous awoke to find themselves virtually surrounded by twice as many troops as the day before. No one expected any kind of resistance from the cold, hungry, and dispirited Indians—that was clear from Forsyth's deployment. Most of his 470 troopers were arranged to form three sides of an open square, in front of a heated army tent in which Big Foot had spent the night. (Any trouble would have resulted in the soldiers firing into each other, a clear indication of Forsyth's desire to disarm the Minneconjous without a fight.) Most of the other four companies were stationed south of the Indian camp on the far side of the ravine. On a low hill to the north sat a battery of four rapid-fire Hotchkiss guns, their barrels pointed at the Sioux village. The guns were capable of rapidly firing 2.6-pound exploding cartridges more than 4,000 yards.

The 120 Minneconjou warriors were gathered to begin the disarmament. A medicine man painted blue, green, and yellow leaped among them in the Ghost Dance maneuvers, exhorting them to resist and telling them that the Ghost Shirts that most of them wore would repel the soldiers' bullets. The warriors gave up a few old rifles, but none of the Winchester repeaters that the soldiers had seen the day before. The prostrate chief was carried out and placed on a pallet in front of the tent in hopes that he would command his fighting men to cooperate. When Big Foot insisted they had no guns, Forsyth ordered the tepees searched, and Captains Varnum and Wallace each took fifteen men and started on either side of the village. Eventually, about fifty guns were discovered hidden in the lodges or beneath the skirts of the women and thrown into piles. The tension increased, particularly among the young men on both sides: the Minneconjous were terrified that after the soldiers had disarmed them, they would kill them all; the inexperienced troopers were generally scared and on edge. Forsyth ordered the young warriors searched about 9:30 a.m. When Wallace attempted to take a gun from one especially hot-headed warrior (some later said he was deaf and did not understand what was required), he resisted. In the struggle, the Indian raised his rifle high and fired a shot.

At that moment, the medicine man took a handful of dirt and tossed it into the air. A nearby group of Indians threw their blankets up to reveal their hidden rifles and may or may not have fired into the surrounding soldiers; no one knows for sure. A lieutenant yelled, "Look out men, they are going to fire!" and more than a hundred troopers fired their carbines at the warriors. All hell broke loose.[13]

The two groups blazed away at each other. Captain Edward Godfrey yelled at his men not to shoot the women and children, but his First Sergeant said, "To hell with the women."[14] Some of the warriors made for the piles of confiscated rifles and grabbed a few. Others pulled knives and hatchets, broke through the line of blue, and ran toward the tepees, where until seconds earlier women had been packing up and small children had been playing in the dirt. Most of the troopers present fired their single-shot Springfields—the same model some of them had used at the Little Bighorn—as fast as they could reload, shooting at anything that moved. Big Foot was killed as he attempted to sit up, and an officer shot the chief's daughter as she rushed to his side. After ten minutes or so of furious gunfire, the field was covered in smoke. Wallace and several other soldiers lay dead, some of them no doubt at the hands of their own comrades across the way.[15] Twenty-five troopers lost their lives that day.[16]

"Scout, we got our revenge now," a lieutenant told an interpreter.

"What revenge?" asked the scout.

"Don't you know? The Custer Massacre."[17]

The Seventh attacked in force, chasing down Indians throughout the valley. The Hotchkiss guns across the way were put to deadly use, firing up to fifty rounds a minute at any Indians in sight and raking the Minneconjou camp after shots were fired from the tepees. The surviving warriors, men and boys, fought fiercely, while most of the women and children escaped into the ravine behind the lodges.

One Hotchkiss round found a wagon loaded with noncombatants, killing or wounding all on board.[18] Troopers pursued those who escaped from the area, chasing them several miles before finding and killing them.[19] Scattered firing lasted for a few more hours.

Godfrey had fought in every major battle involving the regiment—Washita, Little Bighorn, and Bear Paw in September 1877, where his heroic leadership against the Nez Perce would eventually win him the Medal of Honor. In each of the first two actions, he had coolly conducted a textbook retreat while in command of a small contingent of troopers at a distance from the main battlefield. He had been on detached duty when his company had been ordered into the field, and he had rejoined it at Pine Ridge. Now he was out on his own again. His decisions at Wounded Knee—or at least those of the men he commanded—would not reflect well on him.

He was ordered to take fifteen or twenty men and ride west to look for escaping Indians. Three miles from the carnage, his men detected a group hiding behind some brush in a ravine. From fifty yards away, Godfrey yelled for any women and children to come out. When none came forward, he ordered his nervous troopers to fire a volley into the brush. They did, firing half a dozen shots from twenty-five yards away, then heard a child's scream. Godfrey halted the fire. Behind the bushes were a dead woman, two dead little girls, and a motionless and apparently dying boy. When the youth opened his eyes and moved, a trigger-happy recruit put a bullet in his brain.[20]

The day after the engagement, there was more fighting at nearby White Clay Creek with a few thousand other Sioux. Forsyth allowed the regiment to become pinned down in a cul-de-sac valley, and only the arrival of a battalion of Ninth Cavalry buffalo soldiers drove the Indians away. Most of them headed toward the Stronghold. Over the next two weeks, Miles skillfully used a combination of power and persuasion to convince the Indians of the foolishness of further hostilities. By January 16, 1891, the 4,000 refugee Sioux had surrendered, and the situation was under control.

Nelson Miles was furious at the heavy loss of life and the reports of indiscriminate killing of women and children at Wounded Knee. He immediately relieved Forsyth from command and ordered an investigation into the affair.[21] Nine days after the massacre, a court was convened. Not one enlisted man was called to the stand, and only two civilians (an interpreter and a priest) and two Lakotas (by deposition) were asked to testify. Each officer of the Seventh was asked if his troops had deliberately fired on women and children. To a man, they said that they had enjoined their men against shooting women and children, and they claimed that their men had made every effort to avoid firing on noncombatants. Not one of them had seen any instance of indiscriminate firing, they testified, though some of them hastened to add that it was difficult if not impossible to tell the warriors from the women. No one bothered to point out that the army had previously admitted that fewer than thirty warriors had survived the first assault, making this assertion questionable.[22] Some officers mentioned acts of humanity on the part of their troopers.

Their sworn testimony was contradicted by the carnage on the field—one eyewitness said that "it was a terrible and horrible sight to see women and children lie in groups dead"[23]—and by Indian accounts and the reportage of the three newsmen present. "All orders and tactics were abandoned, the object being solely to kill Indians, regardless of age or sex," wrote one reporter. "The battle was ended only when not a live Indian was in sight."[24] Another told the same story: "It was a war of extermination now with the troopers. . . . There was only one common impulse—to kill wherever an Indian could be seen," including old men and women, mothers, and small children.[25] Some 26 children under the age of thirteen were killed, 4 of them babies with crushed skulls.[26] At least 172 Sioux died on the field, more than 60 of them women and children; many others expired from their wounds later. The final toll was most likely 200 or more.[27] Burials were delayed by a blizzard that roared through the region on December 31. The next day, the stiff and frozen Minneconjou bodies were gathered and thrown into a mass grave by a contractor and his crew who were paid $2 per body. Many of the warriors were first stripped of their Ghost Shirts and much of their clothing by souvenir hunters.[28]

After five days of testimony, the two officers of the court took the Seventh at its word. The January 13 opinion exonerated both Forsyth of any faulty disposition of his troops and the entire regiment of any indiscriminate killing of women and children, the latter "ascribed only to the fault of the Indians themselves and the force of unavoidable and unfortunate circumstances."[29] A report by Captain Frank D. Baldwin of Miles's staff, charged to investigate the field of battle several days after the massacre, brought to light facts that contradicted Godfrey's account. Baldwin reported that the dead women and children killed by Godfrey's men all had distinct powder burns on them, indicating deliberate execution from point-blank range.[30] Despite this evidence (which led to a further investigation into the Godfrey incident, in which he was exonerated) and a revised report by the two examining officers that called Forsyth's deployment of his men into question, no action was taken. Years later, however, President Theodore Roosevelt held up Godfrey's promotion to General in the belief that he had ordered or failed to prevent the atrocity.[31]

Miles's recommendation that Forsyth be punished were ignored. The army dismissed the matter as unfortunate but ultimately beneficial and complimented the Seventh on its conduct during the battle. The eastern newspaper coverage was one-sided—of all the major dailies, only the *New York Herald* suggested anything but a regrettable battle with some unavoidable civilian deaths—so there were few voices raised in opposition. To further support the view of an even battle rather than a massacre, the army awarded the Medal of Honor to eighteen men for their actions at Wounded Knee, and Forsyth was promoted to General just a few years later.

Despite his high-handed ways, Miles continued to work to improve conditions on the Sioux reservations and succeeded to a certain extent. Some monetary compensation was arranged, and improvements were made regarding ration issues. But the old way of life for the Lakotas was gone forever, and they would never again fight the white man, or any of their ancestral Indian enemies, on a field of battle.

MANY OF THE SEVENTH'S OFFICERS PRESENT at the Little Bighorn went on to long and successful military careers. Edward Godfrey finally made Brigadier General in 1907, a year and a half after Winfield Edgerly, his handsome Seventh Cavalry comrade and his junior on the army list. Luther Hare, the self-proclaimed "fighting son of a bitch from Texas," beat them both there: he was appointed Brigadier General of volunteers in 1900 while serving in the Philippines during the Spanish-American War. He retired from the regular army as a Colonel, as did Charles Varnum and Edward "Bible Thumper" Mathey.

Most of the regiment's senior officers did not fare as well. Captains Thomas Weir and Thomas French, of course, died not long after the Little Bighorn. Frederick Benteen's final years in the army were a disappointment. In 1883 he was promoted to Major in the Ninth Cavalry, one of the army's two black cavalry regiments—a promotion he had refused in 1866, when he had joined the Seventh. In 1886 he was ordered to oversee the building of a fort in eastern Utah Territory, but he spent more time drinking heavily than making sure the construction went well. (His deteriorating health and accompanying chronic pain may have contributed to his increased alcohol consumption.) After several months, his superiors took notice.[32] Benteen was court-martialed in January 1887 on six charges of drunkenness and one count of "conduct unbecoming an officer and a gentleman." After three weeks, he was found guilty of three counts of drunkenness and the charge of conduct unbecoming. He was sentenced to dismissal from the service. President Grover Cleveland, reminded of Benteen's long and honorable service, mitigated the sentence to a year's suspension at half pay. A year later, he reentered active service, but after a few months he obtained a medical discharge for a variety of ailments, all of which were "incident to the service."[33] He officially retired in July 1888.

Benteen lived another ten years, most of them comfortably in an Atlanta town house. In 1892 he was brevetted a Brigadier General for gallant and meritorious service at the Little Bighorn and Canyon Creek, during the Nez Perce War. Only one officer in the Seventh Cavalry wrote to congratulate him—a much younger man who had joined the regiment after the Little Bighorn.

Publicly, he avoided interviews and questions about the battle, but privately he gave full vent to his feelings about Custer and his mismanagement of the affair. His dislike for his former commanding officer grew to intense hatred. "When the Colonel was lit," remembered one frequent visitor to the Benteen home, "(he) never tired of going over his life in the army, and particularly his grudge against Custer. He sure was venomous."[34] "The Savior of the Seventh" died on June 22, 1898, of a stroke. His funeral was held three days later, on June 25 — twenty-two years to the day after his finest hour as a soldier.

MARCUS RENO'S FALL was even more precipitous. His drinking increased after his wife died in 1874; it became virtually uncontrollable after the Little Bighorn. By the time of his official exoneration in 1879, his life and career were both speedily going downhill. Only a few months after returning to duty from his two-year suspension, ostracized by most of his fellow officers, he began racking up charges of drunkenness and dishonorable behavior. When he made the mistake of peeping into the window of Colonel Sturgis's quarters one night and frightening his pretty young daughter half to death, his goose was cooked. Sturgis pressed charges, and Reno was found guilty on all counts and dishonorably discharged from the service in April 1880.

Reno spent most of the remainder of his life in failed attempts at reinstatement. After more than five years of denials, he took a lowly job in the War Department's Record and Pension Office in Washington, D.C. He had married again in the meantime — an attractive navy widow — but that relationship fizzled in 1887. (She had him arrested on charges of nonpayment of support a year and a half later.) Rumors spread in Harrisburg that he had attempted to commit suicide, prompting the local newspaper to write that "the Major's actions are entirely due to drink."[35]

But it was not demon rum that would ultimately claim the Major. Reno had smoked heavily since his days at West Point, and he developed tongue cancer, which soon became quite painful. In March 1889, he entered a Washington, D.C., hospital for an operation on the growth. Nine days after it was removed, he developed pneumonia in both lungs and died within forty-eight hours, on the morning of March 30. As a result of a misunderstanding involving his wife's family plot, the man who had commanded the initial attack on the great village on the Little Bighorn was buried in an unmarked grave in the nation's capital.[36]

*　　*　　*

RENO'S ACCUSER, FREDERICK WHITTAKER, died six weeks later. After the Reno court of inquiry, he had returned to his home in Mount Vernon and continued to write—dime novels, articles and stories for various publications, songs, and at least one musical comedy—often collaborating with his younger brother, Octave, a musician.[37] With three daughters and a lovely wife, Whittaker seemed to have every reason to be happy. But he became increasingly irascible, and his passionate advocacy of movements such as spiritualism and Volapük (an invented universal language that quickly faded) eventually gained him a reputation, at least among some townspeople, as something of a crank.[38]

On May 13, 1889, Whittaker spent the morning in town, then returned to his house at 11:00 a.m. He greeted his wife and ascended the staircase to his room. His wife heard a shot and ran up the stairs to find her husband near death. Apparently, his walking stick had become entangled in the banister seconds after he had pulled his .38-caliber revolver out of his pocket to put it down, causing him to shoot himself in the head. He expired thirty minutes later. Though the coroner quickly held an inquest, which determined the shooting to be accidental, rumors of suicide—perhaps prompted by an unpleasant business transaction and despondency—gained some legitimacy in the newspapers.[39]

The *New York Sun* added an ironic twist in its story. After the Civil War, the reporter mistakenly wrote, Whittaker "subsequently enlisted under General Custer, and took part in the battle in which Custer was killed."[40] The English-born cavalryman would have been pleased at this posthumous claim of service at the Little Bighorn under the officer he so admired.

JOHN BURKMAN, CUSTER'S STRIKER and most loyal soldier, never got over the death of his idol—and the fact that he did not die with him. He obtained a disability discharge in 1879, worked for some years as a teamster, and eventually retired to Billings, Montana, sixty miles from the battlefield. He subsisted on a pension of $6 a month for almost thirty years, working odd jobs to make ends meet and living alone in a small shack. He never married. Forty-nine years after the battle, he shot himself to death. He was buried in the national cemetery at the battlefield, a stone's throw from what had become known as Last Stand Hill and the mass grave of the troopers who had died with Custer.

THOUGH ELIZABETH CUSTER traveled extensively throughout the United States, Europe, and Asia, she never visited the valley of the Little Bighorn. After fifty-seven years of ceaselessly burnishing her husband's legacy, she died in 1933, four days short of her ninety-first birthday, in her Park Avenue apartment in New York. A few years earlier, she had told a writer that her greatest disappointment was the absence of "a son to bear his honored name."[41] She was laid to rest beside her husband at West Point. Her grave, in the shadow of his obelisk, is marked by a simple gravestone with the words "Elizabeth Bacon, wife of George Armstrong Custer."

THE BATTLEFIELD WAS DESIGNATED a national cemetery in 1879, partly to protect the graves of the hundreds of Seventh Cavalry troopers buried there. The site was officially named the Custer Battlefield National Monument in 1946 and, after much heated debate between traditionalists and Indian rights activists, was renamed the Little Bighorn Battlefield National Monument in 1991. As the nation's outlying regions became laced with roads and railroad tracks, it was an increasingly popular tourist destination, particularly around the anniversary of the battle, June 25, and the week preceding. On the tenth anniversary of the battle, several white survivors, mostly officers, made the journey for a brief reunion. In the years that followed, that reunion became a tradition that blossomed into a weeklong celebration involving 40,000 people in 1926, when veterans of both sides met to set aside their hostilities and to affirm their friendship. Today nearly 400,000 people visit the remote battlefield annually.

Over the years, visitors and employees have reported supernatural occurrences at the battlefield, from ghostly visits by Indian warriors and cavalry troopers to unexplained voices, cold spots, and other spectral phenomena. Some have postulated that the dead rise up occasionally to fight the battle over and over. The area's Crow Indians, watching park rangers lock the gates at night, gave them the name "ghost herders."

After the tourists have gone, the ridges and ravines overlooking the river below are still and eerie. Today, if one stands there alone as the wind sighs through the buffalo grass, it is not hard to believe that the spirits of the men who died there—Lakotas, Cheyennes, Crows, Arikaras, troopers, officers, citizens, scouts—perform their own ghost dance: clasping hands in a circle, moving ever to the right, praying for a chance to walk the earth again in a brotherhood that reaches past race and religion and greed.

ACKNOWLEDGMENTS

The following individuals and institutions were unfailingly gracious and generous with their time and knowledge: Tamara Vidros, Knight Library, University of Oregon; Shannon Bowen, American Heritage Center, University of Wyoming; Irene Adams, Harold B. Lee Library, Brigham Young University; Marty Frogg, Oglala Lakota College; Anthony Tedeschi, the Lilly Library, Indiana University; Terry Black, Indiana State Library; Sister Ruth Boedigheimer, Sisters of the Order of Saint Benedict; Susan A. Harmon, Putnam County Public Library; Ardys Milke, Beatrice Public Library; Joyce Martin, Labriola American Indian Data Center, Arizona State University; Clifford Johnson and George Miles, Beinecke Rare Book and Manuscript Library, Yale University; Patsy Tate, Washington State University; Ellen Zazzarino, Denver Public Library; Heidi Kennedy, McCracken Research Library; Liza Posas, Braun Research Library; Jelena Radicevic and Susanna Garza, Chicago Public Library; Ken Robison, Joel F. Overholser Historical Research Center; Debbie Vaughan at the Chicago Historical Society; Evelyn L. James, Historical Society of Dauphin County; Al Johnson, at Fort Abraham Lincoln, who in his role of Sgt. John P. Ryan personifies the spirit of the Seventh Cavalry; the solicitous staff at the United States American Military History Institute, especially Art Bergeron; the helpful and always patient librarians at the University of Oklahoma Western Collections; the Denver Public Library; the Center for American History, University of Texas at Austin; and the Manuscript Reading Room at the New York Public Library. At the excellent DeGolyer Research Library, Russell Martin, Director, and Kathy Rome were always gracious and accommodating. The folks at Dallas's J. Erik Jonsson Library, a superior example of its kind, were just as helpful, especially the mistress of Inter Library Loan, Marilyn Jackson; librarians David Compos, Patrick Guzik, Terri Huff, Paul Oswalt, Sally Peden, Pat Tackett, and Heather Williams; and Lloyd Bockstruck and his staff at one of the best genealogy centers in the country. The latter two institutions deserve particular praise, as I was an almost daily visitor/pest at one or the other for more than three years.

For reading parts of the manuscript in rough form and/or rendering invaluable advice and assistance, I thank Robert Utley, dean of western historians; Cheyenne expert David Halaas; the all-knowing Bruce Liddic; editor-cum-expert Elisabeth Kimber; Mike O'Keefe, magnanimous with his time, knowledge, and the use of his superlative library; George Getschow and Frank Coffey, editors extraordinaire; the Reverend Vincent Heier, owner of the greatest Custeriana collection, period; and John Doerner, historian at the Little Bighorn Battlefield National Monument, for being generous with his time and expertise. Others much more knowledgeable than I in various fields who patiently answered an endless array of questions and/or were helpful in many other ways included Sandy Barnard, Louise Barnett, Joan Croy, Brice Custer, Chip Custer, Ephriam Dickson, Jeffrey Eger, David Evans, Sam Fore, Gary Gilbert, Jerry Greene, Kenneth Hammer, Dale Kosman, Mike Koury, Shirley Leckie, Darrell Linthacum, Elizabeth McClain Lockwood, Ryan Lord, John Mackintosh, Billy Markland, Jim May, Frank Mercatante, Diane Merkel, Greg Michno, Ron Nichols, Lee Noyes, Jack Pennington, Tim Phelps, Brian Pohanka, Glen Swanson, and Jeff Wilson.

Others I have need to thank: Chip Watts, owner of the Seventh Ranch, for the wonderful ride over much of the battlefield on horseback — now I know how those new recruits felt after a long day in the saddle; Superintendent Darrell Cook of the Little Bighorn Battlefield National Monument, for permitting me to walk the battlefield, from Deep Ravine to Custer Hill and beyond; saddle pal Mike O'Keefe, again, for accompanying me on those two treks; and B. J. Robbins, my agent, who is also my friend.

An author writes the words, but to make of them an actual book — especially one as elegant as this one — takes a talented team. At Little, Brown, that includes Michael Pietsch, publisher, who believed in this book from the start; Geoff Shandler, my editor, who performed as thorough and as pitch-perfect an edit as I've ever seen; Junie Dahn, his assistant, who rendered an excellent line edit and an endless amount of assistance; copyeditor Barbara Jatkola, who gave it that final polish; proofreader Katie Blatt, who rendered an underappreciated but valuable service; cartographer Jeff Ward, whose superb maps are everything I envisioned and more; Renato Stanisic, whose interior design made it elegant within; and Nneka Bennett, whose gorgeous cover design made it elegant without. I thank you all.

Finally, my wife, Judith, and my daughter, Rachel, for putting up with me. Ditto for Caleb and Katie, cat and dog of the first order. Thank you one and all.

Any mistakes, of course, are mine and mine alone.

James Donovan

NOTES

The following abbreviations are used in the notes. These and other sources are listed in the bibliography.

Camp BYU Notes   William M. Camp Papers, Brigham Young University
Camp IU Notes   William M. Camp Papers, Indiana University
Ricker Tablets   Eli Ricker Collection, Nebraska State
                Historical Society

PROLOGUE: A GOOD DAY TO DIE
1. The description of the Crow's Nest scout is based on the following sources: the accounts of the Arikara scouts in Libby, *The Arikara Narrative of Custer's Campaign;* Lieutenant Charles Varnum's story in Carroll, *Custer's Chief of Scouts;* and the story of the Crow scouts as told by them in Dixon, *The Vanishing Race,* and Graham, *The Custer Myth.* Varnum, in his several narratives, claimed to have ridden seventy miles that day, but he may have exaggerated somewhat. Though he never mentioned it, he probably changed horses sometime during the day.
2. Boyer's diminutive stature is from the Joseph White Cow Bull interview, McCracken Research Library; Gray, *Custer's Last Campaign,* 398; and Coughlan, *Varnum,* 10. Other accounts have an Arikara awaken Varnum.

CHAPTER ONE: THE DIVINE INJUNCTION
Chapter title and epigraph: Bryant, *History of the Great Massacre by the Sioux Indians,* Minnesota: North Star Publishing, 1882.
1. Myers, "Roster of Known Hostile Indians at the Battle of the Little Big Horn," 2; Stewart, *Custer's Luck,* 82.

2. Utley and Washburn, *Indian Wars*, 24.

3. Brandon, *Indians*, 196–98; Utley and Washburn, 23.

4. For a thoughtful discussion of this point, see Brandon, 253–54: "In a word, the Indian world was devoted to living, the European world to getting."

5. Merk, *History of the Westward Movement*, 67–69.

6. For specific instances, see Hinsdale, "The Western Land Policy of the British Government," 223.

7. Quoted in Capps, *The Indians*, 157.

8. Ironically, before the Revolutionary War, Washington, the retired officer and Virginia planter, had been in the forefront of those claiming veterans' land warrants (grants of land given in lieu of money). He also bought those of other veterans and helped to found the Mississippi Land Company, a venture into wilderness real estate. By 1770 he had laid claim to 20,000 acres in the West and sent settlers there to hold his claim (Clary, *Adopted Son*, 31).

9. There is some doubt as to whether Little Turtle was present at Fallen Timbers. The Indian forces were badly directed, unlike the impressively led triumph on the Wabash River in 1791 dubbed St. Clair's Defeat.

10. Stephen H. Long, quoted in Prucha, "Indian Removal and the Great American Desert," 299.

11. Prucha, "Andrew Jackson's Indian Policy," 532.

12. Ibid., 532, 537. Jackson acquired a reputation as an Indian hater, but despite his hard-line stance, that seems a harsh assessment. He once took a year-old Indian orphan about to be killed by Indians into his home to be raised along with his adopted son, Andrew. He named the boy Lincoyer and referred to him as one of "my two sons." He may have initially intended Lincoyer as merely a playmate for Andrew, but Jackson grew to care for the young Indian and even aspired to send him to West Point. Lincoyer died at age sixteen, probably of tuberculosis. That relationship is telling, for Jackson consistently treated Indians as children, to be punished harshly when they were "bad." But chiefs of the Five Civilized Tribes often called on him at his home, the Hermitage, for support in their relations with the government; they considered him harsh but fair and honest. See Remini, *Andrew Jackson and His Indian Wars*, 211–12, 228; and James, *Andrew Jackson: The Border Captain*, 311, 357.

13. Prucha, *American Indian Treaties*, 167. In his landmark decision *Johnson v. McIntosh* (1823) and other cases, Chief Justice John Marshall recognized the right of native possession of land and thus established the basic rule of U.S. jurisprudence in regard to Indian land and landownership.

14. Boyer, *The Oxford Companion to United States History*, 379.

15. Act of 1834, quoted ibid., 7.

16. "White persons crossed at will over the Indian's lands, killed his game, seized his land, and even entered his reservation to sell him whisky and steal his annuities" (Welty, "The Indian Policy of the Army," 371).

17. Jackson, quoted in Peters, *Indian Battles and Skirmishes*, 6.

18. Smith, "The Bozeman: Trail to Death and Glory," 35.
19. Journalist John O'Sullivan coined the phrase to justify U.S. expansion into Texas, Oregon, and Mexico. Boyer, 470.
20. Lee, "Lieutenant Phil Sheridan's Romance in Oregon"; Lockley, "Reminiscences of Martha E. Gilliam Collins," 367–68; Cooper, "Benton County Pioneer-Historical Society," 83.
21. It seems likely that Sidnayoh also bore Sheridan a child, a girl named Emma. See Olney, *Who Are You and Who Am I?* 21–22, and Sheller, *The Name Was Olney,* 46–47.
22. Hutton, *Phil Sheridan and His Army,* 8.
23. Ellis, *The History of Our Country from the Discovery of America to the Present Time,* 1483. Sheridan was replying to a Comanche chief, Tosawi, who had just surrendered his band of Indians and said, "Tosawi, good Indian."
24. Utley, *The Indian Frontier of the American West,* 52.
25. This description of the Sioux derives chiefly from White, "The Winning of the West," and Hassrick, *The Sioux.*
26. Lazarus, *Black Hills, White Justice,* 18.
27. Ibid., 41–46.
28. Thomas Fitzpatrick, quoted ibid., 63.
29. Folwell, *A History of Minnesota,* vol. 2, 232.
30. Peters, 7.
31. Camp IU Notes, 437.
32. Ibid., 336.
33. See Calitri, "Give Me Eighty Men," for a well-sourced reinterpretation of Fetterman and his ill-fated band.
34. This summary of Crazy Horse's life is based on Sajna's fine *Crazy Horse;* Hardorff, *The Oglala Lakota Crazy Horse;* Neihardt, *Black Elk Speaks;* Hinman, "Oglala Sources on the Life of Crazy Horse"; Joseph C. Porter, "Crazy Horse, Lakota Leadership, and the Fort Laramie Treaty," in Rankin, *Legacy;* and Eli S. Ricker's interviews in the Ricker Tablets. Only Sieux oral tradition supports his presence with the decoy party.
35. Carroll, *Who Was This Man Ricker?* 48.
36. He Dog, quoted in Sajna, 29.
37. Captain Jesse M. Lee wrote that he was not over five feet six inches (Lee to Camp, May 24, 1910, Camp BYU Collection), but others have said he was five feet eight inches.
38. Hinman, 40.
39. Mrs. Charles Tackett, quoted in Sajna, 29.
40. Smits, "The Frontier Army," 322–23.
41. Utley, "Origins of the Great Sioux War," 49.
42. Vestal, *Sitting Bull,* 110.
43. Thorndike, *The Sherman Letters,* 321.
44. George H. Stuart, quoted in McFeely, *Grant,* 239.
45. Ibid., 306.
46. The 1870 army appropriations bill was amended to prohibit military offi-

cers from holding civil appointments (largely to regain the advantages of patronage). Grant turned all seventy-three agencies over to church groups, a flagrant violation of the nation's doctrine of church-state separation, which was ignored at the time. Smith, *Grant,* 528.

47. Welty, 371.
48. Utley, "The Celebrated Peace Policy of General Grant," 130.
49. Prucha, *The Great Father,* 164–65. Another reason was a growing movement to treat Indians as wards of the government and not equals.
50. One Methodist minister, Dr. Wright, who was appointed Crow Indian agent in 1873, "had always been a good and honest man, until he got into the Indian Department. Dr. Wright's wife . . . was anxious to make money" (Lyndel Meikle, "No Paper Trail: Crooked Agents on the Crow Reservation, 1874–1878," in Walter, *Speaking Ill of the Dead,* 26).
51. For a convincing discussion of this, see Smits.
52. Lee, *Fort Meade and the Black Hills,* 2.
53. Krause and Olson, *Prelude to Glory,* 268. If the search for gold was an official directive of the column, there is no record of it. All of Sheridan's official communications to Custer mention the search for a suitable location for a fort as its purpose. Custer's direct superior, Brigadier General Alfred Terry, denied that the expedition's purpose was the search for gold: "Plunder is not the objective of this expedition. . . . It seeks neither gold, timber nor arable land" (ibid., 3). Also, it's unlikely Custer would have had to pay the two accompanying miners out of his own pocket, or specifically request a geologist (who would go on to disagree publicly with the expedition commander's positive reports of the discovery of gold). Finally, the army sent another expedition into the Black Hills the next year to verify Custer's claims, further proof that the goal of the 1874 expedition was not to find gold. For a convincing discussion of this point, see Jackson, *Custer's Gold,* 82 and chap. 3, "The Scientific Corps."
54. Custer to Barrett, May 19, 1874, quoted in Frost, "The Black Hills Expedition of 1874," 11.
55. Ibid., 3.
56. Ibid., 24.
57. Hutton, *Phil Sheridan and His Army,* 168. For further confirmation hat gold was found, as Custer asserted in one report, "among he roots of the grass," see William H. Wood, "Reminiscences of the lack Hills Expedition," in Cozzens, *Eyewitnesses to the Indian Wars,* vol. 4, 178.
58. Custer, quoted in Slotkin, *The Fatal Environment,* 365.
59. Kime, *The Black Hills Journals of Colonel Richard Irving Dodge,* 11.
60. Lazarus, 78.
61. Lone Horn, quoted in Sajna, 268.
62. Crook, quoted in Andrist, *The Long Death,* 247.
63. Utley, *The Lance and the Shield,* 126.
64. Hutton, *Phil Sheridan and His Army,* 299.

65. Andrist, 85.
66. Lazarus, 83–84; and Gray, *Centennial Campaign*, 23–31.
67. Quoted in Lazarus, 85. White Bull, outstanding Lakota warrior and nephew of Sitting Bull, said that runners from the agency did not reach them to tell them to come to the agency (Hardorff, *Indian Views of the Custer Fight*, 162).
68. Sheridan, quoted in Gray, *Centennial Campaign*, 33. One agent requested an extension of the deadline. It seems that a mixed band of Lakotas had attacked a friendly tribe on the upper Missouri. This assault had prevented the agent's representatives from reaching the other hostiles (John Burke, Standing Rock agent, to Commissioner of Indian Affairs J. Q. Smith, January 30, 1876, in Fay, *Military Engagements Between United States Troops and Plains Indians*). No extension was granted.
69. Stewart, *Custer's Luck*, 80. About three hundred lodges of northern Sioux would come in to Standing Rock Agency in late February, with the promise of more to come (Anderson, "A Challenge to Brown's Sioux Indian Wars Thesis," 40–49).
70. "Annual Report of Lt. General Sheridan, 1874," cited in Merkel, *Unravelling the Custer Enigma*, 86.
71. Beadle, *Western Wilds*, 550.

CHAPTER TWO: "THE BOY GENERAL OF THE GOLDEN LOCK"
Chapter title: quoted in Wert, *Custer,* 85.
Epigraph: William T. Sherman to John Sherman, September 25, 1868, quoted in Thorndike, *The Sherman Letters,* 289.

1. Quoted in Urwin, *Custer Victorious,* 268.
2. Wing, *History of Monroe County, Michigan,* 318.
3. Unless otherwise noted, this account of Custer's upbringing is primarily based on Whittaker, *A Complete Life of General George A. Custer;* Ronsheim, *The Life of General Custer;* Merington, *The Custer Story;* Monaghan, *Custer;* Utley, *Cavalier in Buckskin;* and Wert, *Custer.*
4. *Cincinnati Commercial* story, reprinted in *Big Horn Yellowstone Journal* (Spring 1994, 3).
5. Wing, 318.
6. Wallace, *Custer's Ohio Boyhood,* 20.
7. Bulkley, "As a Classmate Saw Custer."
8. Quoted in Wert, 29.
9. Wert, 34. This disease sometimes led to sterility, which might explain why Armstrong and Libbie had no children despite an active sex life. A classmate, Tully McCrea, also testified to his amorous inclinations; see Crary, *Dear Belle,* 214–15.
10. Merington, *The Custer Story,* 9.
11. Quoted in Wert, 30.
12. Aimore, "U.S. Military Academy Civil War Sources and Statistics." Also, in the letter referenced in note 14 below, Custer claimed that "thirty-seven resigned during the last week. My roommate who is a southerner and a

secessionist intends to resign next Monday." Custer no doubt was referring to all of the Point's classes, not just his.

13. Wert, 39.

14. Custer to Lydia Ann Reed, April 27, 1861, cited in O'Neil, *My Dear Sister,* 14.

15. Joseph Fought, quoted in Merington, *The Custer Story,* 58.

16. Wert, 80, Gregory J. W. Urwin, "Custer: The Civil War Years," in Hutton, *The Custer Reader,* 15.

17. Jacob Greene, quoted in Brady, *Indian Fights and Fighters,* 392.

18. Monaghan, 113, 116, 122. As Monaghan points out, one of Custer's friends later said that Custer never purposely exaggerated; he just saw things bigger than other people.

19. Custer's letters to his family and friends around this time are suffused with contentment and satisfaction with the job of soldiering. Merington, *The Custer Story,* 53–54.

20. Fought, quoted ibid., 60.

21. There seems to be some disagreement on whether Kilpatrick ordered Custer's command to charge or Custer decided himself. Gregory Urwin, in his thorough *Custer Victorious,* blames Custer for the decision and calls it the only incident during the war of true recklessness on his part. Both Jeffrey D. Wert in *Custer* and Edward G. Longacre in *Custer and His Wolverines* fault Kilpatrick for ordering Custer forward (though Longacre cites as his only source Wert). Wert's impeccably researched biography gives the nod to this version.

22. Merington, *The Custer Story,* 62.

23. Pleasanton, quoted in Urwin, *Custer Victorious,* 278.

24. Wert, 201.

25. S. L. Gracey, quoted in Wert, 174.

26. Urwin, *Custer Victorious,* 191.

27. Landis, "Custer at Lacey Spring," 57, 68.

28. Utley, *Cavalier in Buckskin,* 33.

29. George A. Custer to Elizabeth B. Custer, April 11, 1865, quoted in Merington, *The Custer Story,* 162.

30. Wengert, *The Custer Despatches,* 145.

31. For an accurate and balanced account of Custer's discipline measures, see Barnett, *Touched by Fire,* 65–75.

32. Whittaker, *A Complete Life of General George A. Custer,* 344; Custer to President Andrew Johnson, August 11 and 13, 1866, Box 4, Folder 10, Kuhlman Collection.

33. See Carroll, *Camp Talk,* for letters confirming Benteen's randiness.

34. Benteen to General U. S. Grant, August 20, 1866, in *Catalogue: The Personal Collection of Dale C. Anderson,* 62, 63.

35. R. G. Cartwright, a good friend of H Company's Sergeant Charles Windolph after he retired in Lead, South Dakota, wrote the following in his copy of Graham's *The Custer Myth,* p. 201 (Cartwright Collection): "Mrs. Custer states that Benteen was drunk, tangled with his saber, fell down, saluted while prone and was ordered to his quarters. Instead went to Officer's Club

or canteen where he stated he: 'Didn't think he was going to like that pink whiskered S.O.B.'" While Libbie Custer in one of her books did write of a newly assigned officer whose introduction to her husband was identical to this, she also stated that the officer was soon transferred. But the alleged quote likely came from Windolph, who served under Benteen for several years, and sounds very much like a Benteenism.

36. Edward Luce to Charles Kuhlman, January 16, 1939, Box 1, Kuhlman Collection. See also the section titled "A Matter of Drink" in Langellier et al., *Myles Keogh,* 128–29.

37. Leckie, *Elizabeth Bacon Custer,* 102–3.

38. Ibid., 98.

39. For more on alcohol in the Old Army, see Barnett, *Touched by Fire,* 78–79.

40. Even the military-heavy peace commission convened later in the year concluded, after two days of testimony, that the campaign had been unnecessary and disastrous and that it had been "organized and conducted on the basis of false information. Preceding the expedition there had been no major Indian disturbances in Kansas, but in the wake of Hancock's campaign a general uprising occurred." Mattingly, "The Great Plains Peace Commission of 1867," 30.

41. Merington, *The Custer Story,* 205. In January of that year, a group of forty men had deserted together in a single day, and in a two-week period in July, 156 men deserted from six companies of the Seventh.

42. Halaas and Masich, *Halfbreed,* 222. Edmund Guerrier was the guide; he later admitted that he discouraged Custer from pursuing a hot trail and then led the column in the wrong direction, since he had friends in the Cheyenne camp.

43. The officer was Captain Robert M. West, who disliked Custer intensely. Charges quoted in Wert, 262–63.

44. Ibid., 261; Leckie, 97–103.

45. G. A. Custer Court-Martial, 154, 152.

46. Kennedy, *On the Plains with Custer and Hancock,* 128.

47. Libbie Custer to Rebecca Richmond, September 1867, quoted in Merington, *The Custer Story,* 212.

48. Monaghan, 303.

49. Wert, 264; Minnie D. Millbrook, "The West Breaks In General Custer," in Hutton, *The Custer Reader,* 148.

50. Sandy Barnard, "Custer & Elliott: Comrades in Controversy," *14th Annual Symposium,* 19–20.

51. Utley, *Life in Custer's Cavalry,* 258: "The appointment came about because the application of December 1865, despite repeated follow-ups, kept getting lost among all the paper in Washington. Finally, in March 1867, after most of the vacancies in the postwar army had been filled, the powerful wartime governor of Indiana, Oliver P. Morton, called in person on Secretary of War Edwin M. Stanton to urge Elliott's candidacy. Queried by the Secretary, the Adjutant General reported that two vacancies existed for which the young man might qualify: Captain, 9th Cavalry, and Major, 7th Cavalry. The

Secretary at once issued an appointment to the latter post. Only then did Elliott appear before the Hunter examining board, which routinely confirmed the Secretary's appointment."

52. Greene, *Washita*, 61.

53. Sherman, quoted in Camp BYU Notes, Reel 5, 229.

54. Butterfield and Butterfield, *Important Custer, Indian War and Western Memorabilia, April 4, 1995, in San Francisco*, 30.

55. Merington, *The Custer Story*, 217.

56. Cozzens, *Eyewitnesses to the Indian Wars*, vol. 3, 250; Frost, *General Custer's Libbie*, 176.

57. Nepotism was rampant in the postwar army. Wesley Merritt used his influence to gain a commission for his brother and then win him a transfer to Merritt's regiment, according to John W. Merritt, their father: "Charley our seventh son and baby . . . is 24 years old. . . . In September President Grant appointed him through the influence of his brother Wesley for examination as Lieutenant in the regular army. He was examined by a board of officers, passed satisfactorily and was commissioned as 2d Lieut in the 9th Cavalry, his brother's regiment in Texas." John W. Merritt to his niece Josephine, November 22, 1873, Box 3G470, Folder 3, Brininstool Collection.

58. Greene, *Washita*, 79.

59. Ricker, *The Settler and Soldier Interviews*, 290.

60. Hutton, *Phil Sheridan and His Army*, 54.

61. Sheridan's orders are quoted in Wert, 271–72. The information on the Washita battle is chiefly derived from Wert; Godfrey, "Some Reminiscences"; Monaghan, *Custer*; and Custer, *My Life on the Plains*.

62. Foley, "Walter Camp," 23. Other accounts mention as many as 150 warriors.

63. Ibid., 19–20; Ben Clark interview, Camp IU Notes, Box 2, Folder 3: "The trail of warriors we had been following split from it [another party of Indians] near Black Kettle's village and entered the village. When we charged on the village Custer's battalion followed this trail right into the village."

64. Barnitz to W. M. Camp, November 18, 1910, Camp BYU Collection.

65. Ben Clark interview, Camp IU Notes, Box 2, Folder 3.

66. Camp BYU Notes, Reel 5, 186. Ibid., 379: "Killed some squaws in creek" (account of Dennis Lynch). Ben Clark interview, Camp IU Notes, Box 2, Folder 3: "During the heaviest fighting about twenty men, women and children took refuge behind the bank of the river in the bend. When a lull came they were discovered. They refused to surrender and all were killed."

67. Camp IU Notes, 825.

68. Godfrey, "Some Reminiscences," 493.

69. Ben Clark interview, Camp IU Notes, Box 2, Folder 3: "In the afternoon 1,200 or 1,500 warriors massed."

70. Custer, *My Life on the Plains*, 257–58, and Godfrey, in his article in *Winners of the West*, June 30, 1929, both claimed that a detail under the command of Captain Edward Myers rode two miles downriver in search of Elliott. Both Lieutenant Edward Mathey (Carroll, *General Custer and the Battle of the Washita*, 42) and Sergeant John Ryan (Ryan to W. A. Falconer, April 15,

1922, Elizabeth B. Custer Collection) also asserted that a search had been made. ("You claim that Custer never looked after Major Elliott's party that was killed in that battle," wrote Ryan, "but I say that he did and the parties that went in search were driven back.") Finally, another Seventh Cavalry officer, Lieutenant Edward Mathey, also claimed later that "having fruitlessly searched for the Major, it was rightly concluded that he and his party had been attacked and killed, and Custer prepared for his return march" (Cozzens, *Eyewitnesses to the Indian Wars,* vol. 3, 363), though Mathey was with the pack train, which was miles in the rear at that time. In *Sheridan's Troopers on the Borders,* 149–50, DeB. Randolph Keim says twice in one convoluted sentence that no attempt was made. Keim was a newspaper correspondent who was back at Camp Supply with Sheridan and presumably heard Custer and his officers describe the battle.

71. Godfrey, "Some Reminiscences," 499.

72. Greene, *Washita,* 104.

73. Black Kettle himself had admitted only a week earlier that he couldn't control some of his young warriors, and another chief in the village, Little Rock, had admitted the same thing a few months earlier (ibid., 53, 107). Additionally, Sheridan, in his official reports, told of items found in the camp that implicated Black Kettle's warriors in the Kansas depredations: "The mail on his person [an expressman had been killed and mutilated between Forts Dodge and Larned] was found in Black Kettle's camp . . . also photographs and other articles taken from the houses on the Saline and Solomon," though Custer mentioned none in his detailed report of items found in the camp and destroyed. If anyone else saw this evidence, they never wrote about it (Carroll, *General Custer and the Battle of the Washita,* 53; Greene, *Washita,* 186–87). Stanley Vestal, in *Warpath and Council Fire,* 150, claims that "the very day Black Kettle got back to his camp on the Washita, two Cheyenne war parties, led by Black Shield and Crow Neck, came in from Kansas, where they had been committing depredations, and the whole camp prepared for a big scalp dance." Vestal talked to many Indians in researching his books, but he occasionally fictionalized his material and is unreliable. His original interview notes are valuable though somewhat indecipherable. Half-breed scout Edmund Guerrier, in an affidavit, said that young men from the bands of Black Kettle and Little Rock had participated in the massacre on the Solomon and Saline rivers in August 1868 and that one of the two leaders in the party, Man Who Breaks the Marrow Bones, belonged to Black Kettle's band (Carroll, *General Custer and the Battle of the Washita,* 243). Additionally, Trails the Enemy said, "The Cheyenne were having a great dance in honor of the returning war parties" (Hardorff, *Washita Memories,* 346). Finally, according to Sheridan, one of the female captives, Black Kettle's sister Mahwissa, confirmed that war parties had raided and inflicted depredations upon white settlements, returning with scalps (Carroll, *General Custer and the Battle of the Washita,* 53; Custer, *My Life on the Plains,* 266, 251). However, these are all ex post facto justifications. The Indians had a legal right to be where they were. But to Sheridan and his superiors, these

Indians — or some of them — had broken the terms of the 1867 Treaty of Medicine Lodge when they had attacked, killed, raped, and plundered along the Saline and Solomon rivers and deserved punishment. Sadly, Black Kettle had only recently returned from Fort Cobb, eighty miles down the Washita, where he had asked Colonel William B. Hazen for permission to join other peaceful tribes there. Hazen, fearful of another Sand Creek Massacre if Sheridan's troops should find the Cheyennes there, had turned him away, telling him to make peace with Sheridan. Black Kettle would never get that chance (Greene, *Washita*, 104).

74. Custer, *My Life on the Plains*, 241.

75. Greene, *Washita*, 136–37. See also Smith, "Custer Didn't Do It."

76. See Hardorff, *Washita Memories*, 173, for the account of an anonymous correspondent for the *New York Daily Tribune* — likely a Seventh Cavalry officer — who wrote, "A few of the squaws took part in the fight, using pistols"; and ibid., 339–40, where Captain George Yates described a Cheyenne woman firing a pistol. See also Carroll, *General Custer and the Battle of the Washita*, 38, and Greene, *Washita*, 126. For two excellent discussions of the massacre vs. battle controversy, see Greene, *Washita*, chap. 9, "Controversies," and Hardorff, *Washita Memories*, 29–31. For a good discussion of the Indian casualty figures, see Smith, "Custer Didn't Do It," and Hardorff, *Washita Memories*, 403. Scout Ben Clark later estimated the Cheyenne loss at seventy-five warriors and fully as many women and children killed (*New York Sun*, May 14, 1899), though the many Cheyenne estimates averaged less than 20 warriors, 16 women, and 10 children killed (Hardorff, *Washita Memories*, appendix 6). This seems more reasonable than Custer's figure, particularly in light of Godfrey's explanation years later of how it was arrived at. He told researcher Walter Camp: "On second night Custer interrogated the officers as to what Indians they had seen dead in the village and it was from these reports that the official report of the Indians killed was made up. The dead bodies on the field were not counted as a whole, while troops there, but guessed at later, as explained" (Camp BYU Notes, Reel 5, 185). In other words, this was a typical case of the inflated body count so common in U.S. Army reports.

77. Greene, *Washita*, 120.

78. Custer, *My Life on the Plains*, 244. See also Ben Clark's account in the *New York Sun*, May 14, 1899, and D. L. Spotts's account in Box 3G470, Folder 6, Brininstool Collection. In a letter from D. L. Spotts to E. A. Brininstool, Spotts, an enlisted man with the Nineteenth Kansas Volunteer Cavalry, which was part of the main strike force, wrote: "The orders were not to harm the women and children and many of them escaped, others staid [*sic*] in the tents thinking it was safer than venturing outside." In *Sheridan's Troopers on the Border*, 117, Keim, a reporter who remained at Camp Supply, wrote: "A number of squaws also participated in the fight, and were seen fighting with all the energy and precision of warriors. . . . The women and children took up arms." Keim doubtless garnered this information from members of the Seventh upon their return to Camp Supply. However,

Captain Barnitz said that he and his company rode through a "band" of women running, many with infants on their backs and leading children by the hand, and that he and his men did not fire (Camp IU Notes, 541). By contrast, Lieutenant Godfrey told researcher William Camp that when they charged through the village the men "fired through tepees and took no care to prevent hitting women" (Camp BYU Notes, Reel 5, 186) and also "that in charging through the village one of his Sergeants (Claire) killed a squaw" (Camp IU Notes, 445); Private Dennis Lynch told Walter Camp that the troopers "killed some squaws in creek" (Camp BYU Notes, Reel 5, 379); and Clark, in Hunt, "The Subjugation of Black Kettle," 106–7, is quoted as saying, "About twenty men, women and children took refuge in this place [a bend of the river], and hid from sight during the heaviest fighting. When a lull came, they were discovered, and on their refusal to surrender, were all killed." That Custer was capable of cold-bloodedness when it came to non-warriors among the enemy is evinced by his order to Captain Myles Keogh in May 1867: "You will without regard to age, sex or condition kill all Indians you may encounter, belonging to Sioux or Cheyennes, except [if] you are convinced they belong to certain bands of friendly (?) Indians, reported as being on the headwaters of the Republican. . . . it is not proposed to burden your command with prisoners" (Langellier et al., *Myles Keogh*, 108).

79. Wert, 283.
80. Brininstool, *Campaigning with Custer*, 152.
81. Years later, in a letter to a former Seventh cavalryman, Benteen revealed the disingenuousness of his blaming Custer for Elliott's death: "Elliott, like myself, was 'pirating' on his own hook; allowed himself to be surrounded and died like a man." Carroll, *The Benteen-Goldin Letters*, 252.
82. Bates, *Custer's Indian Battles*, 16. However, historian George Grinnell wrote: "Ben Clark, who was in the fight, stated that when the first people appeared from the lower villages, General Custer ordered Major Elliott to take a few men and disperse those Indians" (Grinnell, *The Fighting Cheyennes*, 300), though Clark made no mention of any such orders in any other interviews.
83. George A. Custer to Libbie Custer, November 2, 1868, in the James D. Julia auction catalog *Outstanding Firearm Auction Spring 2007*.
84. Benteen also claimed that he had no idea the letter would be published (Carroll, *The Benteen-Goldin Letters*, 267, 281). Godfrey's account supports Benteen's (Frank Anders to R. G. Cartwright, February 7, 1948, Cartwright Collection).
85. Carroll, *The Benteen-Goldin Letters*, 267; Sklenar, *To Hell with Honor*, 36–38. Sklenar's book, full of fresh insights and conclusions, is one of the best examinations of the Battle of the Little Bighorn yet written. Concerning Custer's failure to mention any officers by name, even his staunchest defender, Godfrey would admit fifty-one years later: "Personally, I was never a 'Custerite.' My grievance was that Custer, in his 'Galaxy' articles, did not give me credit for discovering and giving him, at the battle of the Washita, his first information of the 'big hostile village' below the

battlefield" (E. S. Godfrey to William Ghent, September 8, 1927, quoted in *Research Review* 11, no. 4 [Winter 1972], 76).

86. Sheridan, *Personal Memoirs,* 320. Edward Godfrey later wrote, "We were 'betting' that we should find Elliot with the wagon train — thinking in following the dismounted Indians of whom I wrote you some months ago, he had, on returning, found the hostiles practically surrounding the village and that he thereupon detoured and went on the back trail" (Millbrook, "Godfrey on Custer," 78).

87. E. S. Godfrey to William Ghent, September 8, 1927, Hagner Collection; David L. Spotts to William Ghent, May 26, 1933, Hagner Collection.

88. W. A. Graham to E. A. Brininstool, December 21, 1936, Brininstool Collection.

89. In the years after the battle, some historians insisted that Elliott's death at the Washita had strongly polarized the Seventh, causing a rift that would last until June 25, 1876. There seems legitimate reason to doubt this. Both Godfrey and Spotts, in the letters cited in note 87, stated that they heard no such criticism of Custer for his actions concerning Elliott, and Charles Varnum, who joined the regiment in 1872, later wrote that he had "heard the general story but no criticism of Custer for the abandonment of Elliott" (Colonel T. M. Coughlan to Frederic Van de Water, March 29, 1935, Van de Water Papers). Of course, they may not have talked to the right members of the Seventh. What seems clear is that the rift appeared before the Washita and was more likely the result of the polarizing nature of the antagonistic personalities of Custer and Benteen, exacerbated by Custer's 1868 court-martial and his retaliatory charges against Captain Robert M. West. Years later, in his copy of Custer's *My Life on the Plains,* Benteen penned a revealing note concerning Elliott: "Had party been found after fight of Washita, they would simply have been found dead, as they were two weeks later" — thereby putting the lie to his earlier charges of abandonment (Carroll, *Custer: From the Civil War to the Little Big Horn,* 14). Custer historian William Ghent stated, "No one, so far as I have been able to learn, then spoke of the withdrawal from the field as an abandonment of Elliott" (quoted in Carroll, *The Fred Dustin and Earl K. Brigham Letters,* 15). However, Lieutenant James Bell wrote later, "Major Elliott was missed but careful inquiry developed no knowledge of him. . . . The situation being pressing, the command went off, without investigating, a thing for which Custer was sharply criticized in many quarters afterward" (Hardorff, *Washita Memories,* 167).

CHAPTER THREE: PATRIOTS
Epigraph: Chips, quoted in Carroll, *Who Was This Man Ricker?* 48.

1. Information on the life of Inkpaduta is sketchy and contradictory, both in primary and secondary sources. Mark Diedrich's *Famous Chiefs of the Eastern Sioux* is the best-researched account of his life. Other good sources are Peggy Rodina Larson's "A New Look at the Elusive Inkpaduta"; Joseph Henry Taylor's "Inkpaduta and Sons"; Mrs. Josephine Waggoner's unpub-

lished typescript "Inkpaduta" (though she lifted much of the first half of her paper almost word for word from Taylor's work); and Thomas Teakle's *The Spirit Lake Massacre*, probably the best overall account of that event.

2. Teakle, 68.

3. Larson, 25.

4. Lawrence Taliaferro, quoted in Diedrich, *Famous Chiefs of the Eastern Sioux*, 46.

5. Ibid., 48.

6. Larson, 30. Other death totals listed in other accounts range from thirty-two to forty.

7. Blank, "Inkpaduatah's Great White Friend," 17. For more testimonials, both white and Indian, to Inkpaduta's good character, see Diedrich, *Famous Chiefs of the Eastern Sioux*, 46.

8. Cited in Larson, "A New Look at the Elusive Inkpaduta," 33. Respected Sioux missionary Dr. Thomas S. Sullivan, in a letter in the *St. Paul Pioneer Press*, September 3, 1862, stated that the "utter neglect" of the authorities to punish the Spirit Lake murderers was the "primary cause" of the Great Sioux Uprising of 1862. See also Folwell, *A History of Minnesota*, 225.

9. Vestal, *Sitting Bull*, 55, 57; Utley, *The Lance and the Shield*, 56.

10. This summary of Sitting Bull's life follows Robert Utley's superb *The Lance and the Shield*; Stanley Vestal's elegant but embroidered *Sitting Bull*; and Gary C. Anderson's enlightening *Sitting Bull and the Paradox of Lakota Nationhood*.

11. Vestal, *New Sources of Indian History*, 44.

12. Ibid., 64.

13. Hassrick, *The Sioux*, 15–31.

14. Utley, *The Lance and the Shield*, 30.

15. Lazarus, *Black Hills, White Justice*, 24–25.

16. Sajna, *Crazy Horse*, 135–36.

17. Vestal, *Sitting Bull*, 102.

18. Utley, *The Lance and the Shield*, 86–89.

19. Hinman, "Oglala Sources on the Life of Crazy Horse," 3.

20. Ibid., 14.

21. Vestal, *Warpath: The True Story of the Fighting Sioux*, 139–43.

22. Hanson, *The Conquest of the Missouri*, 179.

23. See George A. Custer, "Battling with the Sioux on the Yellowstone," originally published in *Galaxy*, July 1876, and reprinted in Cozzens, *Eyewitnesses to the Indian Wars*, vol. 4.

24. DeMallie, *The Sixth Grandfather*, 163.

25. Parker, *Gold in the Hills*, 130. See also Brown and Willard, *The Black Hills Trails*; they list about one hundred deaths at the hands of Indians in and around the Black Hills during this period.

26. Milligan, *Dakota Twilight*, 59.

27. Marquis, *Wooden Leg*, 159.

28. Robert A. Marshall, "How Many Indians Were There?" in Carroll, *Custer and His Times*, Book 2, 210–11; Greene, *Battles and Skirmishes of the Great*

Sioux War, 8, 10, 14. Indian accounts (see Marshall's excellent article for the best discussion of the size of the Indian camp) are fairly consistent in reporting between 50 and 60 Cheyenne lodges in the camp and fewer Sioux lodges. Robert Strayhorn, the newspaperman who rode into battle with the army troops at Powder River, mentioned several times in his account of the battle that there were more than 100 lodges in the camp, as did Thaddeus Stanton, another correspondent with Crook's column. Colonel Reynolds himself claimed 105 lodges in his official report. Also, an officer named Charles Morgan told a researcher years later that he had counted 104 lodges in the village (Camp BYU Notes, Reel 5, 133). However, in a 1910 interview (Hammer, *Custer in '76,* 205), He Dog said of the battle, "I was there with a few Sioux," which doesn't sound like 40 or more lodges, and scout-interpreters William Garnett and Big Bat Pourier both claimed that there were only 12 or 14 Sioux lodges (Camp BYU Notes, Reel 5, 287). I have estimated 50 Cheyenne lodges and 15 Sioux lodges.

29. Vestal, *New Sources of Indian History,* 163.
30. Powell, *People of the Sacred Mountain,* 949.
31. Marquis, *Wooden Leg,* 182.

Chapter Four: Outside the States
Epigraph: Custer, quoted in Merington, *The Custer Story,* 277.

1. George A. Custer to Libbie Custer, telegram, February 4, 1873, Harlan Crow Library.
2. Merington, *The Custer Story,* 239.
3. *Bismarck Tribune,* July 16, 1873: "This evening about 70 carpenters arrived from St. Paul, and next week about 80 more will come." In a report of December 1875, the post surgeon reported that "the men have iron bunks and bedsacks filled with hay which is changed once a month. Each man has four or five blankets. In some of the companies the bedsacks are double and two men sleep in a bed, two bedsteads being placed side by side. This is a bad arrangement, but the objections to it cannot be impressed upon the minds of some company commanders" (quoted in O'Neil, *Fort Abraham Lincoln,* 8). Also Al Johnson, Fort Abraham Lincoln, conversation with author, January 8, 2007.
4. Herbert Swett to his parents, June 6, 1875, quoted in *Bonhams and Butterfields Catalogue* of June 28, 2005, 88.
5. John Manion, "Custer's Cooks and Maids," in Carroll, *Custer and His Times,* Book 2, 182.
6. Darling, *Custer's Seventh Cavalry Comes to Dakota,* 148.
7. Felix Vinatieri to Department of Dakota, August 31, 1875, Fort Lincoln, Telegrams Sent, National Archives.
8. O'Neil, *Custer Chronicles,* vol. 1, 22.
9. Barnett, "Libbie Custer and Mark Twain," 19.
10. General Alfred Terry to Custer, March 27, 1875, Department of Dakota, Letters Sent, 1875, National Archives; James Gordon Bennett to Custer, April 4, 1875, Roll 2, Elizabeth B. Custer Collection.

11. Custer to Cheyenne River Indian Agent, March 9, 1875, Fort Abraham Lincoln, Letters Sent, 1875, National Archives.

12. Herbert Swett to his parents, June 30, 1875, quoted in *Bonhams and Butterfields Catalogue* of June 28, 2005, 88. However, a story in the June 2, 1875, *Bismarck Tribune* indicated that Custer was not present at the first treaty signing in late May, which was buttressed by another mention of Custer in the same issue that stated: "Gen. Custer is expected this evening."

13. *Annual Report of the Commissioner of Indian Affairs*, 45.

14. *Bismarck Tribune,* June 30, 1875.

15. Custer to Department of Dakota, March 27, 1875, Fort Lincoln, Telegrams Sent, 1875, National Archives.

16. Milligan, *Dakota Twilight,* 36.

17. Slotkin, *The Fatal Environment,* 426.

18. Ibid., 427.

19. Rickey, *Forty Miles a Day on Beans and Hay,* 70.

20. Wooster, *The Military and United States Indian Policy,* 63.

21. George A. Custer to Libbie Custer, April 10, 1876, Merington Papers; Alberts, *Brandy Station to Manila Bay,* 222.

22. Utley, *Cavalier in Buckskin,* 155.

23. Custer to Terry, January 31, 1876, Department of Dakota, Letters Received, 1876, National Archives.

24. *Our Great Indian War,* 68.

25. Tilford, "Life in the Old Army."

26. George A. Custer to Libbie Custer, January 14, 1869, quoted in Joe Rubinfine, List 152, *American Historical Autographs*.

27. The officer was Edward Godfrey; identified in Millbrook, "Godfrey on Custer," 78.

28. George A. Custer to Libbie Custer, n.d. but probably March 1869, Elizabeth B. Custer Collection.

29. Albert Barnitz, quoted in Wert, *Custer,* 298.

30. Falconer, "Early Notes and Comments," 7.

31. Barnett, *Touched by Fire,* 187–90.

32. Merington, *The Custer Story,* 277.

33. Sheridan to Sherman, March 25, 1875, quoted in Cozzens, *Eyewitnesses to the Indian Wars,* vol. 4, 191.

34. Darling, *A Sad and Terrible Blunder,* 12–15.

35. Wooster, 161.

36. Darling, *A Sad and Terrible Blunder,* 93.

37. Ibid., 41.

38. Wooster, 70.

39. *Annual Report of the Commissioner of Indian Affairs*, 4; *Board of Indian Commissioners, Annual Reports, 1875*, quoted in Gray, *Centennial Campaign,* 20–21.

40. Gray, *Centennial Campaign,* 31–32. Perhaps the best book written about the preparations leading up to the Battle of the Little Bighorn. This discussion owes much to it.

41. Ibid., 33.
42. Ibid., 90.
43. Ibid., 40.
44. Ibid., 43.
45. Cortissoz, *The Life of Whitelaw Reid*, vol. 1, 312.
46. Noyes, "The Guns 'Long Hair' Left Behind," 3.
47. Hynds and Shay, "Reminiscences," 63. However, a story in the March 22, 1876, *Chicago Daily Tribune* related that the train "was stopped 26 miles east of Bismarck by a mountain of snow."
48. Saum, "Colonel Custer's Copperhead," 15.
49. Barnard, *I Go with Custer*, 105.
50. Custer, *Boots and Saddles*, 214; Wert, *The Controversial Life of George Armstrong Custer*, 321–22.

CHAPTER FIVE: BELKNAP'S ANACONDA
Chapter title: New York Herald, March 31, 1876.

1. Brown, *The Plainsmen of the Yellowstone*, 133.
2. Ibid., 135.
3. Morris, *Fraud of the Century*, 24.
4. *New York Sun*, September 14, 1877; *New York Evening Post*, January 20, 1879.
5. It seems that few members of Grant's extended family did not attempt to profit from their relationship to the President. Even a brother-in-law of one of Grant's brothers-in-law was implicated in the post trader scandal. *Chicago Daily Tribune*, March 29, 1876.
6. In testimony before the Clymer committee on March 28, 1876, a former sutler implicated Grant in a very early (1868) post trader arrangement, in which he claimed that yet another Grant brother-in-law had arranged his hiring with the then General of the army for a third of the appointment's profits. The sutler testified that Grant knew all the details. *New York Times*, March 28, 1868.
7. Buell, *The Warrior Generals*, xxix.
8. McFeely, *Grant*, 415. This excellent biography provides a succinct summary of the scandals of the Grant administration and his refusal to admit the malfeasance of his many crooked appointments. See also Prickett, "The Malfeasance of William Worth Belknap."
9. Nichols, *Men with Custer*, 154.
10. Sully, *No Tears for the General*, 204.
11. Walker, *Campaigns of General Custer*, 45.
12. Noyes, "The Guns 'Long Hair' Left Behind," 3.
13. Weymouth, *America in 1876*, 90, 104.
14. Custer, *My Life on the Plains*, 166–68.
15. Wert, *Custer*, 323.
16. Utley, *Cavalier in Buckskin*, 159; Kroeker, *Great Plains Command*, 145; *New York Times*, March 4, 1876, and March 30, 1876.

17. Stewart, *Custer's Luck*, 122–25; *Chicago Daily Tribune*, March 10, 1876; *Nation,* March 16, 1876.
18. Merington, *The Custer Story,* 290.
19. *New York Times*, March 30, 1876.
20. Hart, *Custer and His Times,* Book 2, 25.
21. Hutton, *Phil Sheridan and His Army,* 306. The July 11, 1876, *New York Daily Tribune* recounted the testimony of a former post trader, Caleb Marsh: "The last payment was made by Marsh in person to the present Mrs. Belknap . . . by direction of Mr. Belknap himself. Some of the deposits were made to Mr. Belknap . . . to his order, some were sent to him by express, and some were paid to him by Marsh personally in bank notes." Marsh claimed that Belknap always wrote him with directions on how to send Belknap's share.
22. Hutton, *Phil Sheridan and His Army,* 17.
23. Johnson, *Custer, Reno, Merrill and the Lauffer Case,* 13.
24. Carroll, *The Benteen-Goldin Letters,* 234.
25. Ibid., 275.
26. Johnson, *Custer, Reno, Merrill and the Lauffer Case,* 11. Another reason for the hostility between the two was that Merrill, in testimony before an army examining board (known as the Hancock Board or Benzine Board), supplied details of Custer's harsh discipline. Custer likely knew of that testimony. *New York Times,* April 5, 1876.
27. Stewart, *Custer's Luck,* 177.
28. *Army and Navy Journal,* April 1, 1876, and April 15, 1876.
29. Prickett, "The Malfeasance of William Worth Belknap," 14.
30. Sherman to General Stewart Van Vliet, March 11, 1873: "In reference to the order for the purchase of horses I can only say that it was drafted by [Quartermaster] Genl Meigs himself, approved by the Secretary of War, & if unlawful, that is their business not mine."
31. Hutton, *Phil Sheridan and His Army,* 310; Merington, *The Custer Story,* 245.
32. Merington, *The Custer Story,* 290.
33. Hutton, *Phil Sheridan and His Army,* 308.
34. Ibid., 297.
35. Perkins, *Trails, Rails and War,* 193.
36. Hart, "Custer's First Stand," 28.
37. *Chicago Daily Tribune,* April 19, 1876.
38. Utley, *Cavalier in Buckskin,* 161.
39. Merington, *The Custer Story,* 293.
40. Ibid., 289.
41. Brown and Willard, *The Black Hills Trails,* 133.
42. Whittaker, *A Complete Life of General George A. Custer,* 554.
43. *Big Horn Yellowstone Journal* (Spring 1994), 5; O'Neil, *GarryOwen Tidbits,* vol. 8, 25.
44. Bulkley, "As a Classmate Saw Custer."
45. Whittaker, *A Complete Life of General George A. Custer,* 554.

46. Rives, "Grant, Babcock, and the Whiskey Ring."
47. Nichols, *In Custer's Shadow*, 61.
48. Gray, *Centennial Campaign*, 87.
49. *New York Times*, May 1, 1876. Sherman wrote a lengthy letter of explanation to Grant on May 5 after Grant sent him a copy of the newspaper story and demanded an explanation. Sherman denied the quote and then wrote, "I believe the Army possesses hundreds who are competent for such an expedition" (Sherman to Grant, May 4, 1876, Van de Water Papers).
50. Stewart, *Custer's Luck*, 136.
51. Whittaker, *A Complete Life of General George A. Custer*, 559.
52. Ibid., 560.
53. Noyes, "Captain Robert P. Hughes and the Case Against Custer," 7–8. Though one of the officers present with Ludlow the next morning, George Ruggles, wrote a letter that supported Ludlow's claim, with some disparities between the two accounts (ibid.), questions arise. As one of Custer's officers would later point out, why would Custer reveal such a plan to a member of Terry's staff who was also a close friend of the General's? Further, despite Custer and Ludlow's friendship, the two had publicly disagreed on at least one important subject — the fate of the Black Hills. Custer supported opening them up; Ludlow did not. Ludlow also may have had another reason to besmirch Custer's reputation. In the fall of 1874, soon after the Black Hills Expedition, the two had squabbled over a relatively minor matter involving the expedition's official photographer, William Illingworth, and which of the two had arranged and paid for his services. Ludlow had taken the St. Paul photographer to court for not handing over the prints and negatives, but Custer's telegraphed testimony that Illingworth had discharged his obligations to Custer, who had handled the arrangements, had vindicated him (Custer to Assistant Adjutant General, Department of Dakota, November 26, 1874, Fort Lincoln, Telegrams Sent, 1873–1878, National Archives; and Ludlow to Custer, November 28, 1874, Merington Papers). Clearly, the two were far from close friends at the time. William H. Wood, a surveyor with the Black Hills Expedition, wrote, "I think Ludlow had a small opinion of Custer" (William Wood, "Reminiscences of the Black Hills Expedition," in Cozzens, *Eyewitnesses to the Indian Wars*, vol. 4, 177). Finally, Ludlow later revealed that he hadn't told his superior, Terry, of Custer's brag, though he had the opportunity and claimed to have told several other officers (including George Ruggles) the morning after Terry and Custer had left.
54. Carroll, *A Very Real Salmagundi*, 51.

Chapter Six: "Submitt to Uncl Sam or Kill the 7 Hors"
Chapter title: Sergeant William Cashan to "Cousin Marey," May 6, 1876, in Pohanka, "Letters of the Seventh Cavalry."
Epigraph: W. A. Croffutt, "Our Skeleton Army," *West Point Tic Tacs*, 106.
1. This description of Armstrong and Libbie's parting, as well as the relationship between Custer and Burkman, comes primarily from Glendolin Damon Wagner, *Old Neutriment*, the recollections of Private John Burkman as

recorded by his friend I. D. "Bud" O'Donnell and written in book form by
Wagner, who transformed O'Donnell's notes into a first-person memoir in
Burkman's colloquial speech. I have taken the liberty to eliminate the occasional dialectalism where it was almost surely added by Wagner.

2. Barnard, *I Go with Custer,* 110.
3. Camp IU Notes, 582.
4. Taylor, *Frontier and Indian Life,* 291–92.
5. Scott, *Some Memories of a Soldier,* 32.
6. Libby, *The Arikara Narrative of Custer's Campaign,* 168.
7. Willert, *Little Big Horn Diary,* 3.
8. Stewart, *Custer's Luck,* 244.
9. *New York Herald,* July 11, 1876, in Wengert, *The Custer Despatches,* 51.
    This story was very likely written by *Bismarck Tribune* publisher Clement
    Lounsberry, who would have known of Gerard's newspaper experience.
10. Custer to Alfred Terry, September 22, 1875, Fort Lincoln, Telegrams Sent,
    1875, National Archives.
11. De Trobriand, *Military Life in Dakota,* 312.
12. Information on Gerard (whose name is often spelled "Girard," but who
    signed his name "Gerard") is chiefly derived from Walter M. Camp's
    "Another of Custer's Band Answers the Last Roll Call," *St. Paul Pioneer
    Press,* March 9, 1913, and *Bismarck Tribune,* June 29, 1891.
13. *Chicago Daily Tribune,* February 23, 1879.
14. Ben Ash interview, Hagner Collection.
15. Dunn, *Massacres of the Mountains,* 51.
16. Utley, *The Lance and the Shield,* 73–74; *Inter-Ocean,* January 20, 1879.
17. Vestal, *New Sources of Indian History,* 339; Camp IU Notes, 712.
18. "Report of Persons Hired and Articles Employed and Hired at Expedition in
    the Field," Cartwright Collection. Boston Custer had also been employed as
    a guide on the Black Hills Expedition of 1874.
19. *Bismarck Tribune,* July 19, 1876. Custer has often been criticized for taking a reporter after Sherman expressly told Terry to "advise Custer to be
    prudent, not to take along any newspaper men, who always make mischief"
    (Overfield, *The Little Big Horn, 1876*). But Lounsberry pointed out in one
    of his earliest stories about the campaign that "we are prepared to prove by
    General Terry himself, of whom the writer obtained for Kellogg permission
    to go." Lounsberry later claimed that Custer had asked him to go and he had
    planned to until a family medical problem had prevented him, at which point
    he had hired Kellogg to take his place. Author Sandy Barnard makes a strong
    case for this being revisionist history and an instance of spotlight snatching
    in *I Go with Custer,* chap. 6.
20. Luce, "The Diary and Letters of Dr. James M. DeWolf," 36, 38. Some of
    these doctors would later be assigned to detached duty.
21. Barrett, quoted in Hutton, *The Custer Reader,* 110.
22. Chandler, *Of Garryowen in Glory,* 425–27.
23. MacNeil, "Raw Recruits and Veterans," 7.
24. Utley, *The Reno Court of Inquiry,* 311; Nichols, *Reno Court of Inquiry,* 387.

25. Rickey, *Forty Miles a Day on Beans and Hay,* 106; also Marquis, *Custer, Cavalry and Crows,* 14, wherein a fresh cavalry enlistee writes, "We had some elementary drilling."

26. Coffman, *The Old Army,* 336. In addition, the long, hard winters of the northern plains discouraged most training. A shavetail lieutenant who joined the Seventh Cavalry in the summer of 1876, after the Battle of the Little Bighorn, wrote: "It was not long before the cold and snow stopped all outdoor work. There was no riding hall or hall of any kind, and the barracks were so small and overcrowded that, during the winter, beyond the officers and noncommissioned officers school, there was little or no military instruction" (Carroll, *The Lieutenant E. A. Garlington Narrative,* 26).

27. General Order No. 83, September 23, 1875, AGO, War Department General Orders, 1875, National Archives: "This number to be divided between the carbine and revolver at the discretion of the commanding officer. No greater allowance can be authorized on account of the insufficiency of the appropriations for the manufacture of metallic ammunition."

28. Barry Johnson, "George Herendeen: The Life of a Montana Scout," in Johnson and Taunton, *More Sidelights of the Sioux Wars,* 9.

29. Lieutenant Edward Maguire, in his 1876 report, quoted in Fay, *Military Engagements,* 30.

30. Stewart, *Custer's Luck,* 176. Sergeant John Ryan later wrote: "We had a lot of recruits in that regiment and some of those men never fired a shot mounted up to this battle and some of them was never on a cavalry horse" (Ryan to W. A. Falconer, April 15, 1922, Elizabeth B. Custer Collection).

31. Merington, *The Custer Story,* 239.

32. Marquis, *Custer, Cavalry and Crows,* 16, 14.

33. Quoted in Langellier et al., *Myles Keogh,* 121.

34. Mangum, "The George C. Brown Story," 10.

35. Nichols, *Men with Custer,* 12.

36. Ibid., 105.

37. Barnard, *Ten Years with Custer,* 273.

38. Ibid., 260–66.

39. W. S. Edgerly to Louis Hein, August 19, 1921, Louis Hein Collection.

40. Fred Dustin, quoted in Dixon, "The Sordid Side of the Seventh Cavalry," 12.

41. *New York Daily Tribune,* July 13, 1876.

42. Cecil, "Lt. Crittenden: Striving for the Soldier's Life," 32.

43. Hunt and Hunt, *I Fought with Custer,* 53. The authors clearly added material and heavily rewrote Windolph's account, so any researcher must be careful in assessing the accuracy of any statements in this book.

44. De Trobriand, 62.

45. Marquis, "Indian Warrior Ways," 41–43; Hassrick, *The Sioux,* 96–97.

46. Morris, "Custer Made a Good Decision," 6.

47. Hammer transcript, Camp IU Notes, 114, 441, 632; Grinnell Papers, Field Notebook 332, 92. Braided Locks, who was in the fight, told Grinnell that there "may have been 400 or 500 Sioux and about 40 Cheyenne" (ibid., 93).

Young Little Wolf told Grinnell that "there were many Sioux perhaps 500 or 600 . . . and about 40 or 50 Cheyenne" (ibid.).

48. Greene, "The Hayfield Fight."

49. Information on these fights was derived from Andrist, *The Long Death;* Utley, *Frontier Regulars;* and Potomac Westerners, *Great Western Indian Fights.*

50. Pohanka, "Letters of the Seventh Cavalry."

51. Nichols, *Men with Custer,* 56.

52. Ibid., 154.

53. Ibid., 9.

54. Langellier et al., 97.

55. Bourke, *On the Border with Crook,* 150.

56. Barnett, "Powder River."

57. Vestal, *Warpath: The True Story of the Fighting Sioux,* 179; Camp BYU Notes, Reel 5, 187. See also chap. 3, note 28, for a discussion of the size of the camp.

58. Carroll, *The Eleanor Hinman Interviews,* 38.

59. Camp IU Notes, 280.

60. A reporter who accompanied Reynolds, Robert Strayhorn, claimed in a newspaper story written soon after the battle that "General Crook had especially impressed upon the minds of the officers the importance of saving" the large amounts of dried meat in the village, and "had instructed the officer in command to save all that could be carried off" (Greene, *Battles and Skirmishes of the Great Sioux War,* 14, 18). It was later claimed that Crook had planned on feeding his men with these stores (ibid., xvii). If true, it seems, at least in the comfort of retrospect, to have been quite a risky assumption — to plan, under subfreezing conditions, on provisioning hundreds of troops with food found in the enemy camp.

61. Ibid., 279, 419. See also Hutchins, *The Army and Navy Journal,* 19.

62. Thaddeus Stanton, "A Review of the Reynolds Campaign," in Cozzens, *Eyewitnesses to the Indian Wars, 1865–1890,* vol. 4, 234.

63. Finerty, *Warpath and Bivouac,* 24.

64. Secretary of War J. D. Cameron declared that "these columns were as strong as could be maintained in that inhospitable region or that could be spared from other pressing necessities" — a clear indication of just how important this police action was considered. Hutchins, *The Army and Navy Journal,* 34.

65. Bourke, 296.

66. Finerty, 68.

67. Brady, *Indian Fights and Fighters,* 393.

68. Libby, 58. The mistaken belief that Custer was planning to run for President has its roots in the account of an Arikara named Red Star, whose story is highly questionable. Red Star stated that "there was a rumor of a call to meet Custer at Fort Lincoln, the regular headquarters, but he is not certain of such a meeting." Red Star wasn't there but related what he had heard — that Custer had told the Arikaras that any kind of victory over the Sioux "would make him President, Great Father." Later, on the march west, Red

Star claimed that Custer had told the scouts, through Gerard the interpreter, "When we return . . . I shall go back to Washington. . . . I shall remain at Washington and be the Great Father." There is no other evidence of any presidential aspirations on Custer's part. Indeed, nowhere in the voluminous correspondence between Custer and his wife, Libbie, with whom he shared so many of his dreams, hopes, and concerns, is there any mention of it, and in one of her last letters to him, written only a few weeks before the Democratic convention, she discussed the various presidential candidates and even said, "The radicals have selected such a good man the Democrats stand no show" (Libbie Custer to George A. Custer, June 21, 1876, in O'Neil, *GarryOwen Tidbits,* vol. 8, 33). See also Craig Repass's *Custer for President?*

69. This description of the Dakota column's departure is based on Custer, *Boots and Saddles,* 216–18; Bates, *Custer's Indian Battles,* 28; Godfrey, *Custer's Last Battle,* 5; Hunt and Hunt, *I Fought with Custer,* 53; Graham, *The Custer Myth,* 239; Willert, *Little Big Horn Diary,* 3–4; and Heski, "It Started with a Parade."

70. Almost every history of the campaign fails to include Custer's niece accompanying the column to Heart River. But many years later, she wrote, "My aunts and I went one day's march with them in company of the paymaster; then, the men having been paid at a safe distance from temptation, we returned in the ambulance that had taken us on this little trip" (Buecker, "Frederic S. Calhoun," 22).

71. Libby, 59, 139.

72. Custer, *Boots and Saddles,* 217.

73. Ibid., 218.

CHAPTER SEVEN: "THE HIDE AND SEEK FOR SITTING BULL"
Chapter title: Editorial, *New York Herald,* June 27, 1876.
Epigraph: Gibbon, quoted in Koury, *Gibbon on the Sioux Campaign of 1876,* 64.

1. Custer had directed his subordinates to follow the same orders regarding campaign preparation as he had instituted in the spring of 1874, just before the Black Hills Expedition. See RG 393, Part V, General Orders and Circulars 1876, Fort Rice, General Order No. 40, May 19, 1874, National Archives.

2. Fort Lincoln 1876, Circular No. 21, National Archives.

3. Fort Lincoln 1876, Circular No. 45, National Archives.

4. Bates, *Custer's Indian Battles,* 28. Sergeant Ferdinand Culbertson testified that the new recruits "could not have received much instruction except what Maj. Reno gave them in the spring, which would be about a month's or six week's [*sic*] steady drill" (Utley, *The Reno Court of Inquiry,* 311).

5. Carroll, *The Benteen-Goldin Letters,* 209.

6. Hunt and Hunt, *I Fought with Custer,* 50.

7. Brady, *Indian Fights and Fighters,* 232.

8. This discussion of Reno and his experiences is largely based on information in Ron Nichols's excellently researched *In Custer's Shadow.*

9.   Steinbach, *The Long March*, 50, 52.

10. *War of the Rebellion*, 1st ser., 50: 13, 15.

11. Barnard, *Ten Years with Custer*, 287; Langellier et al., *Myles Keogh*, 154, 225; Charles Scott to his sister, April 23, 1876, quoted in O'Neil, *GarryOwen Tidbits*, vol. 8, 25. The troopers normally were paid every two months, but Scott and other soldiers claimed that they hadn't been paid in four months.

12. Terry to Sheridan, letter, May 15, 1876, quoted in Gray, *Centennial Campaign*, 89.

13. Terry to Sheridan, telegram, May 16, 1876, quoted in Gray, *Centennial Campaign*, 90.

14. Evans, *Custer's Last Fight*, 110.

15. Stewart, "I Rode with Custer," 18.

16. Nichols, *Men with Custer*, 93, 154.

17. Terry to his sisters, May 30, 1876, Terry Family Collection.

18. Bradley, *The March of the Montana Column*, 126.

19. Ibid., 158.

20. DeBarthe, *The Life and Adventures of Frank Grouard*, 116.

21. Gray, *Centennial Campaign*, 120.

22. Vestal, *Warpath: The True Story of the Fighting Sioux*, 186.

23. Charles Eastman, "The Indian Version of Custer's Last Battle," in Cozzens, *Eyewitnesses to the Indian Wars*, vol. 4, 303. In the July 22, 1876, issue of *Army and Navy Journal*, it was reported, "If the estimate of experienced officers who could see the whole field from higher ground further back is to be considered, there were upwards of 700 warriors." White Bull claimed years later that there were 1,000 Indians, of whom 300 had guns (Box 105, Folder 24, p. 45, Campbell Collection).

24. This account of the movements and growth of the hunting bands is based on Gray, *Centennial Campaign*, chaps. 26, 27, 28, and Marquis, *Wooden Leg*, 155–202. The account of the Battle of the Rosebud is based on Utley, *The Lance and the Shield*, 128–42; Vestal, *Warpath: The True Story of the Fighting Sioux*, 177–90; and Marquis, *Wooden Leg*, 193–204.

25. Box 105, Notebook 5, p. 9, Campbell Collection.

26. Utley, *The Lance and the Shield*, 138.

27. Finerty, *Warpath and Bivouac*, 86. Mirrors were also used in other battles, including the Little Bighorn eight days later. One Sioux account of that battle states: "They were signaling from the camp with looking glasses when the sun was getting low in the afternoon, to the warriors" (DeMallie, *The Sixth Grandfather*, 195).

28. Marquis, *Wooden Leg*, 200.

29. Bourke, *On the Border with Crook*, 312.

30. Grinnell, *The Fighting Cheyennes*, 336, 338.

31. Mails, *The Mystic Warriors of the Plains*, 218.

32. Hammer, *Custer in '76*, 205.

33. Evans, 101.

34. Ibid., 320.

35. Ibid., 321.

36. Crook, quoted ibid., 100.
37. Sheridan, quoted in Sarf, *The Little Bighorn Campaign*, 115.
38. Finerty, 93; Evans, 101.
39. Bourke, 286.
40. Ibid., 331.
41. Ibid., 322–23, 333.
42. Crook to Sheridan, July 25, 1876, RG 393, Part I, Orders, Letters Sent, Endorsements and Memorandums, Black Hills and Yellowstone Expedition, May 27, 1876, to October 24, 1876, National Archives.
43. Schmitt, *General George Crook*, 195–96.
44. Utley, *The Lance and the Shield*, 141.
45. Hammer, *Custer in '76*, 205.

Chapter Eight: The Fruits of Insubordination

Epigraph: New York Herald, July 11, 1876, quoted in Graham, *The Custer Myth*, 234–35. Though the story for the *Herald* was unsigned, it is commonly believed to have been written by Custer on June 21, 1876.

Sources for information regarding Reno's scout are scant, chiefly due to the fact that five of the six companies with his wing and all of their officers perished with Custer at the Little Bighorn. One of those officers, Lieutenant James Sturgis, was detailed to keep the itinerary, and his notes were lost. As far as is known, Reno never wrote of the scout or gave any account of it that was recorded. The two primary sources for the scout are a diary kept by Dr. James DeWolf and a diary kept by Sergeant James Hill of B Company. Secondary sources consulted for this chapter include Heski, "Another Look at the Reno Scout"; Stewart, "The Reno Scout"; Gray, *Centennial Campaign*; Stewart, *Custer's Luck*; and Willert, *Little Big Horn Diary*.

1. LeForge, *Memoirs of a White Crow Indian*, 212–13.
2. Ibid., 222.
3. Willert, *Little Big Horn Diary*, 104–5.
4. Libby, *The Arikara Narrative of Custer's Campaign*, 74.
5. *New York Herald*, July 11, 1876, quoted in Wengert, *The Custer Despatches*, 51.
6. Custer, *Boots and Saddles*, 267.
7. Sarf, *The Little Bighorn Campaign*, 135.
8. Gray, *Centennial Campaign*, 128.
9. Joseph White Cow Bull interview, McCracken Research Library.
10. Stewart, *Custer's Luck*, 105.
11. Biographical information concerning Mitch Boyer is from Gray, *Custer's Last Campaign*.
12. Gibbon, "General Gibbon's Comments on Custer's Orders," 4; Camp IU Notes, 494.
13. Camp IU Notes, 135.
14. *Helena Herald*, July 15, 1876, quoted in Gray, *Custer's Last Campaign*, 396.
15. Stewart, *Custer's Luck*, 226.
16. Nichols, *Reno Court of Inquiry*, 41.

17. Gray, *Centennial Campaign,* 127.

18. Ibid., 226.

19. Carroll, *Camp Talk,* 14.

20. Willert, *Little Big Horn Diary,* 118.

21. Ibid., 189; Hardorff, *The Custer Battle Casualties,* 61.

22. Libby, 73–74. Through Gerard, Reno told one Arikara, High Bear, that he couldn't accompany the expedition because his horse wasn't healthy enough. High Bear disagreed and said so; Reno told High Bear that he was a fool if he didn't agree with Reno. High Bear suggested a fight to decide who would go. Reno threatened to shoot him, and High Bear started toward him with a knife. Bloody Knife jumped between them and asked Reno to let High Bear go for his sake. Reno wisely consented.

23. Camp IU Notes, 33.

24. Camp BYU Notes, Reel 5, 389.

25. Gray, *Custer's Last Campaign,* 191–92.

26. A trooper on the scout, Peter Thompson, wrote an account several years later in which he claimed: "Our scout which was Mich Burey was of the opinion that we could overtake the Indians in a day's march" (Brown and Willard, *The Black Hills Trails,* 142). Another trooper claimed that "the night Reno turned back, Mitch told Reno he could take him to the Sioux village in two hours' time. Reno said he did not wish to see it" (Liddic and Harbaugh, *Camp on Custer,* 83). And in a letter from Custer to his wife, Libbie, dated June 21, 1876, and quoted in Wagner, *Old Neutriment,* 193–94, Custer wrote: "The scouts report that they could have overtaken the village in one and a half days."

27. Libby, 70.

28. "Statement of Francis Johnson Kennedy," in Liddic and Harbaugh, *Camp on Custer.*

29. Liddic, *I Buried Custer,* 13.

30. Willis Carland to W. A. Falconer, October 27, 1930, Camp BYU Collection.

31. Godfrey, "Custer's Last Battle," 11.

32. Merington, *The Custer Story,* 307.

33. Forrest, *Witnesses at the Battle of the Little Big Horn,* 47.

34. Camp IU Notes, 623. This was gleaned by Camp from the band director's widow, Mrs. Felix Vinatieri.

35. Lubetkin, "Strike Up 'Garryowen,'" 10–11.

36. Hardorff, *Camp, Custer, and the Little Bighorn,* 37.

37. Custer, *Boots and Saddles,* 273.

38. Ibid., 274.

39. Gray, *Centennial Campaign,* 136.

40. Hunt, *I Fought with Custer,* 64.

41. Gray, *Centennial Campaign,* 137. Some postbattle corroboration that Terry considered Reno's actions insubordinate appeared in a story published in the *Chicago Times,* September 16, 1876. When reporter Charles S. Diehl asked about Reno's disobedience on the reconnaissance, Terry answered, "That is a matter of record" (Knight, *Following the Indian Wars,* 288).

42. Magnussen, *Peter Thompson's Narrative,* 78.
43. *New York Herald,* July 11, 1876, quoted in Graham, *The Custer Myth,*
     234–35. In a letter to Custer, Libbie mentioned the fact that he had been
     sending dispatches to the *Herald:* "I do hope and trust that your communi-
     cations for the Herald & Galaxy were all right" (Libbie Custer to George A.
     Custer, June 21, 1876, Merington Papers).
44. Custer, *Boots and Saddles,* 275.
45. Willert, *Little Big Horn Diary,* 183.
46. Gray, *Arikara Scouts with Custer,* 18, 20.

CHAPTER NINE: THE SEVENTH RIDES OUT
Epigraph: Wallace to his father, June 18, 1876, quoted in *New York Herald,* July
     10, 1876.
 1. Though several participant accounts do not mention Brisbin as being present
     at the conference, at least two men — Lieutenant John F. McBlain, with the
     Montana column (McBlain, "With Gibbon on the Sioux Campaign of 1876,"
     142), and scout George Herendeen (Hammer, *Custer in '76,* 221)—place
     him there. Lieutenant Edward Godfrey mentions that Brisbin was on the
     boat (Godfrey, *Field Diary,* 8), and Brisbin himself, in a letter to Godfrey,
     wrote, "I was on the boat, the steamer 'Far West,' the night of the 21st, when
     the conference took place between Gibbon, Custer and Terry . . . and I heard
     what passed. . . . Terry had a map. . . . Being somewhat near-sighted, as you
     know, Terry asked me to mark the line of march, and I did so with a blue
     pencil" (Carroll, *The Two Battles of the Little Big Horn,* 141–42).
 2. "The maps that we had were what was known as the Reynolds-Maynardier
     [*sic*] Map made 1859 and 1860." Edward Godfrey to Charles Francis Bates,
     March 19, 1926, Ghent Papers.
 3. Carroll, "Diary," 233; Gibbon, "General Gibbon's Comments on Custer's
     Orders," 4; Colonel Robert P. Hughes, "The Campaign Against the Sioux in
     1876," in Graham, *The Story of the Little Big Horn,* 214. In a story published
     in the November 8, 1884, *Los Angeles Times,* Brisbin wrote: "The Indians
     had left the Rosebud and gone no one knew exactly where, but we had a
     pretty good idea, through our Crow scouts. The Sioux were on the big bend
     of the Little Horn." See also Noyes, "A Dispatch from the Battlefield," 28,
     n. 11, for further evidence that Terry believed the Indians to be at the head-
     waters of either the Little Bighorn or the Rosebud.
 4. Several contemporary statements support the fact that Terry's force of four
     hundred men was assigned this duty — to support Custer's attack and act as
     a blocking force to any Indians that attempted to flee north. See Noyes, "A
     Dispatch from the Battlefield," 28, n. 13. For further evidence that there was
     no plan of simultaneous attack, see Walter, "Terry and Custer: Was There a
     Plan?"
 5. Graham, *The Custer Myth,* 261. Though there is no contemporary evidence
     of this date, several accounts written only days after the battle mention it.
     There seems little doubt that the plan called for Custer to rendezvous with
     Gibbon and Terry near the mouth of the Little Bighorn, quite possibly on the

26th. In a report written on July 2, Terry wrote: "I send in another dispatch a copy of my written orders to Custer, but these were supplemented by the distinct understanding that Gibbon could not get to the Little Big Horn before the evening of the 26th" (Graham, *The Custer Myth*, 216). In a letter to General Crook, written on July 9, Terry said: "Custer had been informed that Gibbon's column would reach the mouth of the Little Big Horn on the evening of 26th ultimo" (Overfield, *The Little Big Horn, 1876*, 57). William White, a soldier with Gibbon, later wrote, "It was understood generally we were trying to reach the mouth of the Little Bighorn. There, it was said, Custer was to meet us the next day, the 26th" (Marquis, *Custer, Cavalry and Crows*, 64). Matthew Carroll, Gibbon's wagon master, wrote in his diary on June 26 that Custer "was to meet Terry at the mouth of the Little Big Horn to-day" (Carroll, "Diary," 234). One diarist, Captain Henry Freeman with Gibbon's column, referred to a meeting of the two columns "on the 26th, or [2]7th at latest" (Freeman, "Diary"). Dr. Paulding wrote that "Custer . . . pushed his command ahead, notwithstanding unmistakable directions that he was to await our co-operation & that we could not be near that spot before the 27th" and also that "he was to meet our column at the mouth of the Little Horn on the 27th" (Hudnutt, "New Light on the Little Big Horn," 357, 350). A cavalry officer with Gibbon's column, Lieutenant John McBlain, wrote in a June 1896 *Cavalry Journal* article, "Our commander had vouched for our being at the 'big bend' of the Little Big Horn on the 27th," and forty-four years later, a trooper with Custer, William Slaper, wrote, "It was given out that we were to meet General Terry in the neighborhood of the Big Horn River, with the balance of his command on the morning of June 27th. . . . It seemed to be the general understanding among the men that Custer and Terry were understood to have agreed to meet somewhere in the valley of the Little Big Horn on June 27th" (Brininstool, *Troopers with Custer*, 45–46). Clearly, there was no general agreement on which day the two columns would meet, though the 26th seems probable. See also Evans, *Custer's Last Fight*, 129–33, and Darling, *A Sad and Terrible Blunder*, 66–67.

6.   Terry to Sheridan, dispatch, June 21, 1876, quoted in Gray, *Centennial Campaign*, 140. Terry later claimed that much of the new plan was his idea, which he suggested in the conference. See Gibbon, "General Gibbon's Comments on Custer's Orders."

7.   Gibbon, "Hunting Sitting Bull," 691. This is a variation on Sherman's definition of military glory, "dying on the field of battle, and having your name spelled wrong in the newspaper."

8.   Noyes, *In the Land of the Chinook*, 108.

9.   Graham, *The Custer Myth*, 261.

10.   Ibid. The possibility exists that Kellogg may have received his information from Custer and consequently reported it erroneously. But contemporary accounts almost unanimously support this version of Terry's plans, despite his written letter of instructions tendered to Custer the next morning. For instance: Captain H. B. Freeman of the 7th Infantry with Gibbon told his

friend Anson Mills that "he was perfectly sure that both Terry and Custer understood that it was expected for Custer to surprise and attack the enemy wherever found" (Anson Mills to E. S. Godfrey, August 30, 1918, quoted in O'Neil, *Custer Chronicles,* vol. 1, 32). See also Walter, "Terry and Custer."

11. Gibbon, "Last Summer's Expedition Against the Sioux," 22.

12. *New York Herald,* July 11, 1876, quoted in Graham, *The Custer Myth,* 237. For evidence that at least one of Custer's close subordinates — Captain George Yates — also believed that Custer's orders from Terry constituted "a carte blanche letter of instructions to act on his own initiative and in his own discretion," see Carroll, *A Very Real Salmagundi,* 52.

13. Krause and Olson, *Prelude to Glory,* 268.

14. Noyes, "The Guns 'Long Hair' Left Behind," 6.

15. McClernand, "With the Indian and the Buffalo in Montana," 16.

16. Readers familiar with the story will notice that I have made no mention of the infamous affidavit signed by Custer's cook, Mary Adams, in which she claimed to have heard Terry give Custer supplemental "orders" in person. John Manion, in his excellent book *General Terry's Last Statement to Custer,* makes a convincing case for the existence of the affidavit and Mary Adams's presence on the expedition. Nevertheless, to my mind, there are too many unanswered questions surrounding the affidavit to accept it as factual. See also Francis Taunton's excellent "The Mystery of Miss Adams."

17. *Big Horn Yellowstone Journal* 2, no. 4 (Autumn 1993): 17; Carroll, *The Two Battles of the Little Big Horn,* 175; Urwin, *Custer and His Times,* Book 3, 187, 199.

18. Godfrey, *Custer's Last Battle,* 14.

19. Merington, *The Custer Story,* 309.

20. Hammer, *Custer in '76,* 247.

21. Wagner, *Old Neutriment,* 137.

22. Fougera, *With Custer's Cavalry,* 277.

23. Broome, "In Memory of Lt. James Sturgis," 21.

24. *New York Herald,* July 26, 1876, quoted in Wengert, *The Custer Despatches,* 55. In a letter written to Keogh's sister Margaret on July 15, 1876, Nowlan claimed that he and Keogh had exchanged wills before Keogh rode with the Seventh (Museum of the American West).

25. Camp IU Notes, Box 2, Folder 10.

26. Johnson, "The Seventh's Quartermaster," 16.

27. Camp IU Notes, 606.

28. Willis Carland to W. A. Falconer, October 27, 1930, Camp BYU Collection; Carland to William Ghent, February 2, 1934, Edward S. Godfrey Papers.

29. Hammer, *Custer in '76,* 245.

30. *Los Angeles Times,* November 8, 1884.

31. Nichols, *Reno Court of Inquiry,* 127.

32. Merington, *The Custer Story,* 306–7.

33. For a comparison of the orders to Reno and Custer, see Evans, 453–55.

34. Hammer, *Custer in '76,* 262.

35.   Merington, *The Custer Story,* 307–8. The full text of Terry's orders to
       Custer reads as follows:

       "The Brigadier-General Commanding directs that, as soon as your regi-
       ment can be made ready for the march, you will proceed up the Rosebud
       in pursuit of the Indians whose trail was discovered by Major Reno a few
       days since. It is, of course, impossible to give you any definite instructions
       in regard to this movement, and were it not impossible to do so, the Depart-
       ment Commander places too much confidence in your zeal, energy, and
       ability to wish to impose upon you precise orders which might hamper your
       action when nearly in contact with the enemy. He will however, indicate to
       you his own views of what your action should be, and he desires that you
       should conform to them unless you shall see sufficient reason for departing
       from them. He thinks that you should proceed up the Rosebud until you
       ascertain definitely the direction in which the trail above spoken leads.
       Should it be found (as it appears almost certain that it will be found) to turn
       towards the Little Horn, he thinks that you should still proceed southward,
       perhaps as far as the headwaters of the Tongue, and then turn towards the
       Little Horn, feeling constantly, however, to your left, so as to preclude the
       possibility of the escape of the Indians to the south or southeast by passing
       around your left flank.

       "The column of Colonel Gibbon is now in motion for the mouth of the
       Big Horn. As soon as it reaches that point it will cross the Yellowstone and
       move up at least as far as the forks of the Big and Little Horns. Of course its
       further movement must be controlled by circumstances as they arise, but it is
       hoped that the Indians, if upon the Little Horn, may be so nearly inclosed by
       the two columns that their escape will be impossible. The Department Com-
       mander desires that on your way up the Rosebud you should thoroughly
       examine the upper part of Tullock's Creek, and that you should endeavor to
       send a scout through to Colonel Gibbon's Column, with information of the
       results of your examination. The lower part of the creek will be examined by
       a detachment from Colonel Gibbon's command.

       "The supply steamer will be pushed up the Big Horn as far as the forks
       if the river is found to be navigable for that distance, and the Department
       Commander, who will accompany the Column of Colonel Gibbon, desires
       you to report to him there not later than the expiration of the time for which
       your troops are rationed, unless in the meantime you receive further orders."
       Overfield, *The Little Big Horn, 1876,* 23–24.
36.   Brown, in *The Plainsmen of the Yellowstone,* says 3,000. Nabokov, in *Two
       Leggings,* 155, says that there were 4,100 in 1871.
37.   Information on the Crows comes from Dunlay, *Wolves for the Blue Soldiers,*
       135, and McGinnis, *Counting Coup and Cutting Horses,* 135–38.
38.   McGinnis, *Counting Coup and Cutting Horses,* 138.
39.   Gibbon, quoted in Stewart, *Custer's Luck,* 180.
40.   "White Swan's Story: Interview with Mr. and Mrs. J. S. Burgess in 1894,"
       LBBNM Files; Plainfeather, "A Personal Look at Curly's Life," 18, where
       Curly refers to White Swan as "Biike," meaning "my elder brother"; and

Riebeth, 103, 112, where White Swan is said to be Curly's brother, though in Plains Indian culture, a person often considered his cousin as close as his brother.

41. Custer, *Boots and Saddles*, 275.
42. Hammer, *Custer in '76*, 245.
43. Dixon, *The Vanishing Race*, 159.
44. Gibbon, "Last Summer's Expedition," 293.
45. Libby, *The Arikara Narrative of Custer's Campaign*, 61, 77.
46. Godfrey, in "Custer's Last Battle," wrote that each troop was followed by its pack mules, but this is the only reference that claims such an arrangement.
47. Gibbon, "Last Summer's Expedition," 293. Later, this lighthearted exchange would be misinterpreted in an attempt to prove that Custer's "greed" for glory was evident from the start. But Gibbon's own subordinate, Lieutenant Edward J. McClernand, wrote that Gibbon told him that Gibbon had said essentially the same thing the evening before (McClernand, "With the Indian," 16). It should be abundantly clear that both statements were anything but serious.
48. Hardorff, *The Custer Battle Casualties, II*, 188–89.
49. Holley, *Once Their Home*, 262.

Chapter Ten: The Trail to the Greasy Grass

Epigraph: Coleman, quoted in Liddic, *I Buried Custer*, 81. This is from Coleman's diary entry for June 24, 1876, which was likely filled in at a later date.

1. Vestal, *New Sources of Indian History*, 163.
2. Graham, *The Custer Myth*, 6.
3. A Sioux named Bull Eagle said "emphatically and further that no prominent chief of Minneconjou was at Little Bighorn." Camp IU Notes, 237.
4. Discussions of the village size are plentiful; see Stewart, *Custer's Luck*, 309–12; Gray, *Centennial Campaign*, 346–57; Marshall, "How Many Indians Were There?"; Anderson, "Cheyennes at the Little Big Horn"; and Smalley, *Little Bighorn Mysteries*, chap. 6, "How Large Was the Village?"
5. Milligan, *Dakota Twilight*, 59.
6. Hardorff, *Indian Views of the Custer Fight*, 68.
7. Powell, *Sweet Medicine*, vol. 1, 101; Marquis, *Custer on the Little Bighorn*, 36; Marquis, *Wooden Leg*, 182; Manzione, *I Am Looking to the North for My Life*, 46; Miller, "Echoes of the Little Bighorn," 27. Some or all of these Assiniboines were likely attached to Inkpaduta's group, since much of his wanderings over the past twenty years had been through Assiniboine country.
8. Graham, *The Custer Myth*, 109–11.
9. The consensus of Indian and soldier opinion seems to be somewhere between these figures, though some soldiers who survived the siege thought that most or all of the Indians carried rifles. See Hardorff, *Indian Views of the Custer Fight*, 32; Hammer, *Custer in '76*, 208; Marquis, *Wooden Leg*, 213, 230; Scott et al., *Archaeological Perspectives on the Battle of the Little Bighorn*, 118; Anderson, *Sitting Bull*, 84; Stewart, *Custer's Luck*, 78.

10. Camp IU Notes, 347; Saindon, "Sitting Bull," 7; Grinnell, *The Fighting Cheyennes,* 352; McLaughlin, *My Friend the Indian,* 44; and Hardorff, *Cheyenne Memories,* 154. For a good overview of the subject, see Krott, "Was Custer Outgunned?"

11. Stands in Timber, *Cheyenne Memories,* 194–95. The literature on these suicide boys is disappointingly scant, but oral tradition supports it. See Viola, *Little Bighorn Remembered,* 49, for an account of the suicide boys derived from a battle participant, Louis Dog. For further discussions of suicide vows among the Plains Indians, see Hoebel, *The Cheyennes,* 80, and Stands in Timber, *Cheyenne Memories,* 63.

12. Stands in Timber, *Cheyenne Memories,* 194.

13. Powell, *Sweet Medicine,* 211.

14. Stands in Timber, *Cheyenne Memories,* 193–94.

15. MacLaine, "Our 1876 'Injun Fightin' Cavalry," 80. A cavalry regiment in 1876 was authorized 43 officers and 1 regimental sergeant major, 1 quartermaster sergeant, 1 saddler sergeant, 1 chief trumpeter, and 1 chief musician. Each company comprised 71 enlisted men: 1 first sergeant, 5 duty sergeants, 4 corporals, 2 trumpeters, 1 blacksmith, 1 farrier, 1 saddler, 1 wagoner, and 55 privates. The grand total of authorized personnel was 852 enlisted men and 43 officers — 895 men.

16. Gray, *Centennial Campaign,* 151. Other totals vary about ten troopers either way; there is no definitive total. Several company rosters were lost in the battle, and some men will never be positively located, since it is not clear whether they rode with the Seventh or remained behind on the *Far West* or at the Yellowstone depot. Additionally, four citizen packers were definitely known to be with the column, although there may have been as many as twelve.

17. Details of the column's appearance come from Hutchins, *Boots and Saddles at the Little Bighorn;* Partoll, "After the Custer Battle"; and Godfrey, *Custer's Last Battle.*

18. Coughlan, *Varnum,* 35.

19. Graham, *The Reno Court of Inquiry: Abstract,* 23.

20. Hutchins, *Boots and Saddles at the Little Bighorn,* 30.

21. Details of the regiment's progress up the Rosebud are chiefly derived from Godfrey, *Custer's Last Battle;* Lieutenant Wallace's official report, in *Report of the Chief of Engineer for the Indian Campaign of 1876;* O'Neil, *The Gibson-Edgerly Narratives;* Graham, *The Custer Myth;* Libby, *The Arikara Narrative of Custer's Campaign;* Carroll, *Custer's Chief of Scouts;* and Stewart, *Custer's Luck.*

22. Hutchins, *Boots and Saddles at the Little Bighorn,* 48.

23. This description of setting up camp is derived from Charles K. Mills's well-researched *Harvest of Barren Regrets,* 238.

24. Fougera, *With Custer's Cavalry,* 267; Godfrey, *Custer's Last Battle,* 16.

25. E. S. Godfrey, "Notes on Chapter XXII of Colonel Homer W. Wheeler's 'Buffalo Days,'" in Carroll, *A Custer Chrestomathy,* 71.

26. Brady, *Indian Fights and Fighters,* 372, quoting a letter from Godfrey

discussing the battle: "The time of the arrival of Terry at the Little Big Horn is assumed to be June 26th. What authority there is for that assumption I do not now recall. It is not embodied in the 'instructions.' We of the command knew nothing of it till after the battle; after Terry's arrival, that is." Varnum's testimony (Carroll, *Custer's Chief of Scouts*, 175) also made clear that neither he nor the other officers of the regiment were told of Terry's grand scheme.

27. O'Neil, *In Reply to Van de Water*, 3. Graham told Van de Water, "The probabilities are that Wallace's watch was set by Fort Lincoln time which, I have been informed, was the same as Chicago time." Godfrey testified that their watches had not changed, meaning that they were still operating on the official time of Fort Lincoln, which was Chicago time (Nichols, *Reno Court of Inquiry*, 491).

28. Edgerly to his wife, July 4, 1876, quoted in Clark, *Scalp Dance*, 26.

29. Godfrey, *Custer's Last Battle*, 17. There is also an account by Gerard wherein he stated that Bloody Knife had been "very much under the influence of whisky" and had teased Custer by saying that the General "would not dare to attack" the Indians if he should find them (Holley, *Once Their Home*, 263). This is partly corroborated by one of the Arikaras, Red Star, who said that the scout "was missing, and the scouts waited for him till it was late but he was drunk somewhere, he got liquor from somebody. Next morning at breakfast Bloody Knife appeared leading a horse. He had been out all night" (Libby, 78).

30. Albert Johnson to Theodore Goldin, April 2, 1933, Box 3G469, Albert Johnson Folder, Brininstool Collection.

31. Coughlan, 9.

32. Hammer, *Custer in '76*, 220.

33. Custer, quoted in Gray, *Centennial Campaign*, 156.

34. Libby, 78–79.

35. O'Neil, *The Gibson-Edgerly Narratives*, 6.

36. Stewart, *Custer's Luck*, 265.

37. Graham, *The Custer Myth*, 262.

38. William O. Taylor to Elizabeth Custer, May 29, 1910, quoted in O'Neil, *Custer Chronicles*, vol. 2, 12–14.

CHAPTER ELEVEN: ON THE JUMP

Epigraph: White Man Runs Him, quoted in Graham, *The Custer Myth*, 23.

1. Information on the trips to the Crow's Nest by Varnum and Custer comes from Albert Johnson to Earl Brininstool, January 15, 1933, Brininstool Collection; Coughlan, *Varnum;* Richard Hardorff, "Custer's Trail to Wolf Mountains," in Carroll, *Custer and His Times,* Book 2; and Carroll, *Custer's Chief of Scouts.*

2. Carroll, *Custer's Chief of Scouts,* 61.

3. Barnard, *I Go with Custer,* 207.

4. Graham, *The Custer Myth,* 178–79.

5. William Taylor to Elizabeth Custer, May 29, 1910, quoted in O'Neil, *Custer Chronicles*, vol. 2, 12–14.

6. Godfrey, "The Death of General Custer," 469. The soldier who wrote to Godfrey and included this remembrance did not specify that it was not a song rendered by the officers, but Godfrey wrote that the soldier said "he was thrilled by someone singing in a clear tone," which implies a solitary singer.

7. Davis and Davis, *The Reno Court of Inquiry*, 53.

8. Barnard, *Ten Years with Custer*, 289.

9. Wagner, *Old Neutriment*, 148.

10. Graham, *The Custer Myth*, 136.

11. Graham, *The Reno Court of Inquiry: Abstract*, 211.

12. Brown and Willard, *The Black Hills Trails*, 149.

13. Hammer, *Custer in '76*, 61.

14. Some of the Crow accounts (White Man Runs Him, for instance) state that Custer did not go all the way to the top, just "far enough to see over and down the valley." Graham, *The Custer Myth*, 14–15.

15. Carroll, *Custer's Chief of Scouts*, 88.

16. Libby, *The Arikara Narrative of Custer's Campaign*, 90–93.

17. Nichols, *Reno Court of Inquiry*, 250–51; Hammer, *Custer in '76*, 222.

18. Hardorff, *On the Little Bighorn with Walter Camp*, 147.

19. Nichols, *Reno Court of Inquiry*, 528; Hunt, *I Fought with Custer*, 79.

20. Hammer, *Custer in '76*, 222.

21. Stewart, *Custer's Luck*, 280.

22. Hammer, *Custer in '76*, 64.

23. Carroll, *The Benteen-Goldin Letters*, 30–31, 41; Graham, *The Custer Myth*, 194. There is a different account of this exchange in Schultz's dramatized *William Jackson, Indian Scout*, 133.

24. Godfrey, "Notes on Chapter XXII of Colonel Homer W. Wheeler's 'Buffalo Days,'" in Carroll, *A Custer Chrestomathy*, 74.

25. Liddic and Harbaugh, *Camp on Custer*, 81.

26. Wagner, 151.

27. Hammer, *Custer in '76*, 64; Carroll, *Custer's Chief of Scouts*, 64.

28. Theodore Goldin to E. A. Brininstool, December 3, 1933, Brininstool Collection.

29. Wagner, 152.

30. Most accounts list 24,000 rounds, two for each company, but there were two boxes brought along for the headquarters staff (Hammer, *Custer in '76*, 68).

31. Nichols, *Reno Court of Inquiry*, 439; Edgerly to his wife, July 4, 1876, quoted in Clark, *Scalp Dance*, 26. Besides Edgerly, four others wrote of or testified to these battalion assignments. Myles Moylan wrote of them eleven days after the battle in a letter to Captain Calhoun's brother Fred Calhoun (O'Neil, *Custer Chronicles*, vol. 3, 18); Reno wrote of them in a letter to a newspaper answering an accusatory letter written by Custer's good friend Thomas Rosser (Graham, *The Custer Myth*, 226); Gibson told his wife

about them in his letter of July 4, 1876 (Fougera, *With Custer's Cavalry*, 268); and Sergeant Daniel Kanipe mentioned the two squadrons (Hardorff, *On the Little Bighorn with Walter Camp*, 177).

32. Linderman, *Plenty-Coups*, 175.

33. The actual distance to this first line of bluffs, as ascertained by Roger Darling and revealed in his book *Benteen's Scout-to-the-Left*, is 1.3 miles. Post-battle reports by participants almost unanimously exaggerated the distance; such accounts usually lengthened the distance as time went on. At the Reno court of inquiry in 1879, Benteen testified that the bluffs were "4 or 5 miles away" (Graham, *The Reno Court of Inquiry: Abstract*, 135). In Benteen's personal narrative of the battle, probably written sometime between 1890 and his death in 1898, he estimated the distance at two miles (Graham, *The Custer Myth*, 179). Godfrey in 1892 wrote of "a line of high bluffs three or four miles distant" (Godfrey, *Custer's Last Battle*, 21). The only exception I have found is Lieutenant Edgerly, who testified at the Reno inquiry, "I judge in about a mile distant we came to very high bluffs" (Graham, *The Reno Court of Inquiry: Abstract*, 157).

34. In a letter to his wife written on July 4, 1876, Benteen stated that he was ordered "to go over the immense hills to the left, in search of the valley, which was supposed to be very near by." O'Neil, *Custer Chronicles*, vol. 5, 21.

35. Benteen's several different accounts of these orders were rendered at different times. His earliest accounts — a letter to his wife and his official report, both written on July 4, 1876 — agree on this version of his orders (Hunt, *I Fought with Custer*, 184–87). Gibson's letter to his wife says much the same thing (Fougera, 268).

36. Noyes, "Custer's Surgeon, George Lord," 17–18; *New York Herald*, July 10, 1876.

37. Saum, "Colonel Custer's Copperhead," 45; Theodore Goldin, "The Summer Campaign of 1876," in Cozzens, *Eyewitnesses to the Indian Wars*, vol. 4, 319; Camp IU Notes, 610.

38. Hammer, *Custer in '76*, 231.

39. Ibid., 156. Gerard testified that he thought the Indians were more than three miles away and on the far side of the Little Bighorn (Utley, *The Reno Court of Inquiry*, 125). Hare said that he saw forty or fifty Indians "on rise between us and the Little Big Horn" (Camp BYU Notes, Reel 5, 97).

40. This Sioux warrior had been mortally wounded at the Battle of the Rosebud eight days earlier. At least five different names have been offered for the man. See Hardorff, *Cheyenne Memories*, 153, for a full discussion of this matter.

41. Vern Smalley, "The Lone Tepee Along Reno Creek," *12th Annual Symposium*; Nichols, *Reno Court of Inquiry*, 529.

42. Hardorff, *On the Little Bighorn with Walter Camp*, 6. Not only Daniel Kanipe but also many of the Indian scouts said this.

43. Nichols, *Reno Court of Inquiry*, 84.

44. Utley, *The Reno Court of Inquiry*, 401; *New York Herald*, July 30, 1876.

Though Reno did not mention the Arikaras singing while preparing themselves for battle at the tepees, it seems doubtful that they did so silently. In the *Herald* account, an anonymous Seventh Cavalry officer wrote, "The death song of the Crow Indians rose on the air and floated over the hills," but I believe this officer mistook the Rees' [Arikaras'] death songs for that of the Crows.

45. Utley, *The Reno Court of Inquiry,* 276. That the village Reno was ordered after was the group of fleeing Indians who could be seen a few miles down the trail and not the huge encampment subsequently discovered across the river and two miles down the valley is abundantly clear from the many versions of the orders Reno received. See Darling, *A Sad and Terrible Blunder,* 202–6. In an anonymous account written by a member of the Seventh Cavalry and published in the *New York Herald* on July 30, 1876, the author stated, "The village was just ahead and we were sure it could not get away."

46. Graham, *The Reno Court of Inquiry: Abstract,* 23. There are several versions of these orders. These are from the testimony given by the column's itinerist, Lieutenant Wallace. Years later, Lieutenant Luther Hare told researcher Walter Camp that at the tepees, he "heard Cooke tell Reno to go on in pursuit of the Indians and Custer would follow right behind and support him," which would help explain Reno's later decision to leave the timber. The fact that no one, not even Reno, claimed that Custer said this leaves this just a tantalizing claim (Hammer, *Custer in '76,* 64).

47. Nichols, *Reno Court of Inquiry,* 86. Both Gerard and Herendeen testified that they heard Custer verbally deliver this order and his follow-up about taking the scouts (ibid., 35, 80–81). So did Sergeant Thomas O'Neill (O'Neill to Godfrey, August 17, 1908, Hagner Collection) and Sergeant Daniel Kanipe (Hammer, *Custer in '76,* 92). There are variations in the exact wording of these orders.

48. Libby, 159.

49. Graham, *The Custer Myth,* 13.

50. Hardorff, *On the Little Bighorn with Walter Camp,* 53, 101.

51. Varnum to W. M. Camp, April 14, 1909, Camp BYU Collection.

52. Carroll, *I, Varnum,* 21.

53. Libby, 122.

54. Hammer, *Custer in '76,* 84.

55. Utley, *The Reno Court of Inquiry,* 237, 312, 332. Herendeen testified that they reached the river in five or six minutes (Graham, *The Reno Court of Inquiry: Abstract,* 81).

56. Hammer, *Custer in '76,* 148.

57. There is no testimony that mentions Keogh returning from the river, but when Gerard galloped on the back trail to notify Custer of the enemy's actions, he found only Cooke. I have taken this to mean that Keogh either left earlier than Cooke or outdistanced him enough so that Gerard didn't notice Keogh when he found Cooke.

58. Hammer, *Custer in '76*, 84.

59. Graham, *The Custer Myth*, 263.

60. Nichols, *Reno Court of Inquiry*, 114.

61. Hammer, *Custer in '76*, 112. At least six troopers (Roy, Brinkerhoff, Dono-hue, Petring, O'Neill, and Newell), three officers (Varnum, Wallace, and DeRudio), and one scout (Gerard) later claimed to have seen Custer on the bluffs. Brinkerhoff said that they saw him once or twice on the charge down the valley, and the men waved their hats and cheered (see note 78 for source).

62. Libby, 172–73; Graham, *The Reno Court of Inquiry: Abstract*, 38, 44.

63. Snedeker, "The Porters," 35.

64. Rickey, *Forty Miles a Day on Beans and Hay*, 58–59.

65. Graham, *The Custer Myth*, 345. Porter at least was wearing his, since his bloody buckskin blouse was later found in the deserted Indian village with a bullet hole in the breast area.

66. A few months before the battle, Custer attended a luncheon in his honor in New York, during which he was heard to express exactly these sentiments. Perkins, *Trails, Rails and War*, 193.

67. Ibid., 13. For his superb reconstruction of Custer's trail to Medicine Tail Coulee, I am beholden to Richard Hardorff's "Shadows Along the Little Big Horn," in Hutton, *Garry Owen 1976*.

68. Hardorff, *On the Little Bighorn with Walter Camp*, 53, 101.

69. Daniel Kanipe said that it was "about a half mile from the ford of [the] Little Big Horn to the place where we turned to the right." Quoted ibid., 7.

70. However, two individuals, Curly the Crow scout and Private Theodore Goldin, claimed that they were dispatched about this time with messages to Reno. But Curly's story cannot be reconciled with other independent sight-ings of him. For example, Private Augustus DeVoto, who was with the pack train, stated: "We passed a tepee in which there was a dead Indian. Presently we began to hear firing. Soon afterward we met a Crow Indian coming from the direction General Custer had gone. He could not talk much English. We asked him how about the soldiers. He made motions with his hands saying, 'Much soldiers down,' no doubt meaning killed" (Schoenberger, "A Trooper with Custer," 70). John Burkman also saw Curly two miles east of the Little Bighorn with the Arikara scouts, driving a captured herd of Sioux horses and mules (Camp BYU Notes, Reel 5, 55). Since Curly was the only Crow traveling alone, he did not remain with Custer and Boyer and then escape by riding to the east, as he said in at least one account. Goldin was an incorrigible liar who, until his death fifty-nine years later, told plenty of stories that were provably false. One example: In a letter written years later, Goldin stated that he was in Chicago during the Reno court of inquiry and talked to all the Seventh Cavalry officers there, including Captains Thomas French and Thomas Weir. Neither was anywhere near Chicago at the time — French was confined to quarters during his own court-martial at Fort Lincoln, and Weir died in December 1876.

71. Nichols, *Reno Court of Inquiry*, 397.

72. Hammer, *Custer in '76*, 188.

73. Ibid., 388.

74. In other accounts, Sergeant Daniel Kanipe said that he believed the reason Custer turned north was that the General had seen the band of Indians. See Hammer, *Custer in '76*, 92; Graham, *The Custer Myth*, 249; and O'Neil, *GarryOwen Tidbits,* vol. 8, 27.

75. Camp BYU Notes, Reel 5, 463.

76. Trooper John Sivertsen claimed that Reno immediately ordered a gallop (Coffeen, *Teepee Book 2,* 579), but this is contradicted by all other accounts, and other parts of his account are suspect (see note 78).

77. Barnard, *Ten Years with Custer*, 291; *New York Herald,* July 8, 1876.

78. "California Veteran Writes 'True Story' of Battle of Little Big Horn in 1876," undated newspaper story, probably *Billings Gazette,* clipping file, Billings Public Library; Taylor, *With Custer on the Little Bighorn*, 36. I have combined Brinkerhoff's account of the men cheering (see note 61) with Taylor's account of Reno shouting, as they make sense together. Brinkerhoff, in the first account listed above, also said, "Although he had three miles farther to go we were sure he would be at the lower end of the village to help us in the fight," which suggests that at least some of the men knew what Custer was planning to do. Sivertsen, oddly enough, wrote that Reno encouraged the men's yelling (see note 76).

79. Nichols, *In Custer's Shadow,* 184–85. Reno claimed later that he had only 112 men plus the scouts. Other counts vary. Historian William Ghent counted 146, and latter-day researcher John Gray claimed 175 (140 soldiers and 35 scouts). Another recent researcher, Joe Sills Jr., arrived at 165, which seems the most accurate to me. Since several of the Arikaras were concerned with a small horse herd on the right bank of the river, I have deduced 150 men actually involved in Reno's charge.

CHAPTER TWELVE: THE CHARGE

Epigraph: Smyth, quoted in Brady, *Indian Fights and Fighters,* 66.

1. Gregory Urwin, "Was the Past Prologue? Meditations on Custer's Tactics at the Little Big Horn," in *7th Annual Symposium,* 31.

2. Hunt, *I Fought with Custer,* 82.

3. Hammer, *Custer in '76,* 93–94.

4. Hardorff, *Camp, Custer, and the Little Bighorn,* 86.

5. Hammer, *Custer in '76,* 232.

6. Bateman, "Female Casualties at the Little Big Horn," 121; Graham, *The Custer Myth,* 260.

7. Libby, *The Arikara Narrative of Custer's Campaign,* 96.

8. Overfield, *The Little Big Horn, 1876,* 60–62; Hardorff, "Some Recollections of Custer," 18.

9. Liddic, *Vanishing Victory,* 63; Hammer, *Custer in '76,* 66; Utley, *The Reno Court of Inquiry,* 402.

10. Brininstool, *Troopers with Custer,* 48. Later eyewitness estimates of the enemy force ranged from 50 to 500 and even more. A close reading of these estimates reveals a certain consistency: it appears that 40 to 50 Indians

could be seen harassing the troops several hundred yards away, and many more occasionally could be glimpsed beyond them through the thick dust. Scout Billy Cross stated that about 1,000 Indians attacked Reno (*New York Times,* July 13, 1876), and Sergeant Ferdinand Culbertson testified that there were between 1,000 and 1,200 (Utley, *The Reno Court of Inquiry,* 305). Moylan said that there were no more than 600 to 700 Indians (Camp IU Notes, 112), and Varnum testified: "I don't believe there were less than three or four hundred, and there may have been a great many more" (Carroll, *Custer's Chief of Scouts,* 124).

11.   Michno, *Encyclopedia of Indian Wars,* 258–59.

12.   Brady, 402.

13.   Graham, *The Reno Court of Inquiry: Abstract,* 213.

14.   Ibid., 40. Wallace said that they got within 100 yards of the village (ibid., 18), but no other witness mentioned this degree of proximity. Porter testified that the nearest tepee was a quarter mile away from where he could view the village through an opening in the woods (Nichols, *Reno Court of Inquiry,* 194), though on the next day of testimony, he said that the command was about a mile from the main village (ibid., 196). Scout Billy Cross said that Reno got within 400 yards of the village (*New York Times,* July 13, 1876). Private Edward Davern estimated that it was 1,000 yards to the nearest tepee from the glade in the timber (Nichols, *Reno Court of Inquiry,* 334). Corporal John Hammon claimed that the battalion dismounted about three-fourths of a mile from the village and advanced on foot to within 200 yards of it (Deland, *The Sioux Wars,* vol.1, 483).

15.   Nichols, *Reno Court of Inquiry,* 48, 229; Chandler, *Of Garryowen in Glory,* 69; Libby, 173.

16.   Nichols, *Reno Court of Inquiry,* 382; Graham, *The Custer Myth,* 344. The horse holder assigned to care for the mounts was usually the oldest and most experienced of the four.

17.   Nichols, *Reno Court of Inquiry,* 106, 122.

18.   The carbine extractor problem did exist, though it probably had little impact on the outcome of the battle. DeRudio testified that "the men had to take their knives to extract cartridges after firing 6 to 10 rounds" (ibid., 347), but "the men" seems to have been an exaggeration. Private Daniel Newell mentioned the problem (Carroll, *The Sunshine Magazine Articles*), as did Sergeant William Heyn (Hardorff, *Camp, Custer, and the Little Bighorn,* 61). See also Hedren, "Carbine Extractor Failure at the Little Big Horn," and Reno's official report concerning the problem in Overfield, 60–62.

19.   Graham, *The Custer Myth,* 290; Utley, *The Reno Court of Inquiry,* 313.

20.   Camp BYU Notes, Reel 5, 445.

21.   Graham, *The Custer Myth,* 15.

22.   Ibid., 12–25; Hammer, *Custer in '76,* 174–75. Readers knowledgeable about this part of the battle will have noticed that Curly is uncharacteristically absent from this point on. Ever since the battle, writers and researchers, from Lieutenant Bradley to John Gray, have succumbed to the romance of the young Crow scout and his claim, in many different accounts, to being

the only survivor of Custer's Last Stand — not to mention the comfort factor they have derived from his detail-rich accounts, which provide the only "Custer" voice beyond the point at which trumpeter John Martin was dispatched. But I find his many stories — from carrying a message to Reno (and even delivering a reply!) to fighting hand to hand with a Sioux warrior in the Calhoun area — irreconcilable and highly unreliable far beyond the vagaries of time, translation, and memory. In his last account, given to his friend interpreter Russell White Bear, he refuted his earlier stories and claimed that he left Custer's command somewhere in Medicine Tail Coulee after Custer had dispatched Yates's battalion down the Little Bighorn. There are also several other accounts, from Arikara and Crow scouts to a soldier with the pack train, that place him far away from where he claimed to be. All three of the other Crow scouts with Custer's battalion denied that Curly rode with them past Reno Creek. Hairy Moccasin said in one interview that "Curley left before Custer separated from Reno" (Hardorff, *Camp, Custer, and the Little Bighorn,* 59). White Man Runs Him said, "There were only three of us, Hairy Moccasin, Goes Ahead and myself. We did not see Curley. . . . The Sioux were coming up fast. Curley would have been one of the live ones because he was with the Arikarees and the horses. . . . Curley left us up on Reno Creek. I do not like to quarrel with Curley, but that is the truth" (Graham, *The Custer Myth,* 15, 18). He also said, "I have heard many people say that Curley was the only survivor of this battle, but Curley was not in the battle. Just about the time Reno attacked the village, Curley with some Arikara scouts ran off a big band of Sioux ponies and rode away with them. Some of the Arikaras, whom I met afterwards, told me that Curley went with them as far as the Junction (where the Rosebud joins the Yellowstone)" (ibid., 24). General Hugh Scott, an indefatigable and conscientious Indian researcher, wrote after spending time with Custer's Crow scouts, "Goes-Ahead is sure Curley, the Crow scout, was not with him [Custer]. . . . At this point both Curley and Black Fox, Arikara scout, disappeared" (quoted ibid., 20). Scott also wrote, "Curley & the other scouts do not agree with each other most disagreeing over Curley's movements. . . . They [the other three Crows] say Curley did not come that far but left about the time the Rees [Arikaras] did. . . . The three Crows against Curley hang together. White-Man-Runs-Him impressed me with his honesty by his manner & I believe Curley left long before he says he did" (Scott to Luther Hare, November 28, 1919, quoted in O'Neil, *GarryOwen Tidbits,* vol. 4, 8–9). See also Hardorff, "Shadows Along the Little Big Horn," in Hutton, *Garry Owen 1976,* and Joe Sills Jr., "The Crow Scouts: Their Contributions to Understanding the Little Big Horn Battle," *5th Annual Symposium.* The most likely account of Curly's doings was probably the one he gave to a clerk named Fred Miller at the Crow Agency, in which he said that he left Custer's battalion long before it got near the upper reaches of Medicine Tail Coulee (Marquis, *Custer on the Little Bighorn,* 55–56). Custer's striker, John Burkman, told a writer that Curly's story was "pure fiction. . . . [Burkman] said that about two miles from where they joined Reno, they saw Curly and Billy Cross, a halfbreed and some other scouts, driving along a herd of 80 horses, with Sioux following them. Officers told them to let the horses go as it would draw all the Sioux on them. Curly caught a buckskin horse with a white face and let the others go and the Sioux surrounded the main bunch and drove them back. This in Burkman's opinion was sufficient evidence that Curly left Custer before the fighting began, if he was with him at all" (*Hardin* [Montana] *Tribune Herald,* April 1, 1932).

23. Carroll, *Custer's Chief of Scouts,* 65, 137.
24. Ibid., 142.
25. Hammer, *Custer in '76,* 232.
26. Hardorff, *Cheyenne Memories,* 152.
27. Robinson, *A History of the Dakota,* 430–31; Hubbard and Holcombe, *Minnesota in Three Centuries,* 267–68; Hardorff, *Indian Views of the Custer Fight,* 135.
28. Marquis, *Custer on the Little Bighorn,* 37. The Sioux and Cheyenne accounts overwhelmingly depict a camp surprised by the attack.
29. This account of Wooden Leg's participation is drawn from Marquis, *Wooden Leg,* 215–19.
30. Powell, *People of the Sacred Mountain,* 1009.
31. Stands in Timber, *Cheyenne Memories,* 197; Stands in Timber Manuscript, 356–57.
32. Box 104, Folder 2, Campbell Collection.
33. Hardorff, *Indian Views of the Custer Fight,* 144.
34. Brady, 402.
35. Graham, *The Reno Court of Inquiry: Abstract,* 73.
36. Nichols, *Reno Court of Inquiry,* 53, 249.
37. Hammer, *Custer in '76,* 232; Camp IU Notes, 775; Camp BYU Notes, Reel 4.
38. Mangum, "Reno's Battalion," 5; Carroll, *The Court-Martial of Thomas M. French,* 72; *Atlanta Journal,* May 24, 1897.
39. Barnard, *Ten Years with Custer,* 293. Three troopers claimed that O'Hara was killed on the skirmish line (see Hammer, *Custer in '76,* 118, 143, 148).
40. Carroll, *The Sunshine Magazine Articles,* 11.
41. Brininstool, *Troopers with Custer,* 105. Several Indian accounts mention this adjunct portion of the larger village; see also Brust, "Lt. Oscar Long's Early Map Details Terrain," 6, 10.
42. Coughlan, *Varnum,* 13.
43. Sergeant Ferdinand Culbertson later testified, "I have had men tell me that they fired 60 rounds," and that he himself expended 21 (Nichols, *Reno Court of Inquiry,* 376, 382). Gerard and DeRudio testified that the men expended between 30 and 40 rounds of ammunition (ibid., 104, 344). Moylan thought that the skirmish line stood for forty minutes and fired 50 rounds (Camp IU Notes, 112).
44. Brininstool, *Troopers with Custer,* 106. Unlike some other regiments that carried all their cartridges on their persons, to keep them at hand and avoid their loss if the mounts were stampeded, the troopers of the Seventh had always been ordered to carry theirs in the original packages in their saddle

pockets (R. G. Carter, November 13, 1921, Hagner Collection). Private Peter Thompson wrote: "My belt contained seventeen cartridges for my carbine. . . . I had nearly a hundred rounds in my saddle bags, but owing to the incomplete condition of my prairie belt I was unable to carry more with me. . . . Belts for carrying ammunition were, at this time, just coming into use, and a great many of us had nothing but a small cartridge box as means of carrying our ammunition when away from our horses" (quoted in Brown and Willard, *The Black Hills Trails,* 159).

45. Hardorff, *Indian Views of the Custer Fight,* 101.

46. Dickson, "Reconstructing the Indian Village on the Little Bighorn," 10.

47. Carroll, *I, Varnum,* 13.

48. Graham, *The Reno Court of Inquiry: Abstract,* 38.

49. Ibid., 39.

50. According to an account of the battle written by Francis Gibson, *New York Evening Post,* February 20, 1897. Gibson expressly stated of Reno: "He said the last he saw of Custer was on the crest of the hill we were then on, but that his troops must have been behind the slope, as he did not see them. Custer, he said, after seeing him engaged, waved his hat, which Reno took for a token sign of approval" (ibid.). Reno intimated as much himself on the eve of his court of inquiry in 1879. In an article that appeared in the *St. Paul Pioneer Press* on January 13, 1879, based on an interview with Reno, the correspondent wrote: "I then asked him whether Custer was aware of his [Reno's] engagement with the Indians. The Major said he [Custer] could see from the eminence where he halted for a brief time, that the Indians were fighting my command, but he did not come to my assistance, and had we not retreated just as we did, would have been wiped out." Reno may only have been told of Custer's presence on the bluff later, but this sounds more like a witness than mere hearsay. Though Reno would later claim that he had no idea where Custer was at the time of his retreat from the timber and that no one in his command had told him that they had seen Custer from the timber, it stretches credulity to believe that Reno, who had been so worried about Custer's support, would, when surrounded by hostile Indians in a life-or-death struggle, neither ask if anyone had seen Custer and his command nor be told if someone had. Indeed, the Major would have to have been deaf and blind. At the first fording of the river, just minutes before the charge began, troopers had been openly discussing Custer, whom several had seen on the bluffs opposite. At least ten men with Reno admitted that they had seen Custer. Sergeant Stanislas Roy wrote that Custer's command "was seen by many" (Hardorff, *On the Little Bighorn with Walter Camp,* 38, 43, n. 2), and Private Henry Petring recounted that when he saw Custer across the river on the bluffs, "some of the men said, 'There goes Custer. He is up to something, for he is waving his hat'" (Hammer, *Custer in '76,* 133). Sergeant Brinkerhoff wrote, "As we were going down the Little Big Horn river valley, driving the Indians ahead of us, we saw Custer once or twice very plainly, and at one time we cheered him and waved our hats"

("California Veteran Writes 'True Story' of Battle of Little Big Horn in 1876," undated newspaper story, probably *Billings Gazette,* clipping file, Billings Public Library). Private Dan Newell told Walter Camp that when he saw Custer, he exclaimed, "There he goes! Look at him! And we here a fighting!" (Camp BYU Notes, Reel 5, 464). Private John Donohue wrote in 1888, "Just before we commenced firing we could see General Custer's battle flag on bluffs on the same side of the river we had left" (Saum, "Private John F. Donohue's Reflections on the Little Bighorn," 45). Sergeant Thomas O'Neill stated in 1897, "Custer's band was now a mile and a half distant, and passing behind a high bluff was out of sight, and was never again seen alive" (*Washington Post,* July 12, 1897). Ten years later, he was quoted in the June 23, 1907, *Washington Sunday Star:* "Gen. Custer's command advanced in the same direction as ours, on the opposite side of the river, and, when the fight was begun, Custer and Reno were about a mile and a half apart. The general and his command disappeared behind a high bluff and that was the last we saw of them alive." After interviewing O'Neill in 1919, Walter Camp wrote: "When about half way down to where skirmish line was formed he saw Custer and his command on the bluffs across the river, over to the east, at a point which he would think was about where Reno afterward fortified, or perhaps a little south of this. Custer's command were then going at a trot" (Hammer, *Custer in '76,* 106). O'Neill appears to have seen Custer more than once. An unidentified member of Reno's battalion wrote, "Reno was already engaged in the valley below, and as Custer rode along the ridge above him he raised his hat, and a cheer to their comrades burst from the throats of the 250 men who were following the standard of their beloved commander. On down the ridge with Custer they rode, over a little ridge, disappeared from sight, and we never saw them again alive" (*New York Herald,* July 30, 1876). Gibson's 1897 account quoted above states in no uncertain terms that Reno said he had seen Custer on the bluffs. See also Forrest, *Witnesses at the Battle of the Little Big Horn,* 5, for a letter written by Gibson in which he said of the meeting between Reno and Benteen: "We did not know whose command it was until we came together, and Benteen asked Reno where Custer was, and *when told,* Benteen said — Well, let us make a junction with him as soon as possible" (italics mine). Fred Gerard testified that when he saw Custer's command on the bluffs across the river, "There was quite a cloud of dust coming from it," which would have made it even more unlikely to be missed (Utley, *The Reno Court of Inquiry,* 133). In another account, Gerard stated: "Not more than four rounds had been fired before they saw Custer's command dashing along the hills one mile to their rear. Reno then gave the order: 'The Indians are taking us in the rear, mount and charge.' . . . Reno led his men in Indian file back to the ford above which he had seen Custer's command pass" (Libby, 173). In his article on the battle, Godfrey wrote: "Major Moylan thinks that the last he saw of Custer's party was about the position of Reno Hill"; undoubtedly, he received this information directly from Moylan (Godfrey, "Custer's Last Battle," 182). Lieutenant Edward McClernand, an officer with Gibbon's column, wrote of their finding Reno and the Seventh Cavalry on June 27: "'Where is Custer,' they were asked. Wallace replied, 'The last we saw of him he was going along that high bluff (pointing in a general direction to a point on the bluffs down stream from the position where he had located Reno), toward the lower end of the village. He took off his hat and waved to us. We do not know where he is now'" (McClernand, "With the Indian and the Buffalo in Montana," 27). That Wallace had seen Custer on the bluffs is further indication that Reno either had seen him (as Gibson recounted in two different accounts) or had been told of his presence on the bluffs (by Wallace or one of the many men who had seen him). DeRudio saw Custer five minutes before the retreat from the timber, at a high point on the edge of the bluffs (Utley, *Reno Court of Inquiry*, 284–86), and Varnum saw the Gray Horse Troop on the bluffs while on the skirmish line (Nichols, *Reno Court of Inquiry*, 157–58). Daniel Kanipe, who was with Custer, told Walter Camp that "Custer and all his men proceeded north along the bluffs so far west that they had full view of Reno's men and the Indian village all the time instead of some distance back and out of sight as stated and mapped by Godfrey" (Hammer, *Custer in '76*, 97). Kanipe also told Camp that Custer "struck edge of bluffs [a] few hundred feet north of where Reno afterward corralled, and after going about ¼ mile farther on [Kanipe] was sent back" (Hardorff, *On the Little Bighorn with Walter Camp*, 209). Even allowing for some exaggeration, this shows Custer to have been in full view of Reno's battalion for quite some time. Finally, the Arikara scout Red Star said: "When Custer stood at the bank where Hodgson's stone stands, Curly and Black Fox were there with him" (Libby, 119).

51. Reno offered this reasoning as to why he had not expected support from a flank attack at his court of inquiry in 1879: "I expected my support to come from the direction I had crossed. I did not see how it was possible, on account of the high banks on the other side, for support to come from the flanks. I didn't think it was practicable to get down below me" (Graham, *Reno Court of Inquiry: Abstract*, 228).

52. Mangum, "Reno's Battalion," 5.

53. Even Reno's orderly, Ed Davern — required to stay within calling distance — failed to hear the order. Nichols, *Reno Court of Inquiry*, 336, 348, 355.

54. Hammer, *Custer in '76*, 107; Carroll, *The Seventh Cavalry Scrapbook*, no. 3, 7.

55. Graham, *The Reno Court of Inquiry: Abstract*, 70, 217. Sergeant William Heyn of A Company summarized the nature of the movement when he told researcher Walter Camp, "The men straggled out and started across the flat without any particular command and no bugle being blown, the officers digging spurs into their horses and every man for himself" (Hardorff, *Camp, Custer, and the Little Bighorn*, 61).

56. Graham, *The Custer Myth*, 242.

57. Mangum, "Reno's Battalion," 5.

58. Carroll, *The Sunshine Magazine Articles*, 10.

59. Hammer, *Custer in '76*, 223.
60. Ibid., 262.
61. These orders to mount, dismount, and mount were heard by Herendeen (Graham, *The Reno Court of Inquiry: Abstract*, 82). Private William Taylor later wrote, "All was in the greatest confusion and I dismounted twice and mounted again, all in a few moments, but why, I do not know, unless it was because I saw the others do it and thought they had orders to" (Taylor, *With Custer on the Little Bighorn*, 38). Private Jacob Adams, though with the pack train on June 25, wrote, "Reno ordered his men to dismount. At a second volley from the Indians, the troopers were ordered to remount, whereupon such confusion prevailed that the order was now given for every man to save himself" (Ellis, "A Survivor's Story of the Custer Massacre," 230). The first fully detailed story of the battle appeared in the *New York Herald* on July 8, 1876. Written on the battlefield on June 28, almost certainly by Major James Brisbin, it included this account of Reno's retreat, which Brisbin must have ascertained from an officer in Reno's battalion: "Reno soon discovered that the Indians were working around to his rear and had entered the timber above him, and between him and the reserve. The order was given to mount and charge through the timber toward the reserve. The Indians had already become so strong that it was found impracticable to dislodge them, while mounted, from behind the bushes and the trees, and the command again dismounted and charged on foot. The Indians were every moment getting thicker between the companies on the river bottom and the reserve on the hill. Colonel Reno ordered his men to mount and cut their way through. A wild scramble for life now began." Finally, Lieutenant Charles F. Roe, with the Gibbon column, wrote an account of the expedition and Custer's battle, in which he stated of Bloody Knife's death: "In that emergency, Major Reno lost his head; an officer told me that he gave the command to mount and dismount three times in quick succession" (Roe, *Custer's Last Battle*, 9). See also Whittaker, *A Complete Life of George A. Custer*, 584, where he quotes an officer present with Reno who told much the same story. Significantly, during the Reno court of inquiry, neither Reno nor his counsel objected to or made any attempt to rebut Herendeen's testimony regarding this sequence of orders.
62. Mangum, "Reno's Battalion," 5; Brady, *Indian Fights and Fighters*, 403; Brininstool, *Troopers with Custer*, 51; Rickey, *Forty Miles a Day on Beans and Hay*, 325. In early accounts, Morris identified this trooper as George Lorentz, but a later account (in Brininstool) and other troopers' accounts identify him as Klotzbucher. (See note 66.)
63. Rickey, 5.
64. Carroll, *The Two Battles of the Little Big Horn*, 163. Lieutenant Charles Roe of Gibbon's column, who talked to several of the Seventh Cavalry officers after the battle, claimed that Reno said this (Roe, *Custer's Last Battle*, 9).
65. Carroll, *The Court-Martial of Thomas M. French*, 69, 72.
66. Roe, *Custer's Last Battle*, 5–6; Hammer, *Custer in '76*, 131. There is a

possibility that the wounded trooper whom Morris helped was Henry Klotzbucher. William Slaper told a similar tale of Morris helping another downed trooper shot through the stomach, but in his version that trooper was Klotzbucher (Brininstool, *Troopers with Custer,* 51).

67. Taylor, *With Custer on the Little Bighorn,* 41.
68. Carroll, *Custer's Chief of Scouts,* 180.
69. Carroll, *The Benteen-Goldin Letters,* 47–48.
70. Hardorff, *The Custer Battle Casualties II,* 109–10.
71. Marquis, *Wooden Leg,* 221; Stands in Timber statement, Cartwright Collection.
72. Taylor, *With Custer on the Little Bighorn,* 42.
73. Hammer, *Custer in '76,* 223.
74. Box 105, Notebook 34, p. 24, Campbell Collection; Hammer, *Custer in '76,* 85. Sergeant Stanislas Roy remembered that he saw Reynolds "dismounted and wounded with pistol in hand trying to follow troops in retreat" (Hammer, *Custer in '76,* 112). Fred Gerard told a slightly different version of the death of Reynolds (Graham, *Reno Court of Inquiry: Abstract,* 40).
75. Hardorff, *Camp, Custer, and the Little Bighorn,* 81; Hammer, *Custer in '76,* 85.
76. Hardorff, *Hokahey!* 55.
77. Hardorff, *Lakota Recollections,* 101.
78. Crawford, *Rekindling Campfires,* 155.
79. Utley, *The Lance and the Shield,* 153. In his superb and unrivaled analysis of Indian accounts of the battle, *Lakota Noon,* Gregory Michno makes a good case for this event never happening. But there are too many variables, I believe, to completely eliminate this story, and the Crawford account (see previous note) adds motivation for Sitting Bull's kindness, which as Michno points out was characteristic of the Hunkpapa leader.
80. Hardorff, *Lakota Recollections,* 94–95, 101–2; Greene, *Lakota and Cheyenne,* 42–43. Other accounts claim that the young man was named Deeds. He may have used both names. His sister Eagle Robe was almost certainly also known as Moving Robe and later as Mary Crawler.
81. Hardorff, *On the Little Bighorn with Walter Camp,* 116. Benteen erroneously claimed later that Private John Rapp, McIntosh's orderly, had died in the timber, thus releasing McIntosh's horse, and that Private Samuel McCormick had given up his horse to McIntosh (Carroll, *The Benteen-Goldin Letters,* 42). Several troopers claimed to witness McIntosh's death, and their accounts vary slightly; see Hardorff, *The Custer Battle Casualties,* 131.
82. Marquis, *Wooden Leg,* 222.
83. Brust, 8, 11.
84. Marquis, *Wooden Leg,* 224.
85. Hardorff, *The Custer Battle Casualties,* 155.
86. Marquis, *Wooden Leg,* 224.
87. Carroll, *The Two Battles of the Little Big Horn,* 164.
88. Mangum, "Reno's Battalion," 6. Other accounts mention another trooper, Charles Fischer, as the man whose stirrup Hodgson held on to (Brininstool,

Troopers with Custer, 53; Graham, *The Reno Court of Inquiry: Abstract,* 118–19).

89. Coughlan, 14.
90. Taylor, *With Custer on the Little Bighorn,* 42, 44.
91. Graham, *The Reno Court of Inquiry: Abstract,* 119; Carroll, *Custer's Chief of Scouts,* 91; Nichols, *Men with Custer,* 85.
92. Nichols, *Reno Court of Inquiry,* 351, 365–66.
93. Johnson, "A Captain of 'Chivalric Courage,'" 14; Mangum, "Reno's Battalion," 6.
94. Davis and Davis, *That Fatal Day,* 21.
95. Ibid., 21.
96. Graham, *The Reno Court of Inquiry: Abstract,* 63.
97. Marquis, *Wooden Leg,* 225.
98. Nichols, *Reno Court of Inquiry,* 191, 539–40; Utley, *The Reno Court of Inquiry,* 210. The number of wounded cited ranges from five to ten, with six or seven the most frequently mentioned number.
99. Dixon, *The Vanishing Race,* 174.

CHAPTER THIRTEEN: "THE SAVIOR OF THE SEVENTH"
Chapter title: New York Herald, August 8, 1876.
Epigraph: Custer to Benteen, message, June 25, 1876 (Graham, *The Custer Myth,* 299).

1. Graham, *The Custer Myth,* 290; Nichols, *Reno Court of Inquiry,* 390.
2. Graham, *The Custer Myth,* 289–90; Hammer, *Custer in '76,* 100–1.
3. Marquis, *Custer on the Little Bighorn,* 37: "On a high ridge far out eastward from the Cheyenne camp circle I saw those other soldiers," said Kate Bighead. Several other Indians mentioned seeing soldiers on the high ridges above Medicine Tail Coulee.
4. There is no primary account or other evidence that corroborates this plan, but circumstantial evidence points to it. A short while after Reno's command reached the bluffs and was joined by Benteen, at least two volleys were heard by virtually every officer on the hill and by those left behind in the timber. There were not enough Indians near Keogh's wing to merit volley fire. According to John Stands in Timber in *Cheyenne Memories,* about fifty Cheyenne warriors were in the vicinity but split up to chase the soldiers going to the river and block them from the north. He made no mention of volley fire.
5. Both the archaeological and historical records bear this movement out. See Hardorff, *Lakota Recollections,* 143, in which Two Eagles is quoted as saying that soldiers came down from Nye-Cartwright Ridge to Ford B and were driven to Calhoun Ridge, and other soldiers went directly from Nye-Cartwright Ridge to Calhoun Hill at the same time. See also ibid., 155.
6. Nichols, *Reno Court of Inquiry,* 431.
7. Ibid., 421.
8. Lieutenant Frank Gibson to his wife, July 4, 1876, quoted in Gray, *Custer's Last Campaign,* 259. Also, in an account given twenty-one years later to a New York newspaper, Gibson stated, "Col. Benteen was directed to take

his [battalion] out of column, and proceed with it across the hills to the left, which turned out to be small mountains, and reach the valley of the Little Big Horn as soon as possible" (*New York Evening Post,* February 20, 1897). In 1910, in an interview with Walter Camp, Gibson said that "Benteen told him to keep going until he could see the valley of the Little Bighorn," although Camp also wrote, "He now thinks however that he only went far enough to look down on the valley of the south fork of Sundance Creek," another name for the small valley just east of the Little Bighorn (Hammer, *Custer in '76,* 80). Benteen, in his official report written the same day, described his orders similarly, and he did the same in an early August newspaper interview (ibid.). In their later writings, both Gibson and Edgerly gave similar accounts of Benteen's orders. Gibson, in a letter to his wife, wrote, "We were to hurry and rejoin the command as quickly as possible" (quoted in Gray, *Centennial Campaign,* 304).

9.   Graham, *The Custer Myth,* 187; Hammer, *Custer in '76,* 80, where Gibson said that "Benteen told him to keep going until he could see the valley of the Little Bighorn." See note 27.

10. Graham, *The Reno Court of Inquiry: Abstract,* 157. However, accounts of this scout to the left by Edgerly, Benteen, and Gibson are not consistent.

11. Gray, *Custer's Last Campaign,* 262. See also Darling, *Benteen's Scout-to-the-Left.* Some historians have maintained that the only view Gibson had at his last vantage point did not provide sight of the valley of the Little Bighorn (Dale Kosman, Custer researcher, conversation with author, January 9, 2006). But Gibson, an ardent admirer and defender of Benteen's, emphatically claimed that he could see the valley. In Gibson's account, published in the February 20, 1897, *New York Evening Post,* he wrote: "I got to the valley and found it as quiet as the grave itself. Up the valley I could see a long distance, but in the direction of the village only a short one, owing to the turn in the valley, and the broken character of the country. I hurried back to Benteen, and told him there was no use going any further in that direction." In a letter to Godfrey, written on August 8, 1908, Gibson wrote, "I crossed an insignificant little stream running through the valley, which I knew was not the Little Big Horn, so I kept on to the top of it. I could see plainly up the Little Big Horn valley for a long distance with the aid of the glasses; but in the direction of the village I could not see far on account of the sharp turns in it and I hurried back and reported so to Benteen who altered his course so as to pick up the trail" (quoted in Carroll, *The Anders-Cartwright Letters,* vol. 1, 15). Edgerly also made the same claim (O'Neil, *The Gibson-Edgerly Narratives,* 9), as did Godfrey, who told Walter Camp: "Gibson signaled Benteen that he could see up and down the valley of the Little Big Horn [really South Reno] and could not see any village. When Benteen got this information he made for the main trail, on middle fork of Reno Creek, without going further" (Camp IU Notes, 446).

12. According to Henry M. Brinkerhoff, "Benteen afterwards said he thought Custer had sent him fishing, for no Indians had been reported in that

direction" ("California Veteran Writes 'True Story' of Battle of Little Big Horn in 1876," undated newspaper story, probably *Billings Gazette,* clipping file, Billings Public Library).

13. Brady, *Indian Fights and Fighters,* 404; Godfrey, *Custer's Last Battle,* 22; Nichols, *Reno Court of Inquiry,* 479. Godfrey testified that when they turned toward the trail, their "gait was pretty rapid. My company was in the rear and I had quite often to give the command 'trot' to keep up with the rest of the command." This was likely due to Benteen's fast-walking horse.

14. Kuhlman, *Legend into History,* 88. The regulation cavalry walk, mounted, was four miles an hour.

15. Hammer, *Custer in '76,* 75.

16. Ibid., 69; Camp IU Notes, 79. Some historians have maintained that Boston Custer was assigned to the pack train until he left it to overtake his brother's battalion. But he was employed as a guide, and guides usually rode forward of or with the vanguard of a cavalry column. Besides, if Custer's nephew Autie Reed was allowed to ride with the General, it is hard to believe that Boston was not. Camp wrote, "Boston had two ponies, and was returning to the pack train to get his other pony," but this note is unattributed.

17. Godfrey, *Custer's Last Battle,* 22.

18. Ibid.

19. Hammer, *Custer in '76,* 93, 75.

20. Godfrey recorded their pace in his diary: "After we watered we continued our march very leisurely" (Godfrey, *Field Diary,* 11). Two and a half years later, however, he testified that "our gait was increased to a trot" only after meeting Martin (Nichols, *Reno Court of Inquiry,* 481), and even later he wrote that previous to that, "the column had been marching at a trot and walk, according as the ground was smooth and broken" (Godfrey, *Custer's Last Battle,* 25). Edgerly testified that after they left the water hole, they moved "at a fast walk all the distance" (Nichols, *Reno Court of Inquiry,* 442). It should be kept in mind that horses were rarely galloped unless absolutely necessary, to "husband the powers of our horses as to save them for the real work of the conflict" (Custer, *My Life on the Plains,* 86). On this day, Custer himself had tried not to overexert the animals. He had told Benteen to slow down soon after the Captain had taken the lead at the divide, and he had kept the pace at no more than a walk until they reached the two tepees.

21. Graham, *The Custer Myth,* 299.

22. Two and a half years later, at the Reno court of inquiry, Benteen testified that Martin had told him that the Indians were "skedaddling" (Graham, *The Reno Court of Inquiry: Abstract,* 137). In interviews years later, Martin claimed never to have used the word (Hammer, *Custer in '76,* 101), and it seems an unlikely word for a recent Italian immigrant to use. In an interview thirty-two years after the battle, Martin claimed that Benteen asked him, "Is [Custer] being attacked or not?" Martin replied, "Yes, [he] is being attacked" (Hammer, *Custer in '76,* 101). See also Graham, *The Custer Myth,* 219, for Edgerly's statement, in which he related what Martin said.

23. Godfrey, *Field Diary,* 11.

24. Hammer, *Custer in '76*, 54–55.

25. Graham, *The Reno Court of Inquiry: Abstract*, 137.

26. Martin told two different stories of what happened at this time. This version is what he testified to at the Reno court of inquiry in 1879 (see Nichols, *Reno Court of Inquiry*, 391–92). Forty-seven years later, in another account, he disavowed his original testimony, insisting that he had only exchanged his horse for a fresh one and joined his company. He claimed: "I didn't speak English so good then, and they misunderstood me and made the report of my testimony show that I took an order to Captain McDougall. But this is a mistake." His original testimony encompassing his orders to McDougall went on for ten questions and answers, and then another question referring to McDougall several minutes later (see Graham, *The Custer Myth*, 290–91). Neither Benteen nor McDougall ever corroborated Martin's assignment.

27. See note 9; see also Nichols, *Reno Court of Inquiry*, 405. Edgerly testified that after Martin arrived, the gait was "the same" as before, which was a fast walk (ibid., 442). Godfrey testified that the gait was increased to a trot after meeting Martin and that they kept it up until just before they met the Crow Indians (ibid., 481). Trooper William Morris later wrote: "Miller, of his [Benteen's] troop, who occupied an adjoining cot to mine in the hospital at Fort Abraham Lincoln, told me that they walked all the way, and that they heard the heavy firing while they were watering their horses"; Morris also said that "Benteen, arriving about an hour later, came up as slow as though he were going to a funeral" (Brady, 404). Martin testified that after he gave Benteen the message, Benteen "went a little livelier" (Nichols, *Reno Court of Inquiry*, 392).

28. Ibid., 90, 397.

29. Hammer, *Custer in '76*, 80.

30. Godfrey, *Custer's Last Battle*, 25.

31. Graham, *The Custer Myth*, 181.

32. Lonich, "Blacksmith Henry Mechling," 31.

33. Carroll, *The Seventh Cavalry Scrapbook*, no. 4, 9.

34. *New York Evening Post*, February 20, 1897. I have quoted almost verbatim from this account personally written by Francis Gibson, one of only two officers present at the Battle of the Little Bighorn who were not called to testify at the Reno court of inquiry in January 1879. The other officer, Thomas French, was in the middle of his own court-martial proceedings and thus could not attend the inquiry.

35. Forrest, *Witnesses at the Battle of the Little Big Horn*, 5.

36. These orders and Benteen's response to them — including whether he followed them correctly and whether he was justified in acting the way he did — have been debated since the battle. The fact is that Custer ordered Benteen to come quickly to his aid, and Benteen did not do so. In the Reno court of inquiry, however, recorder Jesse M. Lee seemed to accept that Benteen had placed himself under Reno's direction at the time, and his assumption was not disputed in court or in print.

37. Nichols, *Reno Court of Inquiry*, 189, 399; Godfrey, "Custer's Last Battle," 182.

38. Mackintosh, *Custer's Southern Officer*, 69.

39. Edgerly, Graham, *Reno Court of Inquiry: Abstract*, 160; Nichols, *Reno Court of Inquiry*, 443.

40. Hardorff, *Indian Views of the Custer Fight*, 21. When McLaughlin's five-year hitch expired six weeks later, in August 1876, he reenlisted — but this time in the infantry. In March 1886, he was admitted to the North Dakota Hospital for the Insane, and he died there ten months later.

41. Ibid., 55.

42. Bates, *Custer's Indian Battles*, 33.

43. According to Reno's report, as quoted in Stewart, *Custer's Luck*, 393. Reno later changed his story and said that he had heard no volleys. The only officers on the hill who claimed not to have heard volleys were Reno, Benteen, and Wallace. In his fine biography of Reno, *In Custer's Shadow*, Ron Nichols suggests a seemingly simple reason for this: Reno's and Benteen's service during the Civil War had caused them "considerable hearing loss" (209 n. 23). The problem with this explanation is that nowhere in the voluminous literature on the subject is there even a suggestion — by Reno, Benteen, or anyone else — that this was the case. It's hard to believe that their deafness, if indeed true, would not have been mentioned or noticed during the Reno court of inquiry or any other time.

44. Nichols, *Reno Court of Inquiry*, 352, 361, 365.

Chapter Fourteen: Soldiers Falling

Epigraph: Two Moon, quoted in Graham, *The Custer Myth*, 103.

This narrative of the battle, from the skirmish at Medicine Tail Coulee through the fighting at Calhoun Ridge (the southern end of the long ridge), is primarily drawn from several accounts in Hardorff, *Cheyenne Memories, Indian Views of the Custer Fight, Lakota Recollections,* and *Markers, Artifacts and Indian Testimony;* Powell, *People of the Sacred Mountain* and *Sweet Medicine;* Stands in Timber, *Cheyenne Memories;* Grinnell, *The Fighting Cheyennes;* Michno, *Lakota Noon;* Graham, *The Custer Myth;* Hammer, *Custer in '76;* and Marquis, *Custer on the Little Bighorn,* sec. 6, "She Watched Custer's Last Battle."

1. Hardorff, *Cheyenne Memories*, 49–50.

2. Several Indian accounts make clear that the soldiers rode toward the river on the bluffs along Medicine Tail Coulee. See Marquis, *Wooden Leg*, 226; and Marquis, *Custer on the Little Bighorn*, 37.

3. Michno, *Lakota Noon*, 200; "Yellow Nose Tells of Custer's Last Stand," *Indian School Journal* (November 1905), 40. Yellow Nose told George Bent that he obtained the guidon at Last Stand Hill (Bent to George Hyde, April 10, 1905, Coe Collection). Another Cheyenne, Brave Bear, told Bent that he saw Yellow Nose with the flag during the attack on Calhoun Hill and Keogh's position, but it's unclear whether he meant that Yellow Nose already had the flag or seized it there (Bent to George Hyde, December 1, 1905, Coe Collection).

4. Bordeaux, *Custer's Conqueror,* 57; Joseph White Cow Bull interview, McCracken Research Library.

5. There is abundant oral testimony and archaeological evidence that part of Custer's battalion reached the ford and fought there. See Powell, *People of the Sacred Mountain,* 1023; Hammer, *Custer in '76,* 206; and Greene, *Evidence and the Custer Enigma,* 20–26. He Dog said that the soldiers were six hundred feet away, though other accounts vary from right up on the river's edge to three-quarters of a mile away. Tall Bull said that the soldiers "got onto flat near Ford B within easy gunshot of village" (Hammer, *Custer in '76,* 212). Hollow Horn Bear said, "In the early start of fight, soldiers in front were dismounted and many of their horses were killed" (Hardorff, *Lakota Recollections,* 181).

6. Indian accounts of this skirmish, particularly those of the Cheyennes, proudly state that they prevented the soldiers from crossing the river and attacking the village. But Lights, a Minneconjou Lakota, said later: "The Indians were swarming out of their tepees in such great numbers that he [Custer] appeared to be looking out for the safety of his men more than he did for a chance to cross the river at some other point than at 'B' " (ibid., 166) — further evidence that a crossing was never planned there.

7. Richard A. Fox Jr., "West River Story," in Rankin, *Legacy,* 152.

8. Scott, "Cartridges, Bullets and Bones," 28; Scott and Bleed, *A Good Walk,* 37; Hardorff, *Cheyenne Memories,* 36.

9. "An officer was killed where Custer made his first stand — nearest the river. This officer had a pair of field glasses, and a compass — (wooden box)" (Brust, "Lt. Oscar Long's Early Map Details Terrain," 8). In Hardorff, *Cheyenne Memories,* 126, Two Moon says of the action at Medicine Tail Ford: "Here some soldiers were killed and were afterward dragged into the village, dismembered and burned at [the] big dance that night." White Cow Bull, who was also there, said: "One white man had little hairs on his face and wearing a big hat and a buckskin jacket. He was riding a fine-looking horse, a sorrel with a blazed face and four white stockings. On one side of him was a soldier carrying a flag and riding a gray horse. . . . The man in the buckskin jacket seemed to be the leader of these soldiers, for he shouted something and they all came charging at us" (quoted in Miller, "Echoes of the Little Bighorn," 33). A white scout for General Miles who talked with several Indians present at the battle reported, "Lieut. Sturgis was knocked off his horse, shot and knifed, his body stripped and thrown into the river. It must be Sturgis's death which is thus described, as the Indians tell of this poor fellow as a young warrior who rode with a buckskin coat strapped to his saddle, and it is known he was so equipped" (quoted in Hutchins, *The Army and Navy Journal,* 148). It seems likely that this man was killed near the water, not up on the hill a half mile away. Other Indian accounts mention one or more men shot at or near this ford. One of these men was likely young Lieutenant James Sturgis, of the Gray Horse Troop, whose body was never found or identified. His permanent assignment was to M Company,

but that day he had been detailed to serve with E Company. M Company, Sturgis among them, rode light bay horses, which could easily have been mistaken for sorrels (Smalley, *More Little Bighorn Mysteries,* 18–5). Sturgis had been detailed as acting engineering officer with the Reno scout down the Tongue River two weeks earlier and probably possessed the field glasses and compass to perform his duties. The compass in a wooden box was likely a government-issued one, not a personally owned pocket compass. Private George Glenn told a researcher that one of the heads found in the Indian village "looked to me [to be] that of Lieutenant Sturgis" (quoted in Hardorff, *The Custer Battle Casualties II,* 47). Private Theodore Goldin wrote: "We found a large fire at the lower end of the village, two or three scarred skulls burned beyond recognition, and one of the men picked up a piece of blue flannel shirt with the initials J.C.S. or J.G.S. embroidered on it; this was near where this fire was located" (Theodore Goldin to Walter Mason Camp, July 1908, Camp BYU Collection). If Glenn and Goldin were correct and the head belonged to Sturgis, it is likely that he was killed near the river, since all the other bodies and/or heads found in the village belonged to men from Reno's battalion. It is doubtful that any trooper killed a mile or more from the village would have been carried there. Additionally, Sturgis's buckskin shirt, blue flannel undershirt, underdrawers, and spurs were found in the village, circumstantial evidence that they were taken from his body nearby (Hardorff, *The Custer Battle Casualties II,* 45–47). His sister wrote in 1926 that "his drawers and shirt were found, the shirt with collar button still in the neck" — the inference being that Sturgis had been decapitated, since the collar button was still in place (quoted in Willert, "Does Anomaly Contain Sturgis's Body?" 15). See Willert's article for more circumstantial evidence that Sturgis's head was found in the village, including apparent private disclosures of this fact by Charles Varnum and Francis Gibson.

10. Hardorff, *Indian Views of the Custer Fight,* 140.
11. Stands in Timber, *Cheyenne Memories,* 197–98. See also Fox, *Archaeology, History, and Custer's Last Battle,* chap. 11, "The Cemetery Ridge Episode."
12. Godfrey, *Custer's Last Battle,* 26.
13. Camp BYU Notes, Reel 5, 569.
14. Nichols, *Reno Court of Inquiry,* 206. In a letter to his father dated July 4, 1876, Porter wrote that there were "ten or fifteen wounded" (quoted in Carroll, "The Battles on the Little Big Horn," 3).
15. Camp IU Notes, 579.
16. Godfrey, quoted in Rickey, *Forty Miles a Day on Beans and Hay,* 291.
17. Gray, *Custer's Last Campaign,* 291.
18. Meketa, *Luther Rector Hare,* 22.
19. Nichols, *Reno Court of Inquiry,* 444. Edgerly rendered several accounts of this scene, each with slight differences in wording and timing.
20. Michno, *Lakota Noon,* 153.
21. Merington, *The Custer Story,* 236–37.
22. Dixon, *The Vanishing Race,* 182; Stands in Timber, *Cheyenne Memories,* 199–200.

23. Stands in Timber, *Cheyenne Memories,* 199.

24. There are several Indian accounts of the Indian resistance here. See Hardorff, *Lakota Recollections,* 80, for Red Feather's map, which shows many warriors congregating at Squaw Creek, north of the Cheyenne camp.

25. Kellogg's body was found in a swale near the river in this area. Also, Cheyenne oral tradition speaks of a man riding a long-eared horse down by the river, and at least one resident of the area in the first half of the twentieth century said that Kellogg's family put up a marker for him down by the river; the marker was later pulled up and put in storage (Darrell Linthacum, interview with author, September 6, 2006). See also Moore and Donahue, "Gibbon's Route to Custer Hill"; Donahue, "Revisiting Col. Gibbon's Route"; and Fox, *Archaeology, History, and Custer's Last Battle,* chap. 11.

26. Marquis, *Wooden Leg,* 231–34. Though some historians have placed Wooden Leg's observations of this action — "about forty of the soldiers came galloping from the east part of the ridge down toward the river" — near Last Stand Hill, I believe that his account more accurately points to the vicinity of Calhoun Ridge, since after this part of the battle, Wooden Leg said, "By this time all of the soldiers were gone except a band of them at the west end of the ridge. They were hidden behind dead horses" — a clear reference to Last Stand Hill. Another Marquis-written account by an Indian participant, "She Watched Custer's Last Battle," follows a similar path. However, as Richard Hardorff has pointed out in *Hokahey!* these two accounts of Marquis's are suspect, since it is clear that some of their shared material is suspiciously similar. But Lame White Man's body was found halfway between Last Stand Hill and Calhoun Hill, on the opposite side of the ridge from Keogh's position; it seems more likely that he would have been killed there after leading the assault on the troops at Calhoun Hill. Indeed, that is exactly what Little Wolf, a Northern Cheyenne, said, after stating that there was a skirmish line on Calhoun Hill: "I was there. Lame White Man charged them here and chased them to Keogh where he (Lame White Man) was killed" (Hardorff, *Cheyenne Memories,* 90).

27. Masters, *Shadows Fall Across the Little Big Horn,* 41.

28. Burdick, *David F. Barry's Notes,* 25, 27; McCreight, *Chief Flying Hawk's Tales,* 113.

29. Crazy Horse's rifle is identified as a Winchester in Wiltsey, "We Killed Custer," 26, and Bray, *Crazy Horse,* 216.

30. Vestal, *New Sources of Indian History,* 329.

31. Graham, *The Custer Myth,* 75.

32. Marquis, *Wooden Leg,* 231; Marquis, *Custer on the Little Bighorn,* 38. Although some battle historians have claimed that Lame White Man's charge occurred during the action at Last Stand Hill, it seems more likely from the sequencing in Wooden Leg's account that the Cheyenne chief's charge was at Calhoun Hill. Immediately after Lame White Man's brave action, Wooden Leg made his own move "around the hillside north of the soldier ridge"; the "Indians there were around a band of soldiers on the north slope" — which can only mean Keogh's company. Several pages later,

he discussed the action at the west end of the ridge — Last Stand Hill. In Marquis's other first-person account of the battle, "She Watched Custer's Last Battle" (sec. 6 in *Custer on the Little Bighorn*), Kate Bighead corroborated Wooden Leg's story. After she rode to the south side of the battlefield and witnessed Lame White Man's charge, she "started to go around the east end of the soldier ridge" and watched as "the Indians crowded on westward along the ridge and along its two sides" — a clear reference to Indians moving from Calhoun Hill to Last Stand Hill. However, as Greg Michno has pointed out, these two accounts of Marquis's are so uncannily similar — the same sequence of several events, the same discussions of more general subjects in the same places, even the same wording — that it is clear he used some of the same material in both. Which material is original — or how much of it is Marquis's — is unclear. See Michno, *Lakota Noon*, 258, for further discussion of this problem. Richard Fox has suggested that elements of Cheyenne oral tradition may also have been incorporated into either or both accounts; see Fox, *Archaeology, History, and Custer's Last Battle*, 135–37. Hardorff, in *Hokahey!* 72–73, makes a similar case concerning Marquis's reliability, particularly in these accounts. For Indian accounts that describe Lame White Man's attack at Calhoun Hill, see Wells, "Little Big Horn Notes," 10, and Camp IU Notes, 632.

33. Hardorff, *Camp, Custer, and the Little Bighorn*, 67–69; Ben Ash interview, Hagner Collection; Burdick, *David F. Barry's Notes*, 27, 29.

34. Hardorff, *Markers, Artifacts and Indian Testimony*, 50; Hardorff, *The Custer Battle Casualties*, 102.

35. Hammer, *Custer in '76*, 199. Other Indian accounts state that this group of soldiers, probably Keogh's company with the remnants of C and L, were moving north along the east side of the ridge toward Custer and Last Stand Hill.

36. Hardorff, *Indian Views of the Custer Fight*, 166.

37. Hammer, *Custer in '76*, 207; Hardorff, *Lakota Recollections*, 87–88; Miller, "Echoes of the Little Bighorn," 35–36; Vestal, "The Man Who Killed Custer," 7.

38. Vestal, "The Man Who Killed Custer," 7; Miller, "Echoes of the Little Bighorn," 35.

39. Hardorff, *Lakota Recollections*, 75–76, 86; Hardorff, *Indian Views of the Custer Fight*, 30, 94, 118, 132; Hammer, *Custer in '76*, 199, 201; Vestal, *Warpath: The True Story of the Fighting Sioux*, 200–1; Marquis, *Wooden Leg*, 232; Graham, *The Custer Myth*, 85. These are some of the many Indian accounts of one soldier (or more than one) who rode away from the battle and finally killed himself with his pistol. The fact that Harrington's body was never found — or at least never identified — and that, unlike the other unidentified officers, no trace or article of clothing was found, strengthens the case that Harrington was one of these riders. He was known to have a strong horse (William O. Taylor to Walter Camp, November 19, 1909, Camp BYU Collection), a fact often mentioned in the Indian accounts. One final note:

Indian agent and agency doctor V. E. McGillycuddy said that Crazy Horse had told him "of the officer who did not dismount, struck out East for several miles, pursued by half a dozen young bucks, and being mounted on a powerful horse, would have escaped, had he not become rattled and committed suicide, and was dragged away by his horse, his foot being tangled in the stirrup" (McGillycuddy to E. A. Brininstool, June 1, 1931, Brininstool Collection).

40. Every reconstruction of the final actions of Custer's battalion — the events on and around Last Stand Hill toward the end of the battle — is fraught with difficulty, and none that I have seen is completely satisfactory. There is not enough evidence, historical or archaeological, to come up with a description that satisfactorily incorporates all the Indian accounts and archaeological finds. I have attempted a reconstruction that encompasses most of the known facts and as many of the Indian accounts as possible. Inevitably, some suppositions drawn from the archaeological record do not fit comfortably into this reconstruction; ditto for the many sometimes irreconcilable Indian accounts, some of them based on oral tradition and not primary accounts. That is an inevitable consequence of any such attempt.

41. Many battle researchers deny this movement — troopers moving down into the valley toward Deep Ravine to form what has been termed the South Skirmish Line — by citing several Indian accounts of troopers running down from Custer Hill as explanation. I believe these are two separate movements; the aforementioned accounts are of the final exodus from Custer Hill near the end of the battle. Stands in Timber Manuscript, 423: "Then he [Custer] moved into the center of the big basin and got off the horses." Stands in Timber statement, Cartwright Collection: "By the time some of them (gray horses) did move toward the big ravine on the battlefield (E. Co. ravine), it was too late, and the Indians were all around them in large numbers." Wells, "Little Big Horn Notes," 10: "Two Moon came northeast over hill, yelled, and soldiers ran west down ridge toward river. . . . Cheyennes (charged) from east and chased (soldiers)." Several troopers noticed evidence of a skirmish line. Private Thomas Coleman wrote in his diary, "My Company buried 30 of E Company the[y] were in line not 10 feet apart" (quoted in Liddic, *I Buried Custer,* 124), and John Dolan of Company M, who had been left at the Yellowstone Depot and was not present at the battle, claimed that "the men of companies E and L fell as straight as if they were on a skirmish line" (*New York Herald,* July 23, 1876). His detailed narrative of the battle and the burial of the dead is impressively accurate, suggesting that he probably incorporated accounts from Seventh Cavalry comrades who were present. Two officers with the Montana column later provided descriptions of the battlefield that included a skirmish line. Lieutenant Charles F. Roe wrote that, from the head of a ravine near the river, "dead men and horses were strung along towards the high ridge" (Roe, *Custer's Last Battle,* 10). And Captain Walter Clifford wrote: "An examination of the ground where Custer's five companies perished shows that skirmishers fell on the line, the most of them shot dead. Inside the skirmish line they fell in groups of fours,

and finally Custer and a number of officers inside a circle of forty men, surrounded by slain horses, placed head to tail" (Wheeler, *Tales from Buffalo Land,* 56). While it is possible that Clifford was referring to other parts of the battlefield besides the South Skirmish Line, it certainly appears that he was indeed discussing that area. Luther Hare also thought that E Company had fallen in skirmish order in or near a coulee — which can only refer to Deep Ravine, where they were found (Nichols, *Reno Court of Inquiry,* 304), and Edward Godfrey also believed they were deployed as skirmishers, and told researcher George Grinnell so (Grinnell Papers, Ms. 5, Folder 497). For further discussion of the archaeological evidence supporting the existence of the South Skirmish Line, see Greene, *Evidence and the Custer Enigma,* 68; Gray, *Custer's Last Campaign,* 388–95; Scott et al. *Archaeological Perspectives on the Battle of the Little Bighorn,* 87; and Evans, *Custer's Last Fight,* 292–93 n. 77. See also Bruce Trinque, "The Cartridge Case Evidence on Custer Field," *5th Annual Symposium,* 75; Whittaker, *A Complete Life of General George A. Custer,* 594; and Powell, *Sweet Medicine,* 116.

42.   Stands-in-Timber statement, Cartwright Collection: "When the gray horse soldiers moved south, they were confronted by a large number of Indians in and near the big ravine. Indians coming from the north and from the south forced these gray horse soldiers into the big ravine."

43.   Hardorff, *The Custer Battle Casualties II,* 68; Stands in Timber statement, Cartwright Collection.

44.   Brave Bear: "What soldiers who were not shot down ran towards where one company stood on the knoll" (quoted in George Bent to George Hyde, December 1, 1905, Coe Collection).

45.   Graham, *The Custer Myth,* 291; Brady, *Indian Fights and Fighters,* 375; Forrest, *Witnesses at the Battle of the Little Big Horn,* 5. Though Edgerly claimed that Weir later told him he never asked Reno for permission, several trooper accounts, Gibson's letter quoted in Forrest, and Godfrey's letter quoted in Brady make it clear that Weir did have words with Reno. "Colonel Weir did ask Reno, not Benteen, for permission to go forward and was refused," wrote Gibson. "Weir asked permission to take his troop to reconnoiter in the direction of the firing on Custer, and Reno would not give it." In Edgerly's account of the battle, he wrote: "Weir then said he would ask permission of Reno and Benteen, and moved off in their direction." But he did not reveal what he saw of Weir's request, and he continued: "Soon I saw him returning, mounted and heading down the river" (quoted in Clark, *Scalp Dance,* 19). It is hard to believe that all eyes in D Company — or at least Edgerly's and the noncoms near him — were not on Weir the whole time. Edgerly conveniently avoided revealing what he saw of the confrontation. In an interview conducted by Walter Camp, Edgerly did the same thing; Camp wrote: "Weir went over toward Reno and came back with an orderly and started off and Edgerly supposing Weir had permission followed with the troop. Weir afterward told Edgerly that [he] did not have permission and that he did not ask for any" (Hammer, *Custer in '76,* 55). Another man who claimed to witness the argument between Reno and Weir was the

unreliable Private Theodore Goldin, who wrote: "As we were standing on the bluffs looking down into the valley I heard some loud talk near me, and turning in that direction, I heard Capt. Weir say: 'Well, by God, if you won't go, I will, and if we ever live to get out of here some one will suffer for this.' He strode away" (quoted in Brady, 275). Still later, he contradicted himself, writing to another researcher: "I DID NOT hear it as it was just about over when I climbed the hill after leaving Herendeen the scout and crossing the river while Herendeen went back to guide a larger party of the dismounted men. . . . I heard some loud talking as I approached where the officers were gathered to report my escape, but what it was I cannot say. . . . I was told later by Lieut. Wallace that Weir and Reno had some hot words because Reno refused to advance until the packs came up, and that Weir's action in mounting his troop and moving out was really an act of insubordination and that it was suggested to Reno that he place Weir under arrest, but Reno did not seem disposed to do it" (quoted in Carroll, *The Benteen-Goldin Letters,* 89). A trooper in Weir's D Company, Private John Fox, said in an interview that there was an argument between Weir and Reno about riding to Custer and that "Moylan and Benteen stood by and heard what Weir said and they did not seem to approve of Weir going and talked as though to discourage him" (quoted in Liddic and Harbaugh, *Camp on Custer,* 95). Finally, Lieutenant Edward Godfrey later wrote, "Weir asked permission to take his troop to reconnoiter in the direction of the firing on Custer, and Reno would not give it" (quoted in Brady, 375).

46. "Most of the dead soldiers had been killed by arrows as they had arrows sticking in them." Waterman, an Arapaho, quoted in Graham, *The Custer Myth,* 110.

47. Trooper Henry Mechling said that there were "a good many extra shells" where Custer lay (quoted in Camp IU Notes, 431). Sergeant John Ryan said, "Under Custer's body lay some empty shells of special make from his carbine" (quoted in Hardorff, *On the Little Bighorn with Walter Camp,* 182).

48. Though the saying "Save the last bullet for yourself" was a catchphrase on the frontier and the stories of mutilation and torture were many, the Plains Indians did not as a rule torture their captives. That happened far more frequently among the eastern tribes.

49. Graham, *The Reno Court of Inquiry: Abstract,* 161.

50. Nichols, *Reno Court of Inquiry,* 423, 446.

51. Hammer, *Custer in '76,* 129. Flanagan later told researcher Walter Camp that he had seen a lone trooper gallop south toward the river until he was intercepted and killed by Indians. No other person present on Weir Point ever mentioned it, or at least no known account mentions it (Camp IU Notes, 672).

52. Graham, *The Reno Court of Inquiry: Abstract,* 161.

53. Camp IU Notes, 672. This was very likely John Foley, a Corporal from C Company, who was killed near Medicine Tail Ford, or Sergeant James Butler of L Company. Both bodies were found in the low hills near the ford.

54. Hardorff, *Lakota Recollections,* 116.

55. Ibid., 50; McCreight, 114.

56. Stands in Timber, *Cheyenne Memories,* 203; DeMallie, *The Sixth Grand-father,* 186; Hardorff, *Lakota Recollections,* 121.

57. Hardorff, *Lakota Recollections,* 96; Hardorff, *Indian Views of the Custer Fight,* 189.

CHAPTER FIFTEEN: THE HILL

Epigraph: Roy, quoted in Roenigk, *A Pioneer History of Kansas,* 292.

1. Hardorff, *Camp, Custer, and the Little Bighorn,* 42–43, 46; Camp IU Notes, 103. It seems undeniable that Reno was noticeably drunk from the time of the charge until late that night. At least a dozen men — civilians, enlisted men, and officers — related in later years that they had seen Reno drinking or drunk during the battle, from the time he first crossed the Little Bighorn through the morning of June 26. Trooper John Fox told researcher Walter Camp that "Reno appeared to be intoxicated or partially so" at the time the regiment began heading toward Weir Point and Reno was arguing with Weir (Liddic and Harbaugh, *Camp on Custer,* 95). Lieutenant Winfield Edgerly wrote, "I have to say that Col. Reno had the only whiskey that I had any evidence of during the fight. He (Reno) had a bottle of whiskey which he carried quite openly and from which he took an occasional sip" (Graham, *The Custer Myth,* 322). Lieutenant Charles DeRudio also commented on Reno's drinking during the battle. Camp wrote, "After passing lone tepee, DeRudio stopped somewhere to fill his canteen and did not catch up with the command until it reached the river. Here he found Reno and Gerard sitting on horses in the river, Reno drinking from a bottle of whisky" (Hammer, *Custer in '76,* 84). Interpreter Frederic Gerard told Camp, "As Major Reno left the line and passed into the timber, I saw him put a bottle of whisky to his mouth and drink the whole contents" (Hammer, *Custer in '76,* 84), and Camp also wrote, "DeRudio saw him drinking at Ford A, and twenty minutes later Gerard says he saw him finish the bottle at the skirmish line fight and that at that time Reno was intoxicated, etc." (Camp IU Notes, 775). Camp also wrote: "A commissioned officer of 7th cavalry told me that Davern, Reno's orderly, admitted to him that Reno was intoxicated in timber" (Camp BYU Notes, Reel 5). Private William Taylor related that "about 1 pm on the 25th or a little later, we were nearing the Indian skirmishers on our ride toward their village, the Indians were firing and shouting their defiance, and we had been ordered to charge and some of the men began to cheer when Major Reno shouted out 'Stop that noise.' And once again came the command, 'Charge.' Charrrage, was the way it sounded to me, and it came in such a tone that I turned my head and glanced backward. The Major and Lieut. Hodgson were riding side by side in the rear of my company (A) perhaps 30 or 40 feet away, possibly more but certainly a very short distance. As I looked back Major Reno was just taking a bottle from his lips and passed it to Lieut. Hodgson. In appearance I should say it was a quart flask, about one half or two thirds full" (WM Camp Collection, BYU Library, box 6, folder 2). After interviewing Lieutenant Edward Mathey, Camp wrote that soon after Mathey got to

Reno Hill, "Reno then held up a bottle of whiskey and showed it to Mathey and said: 'Look here, I have got half a bottle yet.' Mathey was then under the impression that Reno was under the influence, but does not wish to be quoted. Says also that Reno was much excited" (Hardorff, *Camp, Custer and the Little Bighorn,* 42–43). Camp also wrote that "a commissioned officer of the 7th Cavalry who was present at the Battle of the Little Big Horn, and who was not unfriendly to Reno, has told me that about the time of the arrival of the pack train, Major Reno saluted him by holding up a flask of whiskey and that his remarks and manners were silly. Said officer stated that the incident remained distinct in his memory for one reason because the bottle was then half full and Reno did not invite him to take a drink of it" (Camp IU Notes, 103). Mathey also testified at the Reno court of inquiry that "on the 26th I saw Major Reno had a bottle with a little in it [whiskey]. Someone spoke of being thirsty and he said he had some whiskey to wet his mouth with and to keep from getting dry, to quench his thirst. It was a flask, I don't know whether a quart or a pint. There was very little left in it then. . . . on the morning of the 26th" (Nichols, *Reno Court of Inquiry,* 521). Trooper John Burkman remembered that, during the retreat from the timber to the river, "Reno was excited, he was skeered out o' his wits and he was half drunk" (Wagner, *Old Neutriment,* 160). Packers John Frett and B. F. Churchill both claimed that Reno was staggering drunk on the evening of the 25th, a statement that was not disputed by Reno or his counsel. They testified that he was carrying a bottle of whiskey and struck Frett in the face with the other fist. Reno admitted this: "I had some whiskey which I obtained at the mouth of the Rosebud. . . it was carried in a flask . . . in the inner breast pocket of my coat. I think [it contained] between a pint and a quart. Probably nearer a pint than a quart, I don't know" (Nichols, *Reno Court of Inquiry,* 525). Private John Corcoran told Camp that "he saw Reno have a quart bottle of whiskey and saw him take a big drink out of it in hospital on morning of 26th" (Hammer, *Custer in '76,* 150), and it was probably Corcoran of whom Camp wrote: "A man who lay wounded on the hill on morning of 6/26 told me that Reno spoke to him regarding his wound and then drew a quart bottle of whiskey, nearly full, and drank a much larger quantity than was necessary merely to 'wet his lips.' He took special note of the occurrence at the time because he craved a drink himself, but Reno offered him none" (Camp BYU Notes, Reel 4). Trooper Charles White said, of Reno's charge on the village: "The first sergeant of Co. M (Ryan) directed me to go one way and one of the drunken officers another. I am writing this not without proper proof. With my own eyes I saw these officers open a bottle of whisky and drink enough to make any ordinary man drunk. I then witnessed the greatest excitement among the intoxicated officers I ever saw. The only officer who maintained self control and acted like an officer should do was Capt. T. H. French" (Hardorff, *Indian Views of the Custer Fight,* 17). Trooper Henry Lange told Camp flatly that "Reno was drunk all the time on Reno Hill" (Camp BYU Notes, Reel 3). Captain Thomas French told a *New York Times* reporter that Reno had been drunk during the hilltop fight and had hidden himself from the command from the evening of June 25 until noon June 26 (*New York Times,* January 19, 1879).

    Many accounts of his peculiar actions bear out the fact of his drunkenness, from his obsession with Benny Hodgson to his admitted altercation with the civilian packers on the night of June 25. Two men claimed that he was also drunk the night before the regiment left Terry's command (June 21) and the next day (June 22). Additionally, three officers said that Reno carried at least a bottle of whiskey along; Godfrey claimed that he brought a half-gallon keg, and Varnum said that it was a gallon keg (Varnum quoted in T. M. Coughlan to Frederic Van de Water, February 22, 1935, Van de Water Papers). That some of the officers brought whiskey was corroborated by Private Jacob Hetler, who years later said, "We had nothing but a pack train and our most valuable bit of equipment was four demijohns of whiskey, which was taken along for officers only — although I did get a little of it while I was in the hospital tent" (quoted in *Winners of the West,* November 30, 1935). In a letter written by Lieutenant Frank Gibson to his wife on July 4, 1876, he said: "Reno did not know which end he was standing on, and Benteen just took the management of affairs into his own hands, and it was very fortunate for us that he did" (quoted in Fougera, *With Custer's Cavalry,* 272). Longtime Bismarck resident W. A. Falconer wrote: "Dr. Porter told me that if it had not been for Benteen that they would all have been killed. That Reno was drunk, and acted cowardly all through the fight" (Falconer to E. A. Brininstool, July 27, 1923, Brininstool Collection). Finally, a good friend of Reno's, the Reverend Dr. Arthur Edwards, was quoted as saying, "His strange actions at the battle of the Little Bighorn, were due to the fact that he was drunk" (Editorial, *Northwestern Christian Advocate,* September 7, 1904).

2. Nichols, *Reno Court of Inquiry,* 529. McDougall rendered slight variations on the text of Reno's response; see Hammer, *Custer in '76,* 70.

3. McDougall said that seven men were wounded and that some were in blankets, some on horses (Nichols, *Reno Court of Inquiry,* 534). Reno, in his official report, said that seven were injured (Overfield, *The Little Big Horn, 1876,* 45). Varnum testified, "When we arrived at the top of the hill I found there were several men wounded there and two or three of them were of my old company, the first sergeant and one or two others" (Nichols, *Reno Court of Inquiry,* 143). Wallace testified several times that there were five to seven wounded men on the hill at the time (ibid., 28, 38, 53, 58).

4. Hammer, *Custer in '76,* 81.

5. Ibid., 71; Camp IU Notes, Box 2, Folder 10. I have blended the two Camp accounts here.

6. Hammer, *Custer in '76,* 71.

7. Camp IU Notes, 40.

8. Hammer, *Custer in '76,* 292; Graham, *The Reno Court of Inquiry: Abstract,* 95, 179. Hare gave a roundabout account of Reno sending him forward with orders to retreat, but this is the only possible way his testimony at the Reno court of inquiry makes sense: "After I delivered the order to Captain Weir, I returned to the command [Reno, in the rear] and met it

coming down stream. When they got to a high hill, the highest point around there, the Indians returned and attacked. Major Reno said that the position would not do to make his fight in, and he selected a point further up on the bluff [the original position], and ordered Weir's and French's companies to cover the retreat back to that point [Reno sent Hare, his adjutant, to deliver the orders]. They did so up to a few hundred yards of the line [they did no such thing], when Captain Godfrey's company was dismounted. I came back with that company." [When Hare delivered the order to Godfrey, he remained with that troop.]

9. Camp BYU Notes, Reel 5, 190. Edgerly also gave a different account of this scene, which included not Sanders (or Saunders, as Edgerly spelled it) but one of his duty Sergeants, Thomas Harrison.

10. Hammer, *Custer in '76*, 57; Liddic and Harbaugh, *Camp on Custer*, 98. Throughout the rest of his life, Edgerly expressed regret that he hadn't been able to save Charley and later blamed his company commander, Weir. He said that when he had reached Weir on the retreat, he had asked Weir for reinforcements to go back and get Charley, whom he'd promised to save. Edgerly testified at the Reno court of inquiry in 1879 that Weir had said "he was sorry but the orders were to go back on the hill" (Nichols, *Reno Court of Inquiry*, 446).

11. Utley, *Life in Custer's Cavalry*, 158, 172.

12. E. S. Godfrey to Adjutant General, n.d., Godfrey Family Papers, reprinted in O'Neil, *Custer Chronicles*, vol. 10, 20; E. S. Godfrey, "Cavalry Fire Discipline," in O'Neil, *Custer Conundrums*, 12–13; Godfrey, *Custer's Last Battle*, 27–28. Some time later, Godfrey revealed to Walter Camp what might have been the real reason he had dismounted his men when falling back from Weir Point. Camp wrote: "He had, upon looking back, seen the man (Vincent Charley) fall off his horse and his company come on but supposed they would want to send a detachment back to get him. He (Godfrey) therefore thought he ought to make a stand to enable D Company to organize to do this" (Camp IU Notes, 444).

13. It seems safe to assume that at least this number of Indians composed the first wave of attackers. Though some officers supplied greatly inflated figures — Benteen estimated the number at an impossible 8,000 or 9,000 — Moylan claimed that no less than 900 or 1,000 surrounded the hill at all times (Graham, *The Reno Court of Inquiry: Abstract*, 72).

CHAPTER SIXTEEN: "DEATH WAS ALL AROUND US"
Chapter title: Hunt, *I Fought with Custer*, 102.
Epigraph: Carroll, "The Battles on the Little Big Horn," 3.

1. See Willert, *Little Big Horn Diary*, 387, for a discussion of what orders were given and to and by whom during the evening of June 25.

2. Carroll, *The Benteen-Goldin Letters*, 171.

3. Rector, "Fields of Fire," 68.

4. Reno and a few other officers claimed that there were only two or three spades in the entire command. But Private William Taylor later wrote that

each company cook carried one "for the purpose of cutting a trench for his fire" (Taylor, *With Custer on the Little Bighorn*, 74). Several participants talked about the paucity of shovels, putting the number at two, three, or four. But one trooper wrote: "We had no tools to dig graves with, there being only one spade to each company" (quoted in Hardorff, *On the Little Bighorn with Walter Camp*, 131).

5. Barnard, *Ten Years with Custer*, 298.

6. Hammer, *Custer in '76*, 72.

7. Godfrey, *Field Diary*, 14.

8. O'Neil, *The Gibson-Edgerly Narratives*, 13.

9. Godfrey to John Neihardt, January 6, 1924, Hagner Collection; Hammer, *Custer in '76*, 67.

10. Nichols, *Reno Court of Inquiry*, 165.

11. Reno lost fifty-three men (give or take a trooper) on June 25 and 26. Thirty-two of those deaths occurred in the valley fight and retreat. Of the remaining twenty-one, nine or ten of them were killed on June 26, leaving about twelve, the number I have used here. Reno, in his official report, claimed that eighteen men were killed and forty-six wounded from 6:00 p.m. to 9:00 p.m. on June 25, a great exaggeration — at least six more deaths and more than double the number of injured. See also Gray, *Centennial Campaign*, 291–97, for an argument that Reno lost a few more men in the valley fight and a few less on the hill.

12. Hammer, *Custer in '76*, 125.

13. Taylor, *With Custer on the Little Bighorn*, 52.

14. Rickey, *Forty Miles a Day on Beans and Hay*, 291; Wagner, *Old Neutriment*, 164; Liddic and Harbaugh, *Camp on Custer*, 161.

15. Glease, "The Battle of the Little Big Horn," 72; Hardorff, *Camp, Custer, and the Little Bighorn*, 77, 136. Researcher R. G. Cartwright, who knew Charles Windolph very well, wrote this in his copy of Fred Dustin's *The Custer Tragedy*, 192: "Windolph said that Gibson played ostrich. Head in hole, rump protruding. The men hoped that some Indian get [sic] on the target" (Cartwright Collection).

16. Nichols, *Reno Court of Inquiry*, 356.

17. Camp IU Notes, 41.

18. Brady, *Indian Fights and Fighters*, 404. Virtually every account of the hilltop siege, whether by officer or enlisted man, makes it abundantly clear that Benteen was in charge in almost every way that mattered, though officers still asked Reno's permission on relatively minor matters. Dr. Porter summed it up when he testified, at the Reno court of inquiry: "I knew Major Reno was the ranking officer, but I thought that Colonel Benteen was the actual commanding officer" (Nichols, *Reno Court of Inquiry*, 193).

19. Libby, *The Arikara Narrative of Custer's Campaign*, 104, 105.

20. This is evident, since they told everyone in their village that those two and Curly were dead.

21. Viola, *Little Bighorn Remembered*, 116–17.

22. Carroll, *Custer's Chief of Scouts*, 94.

23. Nichols, *Reno Court of Inquiry*, 518–19.

24. Graham, *The Custer Myth*, 322.

25. Hammer, *Custer in '76*, 143.

26. Varnum said that it was a gallon keg; Godfrey said that it was a half-gallon keg. Coughlan to Van de Water, February 22, 1935, Van de Water Papers.

27. Nichols, *Reno Court of Inquiry*, 470–71, 505–6.

28. Graham, *The Custer Myth*, 103. Though some Indians mourned the deaths of friends and relatives, there was also much celebrating in the village. See Ibid., 85, 87; Hardorff, *Indian Views of the Custer Fight*, 54, 79; Hardorff, *Cheyenne Memories*, 112; and Hunt, *I Fought with Custer*, 217.

29. Barnard, *Ten Years with Custer*, 299.

30. Graham, *The Custer Myth*, 123; Godfrey to J. A. Shoemaker, March 2, 1926, Roll 4, Elizabeth B. Custer Collection. Godfrey also related this story in other writings and clearly believed it, as did Moylan, who wrote, "If what Colonel Benteen told me at Meade in 1883 was true, and I know of no reason to doubt it, then Reno ought to have been shot" (Moylan to Godfrey, January 17, 1892, quoted in Kuhlman, *Legend into History*, 130). I have combined Godfrey's two main versions here.

31. *New York Evening Post*, February 20, 1897. Colonel William Graham, in *The Custer Myth*, 337, and others have attempted to explain this suggestion of Reno's as just another option among many discussed. Graham wrote: "I do not for a minute believe . . . that Reno made a bald 'proposal' to abandon his wounded which Benteen at once 'indignantly rejected.' " But this is exactly what Benteen claimed several times to several different people, in no uncertain terms. See also Steven Wright, "Edward Settle Godfrey and the Custer Myth," *6th Annual Symposium*, 11.

32. Barnard, *Ten Years with Custer*, 299.

33. Brady, 404.

34. Hardorff, *On the Little Bighorn with Walter Camp*, 180.

35. Graham, *The Custer Myth*, 182.

36. Carroll, *The Sunshine Magazine Articles*, 13.

37. Hammer, *Custer in '76*, 136.

38. Ibid., 67.

39. Coughlan, *Varnum*, 17.

40. Binder 1, p. 81, Cartwright Collection; Hardorff, *On the Little Bighorn with Walter Camp*, 78. Windolph lived until 1950 and gave many other slightly different versions of this scene.

41. Price, *Sage of the Hills*, 70.

42. Hammer, *Custer in '76*, 114.

43. Godfrey, *Field Diary*, 17; Liddic, *I Buried Custer*, 18; Nichols, *Reno Court of Inquiry*, 344. Both Godfrey and Private Thomas Coleman claimed that Reno led the charge, and Edgerly testified that "he was in advance all the time."

44. Carroll, *Custer's Chief of Scouts*, 152; Godfrey, *Field Diary*, 17.

45. Graham, *The Custer Myth*, 145; Graham, *The Reno Court of Inquiry: Abstract*, 164–65.

46. Hammer, *Custer in '76*, 57. See also ibid., 81, where Gibson is quoted as saying that Benteen's charge (the first) was about 9:00 a.m.

47. Hardorff, *Camp, Custer, and the Little Bighorn*, 179.

48. Ibid., 78; Hunt, *I Fought with Custer*, 104–5; Brininstool, *Troopers with Custer*, 57.

49. Though several accounts exist of this occurrence and Madden's request, they may be apocryphal. Private Dan Newell later wrote, "I saw and heard the whole performance and that just wasn't what Mike said, but I don't want to spoil a good story." Carroll, *The Sunshine Magazine Articles*, 14.

50. Liddic and Harbaugh, *Camp on Custer*, 110. See Liddic, *Vanishing Victory*, 170–71, for a discussion of whites and/or half-breeds in the Sioux camp.

51. Hardorff, *Camp, Custer, and the Little Bighorn*, 83.

52. Private George Glease later wrote: "We only had 15 rounds of ammunition left per man." Glease, 72.

53. Liddic, *I Buried Custer*, 19.

Chapter Seventeen: The Rescue
Epigraph: Coleman, quoted in Liddic, *I Buried Custer*, 123–24.

1. Lieutenant Alfred B. Johnson to General R. W. Johnson, reprinted in *St. Paul Pioneer Press and Tribune*, July 22, 1876. Both Alfred Johnson and Lieutenant Charles Roe stated that they had been rationed for six days. Other accounts claim eight days. See Bradley, *The March of the Montana Column*, 147.

2. Some historians downplay Custer's agreement to send Herendeen to the Montana column and explain away his decision not to do so. Custer may have had legitimate reasons — at least in his own mind — to keep Herendeen with him, but Terry clearly expected Herendeen's arrival, as is clear from the accounts of many of his subordinates. Lieutenant Edward J. McClernand: "General Terry doubtless expected and had every reason to expect, that Custer, as his successor in command, would spare no effort to communicate with him. He seemed surprised and mystified by the fact that no report had been received, and was unmistakably anxious" (McClernand, "With the Indian and the Buffalo in Montana," 24). Lieutenant C. A. Woodruff: "While Terry, with Gibbon's command, was camped at Tullock's Creek, Saturday night and Sunday morning, June 24th and 25th, he was looking for a message from Custer very anxiously, so I was told at the time" (quoted in Brady, *Indian Fights and Fighters*, 382). An anonymous "special correspondent" — clearly an officer with Gibbon's command — wrote on July 3, at the camp at the mouth of the Bighorn, about the night of June 26: "Night had come, and the promised scout from Custer had not reported, although we were far in advance of our position" (*New York Daily Tribune*, July 14, 1876). See also Roe, *Custer's Last Battle*, 4. Though after the battle there was undoubtedly avoidance of blame concerning certain areas of the campaign, this does not seem to be one of them. However, when all was said and done, Herendeen's appearance likely would not have changed much, given any possible scenario.

3. McClernand, 53.

4. Though most accounts agree on this date as the day Terry was to "meet" Custer, some accounts by officers in Terry's command gave other dates. One lieutenant (Lieutenant John F. McBlain) and a doctor (Holmes Paulding) with the column said the 27th, and another officer (Lieutenant Charles F. Roe) said the 25th. Reno, in his official report, wrote that on the morning of the 27th, upon viewing a large cloud of dust and then a large but unidentifiable force of men down the valley: "There was no certainty for some time what they were, but finally I satisfied myself they were cavalry, and if so could only be Custer, as it was ahead of the time I understood that General Terry could be expected" (quoted in Overfield, *The Little Big Horn, 1876*, 48). Whom Reno received his information from is unknown; it could have been Custer, or it could have been another officer with either column. What is clear is that there was very little agreement as to when, how, or where Custer would "meet" Terry, a state of affairs summed up by another officer in Terry's command (Captain Henry B. Freeman) unintentionally in his diary: "It having been arranged that we were to meet him [Custer] at nearly the spot where the battle was fought on the 26th, or 7th at latest." Precisely.

5. McClernand, 20.

6. Bradley, 149; Stewart, *Custer's Luck*, 290–98.

7. Noyes, "The Battle of the Little Big Horn," 10.

8. Ibid.

9. Roe, *Custer's Last Battle*, 4.

10. *Los Angeles Times*, November 8, 1884.

11. Carroll, *The Two Battles of the Little Big Horn*, 149–50.

12. Roe, *Custer's Last Battle*, 5.

13. Most of the Crow scouts rejoined the expedition three weeks later (Freeman, Diary, 23). See also Dixon, *The Vanishing Race*, 157, and Graham, *The Custer Myth*, 16. The Crows were so rattled that when they came upon another band of Crows on the way home, "supposing each other to be Sioux, they had a fight for some time, but no one was hurt" (Hammer, *Custer in '76*, 246).

14. Account of Private George C. Berry, 7th Infantry, *Winners of the West*, September 28, 1942.

15. Roe, *Custer's Last Battle*, 7.

16. Freeman, 17.

17. McClernand, 27.

18. Hudnutt, "New Light on the Little Big Horn," 353.

19. Godfrey, *Custer's Last Battle*, 36.

20. Hammer, *Custer in '76*, 249–50.

21. Wagner, *Old Neutriment*, 181.

22. Nichols, *Reno Court of Inquiry*, 322.

23. Graham, *The Custer Myth*, 220; Hardorff, *The Custer Battle Casualties II*, 15, 17.

24. Langellier et al., *Myles Keogh*, 155.

25. Stewart, *Custer's Luck,* 469; Graham, *The Custer Myth,* 345.

26. Hardorff, *The Custer Battle Casualties,* 100.

27. *New York Herald,* July 14, 1876, quoted in Wengert, *The Custer Des-patches,* 66; Camp IU Notes, 602. Sergeant John Ryan claimed to have seen "five or six shells" underneath Custer's body (Barnard, *Ten Years with Custer,* 303), and Lieutenant John Carland wrote that he found "17 cartridge shells by his side" (Frost, *General Custer's Libbie,* 246). Since Ryan was assigned to bury the General, and thus was one of the last men to see his body before burial, there may have only been five or six left by that time, the others having been picked up. Private Henry Mechling told Walter Camp that where Custer lay, there were "a good many extra shells" (Hardorff, *Camp, Custer, and the Little Bighorn,* 77).

28. Hardorff, *The Custer Battle Casualties II,* 20–21.

29. Hardorff, "Some Recollections of Custer," 16.

30. Though many accounts claim that Dr. Lord's body was not identified, and he is traditionally listed among the missing, at least two of Terry's staff officers who knew the doctor (who had been commissioned a first lieutenant on June 25, 1875) later recalled that they had recognized him. See Noyes, "Custer's Surgeon, George Lord."

31. McBlain, "With Gibbon on the Sioux Campaign," 147.

32. Henry Jones to W. M. Camp, June 2, 1911, Camp BYU Collection.

33. Gibbon, "Hunting Sitting Bull," 665.

34. Godfrey to J. A. Shoemaker, March 2, 1926, Roll 4, Elizabeth B. Custer Collection.

35. Godfrey to John Neihardt, January 6, 1924, Hagner Collection.

36. Barnard, *Ten Years with Custer,* 303.

37. Carroll, *The Seventh Cavalry Scrapbook,* no. 1, 15.

38. Barnard, *Ten Years with Custer,* 304. Gibson gave a different version of their burial. See Fougera, *With Custer's Cavalry,* 271–72.

39. Graham, *The Custer Myth,* 364.

40. Taunton, *Custer's Field,* 23.

41. Hammer, *Custer in '76,* 58; Hardorff, *The Custer Battle Casualties II,* 176.

42. Carroll, *The Benteen-Goldin Letters,* 147. Gibbon also received estimates from the Seventh officers of an Indian force numbering between 1,800 and 2,500 (Overfield, 33). In his article "The Campaign Against the Sioux in 1876," Terry's brother-in-law Captain Robert Hughes wrote that when Terry asked the surviving Seventh Cavalry officers to supply an estimate of the number of Indian warriors, "the replies pivoted about the figure 1,500, and I can recall Colonel Benteen's reply almost verbatim which was as follows: 'I have been accustomed to seeing divisions of cavalry during the war, and from my observations I would say that there were from fifteen to eighteen hundred warriors.' No one in the group at that time, put this estimate above eighteen hundred" (reprinted in Graham, *The Story of the Little Big Horn,* 196). Colonel John Gibbon, in his first written account of the battle, sent on June 28, said, "The Indians were in great strength and were estimated at from 1,800 to 2,500 warriors" (Overfield, *The Little Big*

Horn, 1876, 33). Scout Billy Cross estimated that the village contained about 800 or 900 lodges, which would dictate 1,600 to 1,800 warriors, though there were also many wickiups, used by single men (*New York Times,* July 13, 1876). The Cheyenne Two Moon said that after the battle, the women moved the camp from the bend and "pitched tents helter skelter — some on hills to the west," which points to the little-known fact that many or most of the lodges were moved and then repitched. Later estimates of the number of lodges in the village based on lodge circles were therefore erroneous (Two Moon interview, Campbell Collection). For more recent discussions based on other sources of information, see Stewart, *Custer's Luck,* 309–12; Marshall, "How Many Indians Were There?"; and Gray, *Centennial Campaign,* chap. 29, "The Strength of the Little Big Horn Village."

43.   Graham, *The Reno Court of Inquiry: Abstract,* 34.

44.   Nichols, *Reno Court of Inquiry,* 522.

45.   An officer with Gibbon's column wrote, "I conversed with most of the officers of that command at one time or another, while in the field, and nearly all were pronounced in their severe criticism of Reno" (Brady, 385). Another wrote: "It was in leadership that Custer's lieutenant [Reno] failed, and that he had so failed . . . was heard on all sides from his subordinates when Terry arrived. Many of the criticisms heard were severe. Later, before the Court of Inquiry which followed, many were toned down" (McClernand, 48–50). Herder and *New York Sun* correspondent Dick Roberts later wrote, "From the officers on the steamer I learned very minute details of the battle and appearance of the field and even at that early date they branded Reno and others, cowards" (Roberts, *Reminiscences of General Custer,* 19). Finally, another officer later wrote that two other officers with Terry's command told him that "when they reached Reno's defensive line on the bluff all of Reno's officers talked wildly and excitedly about the fight, and of Reno's cowardice, etc." (Captain Robert G. Carter, memorandum, July 6, 1923, Box 4, Folder 8, Kuhlman Collection).

46.   Wheeler, *Tales from Buffalo Land,* 56; Brady, 35.

47.   Hardorff, *The Custer Battle Casualties,* 122; Hammer, *Custer in '76,* 79, 136. Several other accounts place Kellogg on the hill near Custer; see Barnard, *I Go with Custer,* 146–48.

48.   Hammer, *Custer in '76,* 241; W. H. Sipes to Walter M. Camp, February 1909, Camp BYU Collection. Sipes said that Curly wore a blanket, but not a Crow blanket — a red Sioux blanket. Crow Indians, he said, wore light-colored blankets.

49.   Hanson, *The Conquest of the Missouri,* 274.

50.   Ibid., 275–76.

51.   Ibid., 295–96. Besides the testimony in this biography by the book's subject, Captain Grant Marsh, there are corroborating accounts of Comanche's presence on board. There has been some controversy as to whether Comanche was actually taken aboard the *Far West* on its trip to Bismarck. In a letter from W. A. Falconer to Captain Edward Luce (December 9, 1939, Kuhlman Collection), Falconer, a resident of Bismarck at the time, wrote:

"When Comanche was taken off the Far West at the Bismarck river landing on the night of July 5, 1876, he was put in John W. Mellett's livery stable. I used to deliver oats to this livery stable, and saw Comanche every week until he was taken over to Fort Abraham Lincoln in September 1876." And researcher Walter Camp talked to a trooper named Albright who told him: "Ramsey [Charles Ramsey, of Keogh's I Company] rescued old Comanche by carrying water to him in his hat. Ramsey begged to carry him on the boat and Benteen agreed" (Camp IU Notes, Box 2, Folder 10). Finally, a soldier with Gibbon's command, A. F. Ward, later wrote, "The old warrior was placed upon the Far West with the wounded men and we can assure you he was handled as careful and tenderly as any living being could have been handled. A blacksmith led the old warrior to the boat and in crossing over the gang plank while the tears rolled down his cheeks he said this is all that is left of Custer" (Ricker, *The Settler and Soldier Interviews*, 118).

52. Hanson, *The Conquest of the Missouri*, 298.
53. Overfield, 36–38.

CHAPTER EIGHTEEN: "ALL THE WORLD HAS GONE"

Chapter title: Chicago Daily Tribune, July 10, 1876. In a letter to the editor, a doctor who claimed to have known Libbie Custer from childhood wrote: "I well remember the morning on which he [Custer] started from Winchester for Appomattox. I was standing on the porch. He had kissed his wife goodby and mounted his horse. I shook his hand, and turning into the house, found her sobbing. I said, "Well, Libbie, he has gone.' 'Yes,' said she, 'all the world has gone.'"

Epigraph: Neihardt, *Black Elk Speaks*, 98.

1. *Billings Times,* June 10, 1931.
2. *Chicago Daily Tribune,* July 16, 1876.
3. O'Neil, *Custeriana,* vol. 5, 4–5. This account by the telegrapher Carnahan contradicts Lounsberry's self-glorifying account, in which he claimed that he was the first to send out the news of the disaster. Official army business would naturally come first, making Carnahan's account ring true.
4. Hanson, *The Conquest of the Missouri*, 307–08.
5. Utley, "The Custer Battle in the Contemporary Press," 81.
6. Hanson, *The Conquest of the Missouri,* 306–8.
7. Hammer, *Custer in '76,* 241.
8. Farioli and Nichols, "Fort A. Lincoln," 13. I have based the Bismarck and Fort Lincoln scenes primarily on the following sources: Hanson, *The Conquest of the Missouri,* 311–14; Frost, *General Custer's Libbie,* 227–28; Parmalee, "A Child's Recollection of the Summer of '76," in Coffeen, *The Teepee Book,* part 1.
9. Camp IU Notes, 431.
10. Farioli and Nichols, 14, 15.
11. The number of widows has been mentioned as anywhere from twenty-six to thirty-two, though it is not always clear whether the figure includes all the widows of the regiment or just those whose husbands were stationed at Fort Lincoln. Dr. Kenneth Hammer listed thirty-eight widows of all the men

dead in the battle, regardless of station and including scouts such as Mitch Boyer (*Little Big Horn Associates Newsletter,* February 1987).

12. Hanson, *The Conquest of the Missouri,* 314.

13. Merington, *The Custer Story,* 323. However, in an October 2, 1876, letter from Lieutenant Carland to Libbie Custer, he wrote: "Poor dear Mrs. Calhoun . . . followed [me] out of your quarters to ask if I had nothing to say to her," which leads to the possibility that Carland returned with the *Far West* and accompanied McCaskey's small group to notify Libbie that morning (Merington Papers).

14. Hanson, *The Conquest of the Missouri,* 281–82, 300.

15. Utley, *Custer and the Great Controversy,* 32–35.

16. *New York Herald,* July 7, 1876.

17. Sheridan to Sherman, telegram, July 6, 1876, LBBNM Files.

18. Meketa, "The Press and the Battle of the Little Big Horn," 3–4.

19. *New York Herald,* July 7, 1876.

20. *New York Times,* July 6, 1876.

21. Sheridan, quoted in Graham, *The Custer Myth,* 117.

22. Sheridan, quoted in Sarf, *The Little Bighorn Campaign,* 265.

23. Ibid., 265–66.

24. *New York Herald,* August 2, 1876.

25. Diehl, *The Staff Correspondent,* 107.

26. Utley, *Custer and the Great Controversy,* 43.

27. *New York Herald,* July 7, 1876.

28. Ibid.

29. Colonel Samuel Sturgis, quoted in Whittaker, *A Complete Life of General George A. Custer,* 475.

30. *New York Times,* July 17, 1876.

31. Ibid., July 18, 1876.

32. Much later, serious doubt was cast on the legitimacy of the signatures, as Godfrey discovered in talking to survivors of the battle that many of them could not remember signing the petition. He concluded that they may have been coerced or "ordered" to do so. Eventually, an FBI investigation in 1954 indicated that the petition was padded with the names of "soldiers discharged in May, deserters, and several outright forgeries." At least seventy-six — one-third — were "probable forgeries," likely signed by one man: First Sergeant Joseph McCurry, of Benteen's H Company (Overfield, *The Little Big Horn, 1876,* 74).

33. Nichols, *In Custer's Shadow,* 217–18.

34. Ibid., 99.

35. Swift, "General Wesley Merritt," 836.

36. Hutchins, *The Army and Navy Journal,* 85. No one knew at the time that a Marine had died with Custer. Private John Burke, alias Oscar Pardee, had deserted from the Marine Corps in 1873 and enlisted in the Seventh Cavalry the next day (*Little Big Horn Associates Newsletter,* May 1967).

37. Cozzens, *Eyewitnesses to the Indian Wars,* vol. 4, 399.

38. O'Neil, *GarryOwen Tidbits,* vol. 6, 27. Reno may have shared his liquor

with his fellow officers, though judging from his stinginess atop the hill during the battle, that may be a questionable assumption.

39.   Hugh Scott to Hare, November 28, 1919, quoted in O'Neil, *GarryOwen Tidbits,* vol. 4, 9.

40.   "Summary of Talk with General Scott," Merington Papers.

41.   *New York Herald,* August 13, 1876.

42.   R. G. Cartwright's notes in his copy of Graham's *The Custer Myth,* 196, and Kuhlman's *Legend into History,* 83, Cartwright Collection; Cartwright to Charles Kuhlman, January 13, 1940, Camp BYU Collection.

43.   Carroll, *The Benteen-Goldin Letters,* 219; R. G. Cartwright's notes in his copy of Dustin's *The Custer Tragedy,* 142, Cartwright Collection.

44.   *New York Times,* August 18, 1876; *New York Herald,* August 3, 1876.

45.   Carroll, *The Lieutenant E. A. Garlington Narrative,* 8; Brady, *Indian Fights and Fighters,* 385; Ghent, "Varnum, Reno, and the Little Bighorn"; Nichols, *Reno Court of Inquiry,* 522. Also, Captain Robert G. Carter wrote: "General D. S. Brainard told me this date that he has often heard Capt. (later Gen.) Whelan and Lieut. (later Gen.) C. F. Roe, both of the Second U.S. Cavalry and of Terry's command, say that when they reached Reno's defensive line on the bluff all of Reno's officers talked wildly and excitedly about the fight, and of Reno's cowardice, etc. A little later they shut their mouths like clams and would not talk. It seemed to them . . . that there suddenly sprang up among the Seventh Cavalry Officers an understanding and resolve about that affair which would reflect in any way upon the honor of their regiment or regimental esprit, even if they had to sacrifice their own individual opinions concerning the plan of campaign or the conduct of the battle, either by Reno or Custer. This was later shown by their testimony before the Reno Court of Inquiry, where all but Godfrey refused to charge Reno with cowardice" (memorandum, July 6, 1923, Box 4, MS 1401, Camp BYU Collection).

46.   Graham, *The Custer Myth,* 225.

47.   Ibid., 226.

48.   Knight, *Following the Indian Wars,* 221.

49.   *New York Herald,* August 7, 1876.

50.   On August 11, O'Kelly elected to travel with Miles for a while.

51.   *New York Herald,* September 20, 1876.

52.   *Chicago Daily Tribune,* July 28, 1876.

53.   Hutchins, *The Army and Navy Journal,* 25.

54.   Greene, *Battles and Skirmishes of the Great Sioux War,* 81.

55.   John Finerty, "The Fellows in Feathers," in Cozzens, *Eyewitnesses to the Indian Wars,* vol. 4, 388.

56.   Jeffrey Pearson, "Military Notes, 1876," in Cozzens, *Eyewitnesses to the Indian Wars,* vol. 4, 244, 246.

57.   Struthers Burt, "Dispatches from Crook's Column," in Cozzens, *Eyewitnesses to the Indian Wars,* vol. 4, 376; John Bourke, "The Battle of Slim Buttes," in Cozzens, *Eyewitnesses to the Indian Wars,* vol. 4, 379; *Chicago Daily Tribune,* October 10, 1876. Crook's estimate was thirty-odd lodges (Deland, *The Sioux Wars,* vol. 2, 247). Mills said fifty lodges (ibid., 216). An

Indian named Samuel Charger claimed that there were forty-four families returning to their agency (ibid., 280).

58. Langellier et al., *Myles Keogh,* 157, n. 5.

59. Charles Diehl, "Terry's Tribulations," in Cozzens, *Eyewitnesses to the Indian Wars,* vol. 4, 409.

60. Ibid., 411.

61. Merkel, "Custer's Forgotten Lieutenant," 174.

62. Ibid., 175–76.

63. Carroll, *The Lieutenant E. A. Garlington Narrative,* 23.

64. Mills, *Harvest of Barren Regrets,* 286.

65. Barnard, *Ten Years with Custer,* 310.

66. *Bismarck Tribune,* quoted in Nichols, *In Custer's Shadow,* 235.

67. Nichols, *In Custer's Shadow,* 239.

68. Reno, quoted in Mills, *Harvest of Barren Regrets,* 286. See also Nichols, *In Custer's Shadow,* 239–40.

69. Captain Robert G. Carter, in his July 6, 1923, memorandum, wrote of his "interview with Col. John Merrill (son of Major Lewis Merrill, 7th Cavalry) who as a boy heard the battle discussed in the post trader's store at Fort Abraham Lincoln for months and was astounded to learn that three years later (1879) nearly every officer went before the Reno Court and testified to absolutely nothing which, in 1876 they had uttered as a positive conviction."

70. *Omaha Bee,* September 13, 1875, quoted in Sajna, *Crazy Horse,* 293.

71. *New York Herald,* July 7, 1876.

72. Hutchins, *The Army and Navy Journal,* 88.

73. Bordeaux, *Custer's Conqueror,* 61.

74. Diehl, "Terry's Tribulations," 397.

75. Jesse M. Lee, "The Capture and Death of an Indian Chieftain," in Cozzens, *Eyewitnesses to the Indian Wars,* vol. 4, 529.

76. Utley, *The Lance and the Shield,* 179–80.

77. Neihardt, *Black Elk Speaks,* 104.

78. Ibid.

79. Sources for the last year of Crazy Horse's life include Sajna, *Crazy Horse;* Pearson, "Tragedy at Red Cloud Agency"; Hardorff, *The Surrender and Death of Crazy Horse;* and Brininstool, "How Crazy Horse Died."

80. Jean Louis Legare to Camp, October 27, 1910, Camp BYU Collection; Haydon, *The Riders of the Plains,* 70; McGinnis, *Counting Coup and Cutting Horses,* 163.

81. Sitting Bull, quoted in Utley, *The Lance and the Shield,* 232.

82. Brininstool, "How Crazy Horse Died," 6.

83. Deland, vol. 2, 406–7. In 1881 Terry reported, "It is understood that there are still some thirty-five families of Sioux at Wood Mountain and Quappelle."

84. Hubbard and Holcombe, *Minnesota in Three Centuries,* 268.

85. Smith, "Fort Peck Agency Assiniboines, Upper Yanktonais, Hunkpapas, Sissetons, and Wahpetons," 248.

86. *Army and Navy Journal,* October 7, 1876.

87. Utley, *The Lance and the Shield,* 176, 186. As Long Dog and Inkpaduta

were reported together in the area in September, and Long Dog went to Canada at roughly the same time as Inkpaduta, I have concluded that the two bands remained together during this time. If they were not camping together, they were in the same area.

88. Larson, "A New Look at the Elusive Inkpaduta," 35.
89. Leckie, *Elizabeth Bacon Custer,* 199; *Frank Leslie's Illustrated Newspaper,* July 29, 1876; *Billings Times,* June 10, 1931.
90. Johnson, *The Unregimented General,* 87.
91. *New York Herald,* July 18, 1876.
92. Scott, *Some Memories of a Soldier,* 29.
93. O'Neil, *GarryOwen Tidbits,* vol. 4, 27.
94. Hutchins, *The Army and Navy Journal,* 74; *Big Horn Yellowstone Journal* 3, no. 1 (Winter 1994): 21.
95. O'Neil, *GarryOwen Tidbits,* vol. 5, 3.
96. W. A. Falconer to William Ghent, November 19, 1934, Ghent Papers. However, in a *New York Herald* story, a reporter claimed that the postmaster of the town delivered the news personally to the Custer home.
97. Frost, *General Custer's Libbie,* 234.

CHAPTER NINETEEN: THE LOST CAPTAIN
Chapter title: The Lost Captain was a dime novel written by Frederick Whittaker for Beadle and Adams in 1880.
Epigraph: Al. W. Crowell, "A Dedication to the Works of Capt. Frederick Whittaker, the Prince of Novelists," *Banner Weekly,* November 30, 1895, quoted in Johansen, *The House of Beadle and Adams,* vol. 2, 300–1.

1. Much of the biographical material here is derived from Whittaker's entry in Johansen, vol. 2, 301–2.
2. Hall, *History of the Sixth New York Cavalry,* 318, 349. This book says that Whittaker was "wounded June, 1864 — place not given."
3. Johansen, vol. 1, 8, 33.
4. There is no record of a brevet captaincy for Whittaker, and in the first few years of his writing career after the war, he claimed only the rank of lieutenant (Johansen, vol. 1, 301). See also "Another Campaign Lie Nailed," *New York Times,* October 26, 1884. The subject of the article is apparently a Mount Vernon political squabble in which several citizens of that town signed a card stating: "Whittaker was not a Captain in any regiment, but was made a Second Lieutenant in the Sixth Regiment, Volunteers, in 1865, at the close of the war. . . . Whittaker is regarded in Mount Vernon as a crank." One of the signers was the editor of the *Mount Vernon Argus.*
5. Whittaker, "General George A. Custer."
6. "A subscription volume . . . to be sold by subscription only" (*Publishers Weekly,* September 16, 1876, 466); "sold only by subscription" (*Galaxy,* February 1877, 9).
7. *Army and Navy Journal,* August 5, 1876. That Custer's widow would receive a share of the royalties was affirmed by Sheldon and Company, the

book's publishers, in the company's monthly literary magazine, the *Galaxy* (February 1877, 282).

8. Lindell, "Bringing Books to a 'Book-Hungry' Land"; Thomas, "There Is Nothing So Effective as a Personal Canvass."

9. Though most researchers have concluded that the two never met, Whittaker wrote to Libbie: "Do you remember what I said in verse, before I ever thought I should know Custer's wife and not see her face to face?" Whittaker to Elizabeth Custer, n.d., probably January or February 1877, Brice C. W. Custer Collection.

10. Merington, *Army Lady,* 88; Whittaker to Elizabeth Custer, November 18, 1876, Brice C. W. Custer Collection.

11. Carland to Elizabeth Custer, October 2, 1876, Merington Papers.

12. Utley, *The Reno Court of Inquiry,* 172. Whittaker did not name O'Kelly specifically, but the correspondent's letter to the *New York Herald* is almost certainly the missive referred to. In a letter to Libbie Custer, Whittaker wrote, "Yesterday I met O'Kelly of that paper, who was out, and who published the first account of Reno's incompetency" (November 28, 1876, Brice C. W. Custer Collection).

13. One officer with the Seventh and another with Gibbon's column supplied accounts, though Whittaker never identified them. Whittaker, *A Complete Life of General George A. Custer,* 583–85; Hutchins, *The Army and Navy Journal,* 129; *Chicago Times,* January 23, 1879. One of the officers was likely Lieutenant John Carland, a friend of Custer's who later wrote to Libbie Custer to tell her, "I have written Mr. Whittaker — I hope he may find something" (October 2, 1876, Merington Papers).

14. Whittaker to Elizabeth Custer, November 28, 1876.

15. Merkel, "Custer's Forgotten Lieutenant," 191.

16. Leckie, *Elizabeth Bacon Custer,* 210–11.

17. Frost, *General Custer's Libbie,* 237.

18. Whittaker to Elizabeth Custer, November 28, 1876.

19. Merkel, "Custer's Forgotten Lieutenant," 191–93.

20. Whittaker, *A Complete Life of General George A. Custer,* 1–2.

21. "His knuckles were very bony," wrote Whittaker, describing a scene in which Custer dispatched a miscreant with his fists (ibid., 619).

22. Ibid., 604.

23. Ibid., 608.

24. Slotkin, *The Fatal Environment,* 501–6.

25. *Nation,* March 22, 1877, 180.

26. *Galaxy,* February 1877, 282.

27. *Chicago Daily Tribune,* March 31, 1877.

28. Frost, *General Custer's Libbie,* 240.

29. *Publishers Weekly,* March 10, 1877, and March 17, 1877.

30. Leckie, 210. See also the following letters from Whittaker to Elizabeth Custer: November 28, 1876; n.d., probably January or February 1877; and June 13, 1878, Brice C. W. Custer Collection.

31. Whittaker wrote several articles for the *Galaxy* after his Custer biography was published, among them "The American Army," "Bunker Hill," and "Muhammad the Iconoclast."

32. *New York Times,* June 16, 1878.

33. Whittaker to Elizabeth Custer, June 13, 1878.

34. Nichols, *In Custer's Shadow,* 245–55.

35. *New York Herald,* November 16, 1877.

36. Ibid., November 20, 1877.

37. Hutchins, *The Army and Navy Journal,* 176.

38. Nichols, *In Custer's Shadow,* 270–71.

39. "Men of Mark" manuscript, Camp IU Notes; "Address by Gen. Jesse M. Lee, U.S.A. Retired," 1907, Indiana State Library.

40. "Men of Mark" manuscript, Camp IU Notes.

41. Jesse M. Lee ACP File, National Archives; Jesse M. Lee autobiography, unpublished manuscript, courtesy Ephriam Dickson.

42. *Chicago Daily News,* January 16, 1879.

43. Alberts, *Brandy Station to Manila Bay,* 236–37.

44. Godfrey to Van de Water, May 21, 1931, Van de Water Papers. In a memorandum concerning the Reno court of inquiry, R. G. Carter wrote: "Reno's record during the Civil War, although he was breveted as many others were, was clouded by at least one most discreditable affair, as related by General Wesley Merritt, formerly commanding the regular cavalry under Sheridan, and later the Fifth Cavalry" (August 23, 1932, Hagner Collection).

45. *Chicago Times,* January 11, 1879.

46. Davis and Davis, *The Reno Court of Inquiry,* 21.

47. *Army and Navy Journal,* December 28, 1878.

48. Johnson, "A Captain of 'Chivalric Courage,'" 44.

49. Davis and Davis, *The Reno Court of Inquiry,* 22.

50. Ibid., 37.

51. Fougera, *With Custer's Cavalry,* 272.

52. Ibid., 17–19.

53. *Inter-Ocean,* January 11, 1879.

54. Davis and Davis, *The Reno Court of Inquiry,* 20.

55. *Washington Post,* January 25, 1879; *New York Times,* January 11, 1879; *Chicago Daily News,* January 11, 1879.

CHAPTER TWENTY: FOR THE HONOR OF THE REGIMENT

1. Utley, *The Reno Court of Inquiry,* 5.

2. Though several of the newspapermen present mentioned being forced to use their memories to write their stories in the absence of notes — the *Chicago Times* man boasted of his "extraordinary retentive powers" — there is abundant evidence that note taking occurred and that the story about using their memories was a badly concealed joke. (The *Times* ran a long, tongue-in-cheek account of the feats of their "memorizer" on January 16, 1879, and the next day claimed that many of the spectators "were attracted by a desire to see *The Times* reporter take his mental notes.")

Inter-Ocean, January 13, 1879: "These rules which have been adopted make it necessary for the representatives of the press to use their memories or their cuffs for notebooks."

Inter-Ocean, January 14, 1879: During a break, "the reporters hastily gathered themselves into obscure corners and fell laboriously to work making cabalistic memoranda upon their note-books, and winking gravely at one or two sapient gentlemen who gave expression in grave asides, to the somewhat apocryphal information that 'the reporters, d'ye see, have to rely on their memories.' "

Inter-Ocean, January 16, 1879: "Either Chicago reporters were to be set down as men of prodigious mentality, or refreshingly cunning fellows, for, if appearance counts for anything in visual tactics, they complied to the letter with the ruling of the court." And when it was announced that notes would be allowed ("Col King: 'The reporters will be allowed to take notes' "), "significant winks flushed from different quarters of the room, and an army of notebooks and pencils forsook the darkness and arrayed themselves in the light of day. It was a delightful moment. The transformation from distrustful secrecy to bold assurance on the part of the reporters was refreshing to contemplate."

Chicago Evening Journal, January 16, 1879: "Lieutenant Lee, the Recorder, who had been holding a whispered consultation with the judges, interrupted the examination, saying: 'I have to announce that the court permits the reporters to take notes.' And thereupon white paper and pencils came out from the overcoat pockets of half a dozen pale and lofty-browed young men [who] stood incog. about the room, and quickly there was heard the music of the reportorial graphites as they merrily went about their work."

Chicago Daily News, January 16, 1879: "The Court, after a few moments of consultation, agreed to the proposition, and the reporters will in the future not be obliged to write in their overcoat pockets, or compelled to cover their copy paper with their hats."

Chicago Daily Tribune, January 17, 1879: "A short whispered consultation was held among the officers of the Court and the Recorder, at the end of which it was announced that the reporters were at liberty to take notes, whereupon a dozen whipped paper and pencils from their pockets simultaneously, and commenced a vigorous scratching upon their knees."

Chicago Times, January 17, 1879: "A consultation was held with reference to the suggestion Mr. Gilbert had made. The result was that an order was promulgated that the newsmen might take notes of the proceedings if they so desired. Hereupon there was considerable rustling of paper, pencils were produced, memories were relieved from all distressing strain, and the scribes prepared to do their duty in their customary manner."

New York Herald, January 17, 1879: "Immediately after this order the notebooks saw the light of day."

St. Paul Pioneer Press, January 17, 1879: "After taking the suggestion under advisement Col. King said the reporters might be allowed to take notes. In a moment half a dozen hats, that had modestly been held in the hands of half a dozen knights of the Faber [a brand of pencil] went under a half dozen chairs and half a dozen notebooks forsook the darkness of the interior of a hat and sought the light of day. The testimony was resumed."

3. *Chicago Daily Tribune,* January 14, 1879.
4. *Chicago Daily News,* January 24, 1879; *Chicago Times,* January 15, 1876; *St. Paul Pioneer Press,* January 15, 1879.
5. *Inter-Ocean,* January 14, 1879.
6. *New York Herald,* January 16, 1879; Graham, *The Custer Myth,* 338–40.
7. Nichols, *Reno Court of Inquiry,* 52.
8. Ibid., 53.
9. Ibid.
10. McClernand, "With the Indian and Buffalo in Montana," 27.
11. That Wallace may have regretted his testimony is indicated by a statement he allegedly made to a good friend years later. That friend told Captain R. G. Carter the following story: "Major Henry Lemly, formerly of the Third Cavalry, told me this day that in a conversation which he had with Lieut. George D. Wallace, Seventh Cavalry, he [Wallace] said, with tears in his eyes, that when Custer separated from Reno, his plan was to march to the lower end of the villages, crossing at one of the lower fords, and make an attack there. His attack was to be the signal for Reno, just as soon as the latter saw or heard him, to press forward, in the reasonable expectation that the combined pressure would stampede the Indians out of the village.

    "Lemly was emphatic as to his recollections of what Wallace had told him and of the latter's knowledge of Custer's plan. The query still remains: Did Custer tell Wallace his plan, or did Wallace merely guess or surmise such an intention on the part of Custer?" R. G. Carter, memorandum, Box 29, Folder 24, Ghent Papers.

    If this statement is legitimate and Wallace somehow knew of such a plan, it throws an entirely different light on all that followed the separation of Reno and Custer. However, this unsupported hearsay account is too tenuous to accept as history.
12. See Sklenar, "The 'Wallace Factor' at the Reno Court of Inquiry," for an excellent and detailed analysis of Wallace's testimony and its effect.
13. Davis and Davis, *The Reno Court of Inquiry,* 47.
14. *New York Herald,* January 18, 1879; *Chicago Daily News,* January 21, 1879; Davis and Davis, *The Reno Court of Inquiry,* 22, 46.
15. Willert, *March of the Columns,* 254, 393–94.
16. Utley, *The Reno Court of Inquiry,* 102.
17. Ibid., 109.
18. Graham, *The Reno Court of Inquiry: Abstract,* 42.
19. Hammer, *Custer in '76,* 237–38. Gerard also claimed that "before the trial began he and Dr. Porter and certain of the officers were called into a room to talk over what information they could give on certain points. Dr. Porter admitted that he could testify thus and so in reference to certain pertinent questions but said he hoped he would not be called upon to do so" (ibid., 238).

20. Ibid., 127.
21. Nichols, *Reno Court of Inquiry*, 115.
22. Utley, *The Reno Court of Inquiry*, 128.
23. Ibid., 135.
24. This exchange appeared in neither the official account nor the *Chicago Times* account. *New York Herald*, January 22, 1879; *Chicago Evening Journal*, January 21, 1879.
25. Davis and Davis, *The Reno Court of Inquiry*, 53.
26. Johnson, "A Captain of 'Chivalric Courage,' " 44.
27. Frost, *General Custer's Libbie*, 237.
28. Davis and Davis, *The Reno Court of Inquiry*, 49.
29. Hardorff, *On the Little Bighorn with Walter Camp*, 54; Carroll, *Custer's Chief of Scouts*, 64–65, 89.
30. *Chicago Evening Journal*, January 22, 1879.
31. Ibid.
32. *Chicago Daily News*, January 21, 1879.
33. Graham, *The Official Record of a Court of Inquiry*, viii–ix.
34. *Inter-Ocean*, February 8, 1879.
35. *Chicago Daily News*, January 17, 1879.
36. Carroll, *Camp Talk*, 120.
37. *Inter-Ocean*, January 21, 1879.
38. *Inter-Ocean*, January 25, 1879.
39. *Inter-Ocean*, January 14, 1879.
40. *New York Sun*, February 26, 1879; Camp IU Notes, 81, 82.
41. Camp IU Notes, 81, 82; Lee to Elizabeth Custer, June 27, 1897, Hagner Collection.
42. Camp IU Notes, 102. According to Camp's notes, DeRudio told him that "at Court of Inquiry there was a private understanding between a number of officers that they would do all they could to save Reno (and De Rudio says they did it when they got on to the stand!)." And at least one newspaperman also commented on the disparity between the officers' admissions in and out of the courtroom: "I cannot refrain," wrote the *St. Paul Pioneer Press* correspondent, "from remarking that the manner some of the officers have talked in private and to their friends in regard to the events of that day has been strangely at variance with their sworn testimony. It shows conclusively that they are either cowardly talking behind Reno's back, or else that they have not courage enough to face his resentment by speaking the truth on the witness stand" (*St. Paul Pioneer Press*, February 3, 1879).
43. Hammer, *Custer in '76*, 238–39.
44. Ibid., 238.
45. Utley, *The Reno Court of Inquiry*, 198.
46. Merkel, "Custer's Forgotten Lieutenant," 189: Soon after the battle, Weir told Reno what he thought of his conduct during those two days. Moylan told Weir, "Weir, you have been in the 7th Cavalry for ten years, and if the gov't hadn't paid you a cent you have earned it all for what you have said." In an 1892 letter to Godfrey, Moylan wrote: "I desire to be understood that my

defense of Reno is entirely <u>confined to his act of taking his three troops out of the bottom</u>. Of his personal conduct in the bottom or subsequently on the hill the least said the better. If what Col. Benteen told me at Meade in 1883 was true, and I know of no reason to doubt it, then Reno ought to have been shot" (Moylan to Godfrey, January 17, 1892, Box 4, MS 1401, Camp BYU Collection).

47. Utley, *The Reno Court of Inquiry,* 205.
48. Ibid., 232–33.
49. Nichols, *Reno Court of Inquiry,* 246.
50. Ibid., 438, 454.
51. Utley, *The Reno Court of Inquiry,* 240.
52. Davis and Davis, *The Reno Court of Inquiry,* 72.
53. The Articles of War in force at the time concerning courts of inquiry specifically stated that "the recorder . . . unlike the judge advocate, is not a prosecuting officer, since the investigation is not a trial, nor will he properly assume the role or manner of a prosecutor."
54. Nichols, *Reno Court of Inquiry,* 283.
55. Ibid., 284.
56. Ibid., January 26, 1879; Davis and Davis, *The Reno Court of Inquiry,* 36–37.
57. Horn, "The Tainted Testimony of Captain Frederick W. Benteen."
58. Utley, *The Reno Court of inquiry,* 338.
59. Kuhlman, *Legend into History,* 132.
60. Ibid., 585; Utley, *The Reno Court of Inquiry,* 420–21; *Washington Post,* February 10, 1879.
61. Nichols, *Reno Court of Inquiry,* 586–87.
62. Ibid., 593.
63. Ibid., 595.
64. Paul Hedren, "Holy Ground," in Rankin, *Legacy,* 199.
65. Nichols, *Reno Court of Inquiry,* 611.
66. Utley, *The Reno Court of Inquiry,* 431.
67. *Chicago Daily Tribune,* February 12, 1879; Utley, *The Reno Court of Inquiry,* 447.
68. Graham, *The Reno Court of Inquiry: Abstract,* 45.
69. *Inter-Ocean,* February 12, 1879; Nichols, *Reno Court of Inquiry,* 630.
70. Nichols, *Reno Court of Inquiry,* 463.
71. Ibid.
72. Hutchins, *The Army and Navy Journal,* 199.
73. Nichols, *In Custer's Shadow,* 285.
74. Graham, *The Custer Myth,* 337; R. G. Carter to A. H. Hepburn, November 9, 1934, Van de Water Papers. Lee later told researcher Walter Camp that Merritt had used almost the exact same words to him as Merritt drew up the court's conclusions: "We will damn Major Reno with faint praise" and "We have politely cursed him and whitewashed it over" (Camp IU Notes, 58, 578; Hardorff, *On the Little Bighorn with Walter Camp,* 191; Jesse M. Lee autobiography, unpublished manuscript, courtesy Ephriam Dickson).

75. Graham, *The Custer Myth*, 325–29.

76. Ibid., 329–32; *Philadelphia Times*, March 30, 1879.

77. See Otto Eisenschiml's excellent and highly readable *The Celebrated Case of Fitz John Porter* for a particularly egregious example.

78. "It was known and proved by Reno's court-martials, that he was a rather vindictive person toward subordinates" (Luce, review of *Echoes from the Little Big Horn Fight*, 61).

79. Whittaker to Elizabeth Custer, March 31, 1877, quoted in Frost, *General Custer's Libbie*, 240.

80. Ricker, *The Settler and Soldier Interviews*, 361.

81. Frost, *General Custer's Libbie*, 254.

82. Barnett, *Touched by Fire*, 371.

CHAPTER TWENTY-ONE: GHOSTS DANCING

Epigraph: Kicking Bear, quoted in Coleman, *Voices of Wounded Knee*, 234.

1. Carroll, *General Custer and the Battle of the Little Big Horn*, 177.

2. I have relied primarily on the following sources for Ghost Dance and Wounded Knee material in this chapter: Mooney, *The Ghost-Dance Religion;* Vestal, *Warpath and Council Fire;* Coleman, *Voices of Wounded Knee;* Kelley, *Pine Ridge, 1890;* Jensen et al., *Eyewitness at Wounded Knee;* McGregor, *The Wounded Knee Massacre;* Huls, *The Winter of 1890;* Utley, *The Last Days of the Sioux Nation;* Tibbles, *Buckskin and Blanket Days;* Carroll, *To Set the Record Straight!* Mattes, "The Enigma of Wounded Knee"; Jensen, "Big Foot's Followers at Wounded Knee"; and "Reports and Correspondence Relating to the Army Investigations of the Battle of Wounded Knee and to the Sioux Campaign of 1890–1891," RG 94, National Archives.

3. Sitting Bull, quoted in Utley, *Sitting Bull*, 269.

4. There is some evidence that the Lakota Sioux added a touch of vengefulness to the religion that espoused death to the whites. See Vestal, *New Sources of Indian History*, 42–44, 60; Wooster, *The Military and the United States Indian Policy*, 194; Utley, *The Lance and the Shield*, 284.

5. Nichols, *Men with Custer*, 396. Twenty-three of the medals were awarded in 1878; one, to Theodore Goldin, was awarded in 1895. Twenty-seven medals were awarded at Iwo Jima.

6. First Lieutenant Luther Hare was with the regiment at Pine Ridge but was relieved from duty "on account of physical disability" two weeks before the Battle of Wounded Knee and returned to Fort Riley (*Army and Navy Journal*, December 27, 1890, 296). Captain Frank Gibson had been on sick leave since October and would remain on it until he retired from the service in December 1891 (*Army and Navy Journal*, October 4, 1890).

7. Utley, *The Last Days of the Sioux Nation*, 202; the chapter on Wounded Knee in Ricker, *The Settler and Soldier Interviews;* the chapter on the Ghost Dance and Wounded Knee in Ricker, *The Indian Interviews;* and Wells, "Ninety-Six Years Among the Indians."

8. Coleman, 234.

9. Northrop, *Indian Horrors,* 548: In a letter, a Seventh Cavalry trooper wrote, "There were about fifty tepees set up."

10. Coleman, 275.

11. Kelley, 103; McGregor, 89.

12. *Beatrice* (Nebraska) *Daily Express,* December 30, 1890.

13. Coleman, 294–98. The officer's identity was never ascertained. See also Miss Elaine Goodale's report to the Bureau of Indian Affairs as detailed in the January 17, 1891, *Washington Post.* Other eyewitness accounts claim that no orders were given; see Northrop, 549.

14. Rickey, *Forty Miles a Day on Beans and Hay,* 289.

15. Coleman, 301. "Reports and Correspondence," 706: "I have reason to believe that some of our men were killed by the fire of other of our troops," testified one of the Seventh's medical officers, assistant surgeon Charles Ewing. "I base it from the position of the troops. . . . Located as the troops were, and firing as they did, it was impossible not to wound or kill each other." Artillery Captain Allyn Capron agreed: "It was unavoidable that some of our troops should have been hurt from our own fire" (Coleman, 363). A Seventh Cavalry private later wrote: "I have no doubt that I was shot by one of my comrades" (quoted in Flood, *Lost Bird of Wounded Knee,* 41). See also McGinnis, "I Was There!" 52; Ricker, *The Indian Interviews,* 94–95, for a second account from a Seventh Cavalry Sergeant who was "sure that his fire was fatal to the soldiers there. Three men in his own troop were killed by the soldiers from the opposite side"; and Northrop, 549, for an account by a trooper who wrote, "From beginning to end I don't think I saw two dozen bucks, and it is a mystery to all where the bullets came from that killed and wounded one-third of my regiment." See also Greene, *After Wounded Knee,* 33–34.

16. One surgeon who was present, Captain Charles Ewing, later reported thirty men killed (Ewing, "The Wounded of Wounded Knee Battlefield," 7).

17. Coleman, 307. A slight variation of this exchange was reported in a story in the February 12, 1891, *Chicago Daily Tribune,* as related by an Episcopalian minister at a Sioux Indian conference in Washington, D.C. According to the minister, the scout-interpreter told him of the following exchange: " 'Now we have avenged Custer's death,' says the officer, to which the scout replies, 'Yes, but you had every chance to fight for your lives that day. These poor Indian people did not have that opportunity to protect and fight for themselves.' " A Seventh Cavalry trooper was later quoted as saying, "The older men of the regiment began regaling we youngsters with stories of the bloody battle of the Little Bighorn. . . . This made us eager to meet the redskins and get revenge for what they had done to our predecessors" (Greene, *Indian War Veterans,* 179). See also Johnson, *Intensely Interesting Little Volume,* 14, for an account by a man who claimed to have been at the scene: "After an effective volley, rose the sullen roar of voices whose cry was, 'Remember Custer.' "

18. Greene, *After Wounded Knee,* 33.

19. For eyewitness accounts of troopers shooting women and children, see
     Coleman, 350, 356, 365; Flood, 41, 45–46; McGregor, 112, 126; Ricker, *The
     Settler and Soldier Interviews*, 20, 33, 38, 39; Ricker, *The Indian Interviews*,
     202, 203, 221; Lindberg, "Foreigners in Action at Wounded Knee," 176;
     and Northrop, where one trooper wrote, "Some of the men went wild; they
     would shoot men or women" (545), and another trooper wrote, "Of course
     the camp-liar was in his glory, but who shot the squaws was not known, at
     least no one bragged of it" (550).

20. In a special investigation into the circumstances connected with the killing
     of these four Minneconjous in March 1891, testimony was taken from God-
     frey, a Sergeant, and three troopers; see Carroll, *To Set the Record Straight!*
     65–72. See Utley, *The Last Days of the Sioux Nation*, 224 n. 43, for further
     discussion of this incident. See also Johnson, "Tragedy at White Horse
     Creek," and Coleman, 329–33, for a later version ("Tragedy at White Horse
     Creek: General Godfrey's Account of an Incident Near Wounded Knee, in
     1890," written in 1903) that was slightly different in small details; and God-
     frey's May 29, 1931, letter to the chief of the historical section, Army War
     College, for another account, again with some minor differences. (A copy
     of the letter is in the Godfrey Family Papers.) In all three versions, Godfrey
     said that his men saw the Indians run into the brush: "Some of my men
     called my attention, that they saw some Indians in the creek bottom" (1891);
     "My return march was down a partly wooded valley containing clumps of
     bushes with dead leaves on them. . . . I put flankers on each side on the high
     ground. As we entered one of these clumps the advance discovered some
     Indians running to a hiding place. I at once dismounted to fight on foot"
     (1931). It seems curious that none of his troopers noticed or said anything to
     the effect that these four Indians were not full-grown men but a woman, two
     children, and a fourteen- or fifteen-year-old boy. (In his initial testimony in
     1891, Godfrey said that the boy was sixteen or seventeen. In 1931 he claimed
     that the boy was fourteen or fifteen. Captain Frank D. Baldwin claimed in
     his report that the boy was about ten years of age, and General Miles wrote
     in one report that the boy was between eight and ten.) In his 1903 account,
     Godfrey stated: "I found a squaw and two small girls . . . [who] were in their
     death struggles"; in his original testimony in 1891, he claimed that they were
     dead when he found them. Another curious fact: in his 1891 testimony, God-
     frey revealed that Baldwin had told him that the boy had only one gunshot in
     his body, meaning that he had not been shot in the initial fusillade (Carroll,
     To Set the Record Straight!, 69). See Johnson, "Tragedy at White Horse
     Creek," for more discussion of this action.

21. This investigative body does not seem to have been a formal court of inquiry
     and was never officially called that, though it has been referred to as such
     many times since. As a matter of fact, when Miles telegrammed the War
     Department that he had detailed a body of officers to inquire into the matter
     and asked if the President directed "that it constitute a court of inquiry with
     power to take testimony under oath," he received the following reply: "I am
     directed by the Secretary of War to inform you that it was not the intention

of the President to appoint a Court of Inquiry, nor to order at this time, in the midst of the campaign, any further inquiry than you could yourself make without the necessity of a court, the purpose being simply to determine whether any officer had been so far derelict in duty as to make it necessary to relieve him from command, such result to follow upon the inquiry which you were expected to cause to be made" (quoted in *Chicago Daily Tribune,* January 7, 1891). The idea was, it seems, to keep any investigation under wraps for as long as possible.

22. Coleman, 362.

23. Dr. Charles Eastman, quoted in the *Chicago Daily Tribune,* January 8, 1891.

24. Quoted in Coleman, 310. See also McGinnis, "I Was There!" 52, in which the author, a Private in K Company, wrote: "There was no discrimination of age or sex. Children as well as women with babes in their arms were brought down as far as two miles from the Wounded Knee Crossing."

25. Coleman, 315.

26. Ibid., 317.

27. The man who was paid to bury the Minneconjous, Paddy Starr, said that he buried 168 in the mass grave (Coleman, 352); 4 more were found several weeks later by Captain Frank Baldwin, victims of a platoon led by Captain Edward Godfrey. Other estimates put the death toll as high as 184 (Ricker, *The Settler and Soldier Interviews,* 46); 185 (Coleman, 365); or even 300 (ibid., 355). Joseph Horn Cloud, a Minneconjou participant, listed 104 survivors in Big Foot's band and 185 killed (Ricker, *The Indian Interviews,* 204–8). One of the three reporters who witnessed the battle, William Fitch Kelley, claimed more than 200 dead and a total of 275 to 300 killed and wounded (Kelley, 223). One trooper claimed "about 115 bucks, and about 75 women and children killed. . . . Some of the men went wild; they would shoot men or women" (Northrop, 545). Nelson Miles wrote in a private letter that "about 200 women and children were killed or wounded" (quoted in Greene, *After Wounded Knee,* 33). For a thorough early discussion of the number of Indians killed, see Mooney, 870–71.

28. Coleman, 352.

29. "Reports and Correspondence," 726.

30. *Chicago Daily Tribune,* February 20, 1891. A report made to the Commissioner of Indian Affairs by a special agent of the Interior Department finished the section on Godfrey's actions with this: "This instance proves the intensity with which the common soldier hates the Indian, and is a disgraceful stain which the army has not erased from its shield, though the murderers are known to Gen. Miles and other officers" ("Reports and Correspondence," 653–54).

31. *New York Sun,* October 10, 1907: "He served at the battle of Wounded Knee and his participation in that engagement nearly cost him his life, and cost him, in the estimation of many of his officers, the rank of Major-General. Certain alleged facts in that engagement, for which President Roosevelt held Gen. Godfrey responsible, made the President his unsparing critic in

later years, and he declared on one occasion that Godfrey should never be promoted under the Roosevelt administration. The President relented after much persuasion on the part of Gen. Franklin Bell, the present Chief of the General Staff, and others who were in the Wounded Knee engagement, and promoted Gen. Godfrey from senior Colonel of the Line to Brigadier-General. This promotion was not made, however, until last January. The charge against Gen. Godfrey was similar to that brought against Gen. John J. Pershing, then a Captain, on account of the Moro campaign — that he permitted the killing of women and children unnecessarily in battle. Gen. Godfrey has been vigorously defended against this charge by Gen. Bell and other participants in the engagement."

32. Mills, *Harvest of Barren Regrets*, 345–58.

33. Ibid., 368.

34. Louis M. Spaulding to Frederic Van de Water, February 18, 1934, Van de Water Papers; Frank Anders to R. G. Cartwright, May 19, 1950, Cartwright Collection.

35. Nichols, *In Custer's Shadow*, 347–48.

36. In November 1966, a great-nephew, Charles Reno, made an official application for reinstatement, which was granted (after much testimony before the Army Correction Board) in May 1967. Reno's remains were disinterred and reburied, with full military honors, in the National Cemetery at Little Bighorn Battlefield National Monument in September 1967.

37. The musical comedy was entitled *Our Club* and credited entirely to Frederick Whittaker ("Music for the Nation: American Sheet Music," Music Division, Library of Congress). A few of the songs credited to him are "The Crutch and the Empty Sleeve" (with his brother Octave) and, from *Our Club*, "Now Is the Time for the Baby to Sleep" and "Oh, Dear! What Will My Wife Say?" Ironically, Whittaker claimed that since his previous publishers, Beadle and Smith, had engaged Ned Buntline as a writer in 1886, "their work has steadily deteriorated," and he denigrated their dime novels as "vicious trash about pirates, detectives, and western desperadoes" (Whittaker to Robert Bonner, April 21, 1886, Bonner Papers).

38. *New York Times*, October 26, 1884; *New York Daily Tribune*, May 16, 1889.

39. *New York Daily Tribune*, May 14, 1889.

40. *New York Sun*, May 14, 1889.

41. *Collier's*, January 29, 1927, 41.

BIBLIOGRAPHY

More has been written on the Battle of the Little Bighorn, it has often been said, than on the Battle of Gettysburg. This may or may not be true (I tend to think it is); in any case, the literature is voluminous. The following list encompasses books and articles read or consulted that provided both general background and specific knowledge and includes all sources cited in the notes.

BOOKS

Alberts, Don E. *Brandy Station to Manila Bay.* Austin, TX: Presidial Press, 1980.

Algier, Keith. *The Crow and the Eagle.* Caldwell, ID: Caxton Printers, 1993.

Ambrose, Stephen. *Crazy Horse and Custer: The Parallel Lives of Two American Warriors.* New York: Doubleday, 1975.

Anders, Frank L. *The Custer Trail.* Glendale, CA: Arthur H. Clark, 1983.

Anderson, Gary C. *Sitting Bull and the Paradox of Lakota Nationhood.* New York: Longman, 1996.

Andrist, Ralph K. *The Long Death.* New York: Macmillan, 1964.

Annual Report of the Commissioner of Indian Affairs to the Secretary of the Interior for the Year 1875. Washington, DC: Government Printing Office, 1875.

Bailey, John Wendell. *Pacifying the Plains: General Alfred Terry and the Decline of the Sioux.* Contributions in Military History 17. Westport, CT: Greenwood Press, 1979.

Barnard, Sandy. *Digging into Custer's Last Stand.* Terre Haute, IN: AST Press, 1998.

———. *I Go with Custer: The Life and Death of Reporter Mark Kellogg.* Bismarck, ND: Bismarck Tribune, 1996.

———. *Speaking About Custer: A Collection of Lectures.* Terre Haute, IN: AST Press, 1991.

————, ed. *Ten Years with Custer*. Terre Haute, IN: AST Press, 2001.

Barnett, Louise. *Touched by Fire: The Life, Death and Mythic Afterlife of George Armstrong Custer*. New York: Henry Holt, 1996.

Bates, Col. Charles Francis. *Custer's Indian Battles*. Bronxville, NY: privately printed, 1936.

Beadle, J. H. *Western Wilds, and the Men Who Redeem Them*. Cincinnati: Jones Brothers, 1881.

Berthrong, Donald. *The Cheyenne and Arapaho Ordeal*. Norman: University of Oklahoma Press, 1975.

Bettelyoun, Susan Bordeaux, and Josephine Waggoner. *With My Own Eyes: A Lakota Woman Tells Her People's History*. Lincoln: University of Nebraska Press, 1998.

Beyer, W. F., and O. F. Keydel, eds. *Deeds of Valor*. Vol. 2. Detroit: Perrian-Keydel, 1907.

Bookwalter, Thomas E. *Honor Tarnished*. West Carrollton, OH: Little Horn Press, 1979.

Bordeaux, William J. *Custer's Conqueror*. N.p.: Smith and Company, n.d.

Bourke, John G. *On the Border with Crook*. New York: Charles Scribner's Sons, 1981.

Bowers, Claude G. *The Tragic Era*. Boston: Houghton Mifflin, 1929.

Boyer, Paul S. *The Oxford Companion to United States History*. Oxford: Oxford University Press, 2001.

Boyes, W., ed. *The Cheyenne Tribal Historian John Stands-in-Timber's Account of the Custer Battle*. N.p.: Little Big Horn Associates, 1991.

————. *Custer's Black White Man*. Washington, DC: South Capitol Press, 1972.

————, ed. *Surgeon's Diary with the Custer Relief Column*. Washington, DC: South Capitol Press, 1974.

Bradley, James H. *The March of the Montana Column*. Norman: University of Oklahoma Press, 1961.

Brady, Cyrus Townsend. *Indian Fights and Fighters*. New York: McClure, Philips, 1904.

Branch, Edward Douglas. *The Hunting of the Buffalo*. New York: Appleton, 1929.

Brandon, William. *Indians*. Boston: Houghton Mifflin, 1961.

Bray, Kingsley M. *Crazy Horse: A Lakota Life*. Norman: University of Oklahoma Press, 2006.

Brill, Charles J. *Conquest of the Southern Plains*. Oklahoma City: Golden Saga Publishing, 1938.

Brininstool, E. A. *Campaigning with Custer*. Reprint, Lincoln: University of Nebraska Press, 1988.

————. *Troopers with Custer*. Reprint, Lincoln: University of Nebraska Press, 1989.

Brown, Jesse, and A. M. Willard. *The Black Hills Trails*. Rapid City, SD: Rapid City Journal Company, 1924.

Brown, Mark H. *The Plainsmen of the Yellowstone*. Lincoln: University of Nebraska Press, 1961.

Brown, Mark H., and W. E. Felton. *The Frontier Years: L. A. Huffman, Photographer of the Plains*. New York: Henry Holt, 1955.

Bryant, Charles S., and Able B. Murch. *A History of the Great Massacre by the Sioux Indians, in Minnesota*. Cincinnati: R. W. Carroll, 1868.

Buecker, Thomas R., and Eli Paul, eds. *The Crazy Horse Surrender Ledger.* Lincoln: Nebraska State Historical Society, 1994.

Buell, Thomas B. *The Warrior Generals.* New York: Three Rivers Press, 1997.

Burdick, Usher L. *The Army Life of Charles "Chip" Creighton.* Paris, MD: National Reform Associates, 1937.

———, ed. *David F. Barry's Notes on "The Custer Battle."* Baltimore: Wirth Brothers, 1949.

———. *The Last Battle of the Sioux Nation.* Fargo, ND: Worzalla Publishing, 1929.

———. *Tales from Buffalo Land.* Baltimore: Wirth Brothers, 1940.

———. *Tragedy in the Great Sioux Camp.* Baltimore: Proof Press, 1936.

Burgum, Jessamine Slaughter. *Zezula; or, Pioneer Days in the Smoky Water Country.* Valley City, ND: Getchell and Nielsen, 1937.

Burkey, Blaine. *Custer, Come at Once!* Hays, KS: Society of Friends of Historic Fort Hays, 1991.

Burt, Struthers. *Powder River: Let 'Er Buck.* New York: Farrar & Rinehart, 1938.

Byrne, P. E. *Soldiers of the Plains.* New York: Minton, Balch, 1926.

Canton, Frank M. *Frontier Trails.* Boston: Houghton Mifflin, 1930.

Capps, Benjamin. *The Indians.* New York: Time-Life Books, 1973.

Carrington, Col. Henry B. *Ab-sa-ra-ka: Land of Massacre.* 5th ed. of his wife Margaret's narrative. Philadelphia: J. B. Lippincott, 1879.

Carroll, John M., ed. *Camp Talk.* Mattituck, NY: J. M. Carroll, 1983.

———, ed. *The Court-Martial of Thomas M. French.* Bryan, TX: privately printed, 1979.

———, ed. *Custer: From the Civil War to the Little Big Horn.* Bryan, TX: privately printed, 1981.

———, ed. *Custer and His Times.* Book Two. Fort Worth, TX: Little Big Horn Associates, 1984.

———, ed. *A Custer Chrestomathy.* Bryan, TX: privately printed, 1981.

———, ed. *Custer's Chief of Scouts.* Lincoln: University of Nebraska Press, 1982.

———. *The Eleanor Hinman Interviews on the Life and Death of Crazy Horse.* New Brunswick, NJ: Garry Owen Press, 1976.

———. *4 on Custer by Carroll.* N.p.: Guidon Press, 1976.

———, ed. *The Frank L. Anders and R. G. Cartwright Correspondence.* 3 vols. Bryan, TX: privately printed, 1982.

———, ed. *The Fred Dustin and Earl K. Brigham Letters.* Vols. 1 and 2. Bryan, TX: privately printed, n.d.

———. *General Custer and the Battle of the Little Big Horn: The Federal View.* Mattituck, NY: J. M. Carroll, 1986.

———. *General Custer and the Battle of the Washita: The Federal View.* Bryan, TX: Guidon Press, 1978.

———, ed. *I, Varnum.* Mattituck, NY: J. M. Carroll, 1982.

———, ed. *The Lieutenant E. A. Garlington Narrative, Part I.* Bryan, TX: privately printed, n.d.

———. *Roll Call on the Little Bighorn.* Fort Collins, CO: Old Army Press, 1974.

———. *The Seventh Cavalry Scrapbook.* Nos. 1–13. Bryan, TX: J. M. Carroll, 1978–1980.

———, ed. *The Sunshine Magazine Articles by John P. Everett.* Bryan, TX: privately printed, 1979.

————. *Thomas J. McDougall Was Just a Wild and Crazy Guy!* N.p.: privately printed, n.d.

————. *To Set the Record Straight! The Real Story of Wounded Knee.* N.p.: privately printed, n.d.

————, ed. *The Two Battles of the Little Big Horn.* Bryan, TX: J. M. Carroll, 1974.

————, ed. *A Very Real Salmagundi; or, Look What I Found This Summer.* Bryan, TX: privately printed, 1980.

————, ed. *Who Was This Man Ricker and What Are His Tablets That Everyone Is Talking About?* Bryan, TX: privately printed, 1979.

Chandler, Lt. Col. Melbourne C. *Of Garryowen in Glory.* Annandale, PA: Turnpike Press, 1960.

Clark, George M. *Scalp Dance: The Edgerly Papers.* Oswego, NY: Heritage Press, 1985.

Clarke, Joseph I. C. *My Life and Memories.* New York: Dodd, Mead, 1925.

Clary, David A. *Adopted Son.* New York: Bantam, 2006.

Coffeen, Herbert. *The Teepee Book, Parts I and II.* New York: Sol Lewis, 1974.

Coffman, Edward M. *The Old Army.* New York: Oxford University Press, 1986.

Coleman, William S. E. *Voices of Wounded Knee.* Lincoln: University of Nebraska Press, 2000.

Cook, John R. *The Border and the Buffalo.* Chicago: R. R. Donnelley & Sons, 1938.

Coppee, Henry. *Field Manual for Courts-Martial.* Philadelphia: J. B. Lippincott, 1863.

Cortissoz, Royal. *The Life of Whitelaw Reid, Volume One.* New York: Charles Scribner's Sons, 1921.

Coughlan, Col. T. M. *Varnum: The Last of Custer's Lieutenants.* Bryan, TX: J. M. Carroll, 1980.

Cox, John E. *Five Years in the United States Army.* Reprint, New York: Sol Lewis, 1973.

Cozzens, Peter Gould, ed. *Eyewitnesses to the Indian Wars, 1865–1890.* Vol. 3, *Conquering the Southern Plains.* Mechanicsburg, PA: Stackpole, 2003.

————, ed. *Eyewitnesses to the Indian Wars, 1865–1890.* Vol. 4, *The Long War for the Northern Plains.* Mechanicsburg, PA: Stackpole, 2004.

————, ed. *Eyewitnesses to the Indian Wars, 1865–1890.* Vol. 5, *The Army and the Indian.* Mechanicsburg, PA: Stackpole, 2005.

Crary, Catherine S. *Dear Belle: Letters from a Cadet and Officer to His Sweetheart, 1858–1865.* Middletown, CT: Wesleyan University Press, 1965.

Crawford, Lewis F. *Rekindling Camp Fires.* Bismarck, ND: Capital Book, 1926.

Custer, Elizabeth B. *Boots and Saddles.* New York: Harper and Brothers, 1885.

Custer, George Armstrong. *My Life on the Plains.* Reprint, Norman: University of Oklahoma Press, 1962.

Darling, Roger. *Benteen's Scout-to-the-Left.* El Segundo, CA: Upton and Sons, 1987.

————. *General Custer's Final Hours: Correcting a Century of Misconceived Mystery.* Vienna, VA: Potomac-Western Press, 1992.

————. *A Sad and Terrible Blunder.* Vienna, VA: Potomac-Western Press, 1990.

David, Robert Beebe. *Finn Burnett, Frontiersman.* Glendale, CA: Arthur H. Clark, 1937.

Davis, Karen, and Elden Davis. *That Fatal Day: Eight More with Custer.* Howell, MI: Powder River Press, 1992.

———. *The Reno Court of Inquiry: The Pioneer Press, St. Paul and Minnesota, 1878–79.* Howell, MI: Powder River Press, 1992.

Day, Carl. *Tom Custer: Ride to Glory.* Spokane, WA: Arthur H. Clark, 2002.

DeBarthe, Frank. *The Life and Adventures of Frank Grouard.* Norman: University of Oklahoma Press, 1958.

Deland, C. E. *The Sioux Wars.* 2 vols. Pierre, SD: South Dakota Historical Collections, 1930, 1934.

DeMallie, Raymond J. *The Sixth Grandfather.* Lincoln: University of Nebraska Press, 1984.

DeMontravel, Peter R. *A Hero to His Fighting Men.* Kent, OH: Kent State University Press, 1998.

De Trobriand, Regis. *Military Life in Dakota.* Lincoln: University of Nebraska Press, 1982.

Diedrich, Mark S. *Famous Chiefs of the Eastern Sioux.* Minneapolis: Coyote Books, 1987.

———. *The Odyssey of Chief Standing Buffalo.* Minneapolis: Coyote Books, 1988.

Diehl, Charles S. *The Staff Correspondent.* San Antonio: Clegg, 1931.

Dixon, Dr. Joseph K. *The Vanishing Race.* Garden City, NY: Doubleday, Page, 1913.

Downey, Fairfax. *Indian-Fighting Army.* Rev. ed. New York: Bantam, 1957.

Du Bois, Charles G. *Kick the Dead Lion.* El Segundo, CA: Upton and Sons, 1987.

Dunlay, Thomas W. *Wolves for the Blue Soldiers.* Lincoln: University of Nebraska Press, 1982.

Dunn, J. P. *Massacres of the Mountains.* New York: Harper and Brothers, 1886.

Dustin, Fred. *The Custer Tragedy.* Reprint, El Segundo, CA: Upton and Sons, 1987.

Eastman, Charles. *Indian Heroes and Great Chieftains.* Boston: Little, Brown, 1918.

Ege, Robert J. *Curse Not His Curls.* Fort Collins, CO: Old Army Press, 1974.

———. *Settling the Dust.* Chinook, MT: Chinook Opinion, 1968.

Ellis, Edward S. *The History of Our Country from the Discovery of America to the Present Time.* Indianapolis: J. H. Wooling, 1910.

Evans, David C. *Custer's Last Fight: The Story of the Battle of the Little Big Horn.* El Segundo, CA: Upton and Sons, 1999.

Fay, George E. *Military Engagements Between United States Troops and Plains Indians, Part IV, 1872–1890.* Greeley: University of Northern Colorado, 1973.

Finerty, John G. *Warpath and Bivouac.* Chicago: Chicago Times, 1890.

Fiske, Frank B. *The Taming of the Sioux.* Bismarck, ND: Bismarck Tribune, 1917.

Flood, Renee Sansom. *Lost Bird of Wounded Knee.* New York: Scribner, 1995.

Folwell, William W. *A History of Minnesota.* 4 vols. St. Paul: Minnesota Historical Society, 1924.

Forrest, Earle R. *Witnesses at the Battle of the Little Big Horn.* Monroe, MI: Monroe County Library System, 1986.

Fougera, Katherine Gibson. *With Custer's Cavalry.* Caldwell, ID: Caxton Printers, 1940.

Fox, Richard A. *Archaeology, History, and Custer's Last Battle.* Norman: University of Oklahoma Press, 1993.

Frost, Lawrence. *Custer Legends*. Bowling Green, OH: Bowling Green University Popular Press, 1981.

——. *General Custer's Libbie*. Hesperia, CA: Superior Publishing, 1976.

Gibbon, John. *Gibbon on the Sioux Campaign of 1876*. Bellevue, NE: Old Army Press, 1970.

Godfrey, Edward. *Custer's Last Battle. 1892*. Reprint, Olympic Valley, CA: Outbooks, 1976.

——. *The Field Diary of Lt. Edward Settle Godfrey*. Portland, OR: Champoeg Press, 1957.

Goldin, Theodore. *With the Seventh Cavalry in 1876*. N.p.: privately printed, 1980.

Goodsell, James. *History of the Great Chicago Fire*. Chicago: J. H. and C. M. Goodsell, 1871.

Graham, Col. William T. *The Custer Myth: A Sourcebook of Custeriana*. Harrisburg, PA: Stackpole, 1953.

——. *Major Reno Vindicated*. Hollywood, CA: privately printed (E. A. Brininstool), 1935.

——. *The Official Record of a Court of Inquiry Convened at Chicago, Illinois, January 13, 1879, by the President of the United States upon the Request of Major Marcus A. Reno, 7th U.S. Cavalry to Investigate His Conduct at the Little Big Horn, June 25–26, 1876*. Pacific Palisades, CA: privately printed, 1951.

——. *The Reno Court of Inquiry: Abstract*. Harrisburg, PA: Stackpole, 1954.

——. *The Story of the Little Big Horn*. New York: Century, 1926.

Gray, John S. *Arikara Scouts with Custer*. Brooklyn: Arrow and Trooper, n.d.

——. *Centennial Campaign: The Sioux War of 1876*. Norman: University of Oklahoma Press, 1988.

——. *Custer's Last Campaign*. Lincoln: University of Nebraska Press, 1991.

Green, Jerry, ed. *After Wounded Knee*. East Lansing: Michigan State University Press, 1996.

Greene, Jerome. *Battles and Skirmishes of the Great Sioux War, 1876–1877: The Military View*. Norman: University of Oklahoma Press, 1993.

——. *Evidence and the Custer Enigma*. Golden, CO: Outbooks, 1986.

——. *Indian War Veterans*. New York: Savas Beatie, 2007.

——. *Lakota and Cheyenne: Indian Views of the Great Sioux War, 1876–1877*. Norman: University of Oklahoma Press, 1994.

——. *Washita*. Norman: University of Oklahoma Press, 2004.

Grinnell, George Bird. *The Fighting Cheyennes*. New York: Charles Scribner, 1915.

Guns at the Little Bighorn. A Man at Arms special publication. N.p.: Andrew Mowbray, 1988.

Halaas, David Fridtjof, and Andrew E. Masich. *Halfbreed*. New York: Da Capo, 2004.

Hall, Hillman Allyn. *History of the Sixth New York Cavalry*. Worcester, MA: Blanchard Press, 1908.

Hammer, Kenneth, ed. *Custer in '76: Walter Camp's Notes on the Custer Fight*. Norman: University of Oklahoma Press, 1990.

Hanson, Joseph Mills. *The Conquest of the Missouri*. Chicago: A. C. McClurg, 1910.

Harcey, Dennis W., and Brian R. Croone, with Joe Medicine Crow. *White-Man-*

Runs-Him: Crow Scout with Custer. Evanston, IL: Evanston Publishing, 1991.

Hardorff, Richard G. *Camp, Custer, and the Little Bighorn: A Collection of Walter Mason Camp's Research Papers on General George A. Custer's Last Fight*. El Segundo, CA: Upton and Sons, 1997.

———. *Cheyenne Memories of the Custer Fight*. Spokane, WA: Arthur H. Clark, 1995.

———. *The Custer Battle Casualties: Burials, Exhumations, and Reinterments*. El Segundo, CA: Upton and Sons, 1989.

———. *The Custer Battle Casualties II: The Dead, the Missing, and a Few Survivors*. El Segundo, CA: Upton and Sons, 1999.

———. *Hokahey! A Good Day to Die: The Indian Casualties of the Custer Fight*. Spokane, WA: Arthur H. Clark, 1993.

———. *Indian Views of the Custer Fight*. Spokane, WA: Arthur H. Clark, 2004.

———. *Lakota Recollections of the Custer Fight*. Spokane, WA: Arthur H. Clark, 1991.

———. *Markers, Artifacts and Indian Testimony: Preliminary Findings on the Custer Battle*. Short Hills, NJ: Don Horn Publications, 1985.

———. *The Oglala Lakota Crazy Horse*. Mattituck, NY: J. M. Carroll, 1985.

———. *On the Little Bighorn with Walter Camp*. El Segundo, CA: Upton and Sons, 2002.

———. *The Surrender and Death of Crazy Horse*. Spokane, WA: Arthur H. Clark, 1998.

———. *Walter M. Camp's Little Bighorn Rosters*. Spokane, WA: Arthur H. Clark, 2002.

———. *Washita Memories*. Norman: University of Oklahoma Press, 2006.

Hart, John P., ed. *Custer and His Times*. Book 4. LaGrange Park, IL: Little Big Horn Associates, 2002.

Hassrick, Royal. *The Sioux: Life and Customs of a Warrior Society*. Norman: University of Oklahoma Press, 1962.

Haydon, A. L. *The Riders of the Plains*. London: Andrew Melrose, 1910.

Hedren, Paul L., ed. *The Great Sioux War, 1876–77: The Best from Montana: The Magazine of Western History*. Helena: Montana Historical Society Press, 1991.

———, ed. *We Trailed the Sioux*. Harrisburg, PA: Stackpole, 2003.

Hein, O. L. *Memories of Long Ago*. New York: Putnam, 1925.

Hoebel, E. Adamson. *The Cheyennes: Indians of the Great Plains*. New York: Holt, Rinehart & Winston, 1960.

Holcombe, Return I. *Minnesota in Three Centuries*. Vol. 1. St. Paul, MN: Publishing Society of Minnesota, 1908.

Holley, Frances C. *Once Their Home; or, Our Legacy from the Dahkotahs*. Chicago: Donohue and Henneberry, 1890.

Hoopes, Alban W. *The Road to the Little Big Horn—and Beyond*. New York: Vantage Press, 1975.

Horn, W. Donald. *Portrait of a General*. West Orange, NJ: Don Horn Publications, 1998.

Hubbard and Holcombe. *Minnesota in Three Centuries*. Publishing Society of Minnesota, 1908.

Huls, Don. *The Winter of 1890*. Chadron, NE: Chadron Record, 1974.

Hunt, Frazier and Robert. *I Fought with Custer*. New York: Charles Scribner's, 1947.

Hutchins, James S., ed. *The Army and Navy Journal on the Battle of the Little Bighorn and Related Matters, 1876–1881*. El Segundo, CA: Upton and Sons, 2003.

———. *Boots and Saddles at the Little Bighorn*. Hardin, MT: Custer Battlefield Historical & Museum Association, 1976.

Hutton, Paul, ed. *Custer and His Times*. El Paso, TX: Little Big Horn Associates, 1981.

———, ed. *The Custer Reader*. Norman: University of Oklahoma Press, 2004.

———, ed. *Garry Owen 1976*. Seattle, WA: Little Big Horn Associates, 1977.

———. *Phil Sheridan and His Army*. Norman: University of Oklahoma Press, 1995.

Innis, Ben. *Bloody Knife! Custer's Favorite Scout*. Fort Collins, CO: Old Army Press, 1973.

Jackson, Donald. *Custer's Gold*. New Haven, CT: Yale University Press, 1966.

James, Marquis. *Andrew Jackson: The Border Captain*. Indianapolis: Bobbs-Merrill, 1933.

Jensen, Richard E., R. Eli Paul, and John E. Carter. *Eyewitness at Wounded Knee*. Lincoln: University of Nebraska Press, 1991.

Johansen, Albert. *The House of Beadle and Adams and Its Dime and Nickel Novels*. Vols. 1 and 2. Norman: University of Oklahoma Press, 1950.

Johnson, Barry. *Custer, Reno, Merrill and the Lauffer Case*. London: English Westerners' Society, 1971.

———. "Dr. Paulding and His Remarkable Diary." In *Sidelights of the Sioux Wars*, edited by Francis Taunton. London: English Westerners' Society, 1967.

———. *Merritt and the Indian Wars*. London: Johnson-Taunton Military Press, 1972.

Johnson, Barry, and Francis B. Taunton. *More Sidelights of the Sioux Wars*. London: Westerners' Publications, 2004.

Johnson, M. L. *Intensely Interesting Little Volume of True History of the Struggles with Hostile Indians. . . .* Dallas: privately printed, 1923.

Johnson, Virginia Weisch. *The Unregimented General: A Biography of Nelson A. Miles*. Boston: Houghton Mifflin, 1962.

Kadlecek, Edward, and Mabell Kadlecek. *To Kill an Eagle*. Boulder, CO: Johnson Books, 1981.

Kansas Corral of the Westerners. *Custer's Last Stand: The Indians' Viewpoint*. Special Publication 1. Abilene: Kansas Corral of the Westerners, 1972.

Kaufman, Fred S. *Custer Passed Our Way*. Aberdeen, SD: North Plains Press, 1971.

Keim, DeB. Randolph. *Sheridan's Troopers on the Borders: A Winter Campaign on the Plains*. 1870. Reprint, Williamstown, MA: Corner House, 1973.

Kelley, William Fitch. *Pine Ridge, 1890*. San Francisco: Pierre Bovis, 1971.

Kennedy, W. J. D. *A Captain of "Chivalric Courage."* London: English Westerners' Society, 1989.

———. *On the Plains with Custer and Hancock: The Journal of Isaac Coates, Army Surgeon*. Boulder, CO: Johnson Books, 1997.

Kime, Wayne R., ed. *The Black Hills Journals of Colonel Richard Irving Dodge*. Norman: University of Oklahoma Press, 1996.

King, W. Kent. *Mappings of an "Unknown" Land.* N.p.: privately printed, 1981.

———. *Massacre: The Custer Cover-up.* El Segundo, CA: Upton and Sons, 1989.

———. *Tombstones for Bluecoats.* Vols. 1–4. Marion Station, MD: privately printed, 1980–1981.

Knight, Oliver. *Following the Indian Wars.* Norman: University of Oklahoma Press, 1963.

———. *Life and Manners in the Frontier Army.* Norman: University of Oklahoma, 1969.

Koenig, Arthur. *Authentic History of the Indian Campaign Which Culminated in "Custer's Last Battle," June 25, 1876.* Milwaukee: Anheuser-Busch Brewing Association, 1896.

Koury, Michael. *Diaries of the Little Big Horn.* Fort Collins, CO: Old Army Press, 1968.

———, ed. *Gibbon on the Sioux Campaign of 1876.* Fort Collins, CO: Old Army Press, 1969.

Krause, Herbert, and Gary D. Olson. *Prelude to Glory.* Sioux Falls, SD: Brevet Press, 1976.

Kroeker, Marvin E. *Great Plains Command.* Norman: University of Oklahoma, 1976.

Kuhlman, Charles. *Legend into History.* Harrisburg, PA: Stackpole, 1951.

Langellier, John P., Kurt Hamilton Cox, and Brian C. Pohanka, eds. *Myles Keogh: The Life and Legend of an "Irish Dragoon" in the Seventh Cavalry.* El Segundo, CA: Upton and Sons, 1999.

Laubin, Reginald, and Gladys Laubin. *The Indian Tipi.* Norman: University of Oklahoma Press, 1957.

Laviolette, Gontran, O.M.I. *The Sioux Indians in Canada.* Regina, Sask.: privately printed, 1944.

Lazarus, Edward. *Black Hills, White Justice.* New York: HarperCollins, 1991.

Leckie, Shirley A. *Elizabeth Bacon Custer and the Making of a Myth.* Norman: University of Oklahoma Press, 1993.

Lee, Bob. *Fort Meade and the Black Hills.* Lincoln: University of Nebraska Press, 1991.

Leforge, Thomas H., as told by Thomas B. Marquis. *Memoirs of a White Crow Indian.* Reprint, Lincoln: University of Nebraska Press, 1974.

Libby, Orin G., ed. *The Arikara Narrative of Custer's Campaign and the Battle of the Little Bighorn.* Norman: University of Oklahoma Press, 1998.

Liddic, Bruce. *I Buried Custer.* Bryan, TX: Creative Publishing, 1979.

———. *Vanishing Victory: Custer's Final March.* El Segundo, CA: Upton and Sons, 2004.

Liddic, Bruce, and Brian Harbaugh. *Camp on Custer: Transcribing the Custer Myth.* Spokane, WA: Arthur H. Clark, 1995.

Linderman, Frank B. *Plenty-Coups: Chief of the Crows.* Lincoln: University of Nebraska Press, 1962.

———. *Pretty-Shield: Medicine Woman of the Crows.* Lincoln: University of Nebraska Press, 1974.

Lounsberry, Clement A. *Early History of North Dakota.* Washington, DC: Liberty Press, 1919.

Mackintosh, John D. *Custer's Southern Officer: Captain George D. Wallace, 7th U.S. Cavalry.* Lexington, SC: Cloud Creek Press, 2002.

Magnussen, Daniel O. *Peter Thompson's Narrative of the Little Bighorn Campaign, 1876.* Glendale, CA: Arthur H. Clark, 1974.

Maier, Larry B. *Leather and Steel: The 12th Pennsylvania Cavalry in the Civil War.* Shippensburg, PA: Bard Street Press, 2001.

Mails, Thomas E. *The Mystic Warriors of the Plains.* New York: Marlowe, 1995.

Maine, Floyd Shuster. *Lone Eagle, the White Sioux.* Albuquerque: University of New Mexico Press, 1956.

Mangum, Neil C. *Battle of the Rosebud: Prelude to the Little Bighorn.* El Segundo, CA: Upton and Sons, 1996.

Manion, John S. *General Terry's Last Statement to Custer.* El Segundo, CA: Upton and Sons, 2000.

Manzione, Joseph. *I Am Looking to the North for My Life.* Salt Lake City: University of Utah Press, 1991.

Marquis, Thomas B. *Cheyenne and Sioux: The Reminiscences of Four Indians and a White Soldier.* Stockton, CA: Pacific Center for Western Historical Studies, University of the Pacific, 1973.

———. *Custer, Cavalry and Crows.* Fort Collins, CO: Old Army Press, 1975.

———. *Custer on the Little Bighorn.* Lodi, CA: End-Kian Publishing, 1967.

———. *Keep the Last Bullet for Yourself.* Algonac, MI: Reference Publications, 1976.

———. *A Warrior Who Fought Custer.* Minneapolis: Midwest Publishing, 1931.

———. *Wooden Leg.* Bison Press, 2003.

Marshall, S. L. A. *Crimsoned Prairie.* New York: Charles Scribner's Sons, 1972.

Masters, Joseph G. *Shadows Fall Across the Little Big Horn: Custer's Last Stand.* Laramie: University of Wyoming Library, 1951.

McChristian, Douglas. *An Army of Marksmen.* Fort Collins, CO: Old Army Press, 1981.

McCreight, M. I. *Chief Flying Hawk's Tales: The True Story of Custer's Last Fight. . . .* New York: Alliance Press, 1936.

———. *Firewater and Forked Tongues: A Sioux Chief Interprets U.S. History.* Pasadena, CA: Trail's End Publishing, 1947.

McFeely, William S. *Grant: A Biography.* New York: W. W. Norton, 1981.

McGillycuddy, Julia. *McGillycuddy, Agent.* Stanford, CA: Stanford University Press, 1941.

McGinnis, Anthony. *Counting Coup and Cutting Horses.* Evergreen, CO: Cordillera Press, 1990.

McGregor, James H. *The Wounded Knee Massacre: From the Viewpoint of the Sioux.* 6th ed. N.p.: Fenwyn Press, 1969.

McLaughlin, James. *My Friend the Indian.* Reprint, Seattle: Superior Publishing, 1970.

Meketa, Ray. *Luther Rector Hare: A Texan with Custer.* Mattituck, NY: J. M. Carroll, 1983.

Merington, Marguerite. *The Custer Story.* New York: Devin-Adair, 1950.

Merk, Frederick. *History of the Westward Movement.* New York: Alfred Knopf, 1978.

Merkel, Captain Charles E., Jr. *Unravelling the Custer Enigma*. Enterprise, AL: Merkel Press, 1977.

Merrill, James M. *Spurs to Glory*. Chicago: Rand McNally, 1966.

Meyer, Roy. *History of the Santee Sioux*. Lincoln: University of Nebraska Press, 1967.

Michno, Gregory. *Encyclopedia of Indian Wars*. Missoula, MT: Mountain Press Publishing, 2003.

———. *Lakota Noon: The Indian Narrative of Custer's Defeat*. Missoula, MT: Mountain Press Publishing, 1998.

———. *The Mystery of E Troop*. Missoula, MT: Mountain Press Publishing, 1997.

Miles, Nelson. *Personal Recollections and Observations*. New York: Werner, 1896.

Miller, David Humphrey. *Custer's Fall: The Indian Side of the Story*. New York: Duell, Sloan, and Pearce, 1957.

Milligan, Edward Archibald. *Dakota Twilight: The Standing Rock Sioux, 1874–1890*. Hicksville, NY: Exposition Press, 1976.

———. *High Noon on the Greasy Grass*. Bottineau, ND: Bottineau-Courant Printing, 1972.

Mills, Anson. *My Story*. Washington, DC: Byron S. Adams, 1918.

Mills, Charles K. *Charles C. DeRudio*. Mattituck, NY: J. M. Carroll, 1983.

———. *Harvest of Barren Regrets*. Glendale, CA: Arthur H. Clark, 1985.

Mishkin, Bernard. *Rank and Warfare Among the Plains Indians*. Monographs of the American Ethnological Society 3. New York: J. J. Augustin, 1940.

Monaghan, Jay. *Custer: The Life of General George Armstrong Custer*. Boston: Little, Brown, 1959.

Mooney, James. *The Ghost-Dance Religion and the Sioux Outbreak of 1890*. 1896. Reprint, Lincoln: University of Nebraska Press, 1991.

Morris, Roy, Jr. *Fraud of the Century*. New York: Simon and Schuster, 2003.

Mulford, Ami Frank. *Fighting Indians in the 7th United States Cavalry, Custer's Favorite Regiment*. 2nd ed. Corning, NY: Paul Lindsley Mulford, 1878.

Nabokov, Peter. *Two Leggings: The Making of a Crow Warrior*. New York: Thomas Crowell, 1967.

Neihardt, John G. *Black Elk Speaks*. Reprint, Lincoln: University of Nebraska Press, 2000.

Nichols, Ronald H. *In Custer's Shadow: Major Marcus Reno*. Fort Collins, CO: Old Army Press, 1999.

———, ed. *Men with Custer*. Hardin, MT: Custer Battlefield Historical & Museum Association, 2000.

———. *Reno Court of Inquiry*. Hardin, MT: Custer Battlefield Historical and Museum Association, 1992.

Northrop, Henry D. *Indian Horrors; or, Massacres by the Red Men*. Philadelphia: National Publishing, 1891.

Noyes, Al J. *In the Land of the Chinook*. Helena, MT: State Publishing, 1917.

Oaks, George W. *Man of the West*. Tucson: Arizona Pioneer Historical Society, 1956.

Olney, Daniel Hoptowit. *Who Are You and Who Am I?* Toppenish, WA: privately printed, 1991.

O'Neil, Alice Tomlinson. *My Dear Sister*. Brooklyn: Arrow and Trooper, 1993.

O'Neil, Tom, ed. *Custer Chronicles*. Vols. 1–10. Brooklyn: Arrow and Trooper, 1998.

———. *Custer Conundrums*. Brooklyn: Arrow and Trooper, 1991.

———, ed. *Custeriana*. Vols. 1–10. Brooklyn: Arrow and Trooper, 1995.

———. *Fort Abraham Lincoln*. Brooklyn: Arrow and Trooper, 1996.

———, ed. *GarryOwen Tidbits*. Vols. 1–10. Brooklyn: Arrow and Trooper, 1989.

———, ed. *The Gibson-Edgerly Narratives of the Little Big Horn*. Brooklyn: Arrow and Trooper, 1993.

———. *In Reply to Van de Water*. Brooklyn: Arrow and Trooper, 1994.

Our Great Indian War. 1876. Reprint, New York: Garland Publishing, 1978.

Overfield, Lloyd, II. *The Little Big Horn, 1876: The Official Communications, Documents, and Reports, with Rosters of the Officers and Troops of the Campaign*. Glendale, CA: Arthur H. Clark, 1971.

Paine, Bayard H. *Pioneers, Indians and Buffaloes*. Curtis, NE: Curtis Enterprise, 1935.

Parker, Watson. *Gold in the Hills*. Lincoln: University of Nebraska Press, 1982.

Parkman, Francis. *The Oregon Trail*. Boston: Little, Brown, 1907.

Pennington, Jack. *The Battle of the Little Bighorn: A Comprehensive Study*. El Segundo, CA: Upton and Sons, 2001.

Perkins, J. R. *Trails, Rails and War: The Life of General G. M. Dodge*. Indianapolis: Bobbs-Merrill, 1929.

Peters, Joseph P., ed. *Indian Battles and Skirmishes on the American Frontier, 1790–1898*. New York: Argonaut Press, 1966.

Pohanka, Brian. *A Summer on the Plains, 1870: From the Diary of Annie Gibson Roberts*. Mattituck, NY: J. M. Carroll, 1983.

Poole, D. C. *Among the Sioux of Dakota*. 1881. Reprint, St. Paul: Borealis Books, 1988.

Powell, Peter J. *People of the Sacred Mountain*. San Francisco: Harper & Row, 1981.

———. *Sweet Medicine*. Norman: University of Oklahoma Press, 1998.

Price, S. Goodale. *Saga of the Hills*. Los Angeles: Cosmo Press, 1940.

Prucha, Francis Paul. *American Indian Treaties: Documents of U.S. Indian Policy*. Berkeley: University of California Press, 1994.

———. *The Great Father*. Lincoln: University of Nebraska Press, 1986.

Rankin, Charles, ed. *Legacy: New Perspectives on the Battle of the Little Bighorn*. Helena: Montana Historical Society Press, 1996.

Reiger, John F. *The Passing of the Great West: Selected Papers of George Bird Grinnell*. New York: Scribner, 1972.

Remini, Robert V. *Andrew Jackson and His Indian Wars*. New York: Viking, 2001.

Repass, Craig. *Custer for President?* Fort Collins, CO: Old Army Press, 1985.

Reynolds, Art. *Collision of Cultures*. Bloomington, IN: 1st Books, 2003.

Ricker, Eli S. *The Indian Interviews of Eli S. Ricker, 1903–1919*. Lincoln: University of Nebraska Press, 2005.

———. *The Settler and Soldier Interviews of Eli S. Ricker, 1903–1919*. Lincoln: University of Nebraska Press, 2005.

Rickey, Don. *Forty Miles a Day on Beans and Hay*. Norman: University of Oklahoma Press, 1963.

Roberts, Richard A. *Reminiscences of General Custer*. Monroe, MI: Monroe County Historical Society, 1978.

Robinson, Doane. *A History of the Dakota or Sioux Indians*. 1906. Reprint, Minneapolis: Ross and Haines, 1956.

Roddis, Louis H. *The Indian Wars of Minnesota*. Cedar Rapids, IA: Torch Press, 1956.

Roe, Charles F. *Custer's Last Battle*. New York: Robert Bruce, 1927.

Roe, Frances. *Army Letters from an Officer's Wife*. New York: Appleton, 1909.

Roenigk, Adolph. *A Pioneer History of Kansas*. N.p.: privately printed, n.d.

Ronsheim, Milton L. *The Life of General Custer*. Cadiz, OH: Cadiz Republican, 1929.

Sajna, Mike. *Crazy Horse: The Life Behind the Legend*. New York: Wiley, 2000.

Sarf, Wayne Michael. *The Little Bighorn Campaign*. New York: Combined Publishing, 1993.

Scharf, J. Thomas. *History of Westchester County, New York*. 2 vols. Philadelphia: L. E. Preston, 1886.

Schmitt, Martin, ed. *General George Crook: His Autobiography*. Norman: University of Oklahoma Press, 1946.

Schneider, James. *Behind Custer at the Little Big Horn: Lieutenant Edward C. Mathey*. Fort Wayne, IN: n.p., n.d.

Schoenberger, Dale. *End of Custer: The Death of an American Military Legend*. Blaine, WA: Hancock House, 1995.

Schultz, James Willard. *Blackfeet and Buffalo: Memories of Life Among the Indians*. Norman: University of Oklahoma Press, 1962.

———. *William Jackson, Indian Scout*. Boston: Houghton Mifflin, 1926.

Scott, Douglas D., and Peter Bleed. *A Good Walk Around the Boundary*. N.p.: National Association of Professional Archaeologists and the Nebraska State Historical Society, 1997.

Scott, Douglas D., and Richard Fox Jr. *Archaeological Insights into the Custer Battle*. Norman: University of Oklahoma Press, 1987.

Scott, Douglas D., Richard Fox Jr., Melissa A. Connor, and Dick Harmon. *Archaeological Perspectives on the Battle of the Little Bighorn*. Norman: University of Oklahoma Press, 1989.

Scott, Douglas D., P. Wiley, and Melissa A. Connor. *They Died with Custer*. Norman: University of Oklahoma, 1998.

Scott, Hugh Lennox. *Some Memories of a Soldier*. New York: Century, 1928.

Scudder, Ralph E. *Custer Country*. Portland, OR: Binfords and Mort, 1963.

Sheller, Roscoe. *The Name Was Olney*. Yakima, WA: Franklin Press, 1965.

Sheridan, Philip H. *Personal Memoirs*. Vol. 2. New York: Charles L. Webster, 1888.

Shields, Kenneth, Jr. *The Little Bighorn: Tiospaye*. Chicago: Arcadia, 2000.

Sklenar, Larry. *To Hell with Honor*. Norman: University of Oklahoma Press, 2000.

Slotkin, Richard. *The Fatal Environment*. New York: Atheneum, 1985.

Smalley, Vern. *Little Bighorn Mysteries*. Bozeman, MT: Little Buffalo Press, 2005.

———. *More Little Bighorn Mysteries*. Bozeman, MT: Little Buffalo Press, 2005.

Smith, DeCost. *Indian Experiences*. Caldwell, ID: Caxton Printers, 1943.

Smith, Jean Edward. *Grant*. New York: Simon and Schuster, 2001.

Smith, R. A. *A History of Dickinson County, Iowa*. Des Moines, IA: Kenyon Printing and Manufacturing, 1892.

Smith, Sherry. *Sagebrush Soldier*. Norman: University of Oklahoma Press, 1989.

Snelson, Bob. *Death of a Myth*. N.p.: Snelson Books, 2002.

Spotts, David L. *Campaigning with Custer*. Reprint, Lincoln: University of Nebraska Press, 1988.

Standing Bear, Luther. *My People the Sioux*. Boston: Houghton Mifflin, 1928.

Stands in Timber, John. *Cheyenne Memories*. New Haven, CT: Yale University Press, 1967.

Steele, S. B. *Forty Years in Canada*. New York: Dodd, Mead, 1915.

Steinbach, Robert. *The Long March: The Lives of Frank and Alice Baldwin*. Austin: University of Texas Press, 1989.

Stewart, Edgar I. *Custer's Luck*. Norman: University of Oklahoma Press, 1955.

Stuart, George H. *The Life of George H. Stuart*. Edited by Robert E. Thompson. Philadelphia: J. M. Stoddart, 1890.

Sully, Langdon. *No Tears for the General*. Palo Alto, CA: American West Publishing, 1974.

Swisher, James. *How I Know; or, 16 Years*. Cincinnati: n.p., 1881.

Tate, Michael L. *The Frontier Army in the Settlement of the West*. Norman: University of Oklahoma Press, 1999.

Taunton, Francis B. *Custer's Field: A Scene of Sickening, Ghastly Horror*. London: Johnson-Taunton Military Press, 1989.

———, ed. *No Pride in the Little Big Horn*. London: English Westerners' Society, 1987.

———. *"Sufficient Reason?"* London: English Westerners' Society, 1977.

Taylor, Joseph Henry. *Frontier and Indian Life, and Kaleidoscopic Lives*. Reprint, Valley City, ND: Washburn's Fiftieth Anniversary Committee, 1932.

———. *Twenty Years on the Trap Line*. Avondale, PA: privately printed, 1896.

Taylor, Rev. Landon. *The Battlefield Reviewed*. Chicago: privately printed, 1881.

Taylor, William O. *With Custer on the Little Bighorn*. New York: Viking, 1996.

Teakle, Thomas. *The Spirit Lake Massacre*. Iowa City: State Historical Society of Iowa, 1918.

Thorndike, Rachel Sherman. *The Sherman Letters*. New York: Da Capo, 1969.

Tibbles, Thomas Henry. *Buckskin and Blanket Days*. New York: Doubleday, 1957.

Trinka, Zena Irma. *Out Where the West Begins*. St. Paul: Pioneer Company, 1920.

Trout, M. D., ed. *Joseph Culbertson's Indian Scout Memoirs, 1876–1895*. Anaheim, CA: Van-Allen Publishing, 1984.

Urwin, Gregory, ed. *Custer and His Times*. Book 3. El Paso, TX: Little Big Horn Associates, 1987.

———. *Custer Victorious*. Edison, NJ: Blue and Grey Press, 1983.

Utley, Robert. *Cavalier in Buckskin*. Norman: University of Oklahoma Press, 1988.

———. *Custer and the Great Controversy*. Pasadena, CA: Westernlore Press, 1962.

————. *Frontier Regulars: The United States Cavalry and the Indian, 1866–1890.* New York: Macmillan, 1973.

————. *The Indian Frontier of the American West, 1846–1890.* Albuquerque: University of New Mexico Press, 1984.

————. *The Lance and the Shield.* New York: Holt, 1993.

————. *The Last Days of the Sioux Nation.* New Haven, CT: Yale University Press, 1963.

————. *Life in Custer's Cavalry.* Lincoln: University of Nebraska Press, 1987.

————. *The Reno Court of Inquiry: The Chicago Times Account.* Fort Collins, CO: Old Army Press, 1972.

Utley, Robert, and Wilcomb E. Washburn. *Indian Wars.* Boston: Houghton Mifflin, 1977.

Van Nuys, Maxwell. *Inkpaduta: The Scarlet Point.* Denver: privately printed, 1998.

Vaughn, J. W. *With Crook at the Rosebud.* Harrisburg, PA: Stackpole, 1956.

Vestal, Stanley. *New Sources of Indian History, 1850–1891.* Norman: University of Oklahoma Press, 1934.

————. *Sitting Bull: Champion of the Sioux.* Norman: University of Oklahoma Press, 1957.

————. *Warpath: The True Story of the Fighting Sioux.* Boston: Houghton Mifflin, 1934.

————. *Warpath and Council Fire.* New York: Random House, 1948.

Viola, Herman J. *Little Bighorn Remembered.* New York: Crown, 2000.

Voices of the Little Bighorn. Bismarck, ND: Bismarck Tribune, 1996.

Wagner, Glendolin Damon. *Old Neutriment.* Lincoln: University of Nebraska Press, 1989.

Waldo, Edna LaMoore. *Dakota.* Caldwell, ID: Caxton Printers, 1936.

Walker, Judson. *Campaigns of General Custer.* Reprint, New York: Promontory Press, 1966.

Wallace, Charles B. *Custer's Ohio Boyhood.* Cadiz, OH: Harrison County Historical Society, 1987.

Walter, Dave, ed. *Speaking Ill of the Dead.* Guilford, CT: Twodot, 2000.

War of the Rebellion: The Official Records of the Union and Confederate Armies. Washington, DC: Government Printing Office, 1896.

Weibert, Don. *Custer, Cases and Cartridges: The Weibert Collection Analyzed.* Billings, MT: Weibert, 1989.

Weibert, Henry, and Don Weibert. *Sixty-six Years in Custer's Shadow.* Billings, MT: Falcon Press, 1988.

Wengert, James. *The Custer Despatches.* Manhattan, KS: Sunflower University Press, 1987.

Wert, Jeffrey D. *Custer: The Controversial Life of George Armstrong Custer.* New York: Simon and Schuster, 1996.

Weymouth, Lally. *America in 1876: The Way We Were.* New York: Vintage, 1976.

Wheeler, Homer W. *Buffalo Days.* Reprint, Lincoln: University of Nebraska Press, 1990.

White, Richard. "Animals and Enterprise." In *The Oxford History of the American West,* edited by Clyde A. Milner, Carol A. O'Connor, and Martha A. Sandweiss. New York: Oxford University Press, 1994.

Whittaker, Frederick. *A Complete Life of General George A. Custer.* New York: Sheldon and Company, 1876.

Willert, James. *Little Big Horn Diary.* El Segundo, CA: Upton and Sons, 1997.

———. *March of the Columns.* El Segundo, CA: Upton and Sons, 1994.

Wing, Talcott. *History of Monroe County, Michigan.* New York: Munsell, 1890.

Winthrop, William. *Military Law and Precedents.* Reprint, New York: Arno Press, 1979.

Wooster, Robert. *The Military and United States Indian Policy, 1865–1903.* New Haven, CT: Yale University Press, 1983.

Zeisler, Karl. *Custer Observed: General Custer as Seen Through the Eyes of the Monroe Evening News.* Monroe, MI: Monroe County Library System, 1988.

ARTICLES

Aimore, Alan. "U.S. Military Academy Civil War Sources and Statistics." *Military Collector and Historian* 54, no. 3 (Fall 2002).

Anderson, Harry H. "A Challenge to Brown's Sioux Indian Wars Thesis." *Montana* 12, no. 1 (January 1962).

———. "Cheyennes at the Little Big Horn: A Study in Statistics." *North Dakota History* 27, no. 3 (Summer 1960).

Athearn, Robert G. "War Paint Against Brass." *Montana* 6, no. 3 (July 1956).

Bailly, Edward C. "Echoes from Custer's Last Fight." *Military Affairs* 17, no. 4 (1953).

Baker, Miriam Hawthorn. "Inkpaduta's Camp at Smithland." *Annals of Iowa* 39, no. 2 (Fall 1967).

Barnett, Louise. "Libbie Custer and Mark Twain." *Research Review* 11, no. 2 (Summer 1997).

———. "Powder River." *Greasy Grass* 16 (May 2000).

Bateman, Gordon. "Female Casualties at the Little Big Horn." *Little Big Horn Associates Newsletter* 1 (November 1967).

Bates, Col. Charles Francis. "The Red Men and the Black Hills." *Outlook,* July 27, 1927.

Beck, Paul. "Military Officers' Views of Indian Scouts." *Military History of the West* 23, no. 1 (Spring 1993).

Bentley, Charles A. "Captain Frederick W. Benteen and the Kiowas." *Chronicles of Oklahoma* 56, no. 3 (Fall 1978).

Blank, Vernon. "Inkpaduatah's Great White Friend." *Iowan,* December–January 1961.

Bray, Kingsley M. "Teton Sioux Population History, 1655–1881." *Nebraska History* 75, no. 2 (Summer 1994).

Briggs, Harold E. "The Black Hills Gold Rush." *North Dakota Historical Quarterly* 5, no. 2 (January 1931).

Brininstool, E. A., et al. "Chief Crazy Horse: His Career and Death." *Nebraska History* 12, no. 1 (January–March, 1929).

———. "Unwritten Seventh Cavalry History." *Middle Border Bulletin* 4, no. 4 (Spring 1945).

Britt, Albert. "Custer's Last Fight." *Pacific Historical Review* 13, no. 1 (March 1944).

Broome, Jeff. "In Memory of Lt. James Sturgis." *Guidon* 3, no. 3 (June 2000).

Brust, James. "Lt. Oscar Long's Early Map Details Terrain, Battle Positions." *Greasy Grass* 11 (May 1995).

Buecker, Thomas R. "Frederic S. Calhoun: A Little-Known Member of the Custer Clique." *Greasy Grass* 10 (May 1994).

Bulkley, John M. "As a Classmate Saw Custer." *New York Evening Post,* May 28, 1910.

Calitri, Shannon Smith. "Give Me Eighty Men." *Montana* 54, no. 3 (Autumn 2004).

Carroll, Matthew. "Diary of Matthew Carroll." *Contributions to the Historical Society of Montana* 2 (1896).

Cecil, Jerry. "Lt. Crittenden: Striving for the Soldier's Life." *Greasy Grass* 11 (May 1995).

Connolly, James B. "Father DeSmet in North Dakota." *North Dakota History* 27, no. 1 (Winter 1960).

Cooper, Grace E. "Benton County Pioneer-Historical Society." *Oregon Historical Quarterly* 57 (March 1956).

"Custer's Battle from the Indian Viewpoint." *American Indian Journal* 1 (1929).

Daubenmier, Judy. "Empty Saddles: Desertion from the Dashing U.S. Cavalry." *Montana* 54, no. 3 (Autumn 2004).

Deming, Edwin Willard. "Custer's Last Stand." *Mentor,* July 1926.

Dickson, Ephriam. "Reconstructing the Indian Village on the Little Bighorn." *Research Review* 22 (May 2006).

Dixon, David. "The Sordid Side of the Seventh Cavalry." *Research Review* 1, no. 1 (June 1987).

Dobak, William A. "Yellow-Leg Journalists." *Journal of the West* 13, no. 1 (January 1974).

Donahue, Michael. "Revisiting Col. Gibbon's Route." *Greasy Grass* 19 (May 2003).

Dunn, Adrian R. "A History of Old Fort Berthold." *North Dakota History* 30, no. 4 (Fall 1963).

Eastman, Charles A. "The Story of the Little Big Horn." *Chautauquan,* no. 31 (July 1900).

Ellis, Horace. "A Survivor's Story of the Custer Massacre on American Frontier." *The Journal of American History* 3, no. 2 (April 1909).

Ellis, Joseph. "Inventing the Presidency." *American Heritage,* October 2004.

Ellis, Richard N. "After Bull Run: The Later Career of General John Pope." *Montana* 19, no. 4 (October 1969).

Essin, Emmett M., III. "Mules, Packs, and Packtrains." *Southwestern Historical Quarterly* 74, no. 1 (July 1970).

Ewers, John C. "Intertribal Warfare as the Precursor of Indian-White Warfare on the Northern Great Plains." *Western Historical Quarterly* 6, no. 4 (October 1975).

Ewing, Charles B. "The Wounded of the Wounded Knee Battlefield, with Remarks on Wounds Produced by Large and Small Calibre Bullets." *Boston Medical and Surgical Journal,* May 12, 1892.

Farioli, Dennis, and Ron Nichols. "Fort A. Lincoln, July 1876." *Greasy Grass* 17 (May 2001).

Fisher, John R. "The Royall and Duncan Pursuits: Aftermath of the Battle of Summit Spring, 1869." *Nebraska History* 50, no. 3 (Fall 1969).

Flandrau, Hon. Charles F. "The Ink-pa-du-ta Massacre of 1857." *Collections of the Minnesota Historical Society* 3 (1870–1880).

Foley, James R. "Walter Camp & Ben Clark." *Research Review* 10, no. 1 (January 1996.)

Frost, Lawrence. "The Black Hills Expedition of 1874." *Red River Valley Historical Review* 4, no. 4 (Fall 1979).

Gibbon, Col. John. "Hunting Sitting Bull." *American Catholic Quarterly Review*, October 1977.

———. "Last Summer's Expedition Against the Sioux." *American Catholic Quarterly Review*, April 1877.

Glease, George W. "The Battle of the Little Big Horn." *Periodical* 20, no. 2 (Summer 1993).

Godfrey, Hon. Calvin Pomeroy. "General Edward S. Godfrey." *Ohio Archaeological and Historical Quarterly* 43 (1934).

Godfrey, Edward. "Custer's Last Battle." *Contributions to the Historical Society of Montana* 9 (1921).

———. "Some Reminiscences, Including the Washita Battle, November 27, 1868." *The Cavalry Journal* 37, no. 153 (October 1928).

Gray, John S. "Custer Throws a Boomerang." *Montana* 11, no. 2 (April 1961).

———. "The Pack Train on George A. Custer's Last Campaign." *Nebraska History* 57, no. 1 (Spring 1976).

———. "Suttler on Custer's Last Campaign." *Nebraska History* 43, no. 3.

———. "Veterinary Service on Custer's Last Campaign." *Kansas Historical Quarterly* 43, no. 3 (Autumn 1977).

Greene, Jerome. "The Hayfield Fight: A Reappraisal of a Neglected Action." *Montana* 23, no. 3 (Autumn 1972).

Hanson, Charles E. "The Post-War Indian Gun Trade." *Museum of the Fur Trade Quarterly* 4, no. 3 (Fall 1968).

Hardorff, Richard. "Some Recollections of Custer: His Last Battle." *Research Review* 4, no. 2 (June 1990).

Harnsberger, John L. "Land Speculation, Promotion and Failure: The Northern Pacific Railroad." *Journal of the West* 9, no. 1 (January 1970).

Harrison, Peter. "The Eyes of the Sleepers: Cheyenne Accounts of the Washita Attack." *Brand Book* 31, no. 2 (Summer 1997).

Hart, John P. "Custer's First Stand: The Washington Fight." *Research Review* 12, no. 1 (Winter 1998).

Hedren, Paul L. "Carbine Extractor Failure at the Little Big Horn." *Military Collector and Historian*, Summer 1973.

———. "Eben Swift's Army Service on the Plains, 1876–1879." *Annals of Wyoming* 50, no. 1 (Spring 1978).

Heski, Thomas M. "It Started with a Parade." *Research Review* 1, no. 1 (June 1987).

Hilger, Sister M. Inez. "The Narrative of Oscar One Bull." *Mid-America* 28, no. 3 (July 1946).

Hinman, Eleanor. "Oglala Sources on the Life of Crazy Horse." *Nebraska History* 57, no. 1 (Spring 1976).

Hinsdale, B. A. "The Western Land Policy of the British Government from 1763 to 1775." *Ohio Archaeological and Historical Quarterly* 1 (December 1887).

Horn, W. Donald. "The Tainted Testimony of Captain Frederick W. Benteen." *Research Review* 15, no. 2 (Summer 2001).

Hudnutt, Dean. "New Light on the Little Big Horn." *Field Artillery Journal* 26, no. 4 (July–August 1936).

Hunt, Fred. "A Purposeful Picnic." *Pacific Monthly,* March–April 1908.

———. "The Subjugation of Black Kettle." *Overland Monthly,* July 1909.

Hutchins, James S. "Mounted Riflemen: The Real Role of Cavalry in the Indian Wars." *El Palacio* 69 (Summer 1962).

Hynds, A. A., and William J. Shay. "Reminiscences of Sgt. H. A. Hinds." *Research Review* 6, no. 4 (Winter 1972).

Ingham, Harvey. "Sioux Indians Harassed the Early Settlers." *Annals of Iowa* 34, no. 2 (October 1957).

Jensen, Richard. "Big Foot's Followers at Wounded Knee." *Nebraska History* 71, no. 4 (Winter 1990).

Johnson, Barry C. "A Captain of 'Chivalric Courage.'" *Brand Book* 25, nos. 1 & 2 (1987–1988).

———. "The Seventh's Quartermaster." *Crow's Nest* 5, no. 2 (Autumn/Winter 2005).

———. "Tragedy at White Horse Creek." *Brand Book* 19, nos. 3 & 4 (April–July 1977).

Kanipe, Daniel A. "A New Story of Custer's Last Battle; Told by a Messenger Boy Who Survived." *Contributions to the Historical Society of Montana* 9 (1923).

King, Capt. Charles. "Custer's Last Battle." *Harper's,* August 1890.

King, James T. "Wanted: A Re-Evaluation of General George Crook." *Nebraska History* 45, no. 3 (September 1964).

Krott, Rob. "Was Custer Outgunned?"*Military Illustrated,* no. 139 (2004).

Landis, Steven E. "Custer at Lacey Spring." *Columbiad* 2, no. 4 (Winter 1999).

Larson, Peggy Rodina. "A New Look at the Elusive Inkpaduta." *Minnesota History* 48, no. 1 (Spring 1982).

Lee, Minnie. "Lieutenant Phil Sheridan's Romance in Oregon." *Oregonian,* January 2, 1938.

Lindberg, Christer, ed. "Foreigners in Action at Wounded Knee." *Nebraska History* 71, no. 4 (Winter 1990).

Lindell, Lisa. "Bringing Books to a 'Book-Hungry' Land." *Book History* 7 (2004).

Lockley, Fred. "Reminiscences of Martha E. Gilliam Collins."*Quarterly of the Oregon Historical Society* 17 (December 1916).

Lonich, David W. "Blacksmith Henry Mechling: From Pennsylvania to Little Bighorn." *Greasy Grass* 17 (May 2001).

Lubetkin, M. John. "Strike Up 'Garryowen.'" *Research Review* 20, no. 2 (Summer 2006).

Luce, Edward S. "The Diary and Letters of Dr. James M. DeWolf." *North Dakota History* 25, no. 3 (April–July 1958).

———. Review of *Echoes from the Little Big Horn Fight. Montana* 3, no. 4 (Autumn 1953).

MacLaine, Bob. "Our 1876 'Injun Fightin'' Cavalry." *Little Big Horn Associates Newsletter* 1 (August 1967).

MacNeil, Rod. "Raw Recruits and Veterans." *Little Big Horn Associates Newsletter* 21 (October 1987).

Mangum, Neil. "The George C. Brown Story." *Research Review* 13, no. 2 (Summer 1999).

———. "Reno's Battalion in the Battle of the Little Big Horn." *Greasy Grass* 2 (May 1996).

Marquis, Thomas B. "Indian Warrior Ways." *By Valor and Arms* 2, no. 2 (1977).

Mattes, Merrill J. "The Enigma of Wounded Knee." *Plains Anthropologist* 5, no. 9 (May 1960).

Mattingly, Arthur H. "The Great Plains Peace Commission of 1867." *Journal of the West* 15, no. 3 (July 1976).

McBlain, John F. "With Gibbon on the Sioux Campaign of 1876." *Journal of the United States Cavalry Association* 9, no. 33 (June 1896).

McClernand, Edward J. "With the Indian and the Buffalo in Montana." *The Cavalry Journal* 36, no. 36 (January–April 1927).

McGinnis, Anthony. "A Contest of Wits and Daring: Plains Indians at War with the U.S. Army." *North Dakota History* 48, no. 2 (Spring 1981).

McGinnis, Hugh. "I Was There! The Wounded Knee Massacre." *True West* 8, no. 4 (March–April 1961).

Meketa, R. T. "The Press and the Battle of the Little Big Horn." *Research Review* 1, no. 1 (March 1984).

Merrick, Henry S. "Was There a White Survivor of Custer's Command?" *Military Affairs* 20, no. 1 (Spring 1956).

Millbrook, Minnie D. "Godfrey on Custer." *Research Review* 6, no. 4 (Winter 1972).

Miller, David Humphreys. "Echoes of the Little Bighorn." *American Heritage* 22, no. 4 (June 1971).

Montravel, Peter R. "General Nelson A. Miles and the Wounded Knee Controversy." *Arizona and the West* 28, no. 1 (Spring 1986).

Morris, Major Robert E. "Custer Made a Good Decision: A Leavenworth Appreciation." *Journal of the West* 16, no. 4 (October 1977).

Munn, Fred M. "Fred Munn, Veteran of Frontier Experiences, Remembered the Days He Rode with Miles, Howard, and Terry." *Montana* 16, no. 2 (Spring 1966).

Murphy, James P. "The Campaign of the Little Big Horn." *Infantry Journal* 34 (June 1929).

Myers, Steven W. "Roster of Known Hostile Indians at the Battle of the Little Big Horn." *Research Review* 5, no. 2 (June 1991).

Newcomb, W. W., Jr. "A Re-examination of the Causes of Plains Warfare." *American Anthropologist* 52 (July–September 1950).

Nihart, Brooke. "Oral History c. 1909: Recollections of Dennis Lynch." *Military Collector and Historian,* Summer 1973.

Noyes, C. Lee. "The Battle of the Little Big Horn: Reno, Terry and a Variation of a Major Theme." *13th Annual Symposium.*

———. "Captain Robert P. Hughes and the Case Against Custer: An Early Perspective of the Little Big Horn." *Little Big Horn Associates Newsletter* 33, no. 1 (February 1999).

———. "Custer's Surgeon, George Lord, Among the Missing at Little Bighorn Battle." *Greasy Grass* 16 (May 2000).

———. "A Dispatch from the Battlefield." *Research Review* 18, no. 2 (Summer 2004).

———. "The Guns 'Long Hair' Left Behind: The Gatling Gun Detachment and the Little Big Horn." *Brand Book* 33, no. 2 (Summer 1999).

Ostler, Jeffrey. "They Regard Their Passing as *Wakan*." *Western Historical Quarterly* 30, no. 4 (Winter 1999).

Palais, Hyman. "Some Aspects of the Black Hills Gold Rush Compared with the California Gold Rush." *Pacific Historical Review* 16, no. 1 (March 1946).

Partoll, Albert J. "After the Custer Battle." *Frontier and Midland* 19, no. 4 (1938–1939).

Pearson, Jeffrey V. "Tragedy at Red Cloud Agency." *Montana* 55, no. 2 (Summer 2005).

Pennington, Robert. "An Analysis of the Political Structure of the Teton-Dakota Indian Tribe of North America." *North Dakota History* 20, no. 3 (July 1953).

Plainfeather, Mardell Hogan. "A Personal Look at Curly's Life After the Battle of the Little Big Horn." *Research Review* 4 (May 1988).

Pohanka, Brian. "Letters of the Seventh Cavalry." *Little Big Horn Associates Newsletter* 10 (February 1976).

Prickett, Robert C. "The Malfeasance of William Worth Belknap." *North Dakota History* 17, no. 1 (January 1950).

Prucha, Francis Paul. "Andrew Jackson's Indian Policy: A Reassessment." *Journal of American History* 56, no. 3 (December 1969).

———. "Indian Removal and the Great American Desert." *Indian Magazine of History* LIX (December 1963).

Ralston, Alan. "The Yellowstone Expedition of 1876." *Montana* 20, no. 2 (Spring 1990).

Rector, William G. "Fields of Fire: The Reno-Benteen Defense Perimeter." *Montana* 16, no. 2 (Spring 1966).

Rives, Timothy. "Grant, Babcock, and the Whiskey Ring." *Prologue* 32, no. 3 (Fall 2000).

Sage, Walter N. "Sitting Bull's Own Narrative of the Custer Fight." *Canadian Historical Review* 16, no. 2 (June 1935).

Saindon, Bob. "Sitting Bull: Old Fort Peck's Famous Visitor." *Hoofprints* 18, no. 2 (Fall–Winter 1988).

Saum, Lewis O. "Colonel Custer's Copperhead: The Mysterious Mr. Kellogg." *Montana* 28, no. 4 (Autumn 1978).

———. "Private John F. O'Donohue's Reflections on the Little Bighorn." *Montana* 50, no. 4 (Winter 2000).

Schoenberger, Dale T., ed. "A Trooper with Custer: Augustus DeVoto's Account of the Little Big Horn." *Montana* 40, no. 1 (Winter 1990).

Schulenberg, Raymond F. "Indians of North Dakota." *North Dakota History* 23, nos. 3 & 4 (July–October 1956).

Scott, Douglas. "Cartridges, Bullets and Bones." *Research Review* 18 (May 2002).

Scott, Gen. Hugh. "Custer's Last Fight." *New York Times*, January 6, 1935.

Shoemaker, Col. John O. "The Custer Court-Martial." *Military Review* 51, no. 10 (October 1971).

Sklenar, Larry. "The 'Wallace Factor' at the Reno Court of Inquiry." *Research Review* 14, no. 1 (Winter 2000).

Smith, Duane A. "Where a Bird Could Hardly Obtain a Footing." *Colorado Heritage*, Spring 1999.

Smith, Jay. "Custer Didn't Do It." *Little Big Horn Associates Newsletter* 9, no. 2 (February 1975).

Smits, David D. "The Frontier Army and the Destruction of the Buffalo, 1865–1883." *Western History Quarterly* 25, no. 3 (Autumn 1994).

Snedeker, Lenora A. "The Porters: A Star-Crossed Couple." *Nomad and Standby*, no. 4 (1995).

Stewart, Edgar I., ed. "I Rode with Custer!" *Montana* 4, no. 3 (Summer 1954).

———. "The Reno Court of Inquiry." *Montana* 2, no. 3 (July 1952).

———, and Major E. S. Luce. "The Reno Scout." *Montana* 10, no. 3 (Summer 1960).

Swift, Eben. "General Wesley Merritt." *Journal of the United States Cavalry Association*, March 1911.

Talbot, James Joseph. "Custer's Last Battle." *Penn Monthly*, September 1877.

Taunton, Francis B. "The Mystery of Miss Adams." *Brand Book* 28, no. 2 (Summer 1991).

Taylor, Joseph Henry. "Bloody Knife and Gall." *North Dakota Historical Quarterly* 4 (July 1947).

———. "Inkpaduta and Sons." *North Dakota Historical Quarterly* 4 (April 1930).

———. "Lonesome Charley." *North Dakota Historical Quarterly* 4 (July 1930).

Thomas, Amy M. "There Is Nothing So Effective as a Personal Canvass." *Book History* 1 (1998).

Tilford, James D., Jr. "Life in the Old Army." *Research Review* 4, no. 1 (January 1990).

Trennert, Robert A. "Centennial Indian Exhibition of 1876." *Prologue* (January 1972).

———. "Popular Imagery and the American Indian: A Centennial View." *New Mexico Historical Review* 51, no. 3 (July 1976).

Utley, Robert M. "The Celebrated Peace Policy of General Grant." *North Dakota History* 20, no. 3 (July 1953).

———. "The Custer Battle in the Contemporary Press." *North Dakota History* 22, nos. 1 & 2 (January–April 1955).

———. "Origins of the Great Sioux War." *Montana* 42, no. 4 (Autumn 1992).

Vestal, Stanley. "The Man Who Killed Custer." *American Heritage* 8, no. 2 (February 1957).

Walter, Denton. "Terry and Custer: Was There a Plan?" *Little Big Horn Associates Newsletter* 22 (October 1988).

Wedel, Waldo R. "Notes on the Prairie Turnip Among Plains Indians." *Nebraska History* 59, no. 2 (Summer 1978).

Wells, Philip. "Ninety-six Years Among the Indians of the Northwest." *North Dakota History* 15, no. 2 (1948).

Welty, Raymond L. "The Indian Policy of the Army, 1860–1870." *The Cavalry Journal* 36, no. 148 (July 1927).

White, Richard. "The Winning of the West: The Expansion of the Western Sioux in the Eighteenth and Nineteenth Century." *Journal of American History* 65, no. 2 (September 1978).

Whittaker, Frederick. "General George A. Custer." *Galaxy*, September 1876.

Willert, James. "Does Anomaly Contain Sturgis's Body?" *Research Review* 11, no. 2 (Summer 1997).

Wiltsey, Norman B. "We Killed Custer." *Real West* 11, no. 60 (June 1968).

Yarborough, Ralph W. "General Custer Learned Sign Language at Texas State College." *Frontier Times* 29, no. 5 (February 1952).

OTHER PERIODICALS

Annual Symposium, Custer Battlefield Historical & Museum Association, nos. 1–19

Army and Navy Journal

Battlefield Dispatch

Big Horn Yellowstone Journal

Brand Book

Crow's Nest

English Westerners' Society Tally Sheet

Greasy Grass

Guidon

Little Big Horn Associates Newsletter

Research Review

NEWSPAPERS

Bismarck Tribune

Chicago Daily News

Chicago Daily Tribune

Chicago Evening Journal

Chicago Times

Inter-Ocean

New York Herald

New York Sun

New York Times

Philadelphia Times

St. Paul Pioneer Press

Washington Post

Winners of the West

UNPUBLISHED MANUSCRIPTS

Blummer, J. Manuscript. Little Bighorn Battlefield National Monument Collection, Crow Agency, MT.

Brininstool, E. A. *The Thrilling Escape of Lieut. C. C. De Rudio and Sergt. Thos. O'Neil in the Battle of the Little Big Horn, June 25–26, 1876.* Los Angeles: privately bound, 1923. (From the original manuscript of Sergeant O'Neill.) Brininstool Collection, Center for American History, University of Texas, Austin.

Falconer, W. A. "Early Notes and Comments." Van de Water Papers, New York Public Library.

Freeman, Henry J. Diary. Wyoming State Archives, Cheyenne.

Lee, Jesse M. Autobiography. Ephriam Dickson Collection.

Merington, Marguerite. *Army Lady: Mrs. Custer—Wife, Widow of General George Armstrong Custer.* Unpublished manuscript. Hagner Collection, New York Public Library.

Merkel, Chuck. "Custer's Forgotten Lieutenant: Thomas B. Weir." History diss., Florida State University, 1996.

Nelson, Clifford L. "The Custer Battalion at the Little Bighorn." History honors thesis, Concordia College, 1969.

Rickey, Donald. "Interview with John Stands in Timber, August 18, 1956." Little Bighorn Battlefield National Monument Collection, Crow Agency, MT.

Stands in Timber, John. Manuscript. Margot Liberty Collection.

Waggoner, Mrs. Josephine. "Inkpaduta." Brininstool Collection, Center for American History, University of Texas, Austin.

COLLECTIONS AND ARCHIVES

Bonner, Robert. Papers. New York Public Library.

Brininstool, Earl Alonzo. Collection. Center for American History, University of Texas, Austin.

Camp, William M. Papers. Denver Public Library.

Camp, William M. Papers. Harold B. Lee Library, Brigham Young University, Provo, UT.

Camp, William M. Papers. Lilly Library, Indiana University, Bloomington.

Campbell, Walter Stanley. Collection. Western History Collection, University of Oklahoma, Norman.

Cartwright, R. G. Collection. Phoebe Apperson Hearst Library, Lead, SD.

Custer, Brice C. W. Collection. Privately owned.

Custer, Elizabeth B. Collection. Little Bighorn Battlefield National Monument, Crow Agency, MT.

Custer Collection. Monroe County Historical Museum, Monroe, MI.

Custer File and Scrapbooks. Montana Room, Billings Public Library, Billings, MT.

Frost, Lawrence A. Collection. Monroe County Historical Museum, Monroe, MI.

Ghent, William J. Papers. Library of Congress, Washington, DC.

Godfrey, Edward S. Papers. Library of Congress, Washington, DC.

Godfrey Family Papers. U.S. Army Military History Institute, Carlisle, PA.

Grinnell, George Bird. Papers. Braun Research Library, Institute for the Study of the American West, Autry National Center, Los Angeles.

Hagner, Francis R. Collection. New York Public Library.

Harlan Crow Library, Dallas.

Hein, Louis. Collection. Special Collections Division, Georgetown University Library, Washington, DC.

Kuhlman, Charles. Collection. Harold B. Lee Library, Brigham Young University, Provo, UT.

McCracken Research Library, Buffalo Bill Historical Center, Cody, WY.

Merington, Marguerite. Papers. New York Public Library.

National Archives, Washington, DC.

Order of the Indian Wars Papers. U.S. Military History Institute, Carlisle, PA.
Ricker, Eli. Collection. Nebraska State Historical Society, Lincoln.
Terry Family Collection. Beinecke Library, Yale University, New Haven, CT.
Van de Water, Frederic. Papers. New York Public Library.
Wyoming State Archives, Cheyenne.

INDEX